# Broadcast Engineering and IT Conference 2023



Las Vegas, Nevada, USA
15 – 18 April 2023

ISBN: 978-1-7138-7264-1

**Printed from e-media with permission by:**

Curran Associates, Inc.
57 Morehouse Lane
Red Hook, NY 12571

**Some format issues inherent in the e-media version may also appear in this print version.**



National Association of Broadcasters (NAB)
1 M Street SE
Washington, D.C. 20003

Phone: (202) 429 5300

www.nab.org

**Additional copies of this publication are available from:**

Curran Associates, Inc.
57 Morehouse Lane
Red Hook, NY 12571 USA
Phone: 845-758-0400
Fax: 845-758-2633
Email: curran@proceedings.com
Web: www.proceedings.com

# NAB Broadcast Engineering and Information Technology Conference

# PROCEEDINGS 2023

A collection of papers from the
2023 NAB Broadcast Engineering and
Information Technology (BEIT) Conference

NATIONAL ASSOCIATION OF BROADCASTERS

These Proceedings contain technical papers presented at the
2023 NAB Broadcast Engineering and Information Technology (BEIT)
Conference, April 15 – 18, 2023.

Published by the NAB Technology Department.



Additional access to the 2023 Proceedings is available through nabpilot.org.

NAB
NATIONAL ASSOCIATION OF BROADCASTERS
100 YEARS

Foreword

2023 marks the 77th NAB Broadcast and Engineering and Information Technology (BEIT) Conference and this year we are also celebrating the 100th anniversary of NAB. In the spirit of that rich history, it's interesting to look back and see how far we've come. Twenty-five years ago, some of the first commercial DTV stations were just coming on the air and this year we are in the midst of the transition from DTV to ATSC 3.0 television broadcasting. HD Radio was authorized by the FCC a little over 20 years ago and this year we are seeing hybrid radio gaining a foothold in the market. The times are definitely changing, but we are now certainly in a critical period for broadcasting as we improve broadcast technology and converge with other media technologies.

This year the NAB BEIT Conference Proceedings is a microcosm of broadcasting's technological evolution. Papers on ATSC 3.0 use cases and applications, hybrid radio developments, cloud workflows, media convergence, RF technology and other timely topics are all solidly represented. We hope that this contemporary collection of technical papers will serve as an important reference for you.

The NAB BEIT Conference was developed under the guidance of the NAB BEIT Conference Committee that has the difficult task of selecting the papers for presentation among the many qualified proposals. It is gratifying to see that their hard work has resulted in a great conference lineup and a worthy Proceedings publication. And we sadly note here the passing of one of the conference committee members for the past several years—consultant Gary Kline, known to many attending this conference, and a good friend to NAB over the years.

We'd also like to thank our partner organizations in producing the conference—the Society of Broadcast Engineers (SBE), the Society of Cable Telecommunications Engineers (SCTE) and the North American Broadcasters Association (NABA)—for their support, ideas and follow-through.

If you have ideas on ways to improve the conference or the Proceedings, we'd welcome your thoughts.

Sincerely,

*Ling Ling Sun*

Ling Ling Sun, Nebraska Public Media
2023 NAB BEITC Committee Chair

Sam Matheny, NAB
Executive Vice President and CTO

1 M Street SE
Washington DC 20003 3512
Phone 202 429 5300
nab.org

Advocacy Education Innovation

# 2023 NAB Broadcast Engineering and IT Conference

## Program Committee

Ling Ling Sun **(Chair)**
Chief Technology Officer
Nebraska Public Media
Lincoln, Neb.

Rick Ackermans
Director, RF and Transmissions Engineering
CBS Operations and Engineering
New York, N.Y.

Ben Husmann
Product Manager
Quu, Inc.
Asheville, N.C.

Jim Kauffman
Executive Director, Engineering & Ops
Cox Media Group
Orlando, Fla.

Gary Kline
President
Kline Consulting Group
Atlanta, Ga.

J. Brian Morris
Vice President, Chief Information Security Officer
Gray Television, Inc.
Montgomery, Ala.

Sherri Powers
Chief Engineer
Beasley Media Group, Detroit
Ferndale, Mich.

Sun Sachs
Senior Vice President, Product, Digital and Engineering
Townsquare Media
Purchase, N.Y.

Joe Seccia
Regional Director, RF Transmission
TelevisaUnivision, Inc.
Miami, Fla.

Conrad Trautmann
Chief Technology Officer
Cumulus Media
New York, N.Y.

Dave Siegler
Treasurer
IEEE Broadcast Technology Society
Atlanta, Ga.

### Partner Organization Representatives

***NABA:***
Michael McEwen
Executive Director
North American Broadcasters Association
Toronto, Ontario, Canada

***SBE:***
Jim Ragsdale
Executive Director
Society of Broadcast Engineers
Indianapolis, Ind.

Tom Mikkelsen
Chief Transition Director
BitPath, LLC
Arlington, Va.

***SCTE:***
Dean Stoneback
Senior Director, Engineering and Standards
SCTE
Exton, Pa.

NAB® 100 YEARS
NATIONAL ASSOCIATION OF BROADCASTERS

# Proceedings of the 2023 NAB Broadcast Engineering and IT Conference

Table of Contents

NAB® 100 YEARS
NATIONAL ASSOCIATION OF BROADCASTERS

# Proceedings of the
# 2023 NAB Broadcast Engineering and IT Conference
Table of Contents

## Proceedings of the
# 2023 NAB Broadcast Engineering and IT Conference
Table of Contents

## Proceedings of the
# 2023 NAB Broadcast Engineering and IT Conference
Table of Contents

## Proceedings of the
# 2023 NAB Broadcast Engineering and IT Conference
Table of Contents

## Sustainability and 5G

# ATSC 3.0 and Public Broadcasting; A Case for Flash Cut

**Don Smith, Fred Engel**
**PBS North Carolina**
**Research Triangle Park, N.C., United States**
dsmith@pbsnc.org, fengel@pbsnc.org

**Bill Hayes**
**Iowa PBS**
**Johnston, Iowa, United States**
hayes@iowapbs.org

**Abstract** – ATSC 3.0, often referred to as "NEXTGEN TV," is gaining traction and is now being broadcast in over 60 markets in the United States. There are many challenges for broadcasters to adopt this technology and this is especially a concern for Public Broadcasters who may not have a necessary simulcast partner in their markets to continue ATSC 1.0 transmissions while beginning ATSC 3.0 operations. This paper presents a potential roadmap for stations, with an emphasis on statewide networks, to deploy ATSC 3.0. Examples in this paper will focus on two PBS North Carolina broadcast facilities and one Iowa PBS broadcast facility, but the criteria used could easily be adapted for other stations.

## Background

The Federal Communications Commission (FCC) approved the first Digital Television (DTV) standard in 1996. Now commonly known as ATSC 1.0, it was designed around then state-of-the-art video and audio encoding technology and the "8VSB" modulation standard. The FCC developed a transition plan for all broadcasters allowing them to add a second broadcast channel for ATSC 1.0 to complement their analog channel. Through a program administered through the U.S. Department of Commerce and the National Telecommunications and Information Administration (NTIA) a coupon program was initiated to incentivize viewers to purchase Set-Top-Boxes to convert ATSC 1.0 broadcast signals to analog for them to use on their existing television receivers. In late 2009 full power analog broadcast facilities ceased operation in the United States.

ATSC 1.0 was a significant development. It allowed for much higher resolution, High Definition (HD) video, surround sound audio, and the ability to include multiple video/audio streams into one broadcast television channel. However, the standard has been plagued by reception issues caused by multi-path signal reflections that causes video disturbances. ATSC 1.0 is also a technology locked in time; although some innovations with the technology were developed, some of those improvements were not adopted. To remain competitive in media distribution and better serve their audiences, broadcasters needed a better system.

In 2013 the Advanced Television Systems Committee (ATSC) issued a call for papers for a new television standard. The President of ATSC at that time, Mark Richer, noted that "Technology continues to advance, and we are always looking to the horizon. Internet technology now permeates the consumer experience, and mobility has become a requirement. As we look forward to next-generation

---

This paper is excerpted from the Proceedings of the 2023 NAB Broadcast Engineering and Information Technology (BEIT) Conference, © 2023, National Association of Broadcasters, 1 M Street SE, Washington, DC 20003 USA.

television standards, we want to take advantage of advances in compression and transmission technologies that will keep millions of people informed and entertained through broadcasting's inherently efficient one-to-many architecture." [1] The ATSC began developing the ATSC 3.0 standard, which is in reality a suite of standards, to address all aspects of the new technology.

The FCC, through its November 20, 2017 report and order, FCC 17-158, authorized the voluntary adoption of ATSC 3.0 [2]. In that Report and Order ATSC 1.0 simulcast and coverage requirements are set forth, amongst a myriad of other mandatory needs. In June 2020, through the release of FCC 20-72 [3], the FCC provided additional guidance regarding the transition from ATSC 1.0 to ATSC 3.0. In June 2022 the FCC requested comments on the current status of ATSC 3.0 in the marketplace and whether the simulcast requirement should be allowed to sunset in 2023 [4].

Currently there are a number of guidelines that must be met for stations to begin ATSC 3.0 operations. Below is a summary of most of those requirements [3 & 4]. Stations are **strongly urged** to contact their legal counsel to discuss their situation prior to making any decisions.

- Simulcast Partner
    - All stations in the partnership must be licensed in the same market.
    - The ATSC 1.0 host station must have 95% of its population within its coverage area of the ATSC 3.0 partner station carrying its primary program service.
    - Only requires broadcasting the ATSC 3.0 Primary Program Service on an ATSC 1.0 station. However, it is preferable if all ATSC 3.0 program services were available on an ATSC 1.0 station.
    - TV translators and Low Power stations are excluded from the simulcast requirements.
- Waivers are considered on a case-by-case basis.
- Flash Cut Possibilities – Switching from ATSC 1.0 to ATSC 3.0 without a simulcast partner.
    - If fewer than 3 full power stations in a market meet the community of license requirement. The community of license requirement for full power stations is the ATSC 1.0 host signal completely covering the partner station's community of license.
    - Providing program delivery to at least 95% of the population served by the ATSC 1.0 signal is still required. Low cost ATSC 3.0 receive devices are mentioned in one of the FCC proceedings as being acceptable to meet this requirement in lieu of a receivable ATSC 1.0 signal.
- Vacant channels cannot be used to meet audience coverage requirements.
- MVPD carriage
    - Must carry is based on the original ATSC 1.0 signal. No expansion due to changes in the coverage area of the ATSC 1.0 host partner.
    - A good quality signal is still required.
    - ATSC 3.0 signal currently has no must carry rights.
    - Must negotiate carriage if the station flash cuts from ATSC 1.0 to ATSC 3.0, currently no carriage rights exist for these stations.

## Benefits

With the deployment of ATSC 3.0, new and improved services will become available to not just viewers but the entire community. It goes beyond an improved viewing experience with the delivery of 4K Ultra HD video with immersive sound. There's also the addition of interactive video, extended education initiatives [5], automotive mobile data [6], improved emergency and first responder communications [7], in addition to the potential of more services in the future.

## Simulcast Partnership Overview

The accepted means of adopting ATSC 3.0 in a market is through an effort called a "Simulcasting Partnership." Complex legal, business and technical work as well as cooperation among multiple broadcasters in a market may enable an ATSC 3.0 facility to be launched.

For our example we will look at two broadcasters in a market. One broadcasts on Channel 25 and the other on Channel 30 and each station carries one HD and two SD program services. See Figure 1.

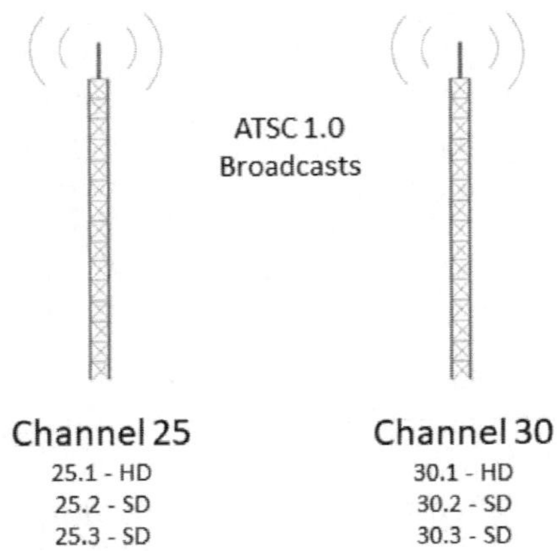


FIGURE 1.

To enable ATSC 3.0 in this market the owners of Channels 25 and 30 will need to engage in a business/legal relationship. From there they will engage the FCC on licensing and build the necessary technology infrastructure to begin the simulcast effort. In our example below, Channel 30 will cease broadcasting in ATSC 1.0 and convert its facility to ATSC 3.0. Channel 25 will continue to broadcast in ATSC 1.0 and will accept Channel 30's three program services, bringing the total number of streams on that facility to six. The Channel 30 facility will become the new ATSC 3.0 facility, carrying at least the two stations' primary services but presumably all six program services. See the example in Figure 2.

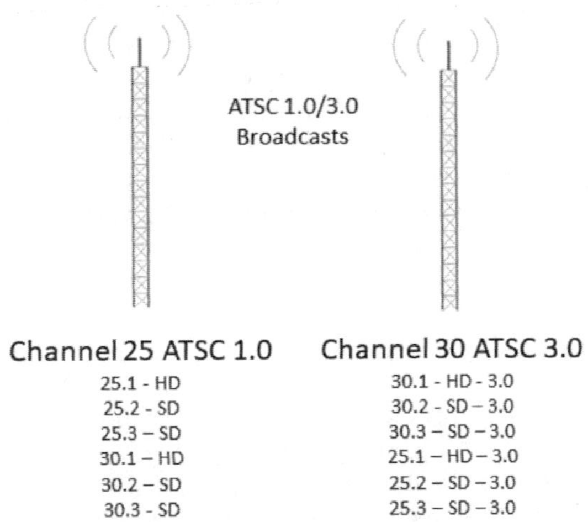


FIGURE 2.

## Population Overlap Determination

One of the simulcast coverage requirements is maintaining ATSC 1.0 coverage to 95% of the population of a station's initial ATSC 1.0 transmission facility. For this paper, the percentage of population overlap is determined by analyzing data created by general purpose studies from the FCC's TVStudy interference analysis software application [7]. This is the RF analytic software used by RF consultants to perform coverage and interference analyses for most television stations.

The application uses a geographic cell grid to determine coverage and interference. The application generates output data files that include information that indicates whether reception is possible for each cell that is inside the station's service contour. With TVStudy configured to use a global grid, a common cell grid is used for calculating all stations' coverage. This allows the output data files to be used to determine where stations have a receivable signal. Those data files also supply area, population and household data for each cell receiving coverage. From this, population overlap percentages can be calculated. If overlap from one or more stations is used to achieve the 95% threshold, the coverage results from each station pair (the planned ATSC 3.0 station and its ATSC 1.0 lighthouse) must be merged and the data consolidated to eliminate counting the same coverage cell area more than once.

## PBS Station Challenges

Although affiliated with the Public Broadcasting Service, PBS stations are independently licensed and operated. They are a mix of community licensed stations, university licensed stations, and stations with governmental licensees. Community licensed stations typically are standalone broadcasters. University and state licensed stations often have multiple transmission sites to serve a state or region. These stations usually broadcast the same program services on each of their stations. This could provide an opportunity for university and state licensed stations to transition to ATSC 3.0.

There are a number of business, legal, and technical hurdles to overcome to create a simulcasting agreement between broadcasters. This is especially true for university and governmental licensees with the statutory restrictions they are required to abide by for any agreement.

Because of the unique mission of public broadcasters to serve the under-served, this results in some stations serving areas not normally served by commercial broadcasters. As a result, simulcast partners that fulfill the requirements don't exist in many cases. In some markets, public broadcasters have joined commercial broadcasters in sharing agreements. However, in several markets, public broadcasters have not had the opportunity to be included in multi-station simulcast partner arrangements, leaving them with little, if any, transition options. There have also been a few markets where public broadcasters have been able to transition to ATSC 3.0 when they partnered with another public broadcaster or had sufficient signal overlap from a co-licensed station to fulfill the simulcast requirement.

## PBS Station Examples

We have examples of three public television stations with ATSC 3.0 transition challenges that we will explore. Each station has its own unique set of challenges. All three stations are part of a state network group. The stations are WUNE-TV, Linville, North Carolina operated by PBS North Carolina; KTIN, Fort Dodge, Iowa operated by Iowa PBS; and WUNU, Lumberton, North Carolina operated by PBS North Carolina.

## WUNE-TV Linville, North Carolina

WUNE-TV Linville, North Carolina is one of 12 full power stations operated by PBS North Carolina. The transmission site is in the mountainous area of northwestern North Carolina and is in the northern corner of the Charlotte television market.

WUNE-TV Linville, NC
1000 kW Directional

| Service Area | |
|---|---|
| Population | 3,146,865 |
| Households | 1,255,782 |
| Area | 14,279.1 sq miles |

| Coverage Area | |
|---|---|
| Population | 2,484,186 |
| Households | 979,361 |
| Area | 11,248.1 sq miles |

TABLE 1: WUNE-TV AREA SERVED.[1]

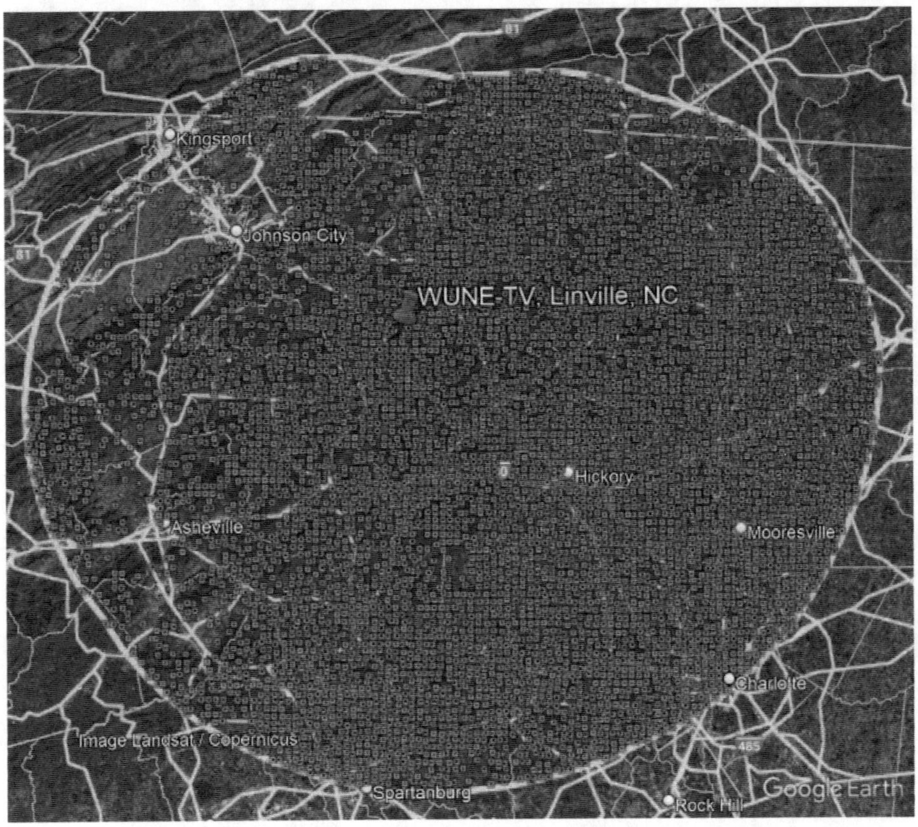


FIGURE 3: WUNE-TV SERVICE AND COVERAGE AREA MAP[2].

[1] WUNE-TV statistics were determined using TVStudy version 2.2.5 with default settings of 2km cell size (4 sq km) and a propagation profile resolution of 1 point per kilometer.
[2] Reception is based on a general purpose study created using TVStudy version 2.2.5 using the default settings of 2km cell size (4 sq km) with a propagation profile resolution of 1 point per kilometer.

The noise limited service contour, the green circle on the map in figure 3, does not mean a station has 100% coverage inside that circle. It simply represents the area where the station receives interference protection. The green blocks inside that circle represent areas where WUNE-TV can be received. In areas like the mountains of western North Carolina, coverage can be significantly reduced due to a number of factors, most notably terrain obstructions.

WUNE-TV was "repacked" as part of the FCC's spectrum incentive auction. A byproduct of that work was the ability to maximize the station's coverage. Also, equipment such as transmitters and antennas had to be replaced as part of the repack process. That resulted in making the potential technical transition to ATSC 3.0 for WUNE-TV a relatively simple task. The much larger task is how to fulfill the FCC's guidelines to allow the station to make that transition.

There are three other PBS member stations in the Charlotte television market. They are WUNE-TV's sister station WUNG-TV, Concord; South Carolina ETV's WNSC-TV, Rock Hill; and Central Piedmont Community College's WTVI, Charlotte. As shown in figure 4, none of these stations meet the community of license requirement for being a simulcast partner for WUNE-TV.

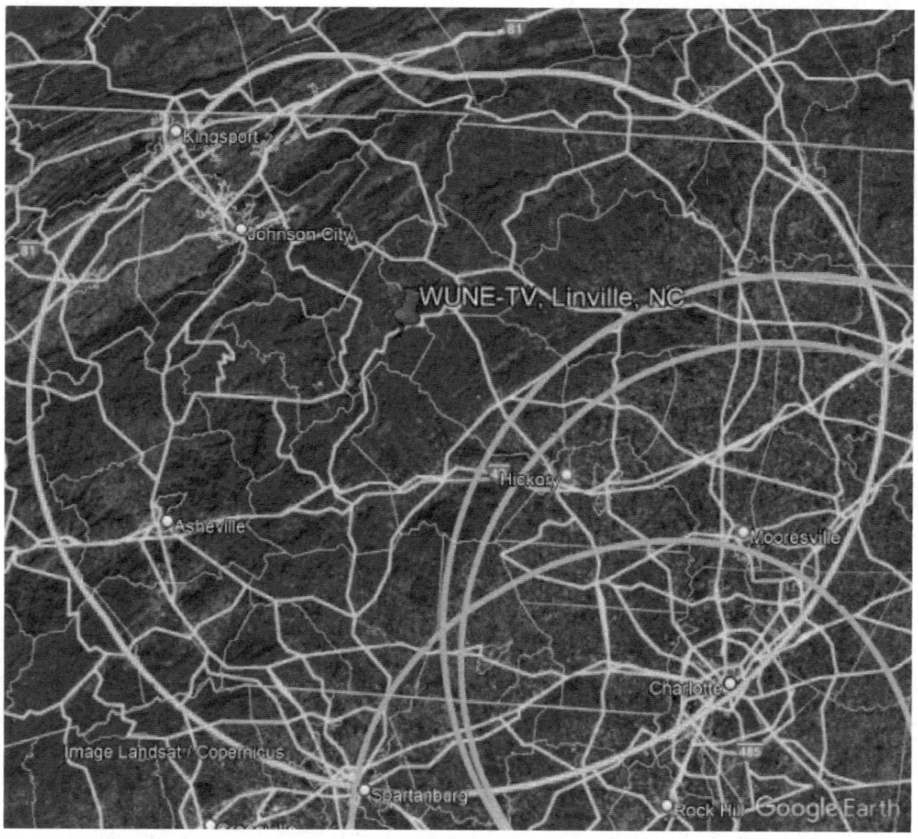


FIGURE 4: CHARLOTTE MARKET PBS MEMBER STATIONS.

There are four commercial stations in the Charlotte television market that appear to meet the community of license requirement for WUNE-TV. They are WBTV, Charlotte (CBS); WCNC-TV, Charlotte (NBC); WHKY-TV, Hickory (IND); and WJZY, Belmont (FOX).

Three of these stations, WBTV, WCNC-TV, and WJZY, are already involved in an ATSC 3.0 simulcast partnership in the Charlotte market. The fourth station, WHKY-TV, Hickory was not considered a viable simulcast partner. While WHKY-TV met the community of license requirement, it only duplicated 66.3%

of the population served by WUNE-TV. Also, with just WUNE-TV and WHKY-TV, there would be insufficient ATSC 1.0 bandwidth to accommodate a total of two high definition program services along with nine standard definition program services on one station.

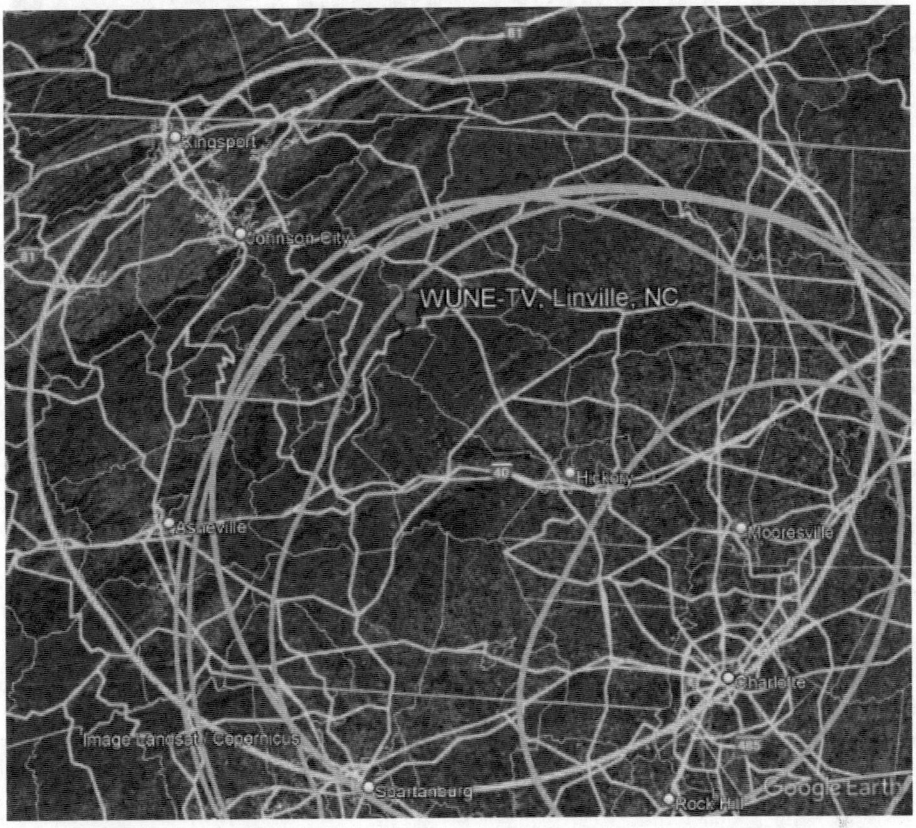


FIGURE 5: WUNE-TV POTENTIAL COMMERCIAL SIMULCAST PARTNERS.

Another potential option for reaching the 95% population duplication threshold is the other PBS North Carolina signals that overlap with the WUNE-TV service area. The PBS North Carolina stations carry the same four program services on all stations. The overlap of other PBS North Carolina stations includes four full power television stations and 11 TV translators.

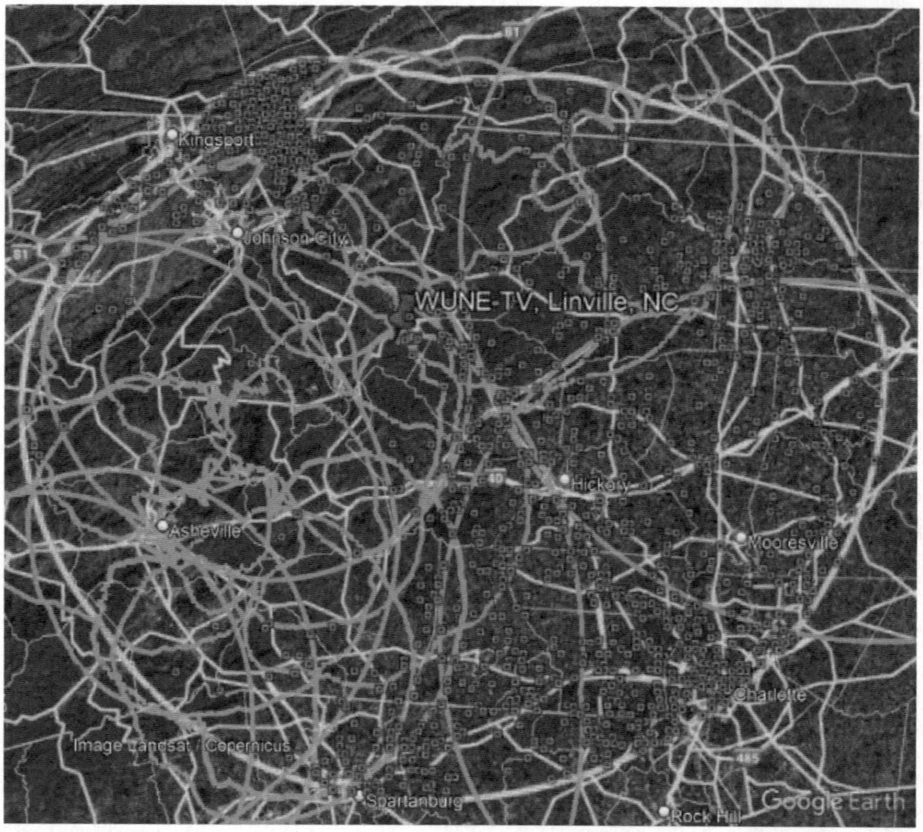


FIGURE 6: PBS NC STATIONS SERVICE CONTOUR OVERLAP WITH WUNE-TV AND WUNE-TV UNIQUE COVERAGE.

The 95% population duplication threshold is not a duplication of service area, but a duplication of population that theoretically can receive the same programming from another signal. In areas like the mountains of western North Carolina, coverage can be significantly reduced due to terrain obstructions.

For WUNE-TV, the population common with the other PBS NC stations is about 1,841,379 (74.1%) or about 724,382 (74.0%) households. For the remaining 642,807 people (25.9%) WUNE-TV is the only PBS North Carolina station serving that area. That would leave those viewers without a PBS North Carolina ATSC 1.0 signal. If PBS North Carolina were to flash cut WUNE-TV, they would need to address the loss of reception at about 254,979 households (26.0%).[3]

## KTIN Fort Dodge, Iowa

KTIN Fort Dodge, Iowa is one of nine full power stations operated by Iowa PBS. The transmission site is in north-central Iowa and is in the northern portion of the Des Moines television market.

[3] WUNE-TV statistics were determined using TVStudy version 2.2.5. with default settings of 2km cell size (4 sq km) with a propagation profile resolution of 1 point per kilometer were used.

KTIN Fort Dodge, Iowa
600 kW Directional

| Service Area | |
|---|---|
| Population | 281,280 |
| Households | 118,800 |
| Area | 10,754.5 sq miles |

| Coverage Area | |
|---|---|
| Population | 278,253 |
| Households | 117,462 |
| Area | 10,657.0 sq miles |

TABLE 2: KTIN AREA SERVED.[4]

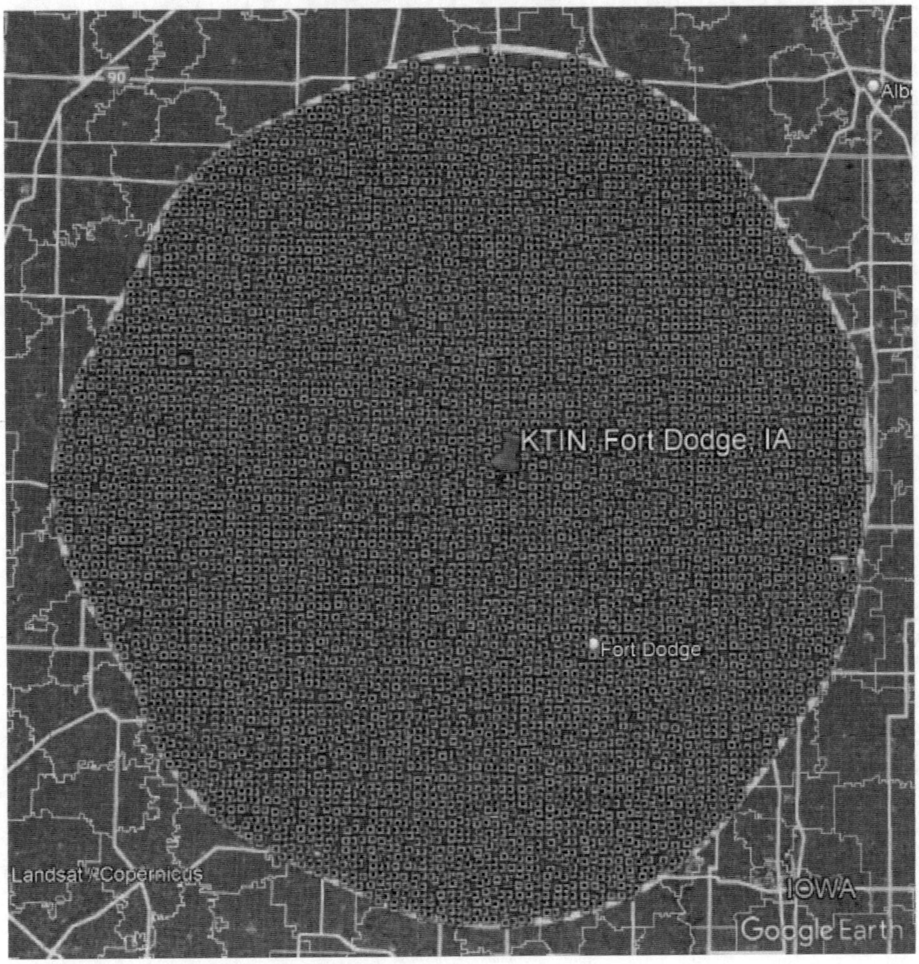


FIGURE 7: KTIN SERVICE AND COVERAGE AREA MAP.[5]

KTIN was not "repacked" as part of the FCC's spectrum incentive auction. As a result, for KTIN to begin broadcasting in ATSC 3.0 will require not just the task of how to fulfill the FCC's transition guidelines,

[4] KTIN statistics were determined using TVStudy version 2.2.5 with default settings of 2km cell size (4 sq km) and a propagation profile resolution of 1 point per kilometer.
[5] Reception is based on a general purpose study created using TVStudy version 2.2.5 using the default settings of 2km cell size (4 sq km) with a propagation profile resolution of 1 point per kilometer.

the station will need to address the various transmitter and antenna system needs that are required to convert the facility to ATSC 3.0 operations.

The Des Moines television market is reportedly scheduled to transition to ATSC 3.0 operations in the spring of 2023. KTIN is not being included in the planned ATSC 3.0 operations.

As shown in Figure 8, there are eight (8) full power stations in the Des Moines television market that meet the community of license requirement for being a simulcast partner with KTIN. They include KTIN's sister station KDIN-TV, Des Moines. The other seven (7) stations are KCCI, Des Moines (CBS); KCWI-TV, Ames (CW); KDMI, Des Moines (TCT); KDSM-TV, Des Moines (FOX); KFPX-TV, Newton (ION); WHO-DT, Des Moines (NBC); and WOI-DT, Ames (ABC). KTIN's most likely simulcast partner is its sister station KDIN-TV.

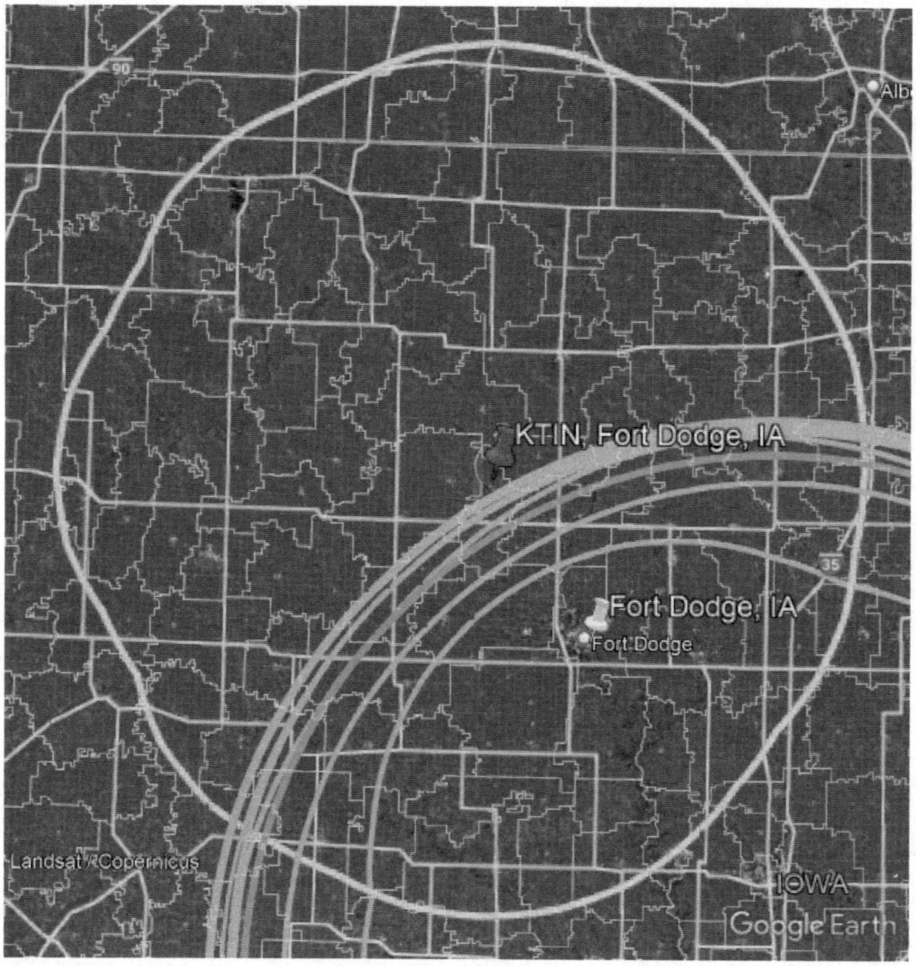


FIGURE 8: KTIN POTENTIAL SIMULCAST PARTNERS.

Iowa PBS also has three other full power stations and one translator that have overlapping coverage with KTIN. See Figure 9.

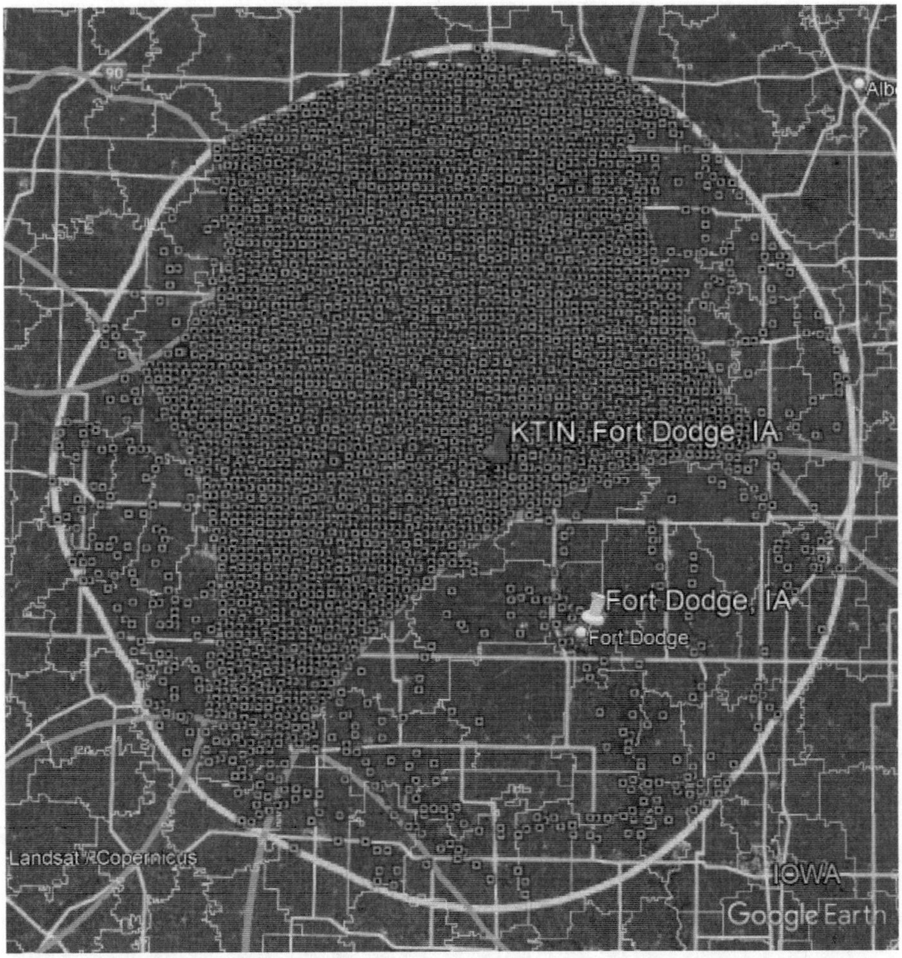


FIGURE 9: IOWA PBS STATIONS SERVICE CONTOUR OVERLAP WITH KTIN AND KTIN UNIQUE COVERAGE.

In the case of KTIN the population common with the other Iowa PBS stations, including KDIN-TV, is about 145,359 (52.2%) or about 59,930 (51.0%) households. For the remaining 132,894 people (47.8%), KTIN is the only full power station serving that area. If Iowa PBS were to flash cut KTIN, they would need to address the loss of reception at about 57,532 households (49.0%).[6]

## WUNU Lumberton North Carolina

WUNU Lumberton, North Carolina is one of 12 full power stations operated by PBS North Carolina. The transmission site is in southeastern North Carolina and is in the northern most portion of the Myrtle Beach-Florence television market.

[6] KTIN statistics were determined by using TVStudy version 2.2.5 with default settings of 2km cell size (4 sq km) and a propagation profile resolution of 1 point per kilometer.

WUNU Lumberton, NC
329 kW Non-Directional

| Service Area | |
|---|---|
| Population | 1,202,495 |
| Households | 456,995 |
| Area | 9,875.0 sq miles |

| Coverage Area | |
|---|---|
| Population | 1,163,925 |
| Households | 441,877 |
| Area | 9,198.6 sq miles |

TABLE 3: WUNU AREA SERVED.[7]

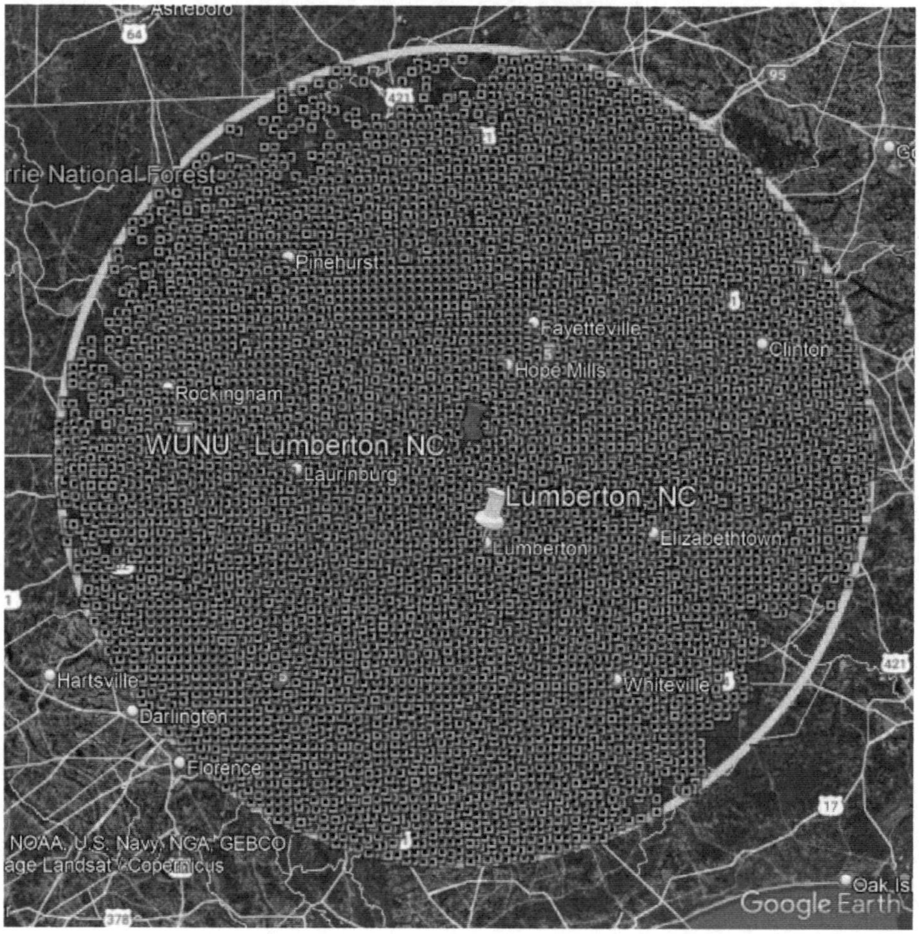


FIGURE 10: WUNU SERVICE AND COVERAGE AREA MAP.[8]

WUNU was "repacked" as part of the FCC's spectrum incentive auction. A byproduct of that work was the ability to maximize the station's coverage. Also, equipment such as transmitters and antennas had to be replaced as part of the repack process. That resulted in making the potential technical transition

[7] WUNU statistics were determined using TVStudy version 2.2.5 with default settings of 2km cell size (4 sq km) and a propagation profile resolution of 1 point per kilometer.
[8] Reception is based on a general purpose study created using TVStudy version 2.2.5 using the default settings of 2km cell size (4 sq km) with a propagation profile resolution of 1 point per kilometer.

to ATSC 3.0 for WUNU a relatively simple task. The much larger task is how to fulfill the FCC's guidelines to allow the station to make that transition.

As shown in Figure 11, there are two other PBS member stations in the Myrtle Beach-Florence television market. They are South Carolina ETV's WHMC, Conway and WJPM-TV, Florence, both in South Carolina. Neither of these stations meet the community of license requirement for being a simulcast partner for WUNU. WHMC's noise limited service contour covers part of WUNU's community of license, Lumberton, NC, but it fails to cover the entire community which is required to meet that requirement.

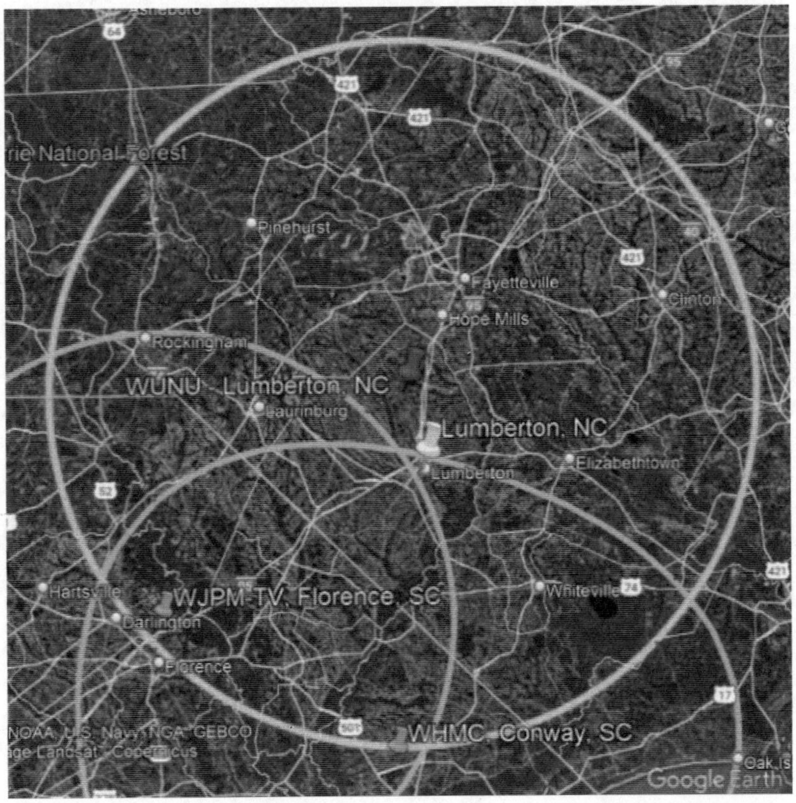


FIGURE 11: MYRTLE BEACH-FLORENCE MARKET PBS MEMBER STATIONS.

Figure 12 shows that PBS North Carolina has four (4) other full power stations with service areas that overlap with the WUNU coverage area. That common coverage area includes a population of 854,993 (73.5%) living in 324,797 households (73.5%). Even with the significant signal overlap of PBS North Carolina signals, if PBS North Carolina were to flash cut WUNU, it would leave a population of 308,932 (26.5%) living in 117,080 (26.5%) households without the ability to receive a PBS North Carolina ATSC 1.0 over-the-air signal.[9]

[9] WUNU statistics were determined using TVStudy version 2.2.5 with default settings of 2km cell size (4 sq km) and a propagation profile resolution of 1 point per kilometer.

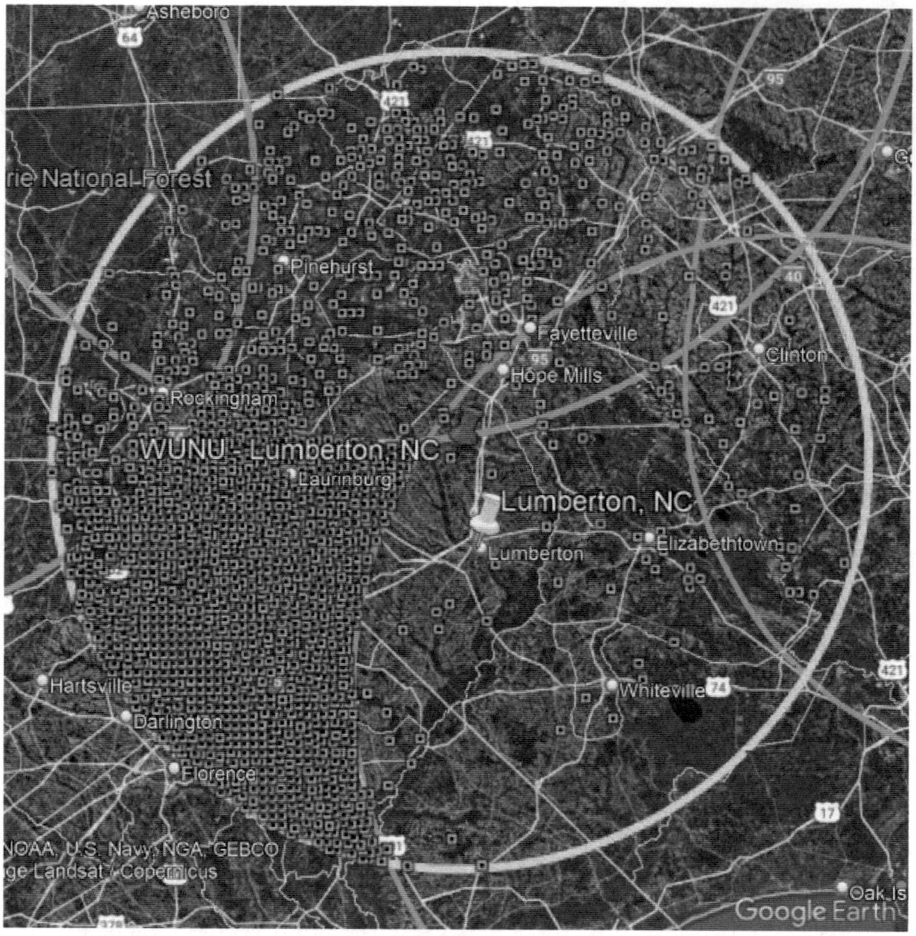


FIGURE 12: PBS NC STATIONS SERVICE CONTOUR OVERLAP WITH WUNU AND WUNU UNIQUE COVERAGE.

Another option to achieve the 95% population duplication threshold would be the use of a simulcast partner. As shown in Figure 13, there are four full power commercial stations in the Myrtle Beach-Florence television market that meet the community of license requirement for WUNU. They are WBTW, Florence (CBS); WFXB, Myrtle Beach (FOX); WPDE-TV, Florence (ABC); and WWMB, Florence (DABL). There is also a Class A television station, WTNG-CD, Rockfish, North Carolina. This station is not considered a viable simulcast partner due to the bandwidth requirements necessary to accommodate its 15 program services.

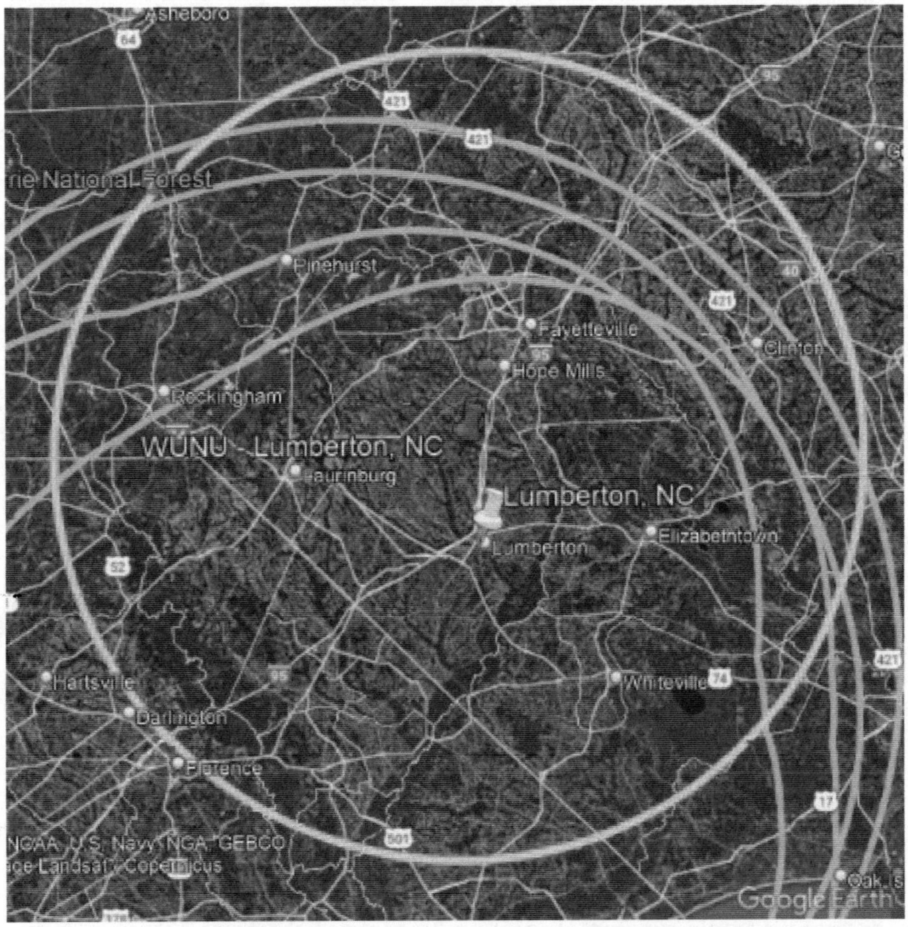


FIGURE 13: WUNU POTENTIAL COMMERCIAL SIMULCAST PARTNERS.

The analysis of the overlap of the four (4) stations indicates that none of the stations meets the 95% population duplication threshold.[10] The WUNU population duplication for each station is:

| Station | Population Duplicated | % of WUNU Coverage |
|---|---|---|
| WBTW | 818,681 | 70.3% |
| WFXB | 661,851 | 56.9% |
| WPDE-TV | 825,983 | 71.0% |
| WWMB | 715,214 | 61.4% |

TABLE 4: WUNU POTENTIAL COMMERCIAL SIMULCAST PARTNERS COVERAGE DUPLICATION.

The analysis was expanded to combine the 73.5% overlap from the four PBS North Carolina stations with each of the potential simulcast partner stations. That combination still failed to meet the 95% population duplication threshold.

[10] The stations' population duplication was determined by using TVStudy version 2.2.5 with default settings of 2km cell size (4 sq km) and a propagation profile resolution of 1 point per kilometer.

| Station | Population Duplicated | % of WUNU Coverage |
|---|---|---|
| WBTW + PBS NC Net | 1,052.613 | 90.4% |
| WFXB + PBS NC Net | 1,027,754 | 88.3% |
| WPDE-TV + PBS NC Net | 1,050,844 | 90.3% |
| WWMB + PBS NC Net | 1,038,014 | 89.2% |

TABLE 5: WUNU COVERAGE DUPLICATION FROM POTENTIAL COMMERCIAL SIMULCAST PARTNERS AND PBS NC STATIONS.

## Other Options

With none of the stations in the three scenarios meeting the 95% population duplication requirement, what other options do these stations have?

### Alternate TVStudy Parameters

One potential option is to investigate alternate study parameters within the FCC's TVStudy application. The FCC's TVStudy application performs Longley-Rice signal analysis by overlaying a grid on a station's service area and then analyzing the station's signal within each cell of that grid. The path profile for calculating path loss can be altered by adjusting the propagation profile resolution. This is defining the number of terrain sample points per kilometer. The TVStudy analysis to determine whether a station is receivable within a cell takes into account interference from other stations as well as path loss. TVStudy's default configuration of a cell 2 kilometers per side or 4 square kilometers, and a propagation profile resolution of 1 sample point per kilometer was used for the initial data presented earlier in this paper.

The FCC has previously accepted application exhibits using TVStudy analyses that used geographic cell sizes and propagation sample profiles other than the default. Typically, exhibits containing analyses using cell sizes ranging from 0.25 square kilometers up to 4 square kilometers have been accepted. The application will also support propagation profile resolutions from 1 to 50 points per kilometer.

We examined what impact utilizing alternate geographic cell sizes and propagation sample profiles can have on the theoretical population duplication. In doing so, would it be possible for a station to meet the 95% population duplication requirement? We looked at cell sizes of 0.25, 1, and 4 square kilometers. We also looked at propagation profile resolutions of 1, 10, 30, and 50 points per kilometer for each cell size.

### WUNE-TV Scenario

For WUNE-TV using the default analysis parameters of 4 square kilometers and a propagation profile resolution of 1 point per kilometer, a 74.1% population duplication from the other PBS North Carolina stations was calculated. When the cell size is changed to 0.25 square kilometers with a propagation profile resolution of 50 points per kilometer, the population duplication increases to 84.5%. See Table 6 for the results of the various cases studied for WUNE-TV.

| Cell Size (sq km) | Propagation Resolution (points per km) | Population % | Households % | Area % |
|---|---|---|---|---|
| 0.25 | 1 | 77.7% | 77.5% | 87.9% |
| | 10 | 84.2% | 84.0% | 91.3% |
| | 30 | 84.1% | 84.0% | 91.5% |
| | 50 | 84.5% | 84.4% | 91.5% |
| 1.0 | 1 | 83.1% | 83.0% | 88.2% |
| | 10 | 84.3% | 84.1% | 91.7% |
| | 30 | 84.2% | 83.9% | 91.8% |
| | 50 | 84.2% | 83.9% | 91.9% |
| 4.0 | 1 | 74.1% | 74.0% | 85.8% |
| | 10 | 83.2% | 82.9% | 91.3% |
| | 30 | 83.4% | 83.1% | 91.6% |
| | 50 | 83.9% | 83.8% | 91.7% |

TABLE 6: WUNE-TV-PBS NC STATIONS DUPLICATION USING VARIOUS TVSTUDY SCENARIOS.

### KTIN Scenario

For KTIN using the default analysis parameters of 4 square kilometers and a propagation profile resolution of 1 point per kilometer, a 52.2% population duplication from the other Iowa PBS stations was calculated. When the cell size is changed to 0.25 square kilometers with a propagation profile resolution of 10 points per kilometer, the population duplication increases to 56.1%. See Table 7 for the results of the various cases studied for KTIN.

| Cell Size (sq km) | Propagation Resolution (points per km) | Population % | Households % | Area % |
|---|---|---|---|---|
| 0.25 | 1 | 51.7% | 50.6% | 46.0% |
| | 10 | 56.1% | 54.9% | 47.5% |
| | 30 | 56.0% | 54.9% | 48.0% |
| | 50 | 55.8% | 54.9% | 48.0% |
| 1.0 | 1 | 52.0% | 50.8% | 45.9% |
| | 10 | 55.1% | 54.0% | 48.0% |
| | 30 | 55.5% | 54.3% | 48.0% |
| | 50 | 55.2% | 54.0% | 47.8% |
| 4.0 | 1 | 52.2% | 51.0% | 46.4% |
| | 10 | 51.8% | 50.9% | 47.8% |
| | 30 | 54.7% | 53.3% | 47.4% |
| | 50 | 54.1% | 52.7% | 47.8% |

TABLE 7: KTIN-IOWA PBS STATIONS DUPLICATION USING VARIOUS TVSTUDY SCENARIOS.

### WUNU Scenario

For WUNU using the default analysis parameters of 4 square kilometers and a propagation profile resolution of 1 point per kilometer, a 73.5% population duplication from the other PBS North Carolina stations was calculated. With the same cell size of 4 square kilometers but the propagation profile resolution changed to 30 points per kilometer, the population duplication increases to 82.1%. See table 8 for the results of the various cases studied for WUNU.

| Cell Size (sq km) | Propagation Resolution (points per km) | Population % | Households % | Area % |
|---|---|---|---|---|
| 0.25 | 1 | 71.3% | 71.5% | 70.6% |
| | 10 | 78.9% | 79.5% | 74.9% |
| | 30 | 79.5% | 79.9% | 75.3% |
| | 50 | 79.5% | 79.8% | 75.4% |
| 1.0 | 1 | 71.1% | 71.2% | 70.6% |
| | 10 | 79.0% | 79.7% | 75.0% |
| | 30 | 79.5% | 80.0% | 75.3% |
| | 50 | 79.6% | 80.0% | 75.4% |
| 4.0 | 1 | 73.5% | 73.5% | 70.7% |
| | 10 | 80.0% | 80.4% | 75.2% |
| | 30 | 82.1% | 82.5% | 75.9% |
| | 50 | 82.0% | 82.3% | 75.8% |

TABLE 8: WUNU-PBS NC STATIONS DUPLICATION USING VARIOUS TVSTUDY SCENARIOS.

The duplication of WUNU's potential simulcast partners were re-evaluated using the 4 square kilometer cell size and a propagation profile resolution of 30 points per kilometer. Again all 4 stations failed to achieve the 95% population duplication threshold.

| Station | Population Duplicated | % of WUNU Coverage |
|---|---|---|
| WBTW | 896,322 | 76.8% |
| WFXB | 711,860 | 61.0% |
| WPDE-TV | 903,699 | 77.5% |
| WWMB | 806,494 | 69.1% |

TABLE 9: WUNU POTENTIAL COMMERCIAL SIMULCAST PARTNERS COVERAGE DUPLICATION.

The simulcast partner analysis was again expanded to include the four PBS North Carolina stations in the population duplication calculations. The combination of any one potential simulcast partner station with the four PBS North Carolina stations meets the 95% population duplication threshold.

| Station | Population Duplicated | % of WUNU Coverage |
|---|---|---|
| WBTW + PBS NC Net | 1,122,753 | 96.3% |
| WFXB + PBS NC Net | 1,127,241 | 96.6% |
| WPDE-TV + PBS NC Net | 1,141,045 | 97.8% |
| WWMB + PBS NC Net | 1,133,355 | 97.2% |

TABLE 5: WUNU COVERAGE DUPLICATION FROM POTENTIAL COMMERCIAL SIMULCAST PARTNERS AND PBS NC STATIONS.

However, further investigation of the potential simulcast partners revealed a potential problem. Each of the four stations being an ATSC 1.0 simulcast partner would create significant coverage expansion for WUNU. The increases in population and coverage areas for PBS North Carolina are shown in Figures 14A through 14D for each station:

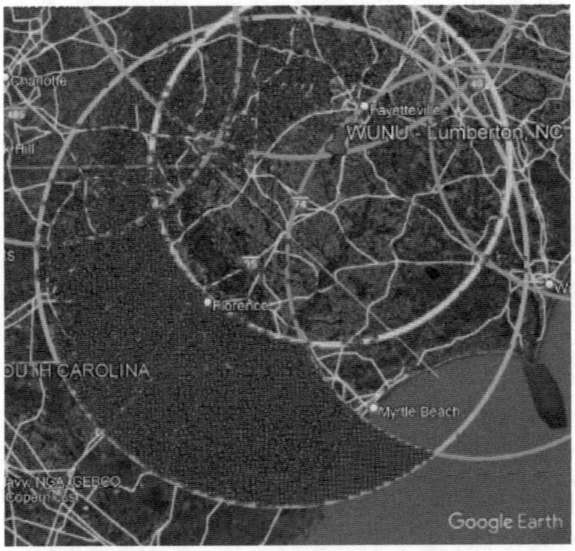


FIGURE 14A: WBTW COVERAGE EXPANSION – 683,412.

FIGURE 14B: WFXB COVERAGE EXPANSION – 428,216.

FIGURE 14C: WPDE-TV COVERAGE EXPANSION – 552,007.

FIGURE 14D: WWMB COVERAGE EXPANSION – 457,426.

This coverage expansion could pose a broadcast rights problem due to the significant increase in coverage area. Further investigation would be required to determine the significance of this problem.

## Other PBS Member Station Partners

We examined what impact including the coverage of neighboring PBS member stations would have on the ability to still receive an ATSC 1.0 signal. During the digital television transition in 2003 WNVT-DT was granted permission by the FCC to become the first digital only full power television station [8]. In their application request they cited the possibility of providing receive devices for the new digital signal. They also believed that the impact of their transition would be minimized since it would not create a white space where PBS programming would not be available to analog viewers.

### WUNE-TV

There are two other PBS member stations in the Charlotte television market. They are South Carolina ETV's WNSC-TV Rock Hill, South Carolina and Central Piedmont Community College's WTVI Charlotte. Adding these two stations to the coverage of the other PBS North Carolina stations, increases the WUNE-TV population percentage to 93.3%.[11] This combination is still short of the FCC mandated 95% threshold.

There are also three (3) out-of-market PBS member stations that also have coverage overlap with WUNE-TV. They are Blue Ridge PBS's WBRA-TV Roanoke, Virginia and East Tennessee PBS's two stations, WETP-TV Sneedville and WKOP-TV Knoxville, both in Tennessee. Adding these other three stations increases the WUNE-TV population percentage to 97.4%,[12] possibly meeting the 95% requirement.

### KTIN

While there are several other PBS member stations near the coverage area of KTIN such as Twin Cities PBS, South Dakota Public Broadcasting, and KSMQ-TV, none of the stations have coverage that overlaps with KTIN. As a result, KTIN's population coverage duplication remained unchanged at 56.1%.[13]

### WUNU

There are two other PBS member stations in the Myrtle Beach-Florence television market. They are South Carolina ETV's WHMC, Conway and WJPM-TV, Florence, both in South Carolina. Adding the two South Carolina ETV stations to the coverage of the other PBS North Carolina stations increases the WUNU population percentage to 96.2%,[14] possibly meeting the 95% requirement.

This strategy is not mentioned in the FCC ATSC 3.0 transition guidelines. Stations are **strongly urged** to contact their legal counsel to discuss whether this is a potential strategy for you.

## Conclusions

In the three station scenarios studied, none of the stations met the simulcast partner requirements for transitioning to ATSC 3.0. A Flash Cut is the only option for these stations. With the voluntary adoption of ATSC 3.0 and the current FCC guidelines that must be met to transition to ATSC 3.0, many Public Broadcasters will have significant challenges to overcome to make that conversion. Examples of those challenges were presented here. A number of receiver manufacturers have products in development that will eventually be available to the general public. Once these products are readily available, more viable ATSC 3.0 transition options will become available for broadcasters. The key is for the FCC to provide flexibility in its ATSC 3.0 transition guidelines that will allow more stations to transition.

---

[11] The WUNE-TV duplication percentage was determined using TVStudy version 2.2.5 with settings of 0.5km cell size (0.25 sq km) and a propagation profile resolution of 50 points per kilometer.

[12] The WUNE-TV duplication percentage was determined using TVStudy version 2.2.5 with settings of 0.5km cell size (0.25 sq km) with a propagation profile resolution of 50 points per kilometer.

[13] The KTIN duplication percentage was determined using TVStudy version 2.2.5. with settings of 0.5km cell size (0.25 sq km) with a propagation profile resolution of 10 point per kilometer.

[14] The WUNU duplication percentage was determined using TVStudy version 2.2.5. TVStudy settings of 2km cell size (4 sq km) with a propagation profile resolution of 30 points per kilometer.

In preparing this paper we discovered that utilizing TVStudy data along with simple database analytics made determining population, household, and areas of reception duplication an achievable task. We also determined that the TVStudy default settings did not provide the most optimistic results for showing common coverage areas between stations. We also found that there is no "one fits all" set of alternate study parameters for TVStudy that provides the most optimistic results.

For WUNE-TV we found that a full power station with maximized coverage in a mountainous area is difficult to duplicate coverage when the stations aren't co-located. We determined reaching the 95% population duplication level with simulcast programming wasn't possible. However, we were able to demonstrate that a flash cut of WUNE-TV to ATSC 3.0, 97.4% of the station's viewers would still be able to receive an ATSC 1.0 signal containing PBS programming.

The KTIN scenario is an example of public television stations serving the under-served. Over 40% of the population that receives a signal from KTIN can't receive another television station, both public and commercial stations. Flash cutting KTIN will require a significant number of ATSC 3.0 receive devices in viewers homes to prevent viewers from losing all over-the-air television service.

The WUNU scenario shows a problem resulting from the use of a simulcast partner that has a significantly different coverage area from its partner station. For WUNU, while none of the simulcast partners on their own met the FCC's 95% population duplication requirement, factoring in the duplication of the surrounding PBS North Carolina stations pushed that total over the 95% threshold. However, it was also discovered that PBS North Carolina would increase its population served by over 420,000 people with the inclusion of the simulcast partner's coverage area. PBS North Carolina currently does not have broadcast program rights for its content in this expanded coverage area. In order to move forward with one of these simulcast partners will require determining whether the broadcast rights to the program content can be obtained for that area and at what cost.

We discovered a different approach that could be taken that avoids the program rights problem. We were able to demonstrate that a flash cut of WUNU to ATSC 3.0, 96.2% of the station's viewers would still be able to receive an ATSC 1.0 signal containing PBS programming.

As a reminder, the percentages of duplicated coverages presented here are all theoretical. Even with 100% theoretical overlap, a station in practical terms will have some viewers that will lose reception. The primary cause will be reduced signal level. An example would be a location where an indoor antenna was being used because it was sufficient to receive a good quality signal. However, the simulcast partner's signal is weaker at that location, requiring a higher gain antenna in order to maintain good quality reception. The viewer might need an outdoor antenna to again receive that good quality signal. If that viewer lives in a location like an apartment building where an outdoor antenna isn't a possibility, what do they / you do so the viewer can once again receive the programming? A station needs to be prepared to address this and similar reception challenges.

While the FCC is currently justified in their concern of viewers being deprived of over-the-air television with stations flash cutting to ATSC 3.0, they also need to provide stations flexibility to promote the transition to ATSC 3.0. Not doing so would not only delay the transition process, it would also deprive individuals access to the various services that a station transmitting an ATSC 3.0 signal can provide. Services that were only contemplated a few months ago are now becoming reality. Not allowing stations to transition to ATSC 3.0 deprives individuals access to these helpful, informative, and potentially lifesaving services. There are many benefits that public broadcasters will be able to offer viewers utilizing ATSC 3.0. The question is whether they will be given the opportunity to provide them by transitioning to ATSC 3.0.

## References


[1] "ATSC Invites Next-Gen Broadcasting Proposals," Advanced Television, March 28,2013.

[2] Federal Communications Commission, "Authorizing Permissive Use of the "Next Generation" Broadcast Television Standard, Report and Order and Further Notice of Proposed Rulemaking," GN Docket No. 16-142, FCC 17-158, November 16, 2017.

[3] Federal Communications Commission, "Authorizing Permissive Use of the "Next Generation" Broadcast Television Standard, Report and Order and Order on Reconsideration," GN Docket No. 16-142, FCC 20-72, June 3, 2020.

[4] Federal Communications Commission, "Authorizing Permissive Use of the "Next Generation" Broadcast Television Standard, Third Further Notice of Proposed Rulemaking," GN Docket No. 16-142, FCC 22-47, June 21, 2022.

[5] Engel, Fred, "The Educational Broadcast Gap; A White Paper on Utilizing ATSC 3.0/NextGenTV to Address Remote Learning Needs."

[6] Kurz, Phil, "ATSC 3.0 Set To Roll As Road To Use In Vehicles Becomes Clearer," TVTech, June 10, 2022.

[7] Federal Communications Commission, "TVStudy Interference Analysis Software," version 2.2.5, March 13, 2018.

[8] Federal Communications Commission, Letter to Commonwealth Public Broadcasting Corporation, DA 03-2845, September 3, 2003.

# ATSC 3.0 Hybrid Delivery and Virtual Channels

**Peter Gogas**
**Gray Television**
**Bryan, Tex., United States**
peter.gogas@gray.tv

**Abstract** – This paper introduces the concept of virtual channels and how hybrid delivery can be used to provide additional services to broadband connected consumer receivers when available OTA bandwidth is limited. It also discusses the backend infrastructure, used during testing and development, to distribute the virtual channels. Finally, it proposes the use of virtual channels to launch new services in markets that have transitioned to ATSC 3.0 where over-the-air bandwidth may be limited due to channel-sharing.

## Introduction

While ATSC 1.0 included the ability to transport IP multicast data in the A/92 [1] standard, this capability was not a core feature and was rarely deployed. When designing ATSC 3.0, the development committee early on decided to base the transport layer on the Internet Protocol (IP) and make it a core feature of the new suite of standards. The use of IP allows for some features including the hybrid delivery of content via the over-the-air (OTA) signal and broadband. Hybrid delivery is a core feature of ATSC 3.0 and is defined in A/331 [2]. Hybrid delivery can not only be used to augment over-the-air services with broadband content such as Scalable High efficiency Video Coding (SHVC) overlays or additional audio tracks, but to also deliver virtual channels.

Virtual channels are a type of hybrid delivery where the signaling for a service is sent in the OTA transmission, but the audio/video content is delivered via a broadband connection. Since only the service signaling is sent in the OTA transmission, relatively little bandwidth is needed by the signaling to add virtual channels.

While hybrid delivery and virtual channels are possible with the MPEG Media Transport Protocol (MMTP), this paper focuses solely on ROUTE and DASH.

## Advantages

One of the main advantages of virtual channels is that they can allow broadcasters that cannot otherwise participate in the channel-sharing market transition approach due to bandwidth limitations to still provide their signal to ATSC 3.0 viewers. As broadcasters start to look at smaller markets as the rollout of ATSC 3.0 continues, it is becoming increasingly difficult to find enough spectrum bandwidth to provide an ATSC 3.0 transmission and maintain the required ATSC 1.0 simulcasts due to the fewer number of stations in these markets.

Virtual channels allow broadcasters to launch new ATSC 3.0 channels even when there is limited OTA bandwidth available. These services include the many diginets available on ATSC 1.0 subchannels as well as occasional use and ad-hoc channels.

Unlike traditional Over-The-Top (OTT) streaming channels, virtual channels can take advantage of advanced ATSC 3.0 features such as interactive broadcaster applications just like OTA delivered services.

Finally, since virtual channels are signaled in the OTA broadcast, they appear in the electronic program guide alongside the broadcasters OTA delivered services. This makes it easier for viewers to find and view virtual channels. In fact, except for a slight delay when first tuning in, many viewers will be unaware that the channel they are watching is being mainly delivered via broadband.

## Disadvantages

While virtual channels have many advantages, they also have several disadvantages. Unlike OTA delivered services that have a known, fixed costs, virtual channels have a variable CDN delivery cost based upon the number of viewers watching the service. If there are no viewers, there is a minimal cost to deliver a virtual channel. However, if there is a large influx of viewers the cost to deliver the virtual channel could be significant. One way to help offset the delivery cost of virtual channels is by utilizing dynamic ad insertion. Since virtual channels requires the ATSC 3.0 receiver to be connected to the Internet, this also means that there is an Internet connection available for delivery of ads for dynamic ad insertion.

Another major disadvantage for virtual channels, at least at the time this paper is being published, is that not all ATSC 3.0 receivers can properly receive virtual channels. While work with consumer equipment manufacturers to support virtual channels is ongoing, deployment by broadcasters of virtual channels may be required in order to see further adoption in ATSC 3.0 televisions and receivers.

## System Architecture

Figure 1 shows the signal flow for the delivery of a typical OTA-only ATSC 3.0 service. The video encoder takes the incoming audio/video signal and encodes it into HEVC with AC-4 audio. The encoded audio/video is then sent to the DASH packager which segments the audio/video and generates the manifest. The manifest and DASH segments are then sent to the ROUTE encoder for encapsulation and onward delivery to the scheduler and broadcast gateway.

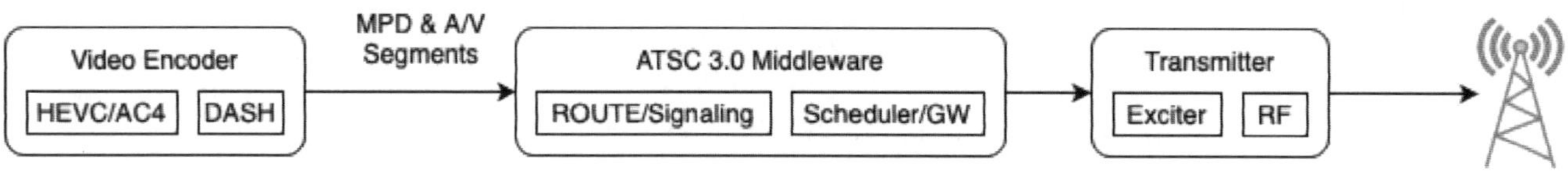


FIGURE 1: ATSC 3.0 OTA-ONLY SIGNAL FLOW.

### Delivery of Virtual Channels

Delivery of a virtual channel differs from an OTA-only service in that there are both OTA and broadband delivered components. Figure 2 illustrates the OTA and broadband paths for the manifest and audio/video segments. Just like an OTA-only service, the audio/video is first encoded into HEVC with AC-4 audio by the video encoder. The HEVC/AC-4 encoded audio/video is sent to the DASH packager for segmentation and manifest generation. The DASH packager then sends the manifest to the ROUTE encoder/signaling generator for onward delivery to the receiver via the OTA transmission.

In addition to sending the manifest to the ROUTE encoder/signaling generator, the DASH packager also sends the audio/video segments to an origin server which is a server or service that hosts the original copy of the audio/video segments and serves as the source for the content delivery network (CDN). The CDN is used to distribute the audio/video segments to the ATSC 3.0 receivers via broadband.

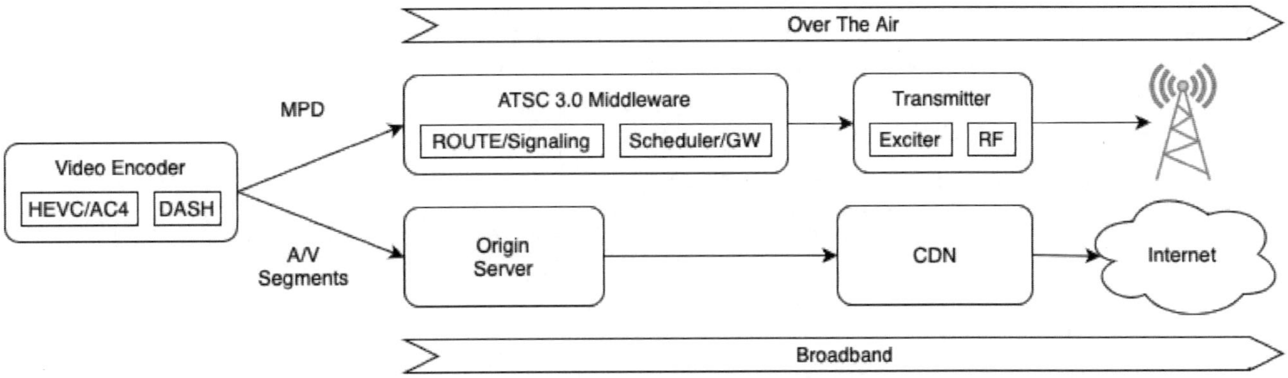


FIGURE 2: ATSC 3.0 VIRTUAL CHANNEL SIGNAL FLOW.

## Reception of Virtual Channels

In order to receive a virtual channel, the ATSC 3.0 receiver must be capable of not only receiving the manifest via ROUTE from the OTA transmission, but it must also be able to request and cache the audio/video segments from the CDN using HTTP.

Figure 3 shows a high-level overview of the signal flow of a virtual channel in an ATSC 3.0 receiver. The receiver receives the manifest from the OTA signal and the audio/video segments from the broadband Internet connection. The manifest and audio/video segments are combined and cached in an internal proxy where they can be retrieved by the DASH player as needed.

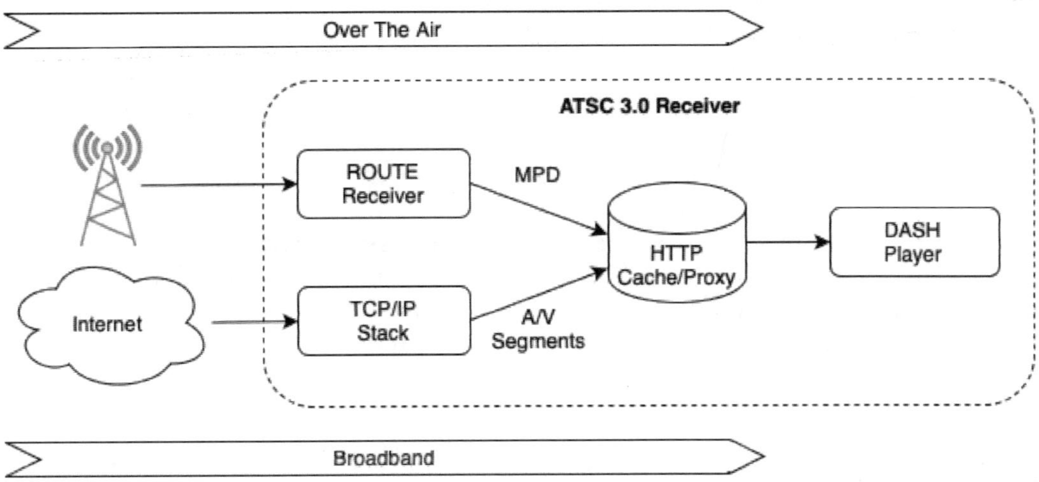


FIGURE 3: ATSC 3.0 VIRTUAL CHANNEL RECEPTION SIGNAL FLOW.

It is important that the CDN is properly configured with a valid Fully Qualified Domain Name (FQDN) and valid SSL certificate. Most receivers that have implemented virtual channels will not request data from insecure webservers.

## Signaling

A/331 [2] defines the signaling tables used for ATSC 3.0 transmissions. The main tables involved with virtual channels are the Service List Table (SLT) and the Service Level Signaling (SLS).

### Service List Table (SLT)

The Service List Table (SLT) is part of the Low Level Signaling (LLS) and provides a list of services contained in the ATSC 3.0 transmission including major/minor channel numbers, global service IDs, service short names, and multicast IP information on the ROUTE session for the service.


```
<?xml version="1.0" encoding="UTF-8"?>
<SLT bsid="10282"
  xmlns="tag:atsc.org,2016:XMLSchemas/ATSC3/Delivery/SLT/1.0/"
  xmlns:xsi="http://www.w3.org/2001/XMLSchema-instance"
xsi:schemaLocation="tag:atsc.org,2016:XMLSchemas/ATSC3/Delivery/SLT/1.0/ SLT-1.0-20211209.xsd">
  <Service serviceCategory="4" serviceId="5001" shortServiceName="ESG" sltSvcSeqNum="0">
    <BroadcastSvcSignaling slsDestinationIpAddress="239.255.50.1"
      slsDestinationUdpPort="5001" slsMajorProtocolVersion="0"
      slsMinorProtocolVersion="0" slsProtocol="1" slsSourceIpAddress="192.168.102.51"/>
  </Service>
  <Service globalServiceID="https://doi.org/10.5239/59E3-0F01"
    majorChannelNo="27" minorChannelNo="1" serviceCategory="1"
    serviceId="5002" shortServiceName="KNXGLD1" sltSvcSeqNum="0">
    <BroadcastSvcSignaling slsDestinationIpAddress="239.255.50.2"
      slsDestinationUdpPort="5002" slsMajorProtocolVersion="0"
      slsMinorProtocolVersion="0" slsProtocol="1" slsSourceIpAddress="192.168.102.51"/>
  </Service>
  <Service globalServiceID="https://doi.org/10.5239/46A4-E6F8"
    majorChannelNo="27" minorChannelNo="2" serviceCategory="1"
    serviceId="5003" shortServiceName="KNXGLD2" sltSvcSeqNum="0">
    <BroadcastSvcSignaling slsDestinationIpAddress="239.255.50.3"
      slsDestinationUdpPort="5003" slsMajorProtocolVersion="0"
      slsMinorProtocolVersion="0" slsProtocol="1" slsSourceIpAddress="192.168.102.51"/>
  </Service>
  <Service configuration="Broadband"
    globalServiceID="https://doi.org/10.5239/0FF8-0C47"
    majorChannelNo="27" minorChannelNo="3" serviceCategory="1"
    serviceId="5004" shortServiceName="KNXGLD3" sltSvcSeqNum="0">
    <BroadcastSvcSignaling slsDestinationIpAddress="239.255.50.4"
      slsDestinationUdpPort="5004" slsMajorProtocolVersion="0"
      slsMinorProtocolVersion="0" slsProtocol="1" slsSourceIpAddress="192.168.102.51"/>
  </Service>
</SLT>
```


FIGURE 4: SERVICE LIST TABLE.

Figure 4 shows a SLT that contains four services. Service 1 is the Electronic Service Guide (ESG). Services 2 and 3 are OTA delivered audio/video services. Service 4 is a virtual channel. The only difference between the OTA and virtual channel services in the SLT is the highlighted section that signifies that the virtual channel service will be delivered via broadband.

### Service Level Signaling (SLS)

Also contained in the LLS is the Service Level Signaling tables. When employing ROUTE for service delivery, the SLS tables associated with each service holds important details about the service, such as a list of its various components, where these components can be found, and the receiver capabilities that are required for proper reception and decoding. In the case of DASH-formatted streaming services being delivered via ROUTE, the SLS tables contain the following elements:

- **DASH Media Presentation Description (MPD):** Provides identifying details for the elements comprising the service.

- **User Service Bundle Description (USBD):** Defines fundamental characteristics of a service such as its name, identifier, delivery mode (broadcast or broadband), and language(s).
- **Service-based Transport Session Instance (S-TSID):** Contains the details on how to obtain the DASH segments specified in the MPD via ROUTE.

The SLS can also contain the following optional elements:

- HTML Entry pages Location Description (HELD)
- Distribution Window Description (DWD)
- Associated Procedure Description
- Regional Service Availability Table (RSAT)

Since the main components of a virtual channel (i.e. audio/video DASH segments) are delivered via broadband, the S-TSID fragment in the SLS is not needed. Instead, a BaseURL pointing to the CDN is added to the MPD so that the receiver knows to retrieve the DASH segments via broadband rather than a ROUTE session in the OTA transmission and location where they can be retrieved from. Figure 5 shows a MPD for a virtual channel and the BaseURL element is highlighted.

```
<?xml version="1.0" encoding="UTF-8"?>
<MPD availabilityStartTime="2023-02-20T15:47:21Z" maxSegmentDuration="PT1.001S" minBufferTime="PT1S"
minimumUpdatePeriod="PT10S" profiles="urn:mpeg:dash:profile:isoff-broadcast:2015" publishTime="2023-02-20T15:48:13Z"
timeShiftBufferDepth="PT6S" type="dynamic"
   xmlns="urn:mpeg:dash:schema:mpd:2011"
   xmlns:cenc="urn:mpeg:cenc:2013"
   xmlns:dashif="https://dashif.org/"
   xmlns:scte35="http://www.scte.org/schemas/35/2016"
   xmlns:xsi="http://www.w3.org/2001/XMLSchema-instance" xsi:schemalocation="urn:mpeg:dash:schema:mpd:2011 DASH-MPD.xsd
http://dashif.org/guidelines/ContentProtection laurl.xsd">
   <Period id="P0" start="PT0S">
      <BaseURL>https://video.gray-nextgentv.com/knxgld3</BaseURL>
      <AdaptationSet contentType="video" id="0" maxFrameRate="30000/1001" maxHeight="1080" maxWidth="1920"
mimeType="video/mp4" minFrameRate="30000/1001" minHeight="1080" minWidth="1920" par="16:9" segmentAlignment="true"
startWithSAP="1">
         <Role schemeIdUri="urn:mpeg:dash:role:2011" value="main"></Role>
         <SegmentTemplate initialization="video-$Bandwidth$-init.mp4" media="video-$Bandwidth$-$Time$.mp4v" timescale="30000">
            <SegmentTimeline>
               <S d="30030" r="2" t="1381380"></S>
            </SegmentTimeline>
         </SegmentTemplate>
         <Representation bandwidth="3000000" codecs="hvc1.1.6.L120.B0" frameRate="30000/1001" height="1080" id="Video1_1"
sar="1:1" scanType="progressive" width="1920"></Representation>
      </AdaptationSet>
      <AdaptationSet contentType="audio" id="1" lang="eng" mimeType="audio/mp4" segmentAlignment="true" startWithSAP="1">
         <Role schemeIdUri="urn:mpeg:dash:role:2011" value="main"></Role>
         <SegmentTemplate initialization="audio-0-$Bandwidth$-init.mp4" media="audio-0-$Bandwidth$-$Time$.mp4a"
timescale="240000">
            <SegmentTimeline>
               <S d="240240" r="2" t="11051040"></S>
            </SegmentTimeline>
         </SegmentTemplate>
         <AudioChannelConfiguration schemeIdUri="urn:mpeg:mpegB:cicp:ChannelConfiguration" value="6">
</AudioChannelConfiguration>
         <Representation audioSamplingRate="48000" bandwidth="96000" codecs="ac-4.02.01.01" id="22"></Representation>
      </AdaptationSet>
      <AdaptationSet contentType="audio" id="2" lang="spa" mimeType="audio/mp4" segmentAlignment="true" startWithSAP="1">
         <SegmentTemplate initialization="audio-1-$Bandwidth$-init.mp4" media="audio-1-$Bandwidth$-$Time$.mp4a"
timescale="240000">
            <SegmentTimeline>
               <S d="240240" r="2" t="11051040"></S>
            </SegmentTimeline>
         </SegmentTemplate>
         <AudioChannelConfiguration schemeIdUri="urn:mpeg:mpegB:cicp:ChannelConfiguration" value="2">
</AudioChannelConfiguration>
         <Representation audioSamplingRate="48000" bandwidth="96000" codecs="ac-4.02.01.00" id="Audio3_3"></Representation>
      </AdaptationSet>
      <AdaptationSet contentType="text" id="3" mimeType="application/mp4" segmentAlignment="true" startWithSAP="1">
         <SupplementalProperty schemeIdUri="http://dashif.org/guidelines/dash-atsc-closedcaption" value="ar:16-9;er:0;profile:0;3d:0">
</SupplementalProperty>
         <Role schemeIdUri="urn:mpeg:dash:role:2011" value="caption"></Role>
         <SegmentTemplate initialization="data-0-$Bandwidth$-init.mp4" media="data-0-$Bandwidth$-$Time$.mp4s" timescale="30000">
            <SegmentTimeline>
               <S d="30030" r="2" t="1381380"></S>
            </SegmentTimeline>
         </SegmentTemplate>
         <Representation bandwidth="50000" codecs="stpp.ttml.im1t" id="Data4_4"></Representation>
      </AdaptationSet>
   </Period>
</MPD>
```


FIGURE 5: DASH MEDIA PRESENTATION DESCRIPTION.

Other optional elements such as an HTML Entry pages Location Description (HELD) may be included in the SLS and utilized for virtual channels.

## Content Security

Ensuring that the virtual channel is only consumed by viewers in the coverage area of the transmitter is mainly accomplished by only allowing access DASH manifest via the OTA signal. Viewers that are unable to receive the OTA signal cannot otherwise receive the manifest and therefor their tuners are unable to retrieve the audio/video segments from the CDN.

Although only sending the DASH manifest in the over-the-air signal provides some protection against out-of-market viewers, it is recommended that encryption is applied to the audio/video segments.

Another method that could be used to prevent out-of-market viewing is to implement a form of rolling tokens that are created in the ROUTE encoder/signaling generator and sent in the service signaling. The receiver could then use these tokens to authenticate with the CDN.

Finally, IP geolocation restrictions can be implemented by the CDN. One issue with this method is that geolocation of IPs is often not precise and may block viewers from within the viewing area from receiving the service.

## Testing

Gray tested virtual channels on WNXG-LD in Tallahassee, Florida and KNXG-LD in Bryan, Texas.

The following is a list of equipment utilized while testing virtual channels:

- **Video Encoder:** ATEME Titan Live
- **ROUTE Encoder/Signaling Generators:** DigiCAP DigiCaster, Triveni GuideBuilder XM
- **Broadcast Gateways:** DigiCAP DigiCaster, Triveni Broadcast Gateway
- **Origin Server:** Amazon S3
- **CDN:** Amazon CloudFront
- **Receivers:** Various models of televisions from three major manufacturers
- **Transmitters:** GatesAir UAXTE-4 (WNXG-LD), Rohde & Schwarz TMU9evo (KNXG-LD, WNXG-LD)

### Video Encoder

The ATEME Titan Live video encoder was configured to encode the virtual service using HEVC for the video and AC-4 for the audio from an SDI source. The video was encoded at 1080p with a bitrate of 3 Mbps. Two audio services were encoded, each with a bitrate of 96Kbps. The video was encrypted using A3SA Widevine encryption.

The Titan Live video encoder also contains the DASH packager. The DASH packager was configured to use time-based segment numbering and a segment time of 1 second. Manual AST was enabled and the current date/time was used.

The output of the DASH packager was setup to publish directly to an Amazon S3 bucket acting as the origin server. Segment Auto Delete was enabled and the Segments in Playlist was set to 8. When using segment auto delete, the Titan Live DASH packager will keep 2 x [Number of Segments In Playlist] + 1 segments on the origin server and automatically delete older segments.

While the Titan Live encoder was used during our testing, any ATSC 3.0 compliant encoder/DASH packager will work when deploying virtual channels as long as the DASH segments can be uploaded to an appropriate origin server.

### ROUTE Encoder/Signaling Generators

Both DigiCaster and GuideBuilder XM were used during our testing.

We first tested using DigiCAP DigiCaster for the ROUTE encoder/signaling generator. We added a standard audio/video service, but we changed the Delivery Method for all components from Broadcast to Broadband. We also added a Base URL pointing to our CDN. Figure 6 is a screenshot from DigiCaster showing the resulting service configuration for a virtual channel.

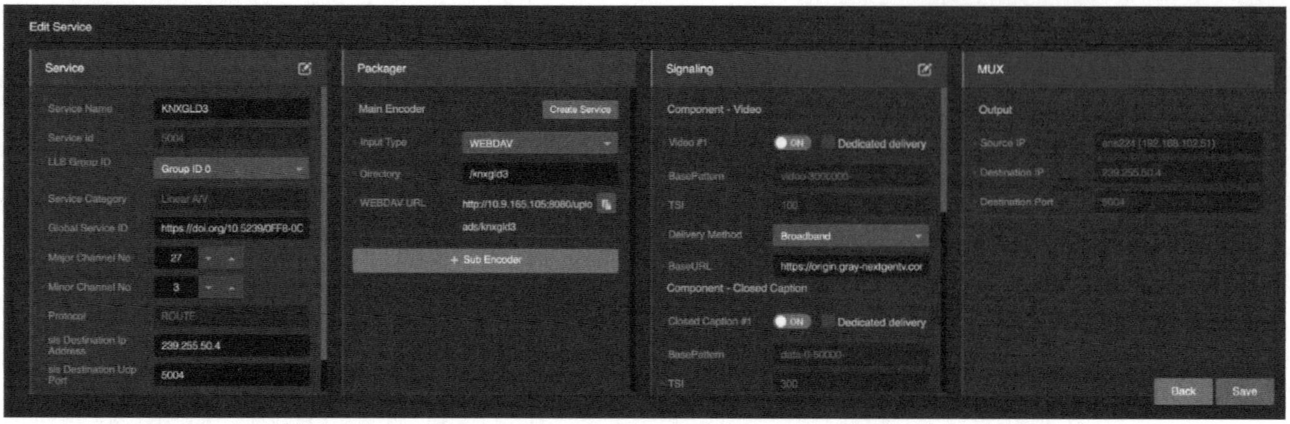


FIGURE 6: DIGICASTER SERVICE CONFIGURATION.

Figure 7 shows an overview of the services configured in DigiCaster during the testing. Note that the total bandwidth used in the OTA transmission for service 3 is approximately 115 Kbps.

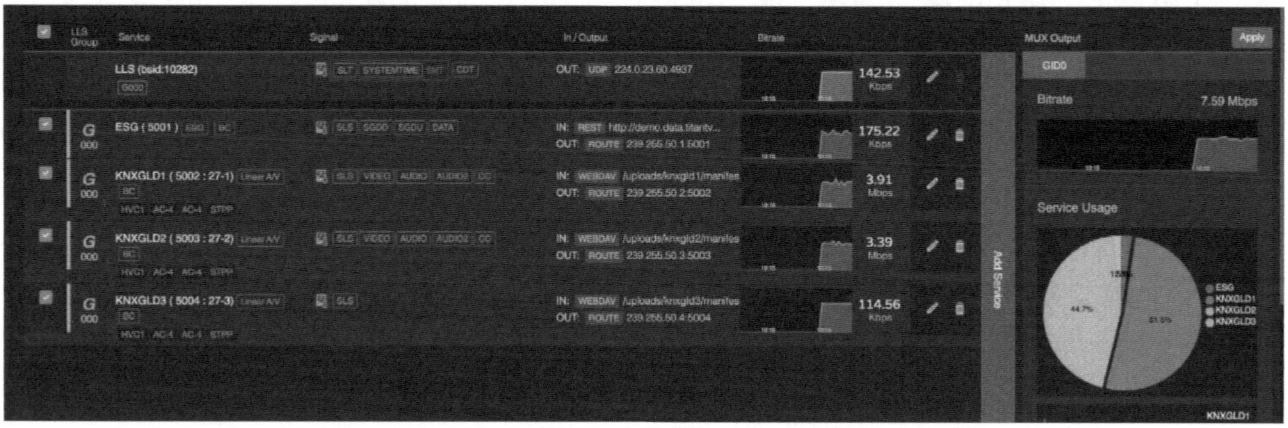


FIGURE 7: DIGICASTER SERVICE OVERVIEW WITH VIRTUAL CHANNEL.

For a comparison, Figure 8 shows the same three services but service 3 has been changed from a virtual channel to a standard OTA delivered service. Note that the total OTA bandwidth used by service 3 has increased to approximately 3.62 Mbps.

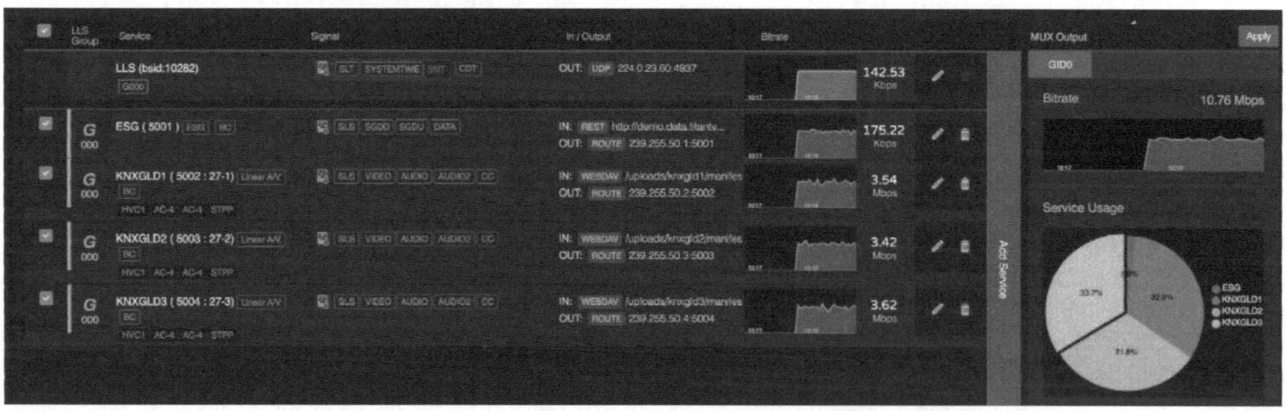


FIGURE 8: DIGICASTER SERVICE OVERVIEW WITH NO VIRTUAL CHANNEL.

In addition to DigiCaster, we also tested virtual channels with Triveni GuideBuilder XM (GBXM). The setup in GBXM is a little different since the ROUTE encoder and signaling generator do not share the same user interface.

We first configured a new service in the GBXM ROUTE encoder and set the SLT Config option to Broadband. Figure 9 shows the relevant service configuration for a virtual channel in the Triveni ROUTE encoder.

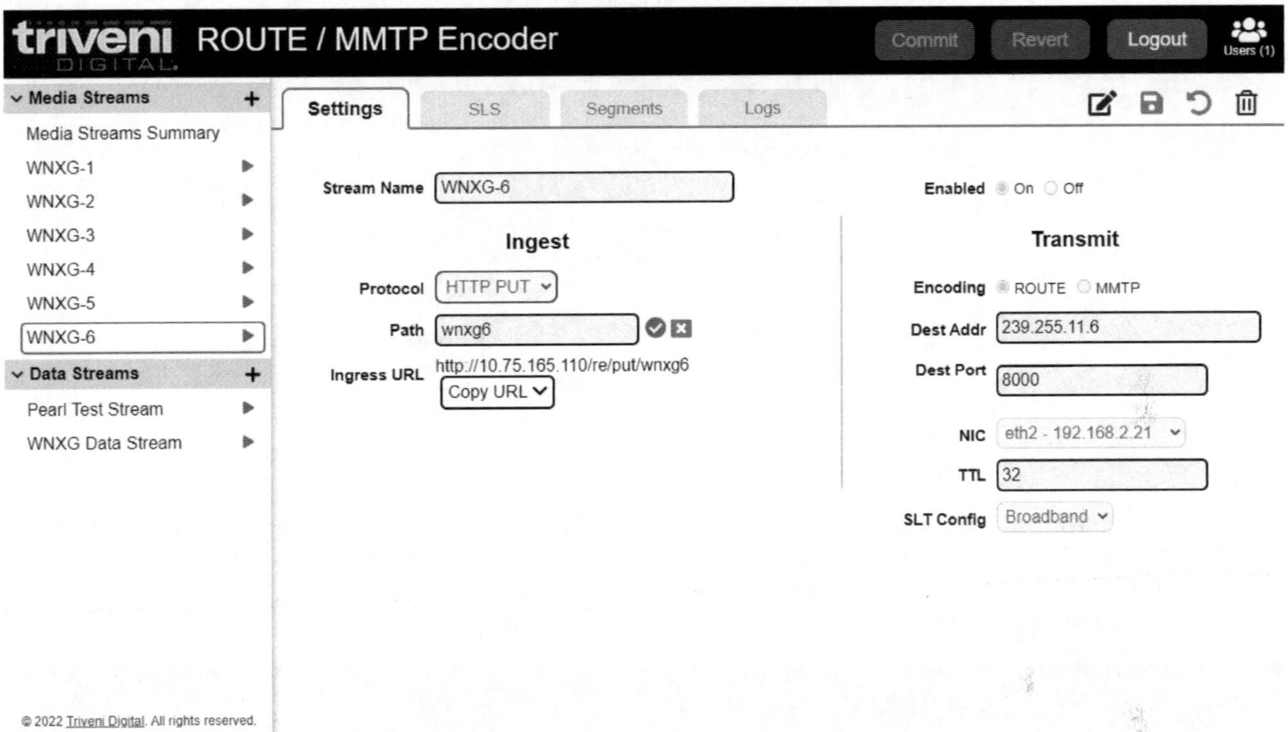


FIGURE 9: GBXM ROUTE ENCODER SERVICE CONFIGURATION.

We then added the Base URL to the service in GBXM. Figure 10 shows the service in the GBXM configuration editor with the Base URL added.

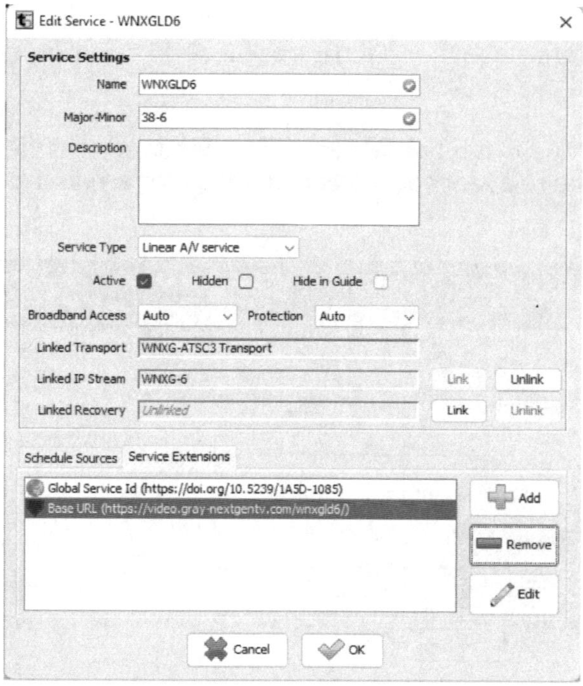


FIGURE 10: GBXM SERVICE BASE URL CONFIGURATION.

We then confirmed that the Base URL was added to the service by looking at the MPD in the GBXM ROUTE encoder. Figure 11 is a screenshot of the virtual channel service in the GBXM ROUTE encoder. The left side shows the MPD as it is ingested from the video encoder/DASH packager. The right side shows the MPD being delivered in the SLS with the Base URL added.

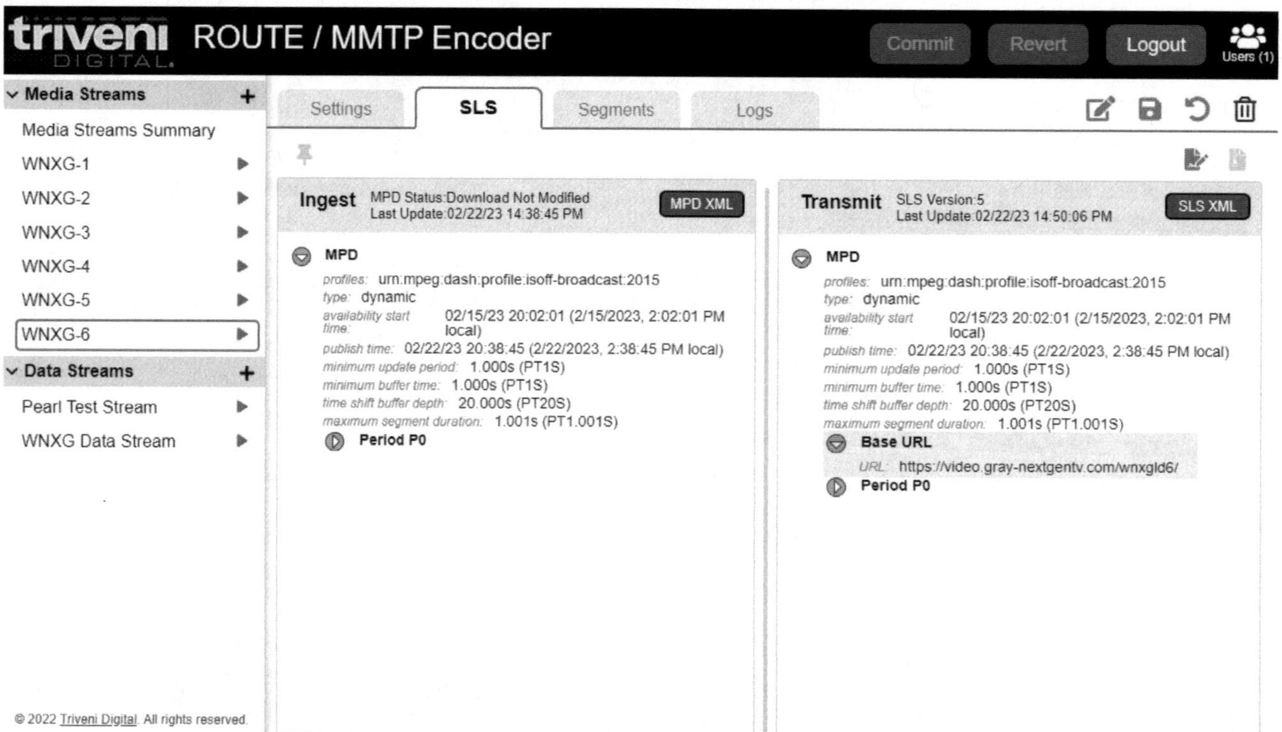


FIGURE 11: GBXM ROUTE ENCODER MPD WITH BASE URL.

### Broadcast Gateway
No changes are needed in the broadcast gateways.

### Origin Server
In our initial testing we used an Amazon S3 bucket as our origin server. The Titan Live DASH packager was configured to upload the DASH segments to the S3 bucket. The bucket was configured with a Fully Qualified Domain Name (FQDN) and a valid SSL certificate. A security policy was configured to block public access to the bucket and only allow requests from the CDN.

### CDN
Amazon CloudFront was configured to use our S3 bucket for the origin server. The cache was set to only keep segments for 60 seconds. A FQDN and valid SSL certificate were added.

Since the Titan Live DASH packager uploads the DASH manifest in addition to the audio/video segments to the origin server, a rule was added in CloudFront to block access to any file with a .mpd extension.

## Results
During our initial testing found only one television that was capable of properly receiving and decoding the virtual channel. Televisions that were unable to receive and decode the virtual channels displayed a message that the channel is unavailable or that the signal level is low.

We tested other televisions from the same manufacturer and discovered that even televisions that were the same model but produced in different years reacted differently to virtual channels. We had three TVs from the same manufacturer and model lineup but produced in 2020, 2021 and 2022. The 2020 model worked out of the box with only minor changes needed to the number of segments kept in the MPD. The 2021 television did not work at all. The 2022 model was a developer board and it was able to start displaying the virtual channel but the audio/video playback was intermittent.

We invited several television manufacturers to our facility in Tallahassee, Florida so that they could access our OTA ATSC 3.0 test signal containing a virtual channel. After taking stream captures, one of the manufacturers was able to write code overnight for their development television so that it could successfully receive and decode the virtual channel. The other manufacturer present has since issued firmware updates for their televisions that greatly improve their performance when receiving virtual channels.

While initial testing utilized Amazon S3 as the origin server and CloudFront for the CDN, we also successfully tested Google Cloud Storage and Cloud CDN. We did not notice any differences in performance between the two services although our testing was limited.

## Conclusion
Virtual channels are an important tool for broadcasters to use when ATSC 3.0 bandwidth is limited but there is a desire to add new services. Virtual channels are superior to standard OTT channels because they appear alongside the broadcaster's other channels in the EPG and they allow for the use of advanced ATSC 3.0 features such as interactive broadcaster applications.

While television support for virtual channels is currently limited, the adoption of virtual channels by broadcasters may encourage broader support for virtual channels by receiver manufacturers.

## Acknowledgments

The author would like to thank Michael Watson from Gray Television and Pete Van Peenen from Pearl for their help and collaboration on this project.

## References

[1] ATSC, "ATSC 1.0 Standard: Delivery of IP Multicast Sessions Over Data Broadcast Standard," Doc. A/92:2002, Advanced Television Systems Committee, Washington D.C., 31 January 2002. https://www.atsc.org/atsc-documents/a92-delivery-of-ip-multicast-sessions-over-data-broadcast-standard/

[2] ATSC, "ATSC 3.0 Standard: Signaling, Delivery, Synchronization, and Error Protection," Doc. A/331:2022, Advanced Television Systems Committee, Washington D.C., 30 November 2022. https://www.atsc.org/atsc-documents/3312017-signaling-delivery-synchronization-error-protection/

# Stretching Elasticity: Traffic Peak Management in an Efficiently Designed Telco-CDN

**Gwendal Simon**
**Synamedia**
**Rennes, France**
gsimon@synamedia.com

**Abstract** – When building a Telco-CDN infrastructure, Internet Service Providers (ISP) first consider the peak throughput and then provision the infrastructure as a function of peak capacity. New network design practices indicate that instead, operators would benefit from dimensioning the infrastructure to cover the traffic demand for a fraction of time, and develop strategies to manage the peaks, which happen when the demand exceeds the capacity of the infrastructure. A peak offloading strategy is particularly effective in online video delivery where demand peaks, often driven by sports events, are transient and significantly higher than average traffic. This paper provides a tour of CDN management, described by a new approach to design Telco-CDN with greater fluidity, mixing appropriate technologies to provide the right elasticity at the right time.

## Introduction

The delivery of video services, whether they are from traditional TV services or from Over-The-Top (OTT) services, is transitioning to an IP-based world. This transition allows the content owners and service providers to add valuable and personalized services and to deliver content for any connected devices in any location. The growth of IP traffic related to video services has thus exploded in recent years and this dramatic growth is expected to continue in the coming years.

This significant growth in traffic is a concern for network operators, who must carry the data from the origin datacenters to the home devices. In addition to the capacity requirements, the video traffic is characterized by tight delay constraints, which call for short connections and fair usage of the resources. Content Delivery Networks (CDN) have emerged to address this traffic growth and this demand for server proximity. A CDN is a distributed infrastructure, which consists of a large number of servers located on the edge of the networks, as close as possible to the end-users.

### Rationale of Telco-CDN

Within the Internet architecture, the Edge Internet Service Providers (ISPs) are the network operators who offer the service to the end-users who consume the video, as opposed to the Transit network operators, who interconnect multiple operators. The ISPs are linked to other networks through two types of links:

- A Point of Presence (PoP), which is a co-located datacenter where any network provider is free to install servers and switches to let the traffic flow from one network to another and vice versa.
- An Internet eXchange Point (IXP), which is a technology company that offers the infrastructure to interconnect multiple network operators.

This paper is excerpted from the Proceedings of the 2023 NAB Broadcast Engineering and Information Technology (BEIT) Conference, © 2023, National Association of Broadcasters, 1 M Street SE, Washington, DC 20003 USA.

In both cases, the network operators have to pay for a *peering* bandwidth capacity (in Gbps) to transfer data from and to other network operators. In the case of PoP, it is fixed cost, while the IXP can be regarded as a variable on-demand monthly fee. For more details about network interconnections for delivery, please refer to the paper from Wohlfart et al. [1].

The growth of video traffic has significantly increased the peering expenses for the ISPs. When one million end-users watch a TV stream at 5 Mbps, the traffic flow from the network operators owning the content aggregates to 5 Tbps. Today's IXP monthly price for a 100 Gbps peering is $3k[1], so the ISP expenses represent $150k monthly. Furthermore, the traffic also increases the burden on the backbone network and requires significant investment in network devices.

To reduce the peering costs, the ISPs often deploy a CDN – or a subset of a CDN -- directly into their own network infrastructure. The CDN edge servers installed in ISPs are called an Edge-CDN or Telco-CDN. It can be owned by the ISP, who then offers the service to the content owners, or it can be part of an agreement between a Public CDN and the ISP, where the Public CDN deals with content owners, while paying the ISP for hosting its CDN servers. In this paper, to simplify the models, we consider the former case, where the ISP deploys its own Telco-CDN. For a typology of CDNs, please refer to the Table 1, which comes from Stocker et al. [2]. The Telco-CDN we consider in this paper corresponds to the second-to-last row of the table (i.e. Licensed).

| CDN Architecture | Examples of Providers | Deployment Strategy | Bandwidth | Latency | Business Model | Typical Applications |
|---|---|---|---|---|---|---|
| Datacenter-based | Limelight, CacheFly, CloudFlare | Servers at strategically connected facilities | High | Medium | Multi-purpose, buy bulk resources | Video Streaming, static Web, software updates |
| Highly Distributed | Akamai | Servers at peering points and inside access networks | High | Very Low | General-purpose, provide global footprint, best quality | Various applications, including dynamic and interactive Web |
| Peer-to-peer | BitTorrent | Serverless, functionality at end-user equipment | Low | High | Multi-purpose, no investment in dedicated infrastructure | File sharing, bulk transfers |
| Hybrid | Akamai NetSession | Dedicated servers combined with functionality at end-user equipment | Low | High | Multi-purpose, partial outsourcing of delivery to end-user equipment | Software updates, file sharing |
| Specialized | Netflix Open Connect, Google Global Cache, Amazon CloudFront | Specialized servers at peering points and inside access networks | High | Low | Single-purpose, reduce delivery costs for specialized service | Video delivery, specialized applications |
| Broker | Conviva, Cedexis | Relies on existing deployments of CDN functionality | Custom | Custom | Opportunistic cost management | Video and Web delivery |
| Licensed | Akamai AURA, Edgecast licensed CDN | Inside access networks | High | Very Low | Telco CDN, or ISP-CDN collaboration | All of above |
| Federated | Edgecast OpenCDN | Relies on existing deployments of CDN functionality | High | Low | Interconnection of CDNs to expand geographic footprint | All of above |

TABLE 1: TYPOLOGY OF CDNS [2].

[1] https://docs.google.com/spreadsheets/d/18ztPX_ysWYqEhJlf2SKQQsTNRbkwoxPSfaC6ScEZAG8/edit#gid=0

### Problem

The ISP, as a Telco-CDN owner, should invest in a fixed capacity infrastructure. It provisions some edge servers, designed to deliver content to the end-users, and some control servers for operations and administration. The number of edge servers is a strategic decision, which is usually related to the overall throughput that the ISP wants to commit to. The number of control servers can be roughly approximated to a linear function of the number of edge servers.

Let us assume for the sake of simplicity that an edge server has a capacity to deliver 100 Gbps of data to end-users. Let us then assume that the number of control servers should be equal to 3 (as a basis of installing a Telco CDN) plus 1 server per 300 Gbps of peak throughput. If an ISP wants to commit to 1.6 Tbps, it must provision 16 edge servers and 9 (3+6) control servers, overall.

The investment in a Telco-CDN is both capital expenditure (CAPEX) when buying the servers and operational expenditure (OPEX) to maintain the infrastructure. Without loss of generality, we assume in this paper that both are a linear function of the number of servers. The ISP should make sure that the Telco-CDN is worth the investment, which is directly related to the throughput commitment.

The problem we attempt to address in this paper is related to the throughput commitment. We aim to evaluate the optimal throughput commitment of the Telco-CDN with respect to the demand of the end-users in the ISP's network.

### Contributions

In this paper, we provide an analysis for the problem of optimizing the Telco-CDN infrastructure capacity.

First, we introduce a model for Telco-CDN, in which we present a model to determine how to design an efficient CDN infrastructure for average typical demand and strategies to deal with peak utilization. We describe the key metrics that should be considered to optimally dimension the CDN while keeping the peak management possible.

Second, we introduce a set of tools to manage the peak demand. A critical component is a peak predictor, which should typically target a peak characterization (time, value) in a one-hour horizon, so that it is possible to orchestrate the CDN offloading. We also show how AI-based techniques have made peak prediction possible.

Third, we describe the different approaches that a CDN operator can leverage to offload the excess traffic during peak. Multiple technologies exist, including multicast ABR, peer-to-peer, cloud-CDN on tap, and Open Caching. We describe these technologies and present a pros/cons analysis.

Finally, we present a use case with optimal infrastructure settings. This real case demonstrates the benefits one can expect from peak offloading strategies for Telco-CDN.

## Telco-CDN Models

We first present the infrastructure component of a Telco-CDN and the concept of peak offloading. We then study the traffic activities. We finally introduce the strategy for building a Telco-CDN infrastructure.

### Telco-CDN Infrastructure

We stick to a simple economic model for Telco-CDN with a target overall egress throughput (say 1.6 Tbps), which is offered by a set of edge servers (with an individual guaranteed target throughput of say

100 Gbps), which are administered through a set of control servers (say 3 default servers and 1 every 3 edge servers).

In this paper, we assume a fixed CAPEX price per server, which can ultimately be translated into a price per Gbps of committed throughput. For example, it would be possible to assume $1k CAPEX for 1 Gbps of deployed CDN capacity (including edge and control servers).

We should then add a fixed OPEX price, which is also related to the number of servers, and thus also translated into a price per Gbps of committed throughput. For example, it would be possible to assume that yearly OPEX represents 0.15 of the initial CAPEX, or $150 per Gbps.

The sum of the CAPEX and the OPEX cumulates as the total expenditure over a course of several years. For example, based on the aforementioned prices, which are indicative prices for back-of-the-envelope calculations, the total expenditure for a Telco-CDN of 1.6 Tbps for 3 years would be $2.3M. It is obvious that the throughput commitment has a direct impact on financial investment. It makes capacity planning a key activity prior to any install of Telco-CDN.

To sum up, the investment into a Telco-CDN is a fixed price in $ per Gbps of committed throughput over a time horizon.

## Peak Offloading

The ISP expects its CDN to fulfill the demand from its end-users. At a given time, the number of end-users who consume a video service that is delivered from the Telco-CDN is a rough estimation of the traffic. If the traffic demand exceeds the capacity of the Telco-CDN, the ISP should run an offloading strategy to guarantee the service to the end-users. We do not go into the details of offloading execution by now. We will describe later in this paper various strategies for traffic offloading.

Regardless of the chosen strategy, the traffic offloading has a cost. For the sake of simplicity, we consider here the most popular offloading strategy, which consists in requesting a third-party CDN to deliver content in complement to the Telco-CDN. In the vast majority of cases, the price is expressed as a function of a data volume, which means that the third-party CDN charges the ISP for every single bit of delivered data. This volume is also generally offered with respect to tiers.

The price per Giga Byte of delivered data is a public information for some Public CDNs (without negotiation) and it is obvious that it depends on a wider scale agreement between a public CDN and an ISP. We consider a price structure which corresponds to an indicative price as shown in Table 2.

| Tier Limits | From (TB) | To (TB) | Price $ per GB |
|---|---|---|---|
| 10 TB / month | 0 | 10 | 0.04 |
| 50 TB / month | 11 | 50 | 0.03 |
| 150 TB / month | 51 | 150 | 0.025 |
| 500 TB / month | 151 | 500 | 0.018 |
| 1 PB / month | 501 | 1,000 | 0.015 |
| 5 PB / month | 1,001 | 5,000 | 0.01 |
| 10 PB / month | 5,001 | 10,000 | 0.005 |
| above | 10,001 | | 0.003 |

TABLE 2: INDICATIVE PRICE FOR PUBLIC CDN OFFLOADING.

To sum up, the price for delivering any data that exceeds the committed capacity of the Telco CDN is a price that depends on the volume of data.

## Traffic Demand

An ISP is by nature a local actor, spanning generally over a country. Most countries in the world are in a single time zone for the vast majority of their population, or have temporal activities shift between work and leisure that are overall synchronized. This has a direct impact on the shape of the traffic that an ISP can expect on its Telco-CDN, since these video services are mainly for entertainment at home, where day and night patterns are highly visible. For example, a day in a local CDN could resemble the pattern in Figure 1.

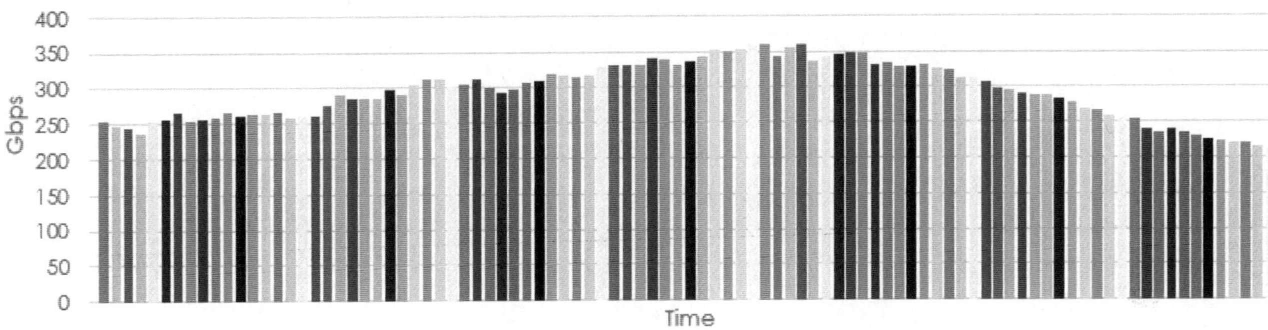


FIGURE 1: AN INDICATIVE DAY IN A LOCAL CDN.

In the case of Figure 1, the peak is at 360 Gbps although the valley is at 210 Gbps. This pattern, which experts would regard as a quite low day-to-night gap, corresponds to a Telco-CDN, which the ISP manages to exploit for a continuous high traffic delivery.

We capture the usage of a Telco-CDN by a metric: the *capacity-to-average ratio*. The common metric is peak-to-average, but we want to emphasize here that other factors have to be considered. First the safety margin that the ISP usually takes when planning the capacity. Second the policies for disaster recovery, which often come with redundancy and extra-capacity. As a matter of fact, the infrastructure capacity is generally between 1.2 and 1.4 of the actual peak when the ISP has a good knowledge of the traffic demand.

The nature of the video services that are delivered by the mean of the Telco-CDN has a critical importance in the patterns that the ISP can expect. We distinguish two types of video services:

- A **TV-like service** over the Internet. It can come with cDVR, with live TV channels, and some other typical VoD sources, which can possibly include major OTT services. Such a video service is the mainstream source of entertainment for regular homes, and it thus corresponds to sustained patterns. In our analysis, we observed that, for a TV-live service, the capacity-to-average ratio ranges from 2.2 to 3.5.
- An **OTT Sport Event video service**, which is generally owned by rightsholders who have paid a significant amount of money to acquire the rights to stream a popular event. Despite the attempts to generate content 24/7, these OTT services generally fail in attracting viewers between events, while they can result a massive amount of traffic during the events. In our analysis, Sport Event OTT services can be characterized by capacity-to-average ratio ranging from 10 to 15.

To sum up, the capacity-to-average ratio captures the burstiness of the traffic, which highly depends on the type of video services that the CDN delivers.

### Telco-CDN Strategy
By aggregating the previous subsections, it is possible to derive a common optimization problem. The goal is to minimize the expenses over a time horizon by combining a well-dimensioned Telco-CDN and an offloading strategy from a third-party CDN.

In practice, some operational constraints may prevent configurations, especially the capacity of the third-party CDN to complement the traffic delivery on demand can be bounded by peering constraints. For example, a third-party CDN may not be able to deliver more than, say, 400 Gbps to an ISP, unless specific agreements. However, we will assume no specific operational constraint in this paper to establish a theoretical technical and economic analysis.

As a preliminary analysis, we can compare the price of a Telco-CDN against opting for a full offloading strategy where the Telco-CDN has zero capacity. It is represented in Figure 2.

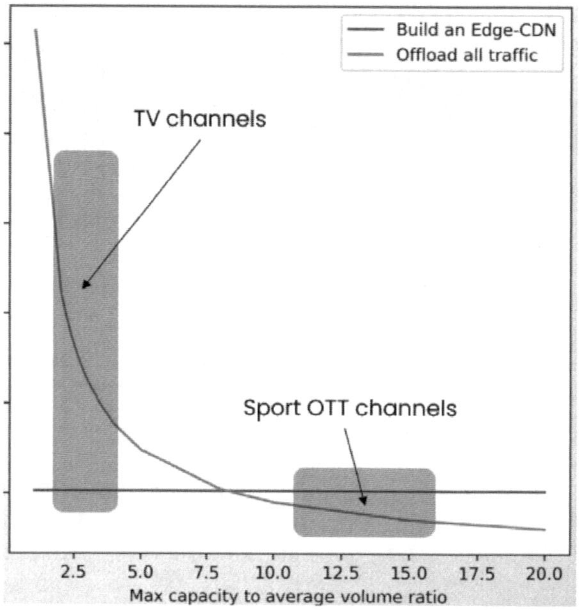


FIGURE 2: COST COMPARISONS (Y-AXIS ON A LINEAR SCALE IN $) BETWEEN A FULL TELCO-CDN INSTALL AND A STRATEGY OF OFFLOADING ALL TRAFFIC FROM A THIRD-PARTY CDN.

For a TV-like service, the benefits of deploying a Telco-CDN are significant (3x to 5x cheaper). For Sport OTT channels, the reality is different. The global volume of traffic per month is small although the peak capacity is large. In that case, the cost of volume delivery can be less than the cost of installing a dedicated infrastructure. Overall, we need a smarter combination of Telco-CDN and peak offloading.

## Peak Offloading
We first provide a background on peak prediction tools, and then we present some peak offloading strategies. Finally, we introduce some results for optimal peak offloading.

### Peak Prediction
When a peak happens, and when this peak exceeds the capacity of the Telco-CDN, the ISP should run a peak offloading strategy, for example connecting to a third-party CDN to get server resources. Unfortunately, this strategy does not come instantaneously. Most peak offloading strategies require a minimum of anticipation and preparation to guarantee that the resources are available to ensure a

smooth and complementary delivery system re-organization. Traffic prediction aims at offering this anticipation.

The simplest solution is to consider the actual global throughput (in Gbps) as a time series and to use the algorithms that have been proposed in the literature for time series forecasting. In the past, the scientific community has studied various stochastic algorithms, such as the popular Autoregressive Integrated Moving Average (ARIMA) method [3]. It takes in input the past measures of throughput, and it generates the prediction based on a consistent learning approach for the weight parameters of the moving average function. It has proven to be efficient in many networking use cases.

More recently, the scientific community has studied the benefits one can expect from the implementation of deep learning strategies for time series forecasting. Here approaches such as Long-Short-Term Memory (LSTM) have demonstrated that they can be efficient [4].

Another approach comes from the big-data oriented Prophet system (which is originally from Facebook) [5]. Here the objective is to scale the computation and to deal with irregular data collection, which are two concerns in the CDN community where many servers are expected to collect, gather, and exports logs and where errors can frequently happen. Prophet does not implement immediate time-series forecasting; it rather learns from observing past measures and it infers long-term variations while taking into account possible holidays and events.

To sum up, sophisticated techniques exist to predict traffic variations, which can also be used to anticipate peak and thus give time to the ISP for an implementation of an efficient offloading strategy.

### Peak Offloading Strategies

We list below various approaches for offloading traffic when a peak exceeding the capacity of the Telco-CDN happens.

- The most popular approach is to leverage **a third-party CDN**. As previously said, the ISP should first assess the capacity of this CDN to deliver multiple hundreds of Gbps of data with respect to peering limitations. It is however often the case for giant Public CDN operators. The second preliminary action the ISP should perform is a dual technical and business agreement with the CDN operator to ensure that the offloading can happen as smoothly as possible and without business disputes. Then the ISP can run its multi-CDN approach, typically following approaches in the literature [6]. Drawbacks include the fact that the ISP collects data from multiple sources (at least two CDNs).
- Another approach is to deploy **virtual edge servers into a datacenter administered by a third-party Cloud provider**. Here again the limitations can come from the peering agreements between the ISP and the Cloud provider. The benefits include the fact that the virtual servers may be regarded as being part of the Telco-CDN, and thus can contribute to the unified log management system. Here again, the literature includes papers that deals with the management of such a transient virtual infrastructure [7].
- The network operators have promoted the implementation of multicast solutions for several years, in the wild Internet and Adaptive Bit-Rate (ABR) world, the solution is **multicast ABR** (or mABR), which has been studied for a decade [8]. This solution requires the ISP network to be multicast compliant and the client devices to be able to subscribe to a multicast group. It is efficient if a few video stream (a profile of a channel) is very popular, which is often the case for popular OTT events. Weaknesses of multicast ABR include the lack of support for watermarking and content protection, the challenges of implementing target advertisement, the need for a backup unicast-based system for error repair and trick mode implementation. Multicast can however complement a unicast Telco-CDN efficiently for peak management.
- The academic community has studied **peer-to-peer (or peer-assisted) solutions** since the early 2000s. It is known as being an efficient strategy for Video on Demand (VoD) [9], but it is

more challenging for live streaming, especially for low-latency scenarios. It suffers from the same weaknesses as multicast since it is a group communication so the server cannot personalize the delivery. It also includes the lack of support for log management, which makes the overall offer not very suitable for a controlled delivery system. However, it is the cheapest solutions, since it exploits the resources that the client themselves offer to the community.

All these strategies complement, transiently, the unicast Telco-CDN that the ISP installs in its network.

### Optimal Cost Management

We study the benefits peak offloading strategies can bring to the ISP. Here we used the result of a typical ISP running a Telco CDN for a TV-like service in its network. It corresponds to the mainstream scenario in which practical limitations are unlikely to happen and significant savings can occur.

We consider two third-party CDN partners, with different price structures, for the offloading. The peak corresponds to 1.52 Tbps and the capacity of the Telco-CDN is fixed at 1.85 Tbps. The results are shown in Figure 3. Any point below 1.0 means that the offloading strategy is beneficial on the course of three years. Any point above 1.0 means that the offloading is economically detrimental for the ISP.

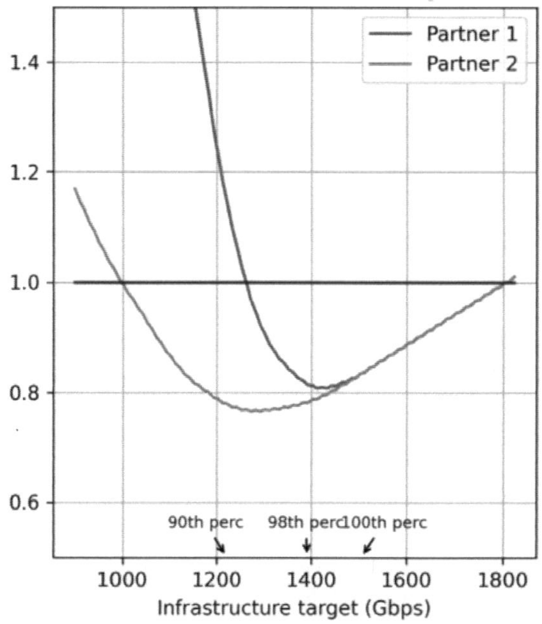


FIGURE 3: COMPARISON BETWEEN A PEAK OFFLOADING STRATEGY AND A TELCO-CDN APPROACH. ON THE Y-AXIS, THE RATIO BETWEEN THE COST OF THE OFFLOADING STRATEGY TO THE COST OF THE REGULAR TELCO-CDN.

The offloading strategy can be efficient. It is however noteworthy that it is far from being always the case. In particular, with the partner 1, the offloading strategy is not to recommend for any Telco-CDN infrastructure below 1.3 Tbps. One of the main lessons learned from this analysis is that the optimal configuration is when the Telco-CDN infrastructure is not far from the peak. It means that the volume of data to offload stays relatively small, so the extra-cost of offloading is limited, while the ISP does not invest for extra-capacity which are too rarely used (less than 5% of the time).

## Conclusion

In this paper, we have studied peak offloading strategy for Telco-CDN. We have first explained the rationale behind the deployment of Telco-CDN. We have then presented a model which combines capacity investment and traffic modeling. We have presented the techniques that are necessary for the implementation of the peak offloading strategy. Finally, we have shown on an example that the cost reduction up to 25% can be obtained on a real case.

## References


[1] Wohlfart, F., Chatzis, N., Dabanoglu, C., Carle, G., and Willinger, W. "Leveraging Interconnections for Performance: The Serving Infrastructure of a Large CDN". *Proceedings of ACM Sigcomm Conference*, 2018.

[2] Stocker, V. Smaragdakis G., Lehr, W, and Bauer S. "The growing complexity of content delivery networks: Challenges and implications for the Internet ecosystem". *Telecommunications Policy*, 41(10), 1003—1016, 2017.

[3] Shumway, R. H., Stoffer, D. S., Shumway, R. H., and Stoffer, D. S. "ARIMA models". *Time Series Analysis and Its Applications: With R Examples*, 75-163, 2017

[4] Torres, J.F., Hadjout, D., Sebaa, A., Martínez-Álvarez, F. and Troncoso, A. "Deep learning for time series forecasting: a survey". *Big Data*, 9(1), pp.3-21, 2021.

[5] Taylor SJ, and Letham B. "Forecasting at Scale". *The American Statistician*. Jan 2;72(1):37-45. 2018.

[6] Akpinar K, and Hua KA. "PPNet: Privacy protected CDN-ISP collaboration for QoS-aware multi-CDN adaptive video streaming". *ACM Transactions on Multimedia Computing, Communications, and Applications (TOMM)*. May 19;16(2):1-23, 2020.

[7] Aldwyan Y, Sinnott RO, and Jayaputera GT. "Elastic deployment of container clusters across geographically distributed cloud data centers for web applications". *Concurrency and Computation: Practice and Experience*. Nov 10;33(21):e6436. 2021.

[8] Arsham F., Nilsson M., and Appleby S.. "Adaptive media streaming over IP multicast (mABR) a data analytic evaluation." In *Proceedings of the 2nd International Workshop on Design, Deployment, and Evaluation of Network-Assisted Video Streaming*, pp. 14-20. 2022.

[9] Huang, C., Li, J. and Ross, K.W.. Peer-assisted VoD: Making internet video distribution cheap. In *6th International workshop on Peer-To-Peer Systems (IPTPS), Bellevue, WA, USA*. 2007.

# Perceptually-aware Live VBR Encoding Scheme for Adaptive AVC Streaming

**Vignesh V. Menon,[1] Prajit T. Rajendran,[2] Christian Feldmann,[3] Martin Smole,[3] Mohammad Ghanbari,[1,4] Christian Timmerer[1]**

**[1]Christian Doppler Laboratory ATHENA, Alpen-Adria-Universität**
**Klagenfurt, Austria**

**[2]CEA, List, F-91120 Palaiseau, Université Paris-Saclay**
**France**

**[3]Bitmovin**
**Klagenfurt, Austria**

**[4]School of Computer Science and Electronic Engineering**
**University of Essex, United Kingdom**

**Abstract** – Currently, a fixed set of bitrate-resolution pairs termed a "bitrate ladder" is used in live streaming applications. Similarly, two-pass variable bitrate (VBR) encoding schemes are not used in live streaming applications to avoid the additional latency added by the first-pass. Bitrate ladder optimization is necessary to (i) decrease storage or delivery costs or/and (ii) increase Quality of Experience. Using two-pass VBR encoding improves compression efficiency, owing to better encoding decisions in the second-pass encoding using the first-pass analysis. In this light, this paper introduces a perceptually-aware constrained Variable Bitrate (cVBR) encoding Scheme (Live VBR) for HTTP adaptive streaming applications, which includes a joint optimization of the perceptual redundancy between the representations of the bitrate ladder, maximizing the perceptual quality (in terms of VMAF) and optimized constant rate factor (CRF). Discrete Cosine Transform (DCT)-energy-based low-complexity spatial and temporal features for every video segment, namely, brightness, spatial texture information, and temporal activity, are extracted to predict a perceptually-aware bitrate ladder for encoding. Experimental results show that, on average, Live VBR yields bitrate savings of 7.21% and 13.03% to maintain the same peak PSNR and VMAF, respectively, compared to the reference HTTP Live Streaming (HLS) bitrate ladder Constant Bitrate (CBR) encoding using x264 AVC encoder without any noticeable additional latency in streaming. Additionally, Live VBR results in a 52.59% cumulative decrease in storage space for various representations, and a 28.78% cumulative decrease in energy consumption, considering a perceptual difference of 6 VMAF points.

## Introduction

In video streaming, video encoding is optimized per-title to increase Quality of Experience (QoE) for end-users and reduce streaming costs for service providers, mainly in Video on Demand (VoD) applications. In live streaming applications, due to the sensitivity to latency, video contents usually use a fixed set of encoding parameters without considering optimization in the process.

---

## Background of Per-title Encoding

The video sequences are encoded at a fixed set of bitrates and resolutions (referred to as the bitrate ladder) to adapt to the network conditions of end-users. Traditionally, a fixed bitrate ladder, e.g., HTTP Live Streaming (HLS) bitrate ladder [1], is used for all video contents. However, due to the vast diversity in video content characteristics and network conditions, a "one-size-fits-all" approach does not exist and, thus, the encoding is optimized per title to increase the QoE or decrease the bitrate of the representations as introduced for VoD services [2]. Per-title encoding schemes are based on a particular resolution performing better than others in a specific region for a given bitrate range. Furthermore, the selected bitrate-resolution pairs from the convex-hull for the bitrate ladder may not always be perceptually different in video quality.

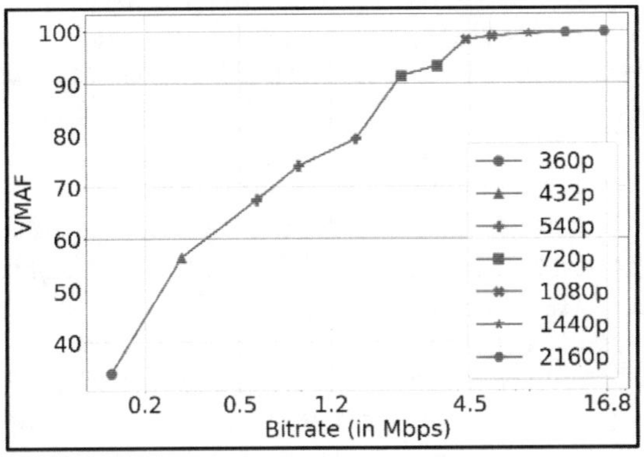


FIGURE 1: RD CURVE OF THE HLS CBR ENCODING OF CHARACTERS_S000 VIDEO SEQUENCE (SEGMENT) OF VCD DATASET [5] USING X264 ENCODER AT ULTRAFAST PRESET. THE POINTS WITH A BITRATE GREATER THAN 3.6 MBPS ARE IN THE PERCEPTUALLY LOSSLESS REGION. HENCE, THERE IS SIGNIFICANT STORAGE WASTAGE WHILE STORING THESE REPRESENTATIONS.

For example, Figure 1 shows the selected resolution-bitrate pairs and their video multimethod assessment fusion (VMAF) scores of Characters sequence using the HLS bitrate ladder. It is observed that there are multiple representations with the same video quality (i.e., VMAF close to 100). There are also representations with similar quality at mid-range bitrates. Selecting similar-quality representations for the bitrate ladder does not result in improved QoE, but it will lead to increased storage and bandwidth costs. Compression gain can be achieved by removing the perceptual redundancy information compared to traditional video coding methods [3, 4].

Though per-title encoding schemes [2, 6, 7] enhance the quality of video delivery, determining the convex-hull is computationally costly, making it suitable for only VoD streaming applications. Some per-title encoding methods pre-analyze the video contents to avoid a brute force encoding of all bitrate-resolution pairs. Katsenou, et al. [8] introduced a content-gnostic method that employs machine learning to find the bitrate range for each resolution that outperforms other resolutions. The authors claimed an average Bjøntegaard Delta Rate (BDR) [9] loss of 0.51% and an average BD-PSNR loss of 0.01 dB compared to the ground truth while significantly reducing the number of pre-encodes required when compared to two other methods (by 81% - 94%). Katsenou, et al. [10] extended the scheme mentioned earlier to predict a content-optimized bitrate ladder for VoD services. The method extracts spatiotemporal features from uncompressed content, trains machine-learning models to predict the Pareto front parameters, and, based on that, builds the ladder within a defined bitrate range. The proposed method claimed an overall 83.83% reduction of required encodings at an average BDR difference of 1.26%. Bhat et al. [11] proposed a Random Forest (RF) classifier to decide the encoding resolution best suited over different quality ranges and studied machine learning-based adaptive resolution prediction. Bhat et al. [6] further proposed a resolution prediction without requiring multiple encoding with the help of machine learning, where two machine learning networks are defined based on the resolution of the previous decision period. Zabrovskiy, et al. [12] predicted an optimized bitrate ladder for each scene using an artificial neural network (ANN). However, these approaches yield latency much higher than the accepted latency in live streaming. To summarize, most related works on per-title encoding yield latency unsuitable for live streaming. Machine learning-based methods are too complex and storage heavy, hence, not suitable for real-time deployments. The plethora of live streaming applications call for low latency approaches to optimize video coding.

## Background of cVBR Encoding

Most streaming service providers use Constant Bitrate (CBR) rate-control mode to encode live videos at a fixed bitrate ladder. The consistency of CBR makes it more reliable for time-sensitive data transport, especially in live streaming applications. Since CBR-encoded files are streamed consistently, there is no concern about the bitrate overshoot, i.e., the encoded bitrate exceeding internet speeds. However, the reliability of this method leads to sacrificing compression efficiency in some situations. In contrast, VoD applications use Variable Bitrate (VBR), where video segments are encoded according to their complexity to optimize the transmission at the cost of adding a pre-processing step to determine the complexity of segments (two-pass encoding). Regarding encoding, bitrate is distributed among segments based on complexity so that the average bitrate remains constant. Constrained Variable Bitrate (cVBR) encoding is the most popular type of VBR encoding. cVBR encoding scheme requires setting a maximum bitrate and a maximum buffer window and uses two encoding passes to process data. Since the target bitrate cannot be specified in Constant Rate Factor (CRF) rate control mode, information achieved in the first-pass is used to identify the optimized CRF to accomplish the target bitrate. In the second-pass, the segment is encoded with the selected, optimized CRF with the maximum bitrate and maximum buffer window constraints. In this manner, the desired target bitrate is achieved with maximum compression efficiency. However, in cVBR two-pass encoding, the encoder processes all segments for the stream twice. Due to the latency introduced by the first-pass to achieve the optimal encoding parameters (i.e., CRF) for the second-pass, two-pass encoding is not used in live streaming applications.

## Goal

This paper targets a cVBR two-pass encoding scheme with a content-adaptive, perceptually-aware, online bitrate ladder prediction optimized for live adaptive AVC streaming applications, as shown in Figure 2. The minimum and maximum encoding bitrates ($b_{min}$ and $b_{max}$), target perceptual difference between representations ($v_J$), and a priori information such as the encoder and its corresponding encoding parameters (termed as preset) are input to the scheme. Based on the video complexity features (extracted in real-time) and the input parameters, N (bitrate, resolution, CRF) parameters are predicted for the encoding process. As shown in Figure 3, the tth point of the bitrate ladder is represented as $(r_{t-1}, b_{t-1})$. $(r_{t-1}, b_{t-1})$ and $(r_t, b_t)$ points of the bitrate ladder (where t ≥ 1) have a perceptual quality difference of $v_J$. This encoding scheme increases the overall compression efficiency of the bitrate ladder encoding but also decreases the overall storage required to store the representations.

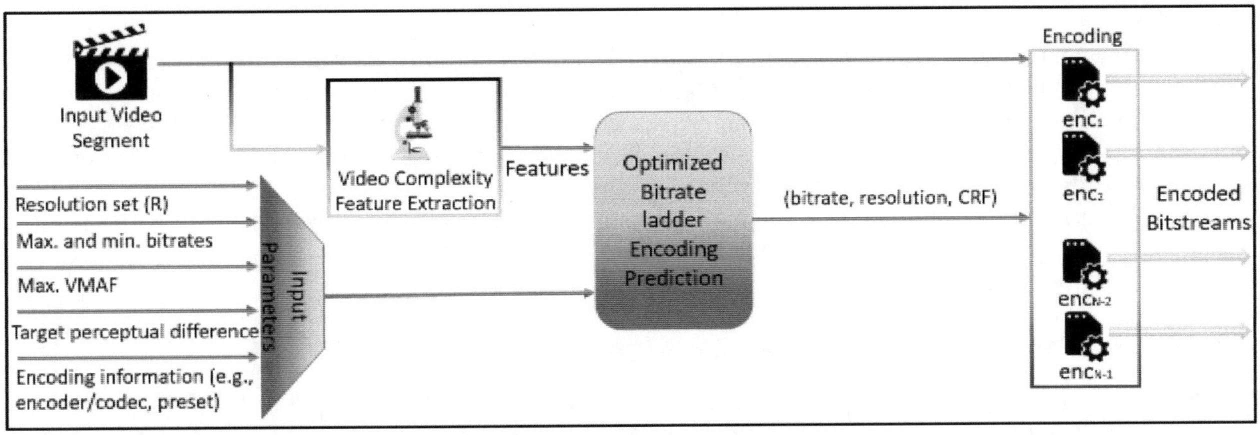


FIGURE 2: THE ENCODING PIPELINE USING LIVE VBR ENVISIONED IN THIS PAPER.

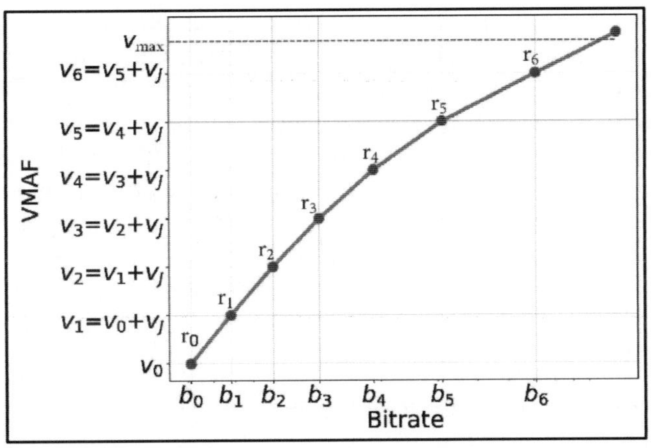


FIGURE 3: THE IDEAL LIVE VBR BITRATE LADDER ENVISIONED IN THIS PAPER. THE BLUE LINE DENOTES THE CORRESPONDING RATE-DISTORTION CURVE, WHILE THE RED DOTTED LINE INDICATES VMAF = $v_{max}$. THE VIDEO STREAM IS DEEMED PERCEPTUALLY LOSSLESS WHEN THE VMAF VALUE IS GREATER THAN VMAX. $v_J$ REPRESENTS THE TARGET PERCEPTUAL DIFFERENCE BETWEEN REPRESENTATIONS.

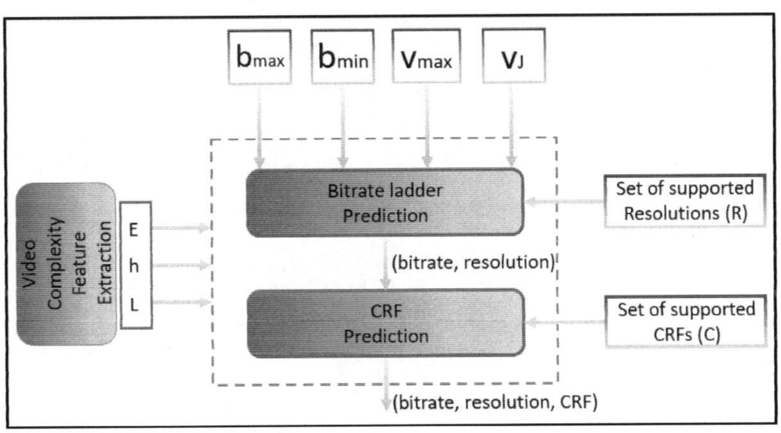


FIGURE 4: LIVE VBR ARCHITECTURE FOR A GIVEN ENCODER CONFIGURATION (TERMED AS PRESET).

### Contributions

In this paper, a low-latency perceptually-aware cVBR encoding scheme termed Live VBR is proposed, which includes an online bitrate ladder prediction for adaptive live AVC streaming. Optimized CRF prediction for each representation further improves the compression efficiency. To predict the bitrate-resolution-CRF pairs, Discrete Cosine Transform (DCT)-energy-based low-complexity spatial and temporal features are extracted. Based on these features, a low-complexity joint-optimization algorithm is proposed to maximize the perceptual quality, minimize the encoding bitrate and maintain the perceptual quality difference between representations.

## Live VBR Scheme

The architecture of the proposed Live VBR scheme for streaming applications is shown in Figure 5. The perceptually aware bitrate ladder is predicted for every segment of the input video sequence such that the adjacent points of the bitrate ladder have a perceptual quality difference of $v_J$. The bitrate ladder is predicted using the video complexity features extracted for every segment and the set of pre-defined resolutions ($R$), minimum and maximum target bitrates (i.e., $b_{min}$ and $b_{max}$, respectively), $v_J$, and the maximum VMAF ($v_{max}$) of the bitrate ladder. $b_{min}$, $b_{max}$, and $v_{max}$ are input to this scheme to ensure that the predicted bitrates and VMAF values are within the specified range of bitrates and VMAF values required by the streaming service provider. This ensures that the scheme can be tuned to accommodate the optimized number of representations in the bitrate ladder by considering the maximum bitrate and VMAF supported in the bitrate ladder of the streaming service provider. $R$ is input to the scheme to ensure that only the resolutions supported by the streaming service provider are selected to generate the encoding set. Live VBR first takes $b_{min}$ and predicts its corresponding VMAF. The VMAF scores for the remaining representations are determined by adding VMAF (until $b_{max}$ or $v_{max}$ is reached) of the previous point of the bitrate ladder with $v_J$. These VMAF values are then used to predict their corresponding bitrate-

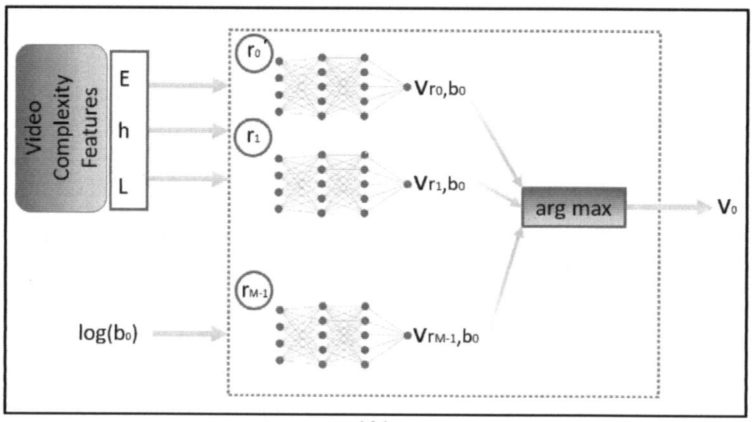


(A)

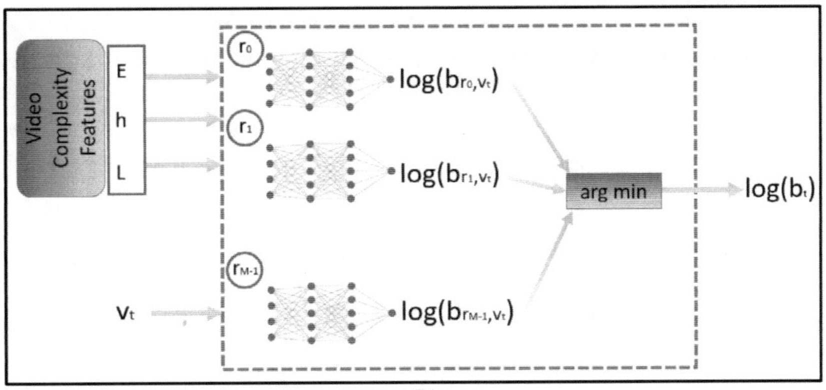


(B)

FIGURE 5: (A) ESTIMATION OF THE FIRST POINT OF THE BITRATE LADDER, (B) ESTIMATION OF THE (T+1)TH POINT OF THE BITRATE LADDER.

resolution pairs. Optimized CRF is also predicted to ensure maximum compression efficiency for the cVBR encoding of the selected bitrate-resolution pairs. The encoding process is carried out only for the predicted perceptually aware bitrate-resolution-CRF triple for each segment, thereby eliminating the need to encode the segments at all resolutions and CRFs to determine the optimized bitrate-resolution-CRF triples for every segment. In this manner, compression efficiency is improved over traditional fixed bitrate ladder encoding schemes and CBR encoding schemes while also decreasing storage costs. Live VBR is clustered into four phases:

(a) Video complexity feature extraction
(b) Perceptually-optimized bitrate ladder prediction
(c) Optimized CRF prediction for the selected bitrate-resolution pairs
(d) cVBR encoding of segments using the predicted bitrate-resolution-CRF triples

## Feature Extraction

In this paper, three DCT-energy-based features, (i) the average texture energy E, (ii) the average gradient of the texture energy h, and (iii) the average luminescence L are used as the spatial and temporal complexity measures [13–17]. The spatial and temporal characteristics of the video segment are used in the following steps to predict the encoding bitrate ladder.

## Bitrate Ladder Prediction

As depicted in Figure 5A, VMAF is projected for $b_o = b_{min}$ for all resolutions in $R$ to find the first point of the bitrate ladder. The highest value is taken into account for the bitrate ladder from the $v_{r,b_0}$ values acquired for various resolutions. The r value that corresponds to the maximum $v_{r,b_0}$ is chosen as $r_0$. The starting point of the bitrate ladder is thus $(r_0, b_0)$.

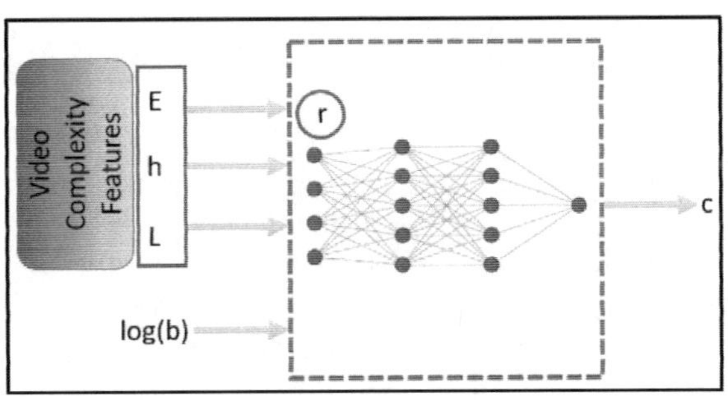


FIGURE 6: ESTIMATION OF THE OPTIMIZED CRF TO ACHIEVE THE TARGET BITRATE USING A PREDICTION MODEL TRAINED FOR A GIVEN RESOLUTION.

For every (t + 1)th point in the bitrate ladder (t > 0), the desired VMAF is $v_t = v_{t-1} + v_J$ , i.e., $v_J$ more than that of the tth point in the bitrate ladder (t > 0). The bitrate to achieve the target VMAF ($v_t$) for each resolution r, i.e., $b_{r,v_t}$, is determined as shown in Fig. 5B. The lowest value is considered as $b_t$ for the bitrate ladder from the $b_{r,v_t}$, values acquired for various resolutions. The chosen value of r is $r_t$, which is the resolution corresponding to this minimum value. The $(r_t, b_t)$ values are predicted iteratively until either $b_t$ is greater than or equal to $b_{max}$ or $v_t$ is greater than or equal to $v_{max}$.

The prediction models are trained for each resolution that the streaming service provider supports. As a result, the design is scalable, i.e., adding a new resolution to the framework does not involve retraining the entire network. In this study, VMAF and log(b) prediction are implemented using random forest models.

### CRF Prediction

The optimized CRF $\hat{c_t}$ is estimated for each $(r_t, b_t)$ using the E, h, and L features once the bitrate ladder has been established. As shown in Figure 6, a prediction model is trained for each resolution r that determines $\hat{c_t}$ based on E, h, L, and $\log(b_t)$ for every video segment. For x264 AVC encoder, the CRF has minimum and maximum values of 0 and 51, respectively ($c_{min}$ and $c_{max}$). For every resolution in $R$, random forest models are trained for CRF prediction.

## Evaluation

### Test Methodology

In this study, 400 sequences (80% of the total sequences) in the Video Complexity Dataset (VCD) [5] are used as the training dataset, and 200 sequences (20% of the total sequences) are used as the test dataset. The sequences are encoded using x264 v1.1 [18] at 30 frames per second with ultrafast preset on a dual-processor server with Intel Xeon Gold 5218R (80 cores, frequency at 2.10 GHz). The segment length is fixed to be four seconds. The resolutions considered in the paper are based on the Apple HLS authoring specifications, *i.e.*, $\boldsymbol{R}$ = {360p, 432p, 540p, 720p, 1080p, 1440p,2160p}. The values for the input parameters $\boldsymbol{b_{min}}$, $\boldsymbol{b_{max}}$, and $\boldsymbol{v_{max}}$ are 0.145 Mbps, 16.8 Mbps, and 94, respectively. In the experiments, the following target perceptual differences between the representations $\boldsymbol{v_J}$ are considered based on current industry practices: two [19], four, and six VMAF [20] points. The features *E*, *h* and *L* are extracted using VCA v2.0 video complexity analyzer [16] run in eight CPU threads using x86 SIMD optimization [21].

Firstly, the pre-processing time, i.e., latency in streaming introduced due to the time taken to extract *E*, *h*, and *L* features, and the inference time of the neural networks to predict the optimized bitrate ladder and CRF is determined to evaluate the first-pass encoding time. Secondly, the prediction accuracy of the VMAF, *log*(*b*), and CRF prediction models are assessed in terms of the $R^2$ score and Mean Absolute Error (MAE). Furthermore, the resulting overall quality in PSNR and VMAF and the achieved bitrate are compared for each test sequence. Rate-Distortion (RD) curves are analyzed for representative video sequences of various spatiotemporal complexities. Bjøntegaard delta rates [9] $BDR_P$ and $BDR_V$ refer to the average increase in bitrate of the representations compared with that of the reference bitrate ladder encoding scheme to maintain the same PSNR and VMAF, respectively. A negative BDR indicates a gain in coding efficiency of Live VBR compared to the reference bitrate ladder encoding scheme. BD-PSNR and BD-VMAF refer to the average increase in PSNR and VMAF, respectively, at the same bitrate compared with the reference bitrate ladder encoding scheme. A positive BD-PSNR and BD-VMAF denote a gain in coding efficiency of Live VBR compared to the reference bitrate ladder encoding scheme. The relative difference in the storage space required to store all representations of the Live VBR bitrate ladder (ΔS) is also evaluated as:

$$\Delta S = \frac{\sum b_{opt}}{\sum b_{ref}} - 1 \qquad (1)$$

where $\sum b_{ref}$ and $\sum b_{opt}$ represent the sum of bitrates of all representations in the reference bitrate ladder encoding and the optimized bitrate ladder encoding, respectively. Furthermore, the relative difference in the energy consumption of the Live VBR bitrate ladder (ΔE) is also evaluated in terms of the overall encoding time difference between the reference bitrate ladder encoding and the optimized bitrate ladder encoding as:

$$\Delta E = \frac{\sum t_{opt}}{\sum t_{ref}} - 1 \qquad (2)$$

where $\sum t_{ref}$ and $\sum t_{opt}$ represent the sum of encoding times of all representations in the reference and optimized bitrate ladder encoding, respectively. This paper considers the following encoding schemes to compare with Live VBR.

1. Ground truth bitrate ladder encoding [2], where videos are brute-force encoded using all of the CRFs that AVC supports for all resolutions to determine the optimized resolution-bitrate-CRF triples. The representations are selected such that there is a perceptual difference of the target $v_J$.
2. HLS CBR encoding [1], which is the CBR encoding of HLS bitrate ladder.

## Experimental Results

This section presents the results of Live VBR. *E, h*, and *L* features are extracted at an average speed of 370 frames per second. The average inference time of the random forest models for the bitrate ladder and CRF prediction is 5 ms. Since the video complexity feature extraction and the encoding bitrate-ladder prediction are executed as concurrent processes, the first-pass encoding speed is the minimum of the speed of the video complexity feature extraction and the encoding bitrate-ladder prediction, i.e., 250 frames per second, which deems it suitable for live-streaming applications.

Figure 7 shows the RD curves of the representative video sequences (segments) of various spatiotemporal complexities with HLS CBR encoding, Live VBR, and the ground truth bitrate ladder. It is observed that Live VBR determines the RD points such that the average quality difference between consecutive RD points is the target $v_J$ (in this paper, $v_J$ is assumed as 6). Additionally, the VMAF achieved is higher than HLS CBR encoding at the same target bitrates. The number of representations in Live VBR for every video segment is lower than the HLS ladder (12 representations for each video segment).

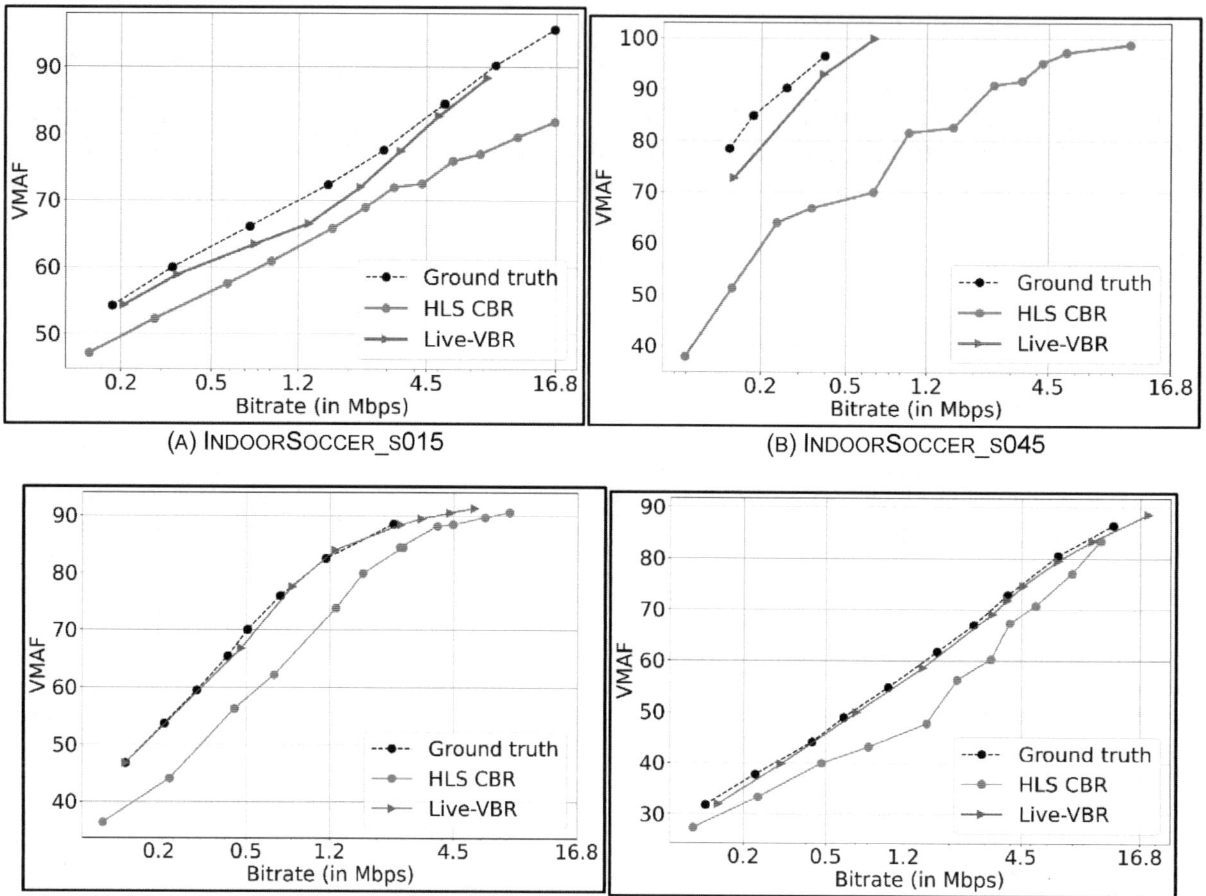


(A) INDOORSOCCER_S015

(B) INDOORSOCCER_S045

(C) SKATEBOARDING_S009

(D) TALLBUILDINGS_S000

FIGURE 7: COMPARISON OF RD CURVES OF REPRESENTATIVE VIDEO SEQUENCES (SEGMENTS) OF VARIOUS SPATIOTEMPORAL COMPLEXITIES USING THE HLS CBR ENCODING (GREEN LINE), AND LIVE VBR ENCODING (RED LINE). PLEASE NOTE THAT THE TARGET $v_J$ IS SIX IN THESE PLOTS.

The bitrate savings findings of the schemes in terms of $BDR_P$, $BDR_V$, and ΔS as compared to the HLS CBR encoding are summarized in Table 1. When forecasts are 100% accurate, ground truth ($v_J$=2), ground truth ($v_J$=4), and ground truth ($v_J$=6) are presented as the best results. As a result, compared to HLS CBR encoding, the ground truth findings represent the maximum bound of the compression efficiency improvement (using VMAF as the quality metric). Compared to the HLS CBR encoding, Live VBR with a target $v_J$=2 delivers bitrate savings of 7.29% and 11.75%, respectively, to retain the same PSNR and VMAF. However, there is a cumulative 12.14% increase in storage space needed for various representations. It is due to an increase in the number of representations when $v_J$=2. The reduction in storage space required is observed as 26.91% and 52.59%, respectively, with a target $v_J$=4 and $v_J$=6. Table 1 also summarizes the qualitative analysis results of the schemes in terms of BD-PSNR and BD-VMAF. Live VBR encoding (with $v_J$=2, $v_J$=4 and $v_J$=6) yields average BD-PSNR of 0.46 dB, 0.38 dB, and 0.34 dB, respectively. Similarly, the schemes yield average BD-VMAF of 1.71, 1.60, and 1.72, respectively.

| Method | $BDR_P$ | $BDR_V$ | BD-PSNR | BD-VMAF | $\Delta S$ | $\Delta E$ |
|---|---|---|---|---|---|---|
| Ground truth ($v_J$=2) | -6.03% | -17.81% | 0.32 dB | 2.82 | -20.42% | 51.95% |
| Ground truth ($v_J$=4) | -6.31% | -22.49% | 0.27 dB | 3.24 | -36.61% | -0.74% |
| Ground truth ($v_J$=6) | -6.59% | -22.44% | 0.32 dB | 3.15 | -54.47% | -29.18% |
| Live VBR ($v_J$=2) | -7.29% | -11.75% | 0.46 dB | 1.71 | 12.14% | 61.31% |
| Live VBR ($v_J$=4) | -6.89% | -11.56% | 0.38 dB | 1.60 | -26.91% | 8.53% |
| Live VBR ($v_J$=6) | -7.21% | -13.03% | 0.34 dB | 1.72 | -52.59% | -28.78% |

TABLE 1: AVERAGE RESULTS OF THE ENCODING SCHEMES COMPARED TO THE HLS CBR ENCODING.

Finally, the relative difference in energy consumption for encoding ($\Delta E$) compared to HLS CBR encoding is discussed. Live VBR encoding (with $v_J$=2, $v_J$=4 and $v_J$=6) yields an average $\Delta E$ of 61.31%, 8.53%, and -28.78%, respectively. Hence, Live VBR ($v_J$=6) is shown to be a green encoding with lower energy consumption compared to HLS CBR encoding.

## Conclusions

The paper introduces Live VBR, an online cVBR encoding technique for HTTP adaptive streaming that considers perceptual factors. Live VBR optimizes the bitrate difference between the representations in the bitrate ladder and maximizes VMAF through joint optimization. The optimized AVC encoding bitrate ladder is predicted based on the spatial and temporal features of the video segment's DCT energy, resulting in resolution-bitrate-CRF triples. This ladder is designed to minimize the perceptual redundancy among the representations by ensuring a defined perceptual difference (in terms of VMAF) between them. Live VBR achieves average bitrate savings of 7.21% and 13.03% for maintaining the same PSNR and VMAF, respectively, compared to the reference HLS bitrate ladder CBR encoding using x264 AVC encoder, without noticeable additional latency in streaming. Furthermore, it results in a 52.59% cumulative decrease in storage space for various representations and a 28.78% cumulative decrease in energy consumption, considering a JND of six VMAF points.

## Acknowledgments

The financial support of the Austrian Federal Ministry for Digital and Economic Affairs, the National Foundation for Research, Technology and Development, and the Christian Doppler Research Association is gratefully acknowledged. Christian Doppler Laboratory ATHENA: https://athena.itec.aau.at/

## References

[1] Apple Inc., "HLS Authoring Specification for Apple Devices," [Online]. Available: https://developer.apple.com/documentation/http_live_streaming/hls_authoring_specification_for_apple_devices, last access: Feb. 28, 2023.

[2] J. De Cock, Z. Li, M. Manohara, and A. Aaron, "Complexity-based consistent-quality encoding in the cloud," in 2016 IEEE International Conference on Image Processing (ICIP), 2016, pp. 1484–1488.

[3] T. Huang, R.-X. Zhang, and L. Sun, "Deep Reinforced Bitrate Ladders for Adaptive Video Streaming," ser. NOSSDAV '21. New York, NY, USA: Association for Computing Machinery, 2021, p. 66–73. [Online]. Available: https://doi.org/10.1145/3458306.3458873.

[4] D. Yuan, T. Zhao, Y. Xu, H. Xue, and L. Lin, "Visual JND: A Perceptual Measurement in Video Coding," IEEE Access, vol. 7, pp. 29 014–29 022, 2019.

[5] H. Amirpour, V. V. Menon, S. Afzal, M. Ghanbari, and C. Timmerer, "VCD: Video Complexity Dataset," in Proceedings of the 13th ACM Multimedia Systems Conference, ser. MMSys '22. New York, NY, USA: Association for Computing Machinery, 2022, p. 234–239. [Online]. Available: https://doi.org/10.1145/3524273.3532892.

[6] M. Bhat, J.-M. Thiesse, and P. Le Callet, "A Case Study of Machine Learning Classifiers for Real-Time Adaptive Resolution Prediction in Video Coding," in 2020 IEEE International Conference on Multimedia and Expo (ICME), 2020, pp. 1–6.

[7] D. Silhavy, C. Krauss, A. Chen, A.-T. Nguyen, C. Müller, S. Arbanowski, S. Steglich, and L. Bassbouss, "Machine Learning for Per-Title Encoding," SMPTE Motion Imaging Journal, vol. 131, no. 3, pp. 42–50, 2022.

[8] A. V. Katsenou, J. Sole, and D. R. Bull, "Content-gnostic Bitrate Ladder Prediction for Adaptive Video Streaming," in 2019 Picture Coding Symposium (PCS), 2019.

[9] G. Bjontegaard, "Calculation of average PSNR differences between RD-curves," VCEG-M33, 2001.

[10] A. V. Katsenou, J. Sole, and D. R. Bull, "Efficient Bitrate Ladder Construction for Content-Optimized Adaptive Video Streaming," IEEE Open Journal of Signal Processing, vol. 2, pp. 496–511, 2021.

[11] M. Bhat, J.-M. Thiesse, and P. L. Callet, "Combining Video Quality Metrics To Select Perceptually Accurate Resolution In A Wide Quality Range: A Case Study," in 2021 IEEE International Conference on Image Processing (ICIP), 2021, pp. 2164–2168.

[12] A. Zabrovskiy, P. Agrawal, C. Timmerer, and R. Prodan, "FAUST: Fast Per-Scene Encoding Using Entropy-Based Scene Detection and Machine Learning," in 2021 30$^{th}$ Conference of Open Innovations Association FRUCT, 2021, pp. 292–302.

[13] V. V. Menon, H. Amirpour, C. Timmerer, and M. Ghanbari, "INCEPT: Intra CU Depth Prediction for HEVC," in 2021 IEEE 23rd International Workshop on Multimedia Signal Processing (MMSP), 2021, pp. 1–6.

[14] V. V. Menon, H. Amirpour, M. Ghanbari, and C. Timmerer, "CODA: Content-aware Frame Dropping Algorithm for High Frame-rate Video Streaming," in 2022 Data Compression Conference (DCC), 2022, pp. 475–475.

[15] V. V. Menon, H. Amirpour, M. Ghanbari, and C. Timmerer, "OPTE: Online Per-Title Encoding for Live Video Streaming," in ICASSP 2022 - 2022 IEEE International Conference on Acoustics, Speech and Signal Processing (ICASSP), 2022, pp. 1865–1869.

[16] V. V. Menon, C. Feldmann, H. Amirpour, M. Ghanbari, and C. Timmerer, "VCA: Video Complexity Analyzer," in Proceedings of the 13th ACM Multimedia Systems Conference, ser. MMSys '22. New York, NY, USA: Association for Computing Machinery, 2022, p. 259–264. [Online]. Available: https://doi.org/10.1145/3524273.3532896.

[17] M. King, Z. Tauber, and Z.-N. Li, "A New Energy Function for Segmentation and Compression," in 2007 IEEE International Conference on Multimedia and Expo, 2007, pp. 1647–1650.

[18] VideoLAN, “x264,” [Online]. Available: https://www.videolan.org/developers/x264.html, last access: Feb. 28, 2023.

[19] A. Kah, C. Friedrich, T. Rusert, C. Burgmair, W. Ruppel, and M. Narroschke, “Fundamental relationships between subjective quality, user acceptance, and the VMAF metric for a quality-based bit-rate ladder design for over-the-top video streaming services,” in Applications of Digital Image Processing XLIV, vol. 11842, 2021, p. 118420Z. [Online]. Available: https://doi.org/10.1117/12.2593952.

[20] J. Ozer, “Finding the Just Noticeable Difference with Netflix VMAF,” Sep. 2017. [Online] Available: https://streaminglearningcenter.com/codecs/finding-the-just-noticeable-difference-with-netflix-vmaf.html, last access: Feb. 28, 2023.

[21] P. Tiwari, V. V. Menon, J. Murugan, J. Chandrasekaran, G. Akisetty, and P. Ramachandran, “Accelerating x265 with Intel® Advanced Vector Extensions 512,” White Paper on the Intel Developers Page, 2018. [Online]. Available: https://www.intel.com/content/dam/develop/external/us/en/documents/mcw-intel-x265-avx512.pdf, last access: Feb. 28, 2023.

# Ultra-low Latency OTT Delivery: The Killer Technology for Betting, Social Networking and Metaverse

**Mickaël Raulet and Khaled Jerbi**
**ATEME**
**France and Canada**
m.raulet@ateme.com, k.jerbi@ateme.com

**Abstract** – Ultra-low latency over-the-top (OTT) video streaming is becoming increasingly important in gaming, metaverse, and gambling applications, enabling social interaction and monetization in live events such as sports and concerts. Moreover, all those applications are conceptually converging. These applications require real-time, interactive experiences that are highly responsive and immersive, and ultra-low latency OTT streaming is essential for delivering this type of experience. Tremendous innovation resources have been invested to build robust OTT delivery systems with ultra-low latency capabilities. Necessary optimizations affect most steps from encoding to packaging and even last mile delivery. In this paper, we explain a setup that leverages the ultra-low latency technology using the Live Media Ingest Protocol and Just-In-Time packaging. We also explore how such setup can be used to enable amazing technologies that have direct impact on the performance of the Content Delivery Network (CDN) and the users' quality of experience (QOE) to achieve the seamless and immersive experience they require.

## Introduction

Over-the-top streaming has revolutionized the way we consume media, enabling us to watch video content on demand and without the need for traditional cable or satellite TV subscriptions. With the rise of gaming, metaverse, and betting applications, the industry requirement to go further and seek ultra-low latency OTT streaming has become increasingly apparent. Ultra-low latency streaming refers to the ability to deliver content with extremely low delay between the source and the end-user, generally required to be under 2 seconds. In the context of gaming, metaverse [1], and betting applications, embedding ultra-low latency video is crucial to ensure a seamless and immersive experience. Users require near real-time interaction with other users, and any lag or delay can significantly impact their mutual experience.

In gaming, we already know that ultra-low latency streaming is critical for competitive online gameplay. An innovative way to improve the experience of gamers would be to mix the game with another event broadcast via OTT, such as an advertisement or a live concert or sports event. The gamer should be able to interact with both events and even with other users at the same time. The latency requirement on the new added event must be under one second. Similarly, in the metaverse, users require real-time interaction with other users and virtual objects to fully immerse themselves in the virtual world. Any lag or delay can break the illusion of being present in the virtual environment. In betting applications, low latency streaming is essential to ensure fair and transparent results. Any delay in the streaming of the event can lead to suspicions of cheating or fraud, which can damage the reputation of the application and deter users from using it in the future. This paper will explore the challenges involved in delivering

This paper is excerpted from the Proceedings of the 2023 NAB Broadcast Engineering and Information Technology (BEIT) Conference, © 2023, National Association of Broadcasters, 1 M Street SE, Washington, DC 20003 USA.

low latency video streaming in a gaming and in a virtual environment, the benefits of achieving ultra-low latency, and the emerging technologies that can help improve the quality of experience.

## OTT Latency Evolution in a Nutshell

OTT delivery has several advantages over traditional satellite or cable delivery of video content. First, it can provide better video quality than traditional satellite or cable. OTT services can deliver high-quality video content in resolutions up to 4K, and they can use adaptive streaming technologies to ensure that users receive the best possible video quality based on their internet connection. Additionally, OTT delivery is more flexible than satellite or cable. With OTT, users can access content on a variety of devices, including laptops, smartphones, tablets, and smart TVs, and they can watch that content anywhere with an internet connection. In contrast, satellite and cable are tied to a physical infrastructure and limited by the availability of cables and satellite signals. We can also add the fact that OTT delivery is often more cost-effective than traditional satellite or cable delivery. While satellite and cable providers often require users to sign long-term contracts, pay for expensive hardware installations, and pay for bundles of channels that may include channels they're not interested in, OTT services typically offer more flexible pricing options for exactly what the user needs to watch.

That said, one of the biggest challenges that video streaming services face is latency. Latency refers to the delay between when a video is captured and when it is played back, and it can be a major problem for live events like sports or news broadcasts. In the beginning of OTT delivery, the overall latency was around 50 seconds: imagine the frustration of hearing your neighbors cheering for a goal that you get to watch 50 seconds later. Considering the video flow, the most important latency factor is the segment duration because that duration also impacts the latency at each delivery step: encoding, packaging, storing, delivering, buffering, and displaying. As shown in Figure 1, an analogy of stream delivery steps is like a fluid that progresses from one container to another. Configurations A and B illustrate how waiting for large containers (large segments) to be filled takes much more time to fill and produce an output than smaller ones.

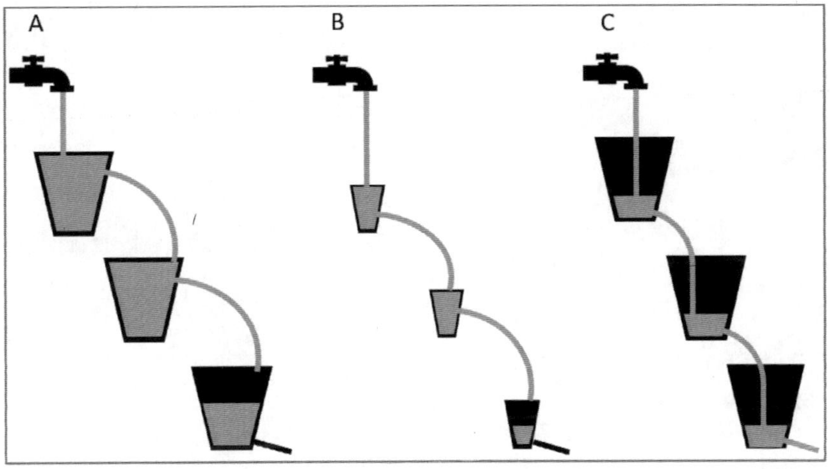


FIGURE 1: VIDEO DELIVERY PIPELINE WITH FLUID ANALOGY: (A) LARGE SEGMENTS, (B) SMALL SEGMENTS, (C) LARGE SEGMENTS WITH CMAF CHUNKS.

Even though it is possible to adopt configuration B and reduce the segment duration to very small values such as 0.5 seconds to get an impressive latency, this manipulation would have a disastrous impact on video quality because it involves putting several data-consuming key frames at the segment's borders. Thus, smarter solutions need to be found. In recent years, the adoption of the

Common Media Application Format (CMAF) [3] and Content Delivery Network (CDN) optimization has helped to solve this issue. CMAF allows for video segments to be delivered in smaller parts called chunks, which improves the efficiency of CDNs in delivering content to end-users while keeping reasonable encoding configurations.

The CMAF chunking is illustrated in configuration C of Figure 1 and enables reducing the bandwidth pipe while keeping reasonable segment durations. CDN optimization, on the other hand, involves strategically placing servers around the world to reduce the distance between the server and the end-user, thereby reducing propagation latency. The combination of these two technologies has led to a significant reduction in latency for OTT video streaming to values around 5 seconds, improving the viewing experience for millions of users around the world.

There is still a need to further reduce latency as new requirements and applications push the limits toward a latency requirement of less than 2 seconds. Indeed, in addition to gambling and gaming, which today have millions of followers, the emergent metaverse technology may be the next big social experience for all generations, following in the heels of social networks that have dominated the previous decade. These new applications require ultra-low latency to produce an engaging and realistic user experience. Figure 2 summarizes the applications involved for each latency interval according to video segmentation technology. Notice the number of new emergent applications in the range of ultra-low latency.

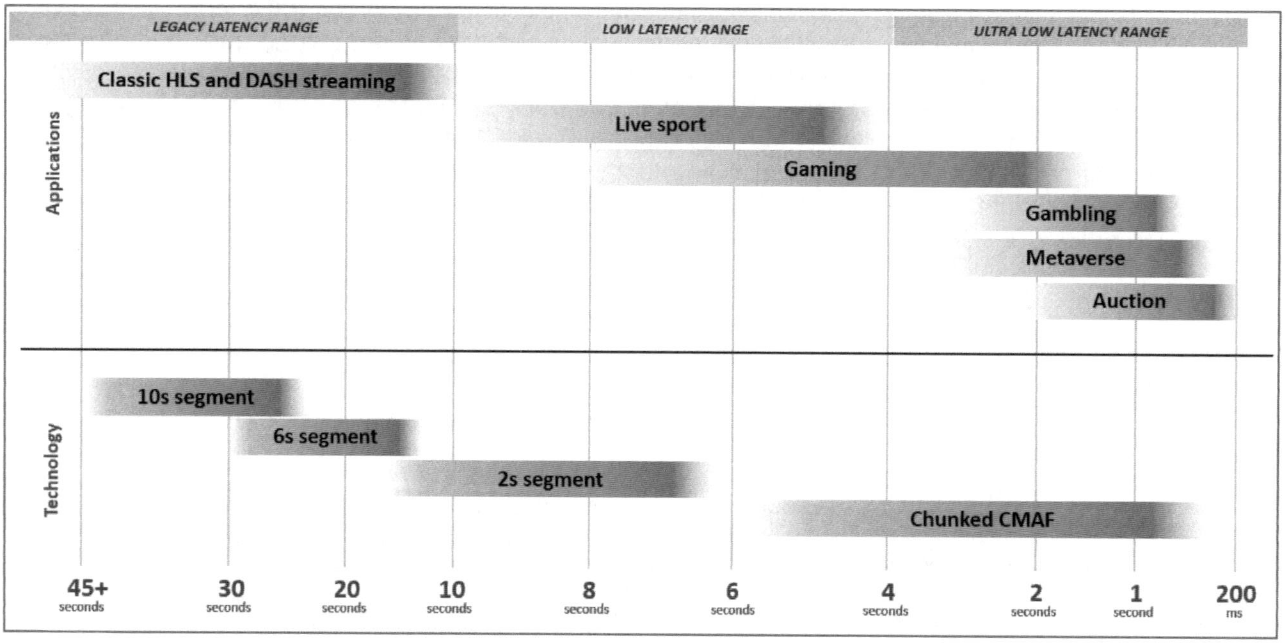


FIGURE 2: EVOLUTION OF APPLICATIONS USING OTT STREAMING, REGARDING LATENCY AND ITS CORRESPONDING TECHNOLOGY FOR VIDEO SEGMENTATION.

## Ultra-low Latency in Practice

Reducing latency in OTT video streaming is an ongoing challenge for streaming providers. One strategy is to combine efficient encoding configuration tuning with packager ingest improvement using the Media Ingest Protocol and optionally CDN caching optimization using byterange technology [5][6]. Additional optimizations can also be added at the player and at the mobile network level [7]. We explore all these aspects in this section.

To begin with, tuning the encoding configuration can help reduce latency by optimizing the video encoding process. Specifically, video encoding settings such as bitrate, resolution, and frame rate can be adjusted to balance video quality and latency. For instance, reducing the resolution and frame rate can lower latency without significantly impacting video quality. Moreover, compression standards offer the possibility to parallelize the compression of frame parts such as slices and tiles. This parallelization is crucial for high resolutions. In addition, using encoding techniques such as GOP (Group of Pictures) alignment, lookahead, frames reordering, and video buffering can significantly help reduce the time it takes to encode the video content. We tested our encoder with 1080x1920 video at 25 frames per second with different presets. In Figure 3, we can see that latency is reduced by a factor of three between the Best Quality preset and the Ultra-Low Latency one. The Lookahead parameter is very important in the encode process because it brings valuable predictive information from future frames to better encode current ones, but using future frames can have a tremendous impact on the latency as shown by the difference between the High Quality and Best Quality presets (yellow line). Note also that the curves are not linear and that dramatic changes in B frames or reordering number are not needed to have a significant latency reduction.

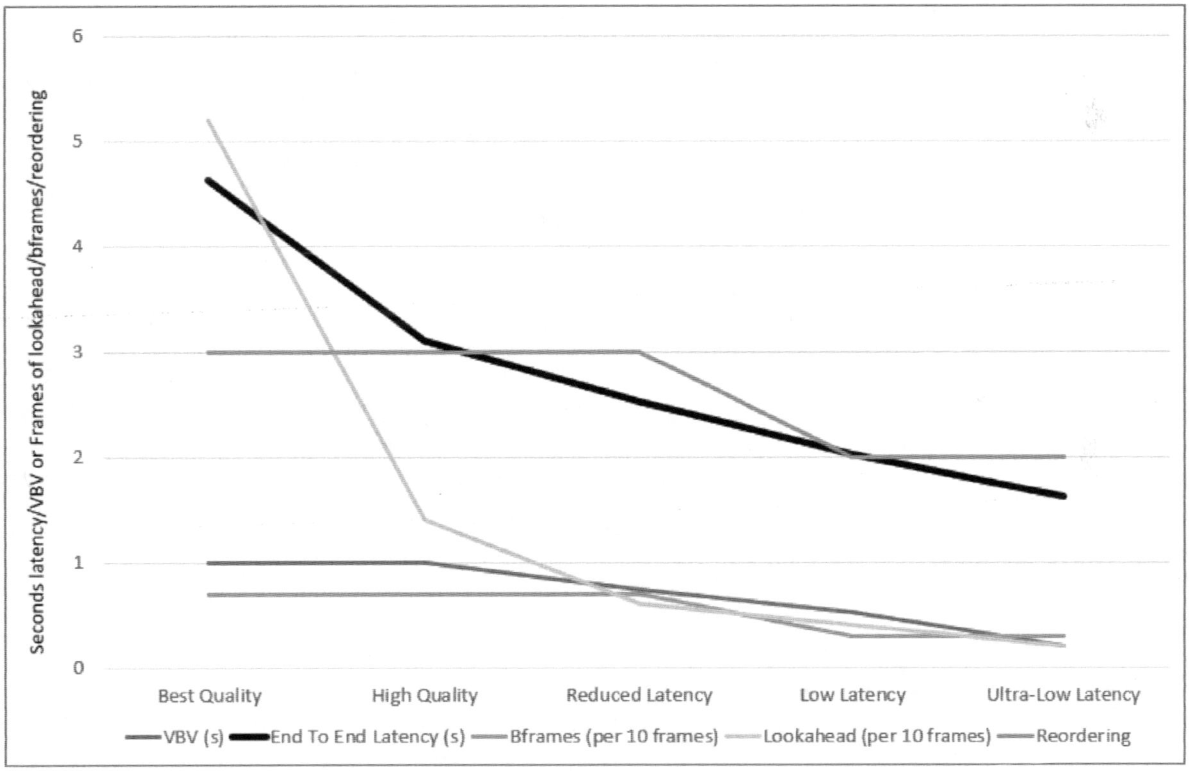


FIGURE 3: END TO END LATENCY EVOLUTION ACCORDING TO ENCODING PARAMETERS.

A related aspect of this setup is the video quality (VQ). In the previous section, we found out that tuning encoder parameters can reduce the encoder latency. However, those parameters can also impact on VQ, and we measure the relative impact using the ratio of the bitrate necessary to maintain same VQ to the original bitrate. Figure 4 shows some results of varying the bitrate. The latency decreases as expected as the relative bitrate increases, though curves are also not linear. For example, moving from 3.5 seconds to 2 seconds – about a 45% latency improvement – requires only a 10% bitrate increase. But, moving from 1.5 to 1.2 second latency – about a 20% improvement – requires about a 65% bitrate increase. Characterizing this nonlinear behavior is very important because we have identified an interval where we can dramatically reduce latency with a very low cost of increased bitrate.

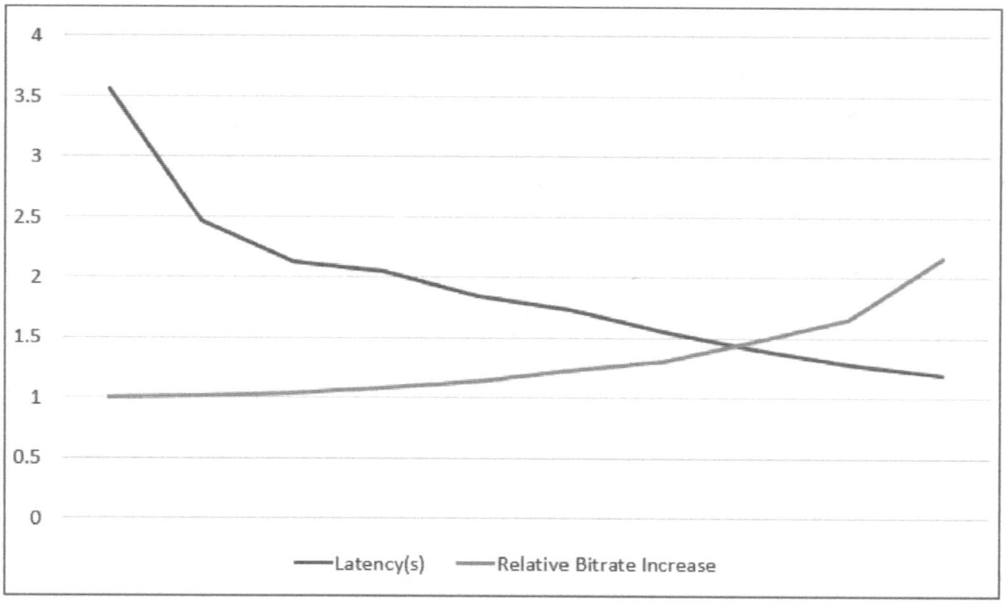


FIGURE 4: REQUIRED BITRATE RATIO TO MAINTAIN VIDEO QUALITY ACCORDING TO LATENCY.

Going beyond the encoder, the next step is the OTT packaging. In this step, we encapsulate the bitstream into an ISO-BMFF format [4] with the required playlists. Traditionally, this step was achieved with MPEG2-TS format. So, the encoder multiplexes the MPEG2-TS, and then packagers must demultiplex it and repackage it into ISO-BMFF format. That process is another source of latency. Recently, the DASH-IF and CMAF-IF developed a new protocol called Live Media Ingest Protocol [2] that allows sending CMAF format directly from the encoder to the packager (more generally, from any sender to receiver entity) and thus removing the MPEG2-TS manipulations from the flow.

Improving the packager ingest with this protocol is another strategy we deployed to reduce OTT video latency. Basically, the protocol defines two interfaces. One is for sending already packaged DASH format segments, and the other is for sending non-packaged CMAF fragments and chunks. The latter is the interface that suits our setup because we use a smart Just-In-Time packager as a receiving entity. Figure 5 shows the pipeline of the improved video flow. We measured around 1.5 second latency gain compared to MPEG2-TS usage.

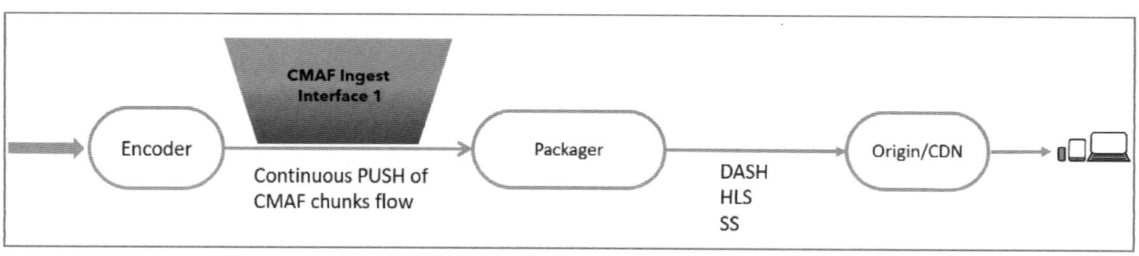


FIGURE 5: VIDEO FLOW OPTIMIZED PIPELINE WITH LIVE MEDIA INGEST PROTOCOL INTERFACE 1 FOR CMAF INGEST.

On the network side, optimizing the CDN cache with *byterange* technology is also crucial to reducing OTT video latency. *Byterange* technology improves the efficiency of the CDN cache and thus improves CDN latency. The technology is basically about delivering video chunks or parts without having them physically in the origin or CDN. OTT video players can be configured for either low latency or classic latency. In the case of classic latency, the CDN should be able to deliver normal segments and in the case of low latency the player will ask for chunks and the CDN should be able to deliver them.

Consequently, both segments and their corresponding chunks will be present in the CDN cache at the same time. Byterange technology allows requesting parts of the segment using their start position in the segment and their size and so the CDN does not require any more to store chunks. Here is an example of an HLS byterange request syntax of file part 6 starting at position 2000 in the file with a size of 100 bytes: `#EXT-X-PART:DURATION=0.2,URI="part6.mp4",BYTERANGE=100@2000`

Another important network breakthrough is the rising 5G network and its capabilities of reducing latency while transferring video from origins or CDNs to the final user. We could benefit from such technology to build promising unicast/multicast/broadcast infrastructures as detailed in [7].

All of the technologies described above combined allowed us to achieve an impressive 1.7 second latency, and we know that further improvement is possible using more buffering and network optimization.

Another important step that has a tremendous impact on latency is the player. In this experiment we are using *avplayer*, the native iOS player. Players have the hard task of managing buffering, dealing with network fluctuations and switching. Basically, if a player buffers a lot, it will create useless latency. However, if it does not buffer enough, any small network interruption would lead to video stuttering and forced buffering which directly impacts the QOE. Players also have another technique to manage networks and buffers using accelerated and slowed playback. More precisely, if a player has enough data in the buffer, it is possible to softly increase the playout speed by 10% or 20% and slowly get to the live edge and that recovery adjustment is hard to distinguish by normal viewers. Similarly, if the player notices a low level of buffer, it can decelerate the playback and keep the edge while having more time to buffer new data. For switching, every time a user changes a channel, the player must switch and wait for the first available segment key frame to be able to start decoding. In this context, technologies like HESP [8] suggest innovative advanced techniques to make that switch fast and seamless, using a sidetrack that has reference-frames only, allowing the decoder to find key frames at any time and quickly start rendering. Notice that a similar effort is being developed at DASH-IF to have fast-switching technology.

## Conclusion

In this paper we presented the concept of ultra-low latency OTT, and we explored the different technologies and applications that helped reduce it. In a practical way, we showed how we could reach about 1.7 second overall latency from encoder to playout, using encoder, packager and network optimizations. Since our contribution cannot cover the whole video delivery flow, we depend on other industrial infrastructures such as 5G networks, CDN, and players. In this context we relied on excellent low latency players that have advanced technologies for handling ultra-low latency streams. We also partnered with CDN and 5G providers that furnished ultra-low latency adapted setups.

These results show that we are holding the killer technology of ultra-low latency and it reveals to be a key for new applications that have strong latency constraints to use OTT. Among these applications, we bring OTT video in gambling, gaming, auctions, and the emergent metaverse technology. With ultra-low latency we should also be able to create new interactions where the gaming universe can cross into another event brought by OTT. It would be more consuming in bandwidth to reduce the latency, but it is worth it. The metaverse is about to revolutionize the way we interact. It is basically going to be Social Network 2.0 where not only texts and images are exchanged but also a full immersive experience that requires video and we believe ultra-low latency streaming is one of the main keys to enter this universe.

## References


[1] Dwivedi et al., 2022 Y. Dwivedi, L. Hughes, A. Baabdullah, S. Ribeiro-Navarrete, M. Giannakis, M. Al-Debei, D. Dennehy, B. Metri, D. Buhalis, C. Cheung, K. Conboy, R. Doyle, D.P. Goyal, A. Gustafsson, I. Jebabli, Y.-G. Kim, J. Kim, S. Koos, D. Kreps, ..., F. Wamba, *"Metaverse beyond the hype: Multidisciplinary perspectives on emerging challenges, opportunities, and agenda for research, practice and policy"*, International Journal of Information Management, 66 (2022), Article 102542.

[2] "*DASH-IF Live Media Ingest Protocol*" Technical Specification, https://dashif-documents.azurewebsites.net/Ingest/master/DASH-IF-Ingest.html

[3] ISO/IEC 23000-19:2018 *Information technology, Multimedia application format (MPEG-A) Part 19: Common media application format (CMAF) for segmented media.*

[4] ISO/IEC 14496-12:2015 - Information technology — Coding of audio-visual objects — Part 12: ISO base media file format.

[5] Web Application Video Ecosystem – DASH-HLS Interoperability Specification (CTA-5005), CTA-Wave.

[6] W. Law, E. Toullec and M. Raulet, "Universal CMAF Container for Efficient Cross-Format Low-Latency Delivery," in *SMPTE Motion Imaging Journal*, vol. 131, no. 6, pp. 17-25, July 2022, doi: 10.5594/JMI.2022.3175955.

[7] C. Burdinat, T. Stockhammer, M. Raulet and T. Biatek, "Network Operator-Provided 5G Streaming Media and Future Broadcast Services," in *SMPTE Motion Imaging Journal*, vol. 131, no. 6, pp. 10-16, July 2022, doi: 10.5594/JMI.2022.3175990.

[8] Pieter-Jan Speelmans. 2022. Low encoding overhead ultra-low latency streaming via HESP through sparse initialization streams. In Proceedings of the 1st Mile-High Video Conference (MHV '22). Association for Computing Machinery, New York, NY, USA, 115–116. https://doi.org/10.1145/3510450.3517294.

# BPS ATSC 3.0 Broadcast Emission Time Stabilization System Proof-of-concept

**Mark T. Corl**
**Triveni Digital, Inc.**
**Princeton, N.J., United States**
mcorl@trivenidigital.com

**Vladimir Anishchenko**
**Avateq Corp.**
**Markham, Ontario, Canada**
vlad_a@avateq.com

**Tariq Mondal**
**National Association of Broadcasters**
**Washington, D.C., United States**
tmondal@nab.org

**Abstract** – The ATSC 3.0 NextGen TV standard defines a precise time stamp of the emission time of each broadcast frame. The time stamp, along with the transmitting antenna location, can be used to determine the distance of the receiver from the transmitter. If at least three such ATSC 3.0 transmissions are available in an area, these broadcasts can be used as a precise positioning system, called a Broadcast Positioning System (BPS) [1], which can be used as a backup system for the Global Positioning System (GPS).

However, providing a precise time stamp is technically challenging due to various delays and variability in the broadcast transmission studio processing chain. This paper describes a proof-of-concept system, developed by multiple partner companies under the direction of NAB Pilot, that provides a closed loop time stabilization system. The paper explores the techniques used to measure the broadcast signal's emission time and to compensate for the processing chain timing variability stabilizing the emission time stamp. The paper also describes the lessons learned and the barriers to further improve the timing accuracy of the BPS system.

## Background

The preamble of an ATSC 3.0 frame carries the bootstrap emission timestamp. If this timestamp is accurate, a receiver can synchronize its clock using the ATSC 3.0 signal. Moreover, since the ATSC 3.0 signal can carry data, the location of the transmitting antenna can be sent with the signal as data. Armed with the precise bootstrap emission time and the location of the transmitting antenna, a receiver at a known location can maintain a very accurate clock.

A receiver can calculate its own location if it receives emission timestamps from three or more ATSC 3.0 transmitting antennas with known locations. A receiver can also improve its past time and location estimates if the past timestamping errors are reported in the data sent over the ATSC 3.0 broadcast.

Finally, location spoofing resiliency increases if an ATSC 3.0 station listens to the signals from neighboring ATSC 3.0 stations and reports the neighbor signal measurements in the data pipe.

Although BPS supports the multiple use cases mentioned above, the goal of the proof-of-concept was to demonstrate an ATSC 3.0-based timing solution with an accurate clock in a lab setting. However, it was also deemed useful to design and test the data structures and transmission so that the timing solution could easily be extended to other use cases in the future.

## Proof-of-concept Prototype Description

The prototype implementation is based on multiple existing products that were enhanced to meet the proof-of-concept objectives and deliverables. These included the Triveni Digital Broadcast Gateway and the Avateq AVQ1022(1st Gen) RF Layer Monitoring Receiver. The use of existing hardware and software platforms allowed the delivery goals of the proof-of-concept to be met. The discussion following the system architecture diagram also describes the products impacted by the function described.

Figure 1 provides a logical diagram of the systems and functions developed. The numbered paragraphs that follow the diagram correspond to the callouts in the diagram.

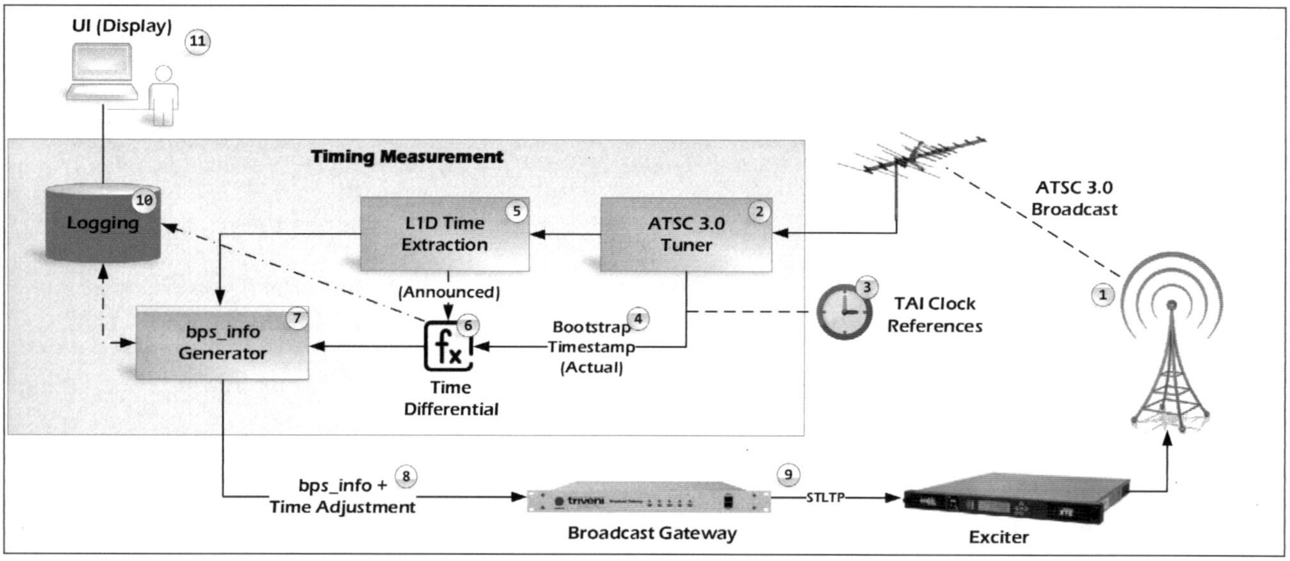


FIGURE 1: BPS PROTOTYPE SYSTEM LOGICAL DIAGRAM

1) **ATSC 3.0 transmission**. Legal transmissions must include a time stamp based on the current TAI time in the detailed preamble (L1D) according to ATSC A/322 [2]. Leap seconds are communicated in other signaling (*i.e.*, LLS). The time represented by the L1D timestamp is referred to as the “Time Information Position,” or “TIP,” which is the instant in time at the center of the leading edge of the first sample of the first symbol of the bootstrap.
2) **ATSC 3.0 tuner**. For the proof-of-concept, this was the tuner currently deployed in the Avateq AVQ1022(1st Gen) RF Layer Monitoring Receiver which has limited capability relative to the desired measurement accuracy. The exact measurement accuracy was determined empirically as part of the prototype development to be near 200 nsec.
3) **Reference clock**. The TAI clock reference used by the receiver is GPS.

4) **Measured time**. The receiver hardware combined with the clock reference results in the Time Information Position measurement. This represents the actual bootstrap emission time accounting for the propagation delay due to the distance from the transmission tower. The accuracy and precision of this value is an outcome of the current Avateq receiver.
5) **L1D Announced time**. The time reported in the preamble is extracted to provide the announced time in the ATSC 3.0 frame. This is created from the L1D_time_sec, L1D_time_msec, L1D_time_usec, and L1D_time_nsec fields in the preamble.
6) **Time differential**. The difference between the measured time and the announced time is calculated. This value is input to a smoothing function to avoid jitter. The filters and methods used to evaluate the overall loop performance are described in detail later in this paper. The resultant values are sent to the bps_info Generator as well as logged.
7) **`bps_info` data generation**. The bps_info Generator uses the latest time differential information along with preset location values to create a bps_info data structure. This data structure is logged and sent to the Broadcast Gateway as an LLS user-defined table. User-defined LLS tables are described in ATSC A/331 [3].
8) **Time adjustment**. The time adjustment information is sent to the Broadcast Gateway through an extension to the products standard control APIs. The time adjustment can be associated with individual transmitters. The bps_info data structure packet is sent to the Broadcast Gateway through using the current gateway interfaces for ingesting LLS.
9) **Broadcast gateway**. The Broadcast Gateway uses the time adjustment information to adjust the emission time in the next available frame for the transmitter. The bps_info data is inserted into a PLP dedicated to the purpose. Note that due to frame buffering within the ATSC 3.0 pipeline, time adjustments will be delayed by multiple frame times.
10) **Log**. The Logging function collects information from the various generation functions and makes it available to the user through the UI interface. The data supplied is also exportable as CSV to allow the data to be ingested into Excel for further evaluation.
11) **User interface**. A user interface (UI) is provided via a web interface (HTTP) to allow logging information to be displayed as well as to allow the system to be controlled. Control connections are not shown to reduce diagram complexity. Of particular interest will be a user interface that provides a graph of the time differential value over time to verify that the system is operating correctly.

## Implementation Details

For the proof-of-concept implementation, the Avateq AVQ1022(1st Gen) RF Layer Monitoring Receiver is used to realize callouts 2) through 6). A laptop computer was provided to collect long-term logs and other information as well as form the bridge between the receiver and the broadcast gateway. The software developed for the prototype running on the laptop provides functions 7), 10), and 11) shown in Figure 1 above. The receiver also provides a user interface which shows details of the reception process. This division allowed more development flexibility between Triveni Digital and Avateq accelerating the availability of the functions for testing.

The resulting prototype implementation is diagramed in Figure 2 below. Descriptions of each callout follow the figure.

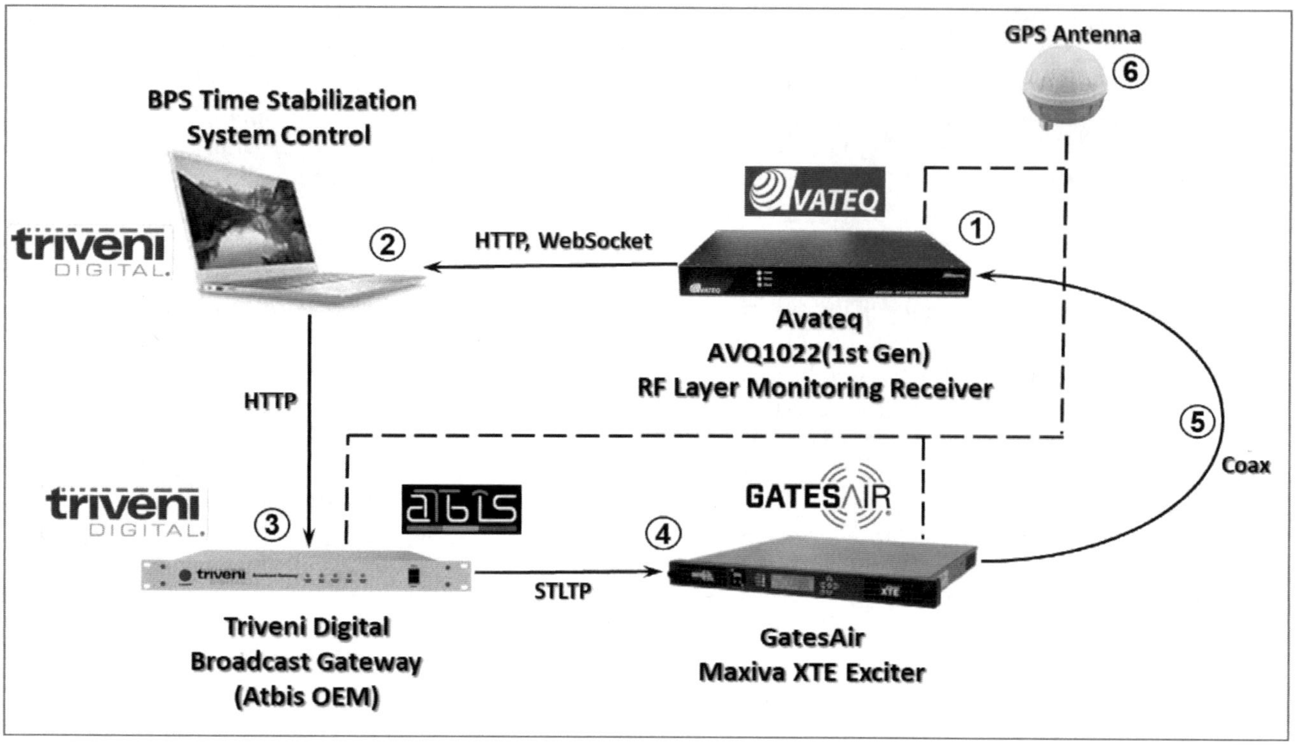


FIGURE 2: PROTOTYPE BPS TIMING LOOP IMPLEMENTATION.

1) Avateq AVQ1022(1st Gen) RF Layer Monitoring Receiver, modified to measure the arrival time of each frame and compare it with the L1D announced time.
2) BPS Time Stabilization system control laptop, providing a convenient user interface to control the various devices in the loop as well as view resulting data. All configuration and control are performed from the user interfaces displayed on the laptop. To ease configuration and avoid conflicts, communication between the components of the loop has been separated into physically disparate networks.
3) Broadcast Gateway, accepting control information from the system control laptop based on measurement data from the receiver and adjusting the emission time of the exciter.
4) Control and baseband packet data are sent to the exciter using scheduler/studio to transmitter link tunneling protocol (STLTP). The exciter in this prototype loop was not modified and is behaving as nominally designed.
5) The prototype system routes the RF output of the exciter directly to the receiver input.
6) GPS is used by the prototype systems to synchronize clocks and provide reference signals.

## Receiver Implementation Details

The Avateq AVQ1022(1st Gen) RF Layer Monitoring Receiver is a central component of the proof-of-concept stabilization loop so details of its implementation and filtering capabilities are provided. Figure 3 provides a functional block diagram of the receiver internal subsystems.

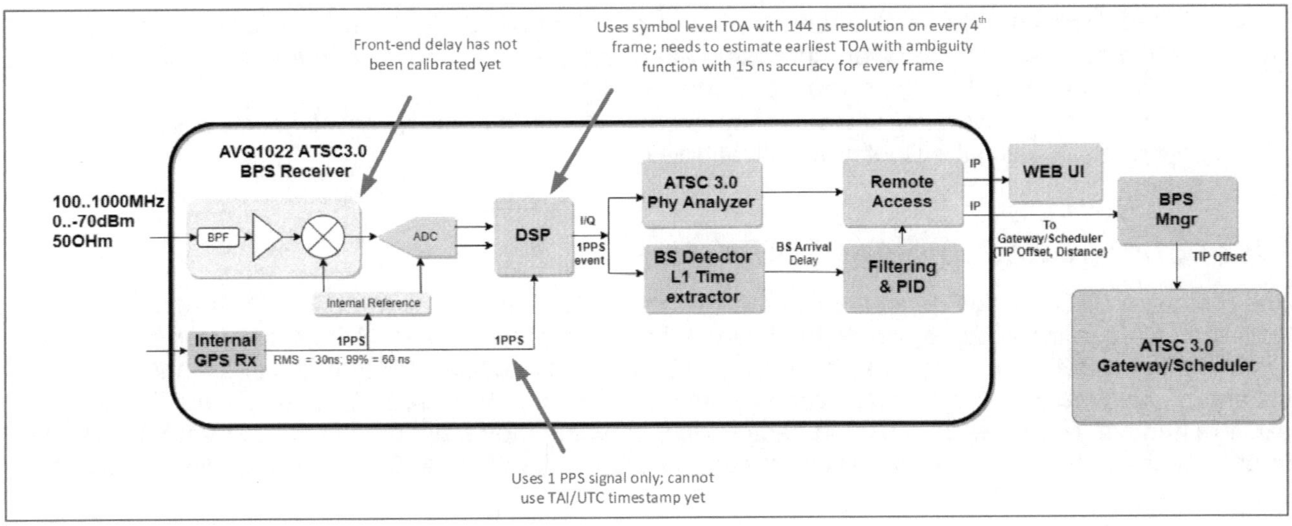


FIGURE 3: BPS RECEIVER LOGICAL DIAGRAM

The AVQ1022 receiver architecture utilizes the software defined radio (SDR) concept with a frequency agile analog front-end, signal digitizing circuitry and digital signal processor (DSP) core implemented in a field-programmable gate array (FPGA). The DSP core outputs I/Q samples for further processing by software based functional blocks. The I/Q samples are marked with a 1PPS event. All frequency converting, sampling and digital processing stages are synchronized with an external or receiver-generated internal GPS module's 1PPS signal.

The software based ATSC 3.0 Phy Analyzer block provides a comprehensive set of measurements and troubleshooting tools to monitor RF signal quality and transmitter system performance.

The Bootstrap Detector block provides a sequence of the Bootstrap arrival delays calculated as a time difference between L1D_time_xxx and the time of receiving the first Bootstrap sample relative to the GPS 1PPS pulse.

The Bootstrap arrival delays are additionally filtered with a moving average FIR, with a user-defined filter length. The filter length is carefully adjusted as it affects both the measurement accuracy and the control loop convergence speed (settling time).

The filter output directly feeds a proportional-integral (PI) controller. The PI Controller is designed with user adjustable proportional and integral path gain coefficients: Kp and Ki.

The resulting PI controller output in a form of TIP adjustment is available through the receiver remote interface and can be used by a BPS controller to adjust the TIP offset in ATSC 3.0 exciter.

An additional parameter, TIP Reference, is introduced to set the TIP Adjustment value as an initial "zero" position, *i.e.*, a position with zero distance from a transmitting antenna and zero Bootstrap arrival delay.

The newly implemented BPS-related functionality provides the following:

- Detecting, estimating, and tracking any difference between the reported L1D_time_xxx and the calculated Bootstrap arrival time.

- Calibrating transmitter-side equipment to account for possible DSP and analog processing delays at a transmitter site and precisely adjusting the L1D_time_xxx time to the instant when the first sample of the first symbol of Bootstrap is transmitted.
- Verification of transmitter equipment synchronization and stability by estimating possible sample rate shifts causing the Bootstrap arrival delay drift.

## Proof-of-concept Prototype Performance

The prototype BPS solution developed by the partner companies demonstrates that a feedback control loop can increase the accuracy of the transmitted timestamps of an ATSC 3.0 transmission chain. We ran two sets of prototype transmission systems with different exciters, and in both cases the instantaneous time delay of the stabilized system was less than 300 nsec. We learned that the different exciters had different time response characteristics, meaning they have different transfer functions. We found that the optimal PI controller settings were different in each case. Our prototypes were stable for many days.

We have also demonstrated that the proposed time stabilization solution can be easily integrated into an existing transmission chain. Most of the elements of the feedback control loop are add-ons, meaning they do not require modifying the existing transmission chain. One impact to the transmission chain is that new gateway software is required that can receive the PI controller output and make necessary adjustments to the timestamps. Note that no changes of any kind were required for either exciter controlled by the prototype systems. The controls provided by the existing broadcast gateway were sufficient.

The solution we have demonstrated is 100% compliant with the ATSC 3.0 standard. No changes to the standard were necessary. We have also demonstrated the solution using transmission equipment from multiple ATSC 3.0 vendors, reinforcing standard compliance.

Finally, we have identified opportunities to make the system more accurate as discussed in a subsequent section below.

### Receiver Prototype Performance

The yellow and blue curves exemplified in Figure 4 correspond to raw measurements of the Bootstrap arrival delay and the filtered and PID-processed TIP adjustment, respectively. The present implementation of the receiver hardware limits the resolution of the time of arrival delay to approximately 144 nsec. However, the sophisticated processing of the raw measurements implemented in the receiver helps constrain the TIP adjustment variations to within approximately ±70 nsec.

The measurement resolution for the prototype is limited by the sampling rate of the baseband signal. The receiver uses the first sample of the first symbol of the bootstrap to calculate the time of arrival. We observed that the time of arrival, denoted by the yellow line, can jump by ±2 samples, or ±288 nsec. Although the time of arrival offset measurements were rather jittery, the averaged values were much smoother, meaning that an external receiver synchronizing its clock to the filtered and/or smoothed time values should achieve much better accuracy.

It is worth mentioning that both the exciter and the time of arrival measurement receiver introduced errors which were found to be ±2 samples, but due the low resolution and accuracy we could not characterize the errors contributed by each individual piece of equipment.

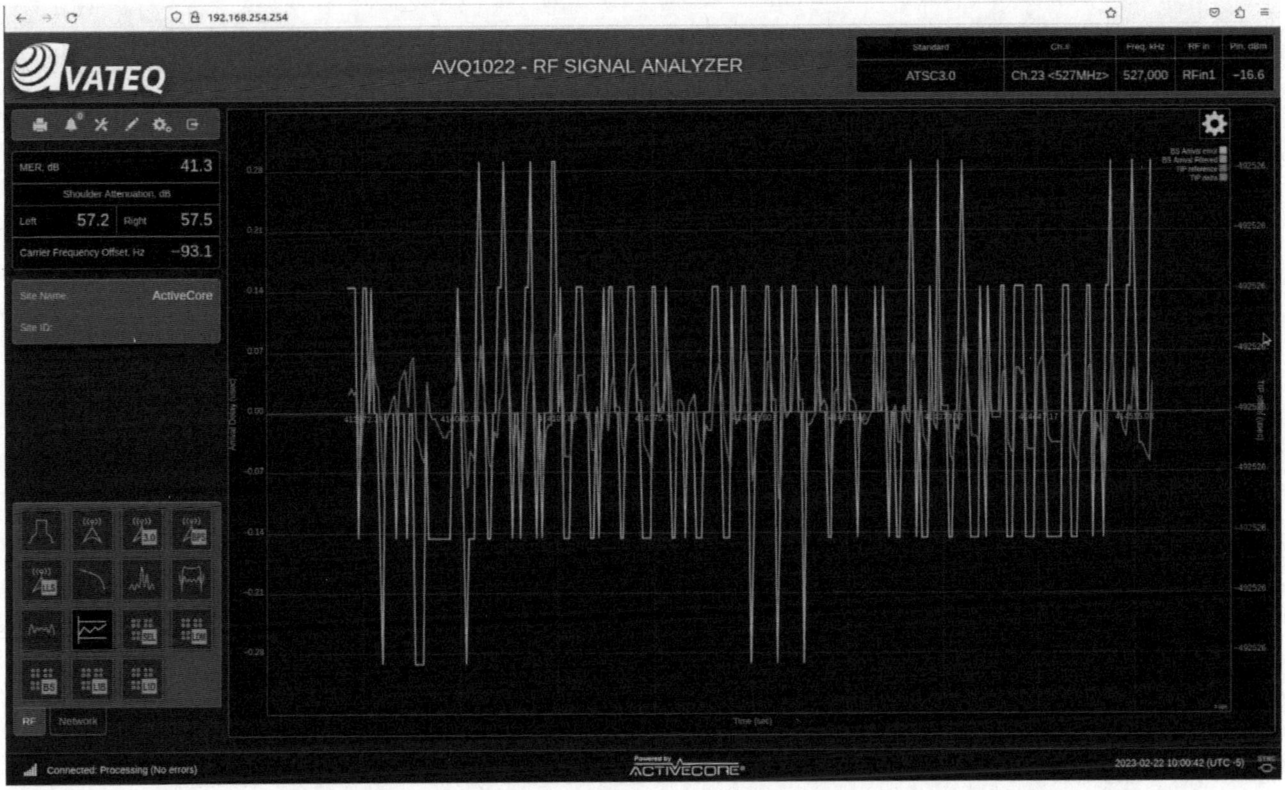


FIGURE 4: EXAMPLE RECEIVER BPS TIME ARRIVAL GRAPH. SEE TEXT.

## System Control Prototype Performance

The purpose of the system control prototype was to obtain measurement data from the receiver, log the data to provide for historical measurement and offline analysis, create the bps_info data structure and interface with the broadcast gateway. The software developed was flexible, anticipating that the proof-of-concept prototype might require changes as the project evolved. This proved to be true, and the resultant user interface is shown in Figure 5.

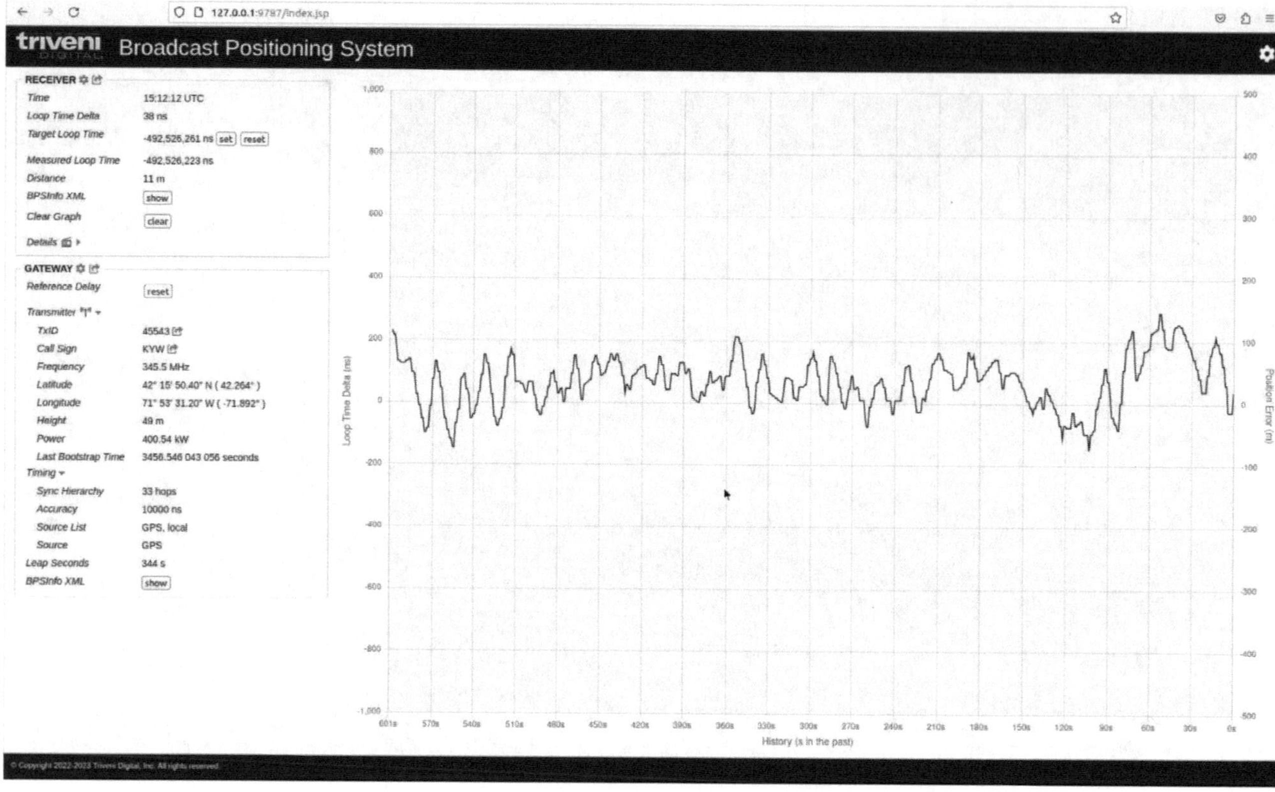


FIGURE 5: EXAMPLE BPS CONTROL SYSTEM USER INTERFACE.

Figure 5 shows a snapshot of the control system during operation. In the left panel, there is data which was either configured through this user interface or obtained from the receiver. The top portion of the panel shows receiver information with buttons to set the "Target Loop Time" shown as the "TIP reference" red line in Figure 4 above, reset that time to zero, and clear the graph. There are also links to launch the receiver user interface and configure the connection to the receiver. Finally, there is a button to view the bps_info data structure read from the receiver after it has passed through the system.

The Gateway portion of the left panel shows information regarding the transmitter, its location, call sign, frequency and other information that is included in the bps_info data structure to identify the transmitter. There is also a button in this panel to access the bps-info structure that will be sent to the broadcast gateway. An example of the dialog shown when this button is clicked is provided in Figure 6 below.

Finally, the graph that makes up much of the control system user interface is a longer time scale version of the blue graph shown in the receiver Figure 4. Note that the snapshots shown in Figures 4 and 5 were not synchronized in time so the illustrative figures cannot be directly compared.

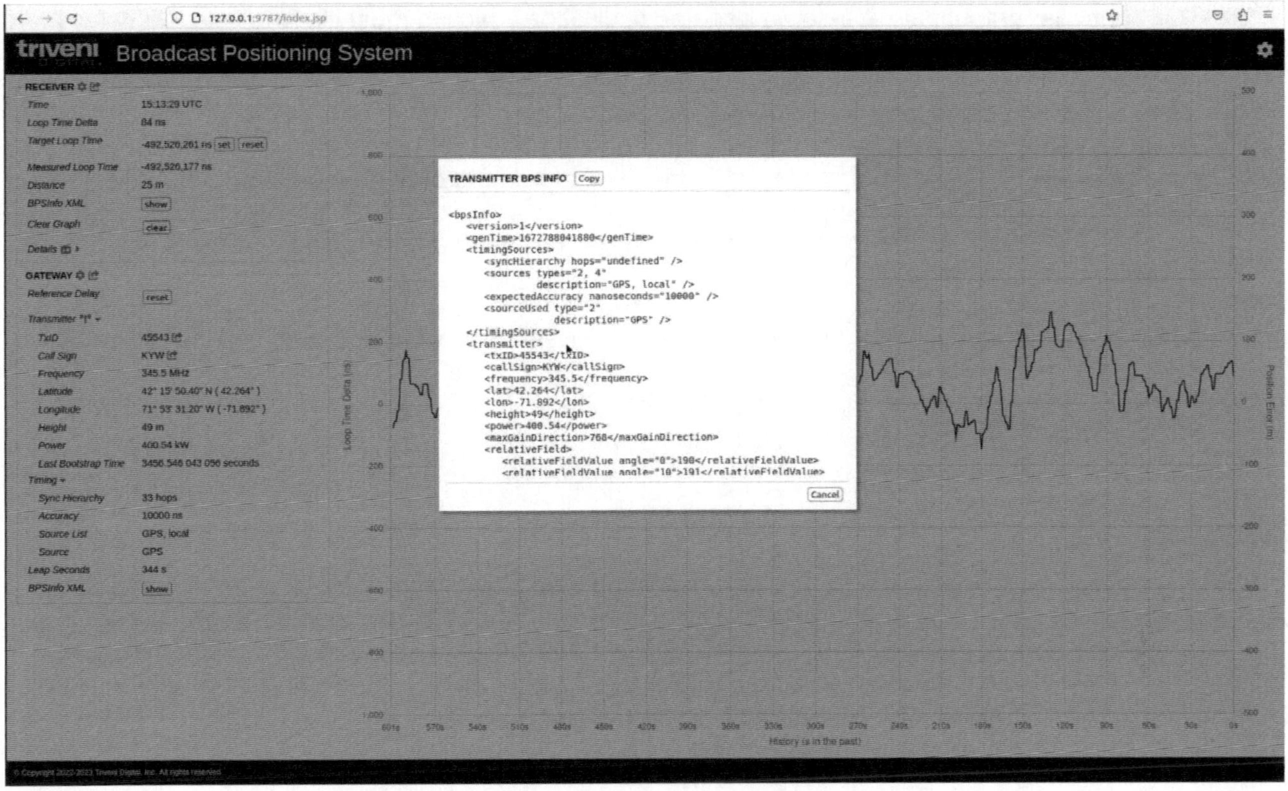


FIGURE 6: EXAMPLE CONTROL SYSTEM BPS_INFO DIALOG.

The bps_info structure, as the dialog shown in Figure 6 exemplifies, was provided to demonstrate the ability to send the data through the control loop. Though not used directly by this prototype, ultimately, the bps_info will be used by other receivers to determine the location of the transmission and be able to determine their distance from that transmitter. In the current implementation, the bps_info data structure was encoded as XML and sent as a user-defined LLS packet [3]. This allows unmodified ATSC 3.0 analyzers to view the data. See Annex A for a detailed description of the bps_info semantics.

## Future Work and Improvement Suggestions

In developing and demonstrating the time stabilization algorithm with existing ATSC 3.0-compliant transmission chains, we identified a number of ways to improve accuracy and efficiency. Our suggestions follow:

1) Develop improved capabilities to timestamp the baseband samples in the receiver with TAI or UTC.
2) The receiver front-end delay needs to be accurately characterized so that we can determine, from the baseband sample timestamps, when the RF signal impinged on the receiver antenna.
3) The time of arrival measurements need to have better resolution and accuracy. One suggestion is to reconstruct the bootstrap waveform in the receiver, correlate with the received signal using an ambiguity function [4] and interpolate between the detection peaks. Using a higher sampling rate will help. Consider doubling the sampling rate for time of arrival measurements.
4) Measure the timestamping errors of every transmitted frame and apply the corrections to every transmitted frame. In other words, add more processing power.

5) The controller output displays some periodic oscillation which is most likely due to the delay in applying the corrections. Reduce the delay in transmission chain with the goal of applying the latest timing corrections before the next frame is transmitted.
6) Once the timing measurement becomes more accurate with higher resolution, experiment with a proportional–integral–derivative controller (PID) in the loop. The derivative part will predict the timing deviations and thus may help with the internal framing delay issues.
7) With more accurate time of arrival measurements, characterize the timing jitter caused by the exciters. If the exciters are too jittery, work with exciter manufacturers and figure out ways to mitigate the timing variability.
8) Populate the API fields for past measurements so that an external receiver can apply those corrections and can achieve a more accurate time reference for past transmissions. This will help with synchronizing the local clock of an external receiver.
9) Consider incorporating the bps_info() message in the ATSC 3.0 standard and making it part of the preamble.

## Conclusion

A proof-of-concept prototype was built that demonstrates time stabilization of a BPS-enabled ATSC 3.0 transmission facility. We used commercial-grade exciters and other transmission chain equipment to prove compliance with the ATSC 3.0 standard. The initial design of the prototype achieved reasonable accuracy and stability but with some timing jitter. We have identified the causes that affected the timing performance and have suggested a number of ideas to improve performance.

## References


[1] Mondal, T., *et al.*, "Broadcast Positioning System (BPS) Using ATSC 3.0," Proceedings of the 2021 NAB Broadcast Engineering and Information Technology (BEIT) Conference.

[2] ATSC, "ATSC Standard: Physical Layer Protocol," Doc. A/322:2022-11, Advanced Television Systems Committee, Washington, DC, 14 November 2022.

[3] ATSC, "ATSC Standard: Signaling, Delivery, Synchronization, and Error Protection," Doc. A/331:2022-11, Advanced Television Systems Committee, Washington, DC, 30 November 2022.

[4] Stein, S., "Algorithms for Ambiguity Function Processing," IEEE Transactions on Acoustics, Speech, and Signal Processing, Vol. 29, Issue 3, Jun 1981, pp. 588-599.

## Appendix A

A mandatory presence in the following table means that if the `bps_info` message is transmitted, those fields must be populated within the message.

| *Syntax* | *No. of bits* | *Format* | *Presence* |
|---|---|---|---|
| bps_info(){ | | | |
| message_length | 16 | unsigned integer | mandatory |
| version | 8 | unsigned integer | |
| | | | |
| timing_source_info(){ | | | |
| sync_hierarchy | 7 | unsigned integer | |
| num_independent_sources | 6 | unsigned integer | |
| for (i=0;i< num_independent_sources;i++){ | | | |
| source_type_list | 4 | unsigned integer | |
| } | | | |
| expected_accuracy | 16 | unsigned integer | |
| source_used | 4 | unsigned integer | |
| } | | | |
| | | | |
| self_measurement_info(){ | | | |
| call_sign | 42 | array of 7 6-bit unsigned integers | |
| tx_id | 13 | unsigned integer | |
| tx_freq | 32 | 32-bit floating point | |
| geodetic_lat | 64 | 64-bit double precision | mandatory |
| geodetic_lon | 64 | 64-bit double precision | mandatory |
| geodetic_height | 64 | 64-bit double precision | mandatory |
| radiated_power | 32 | 32-bit floating point | |
| for (i=0;i<36;i++){ | | | |
| antenna_pattern_relative_field | 252 | array of 36 7-bit unsigned integers | |
| } | | | |
| max_gain_direction | 10 | unsigned integer | |
| prev_bootstrap_time_sec | 32 | unsigned integer | |
| prev_bootstrap_time_msec | 10 | unsigned integer | |
| prev_bootstrap_time_usec | 10 | unsigned integer | |
| prev_bootstrap_time_nsec | 10 | unsigned integer | |
| prev_bootstrap_time_error_nsec | 16 | signed integer | |
| } | | | |
| | | | |
| leap_seconds | 8 | unsigned integer | mandatory |
| | | | |
| num_neighbors | 6 | unsigned integer | |
| for (i=0;i<num_neighbors; i++){ | | | |

| | | | |
|---|---|---|---|
| neighbor_measurement_info(){ | | | |
| call_sign | 42 | array of 7 6-bit unsigned integers | |
| tx_id | 13 | unsigned integer | |
| tx_freq | 32 | 32-bit floating point | |
| geodetic_lat | 64 | 64-bit double precision | |
| geodetic_lon | 64 | 64-bit double precision | |
| geodetic_height | 64 | 64-bit double precision | |
| radiated_power | 32 | 32-bit floating point | |
| for (i=0;i<36;i++){ | | | |
| antenna_pattern_relative_field | 252 | array of 36 7-bit unsigned integers | |
| } | | | |
| max_gain_direction | 10 | unsigned integer | |
| reported_bootstrap_time_sec | 32 | unsigned integer | |
| reported_bootstrap_time_msec | 10 | unsigned integer | |
| reported_bootstrap_time_usec | 10 | unsigned integer | |
| reported_bootstrap_time_nsec | 10 | unsigned integer | |
| bootstrap_toa_offset | 32 | signed integer | |
| prev_bootstrap_time_sec | 32 | unsigned integer | |
| prev_bootstrap_time_msec | 10 | unsigned integer | |
| prev_bootstrap_time_usec | 10 | unsigned integer | |
| prev_bootstrap_time_nsec | 10 | unsigned integer | |
| prev_bootstrap_time_error_nsec | 16 | signed integer | |
| } | | | |
| } | | | |
| | | | |
| reserved_bits | as needed | | mandatory |
| bps_crc | 32 | unsigned integer | mandatory |
| } | | | |

**message_length** – This field indicates the length of the message, including the CRC bits, in units of bytes.

**version** – This field represents the version of the message.

**sync_hierarchy** – This field indicates the number of hops needed to transfer time from a reference ATSC 3.0 tower to the tower that is using neighboring towers' ATSC 3.0 signal as timing reference. If an ATSC 3.0 tower does not use the timing information from any neighboring tower to synchronize its own clock, its hierarchy is 0. For example, towers that receive traceable time from NIST or USNO using satellite, fiber, or other methods but do not use any neighboring tower's signal for synchronization will report 0 in this field. If a tower is using a `sync_hierarchy` 0 tower's signal for timing reference, that tower will report its `sync_hierarchy` as 1. Generally, if a tower is listening to the signals from neighboring towers for clock synchronization, and if n is the lowest `sync_hierarchy` among the received signals, that tower will report n+1 as its own `sync_hierarchy`.

**num_independent_sources** – This field indicates the number of independent timing sources used at the ensemble clock deployed at the tower location for clock synchronization. For example, if a TV station uses GPS, one cesium clock, eLORAN, and 5 neighboring towers as input to the ensemble clock, that tower will report the number 8 in this field. If a tower does not use an ensemble clock but uses another backup clock if its primary clock fails, the reported value will be 1. The corresponding `source_type_list` parameter will be updated accordingly in that case.

**source_type_list** – This field indicates the various timing sources used as reference at the ATSC 3.0 transmission facility. The following table is used to indicate the types:

| *Value* | *Source Type* |
|---|---|
| 0 | UTC from NIST or USNO securely delivered to the TV station |
| 1 | GPS |
| 2 | ATSC 3.0 signal emitted from neighboring towers |
| 3 | Local clock, such as cesium or rubidium |
| 4 | eLORAN |
| 5 | Reserved |
| 6 | Reserved |
| 7 | Reserved |
| ... | ... |
| 15 | Reserved |

If the transmission facility uses an ensemble of clocks, it will list the most accurate timing source of the ensemble as its source.

**expected_accuracy** – This field indicates the accuracy of the TV station clock 99% of the time compared to UTC. The unit is nanoseconds. A value of 200 means that the TV station clock is synchronized in such a way that the local clock is within 200 ns of UTC 99% of the time.

**source_used** – This field indicates the type of timing source used at the transmission facility. If the tower clock is derived from an ensemble of timing devices, a value of 0 will be reported. If the tower uses just one of the clocks available to it, that source will be reported using the table described under `source_type_list` parameter.

**call_sign** – This field states the 3 to 7-letter call sign of the TV station. If the call letters are shorter than 7 characters, the remaining fields are padded with "space" characters. The mapping of 6-bit unsigned integers and the letters in the call sign follows:

| *Binary* | *Character* |
|---|---|
| 000000 | space |
| 000001 | hyphen |
| 000010 | A |
| 000011 | B |
| ... | ... |
| 011011 | Z |
| 011100 | 0 |
| 011101 | 1 |
| ... | ... |
| 100101 | 9 |

| | |
|---|---|
| 100110 | reserved |
| ... | reserved |
| 111111 | reserved |

**tx_id** – This field represents the txid_address field as it is defined in ATSC A/322 with specific codes assigned according to the table at txid.nabpilot.org.

**tx_freq** – This field indicates the middle of the assigned television channel frequency in units of MHz.

**geodetic_lat** – This field represents geodetic latitude of the midpoint of the transmit antenna in WGS 84 LLA convention.

**geodetic_lon** – This field represents geodetic longitude of the midpoint of the transmit antenna in WGS 84 LLA convention.

**geodetic_height** – This field represents geodetic height of the midpoint of the transmit antenna in WGS 84 LLA convention.

**radiated_power** – This field represents ERP of the radiating antenna in units of kilowatts.

**antenna_pattern_relative_field** – This field represents the antenna pattern by the relative field values reported every 10 degrees. The values are arranged clockwise starting at true north, meaning that the 1st value of the 36-element array represents the relative field strength in the direction north, the 2nd value represents the relative field strength in the direction 10 degrees clockwise from north, and so on. The relative field values are scaled such that the maximum value, which is 1.0, is scaled to the integer 127 in fixed point representation.

**max_gain_direction** – This field represents the direction where relative field strength is maximum, i.e., 1.0. The angle is measured clockwise from north. The angle is reported as a fixed-point value such that 360 degrees is scaled to 1023 in fixed point notation.

**prev_bootstrap_time_sec** – This field will be populated with the L1D_time_sec value, as defined in ATSC A/322, of the immediately previous transmitted frame. For self_measurement_info, the transmitting tower will provide this information. For neighbor_measurement_info, the transmitting tower will receive the value in bps_info message from a neighboring tower and report that value in this field.

**prev_bootstrap_time_msec** – This field will be populated with the L1D_time_msec value, as defined in ATSC A/322, of the immediately previous transmitted frame. For self_measurement_info, the transmitting tower will provide this information. For neighbor_measurement_info, the transmitting tower will receive the value in bps_info message from a neighboring tower and report that value in this field.

**prev_bootstrap_time_usec** – This field will be populated with the L1D_time_usec value, as defined in ATSC A/322, of the immediately previous transmitted frame. For self_measurement_info, the transmitting tower will provide this information. For neighbor_measurement_info, the transmitting tower will receive the value in bps_info message from a neighboring tower and report that value in this field.

**prev_bootstrap_time_nsec** – This field will be populated with the `L1D_time_nsec value`, as defined in ATSC A/322, of the immediately previous transmitted frame. For `self_measurement_info`, the transmitting tower will provide this information. For `neighbor_measurement_info`, the transmitting tower will receive the value in `bps_info` message from a neighboring tower and report that value in this field.

**prev_bootstrap_time_error_nsec** – This is the difference between the actual time when the first sample of the first symbol of the bootstrap was transmitted and the reported bootstrap transmission time in the `L1D_time_sec, L1D_time_msec, L1D_time_usec`, and `L1D_time_nsec` fields mentioned in ATSC A/322. The time difference is measured as actual transmission time minus reported transmission time in nanosecond unit. For `self_measurement_info`, the transmitting tower will measure and provide this information. For `neighbor_measurement_info`, the transmitting tower will receive the value in `bps_info` message from a neighboring tower and report that value in this field.

**leap_seconds** – This field represents the current number of leap seconds expressed as TAI – UTC.

**num_neighbors** – This field indicates the number of neighboring signal measurements reported in the message. If this field is set to 0, no `neighbor_measurement_info` will be populated in the message.

**reported_bootstrap_time_sec** – This field will be populated with the `L1D_time_sec` value, as defined in ATSC A/322, of the most recent frame transmitted by a neighbor tower and received at the transmitting tower.

**reported_bootstrap_time_msec** – This field will be populated with the `L1D_time_msec` value, as defined in ATSC A/322, of the most recent frame transmitted by a neighbor tower and received at the transmitting tower.

**reported_bootstrap_time_usec** – This field will be populated with the `L1D_time_usec` value, as defined in ATSC A/322, of the most recent frame transmitted by a neighbor tower and received at the transmitting tower.

**reported_bootstrap_time_nsec** – This field will be populated with the `L1D_time_nsec` value, as defined in ATSC A/322, of the most recent frame transmitted by a neighbor tower and received at the transmitting tower.

**bootstrap_toa_offset** – This field represents the difference between the time of arrival at the transmitting (self) antenna of the neighboring bootstrap signal and the reported timestamp in `L1D_time_sec`, `L1D_time_msec`, `L1D_time_usec`, and `L1D_time_nsec` fields as mentioned in ATSC A/322. The unit of this time offset is nanoseconds.

**reserved_bits** – This field indicates the number of reserved bits, 0 to 7, that is required to byte-align the message.

**bps_crc** – This field will contain the CRC value as computed according to Section 6.1.2.2 of A/322 over the contents of `bps_info` message excluding the `bps_crc` field.

# Delivering Traceable Reference Time for ATSC 3.0-based Broadcast Positioning System (BPS)

**Patrick Diamond**
**Diamond Consulting**
Ayer, Mass., United States

**Tariq Mondal, Robert Weller**
**National Association of Broadcasters**
Washington, D.C., United States

**Andrew Hansen**
**Volpe Center**
Cambridge, Mass., United States

**Abstract** – Delivering accurate and traceable time is important for the operation of critical infrastructure industries. A BPS-enabled ATSC 3.0 TV station can meet the requirements of critical infrastructure industries by transmitting precise time. One of the requirements to do so is to have reliable, robust, and accurate timing sources at the TV stations. This paper describes how a variety of timing sources can be used at TV stations for reference. The paper also outlines how BPS-enabled ATSC 3.0 TV stations can evolve into a self-synchronizing mesh network for timing signals.

## Introduction

BPS is a system and method of estimating time and position at a receiver using ATSC 3.0 broadcast signals [1]. BPS is compliant with the ATSC 3.0 standard which is currently being deployed in the US [2]. One of the features of BPS is its independence and potential for stand-alone use. That is, it can continue to operate when GPS/GNSS, internet, and cellular connectivity are unavailable. The independence of BPS makes it an attractive solution for providing time transfer information to critical infrastructure supporting safety systems, national security functions, and economic activity.

Although BPS can estimate both position and timing at a receiver, this paper focuses on the timing aspect. Reliable timing information can be derived from a single BPS-enabled ATSC 3.0 signal if the receiver location is known. Timing service coverage analysis here shows that the entire continental US can receive reliable timing information from the existing deployment of VHF and UHF television stations.

To transmit timing information, a TV station must have an accurate and trusted timing reference. BPS-enabled TV stations have the flexibility to invoke one or more timing sources to form a robust reference time, *e.g.*, an ensemble of available clocks, cross-checked time sources, etc. BPS-enabled TV stations receive signals from neighboring towers and under the timing service concept, transmit those neighbor stations' identity, timing, and location and affects a self-synchronizing network. This paper discusses methods and algorithms for synchronizing BPS-enabled ATSC 3.0 TV towers.

## High-Precision Position, Navigation and Timing (PNT) as a National Security Concern

U.S. Critical Infrastructure is PNT enabled and per Executive Order 13905 [3] on "Responsible Use of PNT," the 16 Sector Risk Management Agencies (formerly Sector Specific Agencies) are directed to

---

This paper is excerpted from the Proceedings of the 2023 NAB Broadcast Engineering and Information Technology (BEIT) Conference, © 2023, National Association of Broadcasters, 1 M Street SE, Washington, DC 20003 USA.

develop PNT profiles pursuant to the NIST 8323 master profile to identify and mitigate vulnerabilities. The critical infrastructure sectors include the Energy & Power Grid, Communications, Financial Transactions, Transportation (Aviation, Maritime, Rail, Surface, Pipeline), First Responders, Chemical, Dams, Information Technology, Critical Defense Manufacturing, Healthcare and Public Health, and Food and Agriculture to name several. The PNT signals and other data from GPS satellites allow these infrastructure capabilities to function reliably. Without these capabilities, the US economy would come to a standstill. Our adversaries are aware of this weakness and have implemented augmentations within their national boundaries to mitigate this exact same weakness. The US needs to do the same.

The US Government is aware of this issue. This problem has been recognized as critical since at least 2010 as noted in the release of the National Positioning, Navigation, and Timing Architecture: Implementation Plan [4].

The National PNT Advisory Board [5] discusses this issue constantly and has made several recommendations for developing a national resilient precision timing network. So far, nothing has been done beyond "studying the problem." This paper describes a viable infrastructure-ready solution to this national security weakness: namely, a Broadcast Position System based on ATSC 3.0.

## Technical Requirements to Satisfy Critical Infrastructure Usability Needs

Providing an accurate and precise reference clock using ATSC 3.0 is the basic requirement for BPS users. However, critical infrastructure (CI) environments have special needs for this clock signal. The precise clock is used to synchronize critical operations and functions in each CI. A few examples follow:

- **Mobile Wireless Networks** – 4G and 5G radios in the base stations need precise time synchronization to ensure synchrony of their Time Division Duplex (TDD) systems. The requirement for time synchronization in 3GPP radios is a 1 PPS signal, accurate to within 1.1 μsec across the entire network. The 1 PPS signal needs to be traceable to Coordinated Universal Time (UTC).
- **Equity Trading Systems** – Commonly called stock exchanges, there is a legal requirement to apply a time stamp at every step in the processing of a trade. There can be dozens of rapid, independent processing steps in a trade across many systems. In Europe there are Markets in Financial Instruments Directive (MiFID) II rules and in the USA, there are SEC Section 613 rules [6]. A part of each rule set requires time stamps to correlate to UTC within one microsecond. Each trade's entire dataset must be stored for regulatory review for up to 7 years.
- **Power Grid** – Machines called synchro-phasors are used to manage and regulate energy being added to the overall grid from all sources, including conventional power plants, wind farms, and solar panel arrays. Due to the nature of the energy on the grid it is critical to add new energy in a manner that assures it is compatible with the existing energy flow. The technical objective of the synchro-phasor is to ensure the new power is added within one degree of top dead center of the 60 Hz energy carrier. In order for new energy to be successfully integrated, all synchro-phasors need to be time correlated with each other within 1 μsec and correlated to UTC.

These and the other CI industries impose a specific tolerance and accuracy to the time applied to each via the ATSC 3.0 system. This critical level of control requires all ATSC 3.0 clocks to be correlated to UTC. Overall, 200 nanosecond accuracy is adequate for all CI industries, if traceable to UTC.

### Time Sources Available at Individual Stations

BPS-enabled ATSC 3.0 transmission systems designed as a trusted timing source will provide for at least three independent timing sources as illustrated in Figure 1. These stations can then operationally leverage a range of robust timekeeping strategies, *e.g.*, clock ensemble algorithms, redundancy cross-checking schemes, or orthogonal source comparison. The BPS transmitter timekeeping system (TKS) can be used to improve accuracy (UTC offset error), resilience by mitigating faults or threats, and other internal performance needs in the broadcasting sector.

In the U.S., the most reliable timing sources would be UTC obtained from the National Institute of Standards and Technology (NIST) or the U.S. Naval Observatory (USNO) and securely delivered to the TV station via optical fiber, satellite link or microwave link. GPS can also provide reference time, as well as Cesium and rubidium clocks located at the station. Additionally, eLORAN signals, if available, can be used. Significantly, signals from neighboring BPS-enabled ATSC 3.0 stations can be used as reference timing sources.

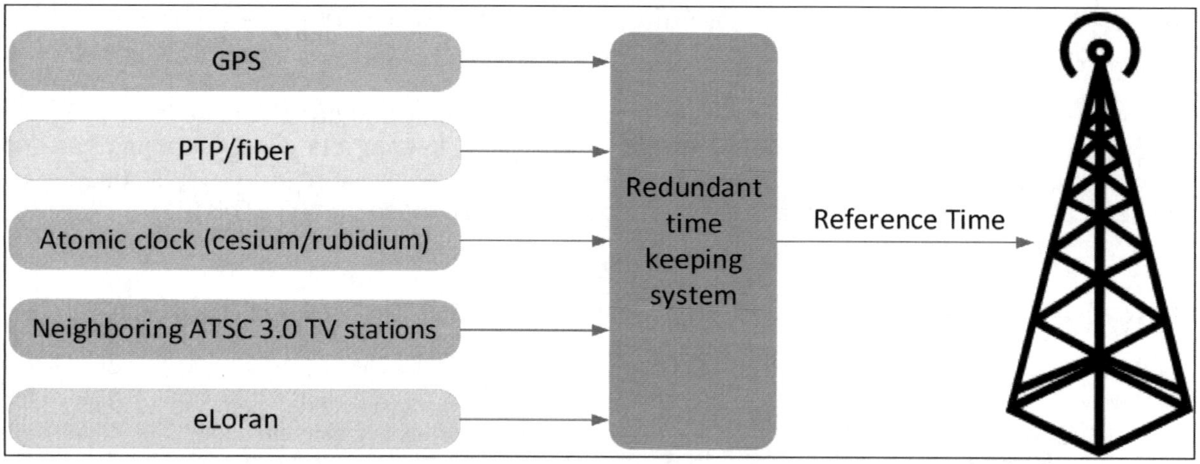


FIGURE 1: MULTIPLE INDEPENDENT TIMING SOURCES CAN PROVIDE REDUNDANCY.

## Time Synchronization Using ATSC 3.0 Signals Only

Television transmission towers are tall, and the transmitted TV signals typically travel about 55 miles before attenuating rapidly due to the Earth's curvature. However, a neighboring TV tower will also be tall and may therefore have line of sight to other tall towers located hundreds of miles away. Thus, using directional receiving antennas, one BPS-enabled station may be able to detect signals emitted from many neighboring towers. If those ATSC 3.0 signals are also BPS-enabled, a TV station can use the neighboring BPS signals as timing references.

ATSC 3.0 TV towers can evolve into a self-synchronizing network with traceable reference time if there are enough master clocks in the network. For example, if a few of the towers in the network have redundant timing sources, then other towers in the network can listen to these "master" towers and synchronize their clocks to them. Receiving antennas mounted high on a typical TV tower may be able to detect signals from many neighboring stations. If there are three or more master clocks in the neighbor list, a slave tower can synchronize its clock using only ATSC 3.0 signals.[1]

The BPS self-synchronization network concept is illustrated in Figure 2. Assume that every tower can receive the signals from the three master towers. In this case, all the slave towers can be reliably synchronized using only ATSC 3.0 signals.

[1] Strictly speaking, only a single master is required for synchronization, but at least three master stations are preferred for reliability and redundancy.

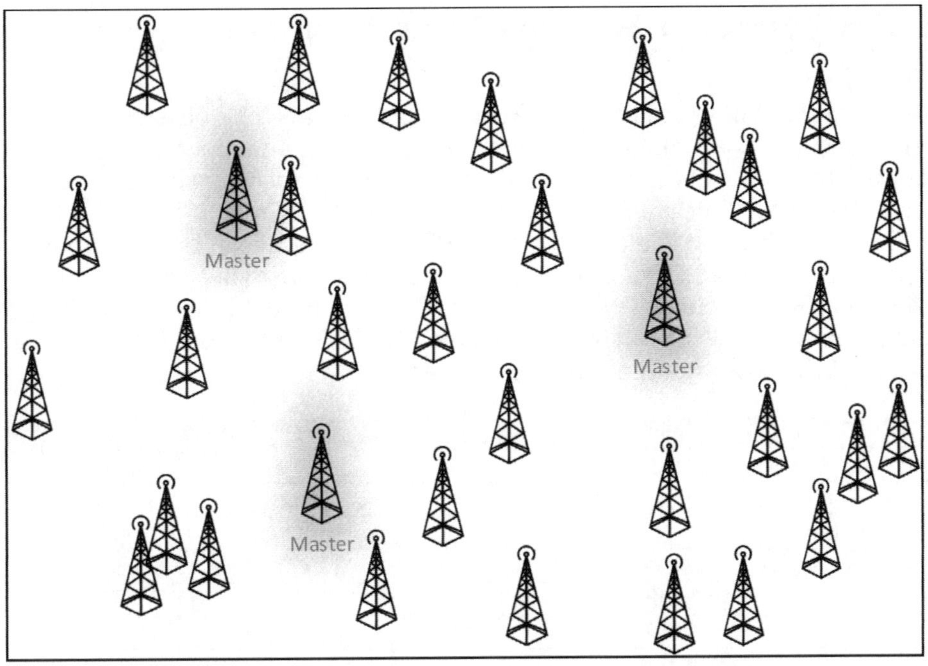


FIGURE 2: IN A SELF-SYNCHRONIZING BPS NETWORK, THE SLAVE STATIONS CAN USE A FEW MASTER STATIONS AS TIMING REFERENCES RESULTING IN ALL STATIONS PROVIDING ACCURATE TIME.

To develop a self-synchronizing network, each ATSC 3.0 broadcast facility will report its clock sources and expected timing accuracy. The `num_independent_sources`, `source_type_list`, and `source_used` parameters, which are described in the Appendix under the `bps_info` message, convey the clock configurations of each BPS-enabled station. The `expected_accuracy` parameter conveys the quality of the timing information. Finally, the `sync_hierarchy` parameter describes the number of "hops" required to trace back to the master clock. Using the described parameters, a synchronization protocol can be developed for the ATSC 3.0 network.

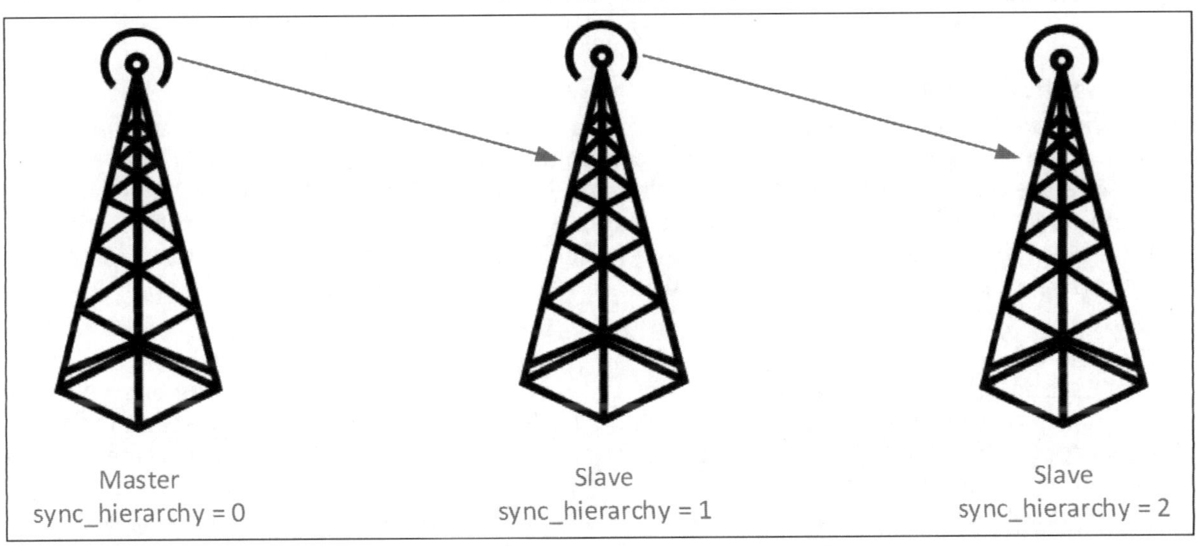


FIGURE 3: EACH STATION REPORTS THE NUMBER OF HOPS IT IS AWAY FROM A MASTER.

## Coverage of U.S. Television Stations Transmitting BPS

### Coverage Definition

In ATSC 3.0, the most robust physical layer pipe (PLP) operates at -5.72 dB signal to noise ratio (SNR) in a Rayleigh fading channel [7]. Simulations shared by the proponents during ATSC 3.0 standards development showed that the bootstrap and preamble signals can be decoded at about -12 and -9 dB SNR, respectively. Therefore, the data PLP carrying the tower location information is the weakest link, requiring the highest signal level. It is expected that BPS will utilize a PLP having robust characteristics, in order to provide usable coverage at great distances from the transmitter site as well as deep indoors and in other challenging environments. We have used -5 dB as the BPS system SNR threshold. This threshold is about 20 dB below what is typically assumed for DTV reception. Other relevant planning factors used to define BPS coverage are tabulated in Table 1.

| Parameter | Value | Unit |
|---|---|---|
| System Bandwidth | 6 | MHz |
| Thermal Noise (kTB) | -106.2 | dBm |
| Frequency of Operation, UHF | 539 | MHz |
| Signal to Noise Ratio | -5 | dB |
| High VHF | 194 | " |
| Low VHF | 69 | " |
| Antenna Gain | 0 | dBi |
| Antenna Factor, UHF | -129.6 | dBm-dBμV/m |
| High VHF | -120.8 | " |
| Low VHF | -111.8 | " |
| Noise Figure | 6 | dB |
| **Required Field Strength, UHF** | **24.4** | **dBμV/m** |
| **High VHF** | **15.6** | **"** |
| **Low VHF** | **6.6** | **"** |
| RX Antenna height, AGL (End-User) | 1.5 | m |
| RX Antenna height, AGL (TV Tower) | 50 | " |
| Location, Time Variability | 50%, 50% | – |

TABLE 1: PLANNING FACTOR VALUES USED TO DEFINE BPS COVERAGE.

### Station Selection

Timing information can be adequately conveyed from a single broadcast station having a primary time reference, but greater reliability and redundancy can be achieved by monitoring signals from several stations. There are a total of 1619 television stations operating 1642 unique transmission facilities licensed and operating in the contiguous United States (CONUS) [8]. U.S. television stations may transmit on low-VHF channels (below 88 MHz), high-VHF channels (between 174 and 216 MHz), and UHF channels (above 470 MHz). All licensed full-power stations are considered in this analysis.

### BPS Coverage Determination

Because of its familiarity to the broadcast industry and because reference software has been published by the FCC, the Irregular Terrain Model (ITM, version 1.2.2) was utilized in its point-to-point mode to predict coverage on a uniform grid covering the United States and its territories [9]. A summary of the ITM, including descriptions of some of its features and peculiarities, is given in McKenna, *et al.* [10] The software implementation of ITM used was the FCC's TVStudy, version 2.2.5, with planning factor values adjusted as indicated above. In particular, the software was first configured to predict field strength at the center point of 10 x 10 kilometer "cells" for general users at 1.5 meters above ground. Coverage was defined as indicated in Table 1 (*e.g.*, 24.4 dBμV/m or greater irrespective of the UHF channel involved) and no consideration was given to clutter or undesired stations (*i.e.*, co-channel and adjacent-channel interference was ignored).

## Results – Predicted Coverage for General BPS Users

The map of Figure 4 shows the predicted aggregate coverage of BPS for general users if transmitted from all full-power and Class A television stations in CONUS. The coverage shown was calculated at some 103,194 grid points (calculation cells) covering about 10.3 million square kilometers. The total land area of CONUS is about 7.7 million $km^2$ [11] and the predicted aggregate BPS coverage includes all of that area, as well as all of the Great Lakes and substantial areas offshore and in the border areas of both Canada and Mexico. Even if coverage is required at 10 or 20 dB above threshold (*e.g.*, because of receiver performance limits or reception indoors), there are only a few pockets of CONUS (mostly rural parts of Nevada, Oregon, Utah, Montana, and Colorado) that are not predicted to receive BPS timing service from at least one station.

While Figure 4 shows predicted reception for general BPS outdoor users in CONUS, broadcast television stations are also located in the states of Alaska and Hawaii, as well as Guam, Puerto Rico, and the US Virgin Islands. If BPS is implemented by television stations in those states and territories, full coverage of the land areas, as well as substantial offshore areas, is predicted, except in Alaska where full-power television service is limited to areas near major population centers.

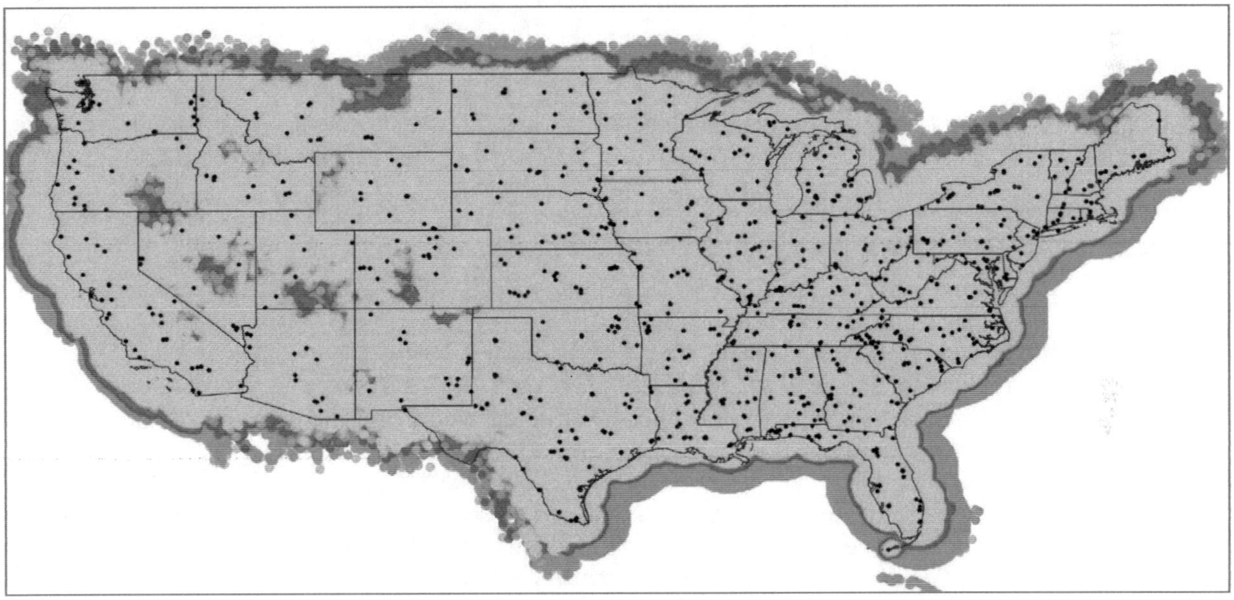

Figure 4: BPS coverage for general users in CONUS. Shaded areas are covered by at least one BPS-equipped television station assuming planning factor values given in Table 1. Coverage equal to or above threshold (Th) is shown in GREEN; ≥Th+10 dB coverage is shown in Red; ≥+20 dB coverage is shown in Orange.

While recovery of a single BPS signal is adequate to provide a timing reference at a given known location, more BPS signals can provide improved accuracy and redundancy at that location. With that in mind, each coverage grid point in Figure 4 was examined to determine how many BPS stations are predicted to provide an adequate signal at that grid point. The histogram of Figure 5 shows the number of grid points covered by 1, 2, 3, 4 and more unique BPS signals. Note that the large number of locations (cells) predicted to receive only one or two BPS signals is attributable to offshore locations where only VHF stations provide coverage. UHF television stations are designed to serve their audience and therefore many stations use directional antennas to limit the energy wasted into offshore or other unpopulated areas. In contrast, most VHF stations use omnidirectional antennas that provide usable signals well offshore [12].

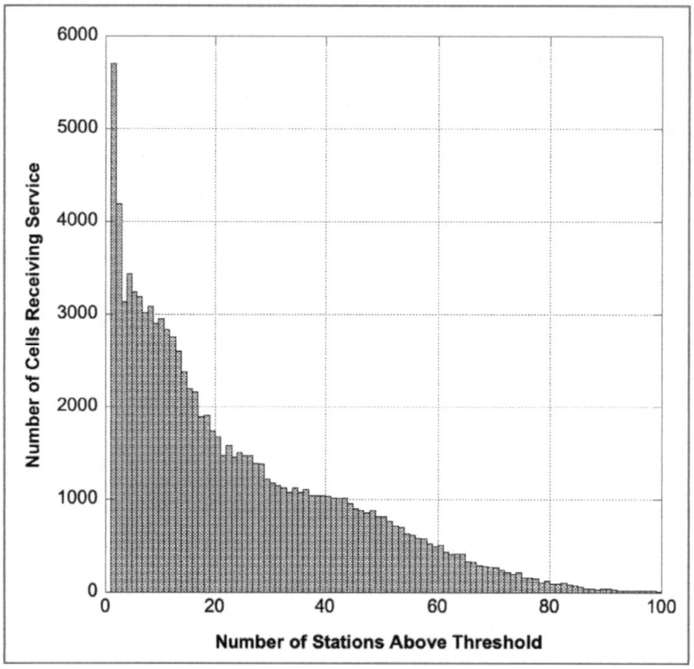


FIGURE 5: NUMBER OF LOCATIONS PREDICTED TO RECEIVE 1, 2, OR MORE BPS STATIONS ABOVE THRESHOLD. THE LOCATIONS (CELLS) PREDICTED TO RECEIVE 1 OR 2 BPS SIGNALS ARE MOSTLY OFF-SHORE. SEE TEXT.

Statistically, Figure 5 shows that a typical (median) location (cell) in CONUS is predicted to receive BPS signals from 17 television stations, although the actual number varies with location, ranging from 1 to 134 stations.

## Results – Predicted Coverage for Networked BPS Slave Stations

As discussed in a previous section, a small number of "master" BPS stations can provide timing to "slave" BPS stations, which then can provide a timing signal derived from one or more master stations. If slave station transmitting towers are used to support antennas for reception of BPS signals from master BPS stations, then the probability of reception from multiple stations improves. This is because TV towers are typically very tall and/or located at prominent geographic locations. A second coverage analysis was performed at the specific locations of all television transmitting stations, assuming the BPS receiving antenna is installed 50 meters above ground on the station's tower. As expected, the number of unique BPS signals predicted to be received increased. A typical (i.e., median) receiving antenna at 50 meters above ground on a TV tower is predicted to receive BPS signals from some 70 television stations, with the actual number ranging from 1 to nearly 150. The median reception figure is over four times that of general users at random locations using antennas just 1.5 meters above ground. A chart showing the cumulative distribution of BPS signals predicted to be received at the location of TV transmitting towers is shown in Figure 6.

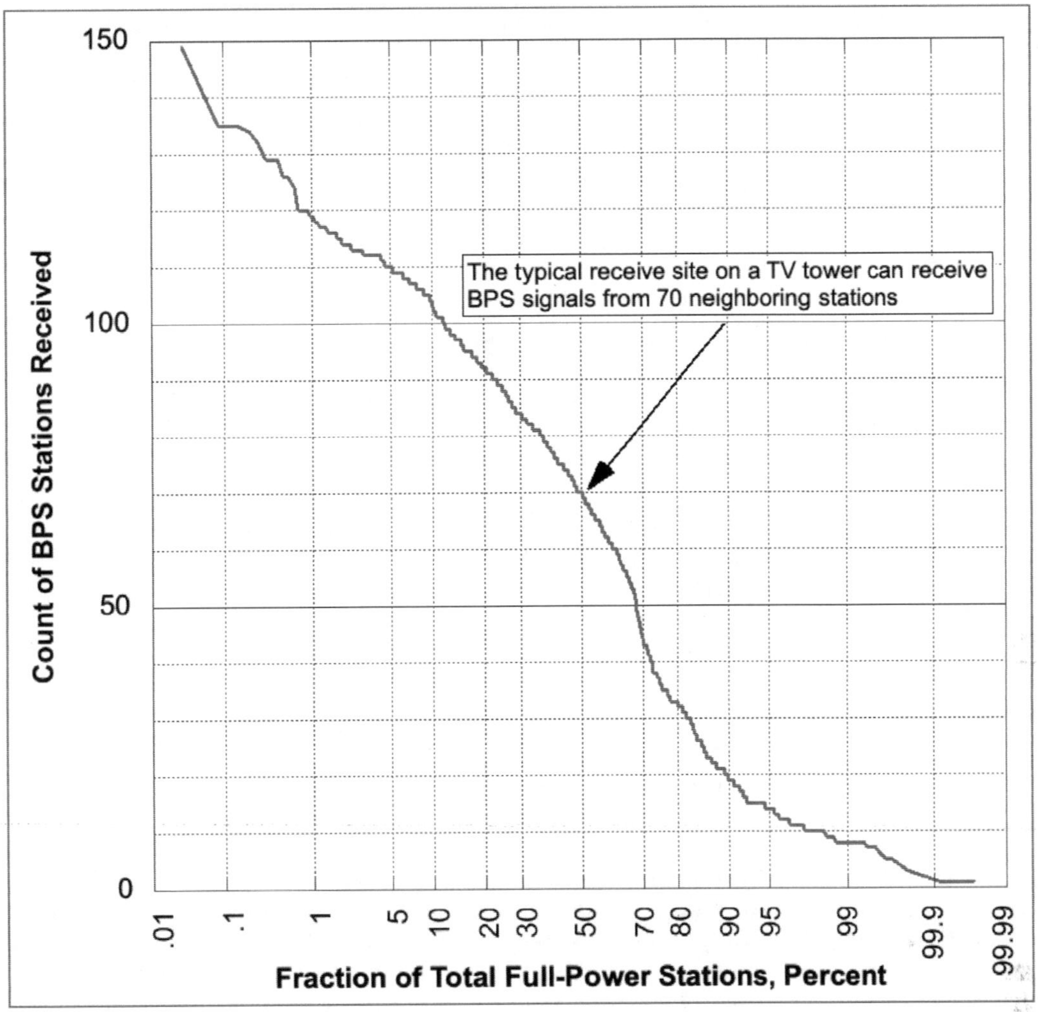


FIGURE 6: CUMULATIVE DISTRIBUTION GRAPH SHOWING THE FRACTION OF TV STATION TOWERS THAT ARE PREDICTED TO RECEIVE THE INDICATED NUMBER OF BPS STATIONS. THE TOTAL NUMBER (100%) OF FULL-POWER STATIONS CONSIDERED IS 1642. SEE TEXT.

## Models for Potential BPS Service Adoption

These initial results confirm that there is potential for not only networked time synchronization to provide accurate, precise, and reliable timekeeping function to support the BPS service(s) but also the provision of end user consumable signals for trusted time transfer. Looking forward, the BPS timekeeping function can be implemented along, at least, two paths for adoption.

Where motivated broadcasters desire an affiliation-oriented path, early transmitter technology investment can follow a vertical integration model and form affiliate network timekeeping systems. An affiliate-driven rollout can be conducted rapidly with closely coordinated management decision processes and provisioning of transmitters.

Where broadcasters pursue a service-oriented path to provide timing and positioning in regions with unmet PNT needs, a horizontal integration model is likely to be effective. Investment under regional agreements for equipage at designated timekeeping transmitters to serve as trusted and traceable UTC anchors opens the door to service level agreements for enhanced monitoring and reliability of the time transfer function station-to-station. Those stations "subscribing" to the trusted-and-traceable time transfer service(s) can then serve as BPS transmitter nodes but at a lower level of expected investment.

Regardless of business model choice, the initial objective is to provide an efficient and cost-effective options for secure trusted time to Critical Infrastructure owners and operators, *e.g.*, fintech, energy distribution, communications networks, and transportation operations. Success in this objective will pave the way for increased service provisioning to higher performance (accuracy, precision, etc.) and new functions (positioning, authenticated services, monitoring and cross-checking of other PNT services).

## Tower Synchronization Method and Algorithm

As noted earlier, the BPS protocol offers the ability of participating towers to synchronize to each other by exchanging timing information plus configuration and performance information for use in the decision model.

The source type list previously noted offers the basis for deciding whether to utilize a tower in the synchronization algorithm. These source types provide the clock quality level for a tower to use in its combining algorithm. The UTC from NIST or USNO are the highest quality, followed by the GPS source. When BPS is being utilized as a backup for GPS time by a Critical Infrastructure provider, these sources are necessary to maintain the critical operation of that provider.

It should be noted that during normal times in which GPS is not interrupted or unavailable, the BPS towers can be synchronized to the GPS signal. In times of interruption or unavailability the BPS tower will provide near GPS equivalent time from the other sources as noted in the source value table. The USNO and NIST sources will be utilized in these times.

An outline of the self-synchronizing method follows. It should be noted that these steps and expected results need to be confirmed through a thorough prototype testing scenario. Steps and processes will be formalized and documented throughout this "shake down" period. If every tower aligns its clock to the mean clock of the neighboring towers, all of them will converge to a self-synchronized value. If the master towers in this group keep their clocks unchanged, then the self-synchronized time will converge towards the master clocks' time.

1. Listen to signals from neighboring towers and extract the `bps_info()` message. Adjust for the propagation delay of each tower and estimate the clocks of all the neighboring towers.
2. Using a tower's own internal clock as a reference, estimate the timing offset of each neighboring tower's clock. This clock is disciplined to either a Precision Timing Protocol source, a GPS source or a master neighbor source.
3. Compute the mean and standard deviation of the neighboring towers' clocks. If there are obvious outliers that are not master towers, remove those towers from the neighbor list. For example, clocks with twice the standard deviation of the neighbor group's distribution can be removed. Do not remove master towers from the list. Let us call the remaining neighboring towers' list "credible towers." If master clocks exist within the neighbor group those shall be utilized by the tower performing the analysis and will be called the "Master BPS network reference time."
4. Using a tower's own internal clock as a reference, align the credible towers' clocks so that all of them refer to the same instant in time. This step will be utilized in the event none of the neighbors reports itself as a master. This step is necessary because the bootstrap signals of the towers may not be aligned in time.
5. Compute the mean of the non-master credible clocks; call it the NM BPS network reference time. If a tower is not a master and is using neighboring towers for synchronization, that tower will align its own clock to NM BPS network reference time.

## BPS Network Reference Time Network

The actual BPS reference time network will be made up of independent but interconnected time distribution "timing domains." The reason for this is that management of the nationwide BPS time distribution network, if it uses all the towers available, will constitute an extremely large number of timing nodes making management decisions and control unwieldy. For this reason, the BPS time distribution network will be segmented into manageable "domains" each with a size making it practical. These domains will interconnect to provide nationwide uniform resilience of time distribution. This technique eliminates the single point of failure such as found in GPS time distribution. This portion of the BPS network reference time distribution network is a work in progress and will be reported on as it evolves.

## Summary

BPS can satisfy the Critical Infrastructure timing needs if GPS becomes unavailable. If all television stations participate, single-tower coverage of BPS signals spans all of CONUS and miles of coastal and border areas. BPS towers can form a self-synchronizing network with a few master stations. A BPS tower synchronization algorithm is proposed to provide the best accuracy to all users throughout the network.

## References


[1] Mondal, T., Weller, R., and Matheny, S. "Broadcast Positioning System (BPS) Using ATSC 3.0," *Proceedings of the 2021 NAB Broadcast Engineering and Information Technology (BEIT) Conference*

[2] https://www.atsc.org/nextgen-tv/deployments/

[3] Presidential Executive Order 13905 "Strengthening National Resilience Through Responsible Use of Positioning, Navigation, and Timing Services," 18 Feb 2020

[4] National positioning, navigation, and timing architecture: implementation plan. (bts.gov) , July 28, 2010

[5] http://gps.gov

[6] 17 CFR §242.613

[7] "ATSC Recommended Practice: Guidelines for the Physical Layer Protocol," *Doc. A/327:2022-03,* March 2022, Advanced Television Systems Committee, Washington, D.C.

[8] FCC LMS data set, downloaded January 23, 2023. Note that some television stations are authorized to operate multiple transmitter sites in a single frequency network configuration.

[9] "Longley-Rice Methodology for Evaluating TV Coverage and Interference," *FCC/OET Bulletin No. 69*, February 6, 2004

[10] McKenna, P. and Najmy, F., "Evaluation of Two Site-Specific Radio Propagation Models," *Proc. ISART, NTIA Special Publication SP-03-401* (2003)

[11] Henry Gannett, "Areas of the United States, the States, and the Territories," *USGS Bulletin No. 302* (1906)

[12] Weller, R., Colombo, M., and Gao, C., "Statistics of Full Power and Class A Television Stations in the United States as of February 22, 2012," *FCC Report No. TAB 2013-01* (July 16, 2013)

## Appendix A

A mandatory presence in the following table means that if the `bps_info` message is transmitted, those fields must be populated within the message.

| *Syntax* | *No. of bits* | *Format* | *Presence* |
|---|---|---|---|
| bps_info(){ | | | |
| message_length | 16 | unsigned integer | mandatory |
| version | 8 | unsigned integer | |
| | | | |
| timing_source_info(){ | | | |
| sync_hierarchy | 7 | unsigned integer | |
| num_independent_sources | 6 | unsigned integer | |
| for (i=0;i< num_independent_sources;i++){ | | | |
| source_type_list | 4 | unsigned integer | |
| } | | | |
| expected_accuracy | 16 | unsigned integer | |
| source_used | 4 | unsigned integer | |
| } | | | |
| | | | |
| self_measurement_info(){ | | | |
| call_sign | 42 | array of 7 6-bit unsigned integers | |
| tx_id | 13 | unsigned integer | |
| tx_freq | 32 | 32-bit floating point | |
| geodetic_lat | 64 | 64-bit double precision | mandatory |
| geodetic_lon | 64 | 64-bit double precision | mandatory |
| geodetic_height | 64 | 64-bit double precision | mandatory |
| radiated_power | 32 | 32-bit floating point | |
| for (i=0;i<36;i++){ | | | |
| antenna_pattern_relative_field | 252 | array of 36 7-bit unsigned integers | |
| } | | | |
| max_gain_direction | 10 | unsigned integer | |
| prev_bootstrap_time_sec | 32 | unsigned integer | |
| prev_bootstrap_time_msec | 10 | unsigned integer | |
| prev_bootstrap_time_usec | 10 | unsigned integer | |
| prev_bootstrap_time_nsec | 10 | unsigned integer | |
| prev_bootstrap_time_error_nsec | 16 | signed integer | |
| } | | | |
| | | | |
| leap_seconds | 8 | unsigned integer | mandatory |
| | | | |
| num_neighbors | 6 | unsigned integer | |
| for (i=0;i<num_neighbors; i++){ | | | |
| neighbor_measurement_info(){ | | | |
| call_sign | 42 | array of 7 6-bit unsigned integers | |

| | | | |
|---|---|---|---|
| tx_id | 13 | unsigned integer | |
| tx_freq | 32 | 32-bit floating point | |
| geodetic_lat | 64 | 64-bit double precision | |
| geodetic_lon | 64 | 64-bit double precision | |
| geodetic_height | 64 | 64-bit double precision | |
| radiated_power | 32 | 32-bit floating point | |
| for (i=0;i<36;i++){ | | | |
| antenna_pattern_relative_field | 252 | array of 36 7-bit unsigned integers | |
| } | | | |
| max_gain_direction | 10 | unsigned integer | |
| reported_bootstrap_time_sec | 32 | unsigned integer | |
| reported_bootstrap_time_msec | 10 | unsigned integer | |
| reported_bootstrap_time_usec | 10 | unsigned integer | |
| reported_bootstrap_time_nsec | 10 | unsigned integer | |
| bootstrap_toa_offset | 32 | signed integer | |
| prev_bootstrap_time_sec | 32 | unsigned integer | |
| prev_bootstrap_time_msec | 10 | unsigned integer | |
| prev_bootstrap_time_usec | 10 | unsigned integer | |
| prev_bootstrap_time_nsec | 10 | unsigned integer | |
| prev_bootstrap_time_error_nsec | 16 | signed integer | |
| } | | | |
| } | | | |
| | | | |
| reserved_bits | as needed | | mandatory |
| bps_crc | 32 | unsigned integer | mandatory |
| } | | | |

**message_length** – This field indicates the length of the message, including the CRC bits, in units of bytes.

**version** – This field represents the version of the message.

**sync_hierarchy** – This field indicates the number of hops needed to transfer time from a reference ATSC 3.0 tower to the tower that is using neighboring towers' ATSC 3.0 signal as timing reference. If an ATSC 3.0 tower does not use the timing information from any neighboring tower to synchronize its own clock, its hierarchy is 0. For example, towers that receive traceable time from NIST or USNO using satellite, fiber, or other methods but do not use any neighboring tower's signal for synchronization will report 0 in this field. If a tower is using a `sync_hierarchy` 0 tower's signal for timing reference, that tower will report its `sync_hierarchy` as 1. Generally, if a tower is listening to the signals from neighboring towers for clock synchronization, and if n is the lowest `sync_hierarchy` among the received signals, that tower will report n+1 as its own `sync_hierarchy`.

**num_independent_sources** – This field indicates the number of independent timing sources used at the ensemble clock deployed at the tower location for clock synchronization. For example, if a TV station uses GPS, one cesium clock, eLORAN, and 5 neighboring towers as input to the ensemble clock, that tower will report the number 8 in this field. If a tower does not use an ensemble clock but uses another backup clock if its primary clock fails, the reported value will be 1. The corresponding `source_type_list` parameter will be updated accordingly in that case.

**`source_type_list`** – This field indicates the various timing sources used as reference at the ATSC 3.0 transmission facility. The following table is used to indicate the types:

| *Value* | *Source Type* |
|---|---|
| 0 | UTC from NIST or USNO securely delivered to the TV station |
| 1 | GPS |
| 2 | ATSC 3.0 signal emitted from neighboring towers |
| 3 | Local clock, such as cesium or rubidium |
| 4 | eLORAN |
| 5 | Reserved |
| 6 | Reserved |
| 7 | Reserved |
| ... | ... |
| 15 | Reserved |

If the transmission facility uses an ensemble of clocks, it will list the most accurate timing source of the ensemble as its source.

**`expected_accuracy`** – This field indicates the accuracy of the TV station clock 99% of the time compared to UTC. The unit is nanoseconds. A value of 200 means that the TV station clock is synchronized in such a way that the local clock is within 200 ns of UTC 99% of the time.

**`source_used`** – This field indicates the type of timing source used at the transmission facility. If the tower clock is derived from an ensemble of timing devices, a value of 0 will be reported. If the tower uses just one of the clocks available to it, that source will be reported using the table described under `source_type_list` parameter.

**`call_sign`** – This field states the 3 to 7-letter call sign of the TV station. If the call letters are shorter than 7 characters, the remaining fields are padded with "space" characters. The mapping of 6-bit unsigned integers and the letters in the call sign follows:

| *Binary* | *Character* |
|---|---|
| 000000 | space |
| 000001 | hyphen |
| 000010 | A |
| 000011 | B |
| ... | ... |
| 011011 | Z |
| 011100 | 0 |
| 011101 | 1 |
| ... | ... |
| 100101 | 9 |
| 100110 | reserved |
| ... | reserved |
| 111111 | reserved |

**tx_id** – This field represents the txid_address field as it is defined in ATSC A/322 with specific codes assigned according to the table at txid.nabpilot.org.

**tx_freq** – This field indicates the middle of the assigned television channel frequency in units of MHz.

**geodetic_lat** – This field represents geodetic latitude of the midpoint of the transmit antenna in WGS 84 LLA convention.

**geodetic_lon** – This field represents geodetic longitude of the midpoint of the transmit antenna in WGS 84 LLA convention.

**geodetic_height** – This field represents geodetic height of the midpoint of the transmit antenna in WGS 84 LLA convention.

**radiated_power** – This field represents ERP of the radiating antenna in units of kilowatts.

**antenna_pattern_relative_field** – This field represents the antenna pattern by the relative field values reported every 10 degrees. The values are arranged clockwise starting at true north, meaning that the 1st value of the 36-element array represents the relative field strength in the direction north, the 2nd value represents the relative field strength in the direction 10 degrees clockwise from north, and so on. The relative field values are scaled such that the maximum value, which is 1.0, is scaled to the integer 127 in fixed point representation.

**max_gain_direction** – This field represents the direction where relative field strength is maximum, i.e., 1.0. The angle is measured clockwise from north. The angle is reported as a fixed-point value such that 360 degrees is scaled to 1023 in fixed point notation.

**prev_bootstrap_time_sec** – This field will be populated with the L1D_time_sec value, as defined in ATSC A/322, of the immediately previous transmitted frame. For self_measurement_info, the transmitting tower will provide this information. For neighbor_measurement_info, the transmitting tower will receive the value in bps_info message from a neighboring tower and report that value in this field.

**prev_bootstrap_time_msec** – This field will be populated with the L1D_time_msec value, as defined in ATSC A/322, of the immediately previous transmitted frame. For self_measurement_info, the transmitting tower will provide this information. For neighbor_measurement_info, the transmitting tower will receive the value in bps_info message from a neighboring tower and report that value in this field.

**prev_bootstrap_time_usec** – This field will be populated with the L1D_time_usec value, as defined in ATSC A/322, of the immediately previous transmitted frame. For self_measurement_info, the transmitting tower will provide this information. For neighbor_measurement_info, the transmitting tower will receive the value in bps_info message from a neighboring tower and report that value in this field.

**prev_bootstrap_time_nsec** – This field will be populated with the L1D_time_nsec value, as defined in ATSC A/322, of the immediately previous transmitted frame. For self_measurement_info, the transmitting tower will provide this information. For neighbor_measurement_info, the transmitting tower will receive the value in bps_info message from a neighboring tower and report that value in this field.

**prev_bootstrap_time_error_nsec** – This is the difference between the actual time when the first sample of the first symbol of the bootstrap was transmitted and the reported bootstrap transmission time in the `L1D_time_sec, L1D_time_msec, L1D_time_usec`, and `L1D_time_nsec` fields mentioned in ATSC A/322. The time difference is measured as actual transmission time minus reported transmission time in nanosecond unit. For `self_measurement_info`, the transmitting tower will measure and provide this information. For `neighbor_measurement_info`, the transmitting tower will receive the value in `bps_info` message from a neighboring tower and report that value in this field.

**leap_seconds** – This field represents the current number of leap seconds expressed as TAI – UTC.

**num_neighbors** – This field indicates the number of neighboring signal measurements reported in the message. If this field is set to 0, no `neighbor_measurement_info` will be populated in the message.

**reported_bootstrap_time_sec** – This field will be populated with the `L1D_time_sec` value, as defined in ATSC A/322, of the most recent frame transmitted by a neighbor tower and received at the transmitting tower.

**reported_bootstrap_time_msec** – This field will be populated with the `L1D_time_msec` value, as defined in ATSC A/322, of the most recent frame transmitted by a neighbor tower and received at the transmitting tower.

**reported_bootstrap_time_usec** – This field will be populated with the `L1D_time_usec` value, as defined in ATSC A/322, of the most recent frame transmitted by a neighbor tower and received at the transmitting tower.

**reported_bootstrap_time_nsec** – This field will be populated with the `L1D_time_nsec` value, as defined in ATSC A/322, of the most recent frame transmitted by a neighbor tower and received at the transmitting tower.

**bootstrap_toa_offset** – This field represents the difference between the time of arrival at the transmitting (self) antenna of the neighboring bootstrap signal and the reported timestamp in `L1D_time_sec`, `L1D_time_msec`, `L1D_time_usec`, and `L1D_time_nsec` fields as mentioned in ATSC A/322. The unit of this time offset is nanoseconds.

**reserved_bits** – This field indicates the number of reserved bits, 0 to 7, that is required to byte-align the message.

**bps_crc** – This field will contain the CRC value as computed according to Section 6.1.2.2 of A/322 over the contents of `bps_info` message excluding the `bps_crc` field.

# How NextGen Broadcasting Improves Public Safety and Community Security by Providing Advanced Emergency Information Service

**Niem Dang, Kevin Wong**
**Sinclair Broadcast Group**
**Hunt Valley, Md., United States**
nhdang@sbgtv.com, kwong@sbgtv.com

**Abstract** – Broadcast television has always done an excellent job of entertaining, educating, and informing us; however, the recent technological advancements in broadcasting that now brings consumers content via multiple platforms and devices can also be leveraged to provide critical, lifesaving emergency information in real time during local, state, or federal crisis situations. The ATSC 3.0 television standard, powered by NextGen Broadcast deployment, combined with its new Internet Protocol functions, can provide first responders and emergency managers with advanced methods to deliver dramatically improved interactive content and targeted Advanced Emergency Information (AEI) alerting to citizens, not just on their televisions, but also to any other device within range of a broadcast television signal or connected to the Internet.

First responders and emergency managers have always battled an array of emergency scenarios, but today they are coming quicker and with much greater intensity whether it be the result of a natural disaster, a technological disaster (e.g., railroad derailment with chemical spill) or a pandemic. Complicating today's task of providing critical messaging and information during emergency events is the challenge of reaching an ever-shifting population demographic that now receives its information from a growing variety of sources and devices. This paper explores how ATSC 3.0 and NextGen Broadcasting enhancements can significantly improve how this task is performed for the betterment of community safety.

## This is What We Need – Wall-to-Wall TV Coverage

Television broadcasting shines during emergency coverage of disasters and related events. Wall-to-wall TV coverage continuously served Floridians having to endure the weather and live through Hurricane Ian. On September 28–29, 2022, that massive storm swept across Florida as one of the most devastating weather events since 1935 to make landfall in the state. In the hours after the storm passed, millions of residential and business customers lost electric power and light [1]. The category-4 hurricane brought sustained winds of 150 miles per hour and several feet of storm surge to the southwestern coast of Florida before dropping more than a foot of rain in vast swaths across the state. Despite several television and radio stations being 'off-the-air' [2], the multiplicity of stations continued to ensure broadcast coverage was available throughout the disaster.

Among the geographic areas impacted by Hurricane Ian, Fort Myers, and Bradenton/ Sarasota were among the worst-hit communities, as shown in Figure 1 (Power outage). While the FCC (Federal Communications Commission) did not identify which TV stations went offline, video footage uploaded to

This paper is excerpted from the Proceedings of the 2023 NAB Broadcast Engineering and Information Technology (BEIT) Conference, © 2023, National Association of Broadcasters, 1 M Street SE, Washington, DC 20003 USA.

social media reported videos and images of WINK-TV (Channel 11, CBS) in Fort Myers submerged in flood water. In hard-hit areas, many lost electricity, wireline/wireless Internet, and mobile cellular connectivity. Despite such destruction, the many TV stations that continued to operate service provided wall-to-wall coverage for real-time updates and emergency communications to local communities, serving as eyes and ears with boots on the ground to help individuals and inform respective TV audience. In addition, spreading timely and relevant information to support initial search and rescue, collaborating, weathering through extreme hardship to save lives, minimizing injuries, and assisting the collective recovery.

Imagine for a moment if these stations had been NextGen Broadcast and mobile and portable devices similarly supported NextGen reception. Despite the loss of power and in some areas with complete swaths of conventional cellular services being unavailable leaving people without conventional mobile device capabilities Figure 2 (Percent Cell Sites Out-of-Service [2]), news and emergency information provided through NextGen Broadcast and AEI could have provided emergency information and other vital services Figure 3 (simulated broadcast coverage without WINK-TV, Channel 11, CBS) and Figure 4 (simulated broadcast coverage after all channels were restored a few days later [3]).

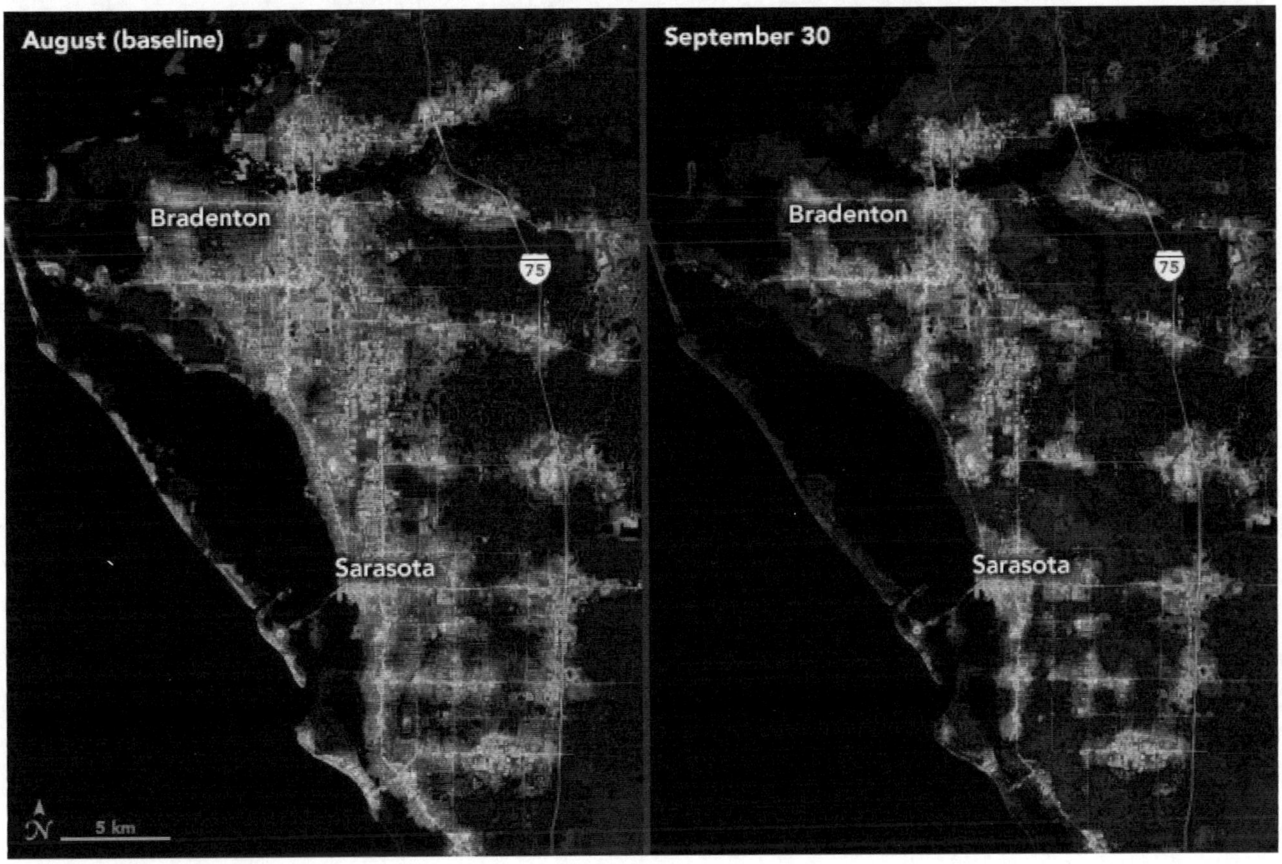


FIGURE 1: NIGHTTIME LIGHT EMISSIONS AND REFLECTIONS BEFORE AND AFTER IAN PASSED THROUGH THE CITIES.

9/29/2022 10:46:57 AM

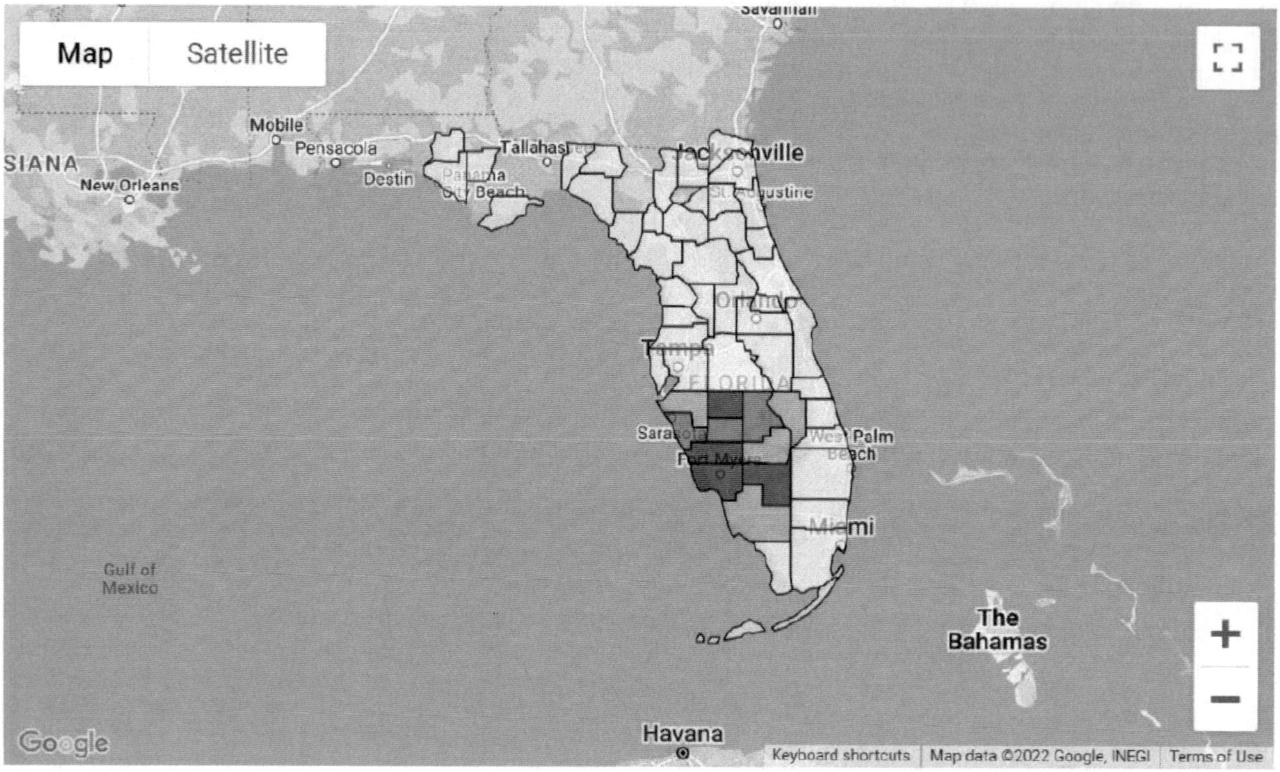


1 - 15 16 - 30 31 - 45 46 - 60 61 - 100

FIGURE 2: PERCENT CELL SITES OUT-OF-SERVICE BY COUNTY AFTER HURRICANE IAN.

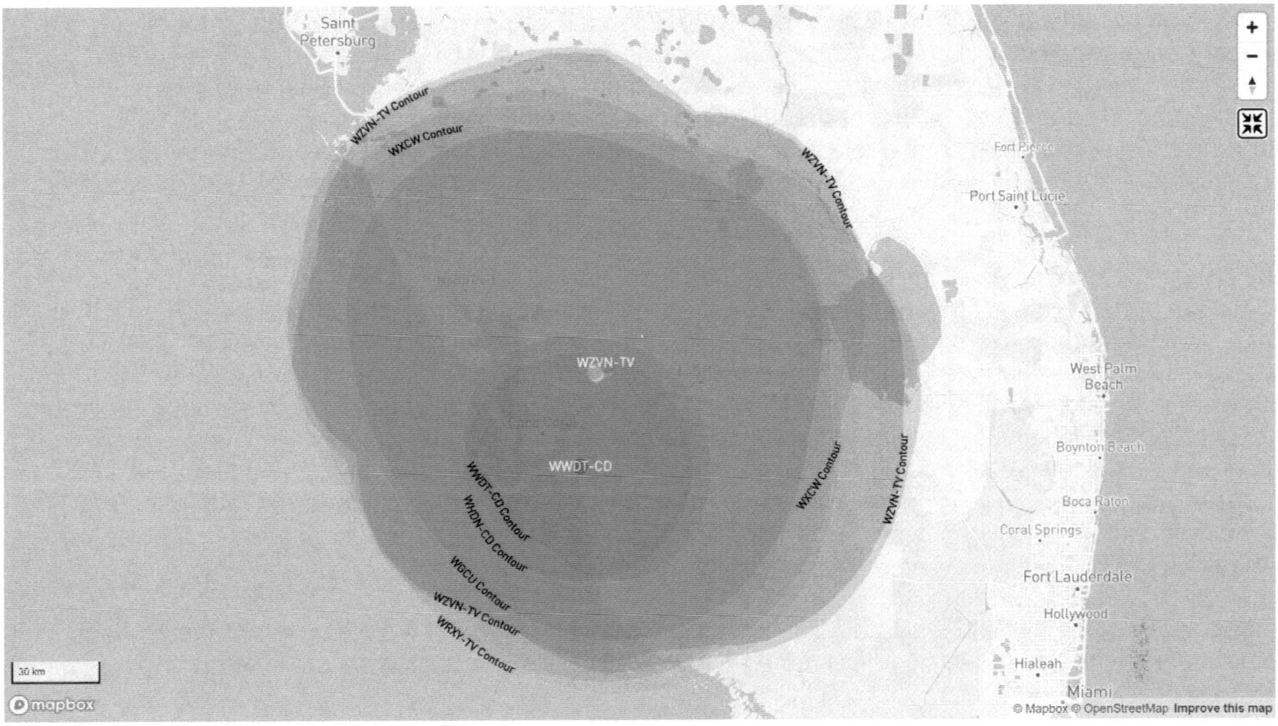


FIGURE 3: SIMULATED STATION CONTOURS FOR FT. MYERS-NAPLES MARKET WITH WINK-TV STATION OFFLINE[1].

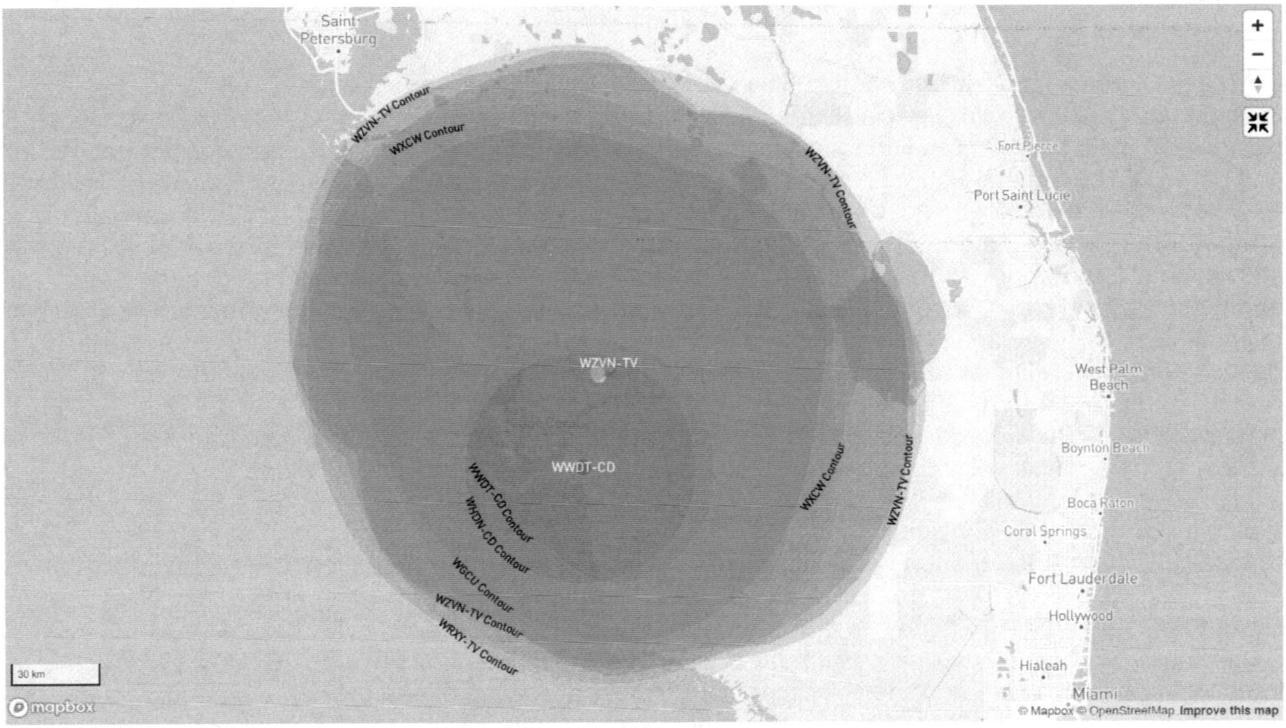


FIGURE 4: SIMULATED STATION CONTOURS FOR FT. MYERS-NAPLES, WITH WINK-TV STATION RESTORED (BLUE CONTOUR)[2].

---

[1] Figure 3 generated with internal tools, available through BitPath. Date generated: February 25, 2023.
[2] Figure 4 generated with internal tools, available through BitPath. Date generated: February 25, 2023.

It was local broadcast journalists who informed and connected those most impacted by the storm with relevant emergency information via radio and television services [4]. For many who watched and monitored Hurricane Ian and its path of destruction from a safer distance, national networks such as The Weather Channel kept concerned audience current on what was happening in Florida [4]. Hurricane Ian served as a "reminder of local broadcasters' vital public safety role during emergencies. Broadcasters are the backbone of the Emergency Alert System and often the first source of detailed news about severe weather, missing children, and other dangerous situations" [5].

Observing the total number of people affected as the sum of injured, requiring assistance, and homeless during a disaster, an estimated 1% of people are affected by various disasters yearly. This is based on the decade average for 2020. Disasters include all geophysical, meteorological, and climate events including earthquakes, volcanic activity, landslides, drought, wildfires, storms, and flooding [6]. But what if the affected individuals were to extend to manufactured disasters, mass events, or extreme inconveniences, including evacuations, closure, and more? The answer would be more about how often and how likely we all would be affected at any moment. As demonstrated throughout the Hurricane Ian disaster, local TV stations, coupled with NextGen Broadcasting for advanced emergency alerting and information, can serve as a complimentary communication mode for when Internet-denied situations.

But again, imagine if NextGen Broadcast services and mobile devices were the norm. Even those without electricity and cellular services could have been provided vital Advanced Emergency Information.

## NextGen Broadcasting Serves as Technology Enabler for Public Safety and Community Security

KSNV (Las Vegas) was the first US television station to support the transmission of ATSC 3.0 signals on December 4, 2015, with 'Special Temporary Authority' from the FCC. It was a historical event when members of the South Korean Broadcaster delegation came together to evaluate and decide the future for what would become the new South Korean broadcast standard – ATSC 3.0. (By May 2017, South Korea was the first to broadcast a 4K signal, paving the way for NextGen Broadcast.) Five years later, South Korea reached more than 70% of the population and the United States more than 60%. With the International Telecommunications Union formally adopting the standard in December 2019 as the fourth international digital terrestrial television standard (and the only one based on the Internet Protocol (IP)), Jamaica and Trinidad-Tobago are next up to transition their countries to the new standard with several other countries testing the standard for adoption there including India and Brazil[3].

Imagine when ATSC 3.0 achieves wall-to-wall coverage through global adoption, and emergency warning and alerting would work anywhere regardless of mobile or connectivity plan.

Driving innovation, the FCC published the report on a Comprehensive Re-imagining of Emergency Alerting [7], where the Communications Security, Reliability, and Interoperability (CSRIC) Working Group 2 (WG2) examined various current and future methods for disseminating emergency alert information to the public[4]. Of the few emergency alert dissemination techniques included, CSRIC WG2 evaluated ATSC 3.0 ("NextGenTV") standards. The evaluation was done by CSRIC WG2 to "hold the potential to not only vastly improve the broadcast television viewing experience and expand programming opportunities but also enhance emergency communications capabilities and create new operational capabilities for broadcast stations." The CSRIC WG2 also discussed ATSC 3.0 Support for Advanced Emergency Alerting services in great depth and as both OTA (Over the Air) and wireless capability, and industry-defined enabler to disseminate emergency alert and information to fixed,

---

[3] Also visit ATSC website for the most status, https://www.atsc.org/nextgen-tv/deployments/.

[4] CSRIC WG2's report also provided details on the difference between ASTC1.0 and 3.0 as it pertains to public warning and emergency alerts.

mobile, and mobile and portable devices. Since the first NextGen Broadcast over KSNV (Las Vegas), the ATSC itself along with broadcasters and consumer electronics manufacturers have collaborated closely to evolve and advance technologies to bring Advanced Emergency Information (AEI) service to NextGen Broadcast receivers and mobile devices.

Figure 5 describes a simplified overview of how TV station leverages NextGen Broadcast and existing EAS ecosystem to provide essential service to the public. In addition to wall-to-wall coverage through hardships, extreme conditions, or basic emergency information to keep the community safer, help parents find missing children, or guide tired souls avoiding traffic delays because of planned or unplanned road closures.

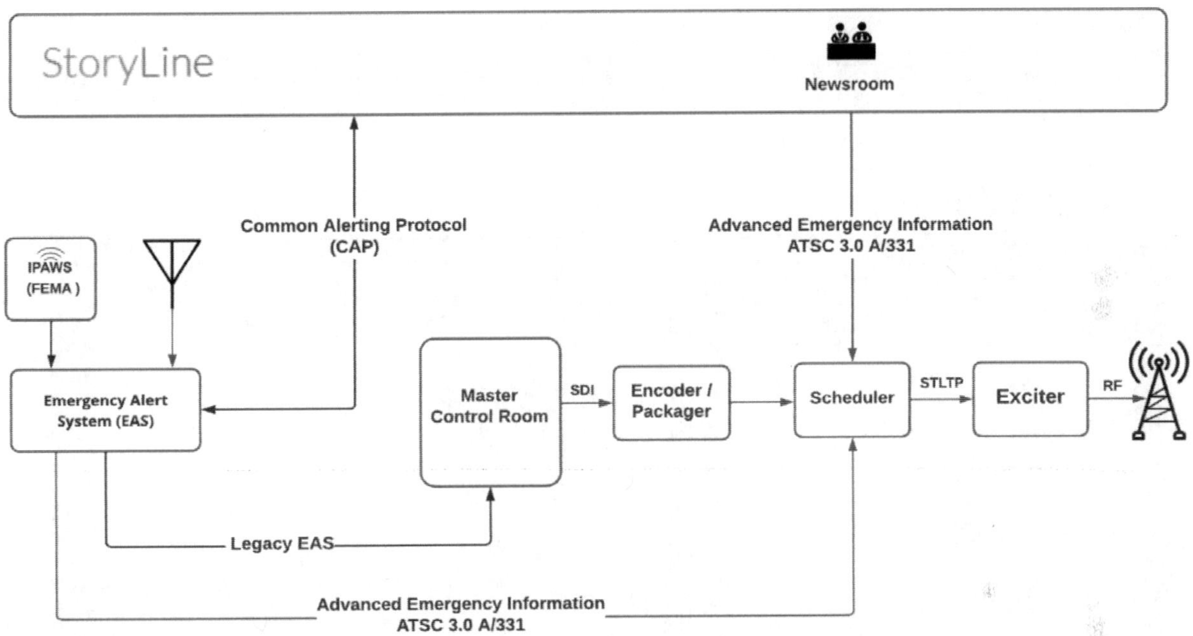


FIGURE 5: SIMPLIFIED ATSC 3.0 SUPPORT FOR EMERGENCY ALERTING AND INFORMATION, INTEGRATED WITH SINCLAIR'S STORYLINE PLATFORM.[5]

## Advanced Emergency Information as a Service

Advanced Emergency Information (AEI) refers to timely, in-depth emergency related information available through Sinclair's Broadcast App that local TV stations offer as a service for their viewers for the benefits of staying warned, alerted, and updated during crisis or inconvenient events [7]. AEI enables the broadcaster community to provide NextGen Broadcast viewers with public safety information that can be personalized and targeted to a viewer's current location and preferences. With these advancements, real-time data can be presented to viewers with location-based attributes for personalized alerts and notifications. In addition to the latter, complementing visuals can include maps of affected areas, evacuation routes, expanded emergency shelters, emergency contacts, and live doppler radar or alternate news streaming and do so in multiple languages. Also, a customized Broadcast Application provides viewers with an intuitive experience that acts as a gateway to accessing life-saving information and entertainment content. AEI continues saving lives by evolving NextGen Broadcasting's capability to transmit and deliver timely and relevant emergency and other critical details.

[5] StoryLine is Sinclair-built and supported media production, metadata management, and delivery system for converging media platform that provides instant publication, syndication, and distribution across all of the Sinclair digital and OTT properties, including live streaming and alerting capabilities for newsroom producers to deliver the right content to the right audience.

As an early developer of the customized Broadcast Application, Sinclair Broadcast Group considered all alert types and sources in developing a functional approach to distributing AEI services. Emergency information (including Emergency Alert System (EAS) messages) contain the data we see in traditional text crawls that appear at the top of the screen and are published by government-regulated agencies. Broadcast station newsrooms are also credible sources for informing and warning the public about natural disasters, matters of public safety, and local news. Broadcast News Flashes (BNF) are notifications newsrooms can issue related to emergency alerts. Broadcast News Alerts (BNA) are newsroom-generated alerts that can drastically vary in priority and nature. Some examples include weather advisories that could potentially threaten public safety, road closures due to a holiday event, or a list of school closings due to inclement weather conditions.

FIGURE 6: THROUGH NEWSROOM INTEGRATION, LOCAL TV STATIONS ARE DELIVERING EMERGENCY ALERT AND INFORMATION TO FIXED, MOBILE AND NEXTGEN BROADCAST RECEIVERS, WHERE TOP: DESKTOP/PC, LEFT: MOBILE AND RIGHT: TABLET.

Newsrooms have typically provided information for all surrounding areas that are part of the FIPS code for the specific market. The recent technology enables alerts to be targeted to a viewer's location and can make communications more efficient and delivered to a specific zip code Figure 7.

FIGURE 7: SINCLAIR'S BROADCAST APP ALLOWS OPTIONS FOR ALERT AUDIENCE THE ABILITY TO DEFINE EMERGENCY ALERT SETTINGS.

Sinclair's AEI solution also considers TV audience preferences. Viewers that supply their zip code can ensure they receive relevant information for their location. If a viewer does not provide their zip code and their TV is connected to the Internet, Sinclair's Broadcast Application will attempt to identify the device's location based on the IP address Figure 8. Alerts can be filtered based on priority, the threat to life level, and, eventually, alert categories Figure 9.

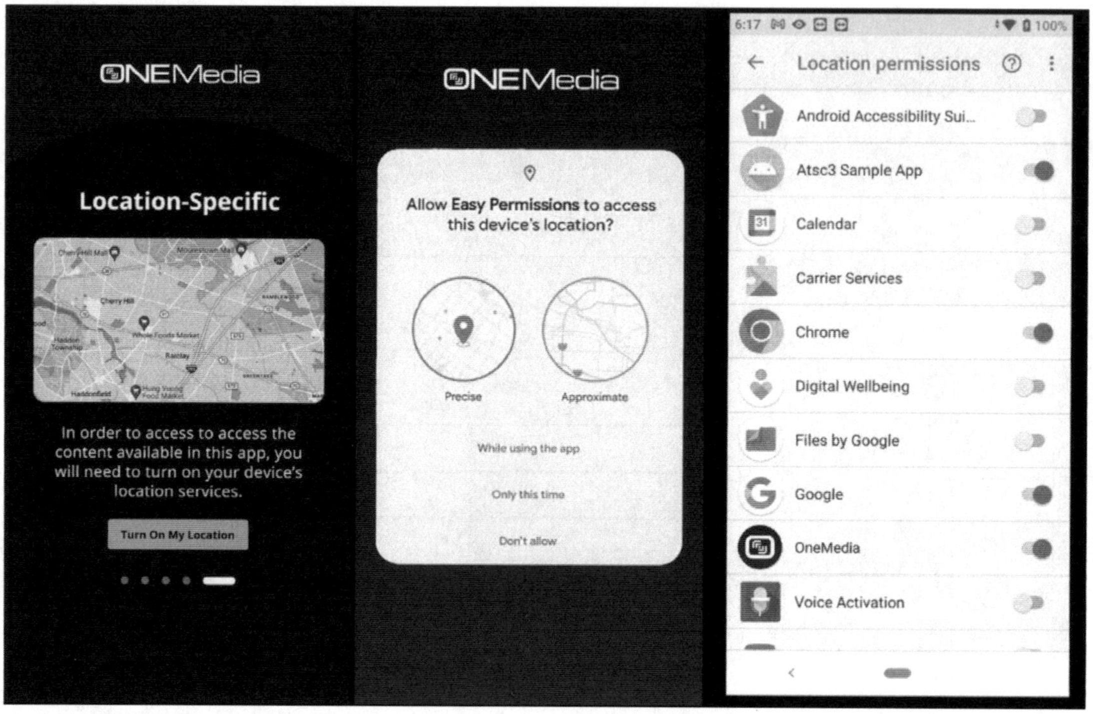


FIGURE 8: BA UI/UX PROTOTYPE FOR ALLOWING LOCATION-BASED EMERGENCY ALERT AND INFORMATION ON MOBILE AND TABLET DEVICES.

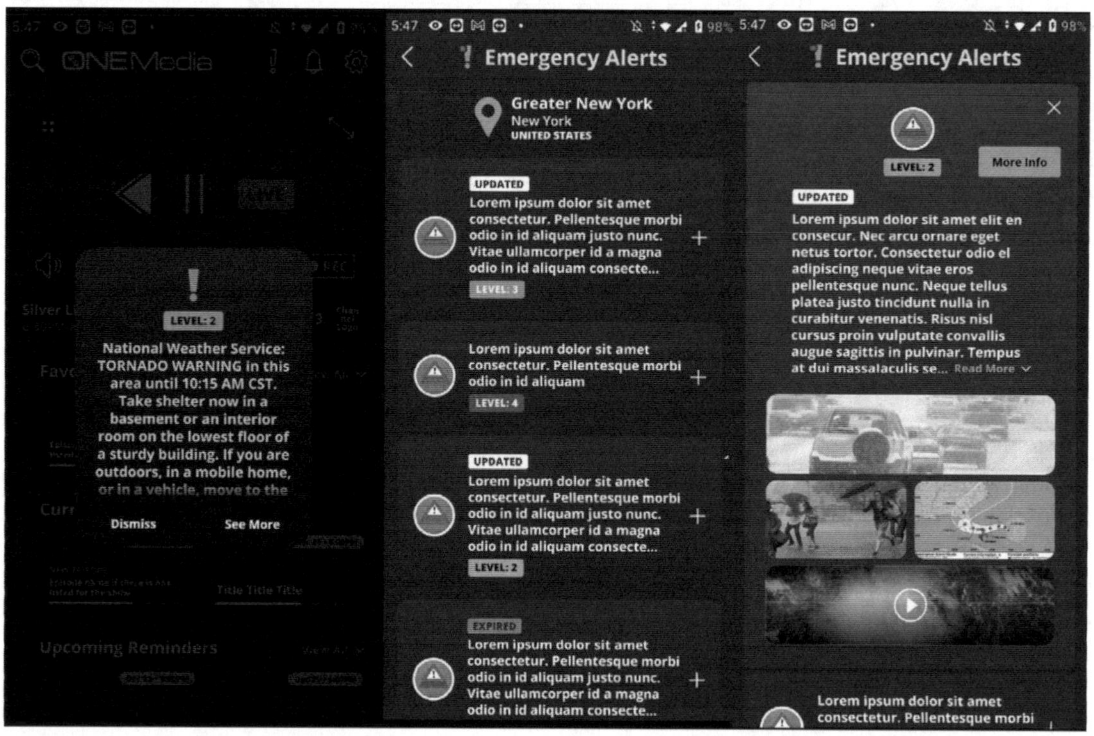


FIGURE 9: BA UI/UX PROTOTYPE FOR MOBILE AND TABLET DEVICES.

AEI Alerts can comprise text and all types of multimedia. For example, Sinclair's AEI solution can deliver video clips, images, text, and QR Codes. In addition, support of live streaming feeds is on the horizon.

AEI not only reaches TV viewers but can reach people on mobile devices. Sinclair has developed a responsive version of the Broadcast Application for smartphones and tablets that features AEI functionality that has parity with the TV version. There are also possibilities for developing AEI support for other mobile and portable devices, like portable and in-car navigation systems.

Of the 21 separate standards and 4 recommended practices that make up the complete ATSC 3.0 standards, Section A/331 (Signaling, Delivery, Synchronization, and Error Protection) allows TV stations to reach alert recipients by allowing key attributes such as – Who gets it, When (and for how long), Where, Alert summary (including rich media for improved clarity), and Urgency [10]. Figure 10 provides key data fields that the Broadcast App (BA) uses today to present emergency information to TV and NextGen Broadcast audience.

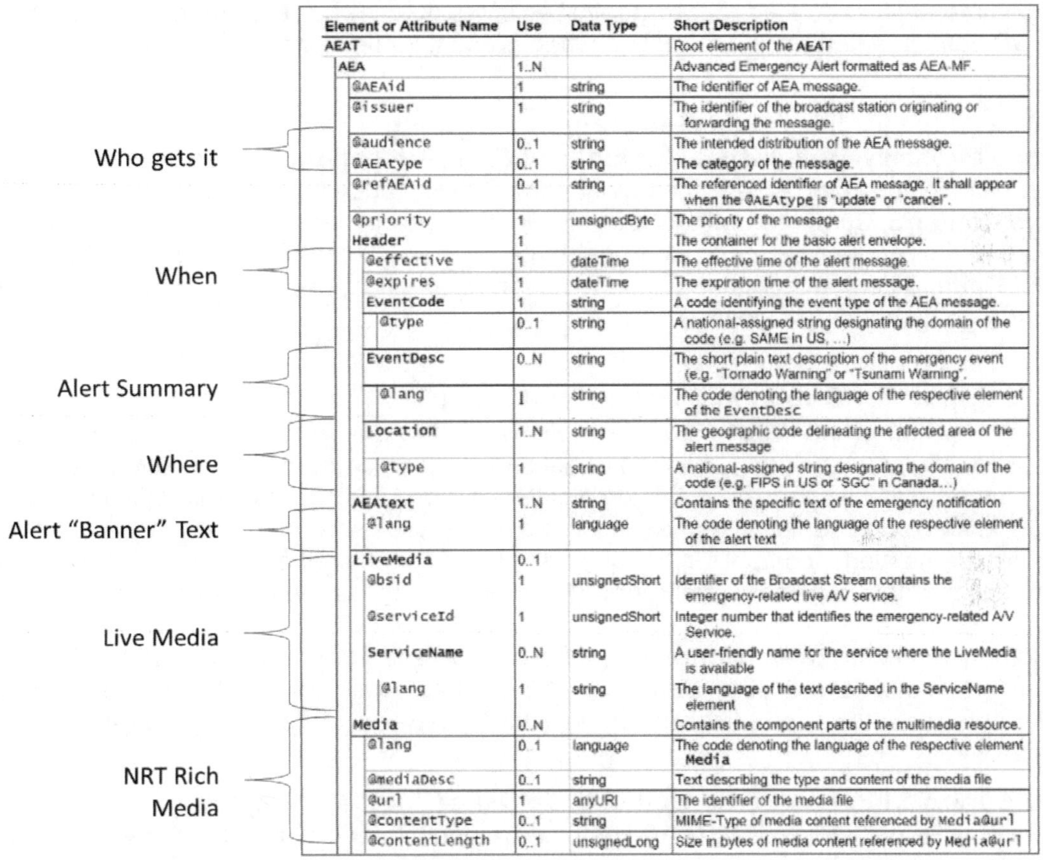


| Element or Attribute Name | Use | Data Type | Short Description |
|---|---|---|---|
| **AEAT** | | | Root element of the **AEAT** |
| **AEA** | 1..N | | Advanced Emergency Alert formatted as AEA-MF. |
| @AEAid | 1 | string | The identifier of AEA message. |
| @issuer | 1 | string | The identifier of the broadcast station originating or forwarding the message. |
| @audience | 0..1 | string | The intended distribution of the AEA message. |
| @AEAtype | 0..1 | string | The category of the message. |
| @refAEAid | 0..1 | string | The referenced identifier of AEA message. It shall appear when the @AEAtype is "update" or "cancel". |
| @priority | 1 | unsignedByte | The priority of the message |
| **Header** | 1 | | The container for the basic alert envelope. |
| @effective | 1 | dateTime | The effective time of the alert message. |
| @expires | 1 | dateTime | The expiration time of the alert message. |
| **EventCode** | 1 | string | A code identifying the event type of the AEA message. |
| @type | 0..1 | string | A national-assigned string designating the domain of the code (e.g. SAME in US, ...) |
| **EventDesc** | 0..N | string | The short plain text description of the emergency event (e.g. "Tornado Warning" or "Tsunami Warning". |
| @lang | 1 | string | The code denoting the language of the respective element of the EventDesc |
| **Location** | 1..N | string | The geographic code delineating the affected area of the alert message |
| @type | 1 | string | A national-assigned string designating the domain of the code (e.g. FIPS in US or "SGC" in Canada...) |
| **AEAtext** | 1..N | string | Contains the specific text of the emergency notification |
| @lang | 1 | language | The code denoting the language of the respective element of the alert text |
| **LiveMedia** | 0..1 | | |
| @bsid | 1 | unsignedShort | Identifier of the Broadcast Stream contains the emergency-related live A/V service. |
| @serviceId | 1 | unsignedShort | Integer number that identifies the emergency-related A/V Service. |
| **ServiceName** | 0..N | string | A user-friendly name for the service where the LiveMedia is available |
| @lang | 1 | string | The language of the text described in the ServiceName element |
| **Media** | 0..N | | Contains the component parts of the multimedia resource. |
| @lang | 0..1 | language | The code denoting the language of the respective element **Media** |
| @mediaDesc | 0..1 | string | Text describing the type and content of the media file |
| @url | 1 | anyURI | The identifier of the media file |
| @contentType | 0..1 | string | MIME-Type of media content referenced by Media@url |
| @contentLength | 0..1 | unsignedLong | Size in bytes of media content referenced by Media@url |

FIGURE 10: A/331 AEAT (ADVANCED EMERGENCY ALERTING TABLE) CONTAINS ESSENTIAL INFORMATION A BROADCAST APP (BA) [10].

## The Last Five Years' Advancement in Emergency Alerting and Informing Towards FCC's Recommendations

This section highlights key technical advancements and improvements developed, piloted, and continuously improved for the betterment of AEI since the FCC first published recommendations for improved emergency dissemination and delivery to subscribed or impacted audiences [8]. The select references included in this section are intended to help facilitate AEI implementation.

## ATSC 3.0 Support for Emergency Alerting and Emergency Information Dissemination

NextGen Broadcasting Serves as Technology Enabler for Public Safety and Community Security section provides a summary of how NextGen Broadcast enables AEI service on NextGenTV receivers. Figure 5 further completes the description for technology enablement with a simplified, and evolving, AEI system currently deployed by Sinclair Broadcast Group.

## Develop Standards for Public Safety Information in Consumer Electronics

Progress on AEI should serve as a model for collaboration, partnership, and technology advancements where members of the ATSC and CTA meet regularly for the purpose of improving and innovating NextGenTV receivers for receiving and rendering emergency alert and information on multi screens. Project CTA-CEB32.6-B (CEB 32.6), Revision of Recommended Practices for ATSC 3.0 Television Sets, Advanced Emergency alert is an example of such collaboration. CEB 32.6 is developed to provide recommendations related to the capabilities of NextGen receivers and how the devices should handle ATSC defined emergency information when present in the signals [11].

## ATSC 3.0 Support for Improved Geographic Targeting

**A/331 (Signaling, Delivery, Synchronization, and Error Protection)** defines how location/geotarget information be included in the AEAT, then delivered to the Broadcast Application through **A/344 (Interactive Content)**. Combined with location finding technology technique, the audience or alert recipient can further provide the Zip code to geotarget alerts subscription through the Broadcast Application. Figure 8 demonstrates an implementation for location-based alert and preferences available through the mobile devices.

## ATSC 3.0 Support for Common Alerting Protocol (CAP) to Convey Impact to Audience

Through CAP/EAS relay, the **A/331 (Signaling, Delivery, Synchronization, and Error Protection)** conveys priority of alert when first published or subsequently updated. When the signal alert or emergency information message is shown on NextGenTV or ATSC 3.0 capable mobile receiver, the Broadcast Application presents the signal according to the issue's priority. The alerts are as follows: Red (urgent/extreme alerts, compelling the alert recipient to seek shelter or safety), Orange, Yellow, and Green (low priority, cautionary, or informative community messages) color scheme.

Figure 9 demonstrates how alert priorities are incorporated and how the BA presents emergency alerts and information on mobile and tablet devices. The Broadcast Application allows alert recipients or NextGenTV audiences to set preferences and selectively view only relevant alert signals.

## ATSC 3.0 Support Increases the Delivery Speed of Alert Information

The amount of time available to issue emergency warnings or alerts depends on the disasters or impending emergencies. Figure 11 maps available warning times to known natural disasters, where for example, earthquakes often occur with no warning time at all [12]. It is imperative that alerting agencies, systems, and local TV stations should operate as one united front to deliver lifesaving and present emergency warning, alert, or information without delay.

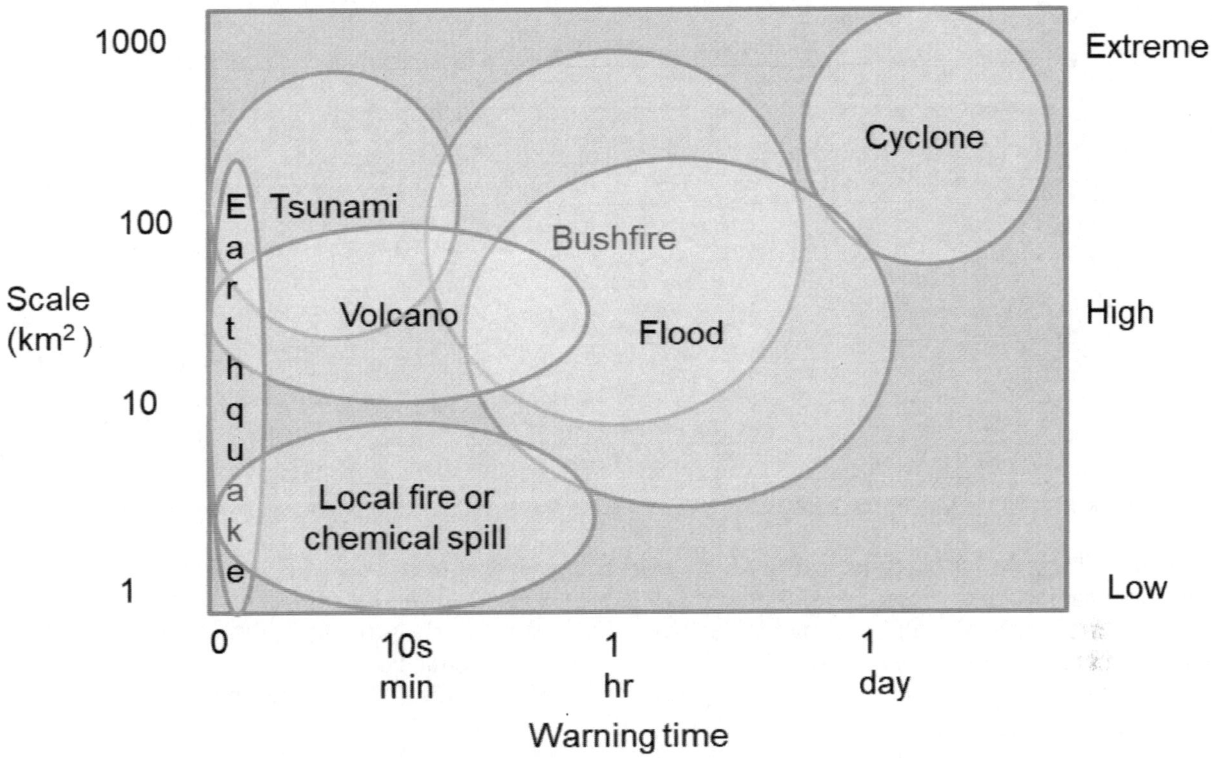


FIGURE 11: WARNING TIMES FOR DIFFERENT TYPES OF DISASTERS.

ATSC 3.0 standards allow emergency messaging to be delivered for timely rendering to alert audience through all connectivity modes – broadband, over the air or faster of either (depending on user preferences and settings.) **A/322 (Physical Layer Protocol)** standard designs RF/transmission of a physical layer waveform that allows flexible and extensible configurations of physical layer resources to target a variety of operating modes [10]. Using the bootstrap, with is the most vital part of the ATSC 3.0 signal, emergency alert wakeup bits are transmitted and delivered to the NextGen Broadcast receivers [14]. The bootstrap signal also plays a crucial role in emergency alerting. For example, a portable receiver in a tablet or cellphone only must turn it on long enough to pick up the bootstrap signal (2 ms). The receiver does not need to decode the preamble or the rest of the frame or turn on additional demodulation circuitry until the bootstrap signals an emergency alert is available, reducing power consumption and thus providing longer battery life. When an alert is received, it can switch on the demodulator and receive and display the emergency message and supplemental data.

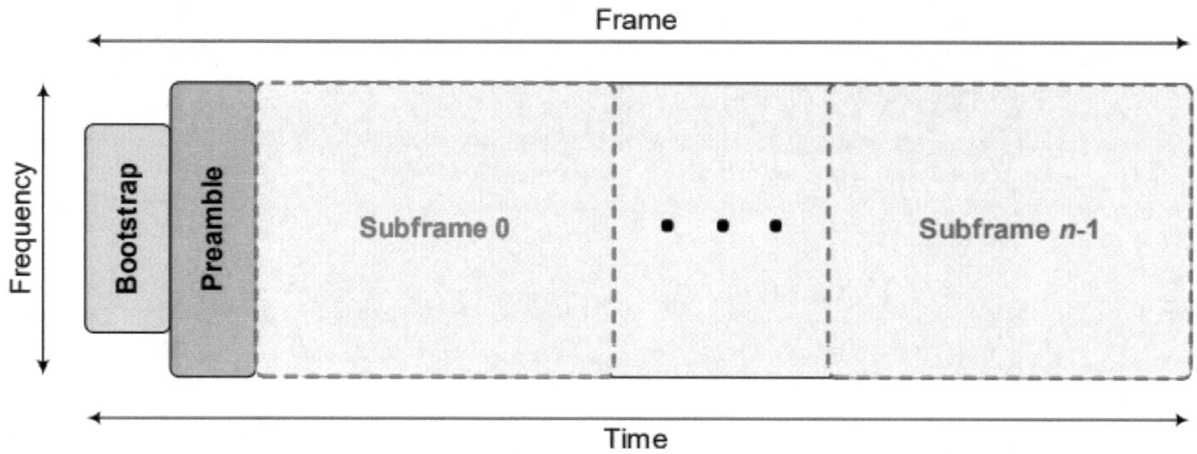


FIGURE 12: SIMPLIFIED VIEW OF FRAME STRUCTURE, WHERE BOOTSTRAP LOCATES AT THE BEGINNING OF EACH FRAME.

**A/331 (Signaling, Delivery, Synchronization, and Error Protection)** allows IP payload to a well-known address/port called Low-Level Signaling (LLS). LLS is designed for rapid channel scans and bootstrapping of service acquisition by the receiver. To detect AEATs arriving at the receiver, it must monitor the LLS payload through a dedicated IP/port. AEAT transmission via LLS is a fast, most reliable, and robust way to deliver emergency alerts and information to the NextGenTV receivers and for presentation by the Broadcast App [15].

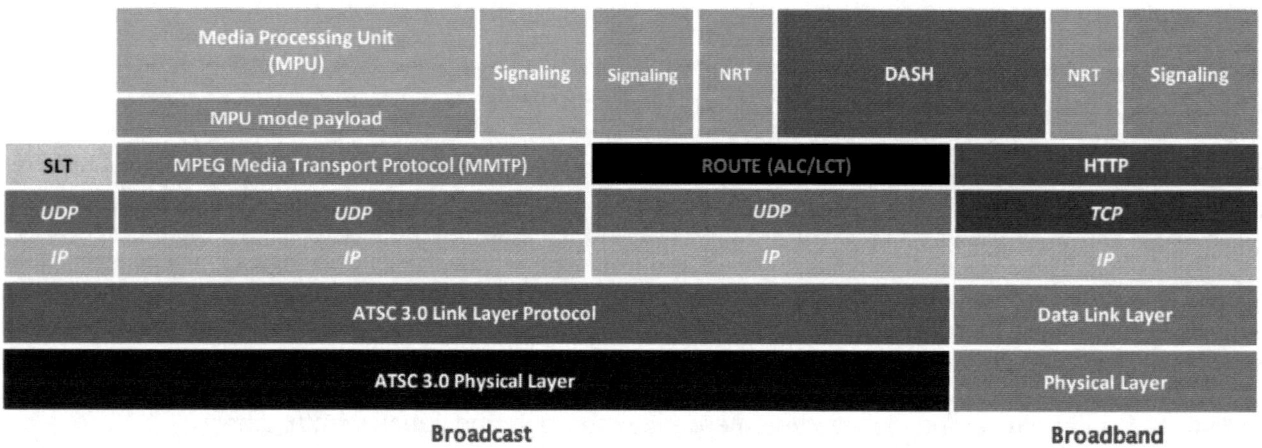


FIGURE 13: NEXTGENTV RECEIVER STACK WHERE AEAT.XML IS CARRIED BY SERVICE LIST TABLE (SLT) AND TRANSPORTED BY LOW-LEVEL SIGNAL FUNCTION.

A/331 also allows files to be delivered non-real-time (NRT), Real-time Object Delivery over Unidirectional Transport (ROUTE) protocol for Broadcast mode, and HTTP (Hypertext Transfer Protocol) for Broadband mode. In either mode, delivering AEAT.XML as a file via NRT is an option, where TV stations can adjust the speed based as needed if spectrum capacity allows.

Several signaling elements are related to advanced emergency messaging paths enabled by ATSC 3.0 standards and systems. However, there may be only one bootstrap and one preamble, but there may be multiple PLPs (Physical Layer Pipe). Figure 14 provides a visual representation of a frame that shows the possible placement of emergency-related signaling or payload to the NextGenTV receivers [16].

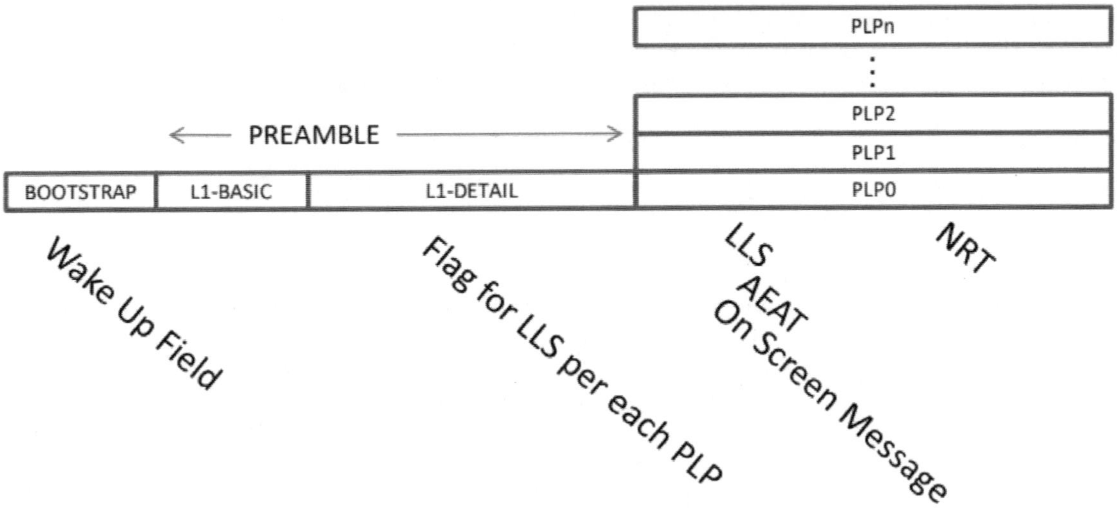


FIGURE 14: ILLUSTRATION OF PLPS AND SIGNALING ELEMENTS [16].

## ATSC 3.0 Support to Improve Public Alerting Systems Resilient and Redundant

It is understood that having durable, reliable, and resilient communications is not enough. Many parts of the world suffer from severe weather such as tornados, severe storms, flooding, wildfires, and winter weather. Broadcast television is native one-to-many instant delivery riding on reliable broadcast television signals is the most efficient way to distribute alerts. In addition, emergency systems should also provide more than one means for emergency messages to be curated, originated, and disseminated to alert audience. ATSC 3.0 standards allow emergency messages to be transmitted and delivered over available internet connections, over-the-air, or both. Further, emergency messages can be manually uploaded to EAS system by local TV stations when internet access is denied. **A/331 (Signaling, Delivery, Synchronization, and Error Protection)** allows carrying AEAT tables via LLS and NRT. The Broadcast Application can listen for notifications for emergency messages delivered through LLS, for example, those issued through an improved EAS system, through NRT in either broadcast or broadband modes. With NextGen Broadcasting and NextGenTV receivers, newsroom integration, TV stations, or alerts. In addition, audiences can receive an emergency alert or information from ten or more paths, presented by the Broadcast App according to emergency preferences and settings. Both Figure 5 and Figure 14 demonstrate ATSC 3.0 support for resilient emergency alerting by providing redundant communication paths. Further, NextGen Broadcasting also can transmit wakeup bits to any receivers capable of listening to the bootstrap signaling.

## ATSC 3.0 Support to Improve the Accessibility of Alert Information for All People

Today, about 20% of the population has a disability and struggle to have access to the same services and products as people without disabilities have. Making AEI accessible or to an able audience is crucial and essential. **A/331 (Signaling, Delivery, Synchronization, and Error Protection) designs AEAT (Advanced Emergency Information Table)** designed AEAT.XML messaging to allow AEI service to prominent audio, visual, vibration, and other techniques to notify the audience and alert recipient of an incoming alert and relevant updates throughout the event.

## ATSC 3.0 Support for the Integration of Public Alert Information Across Consumer Electronics, Electronic Media, and Public Displays

Local TV station news departments have become the most comprehensive source for local news as they now field more news reporters than any other local news organization, including newspapers. Figure 5 is an implementation where Local TV station can leverage newsroom integration for the dissemination of emergency alert and information across website, mobile, tables and

NextGenTV receivers. Figure 13 shows examples of Local TV stations leveraging newsroom integration workflow for real time dissemination of emergency alert and information to news audience. Further, during the AWARN Roundtable hosted by Capitol Broadcasters, moved forward, and expanding adoption with a public demonstration of newsroom integration to include AEI[6].

## Field Report of ATSC 3.0 Technology Enabler for Mass Communications

### SpectraRep's Datacasting Pilot: National Capital Region During July 4th, 2022, Event[7]

The July 4th celebrations in Washington, DC, are magnificent, drawing hundreds of thousands of people into the city. As a result, safety and security are a top priority for District and Federal agencies to strengthen emergency communications and inter-agency sharing; SpectraRep's® IncidentOne™ datacasting solution was deployed and used by DC Homeland Security and Emergency Management and six other federal and local public safety agencies during the celebrations on July 4th, 2022. The datacasting solution utilized NextGen Broadcast spectrum from the WIAV tower in Northwest DC. SpectraRep's July 4th field pilot, Figure 15 detailed the setup, and Figure 16 provided a visual of ATSC 3.0 coverage contour from the WIAV-DC transmission site, which was to demonstrate ATSC 3.0 as a communication enabler to support the Primary, Alternate, Contingency, Emergency (PACE) plan initiatives. In addition to providing situational awareness for multiple organizations responsible for mass communications and emergency management.

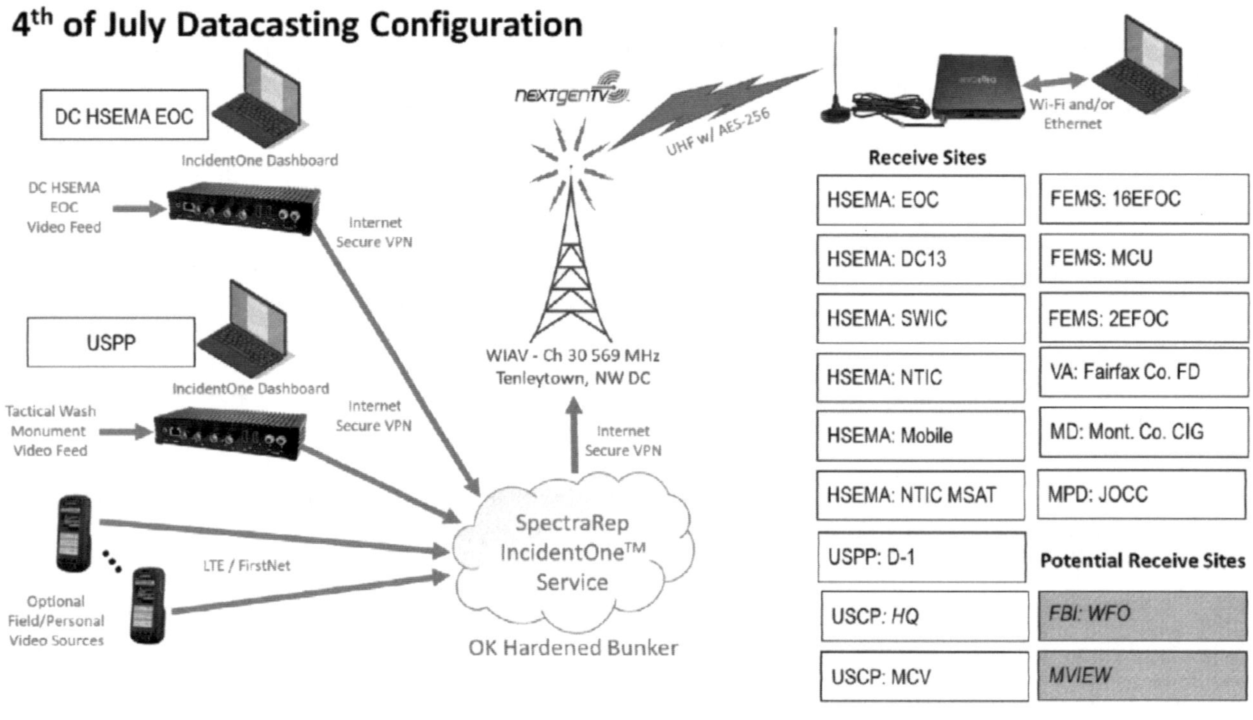


FIGURE 15: FIELD SETUP FOR EMERGENCY COMMUNICATIONS FOR PUBLIC SAFETY AGENCIES TO SUPPORT THE JULY 4TH CELEBRATION AT NATIONAL MALL, WASHINGTON DC [9].[8]

---

[6] AWARN Roundtables are invitation-only event where local TV stations host roundtable discussions with the AWARN Alliance and emergency managers about deploying AEI in specific regions. The AWARN Alliance is an international coalition of broadcasters, consumer electronics makers, B2B tech companies, and trade associations [17].

[7] Republished with SpectraRep's permission [9].

[8] Refer to [9] for acronyms included in Figure 15.

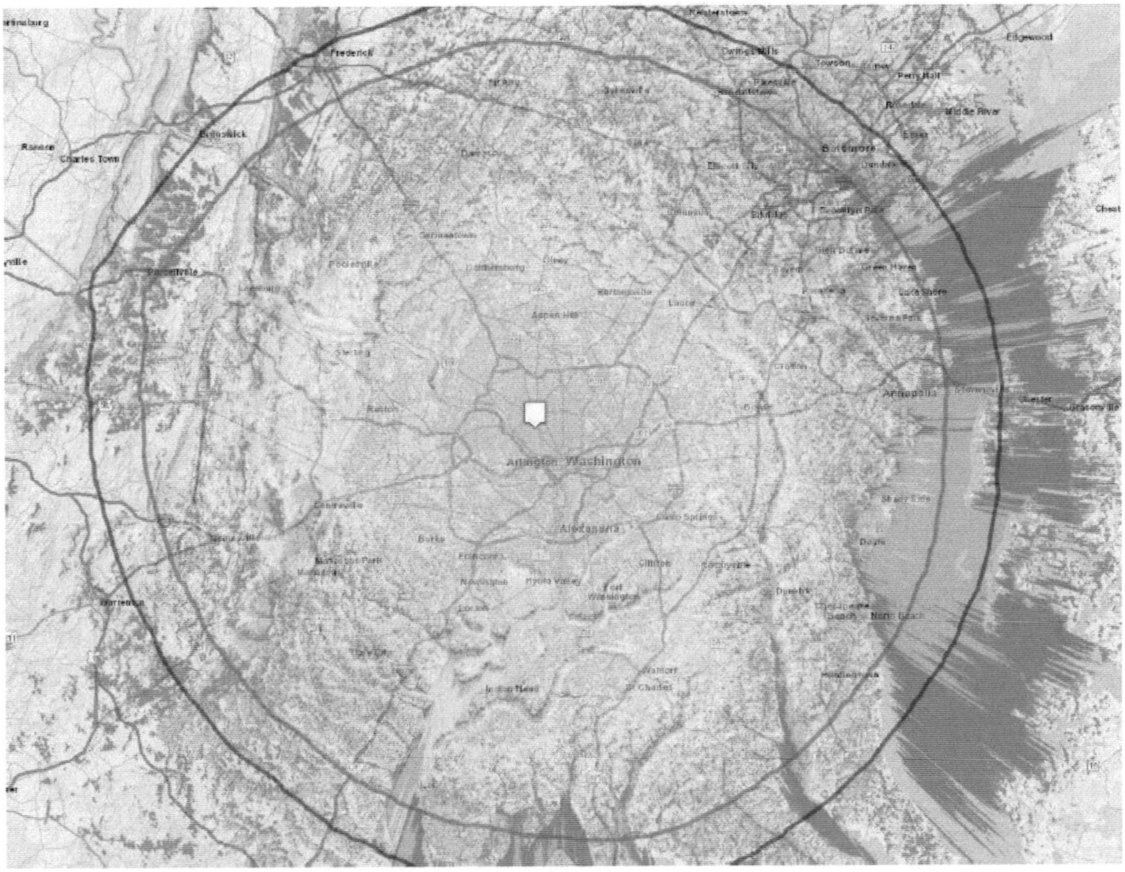


FIGURE 16: SIMULATED CONTOUR COVERAGE OF THE ATSC 3.0 OTA, TRANSMITTED FROM WIAV-DC LOCATION [9].

SpectraRep's pilot during the July 4th celebration demonstrated that multiple agencies could still effectively share critical data as video, messages, and files. This field research also showed that emergency communication during a mass event could not rely solely on LTE/FirstNet; for those feeds was a severe limiting factor as crowds and congestion increased from mid-afternoon onwards. Recognize the shortcomings of LTE (including FirstNet) for critical communications, and ATSC 3.0 infrastructure and technology should be employed as a PACE backup for emergency agencies, first responders, and mass communications. Further, ATSC 3.0 standards allow any portion of these streaming data to be made simultaneously available to NextGenTV receivers for mass communication when situation awareness is vital to safety and personal safety. With the introduction of a Broadcast Core Network or Data Distribution as a Service Platform, ATSC 3.0 is becoming more like a programmable network. Allowing TV stations to configure, dynamically adjust, and dedicate the network to deliver timely information to safeguard life and promote personal safety during unplanned crises.

## Social Impacts

For the first time, CTA had a theme for CES (Consumer Electronics Show) in 2023 focused on Human Security for All (HS4A), partnering with the United Nations and the World Academy of Art and Science. To many, human security refers to freedom from violence and fear of violence. In the broadest sense, HS4A addresses critical issues confronting the world today, including peace, human rights, inequality, health, food, education, jobs, safe communities and personal safety, energy, pollution, biodiversity, and, of course, climate change [19].

Human security is a message that speaks to people beyond basic human needs - to their concerns about everyday security, preserving safety, and having access to aid. More specifically, a safe environment in one's home, community, or when active, is personal and core to fundamental needs. Several keys are important. Those include: 1) Knowing (warned), 2) taking appropriate actions (availability of timely and informed to help individuals move away from dangers), 3) staying alert and informed of ongoing events (when loved ones living across zones, states, or countries are being impacted by disaster) and 4) being equipped with emergency information to seek help during limited connectivity or ill-equipped critical infrastructure (visual cues such as banners to a directly affected zone where help/responders would be). Making AEI available and ubiquitous is more than just saving a life; it also allows participants and recipients involved or impacted by disasters or crises to build a safe, sustainable community.

With the understanding and appreciation that effective communication is the most significant logistical problem during an emergency and for mass communications with much-needed situational awareness, NextGen Broadcasting is a proven solution. NextGen Broadcast enables durable, reliable, and resilient communications by allowing emergency messages to reach mobile, portable, and NextGen receivers. NextGen Broadcast standards support targeting by providing location-based information, maps to allow an impacted person to act and respond accordingly during crises, stressful emergencies, or unexpected moments and allow aggregation and dissemination of diverse communication modes. Further, NextGen Broadcast standards incorporate an interactive experience, and through the Broadcast Application, viewers can now personalize alerts through settings. With AEI service, NextGen Broadcast equips the audience to stay connected with EAS, stay informed with alerts or advisory messages from the newsroom, and prevail safely. An innovation area can be realized through improving smart smoke detectors to alert receivers within Bluetooth range to share and propagate alerts within a home or common space. Through this extension, only the receiver needs to have TV signal reception and can propagate alerts to receivers without good TV reception, e.g., to a receiver in a below-ground basement. Finally, the receiver can also extend alerts directly to mobile phones, tablets, and computers via Bluetooth through a simple app on those devices. Initial production receivers are in pilot deployments now and will be available in quantity for commercial procurement in mid-2023.

## Economic Impacts

It is possible to equate economic damages from natural disasters as a function of GDP9. For example, an estimate of annual damages from decade-based averages was about $78B in 2020 for the United States and $171B worldwide in 2020, Figure 17 [6].

[9] Economic damages from disasters (%GDP): United States: 0.37%, World: 0.20% for 2020 decade. Total World GDP in 2020 is $85.5 Tn, US is $21Tn in 2020.

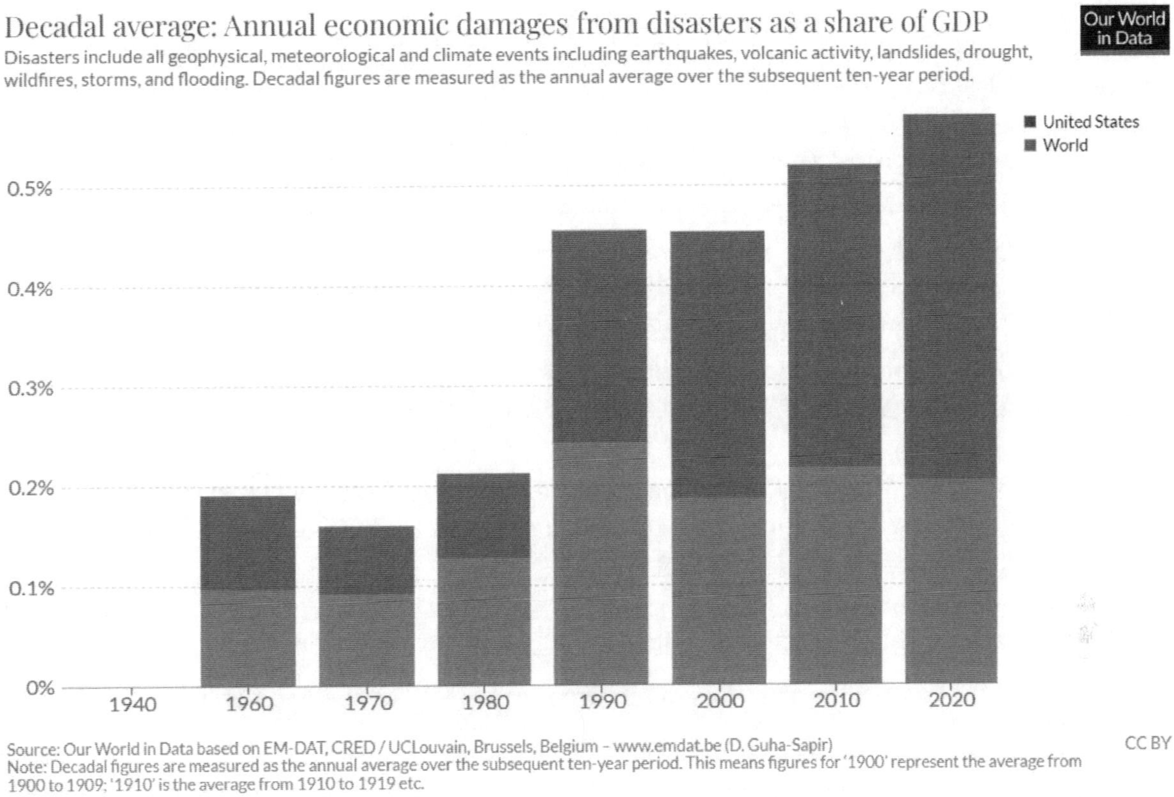


FIGURE 17: ESTIMATED ANNUAL ECONOMIC DAMAGES OF $78B FROM DISASTERS FOR THE UNITED STATES AND $171B FOR THE WORLD IN 2020.

## Conclusion

By delivering time-critical emergency alerting and relevant emergency information, broadcasters can save lives, reduce the number of affected individuals, improve personal safety, and protect properties. AEI service can be offered to any device, anywhere and anytime, when integrated with proven and emerging technologies. While the financial burden of emotional trauma or personal hurt to loved ones is immeasurable, it is possible to equate economic damages from natural or technological disasters. Integrating ATSC 3.0 chips to more mobile and portable devices to make AEI more available and ubiquitous. Coupling with disciplined newsroom integration, AEI is fulfilling an unmet gap – extending emergency alerting to also serve personal safety and community security needs.

## Acknowledgements

The completion of this undertaking could not have been possible without the participation and assistance of many from Sinclair Broadcast Group (Mike Kralec, Drew Sullins, Jason Miller, Louis Libin, Kathleah Obrero and Brandon Amoah), ONE Media 3.0 LLC (Mark Aitken, Jerald Fritz, So Vang, Ian Hoots and Henry McKelvey), BitPath (https://www.bitpath.com), SpectraRep (https://www.spectrarep.com) and PEAK3 (https://www.peak3spectrum.com). Their contributions are appreciated and gratefully acknowledged.

## References


[1] NASA (2022, September 30). Power Outages after Hurricane Ian. Earth Observatory. https://earthobservatory.nasa.gov/images/150431/power-outages-after-hurricane-ian

[2] FCC (2022, September 29th). *Communications Status Report for Areas Impacted by Hurricane Ian September 29th, 2022.* Public Safety and Homeland Security, Media Relations. https://www.fcc.gov/document/hurricane-ian-communications-status-report-september-29-2022

[3] FCC (2022, October 4th). *Communications Status Report for Areas Impacted by Hurricane Ian October 4th, 2022.* Public Safety and Homeland Security, Media Relations. https://www.fcc.gov/document/hurricane-ian-communications-status-report-october-4-2022

[4] Jones, T., (2022), "Who provided the most critical Hurricane Ian coverage?", Poynter., https://www.poynter.org/commentary/2022/who-provided-the-most-critical-hurricane-ian-coverage/

[5] Fowlkes, L. M. (2019, May 20th). Attention Broadcasters: Best Practices for Broadcaster Reliability and Security. FCC. https://www.fcc.gov/news-events/blog/2019/05/20/attention-broadcasters-best-practices-broadcaster-reliability-and

[6] Hannah Ritchie, Pablo Rosado and Max Roser (2022) - "Natural Disasters." Published online at OurWorldInData.org. https://ourworldindata.org/natural-disasters [Online Resource]

[7] Kralec, M. (2022, April). "Interactive NextGen Broadcast TV". Proceedings of the 2022 NAB BEIT Conference.

[8] CSRIC (2018, December 13th). Amended Report on Comprehensive Re-Imagining of Emergency Alerting. FCC. https://www.fcc.gov/file/14854/download

[9] Guddemi, C. (2022, July 27th). DC HSEMA – After Action Report Datacasting Pilot: NCR 4th of July 2022 Event [Report]. Homeland Security & Emergency Management Agency.

[10] ATSC Standard. A/331:2023-02, "Signaling, Delivery, Synchronization, and Error Protection."

[11] CTA. CTA-CEB32.6-A:2022-11. "Recommended Practice for ATSC 3.0 Television Sets, Advanced Emergency Information."

[12] WorldDAB. (2021, July). Factsheet: DAB+ emergency broadcasting and warnings. https://www.worlddab.org/public_document/file/1451/DAB__Emergency_warning_factsheet.pdf?1635785305

[13] ATSC Standard. A/322:2022-11, "Physical Layer Protocol."

[14] ATSC Standard. A/321:2022-03, "System Discovery and Signaling."

[15] ATSC Standard. A/344:2023-02, "ATSC 3.0 Interactive Content".

[16] ATSC Implementation Team Guide. AEA-IT:2019-02. ATSC 3.0 Advanced Emergency Information System Implementation Guide.

[17] Advanced Warning and Response Network (AWARN). https://awarn.org/

[18] The Case for an ATSC 3.0 Advanced Emergency Information Service (A Study from NVISA, The NextGen Video Information Systems Alliance). ATSC3 Advocate. https://www.atsc3advocate.com/aei-webinars

[19] World Academy of Art & Science (WAAS). Campaign on Human Security for All. https://new.worldacademy.org/hs4a/

# Configuring Versatile Video Coding: Technical Guidelines for Broadcast and Streaming Applications

**Łukasz Litwic**
**Ericsson**
**Gdańsk, Poland**
lukasz.litwic@ericsson.com

**Dmytro Rusanovskyy**
**Qualcomm Technologies Inc**
**San Diego, Calif., United States**
dmytror@qti.qualcomm.com

**Sean McCarthy**
**Dolby Laboratories, Inc.**
**San Francisco, Calif., United States**
sean.mccarthy@dolby.com

**Alan Stein**
**InterDigital Communications, Inc.**
**Princeton, N.J., United States**
alan.stein@interdigital.com

**Abstract** – Versatile Video Coding (VVC or H.266) is the latest video coding standard jointly developed by ISO/IEC MPEG and ITU-T VCEG. With best-in-class compression performance, VVC can enhance existing applications and enable new services. As the first VVC implementations enter the market, several application-oriented standards developing organizations and industry fora are defining VVC-based profiles and corresponding receiver capabilities. However, these specifications don't typically prescribe how a service is realized and the impact of the codec's operational parameters on delivered compression performance. To this end, the Media Coding Industry Forum has initiated the development of VVC technical guidelines. These guidelines will serve as a reference for VVC configuration choices to address operational, interoperability, and regulatory needs while achieving optimal compression performance. This paper presents an overview of the guidelines' scope and development process, followed by a discussion of VVC configuration aspects, with focus on new features which are of utmost relevance to broadcast and streaming applications and concludes with analysis of performance for the presented scenarios.

## Introduction

Versatile Video Coding (VVC) was standardized by ITU-T as Recommendation H.266 and in ISO and IEC as International Standard 23090-3 (MPEG-I Part 3) [1]. VVC is the latest generation of open video coding standards developed by the Joint Video Experts Team (JVET) of ISO/IEC JTC 1/SC 29 (known as Moving Picture Experts Group MPEG) and by ITU-T Question 6/16 of Study Group 16 (known as Video Coding Experts Group VCEG). The first release of the standard, published in July 2020, delivered a substantial increase in compression efficiency over its predecessor, HEVC/H.265, achieving around 50% bitrate reduction for the same video quality. VVC also improves on HEVC by including a combination of efficient coding tools designed from the start to support a wider range of video content properties including High Dynamic Range (HDR), Wide Color Gamut (WGC), and computer-generated imagery for gaming and remote screen content sharing. VVC's efficient coding tools and rich functionality target efficient delivery of established and emerging video formats such as Ultra-High Definition (UHD) with 4K and 8K resolutions, VR 360º video, and includes built-in scalability support already at a single layer bitstream level. Additional versatility can be achieved by metadata signaled in supplemental enhancement information (SEI) messages specified in VVC itself and in VSEI (Versatile SEI messages for coded video bitstreams) (ITU-T Recommendation H.274 | ISO/IEC 23002-7 [2]). As a whole, VVC's coding tools, functionality, and metadata signaling capabilities make it the leading state-of-the-art, feature-complete video codec available.

Unlike HEVC, where new functionality and specialized coding tools were added incrementally over time (e.g., 4:2:2 and 4:4:4 chroma formats were added in HEVC edition 2, scalability support in HEVC edition 3, and screen-content coding in HEVC edition 4), VVC includes support for all this functionality already from the first release. Three sets of profiles were included to support a host of video applications:

- **Main 10** and **Main 10 4:4:4** profiles, where **Main 10** is the flagship profile expected to support a wide range of broadcast and streaming applications and includes support for 8- and 10-bit video, temporal sub-layer functionality and spatial scalability through resolution change. **Main 10 4:4:4** includes support for additional chroma sampling formats: 4:2:2 YCbCr chroma typically used in video production and contribution applications and 4:4:4 RGB format for applications operating on content out of graphics frame buffers, e.g., remote desktop
- **Multilayer Main 10** and **Multilayer Main 10 4:4:4** extend **Main 10** and **Main 10 4:4:4** profiles, respectively, with support for multi-layer bitstreams.
- **Main 10 Still Picture** and **Main 10 4:4:4 Still Picture** specialize **Main 10** and **Main 10 4:4:4** profiles, respectively, to support bitstreams comprising a single intra-coded picture.

The second edition of the VVC standard published in April 2022 added new operation range extension profiles supporting bit depths up to 12 bits for YCbCr chroma formats, intra only profiles including up to 16 bits for RGB formats targeting high fidelity content acquisition and studio production applications.

Following VVC finalization, VVC support was enabled in all relevant media transport and systems standards. Encapsulation in MPEG-2 TS for digital television broadcast services is specified in [3]. Encapsulation of VVC bitstreams in MPEG ISO base media file format (ISOBMFF) is specified in [4]. VVC was also added to MPEG Common Media Application Format (CMAF) including baseline VVC media profile and multilayer VVC media profile [5]. For most typical broadcast and streaming applications, Main 10 profile is expected to provide the requisite compression performance and functionality. Such streamlining of available profiles compared with previous generations of codecs like AVC/H.264 and HEVC/H.265 is expected to have a positive impact on the cost of deployment and interoperability across the ecosystem. At the same time, since VVC includes a much richer set of coding tools and functionality than previous codecs, it would be beneficial to have an industry reference for VVC to guide configuration choices that address relevant user profiles and operating points such as those defined in industry leading application specifications. Such a reference for VVC could facilitate cross-industry harmonization and enhance interoperability across the broadcast and streaming ecosystem.

The Media Coding Industry Forum is an open industry forum with the purpose of furthering adoption of MPEG standards initially focusing on VVC, by establishing them as well-accepted and widely used standards for the benefit of consumers and industry [6]. With the strong industry VVC adoption, the MC-IF Interoperability Working Group has launched work on VVC technical guidelines with the focus on broadcast and streaming applications. These VVC technical guidelines aim to provide information to facilitate incorporation of VVC into application-oriented standards, media production workflows, and media distribution to consumers. In addition to covering best practices for VVC configuration, in terms of both functionality and compression performance, the guidelines aim to include up-to-date information on VVC operating bitrate ranges and provide information on the usage of VVC and SEI messages.

This paper attempts to review the status of VVC deployment and adoption in application standards, introduces MC-IF VVC technical guidelines work, and provides in-depth discussion on performance or functionality of selected VVC configuration aspects. The authors of this paper represent companies who are members of the Media Coding Industry Forum and involved in work on MC-IF guideline.

## VVC Deployment Status

Thanks to strong industry interest, VVC has enjoyed a rapid roll-out across different parts of the entire end-to-end video ecosystem with the first reports of optimized decoder implementation made already during VVC standardization [7][8].

### Software Decoding

One of the key enablers of such a speedy implementation cycle is the relatively low complexity of the VVC decoding process which is only about 1.5-2x the complexity of an equivalent HEVC decoder [9]. Several publicly available software decoders and players have been released for various platforms: HD playback on Android [12][11][14] and iOS [10][12] mobile platforms, 4K decoding on laptop/desktop Apple M1 [13] , Intel i7 and Intel i9 processors [9] and 8K decoding with AMD EPYC [9] and Intel Xeon including support for Multilayer Main 10 profile [16]. VVC was also reported to playback HD content in Edge, Firefox and Chrome browsers using a WebAssembly build [14][15].

### Hardware Decoding

While software decoding enables early technology integration and launch of services, in the long term, deployments in broadcast and streaming ecosystem are expected to rely on hardware decoder capabilities especially for 4K and 8K based video formats including high frame rate (HFR) support (100/120 Hz frame rates). Availability of VVC decoder IP core for 8K120 [17] , SoC decoder for set-top boxed [18] and TV chipsets with VVC support for 4K and up to 8K120 were reported [19] while the first news of consumer TV sets supporting VVC were reported for 2023 [20].

### Encoding

On the encoding side, several reports have been made since the launch of VVC. Already in October 2020, a publicly available optimized offline encoder was reported offering performance on par with the VVC reference software encoder (VTM) [8]. Due to inclusion of special encoder features such as adaptive QP, the implementation was demonstrated to outperform the reference VTM encoder in subjective verification tests against HEVC [21] while operating with 100x encoding speed that of the VTM. Several other offline encoders have subsequently been reported offering over 30% performance gains over HEVC [22][23] and have been integrated into cloud-based encoding [24] , transcoding [25] and mobile OTT services [26][27]. VVC encoding software with capabilities up to 8K resolution [28] including capabilities of real-time 8Kp30 encoding were reported [29]. Encoder vendors also reported compression performance gains obtained with VVC encoders using comparable computing resources to currently deployed HEVC encoders. In terms of real-time UHD encoding deployed on a public cloud, VVC was reported to achieve between 15%-30% lower bitrate at the same quality as a commercial HEVC solution at 36% compute cost overhead [30]. Data from another vendor reported VVC real-time implementation to provide between 10%-15% bitrate reduction over HEVC while utilizing the same core coding engine as HEVC encoder [37] for 4K content and on average 20% bitrate reduction for 8K content thus reducing 8K delivery bitrates to fit DVB-T2 or ATSC-3.0 transmission systems at around

35 Mbps [31]. While these performance gains are reported lower than 50% usually expected from new generation of ITU-T and ISO/IEC coding standards, it is important to note that these came from early implementations and encoder complexity in these cases was reported to be between 1x-1.5x of that of equivalent HEVC encoder.

### Interoperability

VVC interoperability with several key technologies used in the broadcast and streaming ecosystem has also been demonstrated in end-to-end trials. Over-the-air (OTA) and Over-the-top (OTT) trials of UHD content with VVC demonstrating encapsulation with MPEG-2 over DVB-S2 and ISOBMFF delivered with DASH were reported in [37]. Live 4K VVC streaming with low latency CMAF packaging was also reported in [37]. Interoperability with CMAF was also reported for Multilayer Main 10 decoder on 8K/4K/HD content [33].

### Conformance Testing

JVET has developed a normative specification *Conformance testing for VVC* as ITU-T Recommendation H.266.1 and ISO/IEC 23090-15 [34]. The specification includes a conformance bitstream test set comprising around 280 bitstreams in over 100 categories to cover all VVC profiles in version 1. DVB released VVC test content for verification and validation of DVB VVC profiles (see also **DVB**) [35]. Commercial conformance and test streams for VVC were also developed already during standardization phased and released shortly after standard completion [36]

In summary, the deployment of VVC seems to have a certain success for such a short term. The annual video developer survey report by Bitmovin, conducted with 424 respondents from over 80 countries [38], indicated that 19% of developer were using VVC in production for live coding and 15% for video on-demand coding, making VVC the third most reported codec in the survey with H.264/AVC indicated by 78% and 85% respondents and HEVC/H.265 indicated by 40% and 42% respondents, respectively. A comprehensive review of reported VVC deployments can be found in [39].

## VVC Adoptions in Applications Standards

Video traffic has been growing exponentially. In mobile networks the share of video traffic is estimated at 70% and is projected to increase to around 80 percent share of the traffic by the end of the decade [40]. This growth is driven in part by the increasing consumer demand for content delivered in high quality formats, which can either mean video delivery in new enhanced and immersive formats (e.g., with 8K resolution) or a larger availability of UHD content delivered to customers. This has led several standards developing organizations (SDO) across broadcast and streaming ecosystem to investigate the benefits of VVC for inclusion into their specification and systems. The Advanced Television Systems Committee (ATSC) has noted their intention to include VVC in the ATSC 3.0 standard. A recent report on ATSC 3.0 and Global Convergence mentions explicitly that *"ATSC is currently specifying Versatile Video Coding (VVC) for inclusion in the ATSC 3.0 suite of standards"* [41]. Streaming industry fora like DASH-IF and CTA-Wave added VVC profiles into their guidelines and specifications [42][43]. Digital Video Broadcasting (DVB) and Sistema Brasileiro de Televisão Digital (Fórum SBTVD) already adopted VVC involving a formal process of verification of compression performance claims against commercial requirements. 3GPP SA43GPP SA4, while has not started a formal adoption of new codecs into its standards, concluded a feasibility study on codecs performance, where initial performance analysis of new codecs such as VVC was investigated. The next paragraphs give a brief overview based on publicly available reports of VVC verification and adoption status in these organizations.

## DVB

**Digital Video Broadcasting (DVB)** started investigations into new commercial requirements for new video codecs in 2020. DVB set out a number of performance related commercial requirements to be met by new codecs, including: the ability to delivery 8K video over legacy broadcast multiplexes at excellent quality; the ability to enable five 4K services in a 40 Mbps DVB-T2 multiplex (compared with three 4K services expected with HEVC); provide at least 27% more efficient live broadcast encoding than HEVC, and over 30% performance gains for 4K streaming use cases while maintaining performance gains for sub 4K resolutions[44]. As reported in [46], DVB did not perform internal tests but relied on testing done externally. Within just a year DVB verified VVC meeting its commercial requirements and adopted VVC into its codec toolbox and released the Bluebook specification in February 2022 [45]. Four VVC-based operating points for MPEG-2 transport stream and DVB-DASH delivery were defined. All four operating points include UHD with 4K resolution and frame rates up to 60Hz. All operating points are also HDR-capable and progressive only. Maximum capability is defined for 8K resolution with frame rates up to 120Hz. VVC support in DVB specification also includes a new functionality to allow dynamic changes of bitstream resolution within a single-layer Transport Stream programme. VVC also provides support for bitstream accessibility such as composition of additional sign-language video within a main video bitstream [46]

## Fórum SBTVD

**Sistema Brasileiro de Televisão Digital** (aka Forum SBTVD) is the organization charged with creation of broadcast and hybrid broadcast-broadband television standards in Brazil. SBTVD has been working toward a new standard for Brazil known as **TV 3.0**. The process consisted of a call for proposals published in July 2020, [47], candidates' responses, and testing and evaluation, followed by selection. Use cases and requirements in the CFP include delivery of 4K OTA and 8K via OTT, native HDR/WCG support, HFR and a reduced-resolution portrait-mode closed second video service. for sign language purposes. For video, VVC was selected as the Video Base Layer Codec, for both OTA and OTT delivery.

Remaining work (on the application layer) involves drafting specification for audio and video coding and determining operating points based on subjective assessment of video coding quality. End-to-end demonstration of TV 3.0, which would include additional system components, i.e., physical and transport layer, is expected in August 2024 [48].

## 3GPP SA4

Assessing a potential dominance of video traffic in 5G networks reaching from 65% to 90% of total traffic, 3GPP SA4 working group developed a comprehensive analysis of the 3GPP-defined video compression technologies in terms of their suitability for existing and emerging 5G services. Based on the extensive framework SA4 working group also evaluated the performance of the new video compression technologies, including VVC. Results of this study were published in 3GPP TR 26.955 [59]. In this document, the working group reviewed requirements of its relevant profiles defined in 3GPP specifications, including TV, VR, 360º video VR and streaming video profiles and defined 5 test scenarios in which widely adopted video coding standards, such as H.264/AVC, H.265/HEVC as well as new generation of video coding standards, including H.266/VVC were evaluated. The test scenarios included HD and UHD 4K Streaming (SDR/HDR), Screen Content, Messaging and Social Sharing and Online Gaming. Scenarios definition included typical parameters including resolution, frame rates, target bitrates and recommended encoder configuration suitable for the application. Performance of the codecs under study was assessed at the target bitrate against the set of defined objective quality metrics using BD-rate measurements where BD stands for Bjontegaard delta [54]. Test simulations were conducted over more than 50 test sequences of different characteristics. The results reported in [59] demonstrated superior characteristics of the VVC over other video coding technologies under the categorization in SA4. Comparing to HEVC, VVC demonstrated around 37% and 39% of BD-rate reduction in PSNR (wPSNR for HDR) metrics on average for HD and UHD streaming scenarios, respectively. For Screen Content coding scenario, average BD-Rate gain around 57% in PSNR metric over HEVC was observed. For test content in Messaging and Social Sharing scenario and Online Gaming scenarios, average BD-rate gain of 27% and 32%, respectively, have been reported. With these results, VVC outperformed any other video codecs under study in all scenarios and all test configurations.

## MC-IF VVC Technical Guidelines

The reported scale of investigations and evaluation processes conducted in applications standards SDOs, points to the importance of assessment true capabilities new video coding technologies with respect to legacy codecs as well as alternative coding technologies. Once the new industry profiles are standardized, the assessment of these new profiles against business needs falls on operators and service providers. A comprehensive set of advanced compression tools, rich functionality, flexibility of high-level bitstream operations, and interoperability with associated metadata, contribute to the versatility of VVC and provide very flexible codec configurations options. In order to facilitate the industry adoption of VVC into standards, workflows, and services, MC-IF has launched work on VVC technical guidelines for broadcast and streaming applications. Figure 1 shows a high-level diagram of end-to-end broadcast and streaming ecosystem. The initial scope of the guidelines work is outlined and concerns primarily final emission to end-users as well as primary distribution. For this initial scope, focus is on the use of VVC Main 10 profile. However, other profiles may also be of interest e.g., Multilayer Main 10 which was reported to be used in 8K delivery scenarios and Main 10 4:4:4 in case of primary distribution of video content with YCbCr 4:2:2 chroma format. The first release of the guidelines is expected in 2023 and will be preceded by an open community review process. Further details on the process and all updates regarding guidelines work will be available through MC-IF website [6].

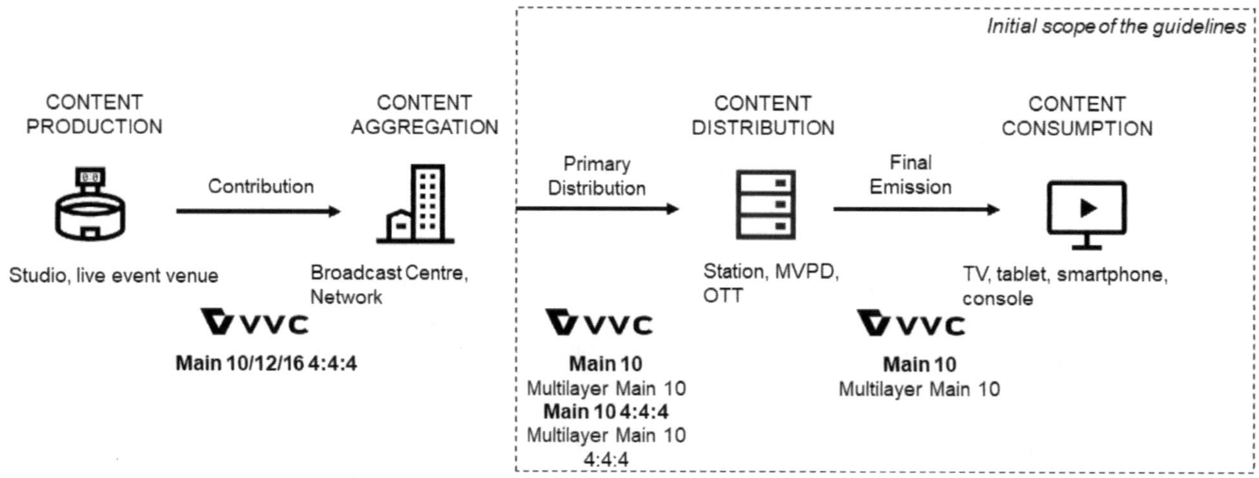


FIGURE 1 SIMPLIFIED END-TO-END BROADCAST AND STREAMING ECOSYSTEM WITH CONTENT CONTRIBUTION, DISTRIBUTION AND FINAL EMISSION STAGES. DASHED PART HIGHLIGHTS THE INITIAL SCOPE OF THE GUIDELINES. VVC PROFILES RELEVANT FOR RESPECTIVE PARTS OF THE ECOSYSTEM ARE HIGHLIGHTED.

The guidelines aim to describe relevant VVC configuration options, in reference to relevant industry VVC profiles, which span through the following areas:

- examples of application of VVC coding tools and VVC performance, including references to industry best practices, relevant external performance results and studies.
- examples of application of VVC functional features including discussion of their benefits and interoperability aspects.

- examples of VVC high-level bitstream operations and signaling.
- examples of VVC usage with associated metadata.

In the following sections we discuss selected examples across these four categories which are investigated for the inclusion in the guidelines. The presented examples do not represent the full set of VVC options and capabilities. For a comprehensive description of VVC please refer to the excellent overview in [49].

## VVC Coding Tools and Performance: HDR Video

High Dynamic Range (HDR) video became a widespread video format in recent years. Multiple online streaming services such as Netflix, Amazon, Disney+ and others are offering HDR content with hundreds of titles. HDR video services are also defined in specifications of the TV broadcasts SDOs, such as ATSC, DVB and others. Rapid deployment of HDR video services was enabled by development of HDR video formats in SMPTE, ITU-R and HEVC. (HEVC Main 10 profile is capable of compressing 10-bit data and encapsulating HDR metadata into the coded bitstream. Although originally designed without HDR-specific coding tools, HEVC encoders can still be configured for efficient compression of HDR video data as well as signaling HDR-specific metadata. Operational practices of handling HDR video data and tools configurations in HEVC are documented in ITU-T Technical Reports (Supplements) [50] and [51].

The practices documented in [50] and [51] are also relevant for VVC, but VVC takes HDR support to a different level. In VVC, all coding tools are applicable to both SDR and HDR video. The distinction between SDR and HDR is made only in high level syntax. Specifically, the colour primaries and optical-electronic transfer characteristics functions that distinguish SDR, hybrid-log gamma HDR (HDR HLG), and perceptual quantizer HDR (HDR PQ) are signaled in the VVC bitstream using video usability information (VUI) metadata specified in VSEI. VSEI also specifies mastering display colour volume (MDCV) and content light level indication (CLLI) SEI messages that provide metadata that are used to optimize display of SDR and HDR coded video on consumer displays. (See the section **Metadata for VVC** for more information.)

Although all VVC coding tools apply to both SDR and HDR, it is worth noting that some new VVC coding tools were originally studied in the context of HDR and later shown to also benefit SDR. In particular, the coding tools called luma mapping with chroma scaling (LMCS) and luma-intensity based deblocking filtering adjustment were aimed at facilitating compression of HDR video data. The luma mapping of the LMCS adjusts the dynamic range of the input video signal by redistributing the codewords across the dynamic range to improve compression efficiency. The chroma residual scaling of LMCS is utilized to compensate for the interaction between the luma signal and its corresponding chroma signals and reduce visual distortions in coded video with WCG representation (BT.2100) [52]. Example encoding algorithms to derive LMCS and luma intensity deblocking parameters are implemented in the VVC reference software (VTM) with specific optimizations for SDR, HDR HLG, and HDR PQ video data. For more details see sections 3.7.2 and 3.7.3 of [53].

Objective quality metrics used during HEVC and VVC development for HDR video data have been documented in [54]. It was determined that calculating the PSNR for the luma and chroma codewords, as is typically done for SDR video, is still appropriate for some HDR HLG video formats. For HDR PQ video, additional metrics were determined to be more suitable. These metrics include: PSNRL100, wPSNR and DE100, as described below and in more detail in [55].

- PSNRL100: This metric is calculated using the luminance values rather than the luma codewords. It is based on the CIELab colour space representation of the input and output sample values of the codec.

- wPSNR: This is a PSNR-like metric calculated from the codewords that attempts to compensate for the more significant distribution of luma codewords to the darker regions by performing a weighting of the codewords before calculating the PSNR.
- DE100: This is a metric based on the CIELab colour space representation of the input and output sample values of the codec. It is specifically targeted at chrominance fidelity.

The performance of VVC for coding of HDR video data compared to HEVC and other codecs has been assessed on multiple occasions. In document [59], VVC performance assessment was conducted by the 3GPP SA4 working group. The coding performance of VVC for HDR PQ material was compared to the coding performance of HEVC, with both encoders using reference software implementations of JVET. For the set target bitrates, the resulting quality was assessed using objective quality metrics, namely wPSNR, PSNRL100 and DE100 as recommended in [54]. It is reported that VVC provides 39% coding gain on average for the wPSNR metric, 35% for PSNRL100, and around 57% for the DE100 metric.

While objective results provide a good indication of performance, subjective assessment of quality of coding performance is very valuable not only to understand coding performance in relation to other codecs but also in relation to determining commercially relevant operating points. MPEG leads the industry best practice in this area and produces high quality subjective verification tests for its codecs, performed by independent and qualified laboratories with the participation of naïve test subjects. Such tests follow established assessment protocols specified in ITU recommendations ITU-R BT.500 [56] and ITU-T P.910 [57]. MPEG subjective quality verification test results are reported in [32]. The assessment included 4k UHD test sequences with HDR HLG content and HDR PQ content. Reported MOS-over-bitrate results demonstrated overall gain of about 49% for the HLG test sequences and an overall gain of about 52% for the PQ test sequences. Figure 2 shows pooled MOS quality assessment data as a function of bitrate for tested VVC and HEVC codecs. The 11-grade MOS scale used in the test represents a full range of video quality impairments present in tested bitstream, from "0" score corresponding to "severely annoying (everywhere)" to "10" corresponding to "imperceptible". "8" corresponds to "slightly perceptible (everywhere)" and can be associated with a broadcast quality. Plots in Figure 2 show that for VVC, averaged bitrates for UHD HDR content range from around 7Mbps for PQ content used in the test to around 12.5 Mbps for HLG content used in the test. This constitutes 50% bitrate reduction compared with HEVC at the same MOS quality achieved with average bitrates from around 15Mbps for PQ content used in the test to around 27Mbps for HLG content used in the test.

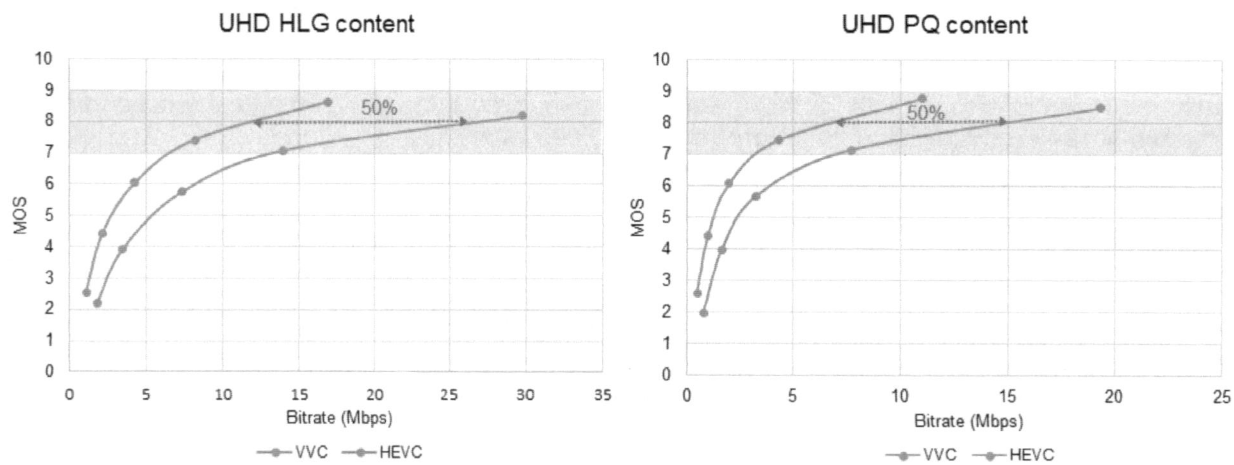


FIGURE 2: MOS QUALITY OVER BITRATE FOR UHD HLG AND PQ CONTENT POOLED OVER 5 TEST SEQUENCES IN EACH CATEGORY. DATA TO CREATE THESE PLOTS WAS USED FROM [32].

## VVC Functional Features: Reference Picture Resampling

Delivery of video services by the means of providing multiple renditions of content at varying resolutions and bitrates has been the backbone of adaptive streaming for broadband (DASH or HLS). Initially, designed to target widely varying end-device display formats and variable available bandwidth, techniques such as "Per-title encoding" were introduced to dynamically select optimal resolutions (from a QoE perspective) for each VOD content. Decoding of short segments of video with different bitrates and resolution could be achieved with the use of closed GOP coding, which inserts IDR (Instantaneous Decoder Refresh) at the start of each segment. In terms of compression performance, the closed GOP configuration is less efficient than the open GOP configuration typically used in broadcast. The coding penalty increases with higher frequency of random access points i.e., shorter segments as IDR frames are less efficiently coded which in effect cause bitrate spikes impacting rate control buffers and makes the penalty higher for low latency streaming. Previous attempts with seamless switching of resolutions with HEVC were reported in [60] with the use of the scalable profile of HEVC and more recently in [61] with the use of Main 10 HEVC profile. However, the former approach could be viable only to applications supporting scalable HEVC profiles, while the interoperability tests with HEVC showed issues at switching since such a functionality had not been tested at the time of deployment.

VVC includes a built-in spatial scalability functionality which allows changing resolution at any inter-coded picture. The mechanism uses reference picture resampling (RPR) which effectively adjusts the resolution of reference pictures used for prediction on the fly. This functionality is supported in the Main 10 profile while Multilayer profiles extend this through efficient high level signaling, however, no additional inter-layer signal processing tools are required [49]. In [62] authors investigated VVC open GOP resolution switching in the adaptive streaming use case and identified potential issues with prediction-error drift in random access skipped leading (RASL) pictures due to change of resolution at RAP (Intra picture) which precede RASL pictures in coding order. It was, however, demonstrated that exercising certain constraints in the encoder mitigated most of the issues and resulted in compression gains up to 9% BD-rate over typical closed GOP setting for low latency live streaming. Reference picture resampling functionality also enables changing resolution within a representation. While VVC allows high flexibility with regards to scaling factors and frequency of resolution change at any picture, application specifications may provide some constraints on how often and which resolutions can be used by the codec. For example, the new revision of DVB TS 101 154 [45] , which allows RPR use in VVC profiles, restricts downsampling scaling factors to 2/3 and 1/2 while new coded resolutions can be introduced at minimum interval of 2 seconds. However, different application standards may choose to adopt different sets of constraints for the use of RPR functionality.

In order to study the benefits of VVC RPR in the context of resolution change within a representation (e.g., as would be used in live broadcast), we used the VTM reference software implementation with RPR encoder functionality from [58]. The encoding algorithm implemented in VTM aims to serve as an illustration of RPR functionality and is configured to limit resolution change at high bitrates while more likely to trigger downsampling at lower bitrates. Resolution change decisions can be made for each reordering segment of pictures (hierarchical B pictures structure) and can use scaling factors: 4/5, 2/3 and 1/2. For the test content we used sequences from 3GPP SA4 5G video test set from the study described in section **3GPP SA4**. Sequences used were from the SDR set of 4K-TV scenario, (HDR results were reported in the section above), for which overall VVC performance gains achieved with reference encoder VTM were reported as 37% BD-rate with PSNR-YUV, 33% BD-rate with PSNR-Y, 33% BD-rate with MS-SSIM and 38% BD-rate with VMAF metrics respectively. Details of these metrics as used in the 3GPP 5G codec study are detailed in section 5.5 of [59]. In our test, we used 4 fixed QP settings (22, 27, 32 and 37) for VTM software as in the original study plus QP 42 at the low end of bitrate scale to align VVC and HEVC quality at the lowest bitrates.

Our tests showed substantial coding gains could be achieved for two out of eight sequences from the test set: Soccer [63] and Tunnel Flag [64]. For three of the sequences, either negligible gain or loss were observed and for the remaining three sequences RPR functionality was not triggered at all which is a correct behavior in case encoder does not predict content benefiting from change of resolution. However, this is still an interesting result since the sequences in the test set were not pre-selected towards showcasing RPR functionality and RPR gains are expected to be content dependent.

Results in Table 1 show extra coding gain can be achieved over HEVC with the use of the RPR coding tool in VVC. Coding gain was consistent for all reported metrics, smaller difference reported by PSNR-based metrics and higher with MS-SSIM and VMAF. Looking at the rate-distortion plots in Figure 2, we notice that coding gain is contributed through a higher quality metric value rather than shifted bitrates. Visual inspection showed that VVC is generally cleaner around the players than HEVC while VVC with RPR looks more consistent than VVC and suffers less from visible artefacts in the background and textured areas like the one highlighted in Figure 3 for Soccer sequence. Figure 4 shows RPR operation for Tunnel Flag sequence at 5.2 Mbps. The sequence comprises two parts, first part which is drive through a tunnel which then cross-fades into a waving flag part. As it is shown in Figure 5, RPR encoding algorithm utilizes three different scaling factors: 4/5 and 2/3 for the tunnel part and 1/2 scaling for the flag part, where the change occurs right after the cross-fade. While we did not conduct a detailed analysis of encoder complexity impact (encodings were run on a cluster with a mix of CPUs), ballpark results showed a decrease of about 15%-20% in computing resources when RPR was employed.

| | BD-rate gains | | | |
|---|---|---|---|---|
| Test | PSNR-Y [%] | PSNR-YUV [%] | MS-SSIM [%] | VMAF [%] |
| **Soccer** | | | | |
| VVC vs. HEVC | 40.34% | 39.27% | 39.26% | 40.23% |
| VVC with RPR vs. HEVC | 44.10% | 43.02% | 43.67% | 48.77% |
| **Tunnel Flag** | | | | |
| VVC vs. HEVC | 49.57% | 52.64% | 52.86% | 55.19% |
| VVC with RPR vs. HEVC | 51.08% | 54.38% | 57.21% | 61.55% |

TABLE 1: BD-RATE GAINS FOR VVC AND VVC WITH RPR FUNCTIONALITY OVER HEVC.

RPR is a new promising functionality offered by VVC which could benefit both resolution switching in ABR video delivery as well as introduce dynamic changes of resolution within a bitstream or representation. In the latter case, it can either provide coding gain or optimize bitrate delivery for the same QoE, e.g., in statistical multiplexing by allowing greater flexibility in allocating bitrates across programs. When employed, RPR can also have an impact on CPU encoder complexity and therefore could contribute to reducing power consumption in the headend. The functionality is supported with some operational constraints in the DVB codec specification [45] and scalability is also considered for SBTVD TV 3.0 specification requirements [47].

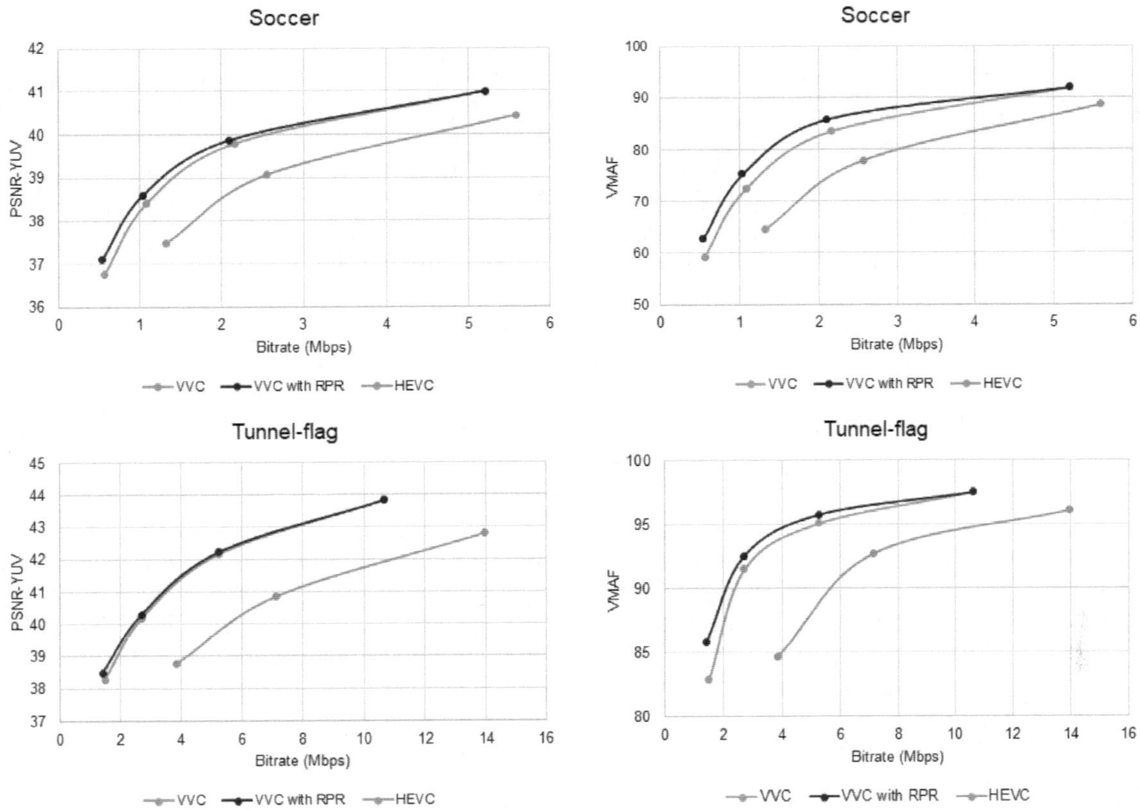


FIGURE 3: RATE-DISTORTION PLOTS FOR SOCCER AND TUNNEL FLAG SEQUENCES FOR PSNR-YUV AND VMAF METRICS.

FIGURE 4: SCREEN SHOT FROM DECODED SEQUENCE FROM HEVC BITSTREAM (LEFT), VVC BITSTREAM (MIDDLE) AND VVC BITSTREAM WITH RPR (RIGHT). VVC WITH RPR DECODED PICTURES WERE UPSCALED TO THE ORIGINAL 4K RESOLUTION. HIGHLIGHTED AREAS POINT TO VISIBLE ARTEFACTS: HALO AROUND PLAYER'S SHOULDER (LEFT) AND SOFT PATCH IN THE ASTRO TURF (MIDDLE) SEQUENCE USED IN THIS TEST IS FROM [63].

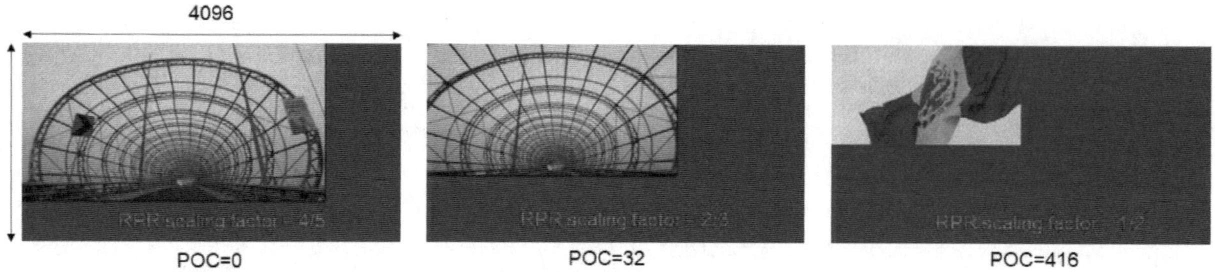


FIGURE 5: VISUALIZATION OF RPR OPERATION FOR TUNNEL FLAG SEQUENCE AT QP 32 (5.2 MBPS). 4096X2160 IS THE ORIGINAL RESOLUTION OF THE SEQUENCE WHICH IS REPRESENTED WITH THE GREEN-PADDED AREA. IMAGES REPRESENT DECODED PICTURES RESOLUTION WITH POC (PICTURE ORDER COUNT) REPRESENTING TIMINGS WHERE CHANGES OF RESOLUTION OCCURRED. SEQUENCE USED IN THIS TEST IS FROM [64].

## High-Level Bitstream Operations: VVC Subpictures

Improved service accessibility is one of increasingly important requirements for video delivery systems. One example is provision of supplemental video bitstream with sign language interpreter [47], where the supplemental video is displayed on request from the end-user. VVC provides functionality for flexible bitstream extraction and merging operations. This functionality is essential in VVC design and provides significant improvement for coding high resolution immersive video such as in VR 360º video applications. Bitstream extraction and merging can be supported with the use of VVC subpictures which are one of the picture partitioning tools available in VVC. Subpictures may be coded independently of other subpictures and can be flexibly rearranged. A detailed overview of VVC subpictures functionality is available in [65].

One way to use this feature is to provide two video bitstreams, main video bitstream which includes sub-pictures arrangement which corresponds to the desired composition, and a supplemental video at lower resolution which can be composed into the main video bitstream mapping directly into the subpictures arrangement in the main video. Such a bitstream operation is performed before video decoding. Restrictions on ensuring the same video characteristics such as bit depth, frame rate, colour space etc., need to be observed. More information on the usage of VVC subpictures in the context of accessibility and personalization for video services can be found in Annex M of [45].

## Metadata for VVC

With a few special exceptions, the VVC standard only specifies the syntax, semantics, and decoding processes required for conforming video decoders. Information about how video is intended to be post-processed, displayed, or otherwise used is specified mostly in the VSEI standard. VSEI specifies two kinds of metadata: video useability information (VUI) and SEI messages.

VUI parameters provide information for the correct display of coded video. For example, VUI parameters indicate that the coded video is progressive or interlaced; SDR, HDR HLG, or HDR PQ; that the source video has a particular aspect ratio; and any other parameters necessary for correct interpretation of the coded video.

SEI messages provide additional information that can assist decoders, displays, and other video receivers perform as desired by the content producer. For example, the display of omnidirectional 360º-video can be assisted by signalling one of the omnidirectional video specific SEI messages in the VVC bitstream. As another example, the annotated regions SEI message can be used to assist video analysis applications by signalling the size and location of objects identified in a video.

As noted previously, several SEI messages were originally developed in the context of HDR and have since become incorporated into application standards. The mastering display colour volume (MDCV) SEI message provides information about how source video looked to creative professionals when the content was created (i.e., mastered). Consumer displays can use the information in the MDCV SEI message to adjust how coded video is displayed so that it matches the source look as closely as possible. The content light level information (CLLI) SEI message indicates how bright the source video was when mastered. Information in the CLLI SEI message can also be used to optimize the look of displayed video and has the potential to enable consumer displays to improve power management. Other SEI messages including the content colour volume (CCV), ambient viewing environment (AVE), and alternative transfer characteristics (ACT) SEI messages can also enable consumer displays to process coded video content to provide better consumer experiences. It is worth noting that although many of the mentioned SEI messages were developed initially for HDR, they have become increasingly applicable to SDR video data as the brightness of SDR consumer displays has increased.

The film grain characteristics (FGC) SEI message has also become increasingly significant with the increase of film grain synthesis in high-value streaming services [65]. The FGS SEI message signals the statistical characteristics of spatial temporal grain added to decoded video. There are two main use cases – one old and one new – for which adding grain to decoded video can be beneficial. The first and original use case was to replace actual film grain that had been filtered out of source video prior to encoding to save bandwidth. The newer use case is to subtly mask compression artefacts (even for source video that did not have original film grain) to reduce bitrate and improve perceived sharpness. A Technical Report on use of film grain technologies is currently in development in ITU-T and ISO/IEC with publication expected in the 2nd half of 2023. Software illustrating the use of the FGS SEI message are available in the AVC, HEVC, and VVC reference software. Open-source film grain synthesis implementations are available in GitHub repositories [67][68].

Although not yet finalized, a pair of neural-network post-filter (NNPF) SEI messages [69] have attracted significant attention by enabling the use of neural networks for post-processing operations such as super-resolution, frame rate upsampling, chroma format conversion, and colourization. The NNPF characteristics (NNPFC) SEI message signals neural-network parameters/weights (contained in an ISO/IEC 15938-17 bitstream [70] or identified by a universal resource identifier [71]) and additional information needed for a receiver to determine if it can implement the indicated neural network. Several neural networks can be signalled using multiple NNPFC SEI messages to support different receiver capabilities and different post-processing operations. Specific neural networks are invoked from the available neural networks using an NNPF activation (NNPFA) SEI message. It is expected that the NNPFC and NNPFA SEI messages will be finalized in VSEI in the 2nd half of 2023.

## Conclusions

Since its finalization in 2020, VVC has enjoyed a steady adoption progress across various implementations spanning the whole end-to-end chain. Also, application layer SDOs are looking into advancements in video codecs in order to further improve penetration of existing services while creating new operating points for delivery of enhanced video services with formats such as 8K. While first adoptions of VVC into application specifications for broadcast and streaming, MC-IF has launched work on VVC technical guidelines. Such guidelines are aimed to cover VVC configuration aspects including its rich combination of coding tools, functionality and associated metadata, to facilitate VVC adoption and facilitate VVC interoperability across products and services. In this paper we provided an overview of VVC's deployment status across implementation and standards, discussed the scope of the launched work in MC-IF on VVC technical guidelines and provided selected examples of VVC configuration aspects which demonstrate VVC superiority in terms of coding performance and functionality against the needs of broadcast and streaming industry, and together with other aspects of VVC are being investigated for inclusion in the MC-IF VVC technical guidelines.

## References


[1] ITU-T | ISO/IEC, "Rec. ITU-T H.266 | ISO/IEC 23090-3 "Information technology Coded representation of immersive media - Part 3: Versatile Video Coding"," 2022.

[2] ITU-T | ISO/IEC, "Rec. ITU-T H.274 | ISO/IEC 23002-7 "Versatile supplemental enhancement information messages for coded video bitstreams"," 2022.

[3] ITU-T | ISO/IEC, "Rec. ITU-T H.222.0 | ISO/IEC 13818-1: "Information technology - Generic Coding of moving pictures and associated audio information: Systems"," 2022.

[4] ISO/IEC, "ISO/IEC: 14496-15:2017: "Information technology -- Coding of audio-visual objects -- Part 15: Carriage of network abstraction layer (NAL) unit structured video in ISO base media file format"," 2022.

[5] ISO/IEC, "ISO/IEC 23000-19:2019/FDIS: "Information technology -- Multimedia application format (MPEG-A) -- Part 19: Common media application format (CMAF) for segmented media (2nd edition)"," 2022.

[6] Media Coding Industry Forum, https://www.mc-if.org/.

[7] Bossen, F., "Performance of a reasonably fast VVC software decoder", *JVET-S0224* , July 2020.

[8] Wieckowski, A., et al., "Open optimized VVC encoder (VVenC) and decoder (VvdeC) implementations," *JVET-T0099,* October 2020.

[9] Bossen, F., Sühring, K., Wieckowski, A., Liu, S., "VVC Complexity and Software Implementation Analysis," *IEEE Transactions on Circuits and Systems for Video Technology*, Vol. 31, Issue 10, October 2021, pp. 3765–3778.

[10] Li., Y., et al., "Performance of a VVC Software Decoder on Mobile Platform," *JVET-U0071,* January 2021.

[11] Yu, L., et al., "VVC software decoder implementation for mobile devices," *JVET-V0132,* April 2021.

[12] Feng, W.-L., et al., "VVC Software Decoder for Mobile Platforms," *JVET-V0070,* April 2021.

[13] Li, L., et al., "Update on a VVC software decoder, BVC, for heterogeneous CPU plus GPU systems," *JVET-Y0054,* January 2022.

[14] Wieckowski, A., et al., "Update on open, optimized VVC implementations VVenC and VVdeC" *JVET-AB0044,* October 2022.

[15] Fraunhofer HHI, "VVdeC Web Player," https://github.com/fraunhoferhhi/vvdecWebPlayer, accessed February 2023.

[16] Spin Digital, "Spin Digital Announces a VVC 8K Decoder and Media Player", June 2021

[17] Allegro DVT, https://www.allegrodvt.com/products/al-d320-decoder-ip/, accessed February 2023.

[18] Realtek, "Realtek Launches World's First 4K UHD Set-top Box SoC (RTD1319D) Supports VVC/H.266 Video Decoding, GPU with 10-bit Graphics, Multiple CAS, and HDMI 2.1a", 29 August 2022.

[19] MediaTek, MediaTek | Pentonic 2000 | Flagship 8K TV SoC, accessed February 2023.

[20] Larsen, R., "Sony and Philips will be the first TV makers to use MediaTek Pentonic chips", "*FlatPanelsHD*", 9 January 2023.

[21] ITU-T | ISO/IEC Joint Video Experts Team (JVET), "VVC verification test report for UHD SDR video content," *JVET-T2020* , October 2020.

[22] Cui, J., et al., "An optimized VVC encoder implementation," *JVET-V0127*, April 2021.

[23] Dong, X., et al., "Update on the progress of the optimized VVC encoder implementation, Ali266" *JVET-X0104,* October 2021.

[24] Bitmovin, "Bitmovin to Unveil Next-Generation VOD Encoder at the 2022 NAB Show", press release, 30 March 2022.

[25] Tencent, "Tencent Cloud Becomes First Cloud Service Provider to Support H.266/VVC Standard", press release, July 16, 2021.

[26] Jia, Y., et al., "Ali266 @ Youku: trial deployment of VVC for video streaming," *JVET-Y0122,* January 2022.

[27] "MX Player becomes first OTT to deploy H.266, cuts down video streaming data consumption into half", *Best Media Info,* 16 June 2021.

[28] *TVNewsCheck* "IBC 2022: MainConcept Launches VVC/H.266 SDK Beta And Demos Cloud-Ready 8K Broadcast Technology",*TVNewsCheck*, 31 August 2022.

[29] Sanz-Rodriguez, S., Alvarez-Mesa, M. and Ching Chi, Ch., "A VVC/H.266 real-time software encoder for UHD live video applications," *JVET-AB0043*, October 2022.

[30] Le Tanou, J., "MediaKind enables live UHD OTT VVC streaming", "https://www.mediakind.com/blog/mediakind-enables-live-uhd-ott-vvc-streaming-on-a-public-cloud/", 21 September 2022.

[31] Biatek, T., Abdoli, M., Guionnet, T., Nasrallah, A., and Raulet, M., "Future MPEG standards VVC and EVC: 8K broadcast enabler," *IBC*, 2020.

[32] ITU-T | ISO/IEC Joint Video Experts Team (JVET), "VVC verification test report for high dynamic range video content," *JVET-W2020*, July 2021.

[33] NHK, "CMAF Multilayer-compatible VVC Decoder", press release, https://www.nhk.or.jp/strl/english/news/2022/5.html, 2022.

[34] ITU-T | ISO/IEC, "Rec. ITU-T H.266.1 | ISO/IEC 23090-15 " Information technology — Coded representation of immersive media — Part 15: Conformance testing for versatile video coding"," 2022.

[35] DVB, "VVC test content", https://dvb.org/specifications/verification-validation/vvc-test-content/, 2 February 2023.

[36] Allegro DVT, H266 VVC Standard JVET Syntax Compliance Bitstreams Validation Decoder (allegrodvt.com), accessed February 2023.

[37] W. Hamidouche et al., "Versatile Video Coding Standard: A Review from Coding Tools to Consumers Deployment," *IEEE Consumer Electronics Magazine*, vol. 11, no. 5, September 2022, pp. 10-24.

[38] Bitmovin, "The 6th annual Bitmovin Video Developer Report," December 2022.

[39] Sullivan, G.J., "Deployment status of the VVC standard," *JVET-AC0021*, January 2023.

[40] Ericsson, "Ericsson Mobility Report," November 2022.

[41] ATSC, "ATSC Planning Team Report: ATSC 3.0 and Global Convergence", December 2022.

[42] DASH Industry Forum, "DASH-IF Interoperability Points; Part 7: Video," May 2022.

[43] CTA, "CTA Specification, Web Application Video Ecosystem – Content Specification, CTA-5001-D," 2021.

[44] Power, J., "New video codecs for DVB services: fast-forward to 2024…," *DVB Scene,* Issue 58, September 2021.

[45] DVB, "Specification for the use of Video and Audio Coding in Broadcast and Broadband Applications," *DVB Document A001 Rev.21*, November 2022.

[46] Drugeon, V., "New in the DVB codec toolbox: Versatile Video Coding (VVC)," *DVB Scene*, Issue 59, March 2022.

[47] SBTVD Forum, TV3.0 Call for proposals, https://forumsbtvd.org.br/wp-content/uploads/2020/07/SBTVDTV-3-0-CfP.pdf.

[48] SBTVD Forum, Fórum SBTVD | TV 3.0 Project (forumsbtvd.org.br), accessed February 2023.

[49] B. Bross et al., "Overview of the Versatile Video Coding (VVC) Standard and its Applications," *IEEE Transactions on Circuits and Systems for Video Technology*, vol. 31, no. 10, October 2021 pp. 3736-3764.

[50] ITU-T, "H. Sup15: Conversion and coding practices for HDR/WCG Y'CbCr 4:2:0 video with PQ transfer characteristics," 2017.

[51] ITU-T, "H. Sup18: Signalling, backward compatibility and display adaptation for HDR/WCG video coding," 2017.

[52] ITU-R, "Rec. ITU-R BT.2100: Image parameter values for high dynamic range television for use in production and international programme exchange," 2020.

[53] ITU-T | ISO/IEC Joint Video Experts Team (JVET), "Algorithm description for Versatile Video Coding and Test Model 18 (VTM18)," *JVET-AB2002*, October 2022.

[54] ITU-T, "Technical Paper ITU-T HSTP-VID-WPOM (07/2020): Working practices using objective metrics for evaluation of video coding efficiency experiments," 2020.

[55] ITU-T | ISO/IEC Joint Video Experts Team (JVET), "VTM and HM common test conditions and evaluation procedures for HDR/WCG video," *JVET-AC2011*, January 2023.

[56] ITU-R, "Rec. ITU-R BT.500: Methodologies for the subjective assessment of the quality of television images," 2019.

[57] ITU-R, “Rec. ITU-T P.910: Subjective video quality assessment methods for multimedia applications,” July 2022.

[58] Andersson., K., et al., “GOP-based RPR encoder control,”*JVET-AB0080,* October 2022.

[59] 3GPP, “TR: 26.955: Video codec characteristics for 5G-based services and applications,” June 2022.

[60] Yan, Y., Hannuksela M. M., Li, H., "Seamless switching of H.265/HEVC-coded dash representations with open GOP prediction structure,” *2015 IEEE International Conference on Image Processing (ICIP)*, 2015, pp. 4121-4125.

[61] Ducloux, X., Diascorn, J-L., Fautier, T., “Exploring the benefits of dynamic resolution encoding and support in DVB standards," *IBC*, 2022.

[62] Skupin, R., et al., “Open GOP resolution switching in HTTP adaptive streaming with VVC,” *Proc. 35th Picture Coding Symp. (PCS)*, June 2021, pp. 1–5.

[63] Cable Labs, “Soccer,”, https://dash-large-files.akamaized.net/WAVE/3GPP/5GVideo/ReferenceSequences/Soccer/Soccer.json, accessed February 2023.

[64] Netflix, “Tunnel flag”, https://dash-large-files.akamaized.net/WAVE/3GPP/5GVideo/ReferenceSequences/Tunnel-Flag/Tunnel-Flag.json, accessed February 2023.

[65] Wang, Y. -K., et al., "The High-Level Syntax of the Versatile Video Coding (VVC) Standard," *IEEE Transactions on Circuits and Systems for Video Technology*, vol. 31, no. 10, October 2021, pp. 3779-3800.

[66] Norkin, A., and Birkbeck, N., “Film Grain Synthesis for AV1 Video Codec,” *2018 Data Compression Conference*, March 2018, pp. 3–12.

[67] Ittiam Systems, “Film Grain Synthesis Library,”, https://github.com/ittiam-systems/libfgs, accessed March 2023.

[68] InterDigital Inc., “VersatileFilmGrain,”, https://github.com/InterDigitalInc/VersatileFilmGrain, accessed February 2023.

[69] McCarthy. S., Deshpande, S., Hannuksela, M. M., Hendry, Sullivan, G. J., and Wang, Y.-K. “Improvements under consideration for neural network post filter SEI messages,” *JVET- AC2032,* January 2023.

[70] ISO/IEC, “ISO/IEC: 15938-17, Information technology – Multimedia content description interface – Part 17: Compression of neural networks for multimedia content description and analysis,” 2022.

[71] IETF, “IETF Standard 66, Uniform Resource Identifiers (URI): Generic Syntax,” http://tools.ietf.org/html/rfc3986

# High-Power Digital FM Field Test Project

**David H. Layer**
**National Association of Broadcasters**
**Washington, D.C., United States**
dlayer@nab.org

**Alan Jurison**
**iHeartMedia, Inc.**
**Syracuse, N.Y., United States**
alanjurison@iheartmedia.com

**Russ Mundschenk**
**Xperi, Inc. (retired)**
**Columbia, Md., United States**
mundschenk55@msn.com

**Steve Shultis**
**New York Public Radio**
**New York, N.Y., United States**
sshultis@nypublicradio.org

**E. Glynn Walden**
**Audacy, Inc. (retired)**
**Philadelphia, Pa., United States**
glynn.walden@audacy.com

**Abstract** – A petition for rulemaking filed at the FCC in October 2022 by NAB and Xperi requests that the FCC adopt an updated formula to determine FM power levels for stations seeking to exceed the currently authorized FM digital ERP of -14dBc. The proposed new formula, which is based on real world, operational experience gained since the FCC last approved a power increase in 2010, will allow more stations to increase digital power above the existing -14 dBc level, without the need for separate FCC authorization. Included in the joint NAB-Xperi filing is information on a field test project conducted by NAB, Audacy, New York Public Radio and Xperi in 2021 to assess the impact on first-adjacent channels of increasing the digital power level from -14 dBc to -10 dBc. The results of this field test demonstrate that the new formula being proposed should adequately protect first-adjacent channels, and are the topic of this paper.

## Background

The FCC authorized in-band/on-channel (IBOC) digital radio broadcasting in the US in October of 2002, recognizing the iBiquity Digital Corporation's HD Radio system as the *de facto* standard for digital radio transmissions in the AM and FM frequency bands.[1] This original authorization was for hybrid digital mode operation, in which both legacy analog and IBOC digital signals are transmitted, and specified that the digital portion of an FM-band HD Radio signal would nominally operate at power level of -20 dBc, that is, 20 dB below the power level of a station's authorized analog effective radiated power (ERP).[2]

Operational experience with FM-band HD Radio gained between 2002 and 2008 demonstrated that the authorized -20 dBc digital power level was insufficient in many instances to replicate the analog coverage of HD Radio stations, especially in mobile and indoor environments. Consequently, a group of

[1] At the time of adoption, the developer and licensor of HD Radio was iBiquity Digital Corporation. iBiquity was subsequently acquired by DTS which was then acquired by Xperi, the current developer and licensor of HD Radio.
[2] -20 dBc is equivalently expressed as 1% of the power in the unmodulated analog FM carrier.

This paper is excerpted from the Proceedings of the 2023 NAB Broadcast Engineering and Information Technology (BEIT) Conference, © 2023, National Association of Broadcasters, 1 M Street SE, Washington, DC 20003 USA.

18 radio group owners jointly filed a petition with the FCC requesting that the nominal power level for FM-band digital carriers be increased to -10 dBc [1]. Concurrently, iBiquity filed a technical report describing the results of their field testing of FM-band HD Radio stations operating at higher digital power levels [2]. The iBiquity report demonstrated that operation at -10 dBc would indeed improve coverage and would not cause a "...meaningful increase in the risk of interference to [1st] adjacent channel analog broadcasts in the vast majority of cases."[3]

Following these filings, National Public Radio (NPR) submitted a report prepared for the Corporation for Public Broadcasting which included the results of NPR's "Digital Radio Coverage & Interference Analysis" (DRCIA) study [3]. While agreeing with the iBiquity report with respect to increased coverage at the -10 dBc power levels, the NPR report suggested that there would be a resulting increase in analog interference greater than that anticipated by iBiquity. A second NPR report, on "Advanced IBOC Coverage and Compatibility Study" (AICCS), further evaluated the impact of increased digital power levels including subjective evaluations by consumers of audio recordings made of analog stations subject to increased power levels of 1st-adjacent channel IBOC stations [4].

After considerable industry deliberation and consultation with the FCC on the proposed power increase, the FCC in January 2010 issued an Order which authorized a blanket power increase of -14 dBc (a 6 dB increase over the original authorization) and included a table, based on a formula from the NPR AICCS study, specifying conditions under which a station may increase its digital power up to a maximum of -10 dBc (Table 1) [5].

| Proponent Analog F(50,10) Field Strength at Protected Analog 60 dBu F(50,50) Contour | Maximum Permissible FM Digital ERP |
|---|---|
| 51.2 dBµ and above | -14 dBc |
| 50.7 dBµ - 51.1 dBµ | -13 dBc |
| 50.3 dBµ - 50.6 dBµ | -12 dBc |
| 49.6 dBµ - 50.2 dBµ | -11 dBc |
| 49.5 dBµ or less | -10 dBc |

TABLE 1. FCC CONDITIONS FOR ALLOWING AN FM DIGITAL STATION TO INCREASE POWER UP TO -10 DBC.

In applying this table, "[a] licensee desiring FM digital ERP in excess of -14 dBc is required to calculate the station's analog F(50,10) field strength at all points on the protected 60 dBu F(50,50) contour of a potentially affected first-adjacent channel analog FM station. This calculation must be done using the station's licensed analog facilities and the standard FCC contour prediction methodology."[4] The most restrictive (*i.e.*, highest) analog F(50,10) value thus calculated is compared to the values in the first column of Table 1 to determine the maximum permissible FM digital ERP (shown in the second column of Table 1).

The 2010 Order further stipulates that "[i]n situations in which the simplified method [just described] is not applicable due to unusual terrain, environmental or technical considerations, or when it produces anomalous FM Digital ERP results, the Bureau will accept applications for FM Digital ERP in excess of -14 dBc. These applications must include a detailed showing containing a complete explanation of the prediction methodology used as well as data, maps and sample calculations. The Bureau will evaluate these applications on a case-by-case basis."[5]

---

[3] With respect to potential interference concerns, the focus is on a digital radio station's 1st-adjacent channel neighbors, as the digital radio station's digital sidebands are centered on a 1st-adjacent channel's center frequencies.
[4] See [5], paragraph 20.
[5] *Id.*

Additionally, the Order specifies a remediation procedure for cases where harmful interference is created to a 1st-adjacent analog signal by an IBOC signal that has increased its FM digital ERP above the originally-authorized -20 dBc level.[6] Briefly, this procedure calls for the following:

- Stations are required to work cooperatively to confirm the instances of interference and attempt to eliminate the interference using voluntary tiered FM digital ERP reductions;
- If stations are unable to resolve the interference, then the affected station may file an interference complaint with the Bureau;
- The complaint must contain at least six reports of ongoing (rather than transitory) objectionable interference.

Many broadcasters believed that the power increase established by the 2010 Order was too conservative and did not provide sufficient opportunities for FM digital broadcasters to replicate their analog coverage area. Even the FCC expressed its concern that the agreed-upon formula was too conservative, noting in their 2010 Order that "The Bureau's experience with higher powered digital experimental authorizations suggests that the formula developed by NPR and endorsed by iBiquity in the Agreement is over-predictive of the potential for interference."[7]

An engineering study conducted by Xperi working in conjunction with Audacy and others, conducted in 2017, served to illustrate just how conservative the 2010 approach was, by studying short-spaced stations operating at -14 dBc, where the digital signal level at the 1st-adjacent channel 60 dBu contour greatly exceeds the limits set in the 2010 formula.[8] Some examples presented in the 2017 study are shown in Table 2.

| IBOC station at -14 dBc | 1st-adj analog station | Actual F(50,10) (dBu) | F(50,10) permitted under 2010 formula (dBu) | Difference - actual vs. 2010 formula (dB) |
|---|---|---|---|---|
| WKTU | WPRB | 72.8 | 51.2 | 21.4 |
| KFRG | KBZT-FM | 63.7 | | 12.3 |
| WJFK | WWMX | 71.5 | | 20.1 |
| WJFK | WWEG | 75.6 | | 24.2 |

TABLE 2. EXAMPLES OF DIGITAL STATION ERP GREATLY EXCEEDING ALLOWED VALUES ESTABLISHED UNDER THE 2010 FCC ORDER.[9]

This table illustrates that, for example, under the 2010 formula, the maximum F(50,10) dBu which WJFK is allowed to have at the 60 dBu contour of 1st-adjacent channel station WWMX is 51.2 dBu, but because of WJFK's grandfathered short-spacing status, the actual value of the F(50,10) contour at this point is 71.5 dBu, over 20 dB higher than the allowed value. For all of the cases illustrated in this table, despite the significantly higher field strengths than allowed by the 2010 formula, there have been no reports of actual interference.

[6] *Id.*, paragraphs 27-28.
[7] *Id.*, paragraph 19.
[8] A description of this study and the results obtained are included in the 2020 NAB-Xperi joint petition as Appendix 1 (see footnote 10).
[9] Other examples of stations that exceed the authorized 2010 power levels are provided in the 2017 study and include KRTH (Los Angeles), KCBS (Los Angeles), KTVW (Los Angeles), KLOS (Los Angeles), KOST (Los Angeles), KSKS (San Francisco), KOIT (San Francisco), KBRG (San Francisco), KMEL (San Francisco), KDON (San Francisco), WZFT (Baltimore), WPRS (Washington, DC), WLZL (Baltimore), WRCJ (Detroit), WFUM (Detroit), WPZR (Detroit), WMDX (Detroit), WAWZ (New York), WUSL (New York), WNSH (New York), WPRB (New York), and WKTU (New York).

## 2022 NAB-Xperi Petition

Given the concerns about analog coverage replication following the 2010 Order, and with an additional 12 years of operational experience to draw upon, NAB and Xperi jointly filed a petition with the FCC in October 2022 proposing relaxed field strength values for determining whether a station can exceed the -14 dBc blanket authorization power level adopted in 2010 [6].[10] These relaxed values derive from a new formula, developed under the previously-mentioned 2017 study; a comparison between the field strength values for determining permissible FM digital ERP under the current and proposed formulas is given in Table 3. A graphical representation of the comparison between the new and old formulas is provided in Figure 1.

| **Proponent analog F(50,10) field strength at desired analog 60 dBu F(50,50) contour** | | | **Maximum permissible FM digital ERP (dBc)** |
|---|---|---|---|
| **Current (dBu)** | **Proposed (dBu)** | **Change (dB)** | |
| 51.2 and above | 57.9 and above | 6.7 | -14 |
| 50.7 - 51.1 | 56.5 - 57.8 | 5.8 | -13 |
| 50.3 - 50.6 | 55.6 - 56.4 | 5.3 | -12 |
| 49.6 - 50.2 | 54.1 - 55.5 | 4.5 | -11 |
| 49.5 or less | 54 or less | 4.5 | -10 |

TABLE 3. COMPARISON OF EXISTING AND PROPOSED CONDITIONS FOR ALLOWING AN FM DIGITAL STATION TO INCREASE POWER UP TO -10 DBC.

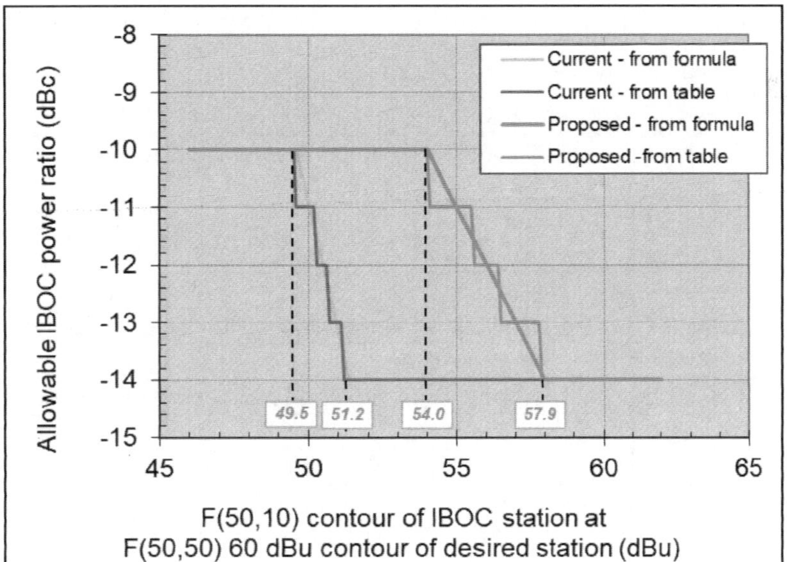


FIGURE 1. GRAPHICAL REPRESENTATION OF VALUES PRESENTED IN TABLE 3.

[10] This petition was placed on public notice by the FCC on November 28, 2022, along with an earlier joint filing by NAB, Xperi and NPR requesting authorization for digital FM radio asymmetric sideband operation. A new docket number was assigned to this proceeding, MB Docket No. 22-405, see FCC document DA 22-1226.

This graph highlights the similarities between the current and proposed methods and depicts how the proposed increase in allowable IBOC power at the F(50,10) contour of the IBOC station is reduced as the IBOC power increases (when compared to the currently allowed increase), highlighting the conservative nature of the NAB-Xperi proposal. Further evidence of this can be found by applying the values derived from the new formula to the extreme, short-spaced station cases described in Table 2, since as with the current formula, none of these cases would be allowed under the new formula (were it not for their grandfathered short-spaced status).[11]

## Field Testing of NAB-Xperi Proposal

Two separate field tests were conducted under FCC experimental authority, one on March 15, 2021 (Connecticut test, CT), and one on March 29, 2021 (New Jersey test, NJ), to determine whether allowing for high-power operation based upon the proposed formula could result in acceptable performance and not create objectionable interference. Briefly, the field test plan involved identifying suitable stations, then collecting audio recordings of FM analog signals in the presence of 1st-adjacent channel IBOC signals operating at both -14 and -10 dBc and conducting subjective evaluations of the recorded audio to determine whether there was objectionable interference attributable to the higher-power adjacent-channel signal. Participating in the planning of this field test project were engineers from NAB, Xperi, Audacy, New York Public Radio (NYPR), iHeartMedia and Cox Media.

### Site Selection and Test Routes

Two station pairs were identified as suitable for the purposes of this field test and are identified in Table 4. These stations are particularly illustrative of the efficacy of the proposed field strength values as under the current formula, -10 dBc operation would be prohibited whereas under the proposed formula, -10 dBc operation would be allowed, as shown in Figure 2. Note that the Audacy stations were able to increase their digital transmit power for the -10 dBc portions of the test without alteration to the broadcast equipment chain.

| Parameter | WZMX | WIP | WNYC |
|---|---|---|---|
| Role | IBOC station (CT) | IBOC station (NJ) | Analog station (CT, NJ) |
| Frequency (MHz) | 93.7 | 94.1 | 93.9 |
| Class | B | B | B |
| Power (kW) | 17.0 | 9.6 | 5.2 |
| Location | Hartford, CT | Philadelphia, PA | New York, NY |
| Licensee | Audacy | | NYPR |
| Program format | Hip-hop | Sports | Public radio |
| LSB | -17.0 | -17.0 | -18.5 |
| USB | -17.0 | -17.0 | -18.5 |
| TX antenna lat | 41.77417 | 40.04167 | 40.74844 |
| TX antenna long | -72.80497 | -75.23614 | -73.98569 |

TABLE 4. RADIO STATIONS USED IN HIGH-POWER DIGITAL FM FIELD TEST PROJECT. NOTE THAT FOR BOTH THE CT AND NJ TESTS, ANALOG AUDIO FROM WNYC WAS RECORDED FOR SUBJECTIVE EVALUATION.

[11] The differences between actual values and allowed values under the proposed formula are 14.8 (WKTU-WPRB), 5.7 (KFRG-KBZT-FM), 13.5 (WJFK-WWMX), and 17.6 dB (WJFK-WWEG).

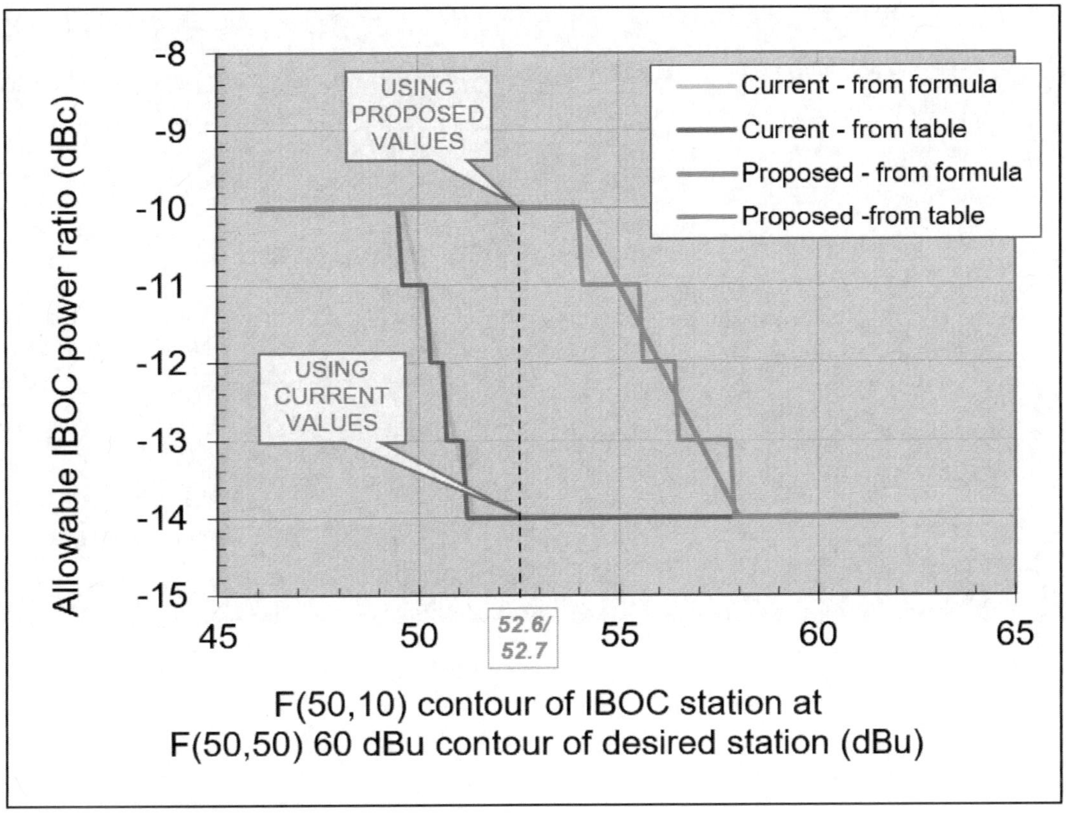


FIGURE 2. ILLUSTRATION OF F(50,10) FIELD STRENGTH VALUES FOR WZMX (52.6 DBU) AND WIP (52.7 DBU) AT 60 DBU CONTOUR OF WNYC, SHOWING THAT UNDER CURRENT FORMULA THESE STATIONS ARE LIMITED TO -14 DBC OPERATION, BUT UNDER THE PROPOSED FORMULA THEY CAN BOTH OPERATE AT -10 DBC.[12]

A map showing the relative locations of these stations is provided in Figure 3 which also shows the general location of the test routes for each test (CT, NJ). Station contours and detailed test routes are provided in Figure 4 and Figure 5. Each test route took approximately 45 minutes of drive time. Following the mobile testing, short stationary recordings of the analog audio were made, as well. Note that in each case, the test route is located at the edge of the analog station's protected contour, at the point closest to the protected contour of the IBOC station, as this is where the interfering IBOC signal will be strongest, and the analog signal being recorded will be weakest.

[12] Field strength values determined using the FCC's FM and TV propagation curves online tool (https://www.fcc.gov/media/radio/fm-and-tv-propagation-curves).

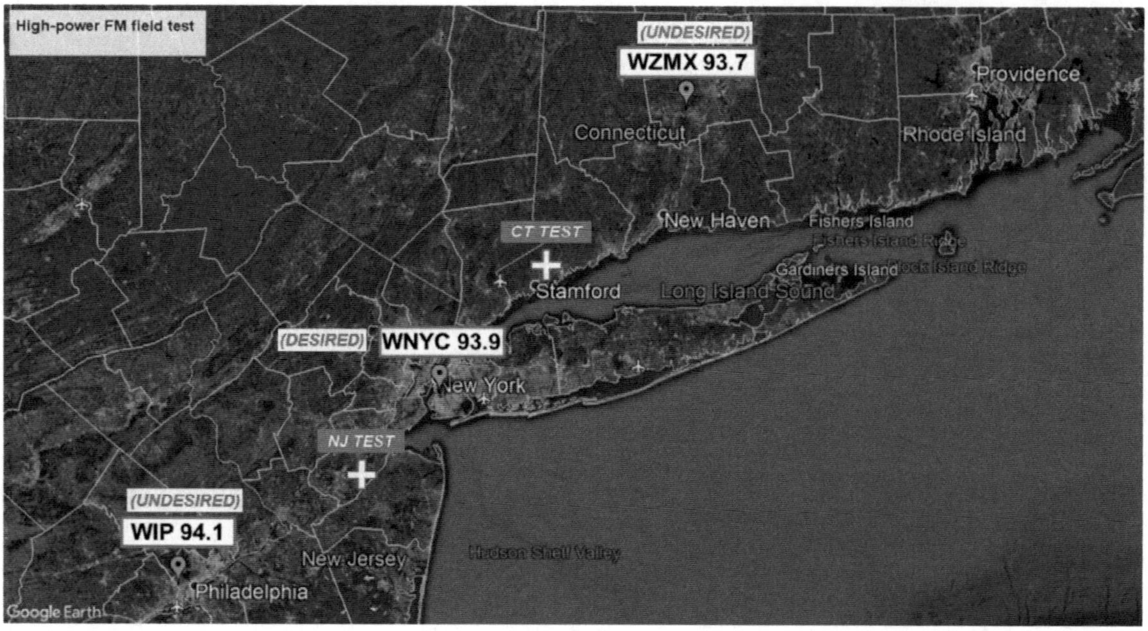


FIGURE 3. MAP SHOWING LOCATION OF TEST STATIONS AND TEST LOCATIONS FOR NJ AND CT TESTS.

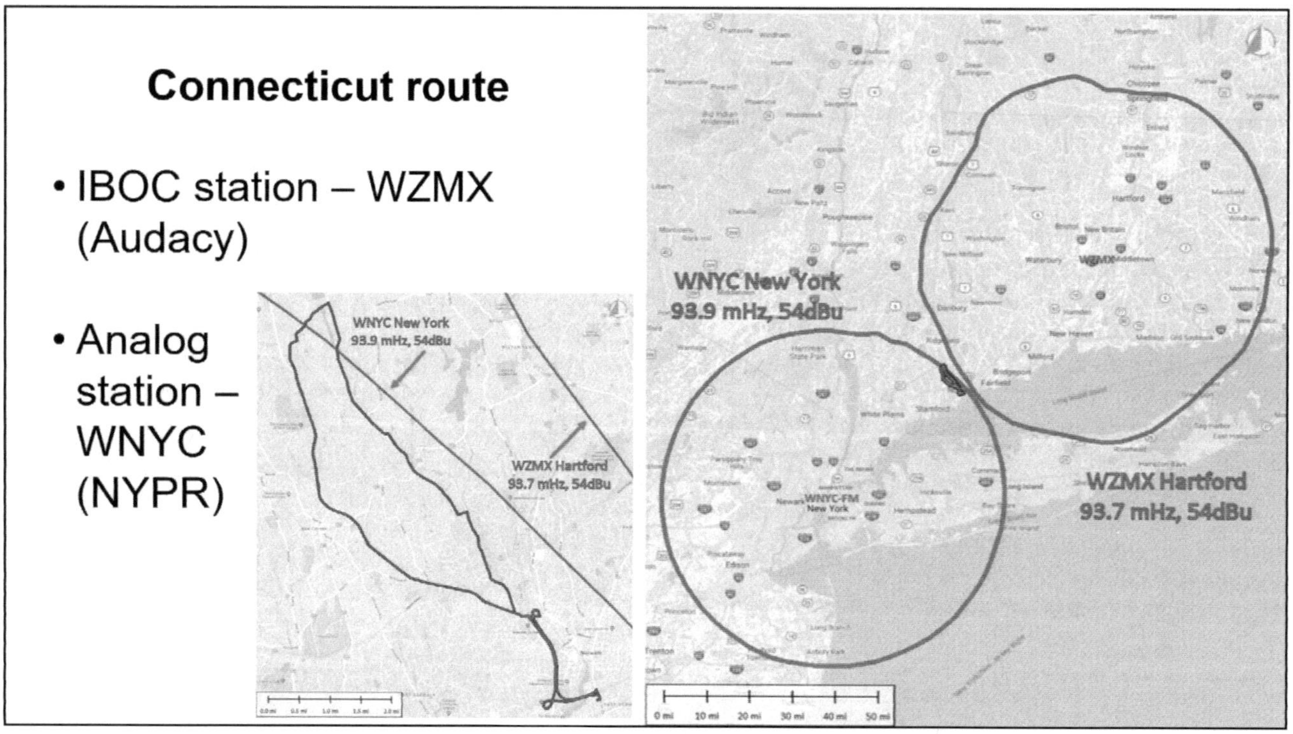


FIGURE 4. STATION CONTOURS AND FIELD TEST ROUTE FOR CONNECTICUT TEST.

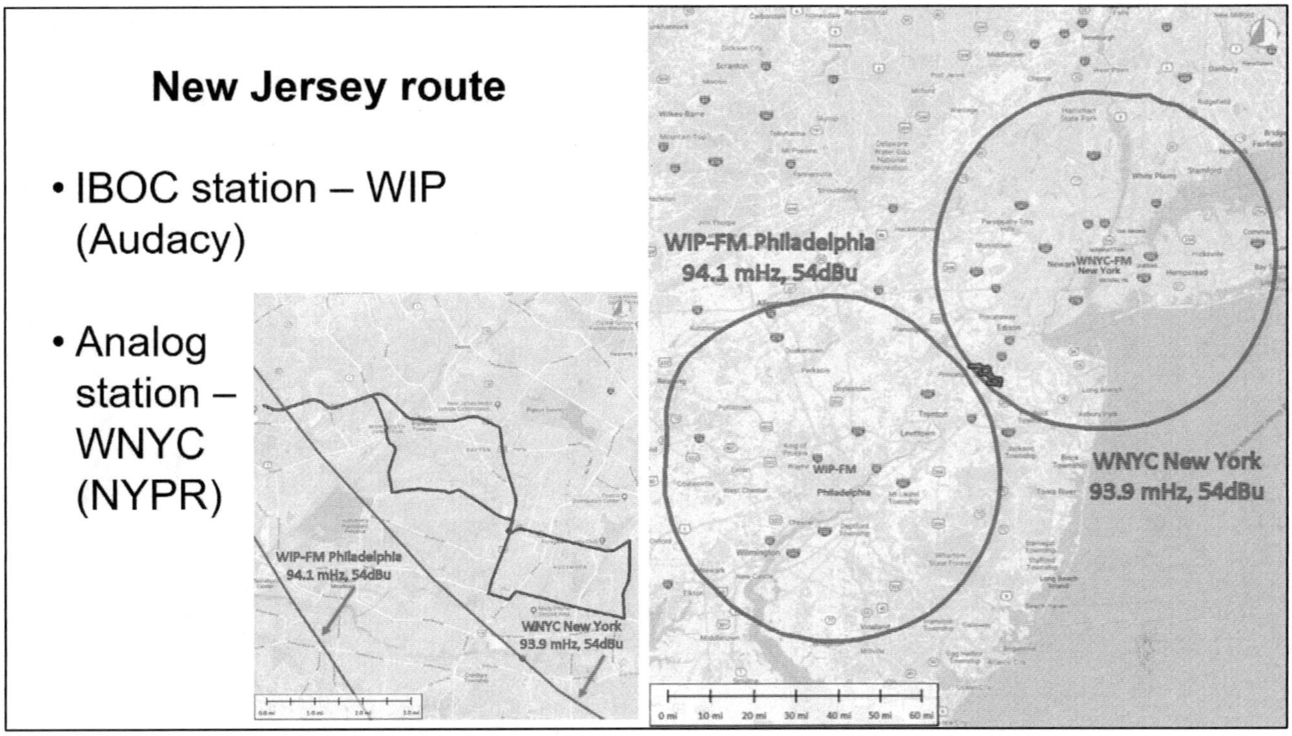


FIGURE 5. STATION CONTOURS AND FIELD TEST ROUTE FOR NEW JERSEY TEST.

## Field Test Vehicle and Test Schedule

Figure 6 is a block diagram showing the field test vehicle equipment configuration; the vehicle used was a stock 2012 Toyota Sienna minivan. For each test, mobile and stationary audio recordings of the analog station (WNYC in both cases) were obtained using 4 different receivers, for two cases of IBOC 1st-adjacent channel operation: at -14 dBc and -10 dBc digital power. Some specifics regarding the field test equipment include the following:

- Receivers 1-3 were automotive aftermarket receivers while receiver 4 was an FM chipmaker's evaluation board which provided access to various control signals and analog and digital reception parameters;
- These receivers were either analog-only or HD Radio receivers operated in analog mode since the goal of the tests was to assess the impact of the 1st-adjacent channel IBOC signal on analog audio performance;
- Analog audio from receivers 1-4 as well as control and status signals from receiver 4, RF signal analyzer information, and GPS location information were all simultaneously recorded on a computer for all mobile and stationary tests.

The field test schedule is outlined in Table 5. Representatives of Xperi, NYPR and/or Audacy were present for all testing. The -10 dBc recordings were collected immediately following collection of the -14 dBc recordings to minimize any differences that might be due to changes in atmospheric or traffic conditions. While the audio content recorded in each case was not identical, it was similar in nature (public radio news and talk programming) and hence comparable for the purposes of subjective evaluation.

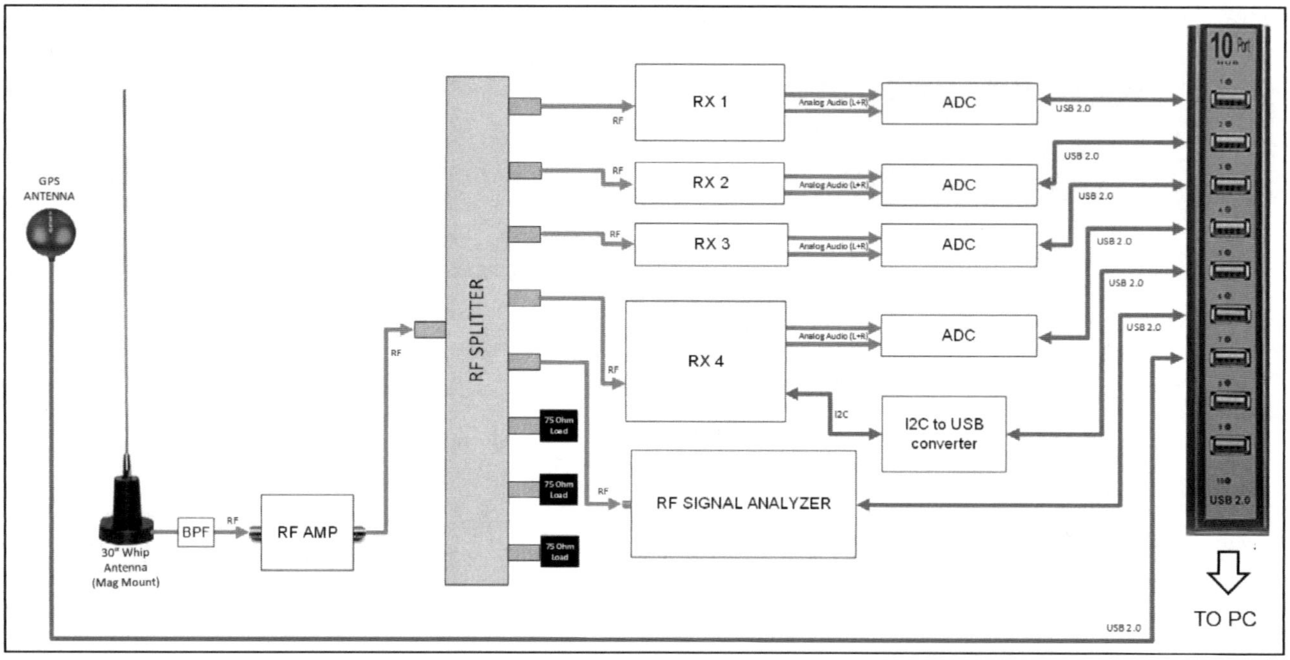


FIGURE 6. BLOCK DIAGRAM SHOWING FIELD TEST VEHICLE EQUIPMENT CONFIGURATION.

| Time | Connecticut test<br>Monday, March 15, 2021 | New Jersey test<br>Monday, March 29, 2021 |
|---|---|---|
| Noon | Start mobile test (-14 dBc) | Start mobile test (-14 dBc) |
| 1PM | WZMX enters -10 dBc operation | WIP enters -10 dBc operation |
| 1:05PM | Start mobile test (-10 dBc) | Start mobile test (-10 dBc) |
| 2PM | Start stationary recording (-10 dBc) | Start stationary recording (-10 dBc) |
| 2:05PM | WZMX enters -14 dBc operation | WIP enters -14 dBc operation |
| 2:10PM | Start stationary recording (-14 dBc) | Start stationary recording (-14 dBc) |
| 2:15PM | End stationary recording | End stationary recording |

TABLE 5. HIGH-POWER DIGITAL FM FIELD TEST SCHEDULE.

## Field Test Results

The principal data collected during these field tests were over 14 hours of audio recordings, summarized in Table 6. For each test condition, recordings from the four receivers were captured simultaneously and stored as .wav files (uncompressed audio). As previously mentioned, additional data was available from the FM chipset evaluation board, but this was ancillary and collected primarily as a reference for future study of the audio files. Also collected was information from an RF signal analyzer, again for future reference.

For purposes of subjective evaluation, the amount and length of audio material to be evaluated had to be significantly reduced. This was done by utilizing a prototype audio analysis tool developed by Xperi for the purpose of evaluating over-the-air (OTA) audio quality to assess when a hybrid (OTA and internet connectivity) radio receiver should switch from the OTA audio to a simulcast, streaming audio source delivered to a hybrid receiver over a mobile broadband channel.[13] Tuner-based RF signal metrics are utilized by the prototype Xperi analysis tool to assess OTA signal quality; these metrics were available for the audio recorded during these tests as part of the ancillary data captured from receiver 4.

| | | -14 dBc | | -10 dBc | |
|---|---|---|---|---|---|
| Description | | # of recordings | Total ET (min) | # of recordings | Total ET (min) |
| CT test | Mobile | 4 | 180 | 4 | 180 |
| | Stationary | 4 | 40 | 4 | 40 |
| NJ test | Mobile | 4 | 180 | 4 | 180 |
| | Stationary | 4 | 40 | 4 | 40 |

TABLE 6. AUDIO RECORDINGS OBTAINED DURING FIELD TESTS (ET IS ELAPSED TIME). A TOTAL OF 14.7 HOURS OF AUDIO RECORDINGS WERE OBTAINED.

In its intended application, the Xperi analysis tool identifies the point at which a hybrid receivers' OTA audio is sufficiently poor in quality so as to necessitate switching to the simulcast streaming audio signal available in the hybrid receiver (so-called "service following"). This is an important feature of a hybrid receiver in that it is desirable to use the streaming audio only when absolutely necessary as the broadcaster incurs additional costs when streaming audio is consumed as compared to OTA audio.

This prototype Xperi analysis tool was applied to the audio obtained during this field test as follows:

- The full 45-minute audio recordings from receiver 4 were analyzed and in this way segments of "listenable" audio were identified. These listenable portions are indicated by the blue waveforms in Figure 7 (CT test data shown). The relatively small portion of listenable audio identified is a reflection of the fact that the mobile test route was located at the edge of the WNYC protected contour and as such the analog audio quality experienced was generally poor. Similar results were obtained when the NJ test results were analyzed;
- A closer comparison of the listenable regions for the -14 and -10 dBc cases reveals that for approximately 60 seconds, the audio recorded in the -14 dBc test was listenable at the same time and location where the audio recorded in the -10 dBc test was *not* listenable, as illustrated in Figure 8 (for both CT and NJ tests). These were the excerpts that were extracted from the collected audio recordings for subjective evaluation.

[13] The use of the term "hybrid" in the context of hybrid (OTA plus internet connectivity) is not to be confused with hybrid digital radio which describes digital radio technology that uses both analog and digital signals, as is the case with hybrid HD Radio signals.

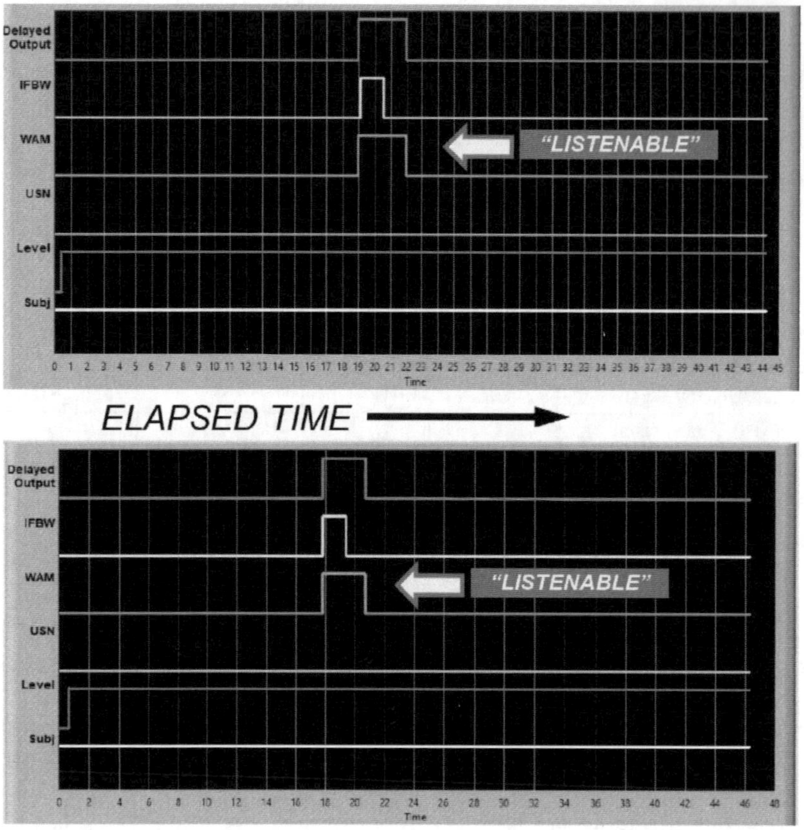


FIGURE 7. RESULTS OF ANALYSIS OF WNYC ANALOG AUDIO FROM THE CT TEST WHEN SUBJECT TO 1ST-ADJ IBOC SIGNALS FROM WZMX AT -14 DBC (TOP) AND -10 DBC (BOTTOM). BLUE WAVEFORMS INDICATE LISTENABLE PORTION OF AUDIO AS DETERMINED BY THE PROTOTYPE XPERI ANALYSIS TOOL.

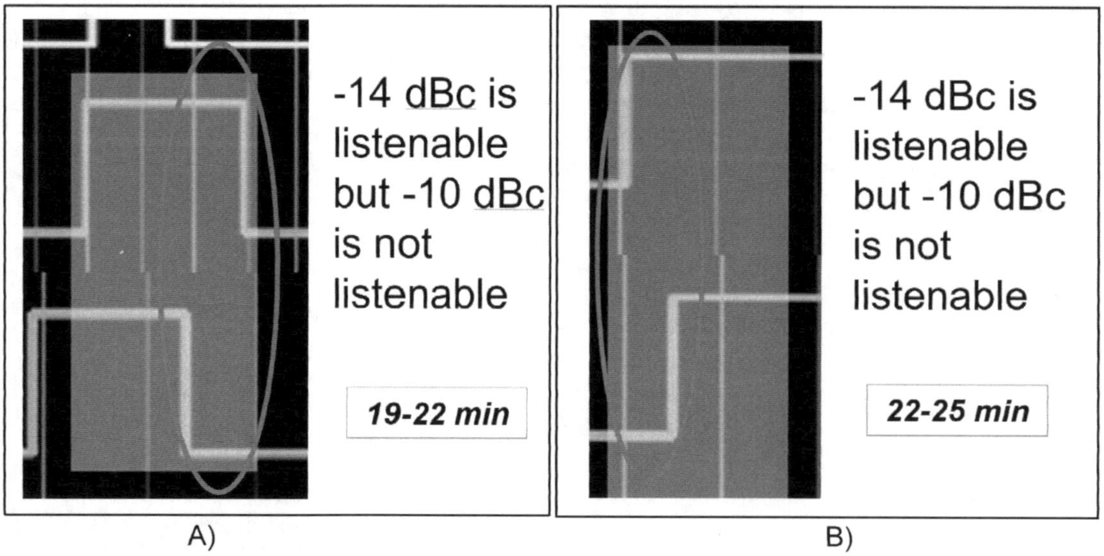


FIGURE 8. EXCERPTS OF WNYC AUDIO FILE ANALYSIS FOR CT (A, FROM 19-22 MINUTE MARKS) AND NJ (B, FROM 22-25 MINUTE MARKS).

With sufficiently short audio segments thus defined, 16 mobile audio files (2 test locations, 4 receivers at each, two power levels at each) were extracted, anonymized and subjectively evaluated:

- For each test, the start and stop locations of the audio excerpts were precisely aligned using the GPS data recorded simultaneously with the audio and ancillary data. The travel times between these locations were slightly different for the -14 and -10 dBc test runs, resulting in a 7- and 4-second difference between the -14 and -10 dBc audio excerpts, for the CT and NJ tests, respectively;
- The final length of the audio clips evaluated were 1 minute 16 seconds (-10 dBc case) or 1 minute 23 seconds (CT test), and 1 minute 11 seconds (-10 dBc case) or 1 minute 7 seconds (NJ test).

Two subjective evaluations were conducted using 5 panelists each, who listened to the 16 audio files and rated each from 1 (unlistenable) to 5 (excellent quality). The results from each panel are presented in Figure 9. A summary of these results is shown in Table 7. As previously noted, in that the field test routes were located at the edge of WNYC's protected contour at the point nearest the protected contour of the 1st-adjacent channel IBOC station, it is not surprising that the perceived audio quality was in the poor to fair range.

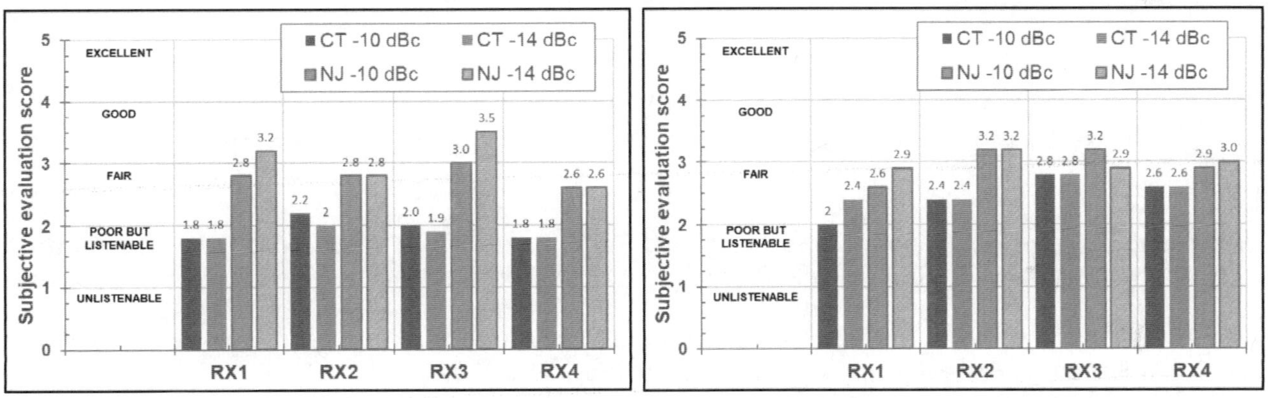


FIGURE 9. SUBJECTIVE EVALUATION RESULTS FROM TWO LISTENER PANELS.

| | Panel 1 | | Panel 2 | |
|---|---|---|---|---|
| | CT | NJ | CT | NJ |
| RX1 | -0.4 | -0.3 | 0 | -0.4 |
| RX2 | 0 | 0 | 0.2 | 0 |
| RX3 | 0 | 0.3 | 0.1 | -0.5 |
| RX4 | 0 | -0.1 | 0 | 0 |

Key:
- -10 sounds worse than -14
- -10 and -14 sound the same
- -14 sounds worse than -10

*(Numbers are difference in subjective eval score)*

*(Subjective eval score ranges from 1=poor to 5=excellent)*

TABLE 7. SUMMARY OF SUBJECTIVE EVALUATION SCORES.

## Analysis and Summary

The subjective evaluation results obtained from the analysis of the field test audio excerpts indicates that for both the CT and NJ tests, it was difficult or impossible to tell the difference between the analog audio recorded when in the presence of a -14 dBc IBOC 1st-adjacent channel interferer versus a -10 dBc interferer. The conclusion is that WNYC's 1st-adjacent channel neighbors, WZMX and WIP could increase their digital power from -14 to -10 dBc with no noticeable impact on the quality of WNYC's analog signal.

These results serve to confirm the efficacy of the proposed NAB-Xperi formula for determining whether a station can increase digital signal power above the blanket authorized -14 dBc value. Comments filed in the FCC proceeding established for considering the NAB-Xperi proposal have been overwhelmingly in favor of moving the proposal forward and the authors are hopeful that an FCC Notice of Proposed Rulemaking to adopt the proposed formula will be forthcoming.

## Acknowledgments

This field test project spanned a nearly 5-year period (due in part to delays caused by the Covid-19 pandemic) and the authors are grateful to the following individuals for their help with and support of the project during this time: Lynn Claudy (NAB), Ashruf El-Dinary (Xperi), Jeff Littlejohn (iHeartMedia), Roswell Clark (Cox Media), and Jim Stagnitto and Dannie Raghunath (WNYC).

## References

[1] *Letter to FCC*, American Public Media Group *et.al.*, Re: MM Docket No. 99-325, filed June 10, 2008.

[2] *HD Radio System Test Report, Compatibility and Performance Tests at Elevated FM Digital Power Level*, MM Docket No. 99-325, May 2008, iBiquity Digital Corporation.

[3] *Report to the Corporation for Public Broadcasting, Digital Radio Coverage & Interference Analysis (DRCIA) Research Project*, National Public Radio, May 19, 2008.

[4] *Report to the FCC on the Advanced IBOC Coverage and Compatibility Study*, National Public Radio, November 3, 2009.

[5] *Order, In the Matter of Digital Audio Broadcasting Systems and Their Impact on the Terrestrial Radio Broadcast Service*, MM Docket No. 99-325, adopted January 27, 2010.

[6] *Petition for Rulemaking Requesting Authority to Increase the Maximum Power of Digital FM Radio*, National Association of Broadcasters and Xperi Inc., MB 22-405, October 26, 2022.

# Advanced FM HD Radio™ Service Modes WTLP Field Test Results

**Paul Peyla**
**Xperi Inc.**
**Columbia, Md., United States**
paul.peyla@xperi.com

**Dave Kolesar**
**Hubbard Broadcasting, Inc.**
**Washington, D.C., United States**
dave.kolesar@wtop.com

**Abstract** – Several HD Radio™ service modes (MA1, MA3, MP1, MP2, MP3, MP5, and MP6) have been available to AM and FM broadcasters for nearly two decades, and MP11 has also recently been added.[1] However, various HD Radio stakeholders have requested additional options for improved robustness and capacity. A new set of advanced service modes for the FM band has been developed in response to these emerging market demands and opportunities. These advanced service modes use higher-order modulation techniques to afford a significant increase in digital audio and data capacity. Furthermore, special signal processing and coding techniques, including time and frequency diversity, are employed to improve signal robustness and combat adverse effects to the HD Radio signal in a real-world automotive listening environment.

The FCC granted a six-month experimental authorization to Hubbard Broadcasting on March 8, 2022, to conduct a series of tests using commercial FM station WTLP in Braddock Heights, MD. The tests evaluated the performance of the following advanced service modes for FM HD Radio broadcasting for both hybrid and all-digital waveforms: MP1X, MP6OV, DSB1, DSB1OV, and MS5. The purpose of the field tests was to validate the analytical, simulated, and laboratory performance predictions of each service mode by measuring performance in a real-world automotive environment. The tests were performed over nine test routes to expose the signal to a wide variety of terrain, speed, interference, multipath, and terrain shadowing conditions. The field tests successfully validated the predicted performance of the advanced service modes. Besides substantiating relative robustness predictions, the test results also demonstrate the ability of higher-order modulation techniques to reliably deliver enhanced digital data capacity to a significant portion of a station's coverage area.

## Service Modes

Both legacy and advanced FM service modes were transmitted during the field tests. Legacy service modes MP1 and MP6 provide a useful performance baseline for the advanced service modes. Service mode MP1 is widely used by broadcasters to transmit hybrid waveforms with both analog and digital components. Service mode MP6 employs extended digital frequency partitions on each sideband and was used to broadcast a hybrid waveform.

---

[1] All-digital AM operations, which are supported by service mode MA3, were authorized by the FCC in 2020 and have been available for only a few years.

---

This paper is excerpted from the Proceedings of the 2023 NAB Broadcast Engineering and Information Technology (BEIT) Conference, © 2023, National Association of Broadcasters, 1 M Street SE, Washington, DC 20003 USA.

The following advanced FM service modes were tested:

- MP1X: backward compatible with MP1, hybrid waveform
- DSB1: non-backward compatible, hybrid waveform
- MS5: secondary sidebands, all-digital waveform
- MP6OV: layered service mode, backward compatible with MP6, hybrid waveform
- DSB1OV: layered service mode, non-backward compatible, hybrid waveform

MP6OV and DSB1OV employ layered, or hierarchical, modulation. This can provide a backward-compatible means of significantly enhancing capacity by simultaneously broadcasting two service modes, one of which is "overlayed" on top of an existing "base" service mode. Legacy receivers detect the base layer, while newer advanced receivers also detect the overlay for additional capacity. MP6OV is backward compatible with legacy service modes; DSB1OV is not.

Descriptions of all tested service modes are provided in Appendix A. Detailed descriptions of all advanced FM service modes can be found in [1].

## WTLP Configuration

WTLP (Braddock Heights, MD) is a Class A FM station located west of Frederick, MD. The main and auxiliary facilities for the station are collocated on the same tower, with the main facility transmitting an effective radiated power (ERP) of 350 watts using a Shively 6813 antenna (2 bays, full wave spacing) at 35 meters above ground level (AGL), with 400 watts transmitter power output (TPO). The auxiliary facility is authorized for the same ERP, using a Shively 6813 antenna (2 bays, half-wave spacing) at 23 meters AGL, with 533 watts TPO. The antenna configuration is shown in Figure 1.

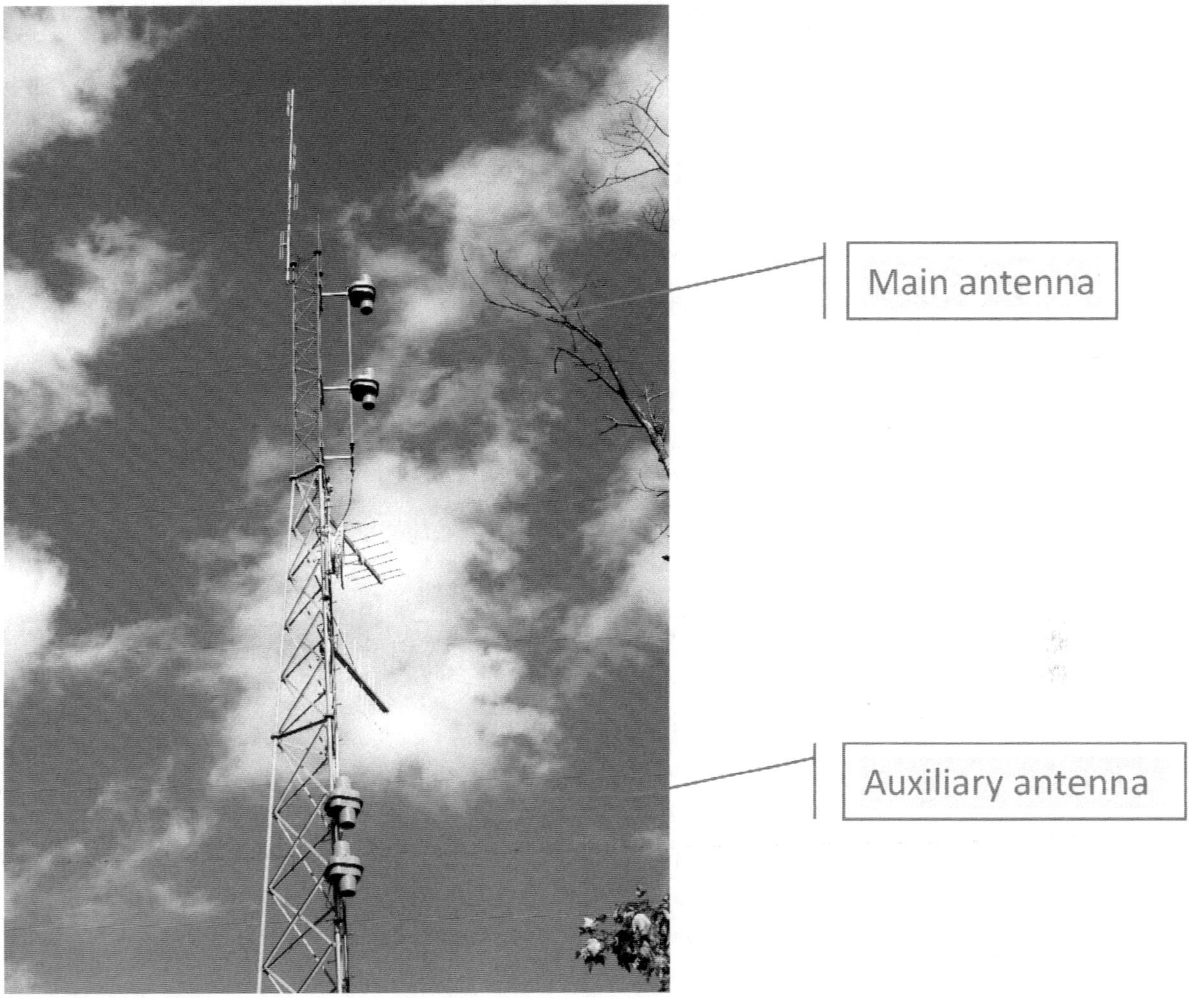


FIGURE 1: WTLP ANTENNA CONFIGURATION.

WTLP simulcasts WTOP-FM (Washington, DC). WTLP normally uses hybrid HD Radio service mode MP3, with two supplemental program service (SPS) channels, combined with the analog signal using a Nautel VS1 transmitter. Even though the station's antennas are omnidirectional, hilly terrain to the north, south, and west obstruct reception. This renders WTLP a good test station for examining the real-world behavior of advanced HD Radio service modes. The terrain to the east of the transmitter site is less hilly and more open, which provides a reference for comparison to the more terrain-compromised directions. The predicted coverage area of WTLP is shown in Figure 2. A Longley-Rice propagation prediction illustrating the terrain shielding of the broadcast signal is shown in Figure 3.

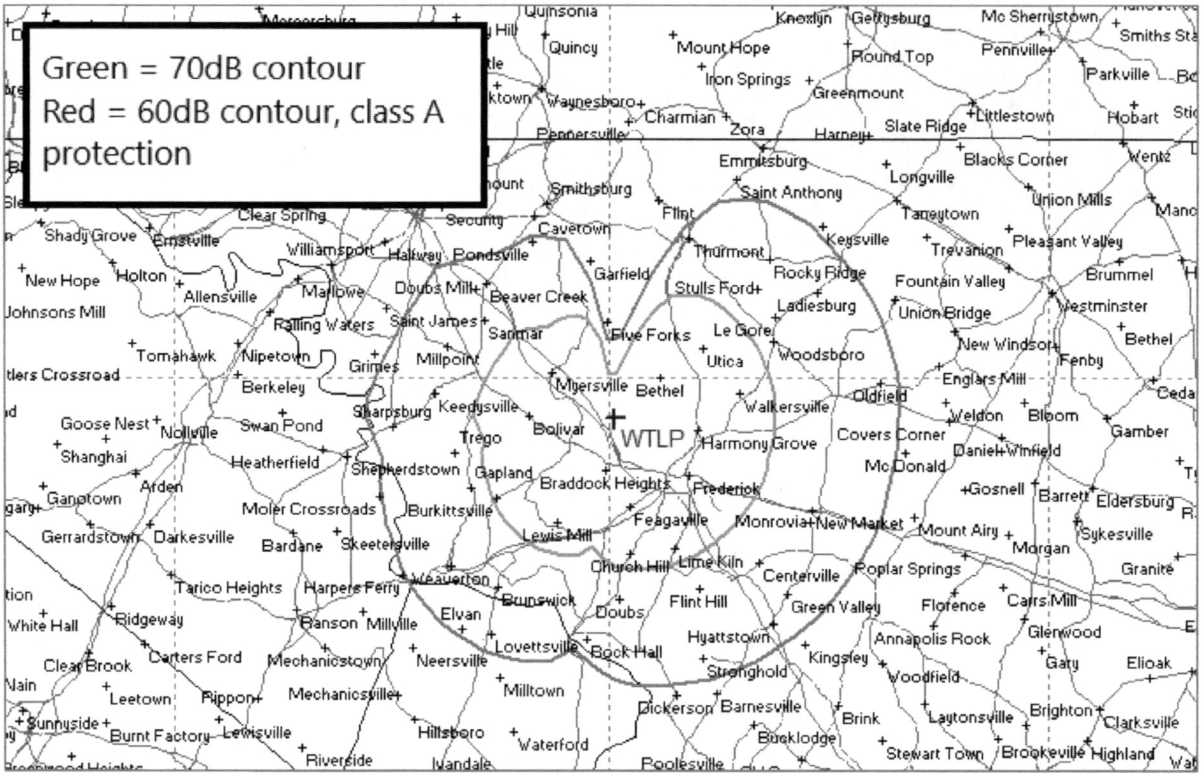


FIGURE 2: PREDICTED COVERAGE AREA OF WTLP.

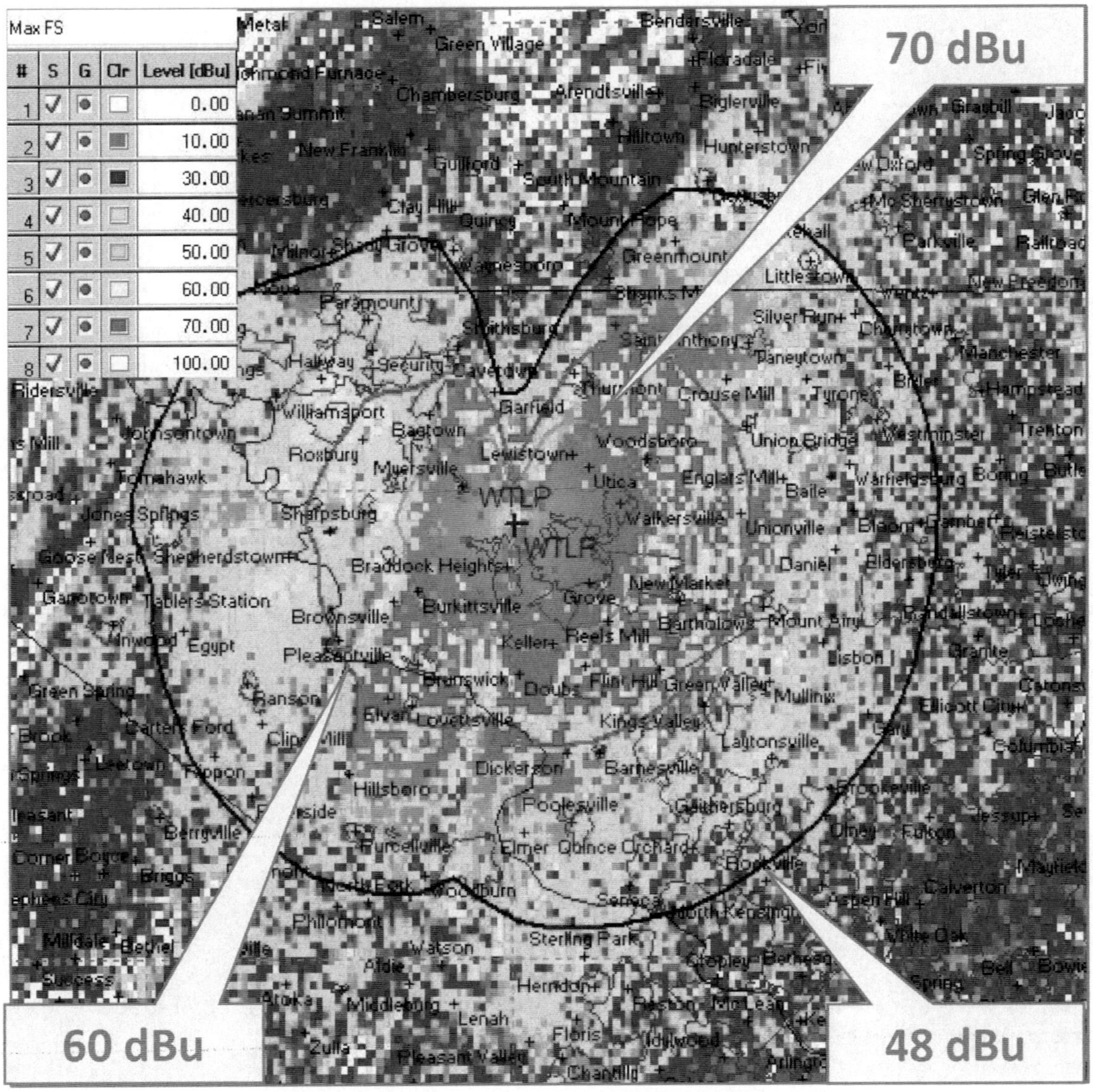


FIGURE 3: LONGLEY-RICE PROPAGATION PREDICTION FOR WTLP.

Although the auxiliary antenna was initially used for advanced service mode dry runs, drive tests quickly indicated significant coverage degradation compared to the main facility. For this reason, all formal testing was performed using the main antenna. It was also determined that the test transmitter (another Nautel VS1) was capable of a maximum of -12-dBc digital injection when operating with the advanced service modes at the licensed TPO; therefore, the test transmitter was set to that injection level for all tests. This permitted a "one-to-one" comparison (same digital injection level, same transmitter, same antenna) between legacy and advanced service modes. The total digital power of the upper and lower primary digital sidebands was identical for each test.

The test configuration is shown in Figure 4. During field trials, the station's main HD Radio broadcast chain was replaced by an auxiliary broadcast chain, in which an Xperi IBEX exciter supplied an HD Radio test signal to a Nautel VSHD exciter via an LVDS interface. The VSHD interfaced with a Nautel VS1 transmitter. The analog portion of hybrid signals was diversity delayed by a Justin 808 time-alignment monitor before being passed into the VSHD.

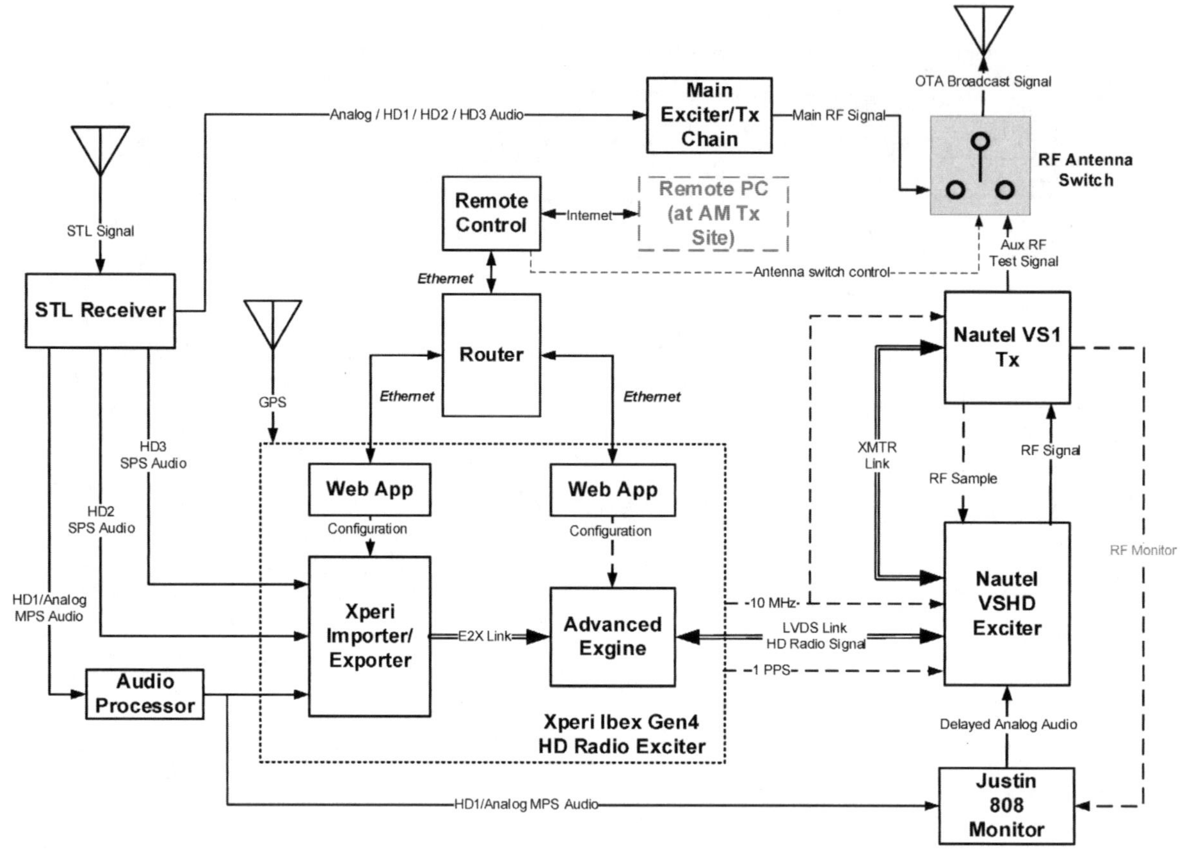


FIGURE 4: WTLP BROADCAST TEST SETUP FOR ADVANCED SERVICE MODE FIELD TESTS.

Hybrid waveform (analog + digital) tests occurred during either the daytime or evening, depending upon whether the service modes were backward compatible with existing HD Radio receivers. Compatible service modes were transmitted during the daytime, and modes not recognized by legacy receivers (and therefore able only to be received in analog) were tested after 7:00 PM.

All-digital service modes, which required the temporary cessation of analog transmissions, were tested between the hours of midnight and 5:00 AM on weekends. The secondary digital sidebands of the all-digital signal were broadcast at a level that was 5 dB below the total power of the primary digital sidebands (which were at -12 dBc).

## Receiver Configuration

The prototype receiver under test (RUT) consisted of an NXP D3 DiRaNa mainboard with an IBOC Digital Module (IDM) daughter board using the NXP Cayman IC for HD Radio baseband processing. The DiRaNa provided radio frequency (RF) tuning, digitization, intermediate frequency (IF) processing, baseband conversion, and an analog FM receiver. The Cayman was selected for its processing and memory resources. Cayman receiver test software was developed for advanced service modes MP1X, DSB1, and MS5, as well as for layered service modes MP6OV and DSB1OV.

The NXP SAF775x tool was used for DiRaNa control, while the Xperi CDM4 controlled and monitored the HD Radio baseband processor. The Xperi Blend Tester7 is a PC-based application that was used to periodically record the contents of specified output variables to a log file as the vehicle traveled along its prescribed course.

Due to limitations in Cayman receiver processing, simultaneous data logging was possible on only a single MPS and a single SPS channel. Therefore, a second NXP Cayman receiver platform was used to support simultaneous field testing of two receivers. This allowed comparison of multiple logical channels within the same broadcast.

A logical channel is a signal path that conducts digital information through the HD Radio system with a specific grade of service, as determined by the service mode. Primary logical channels P1, P2, P3, P4, PIDS, POV, and PIDSOV configure the primary digital sidebands. Secondary logical channels S1 and SIDS configure the secondary digital sidebands. Not all logical channels are used in every service mode, as shown in Table 1. A detailed description of logical channels can be found in [1].

| Service | Logical Channel | | | | | | | | |
|---|---|---|---|---|---|---|---|---|---|
| Mode | P1 | P2 | P3 | P4 | PIDS | POV | PIDSOV | S1 | SIDS |
| MP1 | X | | | | X | | | | |
| MP2 | X | | X | | X | | | | |
| MP3 | X | | X | | X | | | | |
| MP11 | X | | X | X | X | | | | |
| MP5 | X | X | X | | X | | | | |
| MP6 | X | X | | | X | | | | |
| MP1X | X | | | X | X | | | | |
| DSB1 | X | | | | X | | | | |
| MP1XOV | X | | | X | X | X | X | | |
| MP6OV | X | X | | | X | X | X | | |
| DSB1OV | X | | | | X | X | X | | |
| MS5 | | | | | | | | X | X |

TABLE 1: LOGICAL CHANNEL ASSIGNMENTS IN FM HD RADIO SERVICE MODES.

## Test Vehicle

The two prototype HD Radio receivers were integrated into the Xperi test vehicle with diversity antennas employed for maximum ratio combining (MRC). MRC improves reception performance by optimally summing the inputs from two receiver antennas. Only service mode MS5 did not use MRC, since just a single tuner was available on the RUT for receiving secondary sidebands.

Each receiver was connected to the same two quarter-wave whip antennas mounted on the roof of the vehicle, to enable MRC processing. To feed the two receivers, splitters were employed in each antenna path, which reduced the absolute level of each received signal by 3 dB.

Two computers hosted the diagnostic tools described above (one for each receiver). These computers were powered via 120VAC (using a clean sinewave inverter connected to the vehicle battery). The inverter was also used to power a 5-VDC supply for the receivers. A GPS receiver and other standard test equipment (cables, connectors, etc.) were also necessary.

A block diagram of the receiver field test setup within the test vehicle is shown in Figure 5. Photos of the exterior and interior of the test vehicle are shown in Figure 6 and Figure 7, respectively.

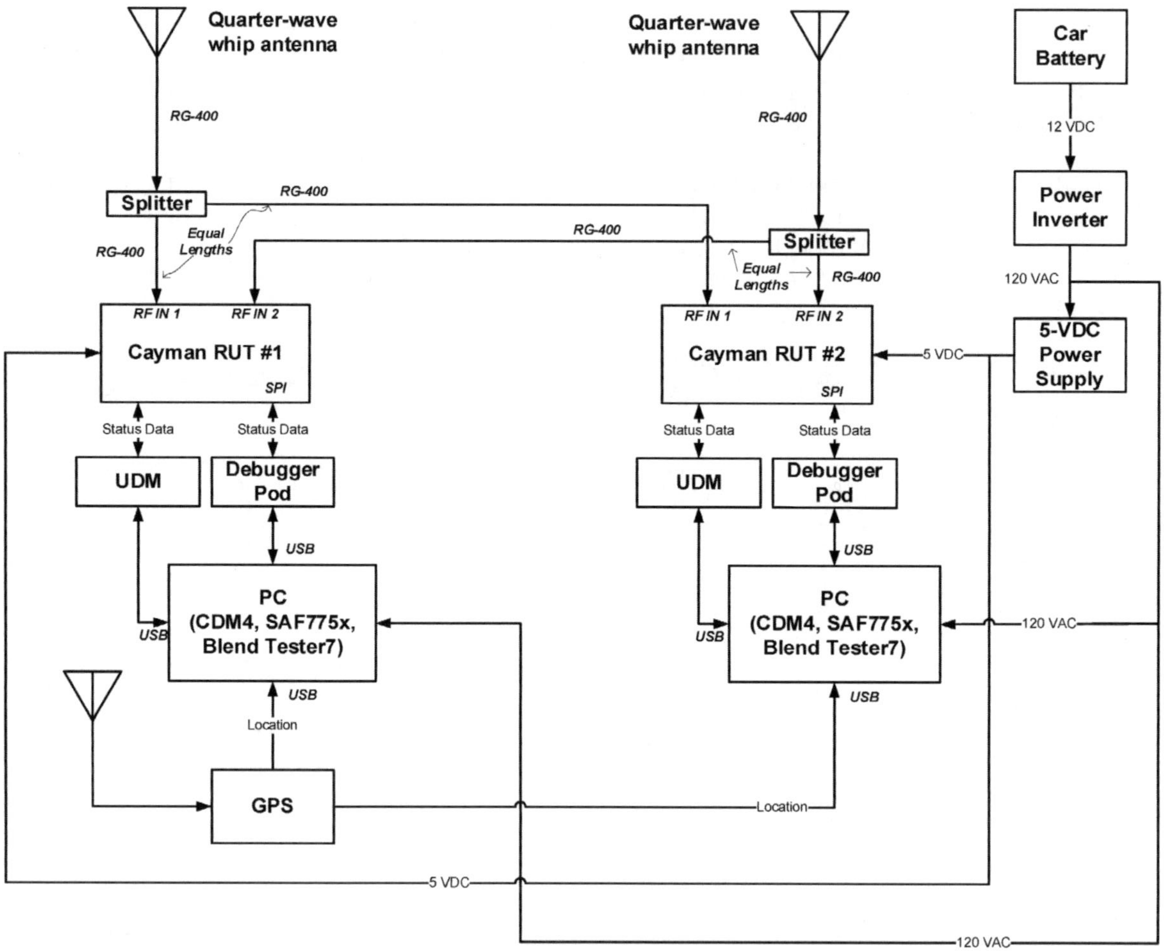


FIGURE 5: RECEIVER TEST SETUP FOR TESTING ADVANCED FM SERVICE MODES WITH DIVERSITY ANTENNAS FOR MRC.

FIGURE 6: XPERI FIELD TEST VEHICLE.

FIGURE 7: RECEIVER SETUP WITHIN XPERI TEST VEHICLE.

## Test Routes

Nine field test routes were used to permit a variety of vehicle speeds and terrain, and widely varying reception conditions. Some routes radiated outward from the test station in different directions and spanned the expected digital coverage area. Others formed test loops that covered more limited geographic areas of specific interest. The Longley Rice propagation predictions for WTLP shown in Figure 3 were used to select routes that could be expected to yield good, marginal, and poor digital audio reception.

The test routes are illustrated in Figure 8 by colored lines. The edge of digital coverage could generally be expected to lie somewhere between the 60-dBu FCC protected contour (black, local coverage) and the 48-dBu FCC contour (navy blue, "fringe" coverage).

Each test radial was traversed in a single direction (moving away from the transmitter, towards the transmitter, or both) to conserve test time and allow for a greater diversity of routes. All test loops were traversed in a counterclockwise manner.

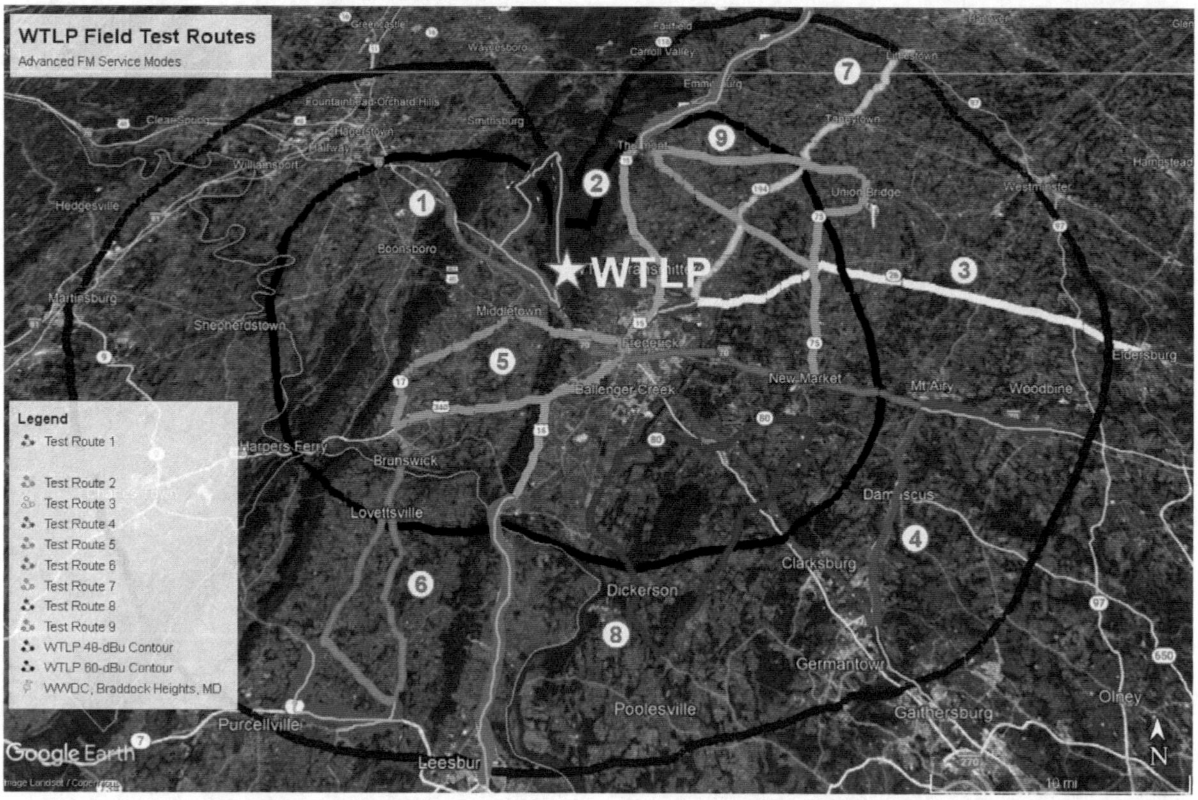


FIGURE 8: FIELD TEST ROUTES FOR ADVANCED SERVICE MODE TESTING.

## Test Results

Following testing, each log file was processed using a Matlab data-reduction script for parsing and plotting the data versus receiver position. The resulting maps use color coding to indicate reception performance at regularly spaced latitude/longitude coordinates along the test route. These maps allow test engineers to draw inferences about receiver performance as a function of terrain and signal level.

Of particular interest in these field tests are maps that display the audio output state, where green indicates digital audio and red indicates analog audio or mute. These maps allow direct visual comparison of the coverage of logical channels in advanced service modes to their legacy counterparts. An example map showing the audio output state of the P1 logical channel in service mode MP1X along Test Route 3 is shown in Figure 9.

FIGURE 9: AUDIO OUTPUT STATE OF MP1X P1 ALONG TEST ROUTE 3.

Although visual inspection of maps can be instructive, making comparisons, inferring trends, and drawing conclusions in this manner can be tedious when comparing multiple logical channels over nine test routes. Fortunately, the graphical performance illustrated in Figure 9 can be conveniently represented by a single performance metric. Digital audio availability (DAA) calculates the percentage of the length of a particular test route where digital audio was output. If all logical channels were recorded over the same route length, DAA provides a figure of merit for comparing the relative robustness of each logical channel on that route.

Table 2 tabulates DAA for each logical channel across all nine test routes. The results are color-coded by quartile: green = 75-100%, orange = 50-74%, magenta = 25-49%, and red = 0-24%. Values of NA represent test cases where DAA was unavailable due to an irregular test route or corrupted/lost test data. A cursory inspection of Table 2 reveals the diversity of test routes (test route 5 was relatively close to the transmitter, while test route 6 was more distant), as well as relative performance differences between the logical channels (MP6 P1 robustness is excellent, whereas DSB1OV POV appears to be more fragile, as would be expected for an overlay channel in a 64-QAM signal).

| Service Mode | Logical Channel | Mod-ulation | Info Bit Rate (kbps) | Simulated Performance (AWGN, dB rel. to MP1 P1) | Test Route 1 (%) | Test Route 2 (%) | Test Route 3 (%) | Test Route 4 (%) | Test Route 5 (%) | Test Route 6 (%) | Test Route 7 (%) | Test Route 8 (%) | Test Route 9 (%) |
|---|---|---|---|---|---|---|---|---|---|---|---|---|---|
| MP1X | P1 | QPSK | 98 | 0 | 84 | 69 | 63 | 56 | 95 | NA | 64 | 59 | 63 |
| | P4 | 16-QAM | 69 | -2.7 | 80 | 67 | 58 | 56 | 93 | NA | 54 | 59 | 59 |
| MP6 | P1 | QPSK | 50 | +2.5 | 88 | 83 | 92 | 81 | 99 | 66 | 91 | 79 | 77 |
| | P2 | QPSK | 49 | 0 | 86 | 77 | 78 | 67 | 96 | 51 | 76 | 68 | 67 |
| MP6OV (16QAM) | P1 | QPSK | 50 | 0.2 | 86 | 77 | 75 | 72 | 99 | 49 | 83 | 71 | 73 |
| | P2 | QPSK | 49 | -3.5 | NA | 67 | 52 | 52 | NA | NA | 61 | 58 | 49 |
| | POV | QPSK | 114 | -4.2 | 76 | 61 | 33 | 37 | 85 | 9 | NA | NA | 22 |
| DSB1 | P1 | 16-QAM | 229 | -2.5 | NA | 63 | 51 | 36 | 91 | 22 | 45 | 44 | 45 |
| DSB1OV (64QAM) | P1 | 16-QAM | 229 | -3.5 | 75 | 63 | 51 | 36 | 85 | NA | 40 | 43 | 40 |
| | POV | QPSK | 114 | -10.3 | 40 | 57 | 24 | 18 | 75 | NA | 24 | 15 | 7 |
| MS5 (-5 dB) | S1 | QPSK | 114 | -2.2 | 85 | 65 | 66 | 59 | 96 | 32 | 55 | 59 | 62 |

TABLE 2: DIGITAL AUDIO AVAILABILITY OF EACH LOGICAL CHANNEL ACROSS ALL TEST ROUTES.

As stated above, the primary goal of these field tests was to validate predicted system performance over a wide range of real-world automotive listening environments. This was effectively accomplished by comparing the median DAA of each logical channel across all test routes to simulated audio frame-error-rate (AFER) performance in additive white Gaussian noise (AWGN, also tabulated in Table 2). This is shown in Figure 10, which illustrates how closely the relative robustness measured in the field agrees with predicted robustness.

The x-axis in Figure 10 represents the logical channel, the left y-axis is the DAA in percent, and the right y-axis is the simulated AWGN AFER performance in dB relative to the simulated AFER performance of MP1 P1 at the digital audio threshold of audibility (1% AFER, which is roughly analogous to the blend point). The dots, color-coded by test route, plot the individual DAA values from Table 2 for each logical channel. The solid blue line represents the median DAA (across all test routes) for each logical channel, while the dashed red line shows the simulated AWGN AFER performance at the threshold of audibility in dB relative to MP1 P1.

Although absolute comparison of the red and blue lines is not possible due to implicit differences in the represented quantities (measured audio availability versus simulated audio frame error rate), the relative predicted and measured robustness of the logical channels can be compared. The similar shapes of the curves clearly indicate agreement in relative performance. This implies that the data collected during the field tests indeed validates the simulated robustness predictions for each logical channel. In other words, the advanced FM service modes appear to perform as expected in a real-world automotive environment.

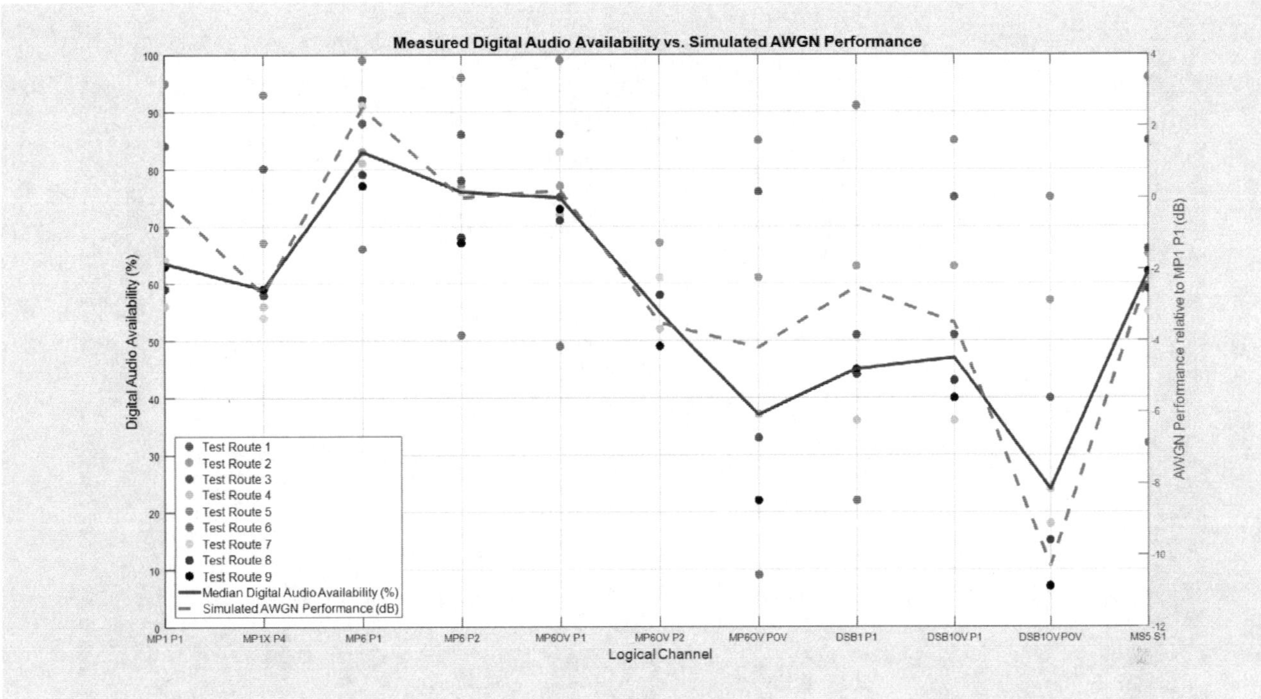


FIGURE 10: COMPARISON OF MEDIAN DIGITAL AUDIO AVAILABILITY WITH PREDICTED AWGN AFER PERFORMANCE.

Another goal of the WTLP field tests was to compare the robustness of specific logical channels in advanced service modes to their legacy counterparts. Of particular interest in this investigation is the relative DAA performance of the following logical channels:

- MP1X P4 versus MP1X P1 (equivalent to MP1 P1)
- MP6 P1 versus MP6 P2 (equivalent to MP1 P1)
- 16-QAM Layered: MP6OV P1 and POV versus MP6 P1, MP6OV P2 versus MP6 P2
- DSB1 P1 versus MP1X P1 (equivalent to MP1 P1)
- 64-QAM Layered: DSB1OV P1 and POV versus DSB1 P1
- All-Digital MS5 S1 versus MP1X P1 (equivalent to MP1 P1)

For the most effective relative comparison, data from both advanced and legacy channels should be captured concurrently. Since simultaneous logging was possible on only a single MPS and a single SPS logical channel, and since logging of the digital audio state was possible for only the selected audio program, a second NXP Cayman receiver platform was used.

Furthermore, some service modes (such as non-backward-compatible DSB1) could not be directly compared to a legacy service mode, since only one advanced logical channel is broadcast. In such cases, although not ideal due to potentially different VHF propagation conditions, comparison was made to legacy channels recorded during other test runs. The use of nine test routes helps to mitigate potential propagation differences.

## MP1X

Since MP1X is backward-compatible with legacy service mode MP1, it will likely be the first advanced service mode to be rolled out by broadcasters. As such, it is important to understand the relative robustness of the new P4 logical channel. Maps showing the audio output states of the P1 and P4 logical channels are shown in Figure 11 and Figure 12, respectively.

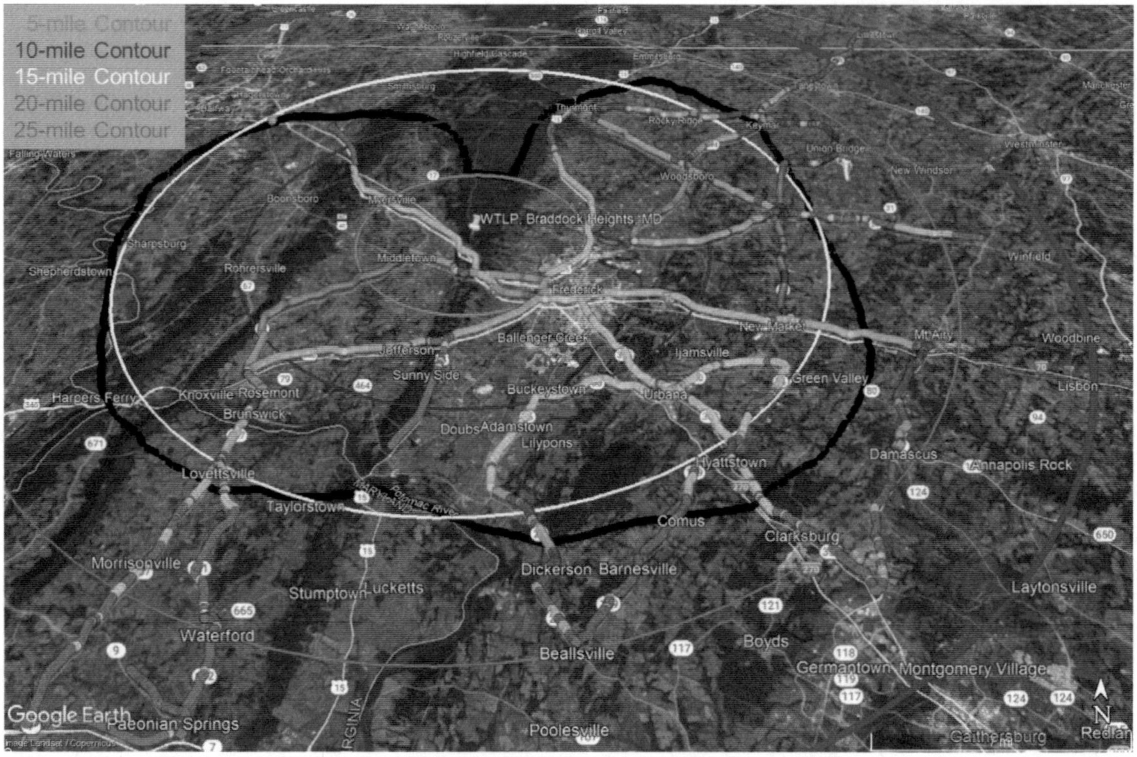


FIGURE 11: AUDIO OUTPUT STATE OF MP1X P1.

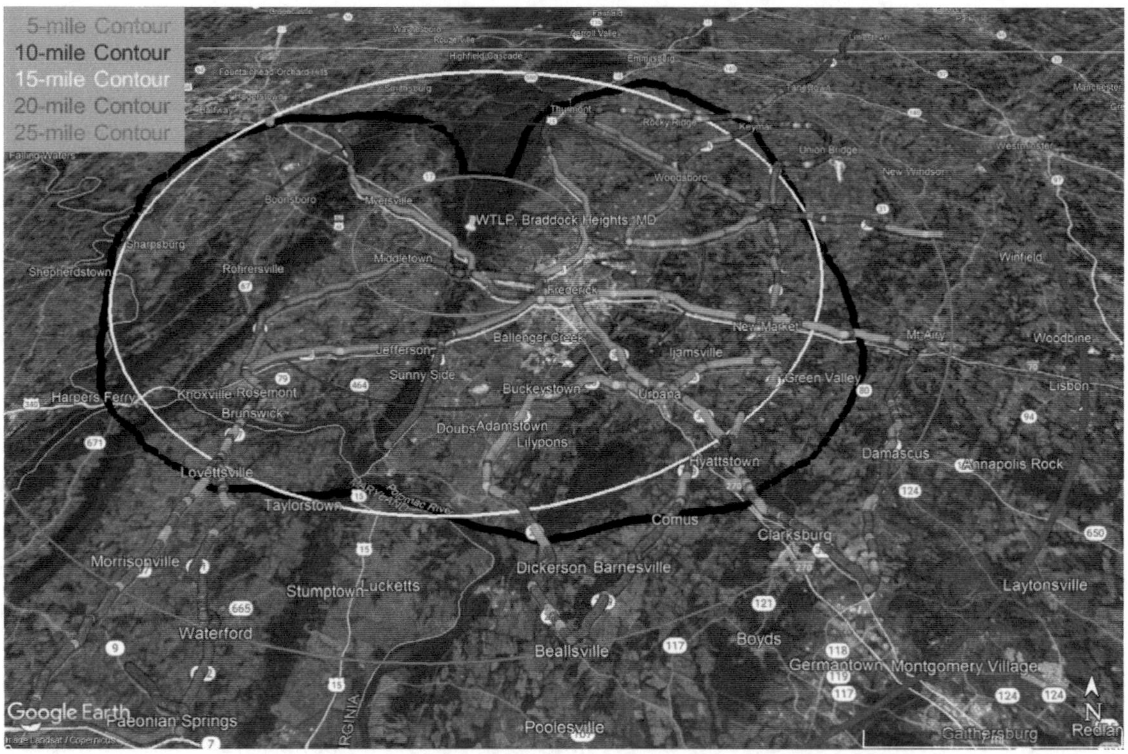


FIGURE 12: AUDIO OUTPUT STATE OF MP1X P4.

A DAA comparison of MP1X P4 with MP1X P1 (equivalent to MP1 P1) is shown in Table 3 (a subset of Table 2). Although the 16-QAM P4 logical channel has consistently lower availability than the P1 channel, the degradation is small enough that it will likely be imperceptible to listeners under most conditions. The additional 69 kbps of P4 digital capacity likely makes this a worthwhile trade for broadcasters.

| Service Mode | Logical Channel | Mod-ulation | Info Bit Rate (kbps) | Simulated Performance (AWGN, dB rel. to MP1 P1) | Test Route 1 (%) | Test Route 2 (%) | Test Route 3 (%) | Test Route 4 (%) | Test Route 5 (%) | Test Route 6 (%) | Test Route 7 (%) | Test Route 8 (%) | Test Route 9 (%) |
|---|---|---|---|---|---|---|---|---|---|---|---|---|---|
| MP1X | P1 | QPSK | 98 | 0 | 84 | 69 | 63 | 56 | 95 | NA | 64 | 59 | 63 |
| | P4 | 16-QAM | 69 | -2.7 | 80 | 67 | 58 | 56 | 93 | NA | 54 | 59 | 59 |
| Difference (% of test route length) | | | | | -4 | -2 | -5 | 0 | -2 | NA | -10 | 0 | -4 |

TABLE 3: DAA COMPARISON OF MP1X P4 WITH MP1X P1 (MP1 P1 EQUIVALENT).

## MP6

The MP6 P1 logical channel, although transmitted in a legacy service mode, is predicted to be the most robust channel due to its low-rate FEC code and its use of time and frequency diversity. Field test results have validated this prediction.

Test results for MP6 P1 and MP6 P2 were collected simultaneously. Maps showing the audio output states of the MP6 P2 and P1 logical channels are shown in Figure 13 and Figure 14, respectively. The MP6 P2 logical channel has the same coding and interleaving as MP1 P1, and their simulated performance in AWGN is identical. Therefore, comparing MP6 P1 to MP6 P2 indicates the relative performance improvement of MP6 P1 versus MP1 P1.

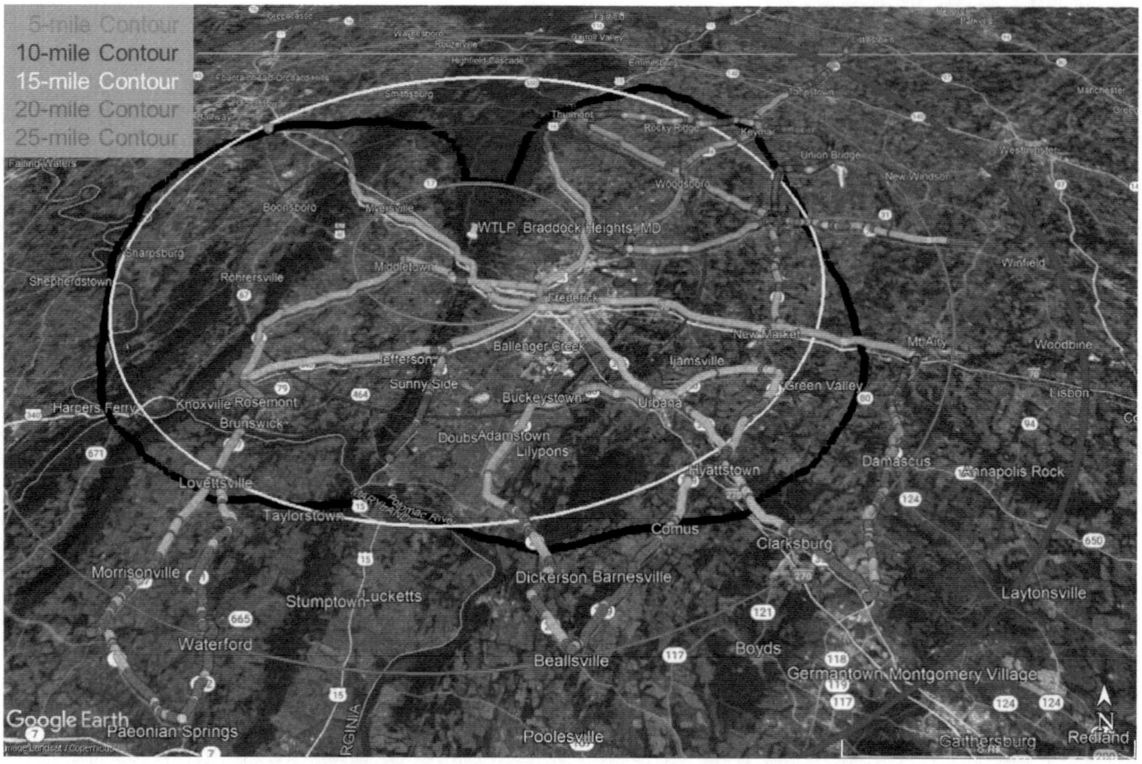


FIGURE 13: AUDIO OUTPUT STATE OF MP6 P2.

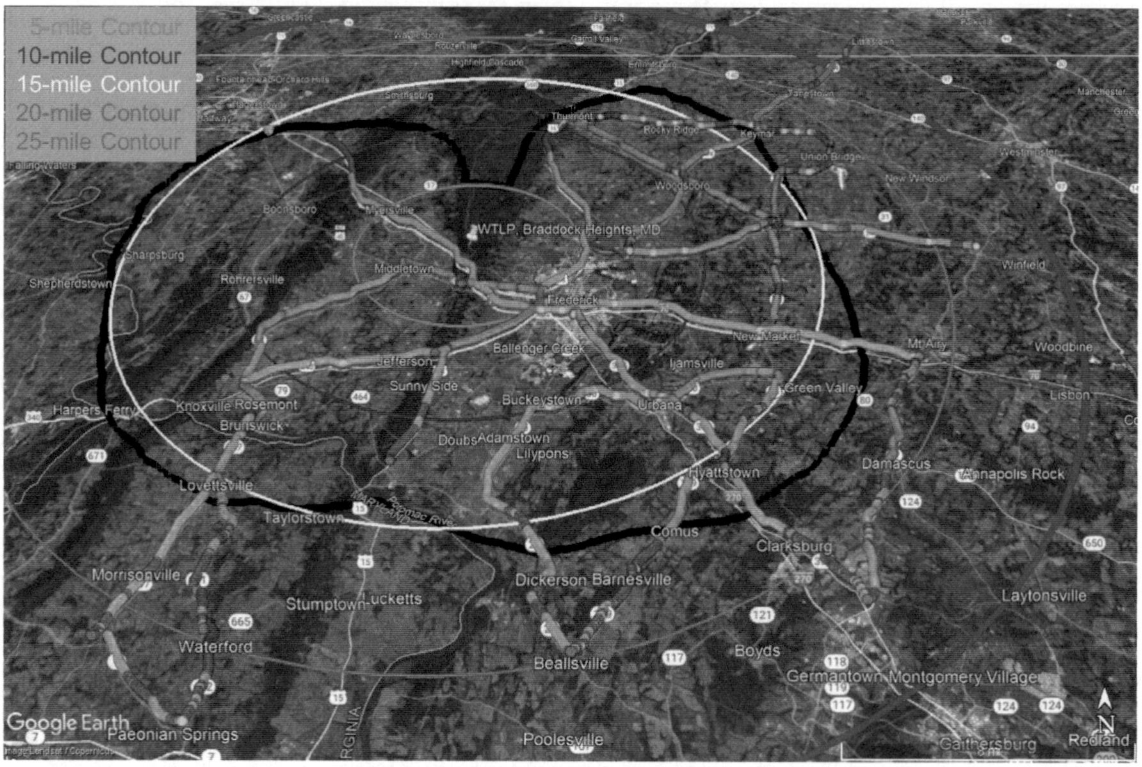


FIGURE 14: AUDIO OUTPUT STATE OF MP6 P1.

Table 4 shows a significant improvement in robustness for MP6 P1 versus MP6 P2 (and therefore the legacy MP1 P1 logical channel).

| Service Mode | Logical Channel | Mod-ulation | Info Bit Rate (kbps) | Simulated Performance (AWGN, dB rel. to MP1 P1) | Test Route 1 (%) | Test Route 2 (%) | Test Route 3 (%) | Test Route 4 (%) | Test Route 5 (%) | Test Route 6 (%) | Test Route 7 (%) | Test Route 8 (%) | Test Route 9 (%) |
|---|---|---|---|---|---|---|---|---|---|---|---|---|---|
| MP6 | P2 | QPSK | 49 | 0 | 86 | 77 | 78 | 67 | 96 | 51 | 76 | 68 | 67 |
| | P1 | QPSK | 50 | +2.5 | 88 | 83 | 92 | 81 | 99 | 66 | 91 | 79 | 77 |
| Difference (% of test route length) | | | | | +2 | +6 | +14 | +14 | +3 | +15 | +15 | +11 | +10 |

TABLE 4: DAA COMPARISON OF MP6 P1 WITH MP6 P2 (MP1 P1 EQUIVALENT).

## MP6OV

MP6OV is a layered service mode that is backward compatible with MP6. The base layer uses MP6, and the overlay uses non-backward-compatible DSB1 (QPSK), forming a 16-QAM waveform. The addition of the overlay to MP6 introduces noise on the P1 and P2 base channels that is predicted to degrade AWGN performance by 2.3 dB and 3.5 dB, respectively. The overlay channel (POV) is expected to be more fragile than the base channels.

Tests were performed using an MP6OV broadcast to measure the degradation caused by an overlay channel in the field. The MP6OV results were compared to MP6 test results collected in an earlier run.

Although field test results indeed indicate a degradation to the P1 and P2 logical channels due to the presence of the overlay, the effects were limited on most test routes, as shown by comparing Figure 14 with Figure 15, and Figure 13 with Figure 16, and as summarized in Table 5. As expected, the impact of the overlay on the P2 channel was somewhat more pronounced. Despite the degradation, this result proves the viability of layered service mode MP6OV as a backward-compatible option to significantly enhance throughput.

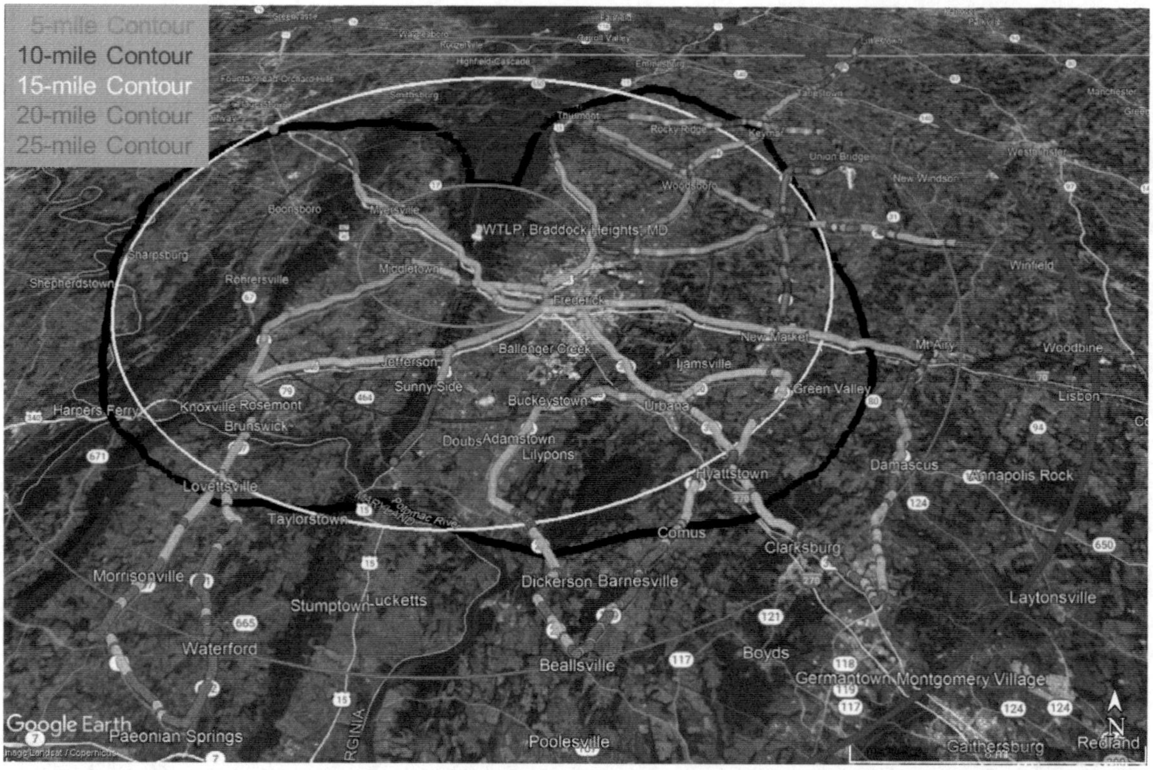


FIGURE 15: AUDIO OUTPUT STATE OF MP6OV P1.

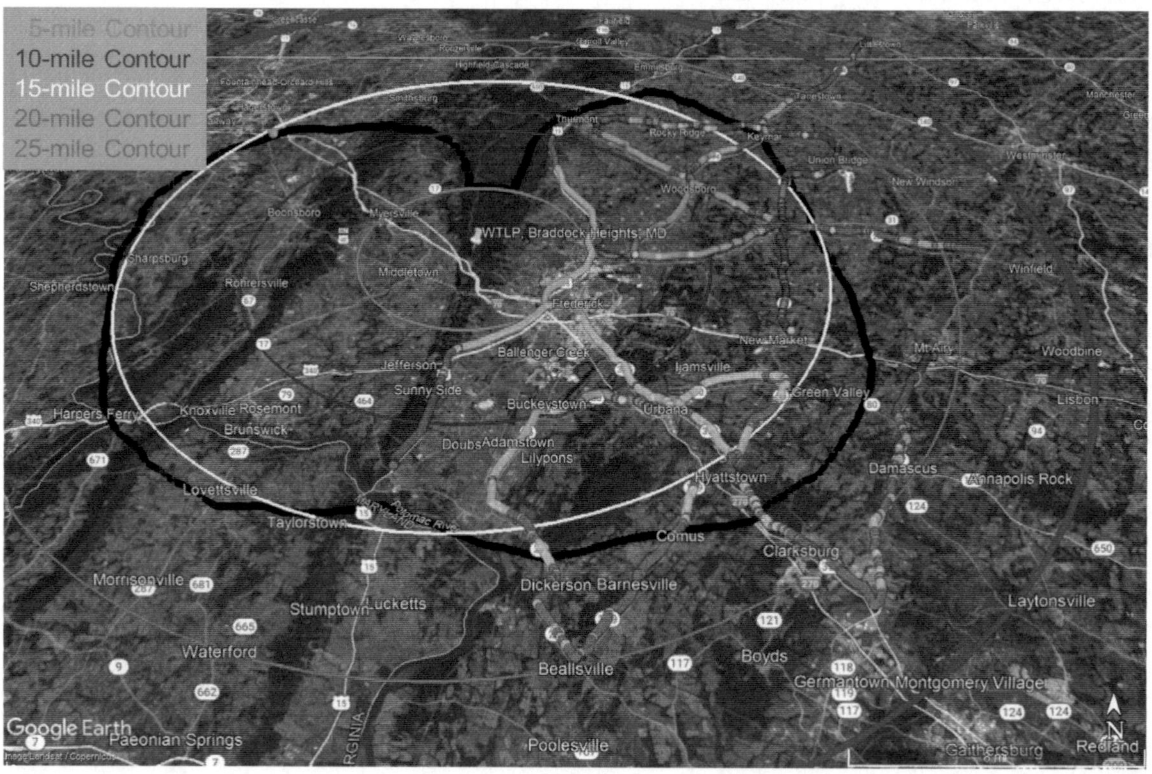


FIGURE 16: AUDIO OUTPUT STATE OF MP6OV P2.

Although the POV overlay channel provides an additional 114 kbps of digital capacity without seriously degrading the base channels, it is itself relatively fragile, as the predicted 6.7-dB AWGN degradation relative to MP6 P1 would suggest. However, on some test routes (*e.g.*, 1 and 5), the degradation to the POV logical channel was relatively minor, as shown in Figure 17 and Table 5. Even on routes where the availability of POV digital audio is significantly truncated, a substantial portion of the coverage area (and population) may still be served. For example, Figure 17 shows that, although digital audio is available on only about one-third of test route 3, one might still expect solid digital coverage as far as 10 miles to the east of the station. In this case, much of the greater Frederick area would have access to 215 kbps of digital capacity.

| Service Mode | Logical Channel | Mod-ulation | Info Bit Rate (kbps) | Simulated Performance (AWGN, dB rel. to MP1 P1) | Test Route 1 (%) | Test Route 2 (%) | Test Route 3 (%) | Test Route 4 (%) | Test Route 5 (%) | Test Route 6 (%) | Test Route 7 (%) | Test Route 8 (%) | Test Route 9 (%) |
|---|---|---|---|---|---|---|---|---|---|---|---|---|---|
| MP6 | P1 | QPSK | 50 | +2.5 | 88 | 83 | 92 | 81 | 99 | 66 | 91 | 79 | 77 |
| | P2 | QPSK | 49 | 0 | 86 | 77 | 78 | 67 | 96 | 51 | 76 | 68 | 67 |
| MP6OV (16QAM) | P1 | QPSK | 50 | 0.2 | 86 | 77 | 75 | 72 | 99 | 49 | 83 | 71 | 73 |
| | P2 | QPSK | 49 | -3.5 | **NA** | 67 | 52 | 52 | **NA** | **NA** | 61 | 58 | 49 |
| | POV | QPSK | 114 | -4.2 | 76 | 61 | 33 | 37 | 85 | 9 | **NA** | **NA** | 22 |
| **Difference (% of test route length): MP6OV P1 vs. MP6 P1** | | | | | -2 | -6 | -17 | -9 | **0** | -17 | -8 | -8 | -4 |
| **Difference (% of test route length): MP6OV P2 vs. MP6 P2** | | | | | **NA** | -10 | -26 | -15 | **NA** | **NA** | -15 | -10 | -18 |
| **Difference (% of test route length): MP6OV POV vs. MP6 P1** | | | | | -12 | -22 | -59 | -44 | -14 | -57 | **NA** | **NA** | -55 |

TABLE 5: DAA COMPARISON OF MP6OV P1 AND MP6OV POV WITH MP6 P1, AND MP6OV P2 WITH MP6 P2.

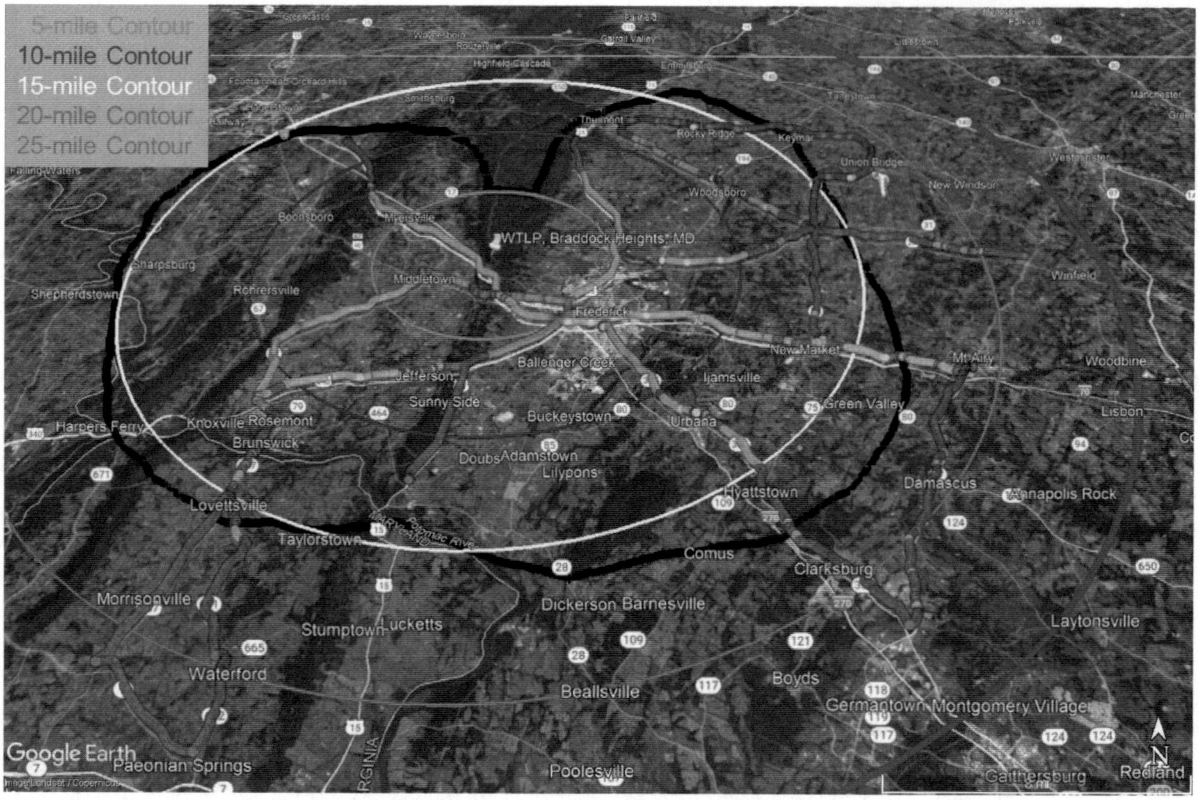


FIGURE 17: AUDIO OUTPUT STATE OF MP6OV POV.

## DSB1

Advanced service mode DSB1 provides a non-backward-compatible (NBC) alternative to legacy service modes for broadcasting new data services or for international applications. Eventually, with sufficient receiver penetration, it could also be used for traditional North American broadcasts. Since DSB1 uses 16-QAM, it provides 229 kbps of digital capacity, an increase of 131 kbps over legacy service mode MP1. But the use of QAM to achieve higher data throughput causes a concomitant reduction in robustness.

Field tests were executed using a DSB1 broadcast to measure P1 digital audio coverage. Results were then compared to MP1X P1 coverage measured in an earlier run. Simulations predict a 2.5-dB degradation in AWGN for DSB1 P1 versus MP1 P1. This degradation manifests itself in the field as a reduction in digital coverage in areas limited by terrain and distance from the transmit antenna, as can be seen when comparing Figure 11 with Figure 18.

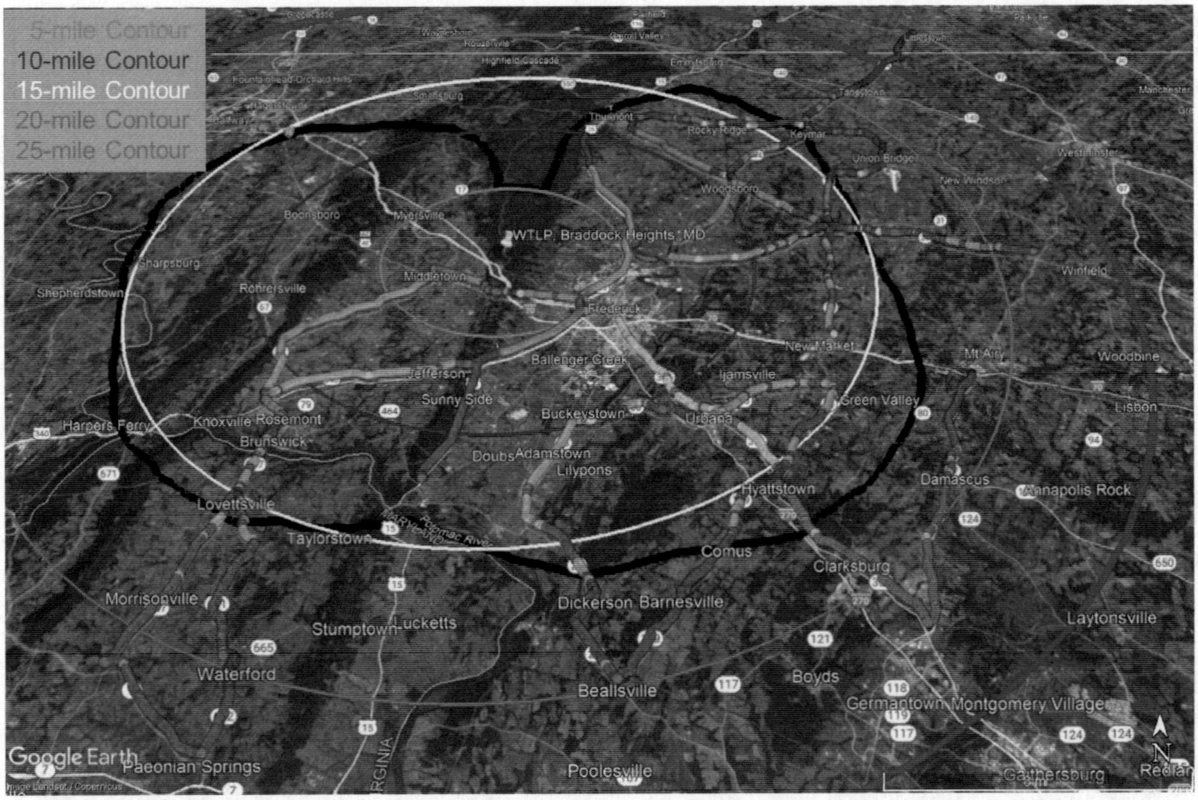


FIGURE 18: AUDIO OUTPUT STATE OF DSB1 P1.

A DAA comparison of DSB1 P1 with MP1X P1 (equivalent to MP1 P1) is shown in Table 6. Although the 16-QAM DSB1 P1 logical channel has consistently lower availability than MP1 P1, trading for the additional capacity may make sense for NBC broadcast data applications since data robustness is often not as critical as audio coverage (due to repeat strategies).

| Service Mode | Logical Channel | Mod-ulation | Info Bit Rate (kbps) | Simulated Performance (AWGN, dB rel. to MP1 P1) | Test Route 1 (%) | Test Route 2 (%) | Test Route 3 (%) | Test Route 4 (%) | Test Route 5 (%) | Test Route 6 (%) | Test Route 7 (%) | Test Route 8 (%) | Test Route 9 (%) |
|---|---|---|---|---|---|---|---|---|---|---|---|---|---|
| MP1X | P1 | QPSK | 98 | 0 | 84 | 69 | 63 | 56 | 95 | NA | 64 | 59 | 63 |
| DSB1 | P1 | 16-QAM | 229 | -2.5 | NA | 63 | 51 | 36 | 91 | 22 | 45 | 44 | 45 |
| **Difference (% of test route length)** | | | | | NA | -6 | -12 | -20 | -4 | NA | -19 | -15 | -18 |

TABLE 6: DAA COMPARISON OF DSB1 P1 WITH MP1X P1 (MP1 P1 EQUIVALENT).

## DSB1OV

DSB1OV is a layered service mode that is not backward compatible with legacy service modes. The base layer uses DSB1 (16-QAM), and the overlay uses DSB1 (QPSK), forming a 64-QAM waveform. The addition of the overlay to DSB1 introduces noise on the P1 base channel that is expected to degrade robustness in AWGN by about 1 dB. The overlay channel (POV) is likely to be much more fragile, with a predicted AWGN degradation of 6.8 dB relative to DSB1OV P1.

Tests were executed using a DSB1 broadcast to measure baseline P1 field performance. The degradation to P1 caused by the overlay channel, along with POV performance, was measured in a different test run using a separate DSB1OV broadcast.

The field test results validated predicted performance, since only a slight degradation was observed on the P1 channel when the overlay was added. This is evident when comparing Figure 18 with Figure 19 and is summarized in Table 7. This degradation should be virtually imperceptible in practice.

As predicted, the coverage of the overlay channel was less robust, and more terrain-limited. However, a significant portion of the greater Frederick area could still receive 343 kbps of digital audio, with just 21 watts of digital ERP, as shown in Figure 20.

Despite its coverage limitations, these results prove that DSB1OV offers a viable means to significantly enhance throughput if backward compatibility were not necessary.

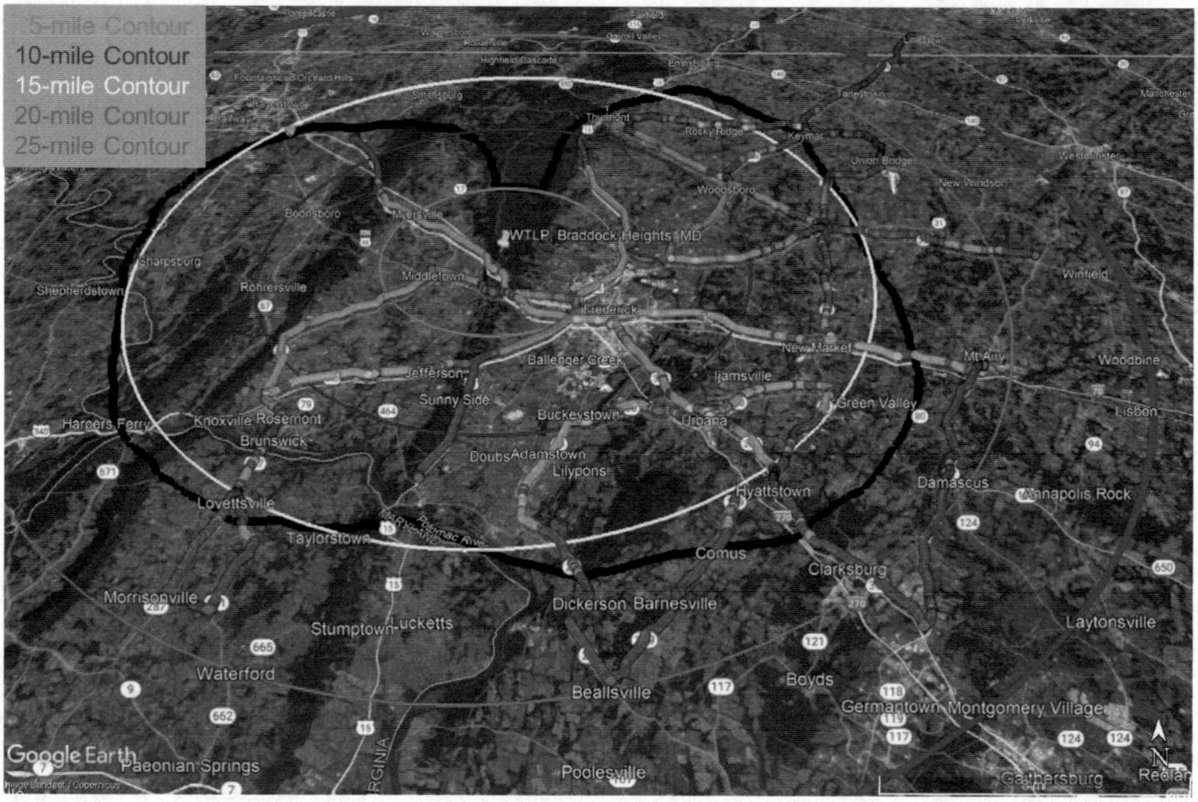


FIGURE 19: AUDIO OUTPUT STATE OF DSB1OV P1.

| Service Mode | Logical Channel | Mod-ulation | Info Bit Rate (kbps) | Simulated Performance (AWGN, dB rel. to MP1 P1) | Test Route 1 (%) | Test Route 2 (%) | Test Route 3 (%) | Test Route 4 (%) | Test Route 5 (%) | Test Route 6 (%) | Test Route 7 (%) | Test Route 8 (%) | Test Route 9 (%) |
|---|---|---|---|---|---|---|---|---|---|---|---|---|---|
| DSB1 | P1 | 16-QAM | 229 | -2.5 | NA | 63 | 51 | 36 | 91 | 22 | 45 | 44 | 45 |
| DSB1OV (64QAM) | P1 | 16-QAM | 229 | -3.5 | 75 | 63 | 51 | 36 | 85 | NA | 40 | 43 | 40 |
| | POV | QPSK | 114 | -10.3 | 40 | 57 | 24 | 18 | 75 | NA | 24 | 15 | 7 |
| Difference (% of test route length): DSB1OV P1 vs. DSB1 P1 | | | | | NA | 0 | 0 | 0 | -6 | NA | -5 | -1 | -5 |
| Difference (% of test route length): DSB1OV POV vs. DSB1 P1 | | | | | NA | -6 | -27 | -18 | -16 | NA | -21 | -29 | -38 |

TABLE 7: DAA COMPARISON OF DSB1OV P1 AND DSB1OV POV WITH DSB1 P1.

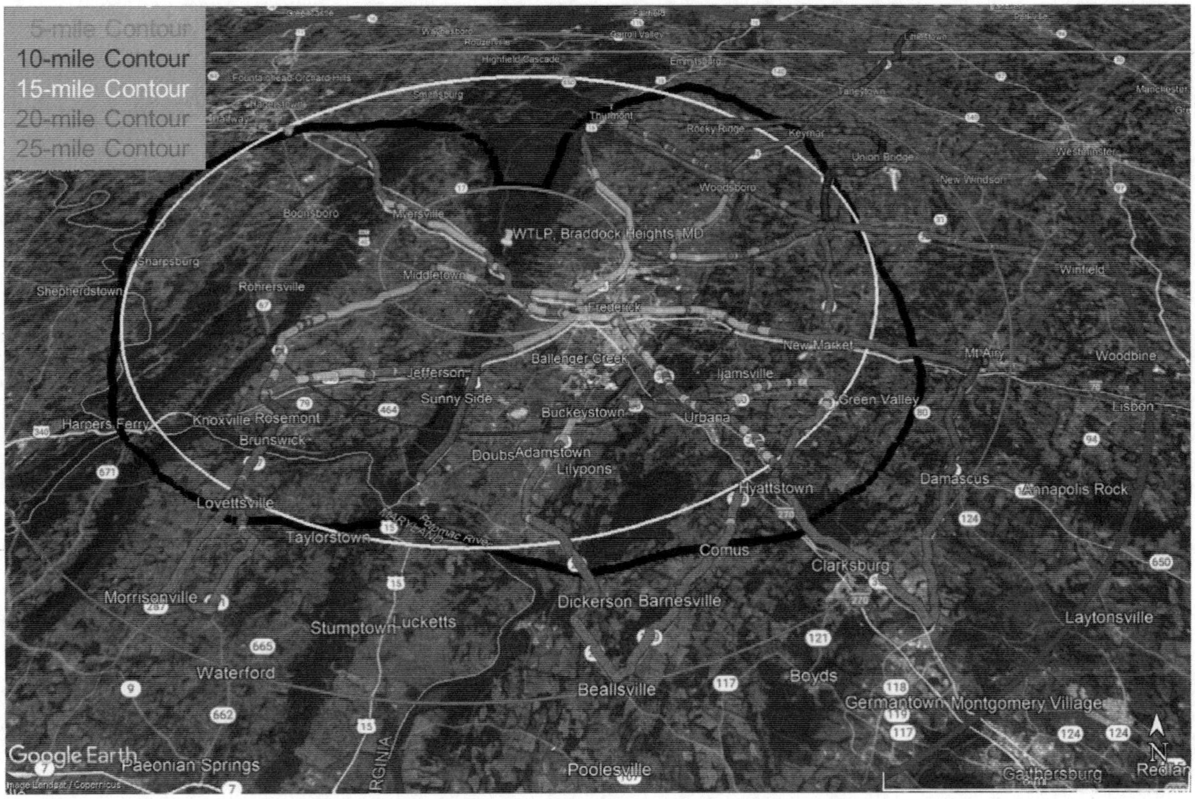


FIGURE 20: AUDIO OUTPUT STATE OF DSB1OV POV.

## MS5

Service mode MS5 is used to configure the secondary digital sidebands in the spectrum vacated by the analog host in all-digital waveforms. These secondary sidebands provide an additional 114 kbps of digital throughput. In the WTLP field tests, MS5 was broadcast with DSB1 configuring the primary sidebands. Test results were compared to MP1X P1 digital audio coverage measured in an earlier run.

The total power in the secondary sidebands was 5-dB below the total power in the DSB1 primary sidebands (and all other tested signals, including MP1X). At this secondary injection level, simulations predict a 2.2-dB degradation in AWGN for MS5 S1 versus MP1 P1. Furthermore, MRC was not enabled in the receiver for MS5, although it was enabled for all primary service modes.

Despite these power and processing disadvantages, robustness of the MS5 S1 logical channel was comparable to the legacy MP1 P1 channel, as may be seen by comparing Figure 11 with Figure 21 and inspecting Table 8. This is likely due to superior FEC coding on the S1 channel and the use of time and frequency diversity. Figure 21 shows that, even on worst-case test route 7, the S1 logical channel is available well beyond the Frederick city limits with just 7 watts secondary digital ERP.

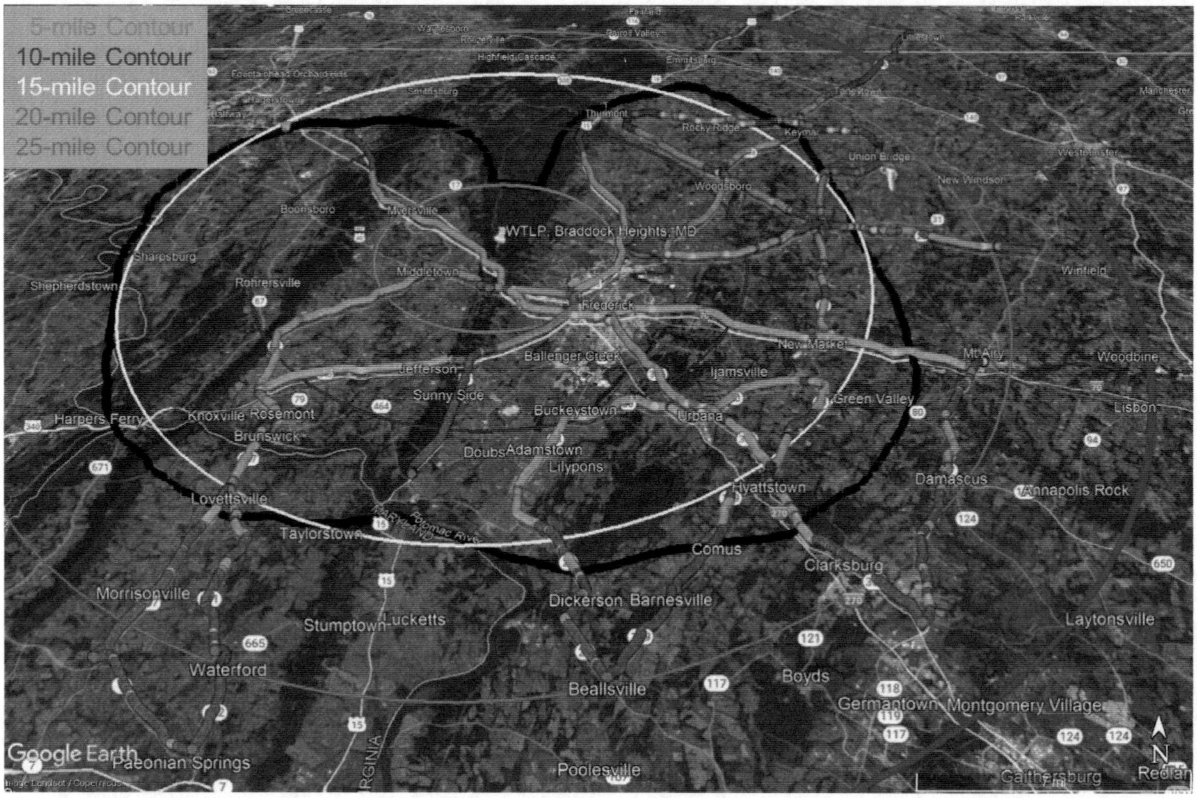


FIGURE 21: AUDIO OUTPUT STATE OF MS5 S1 (-5-DB SECONDARY INJECTION, NO MRC).

| Service Mode | Logical Channel | Mod-ulation | Info Bit Rate (kbps) | Simulated Performance (AWGN, dB rel. to MP1 P1) | Test Route 1 (%) | Test Route 2 (%) | Test Route 3 (%) | Test Route 4 (%) | Test Route 5 (%) | Test Route 6 (%) | Test Route 7 (%) | Test Route 8 (%) | Test Route 9 (%) |
|---|---|---|---|---|---|---|---|---|---|---|---|---|---|
| MP1X | P1 | QPSK | 98 | 0 | 84 | 69 | 63 | 56 | 95 | NA | 64 | 59 | 63 |
| MS5 (-5 dB) | S1 | QPSK | 114 | -2.2 | 85 | 65 | 66 | 59 | 96 | 32 | 55 | 59 | 62 |
| **Difference (% of test route length)** | | | | | +1 | -4 | +3 | +3 | +1 | NA | -9 | 0 | -1 |

TABLE 8: DAA COMPARISON OF MS5 S1 (-5-DB SECONDARY INJECTION, NO MRC) WITH MP1X P1 (MP1 P1 EQUIVALENT).

## Summary and Conclusions

The WTLP field tests met their primary objective, which was to successfully validate the predicted performance of advanced FM service modes. In addition, they demonstrated the ability of higher-order modulation techniques and all-digital secondary sidebands to deliver enhanced digital data capacity over a significant portion of a station's coverage area.

The following general conclusions might be extrapolated from these test observations:

- The relative robustness of advanced FM service modes in an automotive listening environment aligns with expectations established by system simulation.
- Significantly higher bit rates can be reliably delivered over a substantial portion of a station's coverage area. In these tests, WTLP transmitted up to 348 kbps of digital data.
- MP6 P1 robustness exceeds the robustness of all logical channels in both legacy and advanced service modes.
- 16-QAM, 64-QAM, and layered service modes offer feasible means to increase digital capacity.
- MP1X P4 (69 kbps) coverage should be largely indistinguishable from legacy MP1 P1 coverage.
- Trading robustness for capacity could make sense for NBC data applications where data robustness is not as critical as audio coverage.
- All-digital secondary services (114 kbps) with power levels set 5 dB below the primary sidebands and MRC disabled in the receiver provide robustness on par with MP1 P1. With just 7 watts digital ERP, digital audio could be reliably received well beyond the Frederick, MD city limits.
- In layered service modes, degradation to the base signal from the overlay is typically modest. It could be imperceptible to the listener in some cases.
- Overlay coverage may be truncated but is often solid: DSB1OV POV (114 kbps) provided more than 10 radial miles of continuous digital audio coverage on one test route, with just 21 watts of digital ERP.

## Reference

[1] National Radio Systems Committee, In-band/on-channel Digital Radio Broadcasting Standard, Doc. NRSC-5-E, January, 2023, https://www.nrscstandards.org/standards-and-guidelines/documents/standards/nrsc-5-e/nrsc-5-e.asp.

## Acknowledgements

The authors would like to thank Hubbard Broadcasting, Inc. for the use of WTLP, and acknowledge the individual contributions of Brian Kroeger, Gary Cavell, David Layer, Ashruf El-Dinary, Jeff Baird, Mike Raide, Denise Cammarata, Bill Snelling, Alex Davis, Joe Hartgrove, and Charles Whitehead.

# Appendix A – Service Mode Descriptions

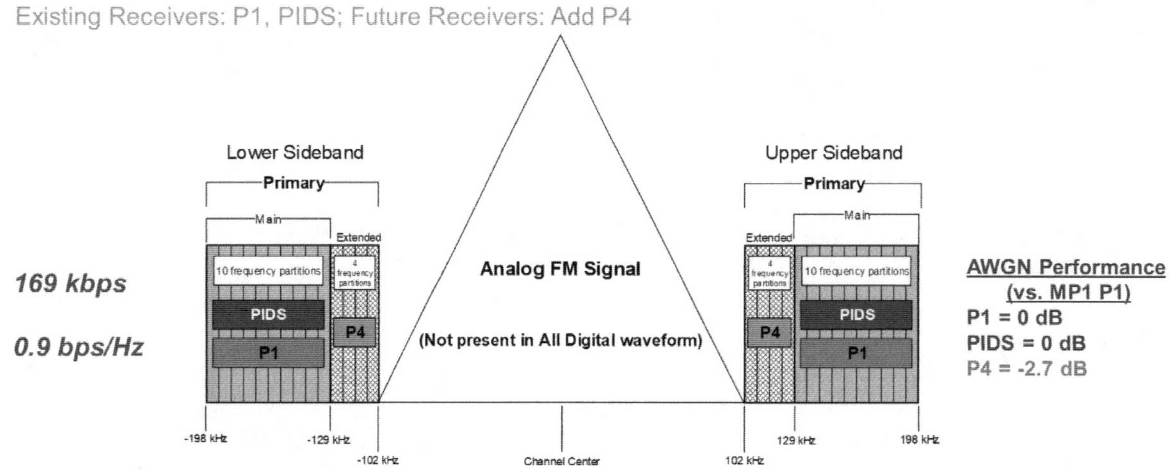


- Adds all four primary extended partitions to each sideband
- 16-QAM P4 = 69 kbps

FIGURE A-1: MP1X (BACKWARD COMPATIBLE WITH MP1, HYBRID ONLY).

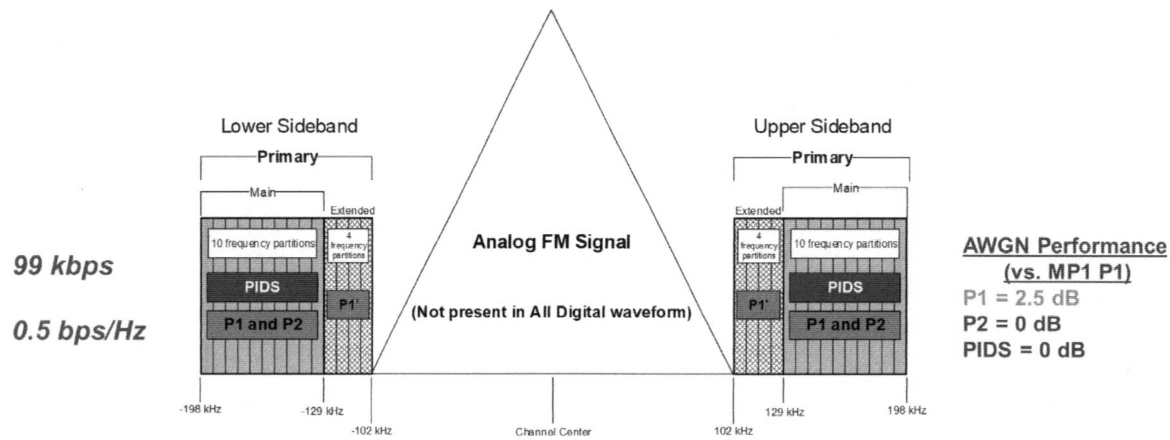


FIGURE A-2: STANDARD HYBRID/ALL-DIGITAL SERVICE MODE MP6.

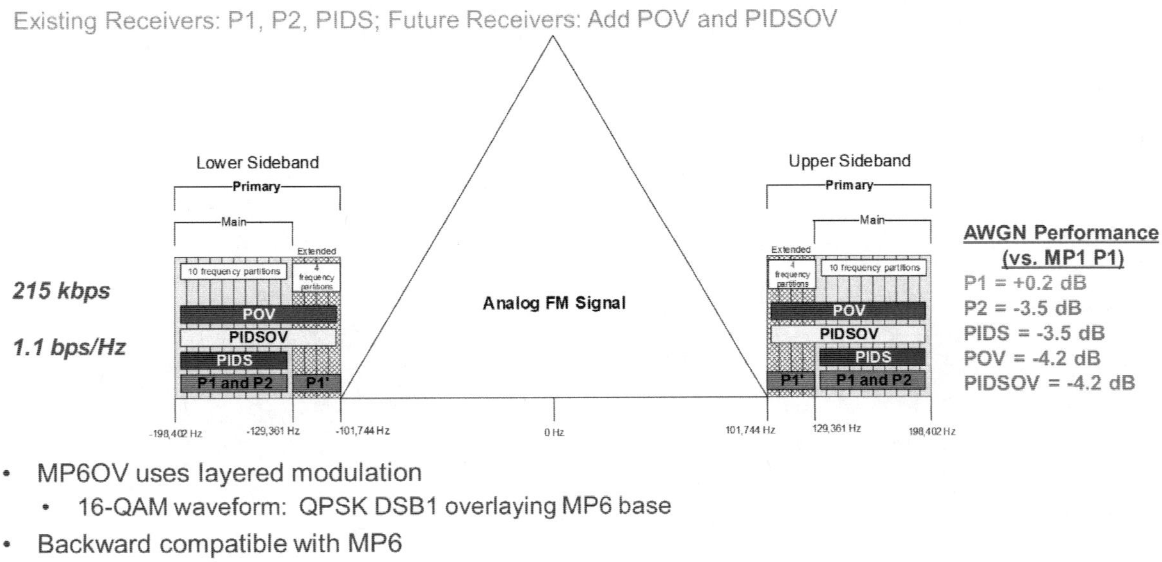


FIGURE A-3: MP6OV HYBRID (BACKWARD COMPATIBLE WITH MP6).

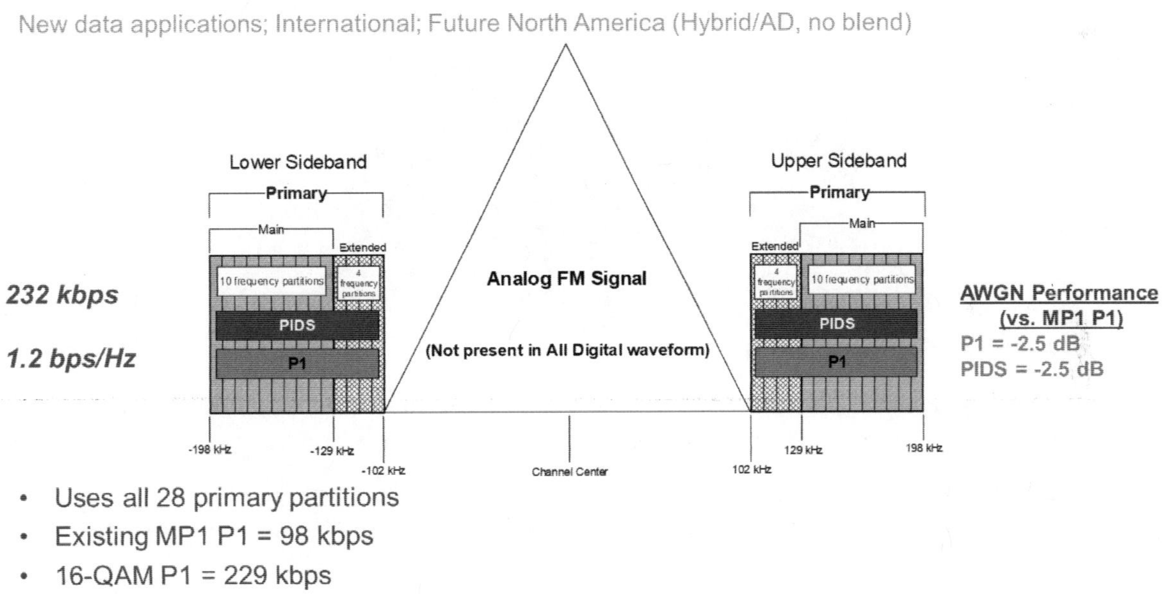


FIGURE A-4: DSB1 (NON-BACKWARD-COMPATIBLE).

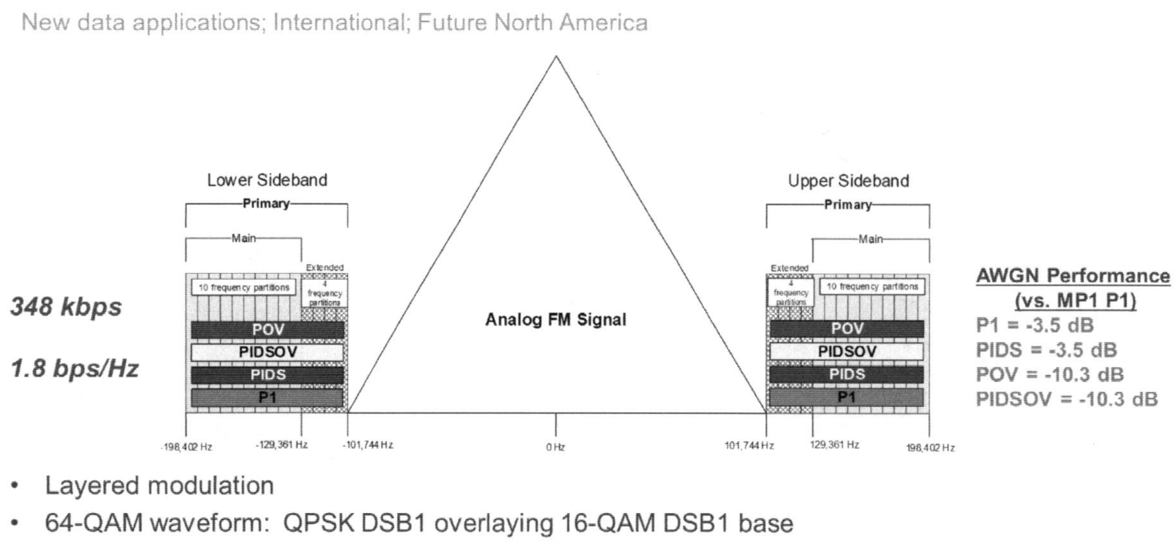


FIGURE A-5: DSB1OV (NON-BACKWARD COMPATIBLE).

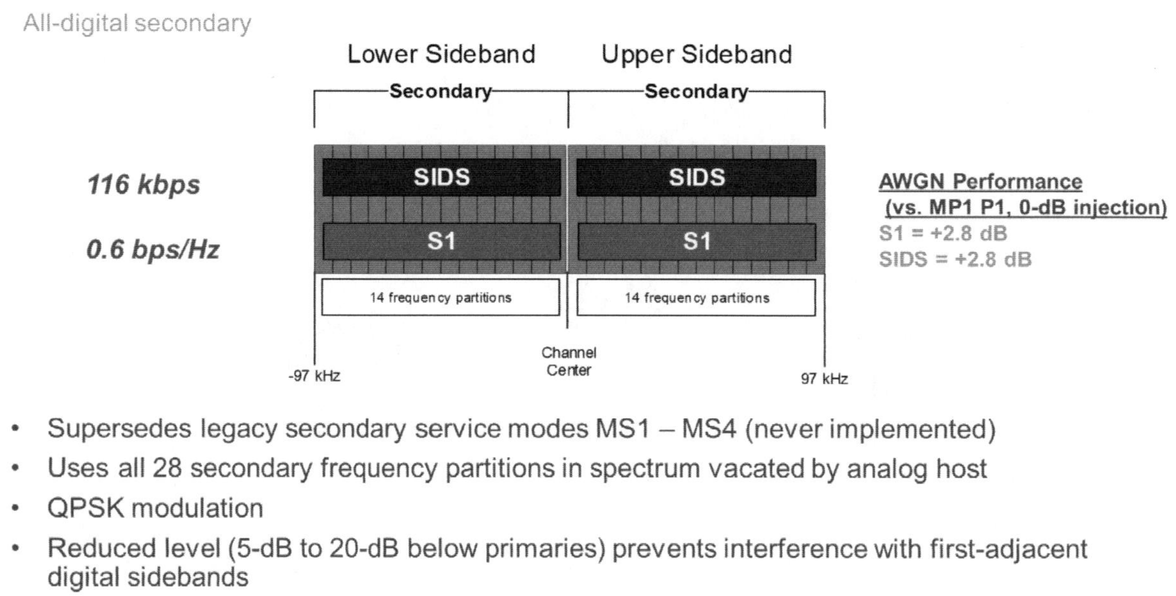


FIGURE A-6: SECONDARY SERVICE MODE MS5.

New data applications; International; Future North America

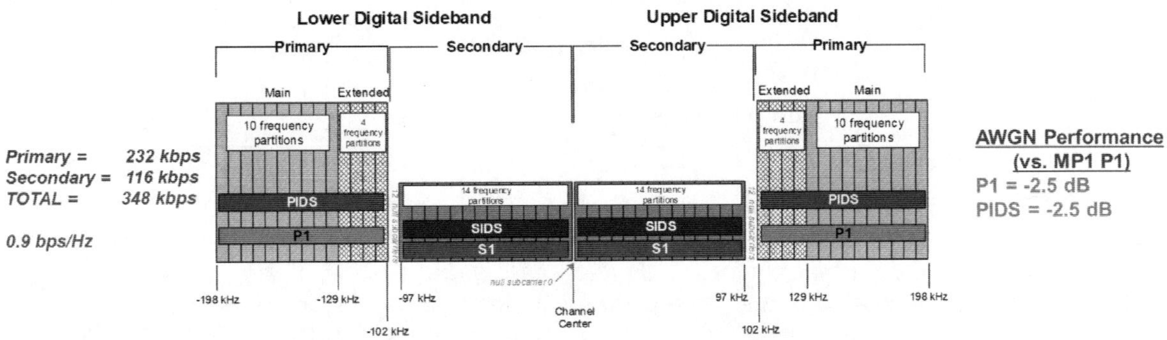


- Uses all 28 primary partitions and all 28 secondary partitions
- DSB1 is identical to MS5, except:
  - Upper/lower sidebands are swapped and located in primary sidebands
  - 16-QAM modulation

FIGURE A-7: DSB1 + MS5 (NON-BACKWARD COMPATIBLE).

# Audio Services over ATSC 3.0: A Proof of Concept

**Liam Power**
**ONE Media**
**Hunt Valley, Maryland, United States**
lpower@sbgtv.com

**Abstract** – This paper provides a proof-of-concept for delivering audio services using ATSC 3.0. It outlines the initial starting requirements for the development of the system. It then covers the determinations made at each step of the process to fulfill these goals: encoding, delivery layer, physical layer, and receiver. Real world results of the tests conducted in the lab and in the Baltimore, Maryland market are then discussed. Finally, next steps in development, as well as potential gaps in the standard to fill are suggested.

## Introduction and Summary

Much attention is given to the better picture and audio capabilities of ATSC 3.0's linear audio-video services, and rightly so, as it provides a significant enhancement over the previous standard. However, there are other tools in ATSC 3.0 that enable broadcasters to bring new value-added services to their viewers. This is in large part due to the broad flexibility with which it was designed. In this paper, an exploration is made that applies this flexibility to a specific goal: the delivery of audio services. The initial requirements laid out were to develop a method of audio service carriage that delivers multiple audio programs at equal or better quality, tuning time, and receivability than analog FM radio, while using as little spectrum as possible, using ATSC 3.0. In particular, the goal was for these multiple audio programs to occupy less spectrum than a single analog FM radio channel.

In this process, several limitations with existing practices were discovered, which forced a look at the core capabilities of ATSC 3.0. Over the course of this paper, the decision-making process will be outlined for each component of the service, utilizing many aspects of the standard.

- **Section 1** presents the overall system architecture of the chosen design.
- **Section 2** covers the encoding choices made to provide the best efficiency with the most client support.
- **Section 3** discusses the various delivery layer options and the benefits and downsides of each.
- **Section 4** examines the approach to the physical layer design, balancing the tradeoffs between spectrum usage and receivability, especially in a mobile environment.
- **Section 5** outlines the real-world drive testing results as well as a comparison to other services in the market.
- **Section 6** looks at some unique receiver features that were required to support this and examines some solutions currently on the market.
- **Section 7** outlines some potential future developments with these services. It also discusses some modifications to the ATSC 3.0 specification that would allow for better implementation of audio services going forward, ensuring consumer receivers can efficiently process these.

## Section 1: PoC Design Overview

Before getting into the fine details in later sections, this section will explain the chosen design for the proof-of-concept (PoC) stage of this project.

On the transmission side, the system does not use the traditional audio-only services design in the standard, for reasons that will be outlined later in this paper. Instead, services are distributed using ProMPEG RTP [1], which provides MPEG transport stream (TS) encapsulated in a real-time transport protocol (RTP) stream. This allows for forward error correction (FEC) to be utilized, while also avoiding the significant extra overhead that would be present in a pure MPEG TS. The encoder pulls the source material from an HTTP live streaming (HLS) feed of the audio source material being used (for the PoC, Stingray Radio services hosted on Stirr are the audio source), but there is nothing that would restrict it to this as a source. For example, tests have been conducted using an Icecast server hosted by FM radio station WTOP (Washington, DC, 103.5 MHz) as the origin instead. Once this is encoded, the encoder then sends out the RTP multicast to the Scheduler (see Figure 1). As there's not a specific major/minor, 239.255.major.201-215 were used as the destination IPs, per 6.1 of [2].

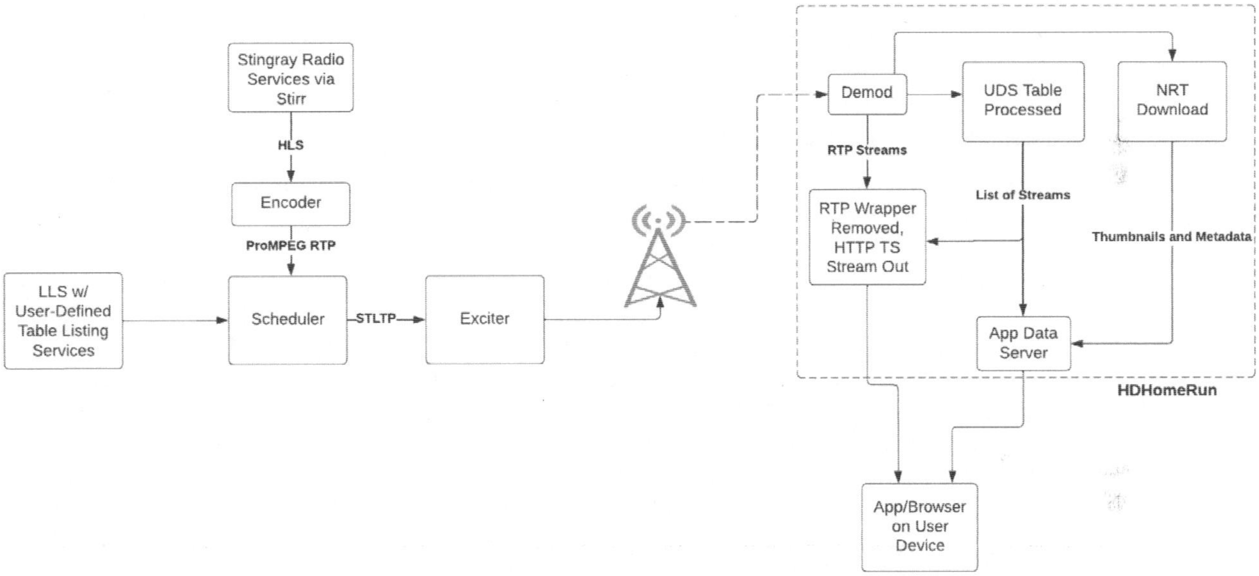


FIGURE 1: ABSTRACTED PROJECT ARCHITECTURE.

To identify these multicast streams to the ATSC 3.0 receiver dynamically, rather than hardcoding them, a schema was created for the UserDefined table per 6.8 of [2], an example of which can be seen in Appendix A. This gives the receiver a way to retrieve the service from the appropriate multicast stream, as well as to distinguish between multiple transmissions of the same service, for potential multiple frequency network (MFN) usage when crossing between markets. It functions very similar in manner to a cut down version of the service list table (SLT) in a traditional broadcast, as seen in Table 6.2 of [2].

All this is then bundled together in the transmission over the air. The physical characteristics, discussed later, are optimized for mobile reception to ensure continuous uninterrupted reception even at highway speeds of 70+ miles per hour.

On the receive side, an HDHomeRun Flex 4K using custom firmware courtesy of SiliconDust is utilized. The firmware allows it to process and list services in the channel lineup based on the info in the UserDefined table. Figure 1 provides a high-level view of this process, where once the streams have been determined using the table, the HDHomeRun then extracts the MPEG TS stream from the RTP stream and supplies that to the client device via HTTP. Simultaneously, it would pull down data being sent via non-real time (NRT) transport, containing supplementary information such as thumbnails and song metadata that the client device can utilize. It also would supply the receiver with the information to host a web server that allows utilizing the app interface in the browser, in addition to the native application on the client device.

When the user is connected to the same network as the HDHomeRun, for example via in-car Wi-Fi, they can then navigate to the hosted web page, or open the native app installed on their device. This then extracts the configuration from the local server, avoiding any need for an internet connection, and uses it to populate the channel listing. The user can then view audio services by selecting them, at which point the MPEG TS supplied by the HDHomeRun begins playing. Linear audio/video services are supplied in the normal manner for a consumer HDHomeRun, though they require adequate receive conditions to play, as the higher bitrate needs make it difficult to place them in a similarly receivable PLP to the audio services.

All this comes together to provide a seamless result to the user. From their perspective, they can drive all over the TV market and obtain mobile reception, selecting any audio service at will with a minimal "tuning time" between each service, as all virtual services are on the same physical channel.

## Section 2: Encoding Choices

One of the earliest considerations was how best to handle the encoding of these audio services. Several audio codecs were considered, namely AC-4, xHE-AAC, HE-AACv1, HE-AACv1, and AAC-LC.

The first assessment was made towards client support. While AC-4 has many benefits, as outlined in other publications around ATSC 3.0, it is the most lacking in client support. This is not as much of an issue when it comes to watching traditional television services on a TV, as ATSC 3.0-capable sets all support AC-4, but when utilizing a gateway device, such as the HDHomeRun, it presents a greater problem. Many TVs, mobile devices, and computers do not have built-in AC-4 support, which means that to decode AC-4, a native app must be used with appropriate licensing and software for decoding. SiliconDust resolves this issue rather elegantly by sending the audio to their servers for transcoding to a compatible codec, then back to the receiver device for playback to the user, all live and on the fly [3]. This allows for a truly device-agnostic playback solution. Unfortunately, because an internet connection cannot be guaranteed in the automotive receive environment, all decoding would have to be done locally.

At the time of the project planning, xHE-AAC was missing client support on Windows, but was otherwise supported in Android, iOS, and macOS. However, since that time, Fraunhofer IIS has announced support for xHE-AAC on Windows 11[4]. HE-AACv2, HE-AACv1, and AAC-LC all have broad support, and indeed are included in a great many standards.

The other primary consideration was bitrate efficiency. After narrowing down the possible codecs, several in-house listening tests were conducted, in addition to examining results from published MUSHRA tests of the various options.[1] Over the course of this testing, it was found that HE-AACv2 achieved the quality standard the project had set for stereo music at approximately 32 kbps, while HE-AACv1 required roughly 48 kbps, and AAC-LC required roughly 64 kbps. AC-4 was found to perform slightly better than HE-AACv1 at 48 kbps for this type of low-bitrate application, but due to encoder restrictions, was unable to be tested at bitrates below 48 kbps. xHE-AAC was able to achieve the

[1] Multiple Stimuli with Hidden Reference and Anchor (MUSHRA) is a methodology for conducting a codec listening test to evaluate the perceived quality.

requirements at 24 kbps. While xHE-AAC performed the best, HE-AACv2 was chosen for the, at the time, device support advantage in exchange for a slightly higher bitrate.

Lastly, one note on a secondary benefit to utilizing xHE-AAC from a feature set perspective. xHE-AAC is designed with both spoken word and music in mind, which is a major divergence from historical trends, where codecs tended to optimize for one or the other when operating in a highly efficient environment. This allows for a single unified codec to satisfy both use cases. While the demonstrated PoC in Las Vegas, Nevada (at the 2023 CES) was conducted using music services for licensing reasons, internal testing with news-talk radio station WTOP's feed backed up Fraunhofer's claims, allowing for even 8 kbps mono speech audio to sound adequate. Upping the bitrate to 14 kbps resulted in what was subjectively described by the evaluation audience as "good" audio in an ad-hoc, non-MUSHRA conformant listening session.

## Section 3: Delivery Layer

Once the codec had been settled on, the conversation turned to the transport method for the audio. Initially, the assumption had been that the services would be delivered using the audio-only service category in ATSC 3.0 described in 3.4 of [2] with the standard real-time object delivery over unidirectional transport (ROUTE) or MPEG media transport (MMT) method. However, this was unexpectedly found to present significant overhead issues, so other options were explored.

Initial testing with a 48 kbps HE-AACv2 stream resulted in significant overhead across all packager options, with scheduler input bitrates ranging from 100-200 kbps above the theoretical media bitrate, thanks to the additional signaling, transport, and protocol needs. On a 3-5 Mbps video service, as is commonly deployed in markets today, this represents minimal overhead, at about 3%, but when running on a theoretical 48 kbps service, this is 200% to 400% of overhead. Such a rate would more than wipe out any gains from codec efficiency, and so other options had to be explored.

One interesting item is the wide variance in bitrates across the three packagers tested: Digicap's Digicaster-M, Enensys's MediaCast, and Triveni's Guidebuilder. One packager operated at nearly 100 kbps less overhead than the other two tested, encoder and scheduler being held equal. In further testing, a significant portion, though not all, of this was due to variation in the default service layer signaling (SLS) repetition rates, all of which fall within the boundaries set by 4.10 of [5]. Simply reducing the SLS repetition rate would help reduce bitrate, but at the cost of tuning time, which was one of the key requirements. As a result, a different delivery solution was required.

Several alternatives were considered, keeping in mind the unidirectional nature of broadcast:

- **QUIC Multicast [6]:** BBC R&D had published some work [12] on integrating dynamic adaptive streaming over HTTP (DASH) with QUIC using a multicast extension to distribute content more efficiently via over-the-top (OTT). Unfortunately, this was constrained by two factors: the unlikeliness of a full implementation in the single quarter timeline allocated to this project, and initial findings of higher overhead than DASH via ROUTE.
- **UFTP [7]:** This is used in some cases to distribute files via one way internet protocol (IP) satellite connections. Importantly for this project, it also does so with a relatively low overhead, at around 10%. However, as segment size decreases, to minimize the impact of loss and reduce tune time, overhead increases due to the increased number of files per second, so this was also ruled out early on.
- **MPEG TS:** Due to the simplicity of implementation, particularly on existing receivers, MPEG TS was next explored. While this worked very reliably, it ran into overhead issues similar to the ones with normal ATSC 3.0 methods, ending up around 150 kbps. This is in large part due to the inability to evenly divide a standard IP packet into 188-byte pieces, as well as the need for stuffing bytes.

- **Muxed MPEG TS:** Given the previous issues, the obvious next option was to multiplex the TS. This resulted in a massive drop in overhead, bringing it to roughly 60 kbps when muxed with 20 streams. While this was an excellent gain in efficiency, it brought about its own challenges, as not all clients process muxed TS well. The other disadvantage was the fewer the streams, the worse the overhead.
- **RTP:** Given its versatility, real time transport protocol (RTP) was another obvious candidate. After all, it underpins even ATSC 3.0. For this, the choice was made to drop the target bitrate to 32 kbps. As this was using full packets, the overhead on each was theoretically 3%, and that was backed up by real-world testing. While full packets meant more tuning delay, it was not significant by any means, as the maximum wait time would be about a third of a second at the bitrate in use. The downside, however, was inconsistent compatibility of clients unless a session description protocol (SDP) file was provided.
- **Pro-MPEG RTP [1]:** This fixed the SDP problem, as it's effectively TS bundled within RTP, so clients handle it just fine. It also did so without an excessive increase in bitrate, at a total of 45 kbps, outperforming even the muxed TS, thanks to the RTP encapsulation avoiding some of the limitations of raw MPEG TS, as a packet can be assembled from fragments efficiently spread in RTP. As a bonus, it allowed for the integration of FEC, which added another 9 kbps.

As a result, Pro-MPEG RTP ended up being the protocol of choice. This would also have a benefit later when it came to the receiver-to-client delivery method, as the stream delivered audio already in MPEG TS, for an easy transfer to a unicast HTTP "last mile."

This is one of the major benefits of ATSC 3.0: the ability to inject regular user datagram protocol (UDP) multicast streams at the scheduler stage. This has already been used by a variety of groups to deliver educational data, public safety data, digital signage, and enhanced GPS, to name a few. It ensures that anything at the delivery layer not thought of in the specification can easily be added for custom solutions like the one described in this paper. Essentially, ATSC 3.0 becomes a unidirectional IP pipe able to be utilized just like it was part of a hardwired network, as the entire RF component can be abstracted away between the scheduler and receiver. The possibilities of this for data delivery are nigh on endless, and well worth exploring.

The downside, however, compared to the audio-only ATSC 3.0 linear service, is the loss of standardized signaling handled by every compatible receiver, as when a multicast is sent to the scheduler directly, the packager is not aware of it, and thus does not list it in the SLT or generate an SLS. Fortunately, ATSC 3.0 provides a table option that handles this precise situation: the UserDefined table, found in 6.8 of [2] and reproduced in Figure 2.

> **6.8 UserDefined**
>
> LLS_table_id 0xFF is available for user-defined usage. This table shall be an XML document that is defined by any user of this Standard and shall have at least one namespace not defined by ATSC.

FIGURE 2: THE FULL TEXT OF THE USERDEFINED SECTION OF A/331.

Table 0xFF allows for the addition of additional signaling to the low-level signaling (LLS) as needed. This provides a way to easily distribute and dynamically update information to a receiver without needing to hardcode non-standard multicast addresses into the receiver. In the case of this project, it was used to distribute information similar to what would be listed in the SLT. An example can be seen in Appendix A, and the reasoning for each element and attribute is explained below:

- **OMLRadio:** This tells the receiver that anything within this element will be related to the audio services.
    - **name:** This provides a friendly name to help with debugging.

- **rsrv:** This denotes an individual service element.
  - **name:** Much like the short service name in the SLT, this provides the receiver with a name to display to the user when listing the service in the lineup.
  - **destIP:** This provides the multicast destination IP, corresponding to one described in the link mapping table (LMT).
  - **destPort:** This provides the multicast destination port, corresponding to one described in the LMT.
  - **mktid:** This provides a globally unique ID for the service on the specific transmitter. This is currently composed by combining the broadcast stream ID (BSID) with the last octet of the IP. This is used to distinguish between transmissions when receiving services from two or more RF channels.
  - **srvid:** Unlike mktid, which is globally unique to the transmission, this presents an ID that is shared across all transmissions that utilize the same media source. In combination with mktid, this allows the receiver to potentially transfer from one transmission to the next as the user travels through different markets. As reception quality begins to degrade from one transmitter, the receiver would be able to locate another transmission with a different mktid but the same srvid and attempt to switch to it.

## Section 4: Physical Layer

Much like the scheduler injection and UserDefined table, the physical layer options are an example of just how flexible the ATSC 3.0 standard can be. There are enough options to allow fine tuning the transmission to almost any use case, and broadcasters already take full advantage of this for all manner of receive environment and payload combinations, resulting in a healthy variety of physical layer pipe (PLP) and subframe combinations across the country. Beyond ensuring the intended receiver will be able to successfully process the transmission, it also allows for a far more efficient transmission, as multiple use cases can be covered by a single RF channel, rather than needing to spread across multiple channels just to handle a different reception situation.

There are two primary groupings to allow tweaking of the physical configuration for the targeted receivability vs bitrate intersection for individual services: subframe and PLP. At the subframe level, deployments so far commonly adjust the guard interval, scattered pilot pattern, pilot boost, and fast Fourier transform (FFT) size. At the PLP level, modulation and code rate are the two primary levers. While others can be tweaked if needed, internal deployments focus on the above settings.

For this project, the spectrum allocation was 16.66% of the total ATSC 3.0 signal capacity (which is 6 MHz), and the bitrate required was 15 services at 45 kbps per for a total of 675 kbps. As will be seen later, the extra 10 kbps for the FEC was deemed unnecessary after field testing. The full 16.66% was also not needed, due to the efficiency at the encoding stage and delivery layer. This is what makes it so critical to plan for efficiency across the entire chain, rather than simply adjusting the physical layer to fit. Had the original service plan been maintained, it would have required approximately 3 Mbps, which would force severe compromises to receivability. All comparisons below are done relative to a baseline of 1.2 Mbps, the bitrate allocated to the PLP in the final scheme.[2]

One note: due to the channel plan in Baltimore, the $C_{red\_coeff}$ of the preamble and subframes is set to 3 to avoid interference due to WBFF's presence on physical channel 26, as this is hosted on WNUV, physical channel 25. This reduces the number of carriers by roughly 4.2%, resulting in a total occupied bandwidth of 5.589844 MHz, rather than the normal 5.832844 MHz. This therefore reduces the bitrates described in the preceding section when compared to a standard deployment.

---

[2] Note that the 1.2 Mbps baseline represents the final bitrate that results from the 16.66% spectrum allocation combined with the physical layer choices.

## Subframe Configuration

The first setting looked to is FFT size. FFT size dictates the available guard interval and scattered pilot pattern options, and so is the natural starting point. It is also the easiest, at three possible choices. 8k is used internally for mobile-targeted services, while 16k is used as an all-around option for generic service reception not targeted at mobile, but not exclusive to 256 QAM. 32k is currently utilized only for exclusively fixed targeted services. Holding all else equal, jumping to 16k would provide only 145 kbps, or 12% in available bitrate,[3] making 8k an acceptable tradeoff given the low bitrate needs, as automotive reception is a priority. Given that cars travel at relatively high rates of speed, it is key to ensure any given symbol has a reduced number of FFT carriers to offset the loss of any given symbol. Half the size means approximately twice the symbols, though also more loss to the guard interval as that's a flat number per symbol, for the same frame time, so a momentary interruption has less impact.

Once FFT size has been determined, guard interval (GI) is the next item to review. At 8k, the GI options range from 192 to 2048 samples, correlating to 27.78-296.30 µs. This one is interesting, as the initial theory internally had been to operate with a GI of 1536 samples as standard practice to avoid multipath issues. However, after a side conversation at an event put together by broadcast engineering consulting firm Meintel Sgrignoli and Wallace (MSW), where it was suggested this may be overcompensating, some field experimentation was conducted. The results lined up with this assertion, as the longest echo measured was still within the 512 sample range. These tests covered the following environments: highway driving, dense urban with tall buildings, indirect reception with no tower line-of-sight, and contour edge reception. One situation where it would be expected to require a greater guard interval would be in a single-frequency network (SFN) deployment, when greater echoes are more likely. This insight avoided a dramatic decrease in available bitrate, 318 kbps or 26.5%.[4]

The last subframe configuration made was scattered pilots and pilot boost. There is an excellent paper, [8], which provides a great reference for optimizing the pilot choices. It has both theoretical information and simulated results to guide these decisions. At 8k/512, the scattered pilot density options are 12_4, 12_2, 6_4, and 6_2. As can be seen in Figure 3, there is a notable gain from the first level of pilot boosting at 8k FFT, sufficiently offsetting the reduction in strength on the rest of the transmission. As can also be seen, there is not a dramatic benefit for 12_2 vs 6_2 density. Given that the higher density of 6_2 would cost 11%,[5] or 137 kbps, it was not deemed sufficiently beneficial, resulting in an optimal configuration of 3.20 dB pilot boost on a 12_2 scattered pilot pattern.

---

[3] 12% when compared to the final PLP bitrate of 1.2 Mbps.
[4] 26.5% when compared to the final PLP bitrate of 1.2 Mbps.
[5] 11% when compared to the final PLP bitrate of 1.2 Mbps.

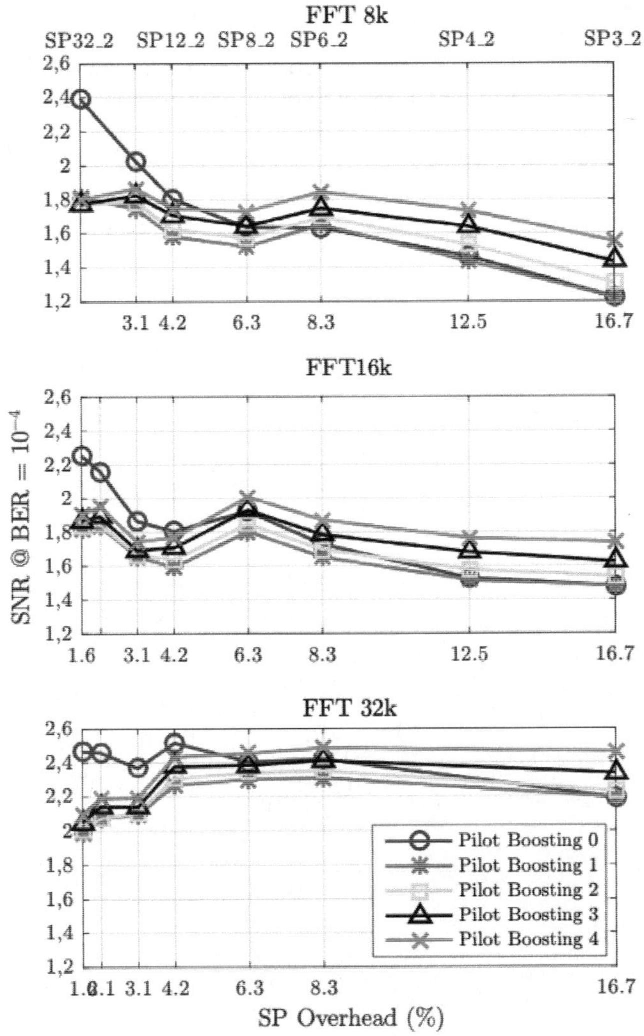


FIGURE 3: SP PATTERN AND BOOSTING IMPACT ON SNR PERFORMANCE FOR MOBILE RECEPTION AT 60 KM/H IN TIME DIVISION MULTIPLEX (TDM) SYSTEMS ($F_C$ = 600 MHZ). REPRODUCED FROM FIGURE 6 OF [8].

## PLP Configuration

While it is among the most impactful for reception, the PLP configuration is also one of the easier decisions to make, as the tradeoffs are very clear and broadly applicable. For signal constellation, there are four options commonly deployed in the field: QPSK, 16QAM, 64QAM, and 256QAM. Code rate varies from 2/15 to 13/15, with mandatory combinations varying depending on constellation and code length. At this point, it is generally a matter of determining the bitrate required for the service, then selecting the most receivable modulation and coding combination (modcod) that is able to supply that bitrate.

For the deployment to the WNUV transmitter, it was decided to leave significant room for future experimentation without necessitating a reconfiguration. This is what brought about the 1.2 Mbps bitrate number for the PLP containing the radio services, pre-hybrid time interleaver (HTI) configuration. For this, the mandatory option that provided the chosen bitrate with the best expected carrier-to-noise (C/N) ratio was QPSK 11/15, at 6.3 dB, per Annex B of [9]. In the truly optimized lab configuration, the chosen modcod would instead be QPSK 7/15, at 2.9 dB.

## Section 5: Real-world Performance

After all the decisions discussed in Section 4 have been made, the next step is to determine the expected field test performance by performing a projection of the anticipated reception area. Those results can be seen in Figure 4 for the Baltimore market (used in the field test described below), with transmissions originating from station WNUV (539 MHz, RF channel 25). For seamless playback, the locations in blue are best suited.

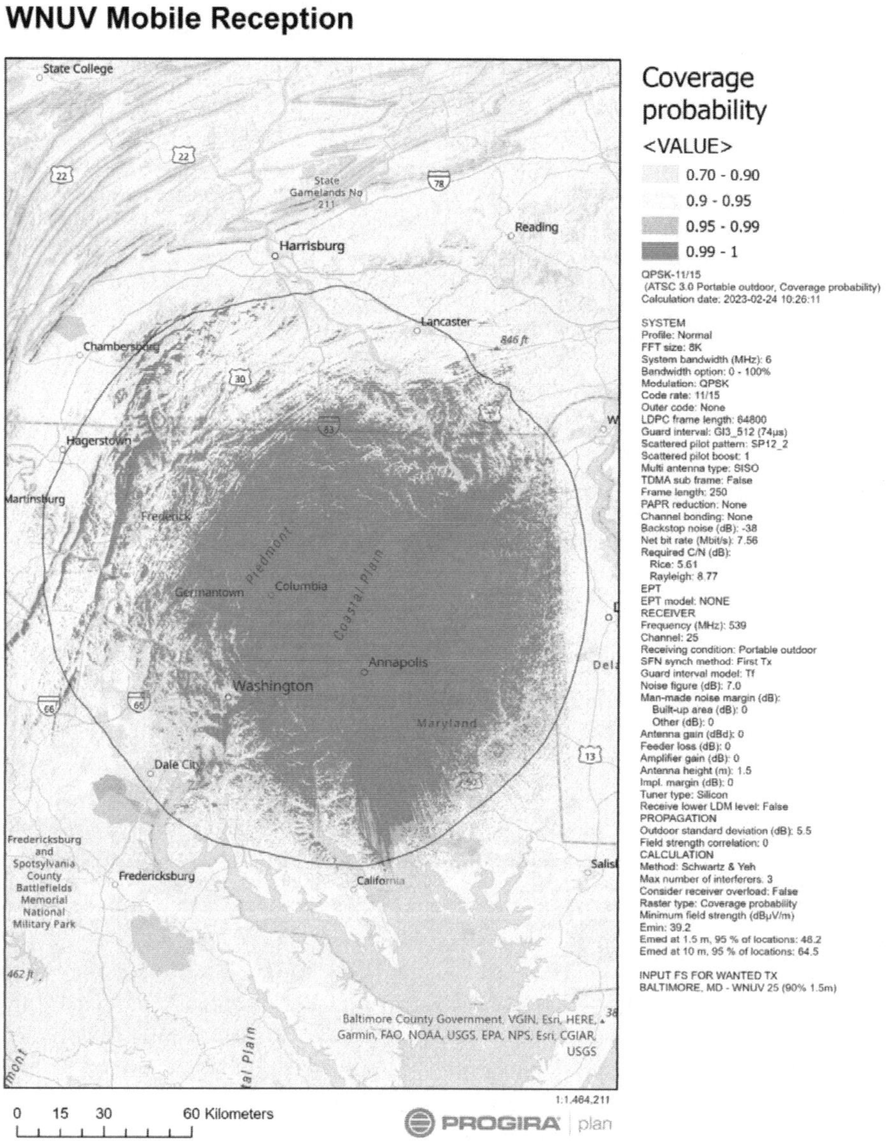


FIGURE 4: THE PROJECTED RECEPTION PROBABILITY OF THE BALTIMORE DESIGNATED MARKET AREA (DMA) FOR THE CHOSEN CONFIGURATION.

Drive test results are shown in Figure 5, including comparative results for analog FM radio stations WYPR and WBJC (discussed below). For WNUV, consistent reception without dropouts was achieved at highway speeds as far north as exit 10, going directly north on I-83, roughly 35 miles from the tower, as far south as Washington, DC going south on I-95, and as far east as the Delaware border going north on I-95. The latter two were used as stopping points because they represent east and west boundaries of the Baltimore DMA, rather than due to a loss of signal (all indicated by black-and-white stars on Figure 5). The reduced northern reception compared to the other two directions is primarily due to the steep peak along the Maryland-Pennsylvania border, which results in little to no line of sight after a few miles north.

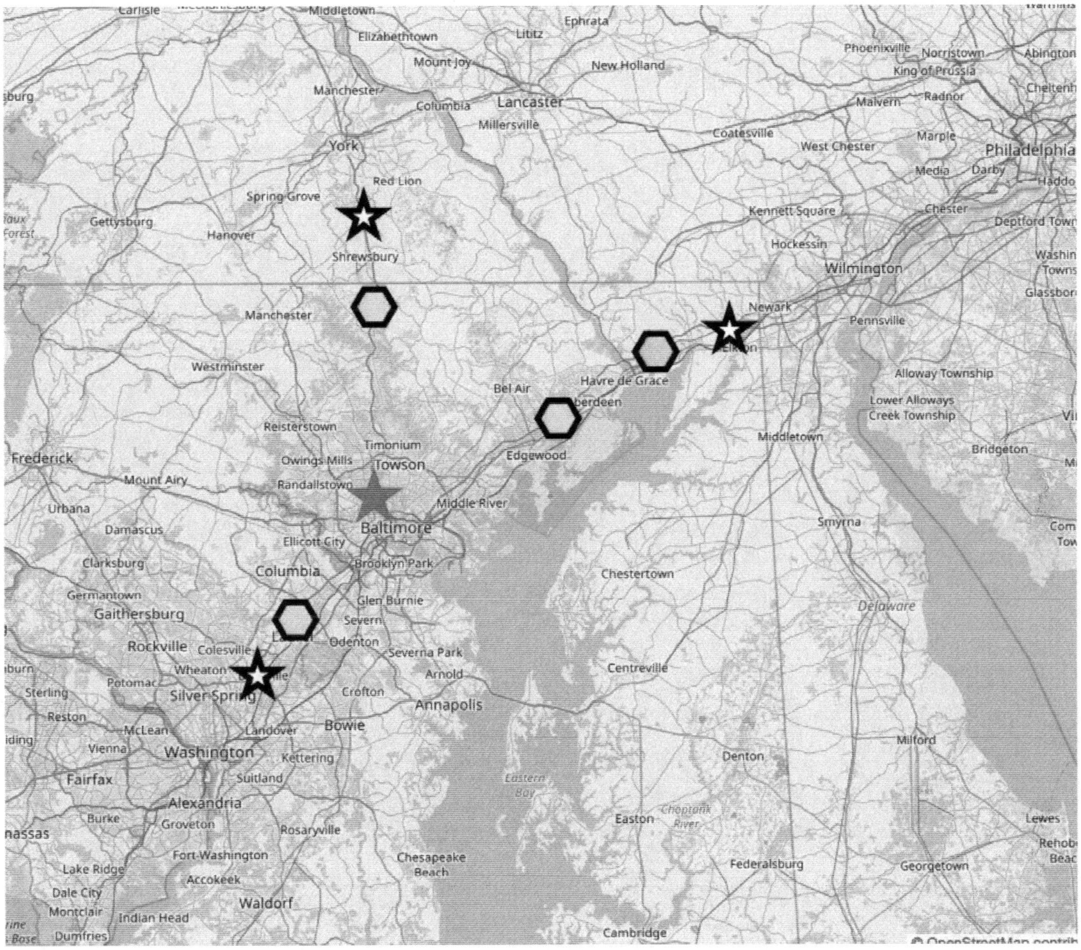


FIGURE 5: A MAP OF THE HIGHWAY DRIVE TEST BOUNDARIES. THE RED STAR SHOWS THE WNUV TOWER LOCATION, WHILE THE BLACK AND WHITE STARS SHOW THE EXTENT OF WNUV RECEPTION FOR EACH TEST ROUTE. THE BLUE HEXAGONS SHOW THE DROPOUT OF WYPR, WHILE THE GREEN HEXAGON SHOWS THE DROPOUT OF WBJC WHEN IT DIFFERED FROM WNUV.

Drive testing in the immediate Hunt Valley, Maryland area was also conducted to assess performance on non-highway speed streets, and near high buildings, wooded areas, and valleys. One example of a route is shown in Figure 6, though additional tests were conducted, such as in the rolling hills to the west, and downtown Baltimore to the south. At no point during these non-highway tests did the audio services experience a failure to decode.

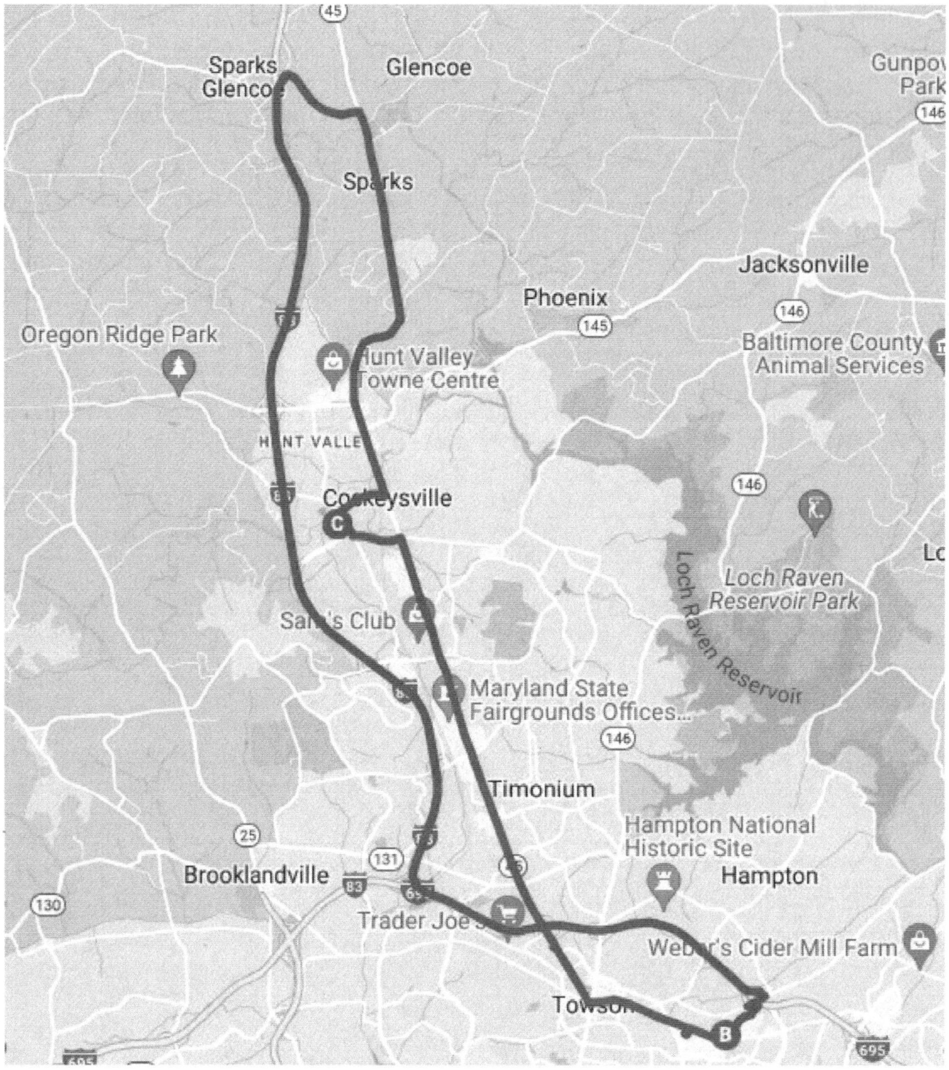


FIGURE 6: AN EXAMPLE OF A NON-HIGHWAY DRIVE TEST ROUTE. ON THIS ROUTE, THERE WERE NO DROPOUTS IN RECEPTION OF AUDIO SERVICES OVER WNUV.

For the FM radio comparison component of the evaluation, two analog radio stations were utilized: WYPR, 88.1 MHz, a 15.5 kW station, and WBJC, 91.5 MHz, a 50 kW station. Their contour maps can be seen in Figure 7. These were received via the built-in car radio and antenna in a 2010 Toyota Prius, while the ATSC 3.0 audio services were received using a 3.5-inch omnidirectional UHF stick antenna, with a magnetic base affixed to the roof of the car, shown in Figure 9. WYPR began to experience breakup just south of the Pennsylvania border, with total loss about a mile over the border (see Figure 5). WBJC performed similarly to the audio services over WNUV, maintaining audible reception until mile 10, though it began to experience breakup a few miles before. East and west, WYPR fell out around Riverside and Laurel, respectively, while WBJC dropped out just over the Susquehanna, while making it all the way to Washington. It must be noted that this is not a truly fair comparison, given the differing signal contours due to the densely packed mid-Atlantic FM radio spectrum.

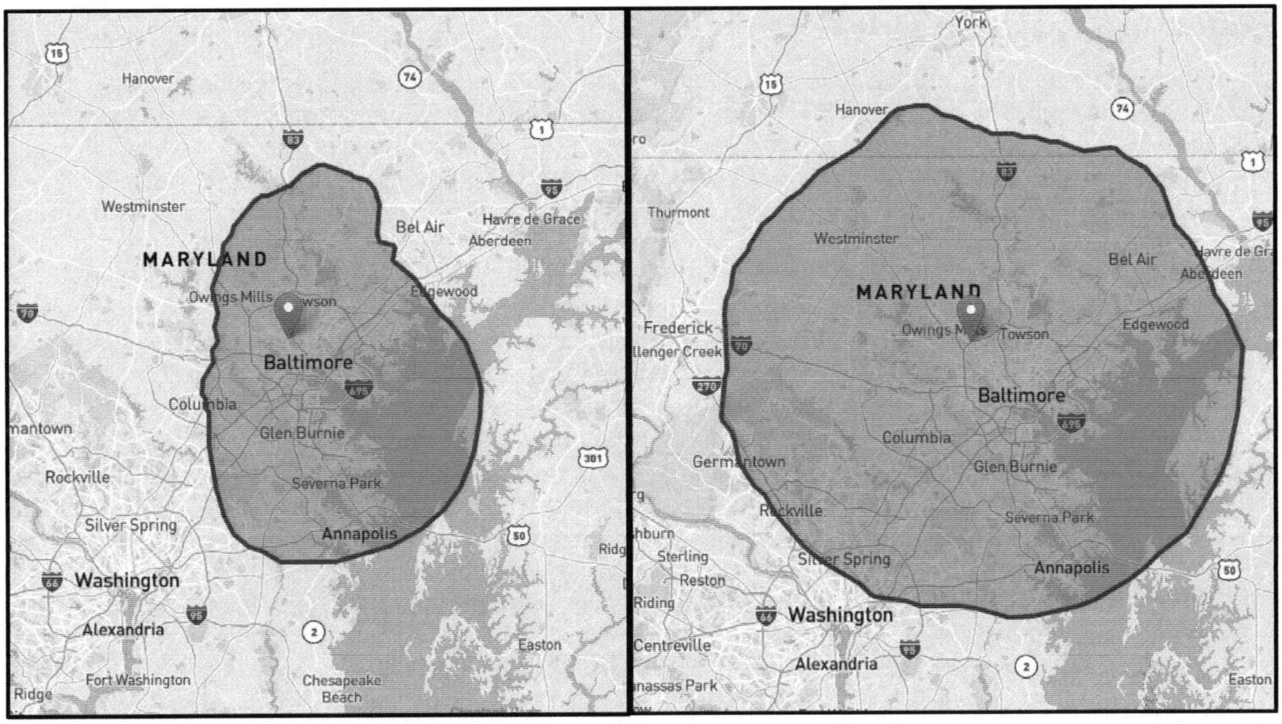


FIGURE 7: THE FCC CONTOUR MAPS FOR WYPR (LEFT) AND WBJC (RIGHT).

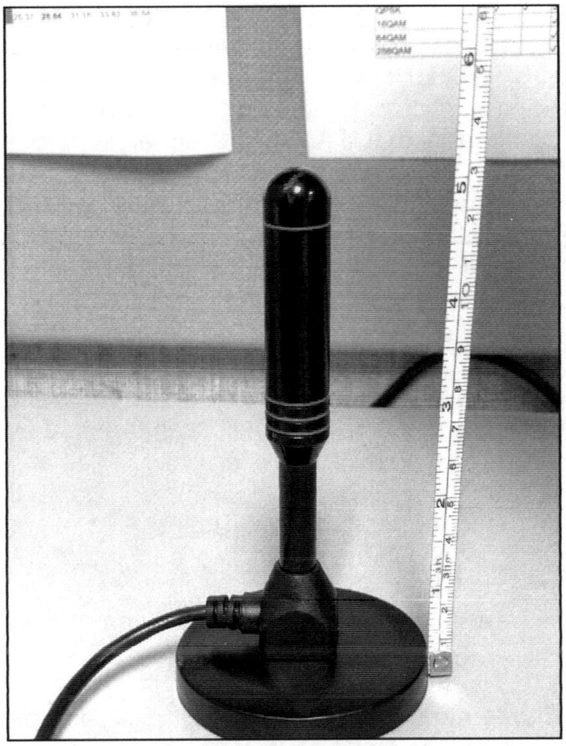

FIGURE 8: THE ANTENNA USED IN DRIVE TESTS.

## Section 6: Receiver Needs

One of the most interesting parts of this project was the receiver component. Even before it was decided to go down the UserDefined/RTP route, it was obvious the requirements of the project would necessitate a specific, and likely unorthodox, receiver. The key needs were as follows:

- **Gateway**: The receiver needs to be able to distribute the incoming services, both the specialized audio services and the regular AV services, to any client devices in the vehicle, such as phones or tablets.
- **Low power:** This would potentially be running off a battery, as it was required to be portable outside the vehicle for demonstration purposes, so it had to be able to run off an FAA-approved battery for a full 8 hours. The FAA restricts lithium ion batteries to 100 Wh, and as this system would have to be transported by plane for trade shows, it could not exceed this limit.
- **Mobile reception:** Not all receivers are equally capable when it comes to handling signals in a mobile environment, which is a key component of an automotive service.
- **Low tuning time:** The delay from the user pushing the button to hearing audio should be comparable to that experienced with analog FM radio.
- **NRT handling:** Metadata and the backend of the application are intended to be transported via NRT in the design, to avoid the need for any external transmission or installation.
- **User interface:** The native and web applications should both have a usable interface that allows easy access to all services.
- **Compact:** The full system should fit in a relatively small portable enclosure.
- **UserDefined/Multicast injection:** The receiver must be able to process the entries in the UserDefined table and use those to extract the data from the injected multicasts.

### Market Options

Due to these unorthodox requirements, the options for receivers were few. Most commercially available receivers are designed for a regular user, and so do not allow for easy external access to low level items like NRT data or multicast streams. However, thanks to the efforts of SiliconDust, OpenZNet, and Digicap, a solution nonetheless arose. Digicap's Autocaster product is incredibly flexible, allowing for easy access to just about any component of the ATSC 3.0 signal, in particular the NRT files and any multicast listed in the LMT, found in 7.1.1 of [10], which can then be redirected as unicast or multicast onto the local network. This was critical to the initial efforts to get a basic prototype up and running, and allowed for rapid testing because it acts as a seamless gateway connecting one multicast network at the transmission end to the network at the receive side. This meant that any unidirectional delivery method that worked in the lab network would work just as well over the air to the Autocaster and the receiving network.

OpenZNet was responsible for design and creation of the web server (used within the vehicle to connect the receiver to user devices) and the native application that tied everything together to create the user experience. This went through several design iterations. The final product assembles the app configuration via an easy-to-use website on the transmission side, then bundles it together into a compressed package that's sent out to the receive side. This is used to populate the web interface on the receiver to user devices, or the options in the native application if accessing that way. At this point, the player then accesses the streams from the receiver. This last part sounds simple but was quite complex to make work in a consistent and responsive way and was only successful due to some heroic efforts on their part.

Lastly, SiliconDust's HDHomeRun formed the core of the final receiver design. Despite the short timeline, the SiliconDust team were able to make several key changes to the stock firmware to enable this project. This allowed the HDHomeRun to read the UserDefined table, retrieve the correct streams, continuously buffer those streams to reduce tune delay, and provide 'virtual tuners' to allow multiple users in the vehicle to simultaneously consume the services while using a single tuner without needing to rework the basic functionality of the device. The other major positive to the HDHomeRun was the excellent performance in a mobile environment. A wide variety of set-top box style receivers were tested in a moving vehicle, and the HDHomeRun consistently was able to retrieve a linear AV service placed in the same PLP as the audio services at higher speeds than any other set top box assessed. Both the device and the development team are remarkably flexible and capable.

### Receiver Challenges

The single greatest challenge, and one that as yet has no satisfactory solution, was AC-4 compatibility. Very few ATSC 3.0 gateway devices support AC-4, as mentioned earlier. While the audio services did not require AC-4, the regular linear AV services do, and part of the requirements given to us was the ability to play AV services. Because the web interface was required within the vehicle to allow users without the app installed to connect to the receiver, this also meant an AC-4 decoder could not simply be supplied with a native app. And as there's no internet connection, the clever solution utilized by the HDHomeRun of transcoding on cloud servers also would not work.

As a result, several different methods were tried to provide AC-4 support to the receiver. The only successful one involved first a Raspberry Pi, then later a NUC (small form-factor PC) with sufficient compute power to continuously take in all the linear services, transcode them to HLS segments with AAC, and serve those HLS streams to the client device. While it worked in a technical sense, it was obviously very impractical, as it was neither low power nor compact. The band-aid in the short term was to utilize only recent Samsung products as client devices, which come with AC-4 support, and to integrate AC-4 decode into the native app.

Tuning time was another major challenge. Initially, all types of services would take 3-5 seconds to begin playback. This is moderately acceptable on video services, but for audio services, the target to achieve a similar delay to analog FM radio. One key point is that the only assessment was made on delay from user interaction to playback. This meant that latency from transmission to the ears was irrelevant, and so the initial solution was to simply have a continuous remux to HLS of all 15 services running. This made for near-instant tuning of the services, as there would always be a segment ready to go. Because it's being transferred over a local network, connection speeds are very fast, so the segment is transferred in a fraction of a second to begin playing. The downside of this approach, however, was the instability, as it layered another single point of failure over each service. Fortunately, SiliconDust was able to devise a solution in which the HDHomeRun would continuously buffer a short section of each audio service being signaled in the UserDefined as long as any audio service was tuned. This meant that after a short initial tune of 1-2 seconds, made faster thanks to some optimizations made to prefer speed over initial stability (the opposite of what would be desired for video), tuning times would be around half a second. Meanwhile, the team at OpenZNet was able to rapidly optimize their player solution to ensure as little delay as possible, dropping the video tuning time from 5 seconds down to 2-3 seconds.

## Section 7: Future Usage

This section discusses a series of potential next steps based on the findings above.

### Physical Layer Fine Tuning

The most immediate and easiest alteration is to adjust the physical layer, as the current configuration outperforms requirements. The bitrate-optimized configuration of QPSK 7/15 is unnecessary, given that QPSK 11/15 is more than adequate. Testing also found that the FEC component of the audio streams was unnecessary. Instead, the number of cells allocated to the PLP can be reduced to only those necessary for the radio service bitrate plus the metadata delivery to lessen the spectrum impact. This would drop usage from 16.66% to 10% of the usable channel bandwidth. This is an effective 600 kHz, though not literally, given the usage of TDM. Divided into 15 channels, this provides 40 kHz per channel. This translates to roughly 20% of the usage by analog FM radio, not considering the added efficiency of HD Radio digital radio, and considering the full assigned channel bandwidth of 200 kHz rather than exclusively the audio component. Further testing could be utilized to reduce receivability of the modcod even further, improving efficiency by finding the optimum operating point.

### MFN Service Deployment

Part of the table design included two sets of IDs, one for the service as a whole, and one for that specific transmission of the service. This could potentially be utilized to transition the listener between two broadcasts of the same service as they move from market to market, with only a momentary interruption. With the coverage results from this test, it would be theoretically possible to drive from Washington, DC to Portland, Maine while remaining in range of an ATSC 3.0 signal the entire time, assuming each market has a 3.0 deployment. This would fulfill a role similar to that of the SLT.Service.OtherBsid element, whose usage is explored by Sony in [11].

### Handheld Usage

Another major potential use case is that of a cellular phone. Due to the ease of receivability, this would be eminently possible using a device like a Mark One, which has an in-built ATSC 3.0 tuner, or using a phone with a USB tuner as Saankhya's Yoga dongle attached. This would also eliminate complexity from the user experience, as no separate receiver would be needed, just their phone. Testing of a video service in the same PLP had favorable results on the ONE Media Mark One, and so integration of the audio services is worth exploring.[6]

### Receiver Market Gaps

As applications like datacasting have become more prominent using ATSC 3.0 technology, one item that has been noted is a lack of receivers designed with datacasting in mind. Simple file transfer via NRT is relatively common, and some even incorporate application layer FEC (AL-FEC). However, some of the most interesting applications of these do not easily fit into basic file delivery, like those mentioned in Section 3. Most of these projects have required extensive custom work to integrate into a receiver, utilizing platforms like Sony's USB ATSC 3.0 tuner dongle, Digicap's Homecaster and Autocaster, and SiliconDust's HDHomeRun as bases. ONE Media's intention is to continue working with receiver manufacturers to better integrate these more advanced datacasting projects. Additionally, work on receivers with better mobile reception will help to alleviate the need for more receivable configurations in the automotive reception environment, allowing for better spectral efficiency.

### Standardization of Audio Services

While the current ATSC 3.0 specification allows for audio-only services, the overhead required to transmit them is simply too high to be feasible on a commercial scale, as mentioned earlier. Additionally, while AC-4 provides many advantages for television, there are other codecs that provide more efficient options in a bitrate-sensitive application like this, especially when it comes to highly compressible content like talk radio.

In addition to the bitrate concerns, a standardized signaling method designed around audio services would provide a clear target for receiver manufacturers, and allow for the easy incorporation of key features, such as song metadata, thumbnails, alerts, and news tickers.

One proposal is to make use of the Digital Radio Mondiale (DRM) standard [13], the development of which has been driven in large part by Fraunhofer IIS. While DRM is deployed as a more traditional digital radio application in countries around the world, there exists a DRM drop-in option that fits neatly into an ATSC 3.0 system, thanks to the option to inject multicast into the scheduler. The signaling,

---

[6] See https://www.tvtechnology.com/news/one-medias-atsc-30-smartphone-becomes-a-reality for information on the Mark One smartphone.

audio encoding, metadata, thumbnails, alerts, and tickers would all be handled by the DRM packager-equivalent, then bundled into a multicast stream. On the receiving side, DRM software would obtain the multicast stream from the ATSC 3.0 receiver and unpack it into the requisite components for the user experience. Incorporating DRM as the standard for audio delivery on ATSC 3.0 would solve many of the issues illustrated throughout this paper and provide a base of support given the existing global adoption. It is better to have a single unified audio services standard, than to end up with a multitude of competing implementations brought about by a gap in the existing ATSC 3.0 standard.

## References


[1] *Pro-MPEG Code of Practice #3 release 2*: Transmission of Professional MPEG-2 Transport Streams Over IP Network, July 2004.

[2] *ATSC Standard:* Signaling, Delivery, Synchronization, and Error Protection, Doc. A/331:2023-02.

[3] "HDHomeRun apps now support ATSC 3.0 audio on more devices, even when they lack the ATSC 3.0 audio codecs," https://mailchi.mp/245e1f09021d/hdhomerun-apps-now-support-atsc-30-audio-on-more-devices

[4] "xHE-AAC Audio Codec now in Windows 11," https://www.audioblog.iis.fraunhofer.com/xhe-aac-windows11

[5] *ATSC Recommended Practice:* Techniques for Signaling, Delivery, Synchronization, and Error Protection, Doc. A/351:2022-03.

[6] Iyengaar, J and Thomson, M., "QUIC: A UDP-Based Multiplexed and Secure Transport," *Internet Engineering Task Force*, RFC 9000.

[7] Bush, D. "UFTP – Encrypted UDP based FTP with multicast."

[8] Garro, E., Gimenez, J., Park, S., and Gomez-Barquero, D. "Pilot configuration optimization for ATSC 3.0," *IEEE Transactions on Broadcasting*, December 2016.

[9] *ATSC Recommended Practice:* Guidelines for the Physical Layer Protocol, Doc. A/327:2022-12.

[10] *ATSC Standard:* Link-Layer Protocol, Doc. A/330:2022-03.

[11] Fay, L. and Clift, G., "ATSC 3.0 File Delivery to Multiple Markets."

[12] Pardue, L. and Bradbury, R., "Hypertext Transfer Protocol (HTTP) over multicast QUIC," *Internet Engineering Task Force Network Working Group*, draft-pardue-quic-http-mcast-11.

[13] Digital Radio Mondiale (DRM); System Specification, ETSI ES 201 980 V4.2.1 (2021-01).


## Acknowledgments


- Marshall Behrmann and the team at ONE Media, for their invaluable work on this project.
- Azita Manson of OpenZNet for handling the front end under tight deadlines.
- Nick Kelsey of SiliconDust for his effort, ideas, and constant revisions of the HDHomeRun firmware.
- Gary Sgrignoli of MSW for his endless knowledge of the physical layer, as well as his willingness to provide feedback on any and all theories.
- Alexander Zink of Fraunhofer IIS for his assistance with all things AAC.

## Appendix A: UserDefined Audio Service Example

Below is an example of the UserDefined table described in Section 3. This one is for the Baltimore market, and so uses the 54 for the major channel and 1409 for the BSID, as it's transmitted on WNUV.


```xml
<?xml version="1.0" encoding="UTF-8"?>
<UDS>
    <OMLradio name="Baltimore Radio">
        <rsrv name="Hit List" destIP="239.255.54.201" destPort="5000"
        mktid="1409201" srvid="10001" />
        <rsrv name="Classic Rock" destIP="239.255.54.202" destPort="5000"
        mktid="1409202" srvid="10002"/>
        <rsrv name="Greatest Hits" destIP="239.255.54.203" destPort="5000"
        mktid="1409203" srvid="10003" />
        <rsrv name="Alternative" destIP="239.255.54.204" destPort="5000"
        mktid="1409204" srvid="10004" />
        <rsrv name="Pop Adult" destIP="239.255.54.205" destPort="5000"
        mktid="1409205" srvid="10005" />
        <rsrv name="Hip Hop" destIP="239.255.54.206" destPort="5000"
        mktid="1409206" srvid="10006" />
        <rsrv name="Hot Country" destIP="239.255.54.207" destPort="5000"
        mktid="1409207" srvid="10007"/>
        <rsrv name="Flashback 70s" destIP="239.255.54.208" destPort="5000"
        mktid="1409208" srvid="10008" />
        <rsrv name="Everything 80s" destIP="239.255.54.209" destPort="5000"
        mktid="1409209" srvid="10009" />
        <rsrv name="Latin Pop" destIP="239.255.54.210" destPort="5000"
        mktid="1409210" srvid="10010" />
        <rsrv name="Karaoke" destIP="239.255.54.211" destPort="5000"
        mktid="1409211" srvid="10011" />
        <rsrv name="Naturescape" destIP="239.255.54.212" destPort="5000"
        mktid="1409212" srvid="10012"/>
        <rsrv name="Qello Concerts" destIP="239.255.54.213" destPort="5000"
        mktid="1409213" srvid="10013" />
        <rsrv name="Classica" destIP="239.255.54.214" destPort="5000"
        mktid="1409214" srvid="10014" />
        <rsrv name="Djazz" destIP="239.255.54.215" destPort="5000" mktid="1409215"
        srvid="10015" />
    </OMLradio>
</UDS>
```

# Case Study: How BBC Studios Leveraged the Cloud for SRT Distribution of Her Majesty the Queen's Funeral

**Paul Calleja**
**GlobalM**
**Geneva, Switzerland**
paul.calleja@globalm.media

**Daniel Maloney**
**Matrox Video**
**Montreal, Quebec, Canada**
daniel.maloney@matrox.com

**Abstract** – BBC Studios televised Her Majesty Queen Elizabeth II's funeral across the UK through its BBC broadcast television network. International broadcast channels with preexisting satellite infrastructures used them to bring the event to their audiences. There were, however, a number of media groups with no existing satellite links to the BBC looking to acquire the rights for rebroadcast to their audiences. This paper will demonstrate why a cloud-based media distribution workflow proved to be the ideal solution for BBC Studios to rapidly augment their distribution footprint for the broadcast of a unique event that captured the attention of the entire world.

## Standard Satellite Distribution

Satellite, by nature, is a multicast network. Traditionally, satellites used for broadcast are high-orbit geostationary satellites (GEOSATs) utilizing a Digital Video Broadcasting (DVB) standardized modulation scheme to carry MPEG transport streams interfaced using Asynchronous Serial Interface (ASI). The mesh topology of GEOSATs allows for a transmission to be uplinked to a transponder for all rightsholders within the satellite footprint to be able to downlink and decode the transmission simultaneously. A satellite footprint, depending on the transponder's spot beam, typically covers a continental area. Therefore, to provide worldwide distribution of an event typically requires the use of at least three satellites, and the original satellite signal needs to be turned around in relay points in geographical locations where satellite footprints overlap.

Satellite distribution has been the standard method for many years, and broadcasters are most comfortable with this technology. However, trends in the satellite contribution and distribution space are changing, and not all broadcasters are equipped with expensive satellite receiving equipment. Costs associated with satellite contribution and distribution have historically restricted such use to events that can afford the occasional use of satellite capacity, satellite uplink and downlink equipment, and costs associated with satellite turnaround relay points. In the case of the Queen's funeral, rightsholders in locations not equipped with satellite receiving equipment still needed to access the signal in the same quality as what would be downlinked from the satellite distribution service.

In consideration of the costs and accessibility associated to satellite contribution and distribution, additional constraints include:

- Satellite capacity is fixed and booked for a certain period of time. If an event over-runs, the temporary channel must be vacated for the next event that has reserved that particular channel or, worse, use another satellite to carry on.
- Encryption such as Basic Interoperable Scrambling System (BISS) originates from the encoder. If a rightsholder is removed from the distribution list, the encryption key needs to be redistributed to all other rightsholders to re-enter into their decoder.
- Satellite is prone to performance degradation associated with weather and sun outages. Heavy rainfall can easily disrupt satellite transmission on either the uplink or reception sides of the network.
- High Earth orbiting GEOSATs are aging, and investments are focused on newer low Earth orbiting (LEO) satellites [1]. This has led to many operators flying GEOSATs past their end of life (typically 15 years), avoiding another 15-year investment cycle. Operators are not investing in GEOSATs that may be rendered obsolete by LEO systems within 5 years [2, 3]. As high Earth orbiting satellites reduce in numbers, the remaining capacity is becoming harder to source and further increasing in price; thus, video applications over GEOSATs are in structural decline [4].

## Private Leased Line Networks

To overcome the limitations of satellite, broadcasters have relied on private leased line networks such as dark fiber or dedicated telecom services (Gigabit per second Ethernet, Optical Carrier level-3, Synchronous Transport Module level-1, Synchronous Transport Module level-4) with specialized network terminal adapters designed for video. While private fiber networks have compensated and often are used in combination with satellite networks on major events, the costs and deployment times of leased line networks still keep them out of reach for a large number of broadcasters.

- Private leased line networks can take several weeks or months to deploy. In some cases, a network provider will need to run new fiber and may need to organize civil works in locations where existing fiber is not available.
- Fiber networks are point-to-point and require a larger investment to include several broadcasters in a network to achieve a multi-distribution scenario.
- Most private fiber networks operate as circuit-switched, therefore requiring a substantial amount of coordination to manage transmissions.

## Software-Defined Video Network

A software-defined video network (SDVN) uses unmanaged networks such as the internet to distribute content to multiple rightsholders without the use of GEOSATs or private leased line networks. This type of network reduces costs and deployment times, and the service availability increases due to the use of Automatic Repeat Request (ARQ) methods such as employed by Secure Reliable Transport (SRT) or Reliable Internet Stream Transport (RIST).

In the case of the BBC studios workflow, the GlobalM network orchestrator manages the creation and deletion of all scheduled network resources and applies all configurations within the cloud (high-level network description illustrated in Figure 1). The gateway architecture treats source and destination streams separately on edge servers (pods), allowing for full distribution and scaling of the network to suit many streams and destinations with worldwide coverage.

Utilizing several points of presence (POP) around the world as shown in Figure 2, the network uses the shortest possible connections via internet (first and last mile) with an ARQ protocol to deliver live content to a receiver pod and multiple stream sender pods. The network utilizes a private IP network backbone between pods in the core of an Amazon Web Services (AWS) cloud. The GlobalM patent-pending architecture allows for significant latency improvements—it reduces the number of internet hops, thus leveraging the power of the cloud by improving the end-to-end throughput between the encoder and each decoder. GlobalM can guarantee true point-to-multipoint internet-based transmissions with detailed monitoring and transmission management from the encoder and every decoder in the network.

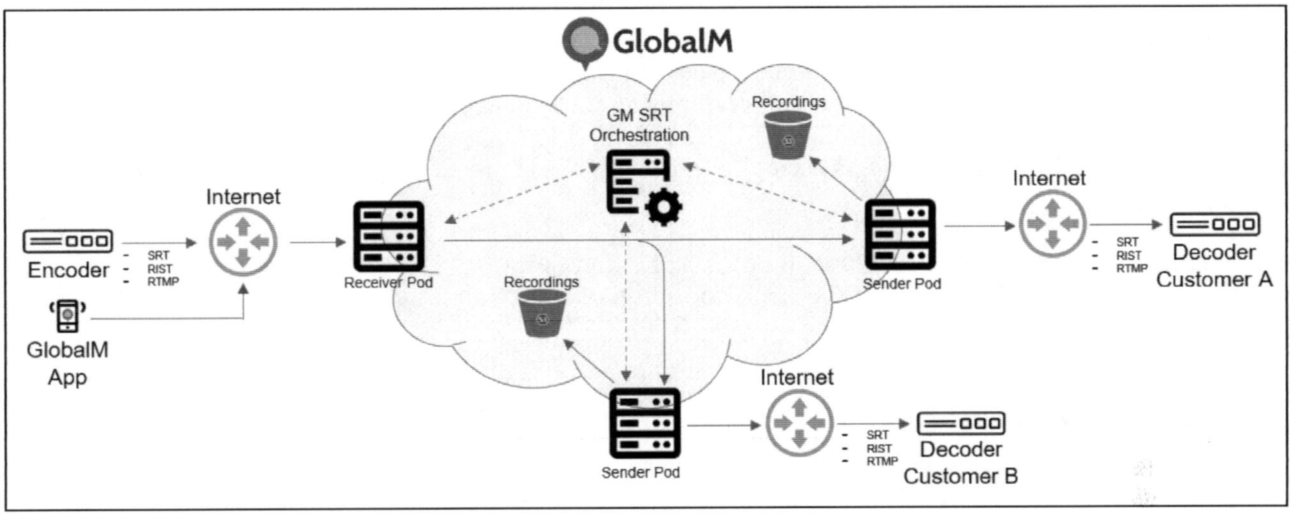


FIGURE 1: HIGH-LEVEL NETWORK DESCRIPTION.

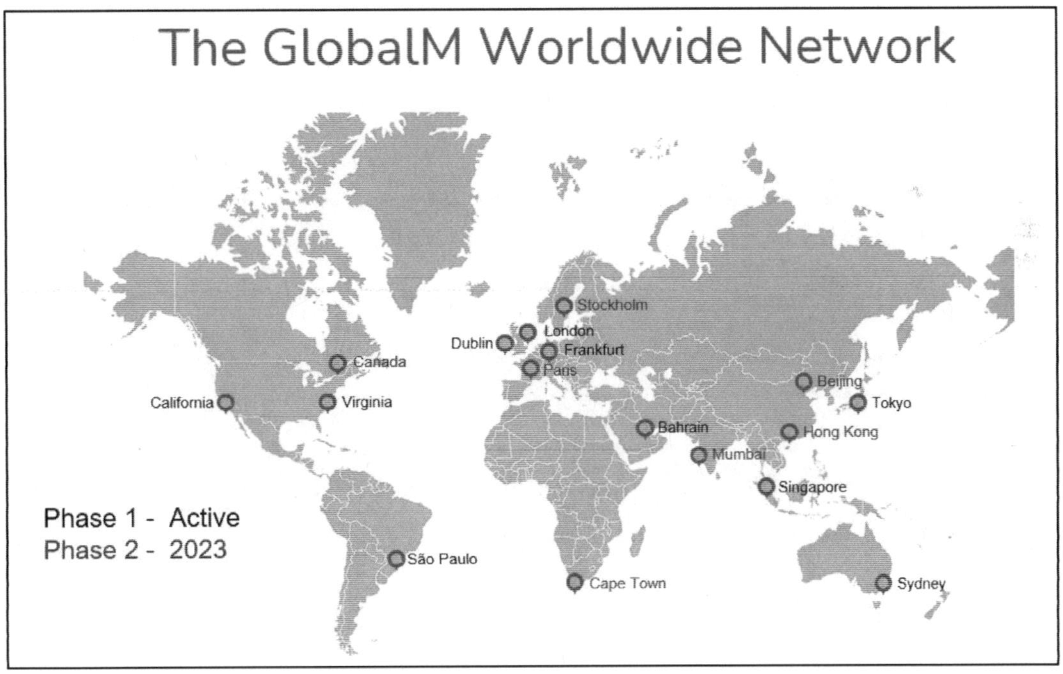


FIGURE 2: NETWORK ACCESS LOCATIONS.

## Encoding Platform

Most of the produced live content ready for distribution comes into the Master Control as SDI feeds. To augment the distribution footprint demanded by the Queen's funeral, the BBC rapidly integrated the Matrox Monarch EDGE E4 encoder. The Matrox Monarch EDGE E4 quad-channel, 4:2:2 10-bit-capable encoder captured and contributed four high-quality, low-latency streams—main and reserve domestic feeds, and main and reserve international feeds—to the GlobalM platform. GlobalM's private IP backbone also ensures low-latency transmission by reducing the number of internet hops an SRT transmission takes, especially on intercontinental routes. This resulted in a zero-packet-loss SRT transmission.

## Pod Architecture and Workflow

The pod architecture is illustrated in Figure 3. A pod is a streaming resource that can be a stream receiver, stream sender, or transcoder. An AWS region runs reservation pools of pods, each with a dedicated, pre-configured Amazon Machine Image (AMI) and machine instance type combination. A pod can be a stream receiver for a service in one region; in another, a pod can be a stream sender for that particular service.

The orchestrator monitors the reservation pools and communicates with the pod's Stream Service Controller (SSC). The SSC controls the behavior of the pod and manages the type of service that pod is running within a network transmission.

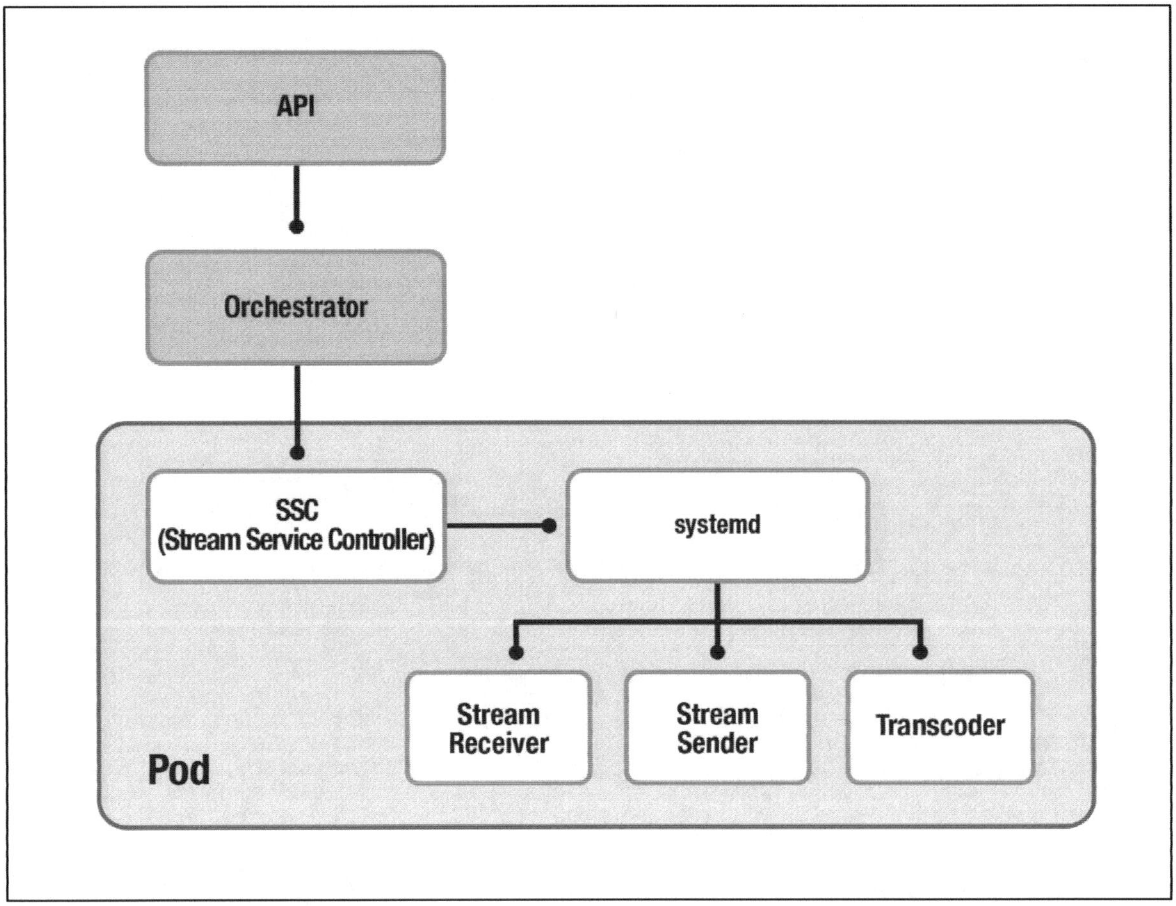


FIGURE 3: POD SCHEMATICS.

As shown in Figure 4, network configuration of a pod starts with the scheduler requesting a new transmission service to the API. The orchestrator then recalls a reserved pod from the appropriate reservation pool. The pod in the reservation pool is replaced to keep an active number of pods always in reserve for fast transmission creation.

The orchestrator then requests the SSC to be a stream receiver, stream sender, or transcoder and configures the pod with the load balancer and virtual private cloud (VPC) network settings.

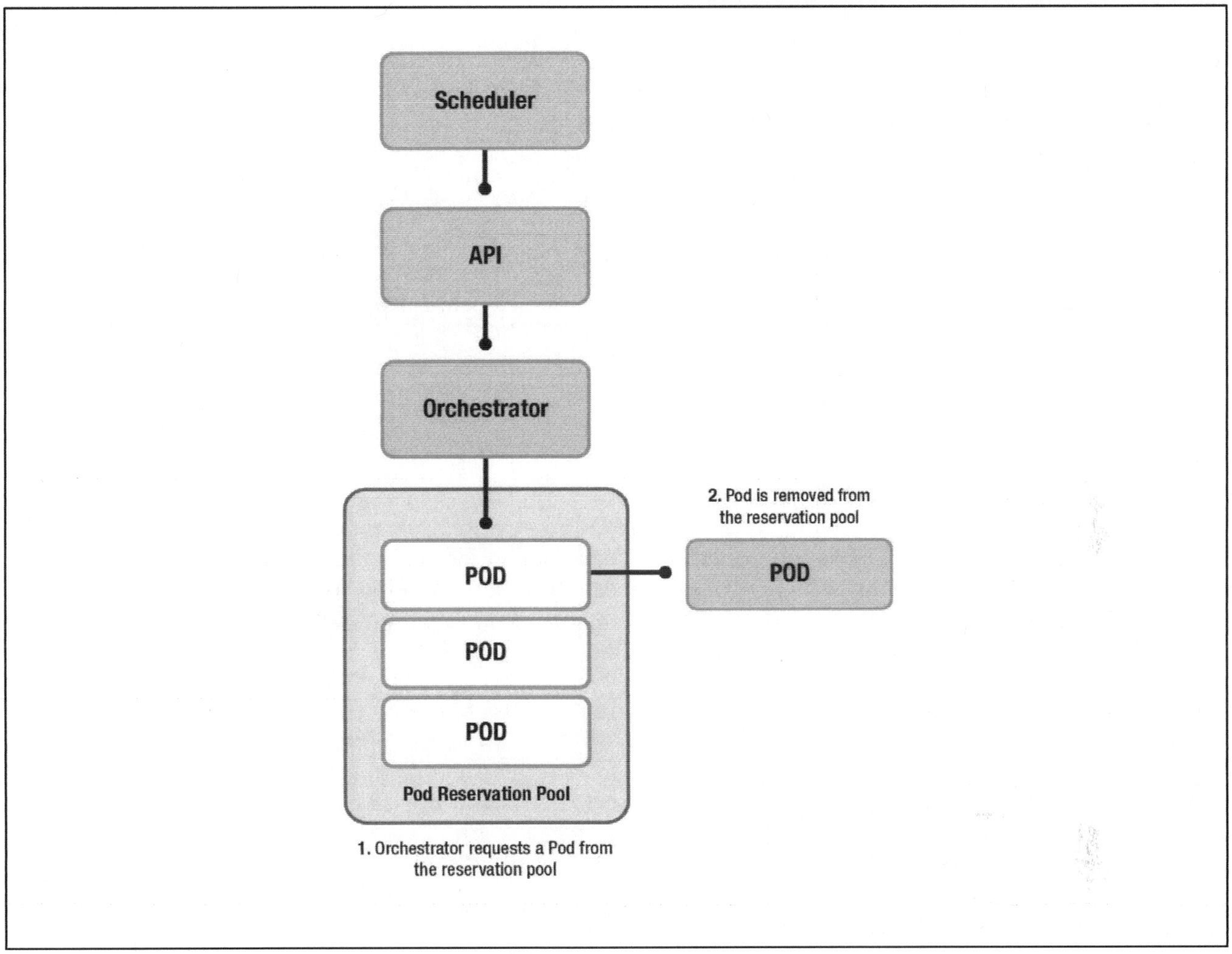


FIGURE 4: ORCHESTRATOR DYNAMIC NETWORK CONFIGURATION.

In each region (data center), pods start and stop based on demands from the orchestrator as illustrated in Figure 5. As discussed earlier, each pod is an edge server resource, acting as a stream receiver, stream sender, or transcoder. The limit to the number of resources that can be applied to pods in any region is the physical limit of what the data center can provide.

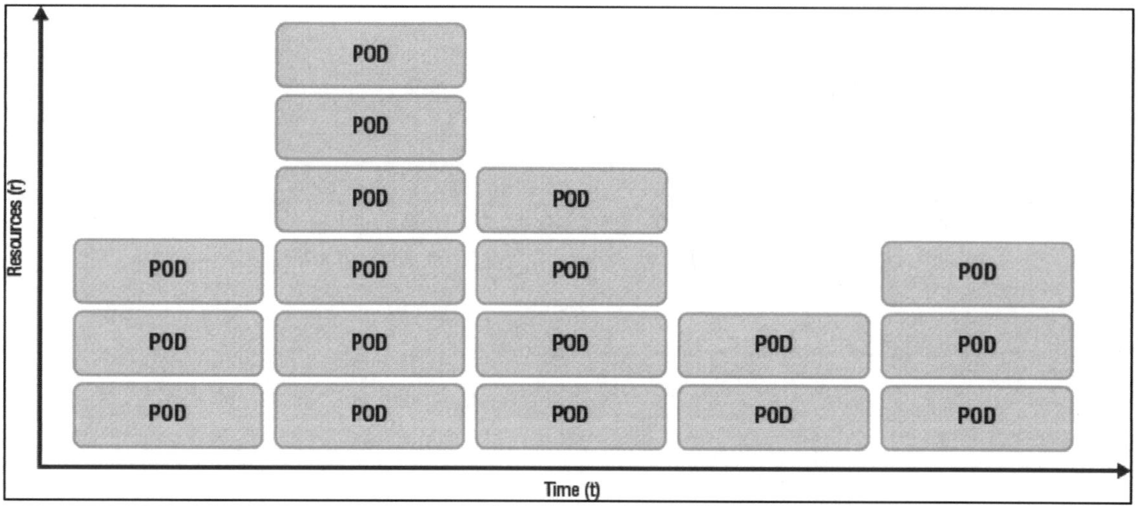


FIGURE 5: ELASTIC RESOURCE DEMAND.

## Cloud Transcoding and Remultiplexing

A major advantage of the pod architecture and cloud is the ability to run simultaneous processing tasks depending on the requirements of each rightsholder endpoint in the network. A transmission in 1080i50 variable bitrate (VBR) can be processed on the sender pods to provide the exact format a rightsholder requires. This is advantageous when rightsholders use decoding equipment that might not necessarily be compatible with the encoding profile of the originating video source.

The example shown in Figure 6 below shows the source Matrox Monarch EDGE E4 encoder sending 1080i50 variable bitrate (VBR). Customer A requires 1080i60 and their decoder is only capable of receiving a constant bitrate stream. Customer B has a decoder only capable of receiving progressive and not interlaced video. In both cases, the sender pods use cloud-based GPUs to remultiplex the video with null packet insertion to provide a muxed CBR and/or transcode the video to the desired video profile for each individual customer.

Utilizing cloud GPUs allows for fast video processing of services at a hardware level and ensures latency introduced by video processing is kept to an absolute minimum. And as with cloud-based services, the GPU pool can scale, providing tailored services to a large number of takers in the network. This workflow avoids broadcasters needing to receive an incompatible video service and having to transcode or remultiplex the video themselves with equipment they may not necessarily have.

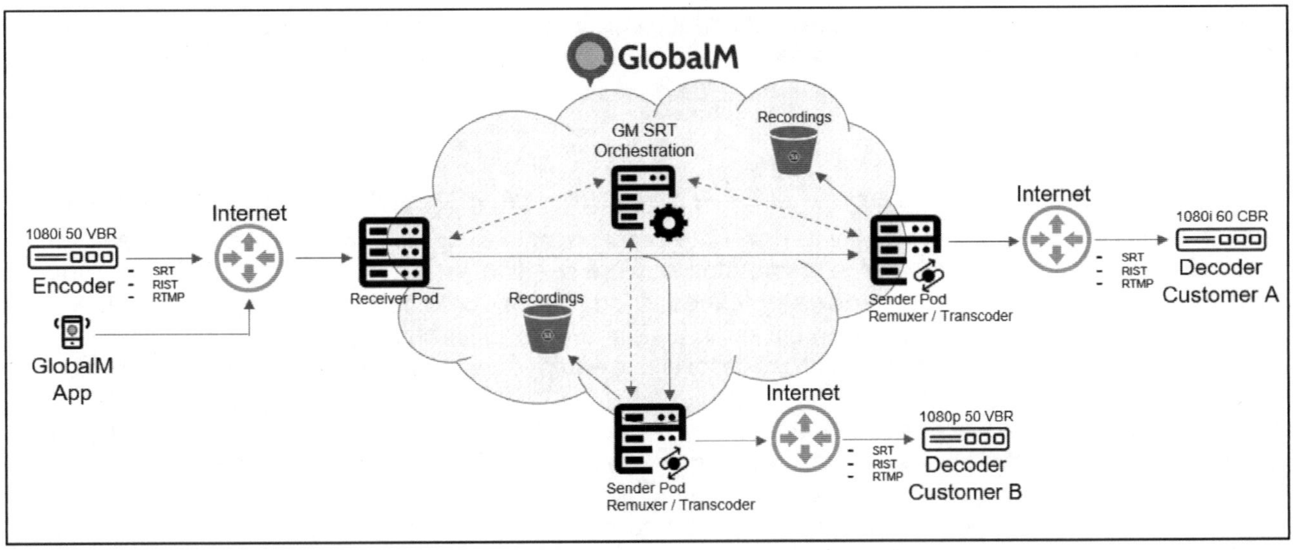


FIGURE 6: EDGE TRANSCODING AND REMULTIPLEXING.

## Monitoring and Control

Monitoring and managing a cloud-based video network without having to be an expert in cloud hypervisors is an important feature for master control rooms accustomed to traditional broadcast workflows. As the orchestrator manages the creation, configuration, and deletion of all cloud resources in the network, operators are only required to schedule and route transmissions in a dashboard that is similar to other resource schedulers. All of the Queen's funeral transmissions were scheduled via the GlobalM dashboard in a matter of minutes. The BBC master control monitored all streams in real time with the monitoring tools built into the GlobalM dashboard as well as return services from the London and Dublin POPs decoded with Matrox Monarch EDGE D4 decoder units.

Packet loss, packet retransmission, bitrates, and link performance measurements are all presented in one table within the GlobalM dashboard. At any moment, the master control room can detect any interruption on any part of all the links in the transmission.

To keep with the familiarity of applying cloud technology to standard broadcast workflows, the dashboard is presented as a video router. All sources are available on one side of the screen, and all destinations are available on the opposite side. This allows pods to be treated as a resource and routed between sources and destinations in such a way. It also allows for the streams' service IDs in the network to be switched without having to retune encoders or decoders in the network by simply dragging and dropping sources and destinations as you would normally do with a traditional video router.

## Service Reception

As SRT has become increasingly popular, many decoder vendors have included support for the format natively. In the case of the Queen's funeral, the receiver sites were already equipped with SRT decoder solutions and did not require a new decoder. Most BBC clients used the Matrox Monarch EDGE 1080i50 SRT-generated stream and distributed the program to the receivers in their native format. One last important element to note about cloud versus satellite primary distribution is that a gateway is not required to bridge cloud-based primary distribution to over-the-top (OTT) distribution. Today's OTT platforms can accept an SRT "contribution" feed for re-distribution. In this case, the OTT platform (many of which also reside in AWS) becomes another receiver, just like the on-premises decoders. In the case of the BBC, existing links were to address this workflow, offering great flexibility.

## Conclusion

In the case of Her Majesty Queen Elizabeth II's funeral, BBC Studios required, in addition to private satellite and fiber networks, the ability to distribute programming to rightsholders that did not have the means to downlink the global satellite distribution or were seeking an alternative backup solution. In combination with the satellite, the software defined video network provided by GlobalM helped to deliver the live service at a contribution bitrate in a standard MPEG transport stream to rightsholders, expanding the reach of the content to broadcasters not equipped with satellite receiving equipment.

During the 12-hour broadcast, the network did not drop a single packet proving its ability to provide a very high service availability over an unmanaged network to multiple rightsholders around the globe. Cloud technology is now proven to be capable of providing real-time, point-to-multipoint video services for contribution and distribution while maintaining a perfect service level at a reduced cost compared to traditional video delivery methods like satellite and private fiber networks. In the future, LEO access points may become yet another point of entry into a cloud-based software defined video network. While this paper prognosticates the continued decline of satellite-based video contribution, this certainly does not mean video data will no longer run through the next-generation of satellite-based internet connectivity.

## References


[1] "NSGO rapidly gaining ground in the satcom industry," *Euroconsult Satellite Connectivity and Video Market,* 29th Edition. https://digital-platform.euroconsult-ec.com/product/satellite-connectivity-and-video-markets-survey

[2] "GEO comsat demand entering a new cycle," *Euroconsult Satellites to be Built & Launched*, 25th Edition. https://digital-platform.euroconsult-ec.com/product/satellites-to-be-built-launched-new

[3] Henry, C., "Companies are flying old satellites longer, study finds," Space News, August 2020. https://spacenews.com/companies-are-flying-old-satellites-longer-study-finds

[4] "Satellite capacity market: video vs data forecast," *Euroconsult Satellite Connectivity and Video Market*, 29th Edition. https://digital-platform.euroconsult-ec.com/product/satellite-connectivity-and-video-markets-survey

# Software-only Facilities Running on an Asynchronous Framework: A Better Approach to Live Cloud Productions

**Dr. Richard Cartwright Ph.D.**
**Matrox Video**
**Montreal, Quebec, Canada**
Richard.Cartwright@matrox.com

**Abstract** – A software-only, asynchronous framework can achieve highly scalable, responsive, easy-to-control, and frame-accurate broadcast media facilities. Both for on-premises and cloud deployments. Contrasting clock-driven and event-driven processing, this paper characterizes virtualization in a live production context. Exploiting learning from other high-performance networking technologies, a new media processing framework is introduced consisting of software-based, composable, and multi-vendor media services. Discussed are details of how this framework governs processing, timing and control, and the consequences for facility designs.

## Virtualizing Facilities

### Clock-driven vs. Event-Driven Architectures

*Clock-driven* denotes linear, synchronous capabilities across point-to-point connected islands. Clock-driven systems rely on a clock signal, the beating heart of a traditional media facility. Each audiovisual signal within that facility is finely tuned to respect a common clock source: synchronized on arrival; delayed and retimed through processing stages; line-timed to present on monitors and outputs. Whether SDI, SMPTE ST 2110, CDI, or NDI, the relationship between a clock and a real-time signal was carried through the transition from analog to digital signals. In the past, the capability to process these signals was only available in specialized hardware.

The Joint Taskforce for Networked Media Reference Architecture [1] provides a framework for the media industry to transition to packet-based networks. Partly, this describes how to recreate the signal-to-clock relationship of a facility using PTP [2], enabling traditional workflows. Additionally, it includes a model of *grains* with timestamps and identity. Using flows of grains, audiovisual content to be treated as streams of data, processed by general-purpose computers in software. Today, pure software systems are capable of processing media streams significantly faster than real-time, whether with 10s of CPU cores or 1000s of GPU cores.

Event-driven implies parallel, asynchronous processing across distributed network fabrics. Event-driven asynchronous programs can exploit all the resources of a multi-threaded, multi-core, distributed system. Code is triggered by events rather than blocked waiting for resources. This achieves a scale of tens of thousands of transactions per second per computer. These programs execute on advanced operating systems that are often *virtualized*, allowing resources to be efficiently shared between processes. In the cloud, one computer may have multiple tenants. Due to virtualization, the business benefits of modern IT innovations – described in the next section – can be realized.

This paper is excerpted from the Proceedings of the 2023 NAB Broadcast Engineering and Information Technology (BEIT) Conference, © 2023, National Association of Broadcasters, 1 M Street SE, Washington, DC 20003 USA.

## Benefits

To virtualize is to benefit from the *–ilities* or IT:

- *agility* – experiment, free from infrastructure constraints
- *scalability* – grow or shrink – use a bigger/smaller computer, or more/less computers, within minutes
- *reliability* – avoid single points of failure and stay on air
- *card-swipe-ability* – pay only for what you use
- *composability* – construct flexible workflows using a chain of micro-services
- *sustainability* – benefit from cross-industry investment in renewables

The challenge is enabling these benefits for live production, where production requirements are both high-quality and low-latency video. This means high data rates with strict timing constraints. Encoding streams at every stage is an option, but takes time, has processing cost and risks introducing encoding artifacts. Instead, this paper focusses on processing uncompressed streams (e.g. HD 1080p50 10-bit 3 GBit/s) across fast networks (e.g. 10 GBit/s+).

## Limitations

Many media applications are more like a computer game than a database or webserver. One single process exploits a large percentage of the resources available. For media streams, processing must deliver-at, or go faster than, a given frame rate. This might include filling the capacity of a PCIe bus with I/O traffic and consuming most of the available network bandwidth. If one application uses most of the resources of a system, what is the benefit of virtualization? What if virtualization degrades performance?

In these situations, automating the management of a system – its drivers, libraries, processes and configuration – provides many of the benefits of *infrastructure as code* [3] claimed for virtualization. As an example, consider a PC games library (e.g., *Steam*) or cellular app store, both of which use automation as a replacement for shrink-wrapped software delivery.

A further limitation is the way software-hosting environments share resources. Ultimately, at any point in time down at a micro-second level, a process is not necessarily being serviced by the operating systems or hypervisor. When the time slices granted to an application are not regular enough to receive real-time media packets, the software cannot keep up. This makes implementation of packet-paced real-time streams synchronized to PTP clocks – like SMPTE ST 2110 – difficult to virtualize.

# An Asynchronous Framework

## The Real-Time Event Horizon

Exploiting event-driven rather than clock-driven architectures, with asynchronous rather than synchronous processing, a modern media facility can benefit from innovations in IT. Is it possible to go beyond the real-time event horizon of clock-driven facilities and still make live television?

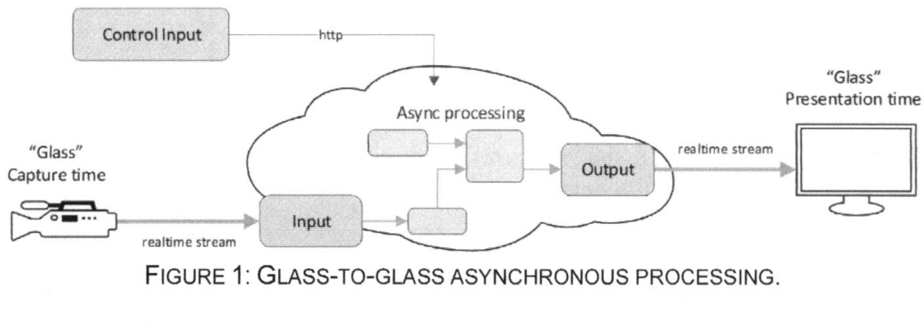


FIGURE 1: GLASS-TO-GLASS ASYNCHRONOUS PROCESSING.

Figure 1 shows an asynchronous approach to media processing for live production. Streams arrive and leave in real-time. Sequences of pictures – grains – are received through the glass of a lens and are displayed through the glass of a screen. Each grain in every input stream is given an identity and capture timestamp. Similarly, each output stream consists of grains with a presentation timestamp. Grains are placed in a content fabric and processed asynchronously, as fast as possible, across one-or-more systems.

Given that capture time is before presentation time, an asynchronous framework must ensure two things:

- Events fire in order to ensure that grains are processed to a deadline
- Control inputs – such as the position of a T-bar – can be related in time to the streams that they refer to

With such an asynchronous media framework, we can go beyond the real-time event horizon and process media streams significantly faster than real-time. Each media processing stage is a media service and flexible workflows can be composed in real-time.

## Media Services

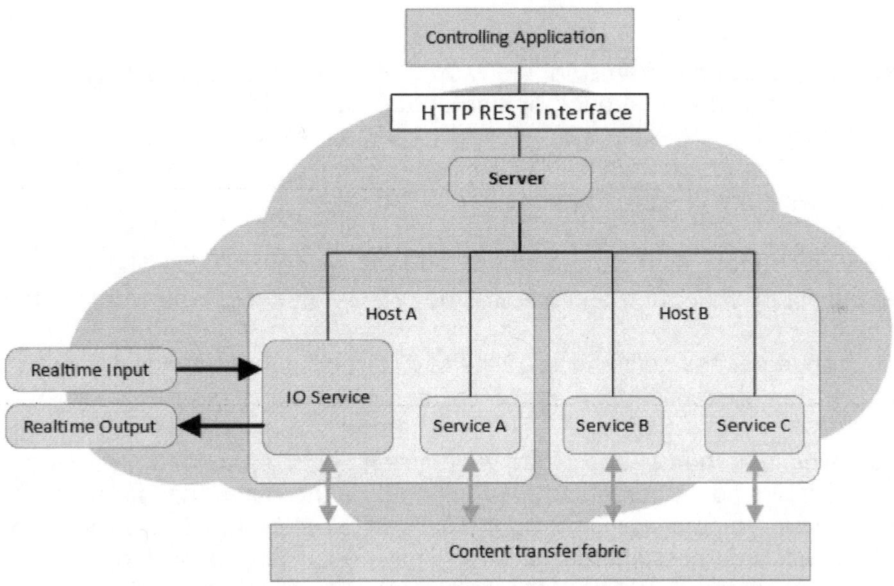


FIGURE 2: MEDIA SERVICES IN AN ASYNCHRONOUS MEDIA FRAMEWORK.

A media service is a specialized, high-quality, uncompressed media-processing capability implemented in software, as a process. Figure 2 shows the context for media services within an asynchronous framework.

In the framework, services are written to a relatively simple interface. The framework fires an event and asks the service to produce a frame for a given timestamp. The service then asks for control information for that point in time. It uses the control values in the response to further request the media sources it requires. Once all the service's requests are satisfied, it produces and writes its output. With the framework defining the media formats and control model, a media service is an isolated component of media processing logic.

How, where, and when the media service runs, and how many copies of the service exist at any given time, is controlled by a *server*. The server manages the lifecycle of *hosts,* where each host includes a shared memory pool and co-ordinates work on a single computer. The server also manages the instance lifecycle of *media services*. Each service has zero-copy access to the local memory pool. If a service on one host needs to consume frames produced on another host, a link is established and grains flow across the *content transfer fabric*.

Multiple instances of the same service can be distributed across two or more hosts, with each instance doing the same work. If one instance fails, the work is still being done by the others and no frames are dropped. In this way, the complexity associated with scaling, migrating, and protecting against failure is the responsibility of the framework. It is not a concern for the implementor of a media service.

Real-time inputs and outputs come in and out of the framework via media services, which can provide multi-path hitless protection with instances distributed across hosts. Input services assign a framework timestamp to each grain, either by creating one from scratch or basing it on one provided, such as a SMPTE timecode. Output services retrieve frames from the fabric and send them out according to their real-time clock. Services may have to deal with clock drift or latency caused by decoding a long-GOP codec. Where suitable hardware is available on-premises, connections to SDI and SMPTE ST 2110 streams are possible.

## Control Tracks

A core concept of an asynchronous framework is its model of control, common to all media services, called the *control track*. Treated as just another kind of track alongside audio, video, and ancillary data tracks, control tracks configure the processing done by a media service at a given point in time. The state of the control track is maintained in the server and queried by the media service for each grain. The result is that media service implementations can be stateless.

Various kinds of service configuration can be controlled from a control track. These could be:

- values that persist throughout the entire lifetime of a service, such as what file to play or bug to render
- values that change occasionally, such as the text to render in an overlay graphic
- values that update constantly, such as the position of an audio fader

One special type of value is a *source*, specifying what stream or streams of data a media service should read from. In combination, source control tracks define the paths that streams take between media services, from inputs to outputs. Enabling the framework to be used as a router, changing the sources a media service reads reconfigures workflows on-the-fly. Source switching with the framework is clean. The consequence is that workflows are orchestrated by the framework in a kind of loosely coupled micro-services architecture.

## Content Transfer Fabric

Other industries are using computers and networks – both on-premises and in the cloud – at data rates that transcend the requirements of a broadcast facility. What can be learned from them? If a network says it is 25 GBit/s or 100 GBit/s and is non-blocking, how can the network connections be filled with media streams? Testing is the place to start, and then replicating successful test environments in our software.

The Energy Sciences Network [4] is building high-performance data processing networks to aid scientific discovery. They publish *fasterdata* [5], advice on how to tune operating systems and software to get full use out of high bandwidth networks and fast computers. By following their instructions with tests on AWS it is possible to achieve close to full bandwidth using TCP/IP sockets. In short, this required distributing network-specific load across multiple threads, a few ports, and a few CPU cores.

Other accelerated networking technologies are available, such as Elastic Fabric Adapters on AWS and network cards supporting remote direct memory access (RDMA). The Open Fabrics Alliance [6] is creating advanced network ecosystems. They have provided *libfabric* [7], a software library that enables developers to gain maximum performance and efficiency from whatever underlying network is available. Anyone familiar with AWS CDI [8] is already using a cloud-specific version of libfabric. However, the scope of the libfabric is much broader than cloud. Tests show the library moves frames of video over TCP/IP networks much faster than real-time, with low CPU impact. The content transfer fabric uses this to transfer only frames that need to move, within and outwith cloud availability zones.

## Journey to Software and the Cloud

### Collective Goal

The collective goal of the industry should be to design systems that work equally well on-premises and the cloud. A transition to software is not going to happen overnight. High-quality live news and sports programs continue to be made and broadcast on a daily cycle from studios, galleries, and equipment rooms. The journey can start by moving to small clusters of on-premises processing, managed through automation with a tool like ansible [9], and connected to legacy SDI and/or IP systems with hardware cards. Over time, as more software capabilities are developed, processing can be virtualized. As fast networks are established between studios and the cloud, processing can be moved from on-premises to the cloud.

### Media-Specific Architecture

Designing a software-only broadcast facility will be different from a traditional broadcast facility. It may be counter-intuitive to design a system without a clock at its core. Instead, asynchronous designs rely on making measurements to show frames moving and processing faster than real-time. Also, when the media services are composed into a workflow, cumulatively they must be able to beat a specified end-to-end deadline. A form of fine tuning, informed by system performance metrics.

An asynchronous framework as described allows services to be duplicated across hosts to protect against a single point of failure. Architects must also understand the shared responsibility model of their cloud provider – e.g., *availability zones* on AWS [10] – or the resiliency inherent in their own data center. This will require having multiple paths from a source to its media input service instances in different availability zones, and from output instances to a destination.

Network bandwidth and the configuration and capability of a network is another consideration. How many streams of video and audio can you fit in each network connection? For example, for a single HD 720p60 4:2:2 video with 64 tracks of 24-bit audio, a network of 1.26 GBit/s is required. Given no other significant network traffic, network bandwidth is bidirectional, and a network is non-blocking, it should be possible to receive and transmit up to 21 streams in each direction on a 25 GBit/s link.

### Benefits Realized

How can we realize the benefits of virtualization with an asynchronous framework? Revisiting the benefits identified earlier:

- *agility* – media services are separate software processes and can be deployed on-the-fly, enabling experimentation
- *scalability* – add or remove services to/from a host and increase or decrease the number of hosts. Live-migrate services between hosts without dropping a frame

- *composability* – the workflow, executed by content flowing between media services, is orchestrated by control tracks, at runtime
- *reliability* – multiple instances of a service distributed across hosts and availability zones, duplicating input and output streams for hitless protection
- *card-swipe-ability* – infrastructure is described as code templates and can be reproduced and deleted as required
- *sustainability* – capitalize on renewable energy investments of cloud providers while minimizing the amount of equipment installed a rack just-in-case it is required

Such a framework can be run 100% on virtual machines. Or directly on on-premises hardware, accessing I/O cards, and managed with automation. Or on local virtual machines.

## Conclusion

Taking advantage of state-of-the-art software development techniques, software can deliver the benefits of virtualization for broadcast workflows. For high-performance video processing applications – ones that use most of the resources available to a computer – automation rather than virtualization delivers infrastructure as code advantages. We can learn from other industries that are using the capabilities of high-performance computers and network fabrics. Moving to exploit these requires an event-driven asynchronous approach, one that may be counter-intuitive to those familiar with synchronous broadcast engineering practices. Knowingly, a media-specific asynchronous framework was introduced. A framework that enables the transition of broadcast workflows to software, benefiting from IT innovations, deploying both on-premises and in the cloud.

## References

[1] https://www.jt-nm.org/reference-architecture

[2] https://standards.ieee.org/ieee/1588/6825

[3] Morris, K., "Infrastructure as code: Managing Servers in the cloud," *O-Reilly*, June 2016, pp. 3-20.

[4] https://www.es.net

[5] https://www.es.net/engineering-services/fasterdata

[6] https://www.openfabrics.org

[7] https://ofiwg.github.io/libfabric

[8] https://aws.amazon.com/media-services/resources/cdi

[9] https://www.ansible.com

[10] https://docs.aws.amazon.com/AWSEC2/latest/UserGuide/using-regions-availability-zones.html

# Sinclair Cloud Media Pipeline

**Mike Palmer**
**Sinclair Broadcasting**
**Hunt Valley, Md., United States**
mpalmer@sbgtv.com

**Abstract** – Sinclair Broadcasting's Cloud Media Pipeline (CMP) brings centralized reception and processing of commercials, syndicated programming and promos to the group's 210 channels by applying cloud-native applications and services to achieve savings, efficiency and speed.

## Problem

Each month Sinclair's 210 channels receive on average 30,000 advertising spots, 6,000 syndicated programs, and create more than 60,000 episodic promos.

Prior to Sinclair's creation of the Cloud Media Pipeline (CMP) this content was received across 60 different physical locations, each with their own hardware, software and operators, where media timing and quality was manually checked (prepped). Though much of the content was also used on other channels, every master control received and prepped their own content. If an exception, such as bad timing, was found at one site, the content had to be manually corrected at all other sites where that same content was also used.

The result was unnecessary duplicated effort by both humans and machines and produced redundance costs, including annual for support, power, cooling, rack space, etc.

Due to the legacy on-prem design, the hardware and software required for processing was sized for a peak load on single day per week, resulting in an underutilized system capacity and support during off-peak days. Even during peak time, the linear nature in which these on-prem systems processed content often resulted in lengthy queues, sometimes lasting hours in duration.

Sinclair wanted to reduce redundant operations and resources through consolidation of hardware, services and workflow. We also wished to produce cost savings as well as cost avoidance, improve the quality and consistency of processed files, and increase average speed.

We would use average cost to process a rendition, and time to make the content available for delivery as metrics.

## Direction Chosen for Solution

Sinclair determined the best course forward would be to consolidate ingest and prep operations into the public cloud, using a limited number of flexible and loosely coupled cloud-native applications and services to ingest, process and deliver content to playout for the entire group.

The chosen system components would be easily integrated and able to flex capacity in response to demand. The resulting system had to be able to support both present on-prem playout and future cloud playout.

## Benefits

Ultimately, cost savings and efficiency drove this project.

The solution would be able to reduce or eliminate reception of duplicate content, resulting in savings in storage and transport, and generally lowering the complexity required to manage many disparate on-prem systems.

Resources needed to receive and process redundant content could be eliminated, reduced in size or repurposed, resulting in savings in manpower, compute, power, cooling and real-estate.

A fundamental shift in compute paradigm, from on-prem sequential processing to cloud parallel processing, would allow us to generally avoid workflow queues and dramatically lower processing times for media during peak periods.

Advanced workflow combined with automated QC would result in fewer exceptions that would require human intervention. Adjustments made to timing or other QC operations made by one Master Control Operator when applied to shared media could be applied everywhere else that content is scheduled to be used.

Services and applications could be managed at a macro level and enable the creation of the CMP Media Bus, to which actions and requests would be published, enabling more flexible and extensible federated workflow.

The system would also be able to automate our episodic promo production process nearly fully.

## Challenges

Our challenges were numerous.

First, workflows required to process content for local stations are much different than those used by the handful of companies who have moved similar operations to cloud before us. Though we found an understanding of other's previous experience helpful, we had a number of local broadcaster-specific challenges to solve.

Many of those challenges stemmed from the fact stations receive content from a very broad range of content producers and distributors, with vastly different technical capabilities, submission methods and experience.

Content Distributors have for many years delivered content directly to individual stations. It was typical for distributors to guarantee delivery of content to multiple individual stations. We wished to change this model to one where Distributors delivered content directly into cloud storage at our central point of ingest. From this point Sinclair, not the Distributor, would handle final delivery to our stations. Though central ingest clearly offered efficiencies to us, it would require some Distributors to make fundamental changes to their business models. As well, technical changes were also needed. For instance, we needed Distributors to attach to every piece of media a side-car containing a list of stations/channels intended to receive the content.

Individual producers who submit content directly and not through a Distributor are considered Contributors. These can range in sophistication from a major production house to an individual working from home. In the past, content from Contributors was received through multiple FTP servers hosted at individual stations and at our headquarters. The continued use of FTP was considered a significant security risk and an alternate method of submission was required.

In addition to capture of metadata at the point of Contributor submission (including distribution end points) we also wished for the system to check media *before it was uploaded* to ensure it fell within a range of acceptable technical parameters. We saw this as necessary to accommodate the wide range of technical abilities and tools used by contributors.

This technical requirement for content to fall within a range of values (driven largely by Contributors), was fundamentally more complex than other similar projects, which required all content to meet a single standard in which each parameter had a single defined value. We found this to be one of the major differences between what Sinclair wished to accomplish and what others before us have implemented through application of more restrictive standards, such as those provided by the DPP.

Sinclair also needed to standardize, to the greatest degree possible, our own internal processes, including those used for spot and program scheduling, as these would need to align with the processed content.

We had a clear requirement for cloud-native systems – meaning we sought either software architected to run in our own cloud tenancy using scalable services responsive to demand, or pure SaaS solutions. Because many broadcast vendors are still relatively early in their cloud journeys and only a small number have produced mature cloud-native solutions, we found it challenging to identify cloud-native software and services that met our functional and cost requirements.

We wished to reduce vendor lock-in and dependency by ensuring our media and a limited amount of descriptive associated metadata were always available together in storage, without being confined behind any one vendor's database or API's. We determined we could best avoid this by adding a requirement that a limited set of descriptive core metadata would be written to a side-car metadata file that accompanied the media file into storage.

This approach provided several benefits, including the ability for multiple systems to simultaneously access the content using only a storage API, the ability for third party systems to directly enrich the content through AI/ML services, future ease in migration of metadata and content from one vendor to another, and the ability to more easily and quickly recover from unlikely/infrequent but catastrophic events which might damage or destroy application databases.

We looked at several large media management systems and found they were capable of a range of tasks much larger than our present need and were rather expensive. We also found that the larger systems were perhaps less nimble and comparatively slower to adapt and evolve than smaller task-focused tools, which could be integrated and were less expensive.

With the potential use of a handful of smaller but integrated systems, we saw potential benefits in reduced training time, reduced support (including dev ops), and the future ability to switch or upgrade task-specific tools individually and incrementally, which can be difficult with more monolithic systems. We felt an initial increase in integration complexity would be offset by expected cost savings and risk reduction.

Though we plan to consolidate on a single playout system, at the outset our CMP needed to support five different types of playout systems, and thus produce five types of file renditions, each with their own format and bit rate. For efficiency, we did not want to produce all five renditions for every file received. Instead, we wanted to produce only renditions needed by the channels who needed the file.

Files needed to be delivered for channel playout in two ways. First, files needed to be delivered, in their channel-specific format, to storage attached to playout through an automated mechanism. Files also needed to be delivered through a UI that allowed an operator to handle exceptions by searching and previewing media before it was downloaded. This needed to work for both on-prem and cloud playout systems.

## Architecture

We broke our architecture into these seven elements: 1) **Cloud Infrastructure** 2) **Ingest Operations**, 3) **Media Processing**, 4) **Media Search & Visibility**, 5) **Media Workflow Orchestration**, 6) **Connectivity** and 7) **Schedule & Playout Integration**

1) **Cloud Infrastructure** - Amazon was chosen to provide cloud services. The Cloud Media Pipeline uses Networking, Simple Notification Service, Simple Queue Service, Compute, Block Storage, Object Storage, Active Directory, Database, Security, Logging and Billing services. These components are in large part managed as infrastructure as code through Terraform.

2) **Ingest Operations** - Signiant's Media Shuttle service was chosen for the Ingest component. Running within Signiant's cloud tenancy, it provides a web portal to enter selected metadata, including Ad-ID/ISCI or Day Code, and a list of channels for which the content is intended.

   Prior to upload, the portal will use the Contributor's computer to check if the file's technical parameters fall within our accepted ranges before the file is allowed to be uploaded. If the media and metadata does not pass this check, the media is not uploaded.

   Initially, a web portal was created for each of more than 60 markets, each directing files to be processed in the correct formats required for renditions used in each market. This was later replaced with a single portal used by all markets which forced contributors to identify the market(s) intended as the destination for the file.

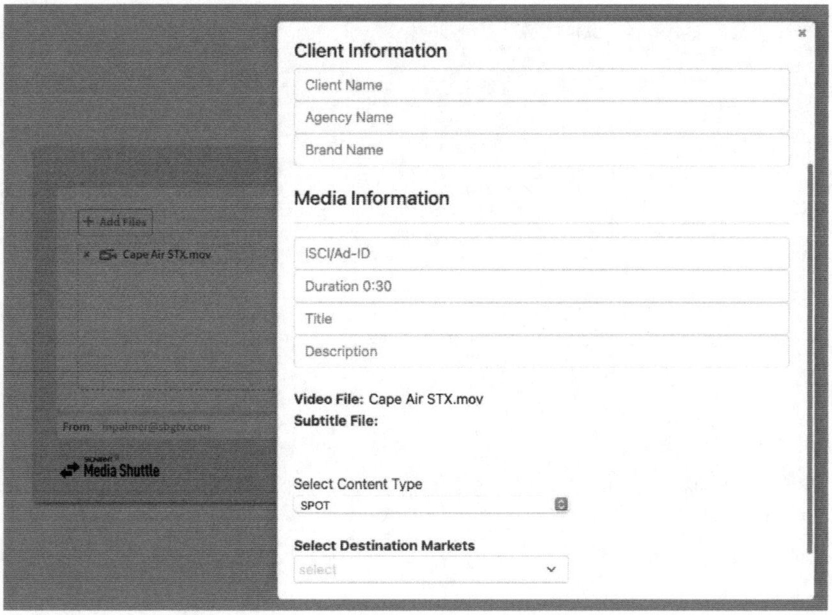


FIGURE 1: THIS IS AN EXAMPLE OF THE WEB-BASED CONTENT SUBMISSION FORM USED BY CONTRIBUTORS TO UPLOAD FILES. TRANSFERS CAN BE MADE WITH OR WITHOUT FILE ACCELERATION. DISTRIBUTORS SKIP THIS STEP AS THEY WORK WITH HIGHER VOLUMES OF CONTENT AND SUBMIT CONTENT DIRECTLY TO AN S3 BUCKET.

Content from Distributors bypasses this portal and is sent to an Amazon S3 bucket assigned to them. Some Distributors are capable of direct delivery to their assigned S3 bucket, while others require content be sent to a legacy server hosted by Sinclair, from which content is forwarded to their S3 bucket. Most, but not all, distributors supply side-car files with timing and other metadata. A few also include distribution end points (lists of stations intended to air the content).

3) **Media Processing** - Sinclair chose Telestream Vantage as the Media Processing engine which ingests and then processes files submitted by Contributors and Distributors.

The Media Processing engine first applies basic QC to files and then checks timing metadata provided by the Distributor or Contributor against the media file. Slight exceptions in timing are corrected automatically. Large exceptions are flagged for manual exception handling. Timing / Trimming is automatically applied to advertising spots which arrive without timing information. Syndicated programs which arrive without timing information are handled as manual exceptions. All timing information is written into a normalized BXF side car file.

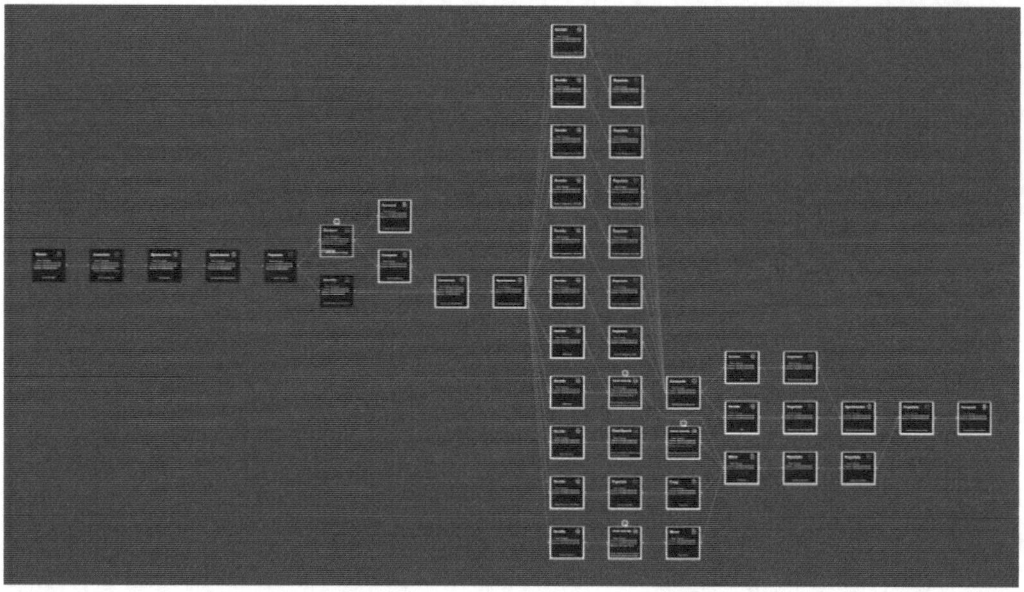

FIGURE 2: THIS IS AN EXAMPLE OF THE COMPLEXITY OF A TYPICAL MEDIA PROCESSING WORKFLOW. THIS PARTICULAR TASK CHECKS TIMING OF A RECEIVED FILE AGAINST THE FILE'S ASSOCIATED BXF SIDE CAR USING BLACK DETECTION.

Using internally and externally provided metadata, the Media Processing engine creates, through transcode, correctly formatted renditions of files specific to a list of end points provided at ingest, and also creates an internal unique ID which captures the Distributor/Contributor file name, point of ingest, time and check sum. Sinclair-specific Day Codes are also synthesized from metadata received from Distributors to match those used by Traffic.

Syndicated Program Sinclair Internal ID Example

**JJudySeason523E33223**synexr**cmpevtml**20220727T191655.173-6**A**

Prefix (26 chars of 80 max)
Program File name received from syndicator: **JJudySeason523E33223**

Content Type & Source (6 chars)
Type: syn (Syndicated)
Distributor: exr (Extreme Reach)

Suffix UID (30 chars)
8-char Ingest Point: **cmpevtml**
21-char Ingest Time: 20220727T191655.173-6
1-char NCDA Checksum: **A**

FIGURE 3: UNIQUE ID'S ARE CREATED FOR ALL FILES RECEIVED FROM DISTRIBUTORS AND CONTRIBUTORS. THE ID FORMAT IS DERIVED FROM THE PROGRAM NAME, PROGRAM TYPE, DISTRIBUTOR, POINT OF INGEST, TIME OF INGEST, AND A CHECKSUM.

The system creates a transcode job for up to five types of renditions used by the end point playout systems based on a list of stations that need the content. For instance, a commercial intended for air by only one station will result in only one transcode job to produce only the single rendition type used by that station's playout system.

As they are created, transcode jobs are sent to a dispatcher. If a transcode processor is not immediately available, a new processor is spun up by the dispatcher to handle the job. After completion, the processor is allowed to run for a short period of time, after which if an additional job is not received, the processor is shut down.

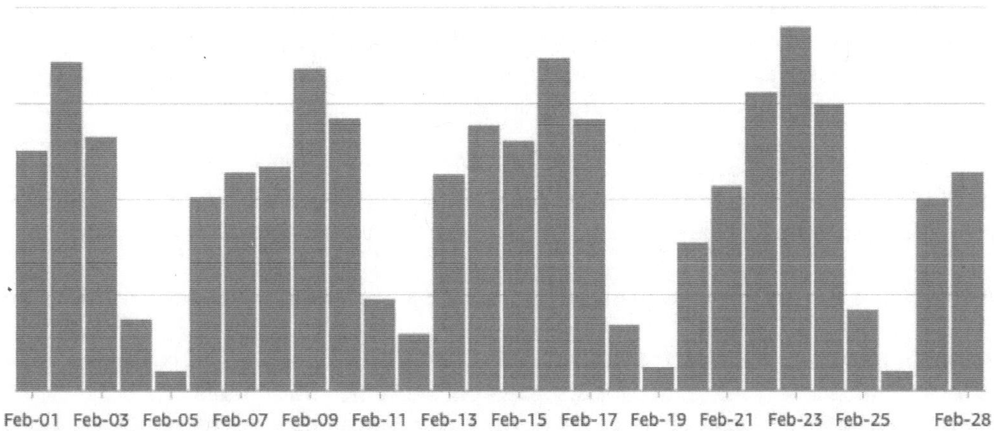


FIGURE 4: THIS GRAPH REPRESENTS ON-DEMAND COMPUTE RESOURCES USED BY TRANSCODE SERVICES IN FEBRUARY OF 2023. NOTE THE VERY LOW USAGE ON WEEKENDS, WITH PROGRESSIVELY HIGHER USAGE THROUGH A PEAK ON THURSDAY. MONOLITHIC OR UNRESPONSIVE SYSTEMS BUILT TO PEAK DEMAND OFTEN WASTE EXPENSIVE PERFORMANCE AT TIMES OF LESS DEMAND.

The Media Processing component transcodes files using containerized transcode engines that are created and destroyed in direct response to demand. At peak times on the busiest days files typically begin the transcode process in only a number of seconds after submission. The older on-prem solution, which was built for peak demand, typically developed a backlog of up to two hours at peak times.

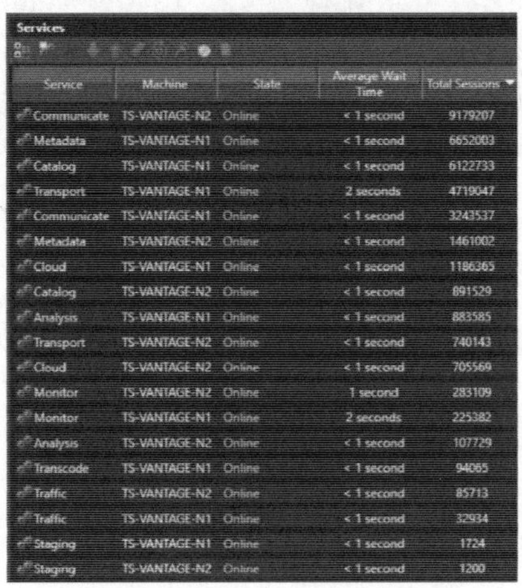
Services

| Service | Machine | State | Average Wait Time | Total Sessions |
|---|---|---|---|---|
| Communicate | TS-VANTAGE-N2 | Online | < 1 second | 9179207 |
| Metadata | TS-VANTAGE-N1 | Online | < 1 second | 6652003 |
| Catalog | TS-VANTAGE-N1 | Online | < 1 second | 6122733 |
| Transport | TS-VANTAGE-N1 | Online | 2 seconds | 4719047 |
| Communicate | TS-VANTAGE-N1 | Online | < 1 second | 3243537 |
| Metadata | TS-VANTAGE-N2 | Online | < 1 second | 1461002 |
| Cloud | TS-VANTAGE-N1 | Online | < 1 second | 1186365 |
| Catalog | TS-VANTAGE-N2 | Online | < 1 second | 891529 |
| Analysis | TS-VANTAGE-N1 | Online | < 1 second | 883585 |
| Transport | TS-VANTAGE-N2 | Online | < 1 second | 740143 |
| Cloud | TS-VANTAGE-N2 | Online | < 1 second | 705569 |
| Monitor | TS-VANTAGE-N2 | Online | 1 second | 283109 |
| Monitor | TS-VANTAGE-N1 | Online | 2 seconds | 225382 |
| Analysis | TS-VANTAGE-N2 | Online | < 1 second | 107729 |
| Transcode | TS-VANTAGE-N1 | Online | < 1 second | 94065 |
| Traffic | TS-VANTAGE-N2 | Online | < 1 second | 85713 |
| Traffic | TS-VANTAGE-N1 | Online | < 1 second | 32934 |
| Staging | TS-VANTAGE-N1 | Online | < 1 second | 1724 |
| Staging | TS-VANTAGE-N2 | Online | < 1 second | 1200 |

FIGURE 5: THIS CAPTURE FROM A MEDIA PROCESSING MONITORING TOOL SHOWS THE AVERAGE WAIT TIME FOR A SERVICE IS LESS THAN 1 SECOND. THE KEY CONTAINERIZED SERVICE HERE IS "CLOUD" WHICH PROVIDES SCALABLE AND RESPONSIVE TRANSCODING. IN ESSENCE, THIS SHOWS US THAT PERFORMANCE OF THE PIPELINE IS NOT SIGNIFICANTLY AFFECTED BY THE AMOUNT OF CONTENT TRANSCODED, *IF* THE TRANSCODE SERVICES ARE CONTAINERIZED AND DYNAMICALLY RESPONSIVE.

The Media Processing engine will also generate formulaic episodic promos. For instance, a syndicated program may air five days a week on five channels. Programming may want to schedule two types of promos ("Tomorrow" and "Today") for each of five episodes, resulting in

10 promos per station. Each promo must be customized with station specific graphics, as well as "Tomorrow on Channel X" or "Today on Channel X" audio voice overs.

Templates are created for each syndicated program which contain spatial and temporal placeholders used by Media Processing automation to drop in station specific graphics and voice overs  In this way we can automate creation of the 50 promos required for the five stations to air this syndicated program Monday through Friday.

Media and side-car files output by the Media Processing engine are placed in the CMP Output S3 bucket and a status messages informing other processes of the newly available files are sent on the CMP Media Bus.

4) **Media Search & Visibility** - Sony Ci was chosen as the tool for Media Knowledge & Visibility.

   This tool detects new files in the CMP Output S3 bucket, ingests and indexes metadata, creates links for download and retrieval, and creates proxies and thumbnails.

   Received media is available through a web UI / lightboard where it can be searched, viewed, checked and downloaded if needed.

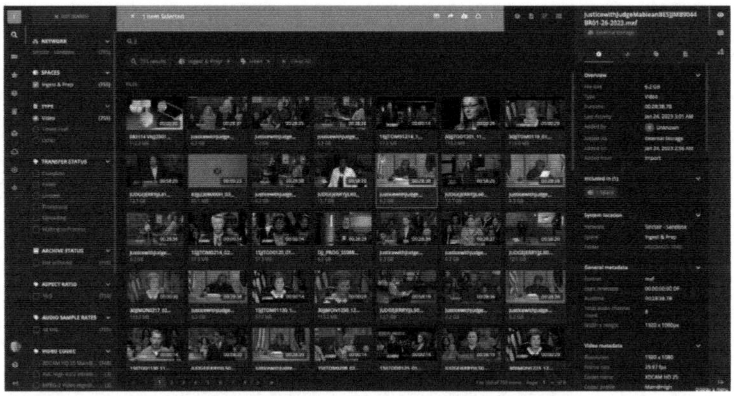

FIGURE 6: THIS IS AN EXAMPLE OF SYNDICATED PROGRAMS DISPLAYED IN THE LIGHT TABLE SEARCH VIEW PROVIDED BY THE MEDIA SEARCH & VISIBILITY TOOL.

Master control operators use this tool for manually handling exceptions. As the central point of truth, changes to media or metadata using this tool are then available globally to both users and API's.

Integrated systems, including automated systems to pull media for playout, use this tool's API to search and retrieve media, primarily using Ad-ID/ISCI and Day Codes. Traffic and scheduling also use this tool to manage ID's and verify content.

Versioning is applied such that previous or earlier versions are also available via UI and API.

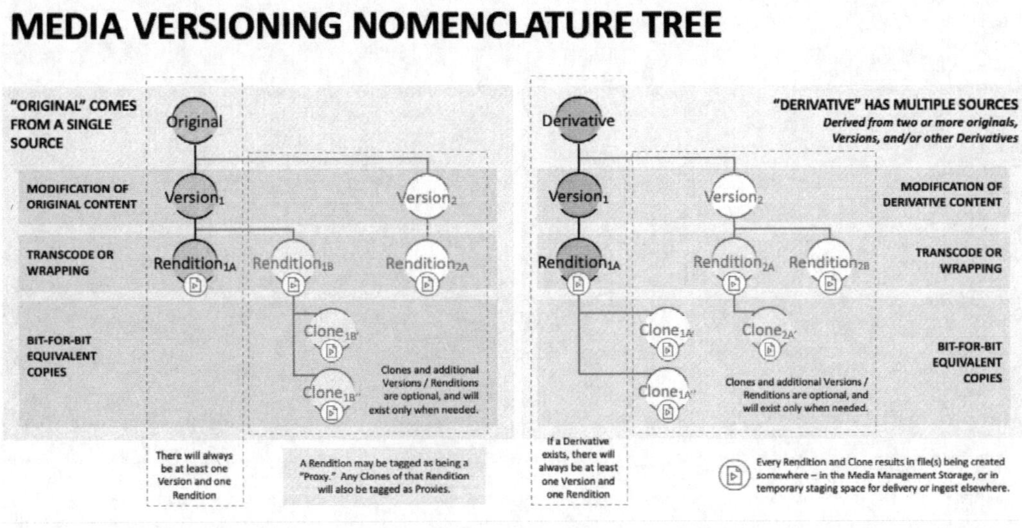


FIGURE 7: DEFINITIONS OF "ORIGINAL", "VERSION" AND "RENDITION" BECOME CRITICALLY IMPORTANT WHEN DISCUSSING MEDIA PIPELINE WORKFLOW – PARTICULARLY WHEN THOSE DISCUSSIONS ARE ACROSS BUSINESS AND TECHNICAL UNITS.

This system currently manages a rolling window of 90 days of content, comprised of about 800,000 renditions. Renditions, thumbnails, side cars and metadata consume about 600TB of storage.

5) **Media Workflow Orchestration** - Embrace's Pulse.it product was chosen as the Orchestration and Workflow Engine. This tool serves two interrelated functions.

   The first function is to translate webhooks and other notifications received from federated systems, such as media management, and repeat those to the CMP Media Bus, embodied in practice as an AWS SNS/SQS Notification/Message queue stack.

   The second function is to provide a low-code graphical method to quickly perform API integration with other services which can be integrated as elements of larger workflows.

   These workflows themselves can be called as REST interfaces by other services. This provides a robust method for linking other services into and out of the CMP.

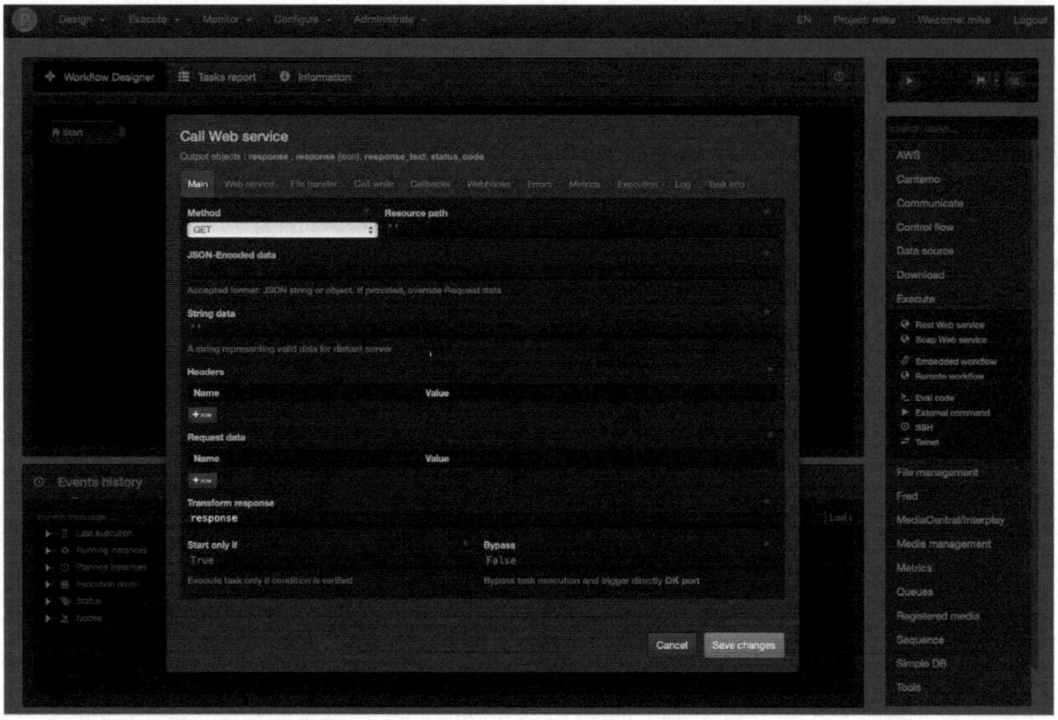


FIGURE 8: MEDIA WORKFLOW ORCHESTRATION ALLOWS INTEGRATION WITH REST AND OTHER API'S WITH LITTLE OR NO CODE. HERE, A REST INTERFACE CAN BE CONFIGURED THROUGH A FORM.

6) **Playout Integration** – though not a part of the CMP, these systems are consumers of CMP output: Crispin, Kumulate/SPA, Amagi

   Day Codes for syndicated and other non-advertising content are generated by the Media Processing engine using a standard template and information provided by the distributor or contributor. Day Codes generated in this fashion match the day codes used by Programming and Traffic.

   Ad-ID/ISCI codes are used for advertising content. Supplied by the person or system who uploaded content, this ID must match that used by Copy/Traffic. If there is no match, this is handled as an exception.

   Care has been taken to create a deconflicted, shared namespace for identifying metadata used by content for all channels. This is particularly important because at the outset channels traffic will be applied independently to all channels.

## Results

The system is operating well, and producing content used by the full enterprise. Full efficiencies will come over time as the environment continues to evolve.

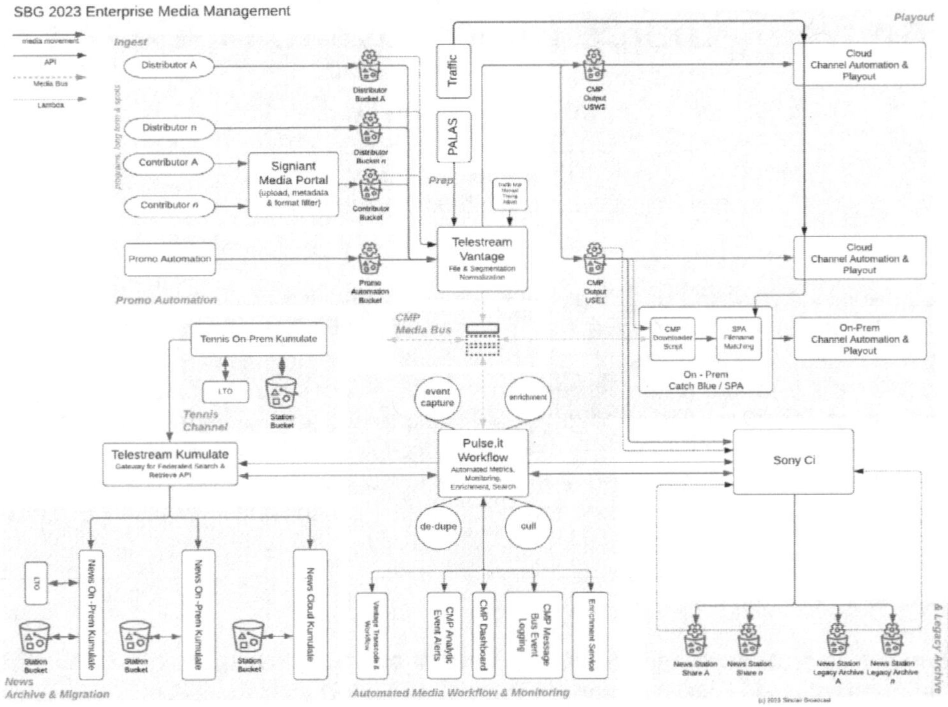


FIGURE 9: THIS DIAGRAM DESCRIBES SOME, BUT NOT ALL, OF THE COMPONENTS THAT COMPRISE THE SINCLAIR CLOUD MEDIA PIPELINE, WHICH IS ITSELF A COMPONENT OF OUR LARGER CLOUD MEDIA MANAGEMENT INITIATIVE.

As more distributors add lists of channel end-points to their spot and syndication metadata the number the number of manual operations to add the end points will also drop.

As we move playout from on-prem to cloud the number of renditions the CMP produces will drop from five to one, resulting in proportional savings in both compute and storage.

We have already demonstrated the ability to produce renditions at 10% of the cost of creating the same renditions on-prem. As we move playout to cloud and reduce the number of required renditions from 5 to 1 we expect to experience even more savings.

Another benefit is increased speed. At peak times on the busiest days files typically begin the transcode process within less than 20 seconds of submission. The older on-prem solution, which was built for peak demand, typically developed a backlog of up to two hours at peak times.

Automated production of episodic promos, once fully deployed, has the potential to reduce the cost of creating our 60,000 promos per month by up to 90%.

Sinclair's next steps include adding further monitoring with automated alerts, orchestrating dynamic deployment of infrastructure through Terraform, and further integration with AI/ML enrichment services.

# Elastic Frame Protocol: An Open-source Alternative to MPEG-2 TS

**Mikael Wånggren**
**Agile Content S.A.**
**Stockholm, Sweden**
mikael.wanggren@agilecontent.com

**Abstract** – This paper looks at the use of framing and multiplexing protocols in broadcast media. In it, we identify several inefficiencies that have arisen from using MPEG-2 Transport Stream (TS) in some areas of modern IP-based media transport and discuss how the new open-source Elastic Frame Protocol (EFP) attempts to avoid these issues. Areas discussed include protocol overhead, timeline and time stamps, error detection and recovery, (de)multiplexing, complex transport architectures and flexibility. MPEG-2 TS has the advantage of being almost universally supported in broadcast media transport. But we found that EFP provided significantly lower overhead, 64-bit timestamps and much improved possibilities to detect packet loss and correct packets that are delivered out of order.

## Introduction

Video and audio media already constitute the majority of all traffic transported over the internet, and their share continues to grow. But IP transport of multimedia extends far beyond YouTube videos and OTT streaming services. Within the broadcast media business, we need to take into account local production facilities, remote production contribution flows, and a plethora of distribution solutions. Each of these have environmental conditions that have influenced the design of the protocols that are used in their IP transport. This paper focuses on the use of framing and multiplexing protocols and how they are best tailored for these different environments, specifically comparing the omnipresent incumbent MPEG-2 Transport Stream (TS) [1] with the new open-source Elastic Frame Protocol (EFP) [2].

A framing and multiplexing protocol may have several purposes:

- **Framing**, i.e. dividing an elementary media stream into suitable chunks for multiplexing.
- **Multiplexing**, which means alternating chunks from several elementary streams into one single stream.
- **Synchronization**, where the timeline of each elementary stream is related to a common time base and that time base may be transported or signaled between sender and receiver.
- **Metadata** can be transported describing all the constituent elementary streams.
- **Error detection and recovery** support can be added on the multiplexed stream.

### Local Production Facilities

It isn't always necessary to use a multiplexing protocol. Take the example of a local production facility, which typically includes television studios, control rooms and networked production machinery such as cameras, microphones, video switchers, audio mixers, etc. Here, there are many media streams produced and consumed in a complex pattern. What's required in this context is very low latency, so often media is transported fully uncompressed – leading to video stream bandwidths measured in the

This paper is excerpted from the Proceedings of the 2023 NAB Broadcast Engineering and Information Technology (BEIT) Conference, © 2023, National Association of Broadcasters, 1 M Street SE, Washington, DC 20003 USA.

gigabit/s each. In this domain, SMPTE ST 2110 [3] and its associated protocols and technologies are gradually replacing legacy SDI production environments.

ST 2110 doesn't rely on a framing and multiplexing protocol. Instead, each elementary stream produced by a media source is made available on its own in the network via unique UDP multicast ports. Error detection and some recovery (such as reordering) are performed on a per elementary stream basis using the Real-time Transport Protocol (RTP) [4], a protocol that also supplies the time stamping functionality. Time synchronization is handled separately using Precision Time Protocol (PTP) [5], and metadata on all available streams is handled out-of-band using the NMOS protocol suite [6] or manually using Session Description Protocol (SDP) [7].

Having separate elementary streams, all available on the shared network over multicast, is useful in this environment because there are plenty of processing devices that are interested either in reading only one single elementary stream, or many streams of the same type from a number of different sources. Examples of the latter type are video switchers or audio mixers. Both types benefit from being able to pick up only the specific streams they are interested in, without having to resort to demultiplexing combined streams first. The cost of not multiplexing is more network resource usage (such as UDP ports) which isn't a problem in a local environment. However, the complexities that arise from the large volume of streams, producers and consumers that make up these environments can prove problematic. One example of this is that the network must be managed so that there are no packet losses, as there are no loss recovery mechanisms in these high bandwidth multicast streams.

## Remote and Distributed Environments

When transporting media streams over longer distances, the approach described above isn't feasible. Instead, the goal is often to multiplex all elementary streams to be transported into one single data stream. Generally, the elementary streams are compressed into a bit stream format in order to reduce the transport and storage requirements. The single multiplexed stream may then be transported over satellite, over-the-air broadcast, ASI, virtual circuit switched connections such as ATM, or packet switched IP networks where network resources such as UDP ports are scarce (or made complicated by enterprise firewall management) and UDP multicast isn't available. We can distinguish between connections that are one-way (simplex) such as satellite and over-the-air broadcast, or two-way (duplex), such as modern internet. This distinction is important, since in a simplex connection it's impossible to give feedback on the connection or to synchronize clocks, meaning the receiver needs to resort to recovering a common clock based on information sent inside the stream.

Today, IP-based contribution flows for remote and distributed production are often transported using the public internet over links that require compression and multiplexing, but that are duplex in nature. Here, media acquired by cameras and microphones in remote locations is transported to a central facility for use in broadcast production. Synchronizing all media sources to a common timing reference is a challenge is these environments.

## Distribution

On the distribution side, what's transported is a finished program consisting of one video stream and one or a few audio streams, as well as subtitles and other metadata, often heavily compressed. Distribution IP transport consists of both UDP-based and TCP-based technologies, where the latter may be segmented. Interestingly, with segmented streaming it has become increasingly common to disregard multiplexing and offer each sub-stream separately in the manifest, so that the client may pick and choose a collection of streams more efficiently. Non-IP distribution technologies relevant to our discussion of MPEG-2 TS are the simplex-based ones mentioned above.

## MPEG-2 Transport Stream

MPEG-2 Transport Stream is a protocol for framing and multiplexing elementary media streams into a format that's suitable for transport and to some extent storage. It was developed in the early nineties and first specified in 1995 in the standard ISO/IEC 13818-1, which is the systems part of MPEG-2, as well as in the ITU-T H.222 [8] specification. In some respects, MPEG-2 built upon the MPEG-1 Systems specification developed to make it possible to store MPEG-1 progressive video in SIF resolution (352x240 or 352x288 pixels for NTSC and PAL respectively) and play it from a disc. MPEG-2 video focused on digital SDTV, which has twice the resolution of SIF and is interlaced. MPEG-2 Systems contain both a Transport Stream (TS) and a Program Stream (PS) specification, where the latter is essentially the same specification as MPEG-1 Systems, i.e. suitable for fairly reliable media such as a storage disc.

When MPEG-2 TS was conceived, IP transport of media was in its infancy, and the focus was instead on error-prone channels with low jitter in delay and often in simplex mode. This had some specific influences on the design of the protocol that are not best suited for modern IP-based transmission. The following sections presents a brief overview of the MPEG-2 TS protocol in order to outline these areas where the protocol would benefit from alterations.

### Elementary Streams

The separate media streams transported using TS are called elementary streams and are generally compressed bit streams of video, audio, subtitles or different forms of metadata. The capture times of elementary stream media samples are recorded relative to a shared time reference.

### Packetized Elementary Streams

Each elementary stream is split into sections or packets which form a Packetized Elementary Stream (PES). For video, a PES packet typically carries one video frame or field, while for audio there's typically a larger number of audio samples in a single PES packet. The idea behind this is to achieve lower packetization overhead, since audio in general uses much less data than video. As an example, AAC encoded audio is often transported wrapped in an Audio Data Transport Stream (ADTS) [9], where 1024 audio samples are collected in one ADTS frame. It is common to put one ADTS frame inside a PES packet, but if the increased latency is acceptable, up to a dozen such frames can be placed in a single PES packet. A further optimization of packaging overhead can be achieved by not requiring alignment of the start of a PES packet with the start of an ADTS frame, and instead letting the ADTS frame start anywhere in the first TS packet of a PES frame. Such optimizations do lower the overhead, but they make stitching and tune-in to a stream much harder.

Each PES packet header contains a Presentation Time Stamp (PTS) and optionally a Decode Time Stamp (DTS). The latter is used to identify the decode timeline when the media samples (typically video) have interdependencies in the forward direction, such as B-frames in MPEG video, where the decode order doesn't match the presentation order.

The PTS and DTS in MPEG-2 TS are represented in 33 bits at a rate of 90 kHz, resulting in a wraparound of about 26.5 hours. The timestamps are not set relative to a fixed real-world time anchor, so they are used solely as a way to synchronize different sub-streams and control the pace of egress in the receiving end. The 90 kHz resolution was constructed to represent many common sample rates with integer valued period lengths. However, this can present a problem when attempting to represent time stamps for video sampled at 59.94 frames per second, as each sample period ends up being 1501.5 long. The workaround for this has become to alternate every second frame to be 1501 or 1502 long, which is far from an elegant solution as it results in slightly inaccurate timestamps and care must be taken to alternate perfectly or drift will occur.

## Transport Streams

The PES packets are subdivided into equal size Transport Stream (TS) packets of 188 bytes, a size that was chosen to harmonize with the ATM cell payload size at the time. It always starts with a 4-byte header, including a specific start byte of 0x47 that can be used to seek in the stream for the start of a TS packet. A flag called 'payload unit start indicator' signals if a PES packet starts in that particular TS packet.

The size of a PES packet is generally not an even multiple of the TS packet payload size of 184 bytes, resulting in a need to add padding to fill out the last TS packet in a PES. It's possible to skip this padding and instead to start a new PES packet inside the TS packet. However, this isn't commonly done, as the transmission of the last bytes of one PES packet would have to be delayed until the next PES packet has been constructed, so that the TS packet can be fully filled, leading to increased latency. Another issue is that the stream becomes more complicated to parse.

For video, each frame or field is typically a PES packet, so for a 50 frame per second video there are 50 PES packet endings per second that need to be padded to a 184-byte multiple. For audio, assuming a low-latency setup with one ADTS frame per PES packet, the PES packet frequency is typically in the same area (46.8 PES packets per second for 48kHz AAC-LC, for example). Thus, the relative impact of this padding is completely dependent on the size of the PES packet.

Consider this theoretical example. Assume that audio is encoded into AAC at 128 kbps and the resulting PES packets are 379 bytes. Dividing this into 184-byte units that constitute the MPEG-2 TS packet payload, the result is two full TS packets and a third TS packet with 11 bytes from the end of the PES packet and 173 bytes of padding. That's 173 bytes of padding added to a 379 byte PES packet, an additional 45.6% of overhead on the AAC coded audio stream! This should be taken with a pinch of salt, as audio bit rates are generally a small part of a stream, compared to the video part. It is however clear that there's significant protocol overhead to be saved here if we could move beyond this archaic fixed packet size of 188 bytes.

Figure 1 sums up the different layers of framing in the MPEG-2 TS standard.

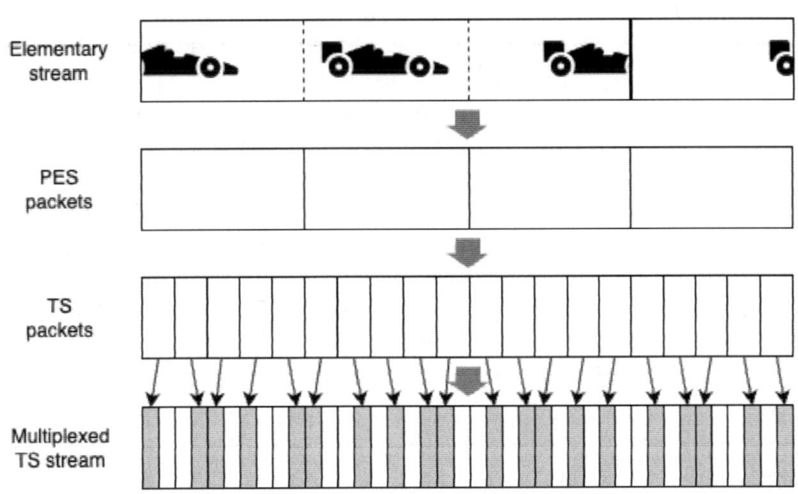


FIGURE 1: MPEG-2 TS FRAMING.

## Transporting TS Packets Over Ethernet

The 188-byte TS packet also causes inefficiencies when transporting TS packets inside UDP/IP over Ethernet transport. Since UDP isn't a reliable protocol, it is common in contribution workflows to wrap a live TS stream in a network resiliency protocol such as SRT [10] or RIST [11] that attempts to recover lost packets and to remove induced network jitter. Ethernet can carry a payload of 1500 bytes, which gives an MTU of 1456 bytes after IPv4, UDP, and SRT headers are added, as demonstrated in Table 1.

| Protocol | Header size (bytes) |
|---|---|
| Ethernet | 14 |
| IPv4 | 20 |
| UDP | 8 |
| SRT | 16 |

TABLE 1: IP/UDP PROTOCOL STACK HEADER SIZES.

MPEG-2 TS packets are always 188 bytes long. But it's common to aggregate several into one IP packet to minimize overhead. The maximum is 7 TS packets constituting a total payload of 1316 bytes. A protocol that can fill the entire payload (MTU) of the ethernet packet would get a higher ratio of useful traffic to total amount of headers. It's clear that TS can't achieve this.

## Additional Sources of Protocol Overhead

- **Start Codes and Checksums:** There are various start codes and checksums distributed in the various levels of protocol headers like PES and TS. For example, PES packets have a PES header starting with a three-byte start code. This makes it possible to find the PES start even if some packet is missing, or if the PES packet starts in the middle of a TS packet. The mentioned mechanisms make it possible to send a MPEG-2 TS stream without a compatible packet framing, since it's possible to search and find the starts of TS packets and PES packets by looking at byte patterns. However, when using a packet-based framing such as UDP, or protocols on top of UDP like SRT and RIST, handling misaligned or partial packets isn't an issue, and such mechanisms could be removed.
- **Null packet stuffing:** Traditionally, MPEG-2 TS streams have been sent using a constant bit rate (CBR). To achieve this from non-constant elementary streams, the multiplexer adds stuffing in the form of null packets to the TS stream. These packets are discarded by the demultiplexer. This is also a source of overhead, typically in the range of 5-10%.
- **Repeating descriptive Metadata:** In MPEG-2 TS, the Program Association Table (PAT) and Program Map Table (PMT) periodically repeat metadata that acts as a table of contents for the transport stream. The reason for this repetition is to enable receivers to start parsing the stream at any point, without communicating with the sender. This approach enables them to determine the content of a stream within a reasonable amount of time. The repetition rate is system dependent, but in Digital Video Broadcasting (DVB) the requirement is once every 500ms [12]. This table-of-contents metadata contains information on all the programs in the transport stream, and all elementary streams in each program. For each type of elementary stream, there are separate specifications that define descriptors, data structures that can be quite lengthy, that also go in the PMT.

## Error Detection and Recovery

For MPEG-2 TS, each elementary stream has its own 4-bit wide continuity counter corresponding to 16 possible values. It can often (but not always) be used to detect that some data has been lost, but reassembling a stream with out of order or duplicated packets is very hard, if not impossible. The fact that up to 7 TS packets from different elementary streams can be combined in each UDP packet only complicates these operations. Therefore, there's often an extra layer of protocols for transporting TS over UDP, such as RTP. This is added to get a sequence number for the whole set of 7 MPEG-2 TS packets. However, the RTP header adds another 12 bytes of overhead and only carries a 32-bit timestamp, so it is not an optimal solution.

### Time Synchronization

When MPEG-2 was first developed, it was very hard to synchronize clocks between sites, so MPEG-2 TS carries a System Time Clock (STC) timeline via 42-bit (27MHz) PCR (Program Clock Reference) time stamps. The PCR time stamps are intended to be used to generate a receiver STC that does not drift relative to the sender STC. This allows the receiver to pace out media samples in the same rate and internal relation as they were created in the producer. The PTS and DTS time stamps in the PES header are expressed in the time base established through the PCR time stamps. Thus, not only PTS and DTS but also PCR time stamps wrap around after roughly 26.5 hours. Clock recovery suited the early environments with low jitter and hardware-based TS protocol implementations, but modern internet transport introduces jitter in both transport and software-based timestamping that makes clock recovery more difficult.

### Complex Buffer Model

A further restriction is a strict buffer model. This was invented to support hardware decoders and set-top-boxes with very small amounts of buffer memory. The standard defines a theoretical system target decoder (T-STD) and a leak or Video Buffer Verifier (VBV) model. This should be used to schedule the TS media packets and insert TS stuffing packets in order to neither underflow nor overflow the receiver buffer. These specifications are neither necessary nor strictly adhered to in many modern software-based implementations.

## Elastic Frame Protocol

The work on EFP was started in 2020, with the aim of creating a lean protocol to only be transported over packet networks. This suits today's conditions of media transport over the Internet. It transports well over modern low latency network resiliency protocols such as SRT or RIST, and avoids as much unneeded complexity as possible in its specification. It takes the approach of an open-source implementation, rather than a standards-body-driven specification.

In the following sections, we will first give an overview of EFP's framing mechanisms. We'll then examine the protocol feature areas that were identified as problematic in MPEG-2 TS, and explain how EFP addresses these.

### EFP Framing

As previously described, in MPEG-2 TS, a media frame (such as a video frame or an ADTS frame containing audio samples) is encapsulated in a PES packet, which is then broken down into TS packets. In a similar way, in EFP the media frame is encapsulated in a Superframe, which is then broken down into fragments. These fragments are the same size as the underlying transport's MTU. For example, when transported using a protocol stack consisting of Ethernet, IP, UDP and SRT, the remaining MTU is 1456, as was shown in Table 1.

There are a few different types of fragments in EFP, as demonstrated in Table 2. A superframe consists of zero or more type-1 fragments and is ended by a type-2 fragment. The type-2 fragment contains the frame metadata (such as timestamps and content type), in addition to the last part of the payload. In rare corner cases having to do with certain superframe sizes, a type-3 fragment is placed between the type-1 and type-2 fragments.

| Type | Header size (bytes) | Description |
|---|---|---|
| 0 | 1 | Real-time fragment |
| 1 | 8 | Regular media fragment |
| 2 | 28 | End of superframe incl. time stamps |
| 3 | 10 | Regular media fragment with size |

TABLE 2: EFP FRAGMENT TYPES.

Type-0 fragments are high priority fragments sent and delivered instantly. Among other uses, they can be used to implement an inline time-transfer functionality.

Figure 2 shows some examples of superframes constructed from different types of fragments.

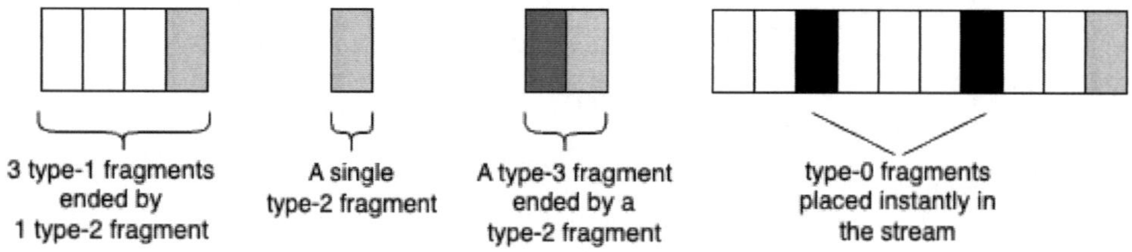


FIGURE 2: EFP SUPERFRAME EXAMPLES.

EFP provides the option to have the superframes delivered in-order or out-of-order (i.e. instantly on arrival of the full superframe). If delivered in-order, one can set a time-out for how long to wait for a missing superframe.

If a fragment of a superframe is lost, the remaining parts of the superframe are still delivered, but the superframe is marked as broken. The timeout to wait for missing fragments is configurable.

The API and protocol also allow for embedding extra data (e.g. metadata) in a superframe.

### Protocol Overhead

EFP attempts to keep protocol overhead low in several different ways. It does not contain start codes or checksums, instead relying on such functionality in the encapsulating lower layer protocols. It also attempts to use the full MTU to make the relative size of the stack of headers as small as possible. However, EFP does not currently put more than one superframe in an IP packet, so in the case of very short superframes (such as for low-latency audio) where the payload is typically in the range of a few hundreds of bytes, the per-Ethernet-packet overhead ratio will be higher than the theoretical minimum.

### Error Detection and Recovery

We saw that the 4-bit continuity counter in TS may be useful for identifying the presence of packet loss or reordering, but that it commonly does not provide enough information to reflect the extent of these errors or how to correct them. EFP on the other hand has a 16-bit counter for superframes and another 16-bit counter for fragments within a superframe. This allows for clear identification of exactly how much data was lost, and for sorting out duplicates and reordering out-of-order packets. In fact, EFP's frame numbering and timestamps means EFP alone goes beyond what MPEG-2 TS + RTP achieve together in this respect. As a bonus, using the EFP frame numbering, it's also possible to insert a thin layer between EFP and the transport stack to do multi-path delivery. This can either be done by duplicating all packets over several separate paths, known as "1+1", "1+N" or "active-active" redundancy, or distributing the stream over several channels in a way that creates one larger combined virtual channel, known as channel bonding. This is possible since identifying each packet uniquely is trivial. The advantage of solving multipath delivery at the EFP layer is that it is independent of the underlying transport protocols of the different data paths.

### Time Stamps and Clock Consistency

EFP does not carry an inline System Time Reference that is recovered on the receiving side. Instead, EFP expects the clocks in the communicating nodes to be synchronized using some external method, such as Network Time Protocol (NTP) [13], Precision Time Protocol (PTP) or some custom time synchronization protocol. There is also a fragment type (type 0) defined in EFP that can be used for building a custom synchronization protocol. This removes a large amount of complexity compared to the MPEG-2 TS specification.

EFP uses a 64-bit timestamp which can be used to carry International Atomic Time (TAI), a monotonic absolute time. The interpretation of the timestamp in EFP is not specified in the protocol, which is both a weakness and a strength. For interoperability purposes, a fixed definition would have been useful, but leaving it to be implementation defined allows for multiple different uses. One can choose a timescale that avoids the MPEG-2 TS issue that the DTS values for 59.94 frames/s video increase by 1501.5 ticks in average, resulting in fluctuating DTS step sizes.

By using 180 kHz, the DTS steps increase evenly by 3003 for each frame. With a monotonically increasing timeline and constant DTS step, one can also make a direct translation to and from MPEG DASH live streams [14] with ISOBMFF [15] segments, since they have a monotonic clock with 64-bit resolution. Having a constant DTS step translates into a constant sample duration in the ISOBMFF fragments which allows for less overhead by conveying the sample duration as a default value in the Track Fragment Header box.

### Descriptive Metadata

MPEG-2 TS transports descriptive metadata repetitively inline. EFP also has a method for sending this kind of table-of-contents metadata in-band in the stream. However, to take advantage of modern duplex-based communication, it can also communicate out-of-band using web sockets. If transported in-band, the metadata can be repetitive or only triggered on changes in the stream. Taking even more advantage of the duplex functionality, EFP also adds the possibility to communicate from a receiver to the sender, filtering settings so that not all content is sent over the link.

EFP has one weakness in relation to MPEG-2 TS. Many elementary stream protocol specifications already contain information on how to map them into MPEG-2 transport streams and exactly what the descriptors should contain, whereas EFP currently has a more limited set of streams and descriptors.

### Open-Source Reference Implementation

While MPEG-2 TS is the de-facto standard today due to its widespread support in legacy products, there's no open-source library that supports the full specification in software, due to its complexities. With EFP, the stated aim is to create a definitive reference implementation that is portable and easily integrated, with a simple, clean, powerful C++ interface, and a friendly license type.

## Experimental Results

In addition to theoretical discussions on protocol overhead, we conducted an experiment to measure the protocol overhead of MPEG-2 TS and EFP when multiplexing a stream consisting of one video and one audio stream. The audio and video sources contained random noise. To achieve a reproducible result, we used FFmpeg to generate H.264 video at 50 frames per second at a series of different bit rates, while keeping the bit rate of the AAC-LC audio constant at 96kbps. In the script (see Listing 1) the bit rate in kbps is represented by $1 and is varied from 500 to 20000 in steps of 500, while the buffer size is represented by $2 with the value $2 = 1.5 ∗ $1.

```
ffmpeg \
−f lavfi \
−i nullsrc=s=1280x720: rate=50 \
−filter complex "geq=random(1)*255:128:128; aevalsrc=−2+random(0)" \
−c:a aac −b:a 96k −ac 2 −ar 48000 \
−c:v libx264 −preset medium −b:v $1k −minrate $1k −maxrate $1k −bufsize $2k \
 −x264opts "no−scenecut : keyint=50 : min−keyint=50 : \
   nal−hrd=cbr : no−open−gop=1 : force−cfr=1 : aud=1" \
−y −f mpegts −t 25 rnd.ts
```

LISTING 1: FFMPEG SCRIPT TO GENERATE DATA.

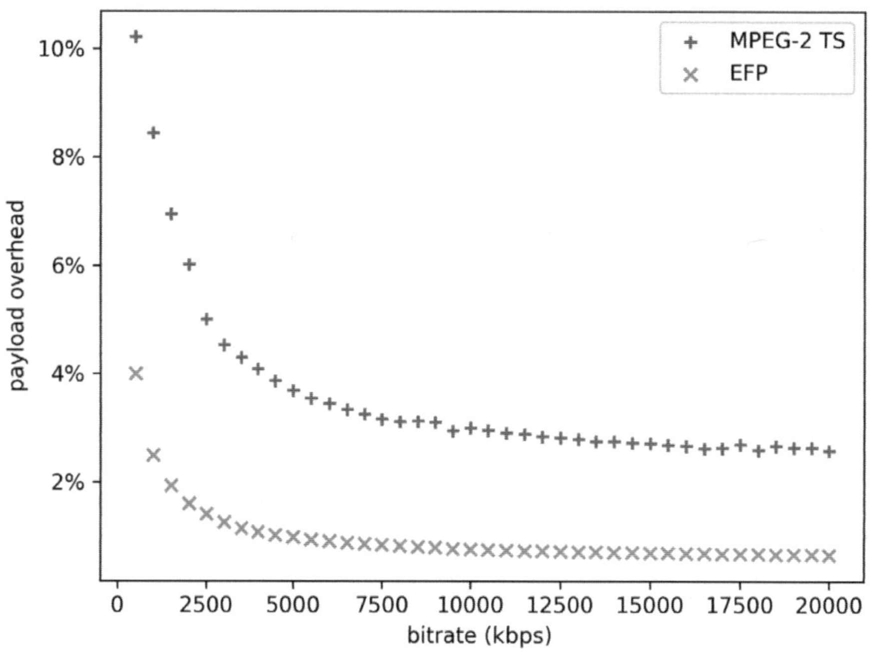


FIGURE 3: PAYLOAD OVERHEAD PER PROTOCOL.

The result is shown in Figure 3. The x-axis shows the video bit rate, while the y-axis shows the payload overhead which is calculated as:

$$payload\ overhead = \frac{media\ bytes + protocol\ bytes}{media\ bytes} - 1 \quad (1)$$

$$media\ bytes = video\ payload + audio\ payload \quad (2)$$

Since all video and audio frames have time stamps and other sample information, the overhead is higher for lower bit rates. For MPEG-2 TS, there is also a high relative overhead from stuffing the end of each frame. As the bit rate approaches higher values, the payload overheads converge to the asymptotic values where the frame endings are negligible, and the overhead can be calculated as:

$$asymptotic\ overhead = \frac{header\ size}{packet\ size - header\ size} \tag{3}$$

This results in the values in Table 3.

| Protocol | Packet size (bytes) | Header size (bytes) | Asymptotic overhead |
|---|---|---|---|
| MPEG-2 TS | 188 | 4 | ≈ 2.2% |
| EFP | 1450 | 8 | ≈ 0.55% |

TABLE 3: ASYMPTOTIC OVERHEAD.

In the above, we didn't consider other effects, like stuffing to constant bit rate and the headers of the transport packet layers. However, it's clear that it is possible to lower the overhead substantially by using a more modern protocol like EFP, compared to MPEG-2 TS.

## Conclusions

The main upside of MPEG-2 is that almost any equipment can handle it. This has no doubt contributed to its popularity in the broadcast media transport world – and has created a sort of 'self-fulfilling prophecy' for its continued use. However, there's no doubt that it's inefficient in modern packet-switched software-based environments. So much so, that the full specification is seldom strictly adhered to any longer.

EFP offers a number of improvements that align better to today's world, including (but not limited to):

- Significantly lower protocol overhead verified through theoretical reasoning and experiments.
- Monotonically increasing timeline with 64-bit timestamps, compared to 33-bit cyclic timestamps.
- The ability to repair of out-of-order packet delivery using dual 16-bit instead of 4-bit counters.

The main downside of EFP at the moment is its lack of interoperability. This can be put down to its relative lack of maturity compared to MPEG-2 TS. However, since it's available as open-source code it can be used and improved freely and simply together with SRT or RIST to achieve a better media transport link between two nodes.

## References


[1] "Information technology - Generic coding of moving pictures and associated audio information - Part 1: Systems", ISO/IEC 13818-1 First Edition, 1995.

[2] Elastic Frame Protocol (EFP), https://github.com/agilecontent/efp

[3] "ST 2110-10:2017 - SMPTE Standard - Professional Media Over Managed IP Networks: System Timing and Definitions,", SMPTE standard ST 2110-10:2017, 2017.

[4] "RTP: A Transport Protocol for Real-Time Applications", IETF RFC 3550, 2003.

[5] "IEEE Standard for a Precision Clock Synchronization Protocol for Networked Measurement and Control Systems", IEEE 1588-2008, 2008.

[6] Networked Media Open Specifications, https://specs.amwa.tv/nmos/

[7] "SDP: Session Description Protocol", IETF RFC 4566, 2006.

[8] "Information technology — Generic coding of moving pictures and associated audio information — Part 1: Systems", Recommendation ITU-T H.222.0 First Edition, 1995.

[9] "Information technology — Generic coding of moving pictures and associated audio information — Part 7: Advanced Audio Coding (AAC)", ISO/IEC 13818-7:2006, 2006.

[10] "Secure Reliable Transport (SRT)" https://github.com/Haivision/srt

[11] "Reliable Internet Stream Transport (RIST), Protocol Specification - Simple Profile", Video Services Forum, 2018.

[12] "Digital Video Broadcasting (DVB); Measurement guidelines for DVB systems", ETSI TR 101 290 V1.3.1, 2014.

[13] "Network Time Protocol Version 4: Protocol and Algorithms Specification", IETF RFC 5905, 2010.

[14] "Information technology — Dynamic adaptive streaming over HTTP (DASH) — Part 1: Media presentation description and segment formats", ISO/IEC IS 23009-1, 2021.

[15] "ISO base media file format", ISO/IEC IS 14496-12, 2021.

# Immersive and Interactive AR Graphics and Environments for Broadcast Applications

**Caroline Stedman Mishra, MA., BSc.**
**Star Lab, Disney Star**
**Mumbai, Maharashtra, India**
caroline.stedman.mishra@disney.com

**Saurabh Ranjan, Btech., Sanjyot Dale, BE.**
**Liminal**
**Mumbai, Maharashtra, India**

**Abstract** – This paper presents a Mixed Reality Toolkit solution for visualisation and interaction with broadcast AR graphics, with a multi-camera spectator camera solution so that the audience can see the same graphics that the presenter is interacting with. This solution was developed by Disney Star's R&D Lab, Star Lab. The purpose of the toolkit is to provide a more immersive experience for both audiences and presenters and to aid in storytelling around sports data in cricket broadcast programming.
This paper describes the background and inspiration for the project which started with the Hololens demos by Epic Games and Microsoft. It then goes on to describe the technical specifications and workflow of the system. There is an evaluation which details the technical roadblocks encountered by the team and steps taken to solve them and/or possible future solutions that will provide improvements to the system. The evaluation also details the results of a subjective user test from both presenter and audience points of view. The paper concludes with a summary of the state of the industry in the field of broadcast augmented reality graphics and how our product is novel in its capabilities and approach and plans for its next stages of development, as well as an outlook for the future of interactive AR graphics and virtual sets.

## Introduction

Broadcast augmented reality graphics are widely used to demonstrate data points which are used for storytelling in programming, largely in factual based shows i.e., weather, news, sports, science etc. They are used in hard set environments as well as in combination with virtual studio green screen environments. So far, their use has been subject to technological restrictions whereby the presenters are unable to see the graphics and must rely on comfort monitors which show their proximity to the virtual objects. Presenters have also been unable to interact directly with the graphics, so any dynamic changes to the graphics must be implemented by an additional graphics operator or a hardware device controlled by the presenter, such as a clicker or gesture band worn on the hand or wrist. In addition, the graphics generally appear as an alpha layer rendered in front of the presenter or a background layer in a green screen set-up, where the presenter is keyed in front of the graphic. If the presenter moves around the studio space, there is a risk of unwanted occlusion which 'breaks the magic' of the virtual object appearing to be a 3D physical object.

These restrictions on visibility to the presenter, interaction and free movement around a virtual object considerably limit storytelling abilities, natural looking interactions and other visual aesthetics.

The above is certainly true of traditional graphics systems like the earlier versions of VizRT. While presenter visualization is still not currently a part of any commercial product, now with the integration of gaming engines into virtual production tools, virtual production software companies are beginning to address the challenges of interaction and un-occluded movement around virtual objects.

This paper describes a novel system for the control of broadcast augmented reality graphics which allows for real time dynamic interactions with data within a multi camera set-up and visualization of AR graphics by a presenter via a HMD with holographic capabilities. The system has been designed with sports broadcast as the focus, specifically for the sport of Cricket. However, it is suitable for other types of non-fiction broadcast.

The system uses the Microsoft Hololens 2 as the primary viewing and interaction device via holographic remoting controlled from within Epic Games' Unreal Engine, integrated with Mosys camera tracking and Awe can calculate ball trajectories based on moving data points produced by presenter interactions with match Hawkeye data, as well as the provision for biomechanics data and bat-ball trajectories from manipulation of 3D player mannequins. The system also allows for fielding analysis based on player positional data integrated into the system as well as templates of commonly used fielding configurations. These can be overlaid with Hawkeye 'wagon wheel' data showing scoring zones for specific players. There are additional features for calling up dynamic player stats and viewing/telestrating on multiple virtual video screens.

The short-term goal of the application development is to enable new and enhanced tools for presenters for storytelling around sports data which are visually appealing for Disney Star's audiences, and an upgrade on what is currently possible with 'off the shelf' virtual production and AR graphics products. In the longer term, the aim is to create the next generation of fully immersive and interactive environments using game engines for presenting television programming content. This would extend beyond singular AR graphics, and we envision a fully interactive, tactile, virtual studio environment for immersive storytelling.

In the nearer future, additional data such as skeletal tracking and pose estimation data will be enabled in order to create 3D AR replays of sporting moments in near real time. These dynamic 3D assets will be fully interactive so that the presenter has the ability to play, pause, rewind and manipulate the model to understand what the result would have been if the player had been in a different pose. For example, we could show how if a bowler had moved his arm higher and made his elbow straighter, his delivery would have landed in an area of the pitch that would have likely got the batsman out.

The use cases of this technology do not stop here, however. While we are at present developing these features for use in the studio, eventually interactive 3D data visualizations and 3D player replays can be pushed out to audiences via mobile or HMD devices. Volumetric video of entire sports arenas can become immersive virtual environments that presenters can move around in and visualize via an HMD, and these same environments can be provided to audiences to experience a match from within, any angle, any position. These same environments have the potential to be gamified and shaped by audience engagement data and feedback/inputs.

The technology also has further use cases outside of sports broadcast and LBE experiences.
As we explore the possible future of a tangible metaverse, we are creating the foundation technology now that can be used to build out such future audience experiences, moving out of the television studios and into our audience's living rooms.

## Background

The Apollo 11 project created by Epic Games was used as an inspiration for our project. The development of the camera tracking system in this project was done in such a way that the system used a combination of 2 tracking data feeds, one coming from an optical tracking system and another from a mixed reality headset, both of which were mounted on top of a real camera. Using a combination of both these values, a virtual camera was controlled inside Unreal Engine. The real camera feed was fed into Unreal Engine and using the Composure plugin, the mixed reality (MR) graphics that were captured by the virtual camera were composited on top of the real camera feed in real-time. In this composition the real camera feed was set as the background and the MR graphics were always set as the foreground. As this compositing system does not include a virtual background, switching the real camera feed to be in the foreground is not possible.

The spectator camera view for Hololens was first introduced in the Hololens 1. It was showcased in Hololens 2 demos by Microsoft where the audience were able to see the Hololens user interacting with the MR graphics from the point of view of a secondary camera. Microsoft later introduced the spectator camera feature for the Unity Engine, using which we can integrate a secondary camera into the MR space to capture all the MR graphics that the Hololens user interacts with. This feature required one Hololens device to be mounted on top of the secondary camera. A major limitation with this system was that the camera parameters like the focal length and aperture of the secondary camera could not be changed once the calibration was done using a set of values.

The spectator view system was not introduced for the Unreal Engine. However, Epic Games created a similar system for the Apollo 11 project using a combination of a mixed reality headset and an optical tracking system mounted on top of the secondary camera. They used the data from both these tracking devices and set a virtual camera to capture the MR graphics from the secondary camera's point of view.

In our project we have eliminated the need of mounting a MR Headset on the secondary camera, instead we use a combination of mixed reality local anchors placed using the user's Hololens device and the Mo-sys camera tracking system to match the virtual camera with the real camera. This system also allows us to change the camera parameters such as focal length and aperture in real-time, as these values are also updated in the virtual camera. Additionally, as our project is designed on a multi-player system, we also have the ability to integrate multiple cameras in the MR space.

## The Mixed Reality Toolkit

The overarching idea of the entire system was to create a real-time interactive mixed reality experience with broadcast quality graphics, which can be showcased to an audience watching via linear television or OTT (without access to a mixed reality headset). The system we created to achieve this can be subdivided into three different parts as follows:

1. Spectator view / Third person view / Production system
2. Hololens operations
3. Pre-show operations and setups using interfaces for Operators.

### Spectator View

The foundation of our Unreal Engine project is based on the multi-player system, through which we are able to separate the Hololens and the broadcast/spectator cameras as independent entities in the system.

The Hololens, as well as each individual spectator camera which is to be connected to the system, has their individual computer running the Unreal Engine project instance. The multiplayer system is based on a server-client model running on a Local Area Network in which the Hololens is always connected to the server computer and all the cameras are connected to the system as client computers.

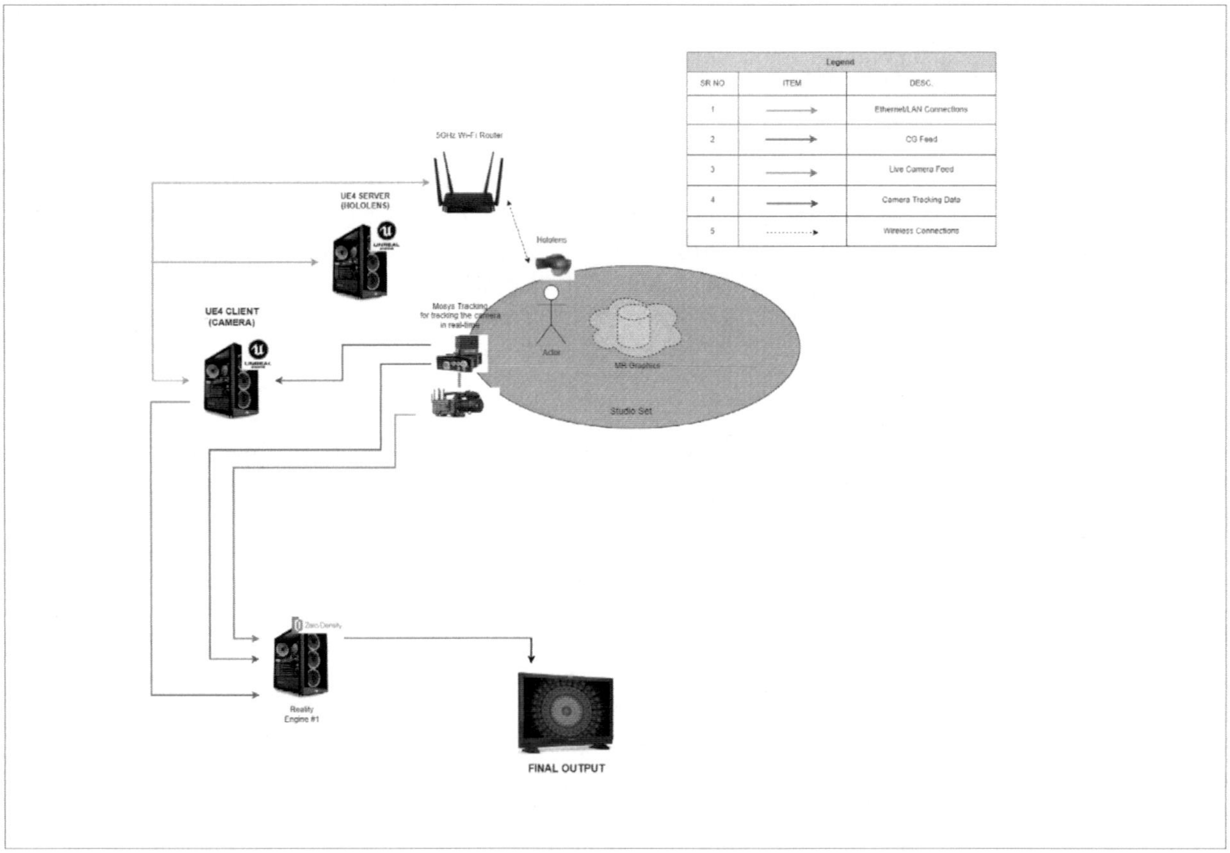


FIGURE 1: SPECTATOR VIEW WORKFLOW.

The computers connected to the cameras receive live camera tracking data from their Mo-sys camera trackers which provide positional and pan, tilt and zoom data of the camera as well as all the intrinsic properties of the camera in real-time.

We use the camera tracking data to place a virtual camera in the MR simulation at the exact position, with all the properties of the real camera. Hence as the virtual camera moves in the MR space it captures the MR graphics with the right perspective and movements.

The captured visuals are processed by the Composure system in the Unreal Engine though SDI and the feed is finally sent to a Zero Density system designated for that camera for compositing with the RGB camera feed.

In this final composition we factored for two situations, one where the talent is standing in a physical set, and the other where the talent is standing in a green screen virtual set. When the talent is standing in a physical set, there is no virtual background and hence the real camera feed becomes the background and the MR graphics become the foreground.

When the talent is standing in a green screen set, we have the virtual background captured by the Zero Density camera, as the background and the talent captured by the real camera is keyed out from the green screen. Hence here we have the ability to choose which feed becomes the foreground between the two remaining feeds, for example, the keyed out real camera feed or the keyed-out MR graphics feed.

Depending on the kind of interactions that we wish to showcase, as well as depending on the position of the talent with respect to the MR graphics, we needed to be able to switch the midground and foreground feeds real-time.

To facilitate this, we created a script using Zero Density's custom scripting language called the Rgraph. Currently this switching between this midground and foreground is triggered on a keyboard button click, but in future updates we plan to automate this switching using technologies like the Zero Density Talent S Traxis, which can provide us the real-time 3D position of the presenters.

## Hololens Operations

When the user wears the Hololens it scans the surroundings of the user and generates a mesh of its surroundings. It uses this mesh for calibration and detects the position of the user as well as Local Anchors in the real-world. Once the calibration is complete, the Windows Mixed Reality plugin allows us to track the user's hands including individual finger joints. The MRTK plugin also allows us to use certain hand tracking gestures like palm detection and pinching, thus allowing the user to interact with the mixed reality graphics. We have used a combination of such gestures to execute different actions like opening the menu and interacting with the ball trajectories, etc.

When the user interacts with the MR graphics i.e. menu, video wall etc. the interaction is received by the server system on which the Hololens is connected (via the WMR plugin), and the result of the action is shared with the client computers connected with the server system using multiplayer setup. Thus upon user interaction, we see the same results on the Hololens as well as on all the spectator cameras.

## Pre-show Operations & Setups Using Interfaces for Operators

The Mixed Reality Toolkit is tailor-made for cricket analysis and cricket-based storytelling; hence it is important to integrate various databases which provide us with the critical data required to visualize specific analytical simulations. We collaborated with Hawkeye to gather this data in the form of JSON files which provided us an exhaustive library of parameters regarding each ball played during different matches. The database from Hawkeye is a mix of historic, as well as real time data. The historic data contains information about each ball delivery since 2018 for all the IPL tournament matches and several other tournament matches. The real-time database provides live match data with a latency of around 2-3 seconds.

We created a custom API to communicate with a remote server that hosts thousands of these JSON files and receives only those data parameters that are required for a particular simulation. To send these API requests from Unreal Engine, we created a front-end GUI for the operator, which they can use to set all the query parameters according to the requirement of the simulation and send an API request. Once the database receives the API request from Unreal, it runs a query that fetches each delivery and its parameters. This data is then sent back to Unreal for further processing of visualization.

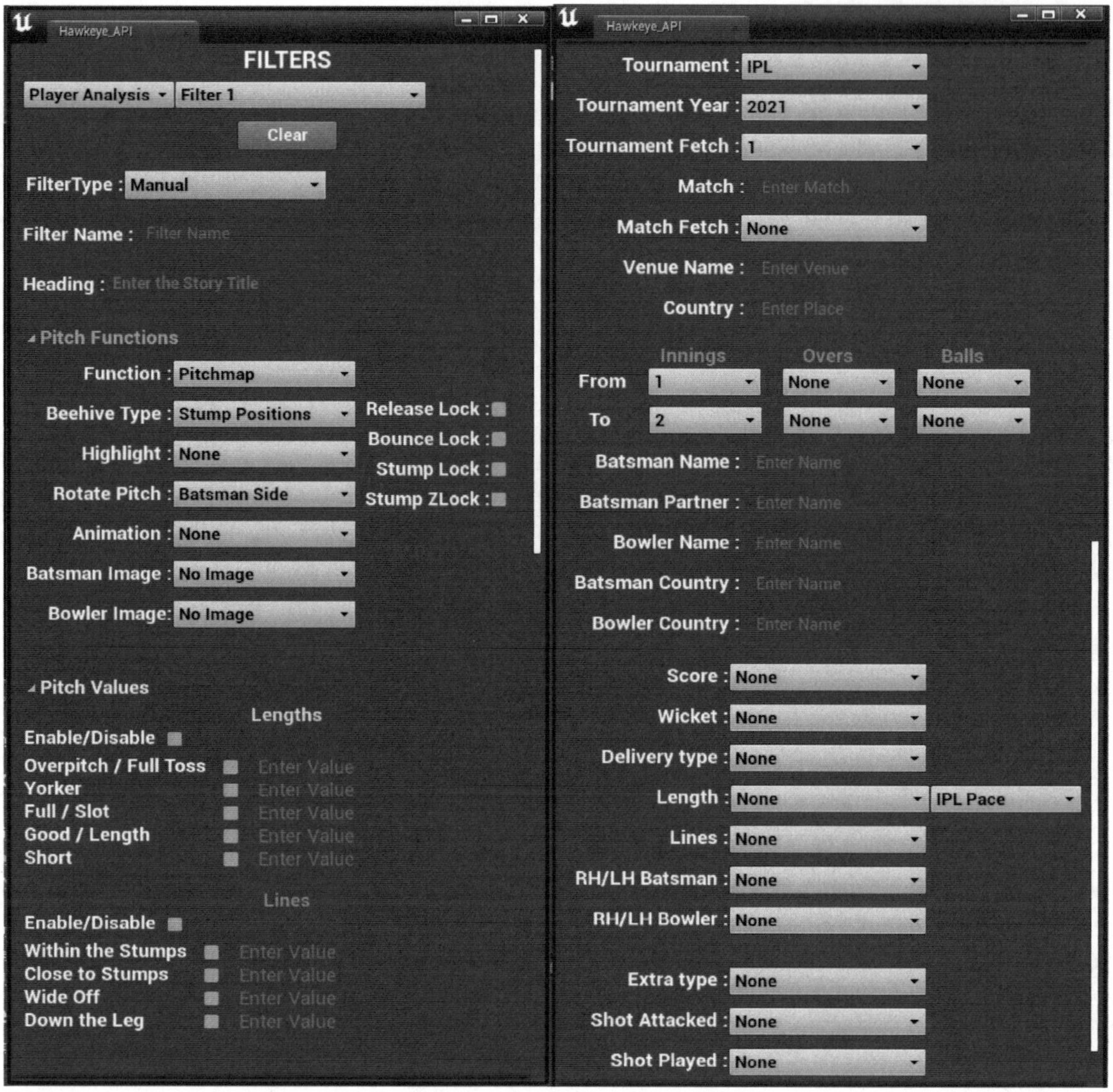


FIGURE 2: DATA FILTERS UI.

The data received by Unreal as a response to the API request is then processed and simulated as MR graphics in the form of ball trails, pitch maps etc.

Once the Unreal Engine receives the data from the Hawkeye API, it processes the data as per the graphics that the operator has selected. The operator can choose between four types of graphics: ball trajectories, pitch maps, beehives, and wagon wheels (with scoring areas). The most important part of the Hawkeye graphics is the virtual pitch, which has been created using accurate real-world values. We have created multiple pitches for visualizing different types of scenarios i.e., pitch for pacers, pitch for spinners, etc. If the operator has selected ball trajectories, multiple parameters are extracted from the JSON files for each ball, for which a trajectory is generated between two or three points on the pitch. The number of points used for creating this trajectory depends on the type of ball that is being showcased i.e., full toss, bouncer, etc. Once the trajectory is generated, the Hololens user has the ability to select a point using hand gestures and manipulate it to modify the trajectory as per their requirements.

Based on the inputs of the user, the trajectories of the balls are re-calculated based on the different parameters of the ball from Hawkeye and Unreal Engine's physics-based calculations, thus giving the ability to the user to not just visualize the trajectory as per the actual ball information, but to also interact and change the trajectory according to the requirements of the story that they are trying to convey.

## Evaluation/Key Findings

In this section we identify any roadblocks encountered during development which may inhibit the short- and long-term progress of the project and present the results of a subjective user test (presenter perspective, audience perspective).

### Roadblocks

Below are some roadblocks and challenges we faced while working on the mixed reality toolkit:

1. No in-engine support for Azure spatial anchors while using Holographic remoting. The Unreal Engine connected to the Hololens crashes the moment we try to place or load any Azure anchors. We have reported this issue to both Epic Games and Microsoft Support, we hope that this issue will be resolved in the future updates of the Hololens plugins.
2. When we use Holographic Remoting with the Windows OpenXR plugin, the Anchors system including Local Anchors or Azure Spatial Anchors do not work in OpenXR. We are currently using the Windows Mixed Reality plugin which supports the Local Anchors.
   Currently the OpenXR plugin is only supported for native Hololens applications, we have reported this issue to Microsoft Support and we hope that this support will also be expanded for applications that use Holographic remoting.
3. We have been using Composure in our project to get an output of the MR graphics that the Hololens user is interacting with. During the play session we have observed that the output stops abruptly and Unreal does not realise this, as the recording buttons/icons in the Composure panel stay active. Hence, we have to manually disable and enable the output using a Blueprint script. We believe that this is a minor bug which would have been fixed in Unreal Engine 5 and we have informed Epic Games of the issue.
4. If we replicate the UXTPessableButton component or if we replicate any of its child components (ex. Static Mesh, Text Render, etc) in a Blueprint, Unreal crashes as soon as that Blueprint is spawned in the Level. As the MRTK plugin is currently in its Beta phase we believe that this issue would be fixed in its future iterations by Microsoft and we have made them aware of the issue.
5. In a scenario where we want to add multiple Hololens HMDs in the ecosystem, especially when the Hololens is connected as a client, the Hololens stops recognising the hands of the user, hence the hand-based interactions are not possible for the second Hololens device. In the current system we can add multiple spectator cameras, but only one Hololens which acts as a server. This is a critical issue that we have reported to Epic Games and we are still in communication with them to find a way to solve this problem.
6. The Mo-sys VP Free plugin that we currently use to get the Mo-sys camera tracking information inside Unreal Engine does not provide us accurate focus and lens distortion data of the camera. We also tried using the Mo-sys VP Pro plugin which provides us accurate data of all the camera parameters, but the format in which the plugin is created hinders us from connecting other devices such as the Hololens in the same environment. We have reported this issue to Mo-sys and they assisted us in creating a system to receive lens distortion data, but we still don't receive accurate focus data. Hence, we have manually set the focus of our virtual cameras at infinity to avoid any issues.

### Subjective User Test

#### Scale

Q1) 1 (very unclear) – 5 (very clear)
Q2) 1 (very unrealistic) – 5 (very realistic)
Q3) 1 (very meaningless) – 5 (very meaningful)
Q4) 1 (very unpleasant) – 5 (very enjoyable)

### Presenter Q&A

#### Question

Q1) Could you please rate the clarity of the information in the scene you just presented?
Q2) How realistic were the graphics in the virtual environment?
Q3) How meaningful were the graphics/interactions in the virtual environment as a storytelling aid?
Q4) How much would you say you enjoyed presenting using the tools provided in the scene?

### Audience Q&A

#### Question

Q1) Could you please rate the clarity of your understanding of the information in the scene you just viewed?
Q2) How realistic were the graphics in the virtual environment?
Q3) How meaningful were the graphics/interactions in the virtual environment as a storytelling aid?
Q4) How much would you say you enjoyed watching the scene?

| PARTICIPANT SN | Q1 | Q2 | Q3 | Q4 |
|---|---|---|---|---|
| 1 | 5.0 | 4.0 | 4.0 | 5.0 |
| 2 | 4.0 | 3.0 | 4.0 | 2.0 |
| 3 | 4.0 | 3.0 | 5.0 | 5.0 |
| 4 | 5.0 | 4.0 | 3.0 | 4.0 |
| 5 | 4.0 | 3.0 | 5.0 | 5.0 |
| 6 | 5.0 | 4.0 | 5.0 | 5.0 |

TABLE 1: AVERAGE AUDIENCE RATINGS.

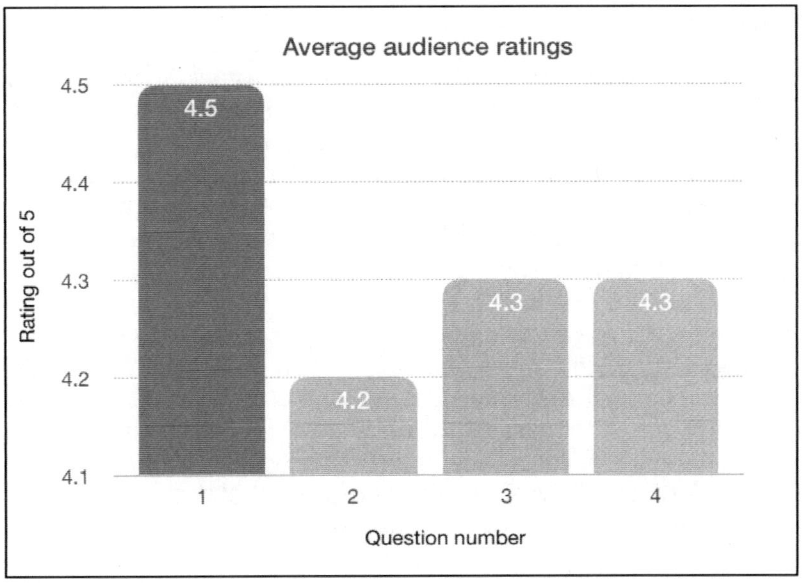


FIGURE 3: SUBJECTIVE USER TEST RESULTS.

| PARTICIPANT SN | Q1 | Q2 | Q3 | Q4 |
|---|---|---|---|---|
| **1** | 5.0 | 5.0 | 5.0 | 5.0 |
| **2** | 5.0 | 4.0 | 5.0 | 5.0 |
| **3** | 4.5 | 4.0 | 4.0 | 3.0 |
| **4** | 4.0 | 4.0 | 3.0 | 4.0 |
| **5** | 4.0 | 3.0 | 5.0 | 4.0 |

TABLE 2: AVERAGE PRESENTER RATINGS.

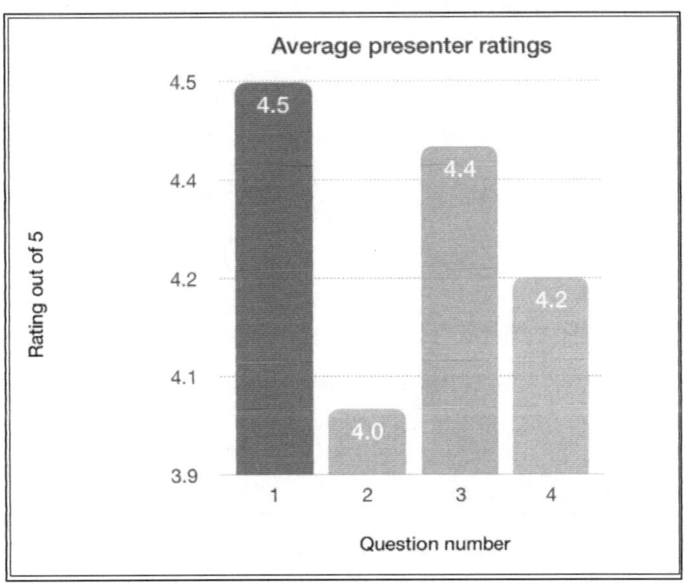


FIGURE 4: SUBJECTIVE USER TEST RESULTS.

## Conclusion & Outlook

Truly interactive graphics are an active area of development for many OEMs and software companies. Broadcast graphics middleware companies built on gaming engines like Zero Density and Pixotope (both based on Unreal Engine), are creating solutions that address talent (presenter) tracking in the 3D space, using either stereo cameras or computer vision. These products also are working on graphics interactions based on presenter body collisions and physics built in to trigger actions in the AR objects. Pixotope recently acquired Trackmen Gmbh, a real-time 3D camera and talent tracking company, to facilitate this goal further and have the provision for multi-person tracking.

These various talent tracking solutions allow for a graphics alpha layer to be switched from foreground to background and visa-versa according to the relative position of the talent to the AR graphic. While our system already has provisions for interactions based on collisions/physics and manual foreground/background switching, automatic switching is an additional functionality that will be added into our system in the near future. The limitations in the commercially available systems, however, are that the talent still has no way of directly visualizing the graphic that they are interacting with and most systems do not support fine interactions as they are based on a bounding box around the skeleton of the talent - whereas our system is novel in that it facilitates this graphics visualization feature as well as fine hand/finger interactions.

A further limitation in the above OEM/software company's solution as well as our own, is that a green screen is required for keying the presenter against the graphic when it is placed as a background element. To solve this so that the system will work in this capacity in a hard-set environment, a real time matting/keying solution is proposed. This can be achieved through the use of depth sensing cameras for depth keying, or a more desirable solution of a computer vision-based system, which must be robust enough to detect and segment fine features such as hands and fingers. This proposed system will also have value in regular scenes which have AR graphics and virtual sets where no holographic visualizations/interactions are present. Our system is also currently limited in that it is restricted to the Microsoft Hololens 2 device. In the future we aim to develop functionality for other HMDs and even AR contact lenses.

The results of the subjective user test are promising and demonstrate that our system is successful in aiding in both the storytelling abilities of the presenter and audience experience and understanding of the content produced using the toolkit. As such we see value in developing the solution further and adding in the functionalities described above as and when the technology becomes available.

We can draw a few more detailed conclusions from the subjective user: The clarity of information for both audience members and presenters scored the highest and realism scored the lowest. We can conclude that the realism of the graphics is something we need to work on as well as developing the ability to add dynamic lighting and shadows and different shaders (currently limited in our system due to software constraints).

Overall, both presenter and audience members scored highly in regards to the experience being meaningful and enjoyable, however there is some room for improvement.

One piece of verbal feedback given by several audience participants was that the menu was difficult to see as it was a mirror image in the camera, and it would be great to have a visual indication as to what the presenter was selecting. This is something we implemented right away to a positive reception.
In regards to the roadblocks encountered as well as the more general challenges of green screen-free keying/real-time matting, we remain optimistic that these will be solved in due course. The OEMs/software companies have been made aware of the issues we encountered during the project, and we continue to work with industry to suggest features, beta test new ones and build new use cases for the technology.

With the release of UE5, OEMs/software companies are updating their plugins and Epic Games has a strong focus on building out the engine for Metaverse applications, so we anticipate they are all incorporating the functionalities required to enable projects such as this.

Our ultimate end goal that we continue to work towards, is for the presenter to be able to see and interact with graphics and virtual sets as naturally as if they were real physical objects and environments, with occlusion solves and physics built into the system, and for this experience to eventually become available for audiences also in the next generation of content, as active participants and not just passive viewers.

## Acknowledgements

I would like to thank the Liminal team for their hard work and expertise in helping the Lab team realize this project and co-authoring this paper. I would also like to thank Epic Games, Zero Density, Microsoft and Mo-sys for their technical support and advice regarding the integration of their products into the workflow. Thanks are also given to my manager Prashant Khanna and leader Sanjog Gupta for supporting the project from its inception. Also thanks to Harshit Baranwal, Rahul Manglik, Rakesh Jha, Pramod Nagdeve, Mahesh Srikanta, Gary Burchett, Harsh Kalan, Saumitra Shankar and Hrushikesh Deo for their inputs and work on refining and testing the product and making it broadcast ready. Also thanks to Aakash Chopra for being our presenter-tester and giving valuable inputs from a talent point of view. Thanks also to the Disney Star IP, legal teams and PR teams for their work enabling the project patent and whitepaper. A very special thanks to Sandra Stedman.

## References and Further Reading

[1] Sharon, Brian. "Apollo 11 Mission AR Project Sample Available Now on the Unreal Engine Marketplace - Unreal Engine." Unreal Engine, Epic Games, 9 Dec. 2019, https://www.unrealengine.com/en-US/blog/apollo-11-mission-ar-project-sample-available-now-on-the-unreal-engine-marketplace. Retrieved on 25th May, 2022.

[2] Epic Games. "Microsoft Hololens Development." Unreal Engine, Epic Games, https://docs.unrealengine.com/4.27/enUS/SharingAndReleasing/XRDevelopment/AR/ARPlatforms/HoloLens/. Retrieved on 17th June, 2022.

[3] Epic Games. "Developing for Hololens." Unreal Engine, Epic Games, https://docs.unrealengine.com/5.0/en-US/develping-for-hololens-in-unreal-engine/. Retrieved on 17th June, 2022.

[4] Kerawala, Sean. Sherer, Tim. Summer, Wu. Ferrone, Harrison. Coulter, David. "Unreal Development Overview." Microsoft, 3 November. 2022, https://docs.microsoft.com/en-us/windows/mixed-reality/develop/unreal/unreal-development-overview?tabs=ue426%2Cmrtk%2Casa%2CD365. Retrieved on 17th June, 2022.

[5] Microsoft. "Mixed Reality UX Tools." Microsoft, https://microsoft.github.io/MixedReality-UXTools-Unreal/README.html. Retrieved on 17th June, 2022.

[6] Mo-Sys. "Mo-Sys VP Free." Unreal Engine, Epic Games, 7 January. 2022, https://www.unrealengine.com/marketplace/en-US/product/mo-sys-tracking. Retrieved on 17th June, 2022.

[7] Epic Games. "Announcing a $1Billion Funding Rount to Support Epic's Long-Term Vision for the Metaverse." Unreal Engine, Epic Games, 13 April. 2021, https://www.epicgames.com/site/en-US/news/announcing-a-1-billion-funding-round-to-support-epics-long-term-vision-for-the-metaverse. Retrieved on 17th June, 2022.

[8] Epic Games. "The LEGO Group and Epic Team up to Build a Place for Kids to Play in the Metaverse." Unreal Engine, Epic Games, 7 April. 2022, https://www.epicgames.com/site/en-US/news/the-lego-group-and-epic-games-team-up-to-build-a-place-for-kids-to-play-in-the-metaverse. Retrieved on 17th June, 2022.

[9] Sullivan, Mark. "Epic Games CEO Tim Sweeney Talks the Metaverse, Crypto, and Antitrust." Fast Company, 25 April, 2022, https://www.fastcompany.com/90741893/epic-games-ceo-tim-sweeney-talks-the-metaverse-crypto-and-antitrust. Retrieved on 17th June, 2022.

[10] Dot. "Body Pose What?" Pixotope, 29 December. 2021, https://blog.pixotope.com/body-pose-what, Retrieved on 17th June, 2022.

[11] Pixotope. "Trackmen Acquisition FAQ." Pixotope, 21 April. 2022, https://www.pixotope.com/trackmen. Retrieved on 17th June, 2022.

[12] Izmir, TR. "Zero Density Releases AI-powered Talent Tracking Product." Zero Density, 16 Novermber. 2021, https://www.zerodensity.tv/zero-density-releases-ai-powered-talent-tacking-product/. Retrieved on 17th June, 2022.

[13] Avid Technology. "Avid Maestro Virtual Set Setup Guide Version 2020.3." Avid Technology, 2020, https://resources.avid.com/SupportFiles/attach/Maestro_Virtual_Set/Maestro_Virtual_Set_Setup_Guide_v2020.3.pdf. Retrieved on 17th June, 2022.

[14] "Pixotope Aquires TrackMen Real-Time 3D Tracking Solutions." Business Wire, 21 April. 2022, https://www.businesswire.com/news/home/20220421005180/en/. Retrieved on 17th June, 2022.

# Unified System Design

**Lukas Odhner**
**NTC, A Deloitte Business**
**Los Angeles, Calif., United States**
lodhner@deloitte.com

**Abstract** – Over the past two decades, the media industry has needed to adapt to new IP delivery methods that enable high-quality content to be delivered over private networks and the internet. More recently the transition to IP has progressed further upstream in the media supply chain with the wide availability of network hardware that can support uncompressed video over IP in the form of SMPTE ST 2110. However, in this transition to a future where all media flows are carried over IP networks, the methods used for design and documentation have not been able to keep up. New approaches and tools are required.

## Introduction

The concept of signal flow has existed even before the first television transmission nearly a century ago in 1927. Since that first broadcast, the specifics of the electrical signals that carried audio and video signals between devices evolved from black and white to color, from analog to digital, and from standard definition to high definition. Through all these technical transitions the concept of signal flow remained consistent: a program signal being carried in one direction over one or more cables. Originally, system design drawings were drafted by hand with each device shown as a rectangle and each cable carrying these signals drawn as a line. When CAD software became available, the drawing process shifted to computers but the format remained. This signal flow-based approach to drawing physical connections has proven very useful to engineers and technicians diagnosing audio and video signals for many decades. However, the more recent transition to media over IP has, for better or worse, completely upended the longstanding paradigm of signal flow and decoupled it from the physical layer, making the physical drawings less and less relevant. It is no longer possible to verify what signals are present on a physical cable by using the age-old method of plugging it into a monitor for troubleshooting or analysis. The bidirectional nature of network connectivity all but eliminates the ability to verify signal presence at the physical layer.

The benefits of the transition to IP-based audio and video have been tremendous and have enabled technical innovation in many ways. However, there are a few things have been lost in the transition and still need to be addressed. Along with the continued obsolescence of signal flow, methods to document logical connectivity and signal flow on the network level are wildly inconsistent across the industry. Tools that are used to manage signal configurations (such as multicast IP flows through a network) are rarely integrated with the physical layer (cables) and the ones that do are not design tools but production control systems. As any experienced engineer knows making changes directly in a production system without planning and checking is a recipe for disaster. One important piece that has been missing from the broadcast industry transition to IP is a design and documentation platform that supports this new paradigm.

This paper is excerpted from the Proceedings of the 2023 NAB Broadcast Engineering and Information Technology (BEIT) Conference, © 2023, National Association of Broadcasters, 1 M Street SE, Washington, DC 20003 USA.

Deloitte has confronted this challenge by employing new data-driven design tools to build and manage media network infrastructure. Specifically, Deloitte has adapted an open-source project called Netbox[1] and used it as the starting point for a completely new approach to broadcast documentation. This customized fork is referred to internally as "Ndox."

The tools described in this paper—whether Netbox or Ndox—make the foundation of a new approach to documentation which is best summarized as "unified system design." This approach utilizes the best tools and practices of multiple industries, bringing both physical and logical data sets together in a structured database that captures the entire system design. Logical design elements (such as IP addresses and signal names) are managed together with existing drawings on a single, integrated platform. Network automation tools[2] that have been proven in enterprise IT are used to manage and deploy configurations to routers and switches. When this previously isolated data is integrated, these documentation solutions organize both the physical and logical information into a searchable, structured, single source of truth.[3]

Deloitte has continually pioneered new ways to work and design media systems. Over the years the tools have changed, but we have always been focused on three fundamental reasons that documentation is important to our industry: to design and build media systems, to communicate changes throughout the life of the system, and to promote understanding of the system by the people who depend on it.

## Building The System

To build broadcast facilities and systems that can support the complex workflows needed for cutting-edge production, many design considerations need to come together in a short time. Just a few elements to be considered include: building layout, cable paths, operator consoles, acoustics, power, and cooling. These details and many other decisions must be made prior to construction. As the media business continually adjusts to address new markets and deliver new types of content, the tools and software that media personnel need to perform their jobs is constantly changing. This means that making every single design decision right down to the last cable before beginning construction is no longer feasible. The design process must adapt to constant change and become more flexible and iterative. By adopting a unified system design approach, equipment orders can be placed much earlier than previous waterfall design approaches that necessitated the completion of all design work—including the final bill of materials—before any orders could be made. This advantage is particularly important considering recent global supply chain issues which have caused significant delays in hardware availability. When device quantities are stored in a database instead of poorly organized spreadsheets, it is much easier to track adjustments made while waiting for equipment to arrive.

[1] https://netbox.dev/

[2] Examples Include: Ansible, Nexus Dashboard Fabric Controller, Cloud Vision

[3] A Single Source of Truth (SSOT) is a model for storing information in an enterprise, where each piece of data is mastered in a specific, well-known place. This model is only effective when the organization trusts that the data it needs always exists in the SSOT and is always current.

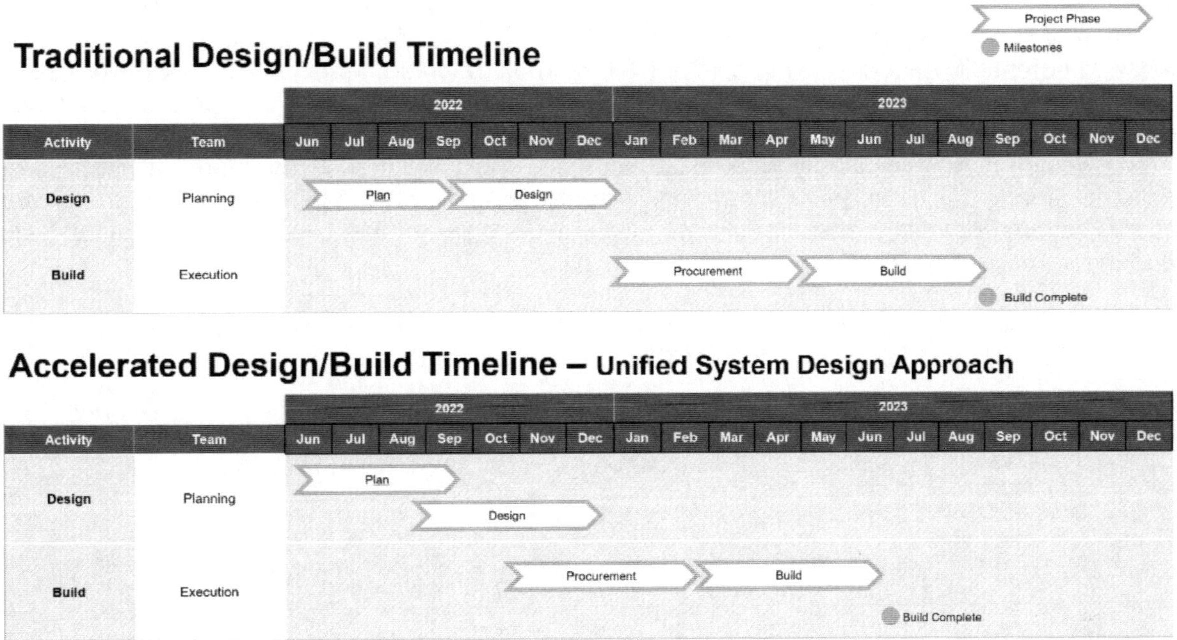


FIGURE 1: ACCELERATED DESIGN TIMELINE.

## Accelerated Procurement

In a recent Esports[4] project designed and built by Deloitte, we adopted the unified system design process that allowed us to track orders on a per-vendor and per-device basis instead of waiting for all design decisions to be finalized before placing equipment orders. As decisions were made, orders were immediately moved into final negotiations and procurement. The centralized database included device quantities and orders, ensuring that the design remained synchronized with procurement. For instance, if a spare intercom was ordered for inventory and later required for installation, the design engineers would be informed and could allocate it to the specific location it was needed. This approach enabled Design Engineers, Procurement Specialists, Logistics Coordinators, Installation Supervisors, and Network Admins to work together seamlessly, resulting in the project being completed in record time. Despite supply chain issues causing some delays, the project was estimated to have been finished 6-8 weeks earlier than with traditional design methods due to the innovative design and procurement process.

## Logistics

The same Esports project also featured a simplified onsite logistics process that utilized asset and location tracking of devices in the design database. This process included the introduction of many new logistics workflows and resulted in a faster onsite build. Upon equipment arrival, the logistics team attached pre-printed labels to each device that indicated its designated installation room, specific rack location, and even the rack unit in which it was to be installed. The labels also included QR codes that enabled the direct entry of serial numbers and asset tags into the database using a handheld barcode scanner connected to a tablet or laptop. This method also allowed real-time installation status data to flow back to project management, enabling resources to concentrate their efforts on areas where all equipment had been received. The labels placed on each box as it was inventoried ensured that devices were installed in the correct location the first time, avoiding wasted time on install mix-ups.

---

[4] Electronic Sports – Competitions with an in-person or remote audience watching players compete in video game matches live.

## Cabling

As anyone who has worked in a large broadcast facility would acknowledge, cabling is one of the most complex and potentially error-prone aspects of system implementation. In a recent Deloitte project, approximately 20,000 cables were installed in just a few months. The cables were organized by the team responsible for installation, allowing for customized exports based on the type of label required. The unified design database directly tracked cable details, including their location and device connections. Storing cables in a structured database, rather than a spreadsheet, enabled immediate error identification. For instance, stringent database checks ensured that two cables did not mistakenly attach to the same port on a specific device.

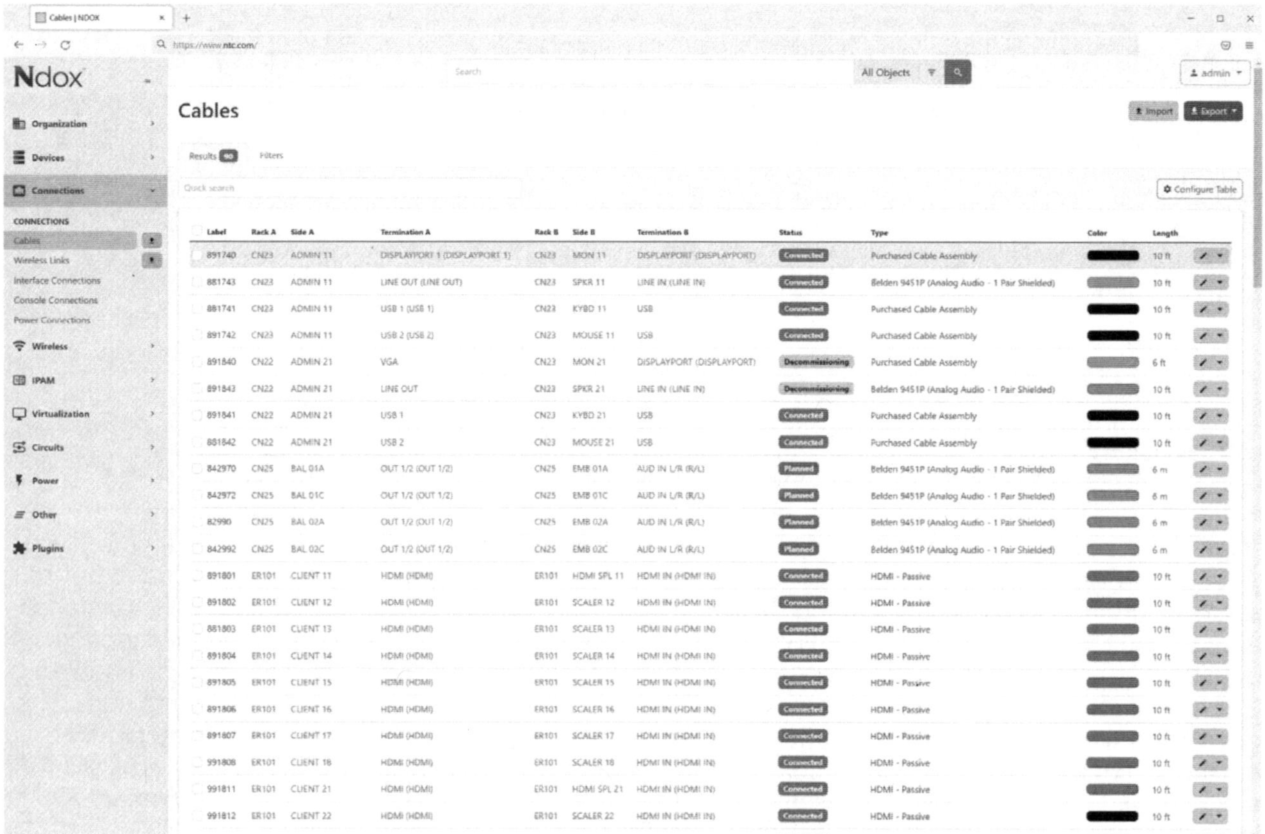


FIGURE 2: CABLE LIST IN DATABASE.

Once cables were installed and cable testing was underway, deployment engineers could report issues to the install team and track the status of cables as they were connected. During final network validation the database provides a centralized record of all physical cables, including multi-segment paths over "horizontal" cables and patch panel cross connects.

Cable trace is a powerful feature that allows the cable "run list[5]" to be directly correlated to network interfaces and logical connectivity to be traced over physical cables. This structured data unlocks powerful network automation that drastically reduces configuration errors. When used to generate network configurations, it cuts deployment times to minutes instead of weeks. The bridge between the physical (cables) and the logical (network) also enhances communication between offsite and onsite engineers. For example, a network engineer can communicate which cable number needs to be

[5] A cable "run list" refers to a list of cables and their respective termination points for an entire system.

checked instead of relying on poorly labeled network appliances with interface names like “Eth1/2/3” or “Eth0” that are not always clearly labeled on the device. This is perhaps the single, most powerful capability that is unlocked with unified system design methods available—using either Ndox or open-source alternatives.

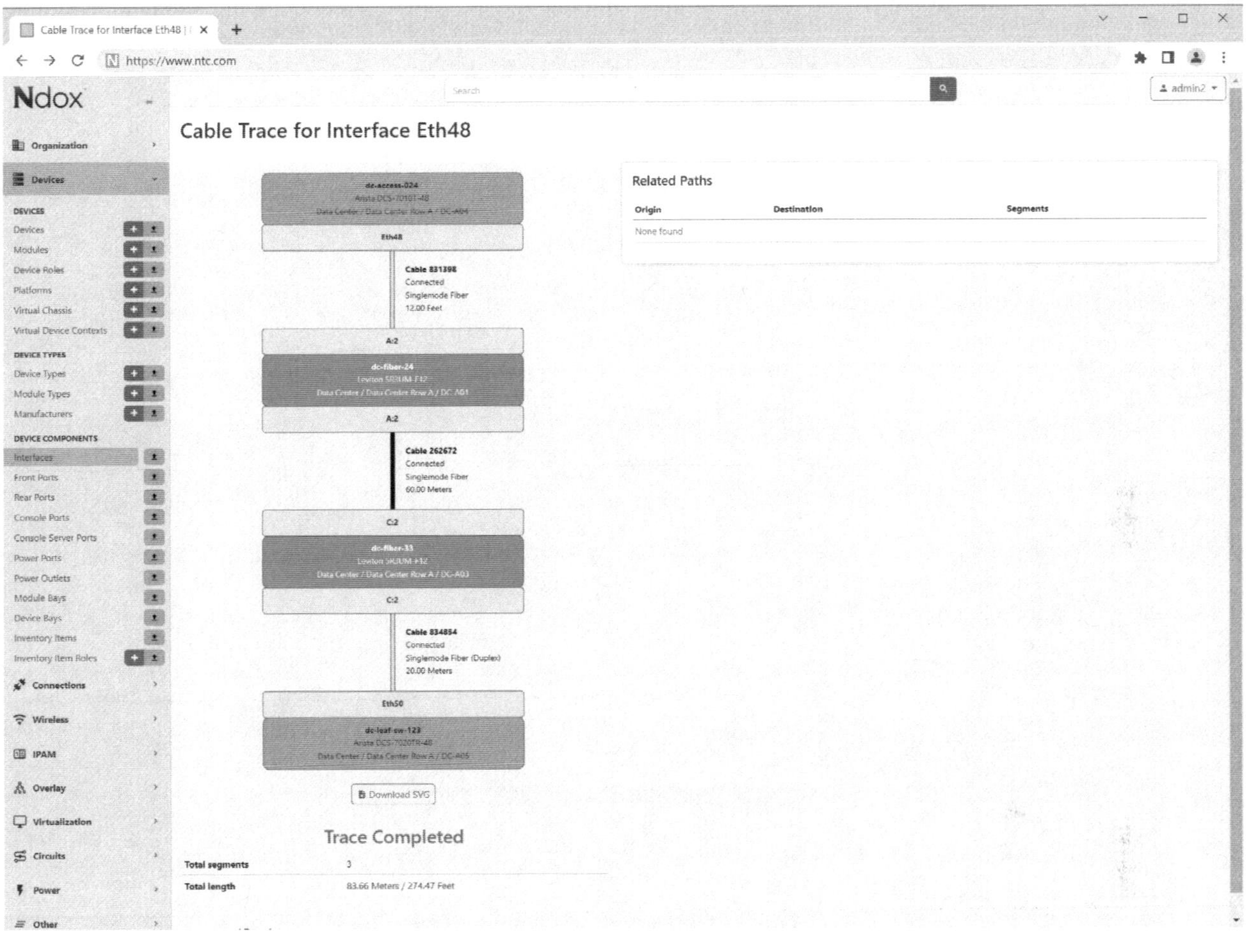


FIGURE 3: MULTI-SEGMENT CABLE TRACE.

## Signal Flow

With the ongoing transition of video and audio signals from SDI to the network, many video and audio signals are often carried over a single cable using standards such as MPEG-TS, SMPTE ST 2022-6, and SMPTE ST 2110. The traditional connection drawings previously used for documenting signal flow no longer provide a useful picture of where signals are routed as VLANs and multicast IPs cannot be easily represented on drawings. Furthermore, many ST 2110 devices lack automated multicast assignment support via NMOS, resulting in an increasing number of statically-assigned multicast signals that need to be managed. Typically this is handled by a dedicated orchestration layer or "broadcast controller," but the planning is usually left to the orchestration vendor. Unified system design allows for logical multicast signals to be defined earlier during design and signal compatibility can be tracked as equipment is tested. For example, ST 2110-21 wide or narrow senders that may not always be compatible can be flagged to avoid issues during system configuration. By documenting signals *ahead* of deployment, devices that do not yet support automatic provisioning standards can be configured in parallel by multiple teams, reducing the time it takes to configure a complex media network.

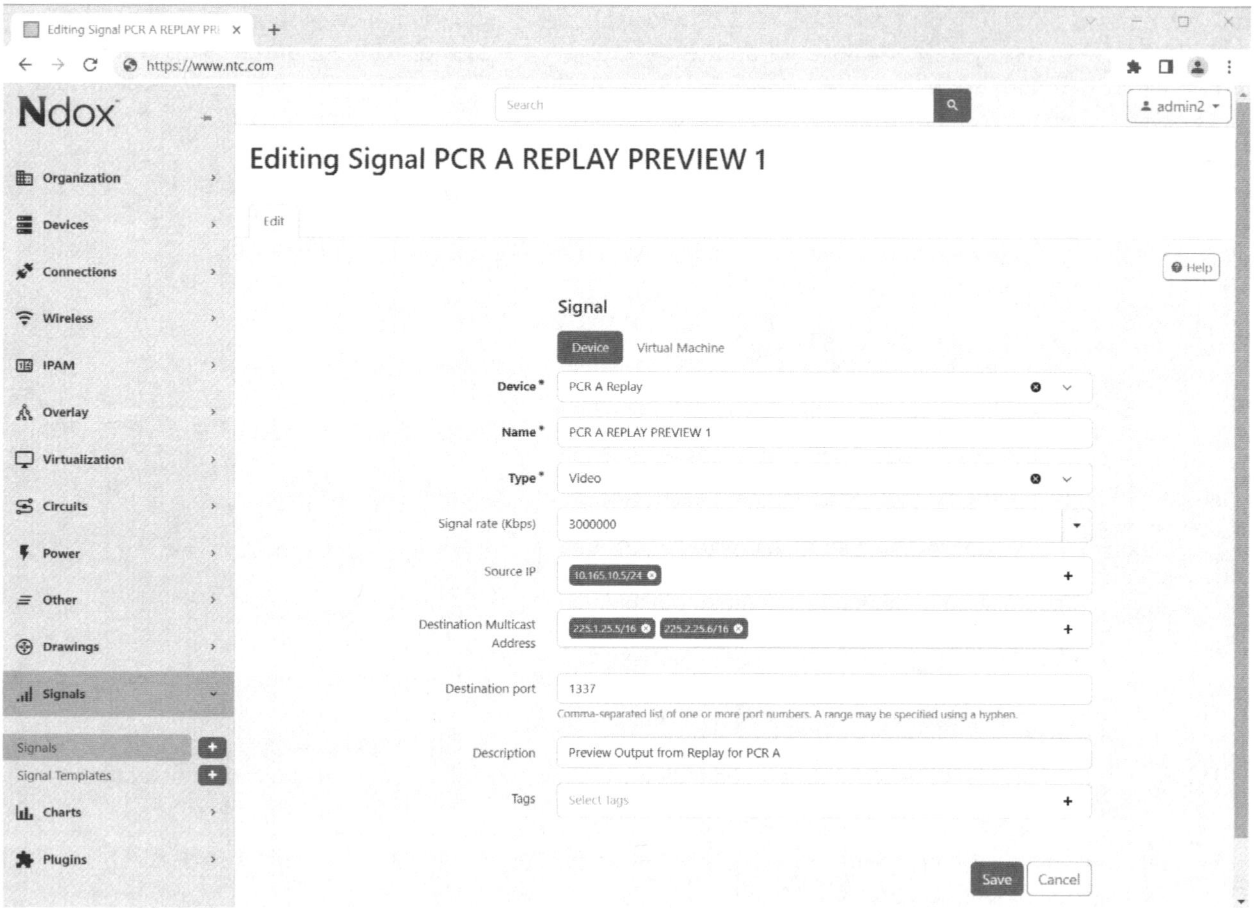


FIGURE 4: MULTICAST SIGNAL DEFINITIONS.

## Maintaining The System

A system's configuration will generally begin to change from the moment that the build is complete. As system configurations change over time, it can be difficult to track and communicate these changes between teams. The unified system design approach provides the centralized source of truth required to track system changes and enables reliable communication between teams.

### Single Source of Truth

A shared "single source of truth" (SSOT) is an agreed-upon, centralized reference point that contains up-to-date information about the "desired" or "ideal" future state of a system. It's important to note that a desired state does not always match the current state. For example, when a device is added to a design document it does not magically appear in the real world. However, if the device is added and marked as "planned" in the single source of truth, it accurately represents both current (actual) and desired (planned) states.

There are also times when possible future states do not qualify as the "desired state," such as when two server models are being considered for a project. Although diagrams, test fits, and cost comparisons are made, the hardware should not be added to the SSOT until the decision is made to move forward with a particular model. Of course, it is also possible that the decision is made but then reversed. Unfortunately, this type of situation is not uncommon. However, when it does occur, any outdated elements are reversed and the SSOT is updated with the current "desired state." Complex hypothetical scenarios can be difficult to manage using any design tools. Unified system design cannot predict future challenges, but it can provide a common reference point from which all teams can work in alignment toward a common goal.

## Change Management

Having a shared data source for design details is essential but equally important is having a structured change management process to flag impacts and coordinate updates with the goal of reducing risk. Substantive modifications to any network or system must be drafted, evaluated, approved, and only then implemented. Managing change is especially crucial when coordinating efforts across different teams. When unified system design approaches are followed, information about the current system is readily available to all teams, allowing accurate data to be tightly coupled with change management systems like Service Now. Only when specific details of the change are documented can stakeholders make informed decisions about risk. Unified system design allows all parties to better understand the nature of the change being requested and make informed decisions about the approach.

Documenting a planned change before it is executed reduces the likelihood of errors, unexpected outcomes, and outdated documentation. With unified system design the paradigm shifts from documentation being an aspirational final step after a change is complete, to being a necessary *first* step that is required to initiate a change. For example, if an engineer needs to install a new cable, they must first enter the connection into the unified system design database, and only then can they export and print the label for the cable being installed. The same rule would apply to VLAN port changes and many other workflows. The "document first" approach becomes a necessity that is enabled and even enforced by unified system design methods. This assures that all stakeholders are notified of planned changes as well as being accountable for changes they make to the system.

## Infrastructure as Code

While physical infrastructure cannot be deployed as code, the rise of virtualized resources has created an opportunity to automate some types of infrastructure deployment. This includes not only the more obvious compute and storage functions, but also historically hardware dependent resources such as network and security appliances can be virtualized and automated. This applies to both on-prem physical network devices as well as public cloud based virtual network resources like firewalls and load balancers. With the ability to deploy an entire network virtually inside a VM for the purpose of testing, it is possible to employ CI/CD[6] processes that have been widely adopted and successful in software development environments to network design and deployment. Infrastructure as Code[7] is a key part of bringing DevOps[8] to the network. This is also referred to as Network DevOps. These methods are being pioneered by many companies, including Deloitte. The specific tools used to automate network test, integration, and deployment may vary depending on factors specific to each project, but unified system design is fully-aligned with the vision of bringing software development processes into the realm of network deployment.

Deloitte has used unified system design approaches to drive both network configurations and monitoring systems directly from the design database. In a recent project, ETL[9] modules were built to connect the design database to broadcast monitoring systems. As new devices and software were added to the design, they were registered for monitoring and alerts. For example, a closed captioning server is installed into a datacenter. Once powered up, it is recognized as coming online. The updated

---

[6] Continuous Integration and Continuous Delivery (CI/CD) refers to the automation of testing and delivering code. An organization that uses CI/CD makes changes more quickly and confidently, knowing that code has been tested and deployed using well documented and automated processes.
[7] Infrastructure as Code (is the managing and provisioning of infrastructure through code instead of through manual processes)
[8] Development Operations is a set of practices that integrate software development and IT operations
[9] Extract, Transform, Load.

device status triggers the inclusion of this new device in the dashboards and monitoring systems of the NOC[10] and sends a notification about the new device coming online. All of this can happen without the need for unnecessary data entry. Since unified system design also captures device subsystem and function the NOC operators can distinguish between critical and non-critical messages directing them where to look when something goes wrong. This workflow directly supports system stability, lowers risk, and reduces costs by quickly surfacing both physical and logical system failures to those responsible for keeping the system running without disruption.

In previous projects, Deloitte has successfully developed automation that generates complete network switch configurations based on both the physical and logical design information in the design database. The software traces cables through patch panels to end devices. The VLAN and router IP addresses are also pulled from the unified system design database instead of being manually input from a spreadsheet. This generates a complete switch config ready to deploy to the switch. This updated configuration can then be queued for approval by network admins and deployed via whatever change management processes are in place.

The power of automatically generated network configurations is that since they are built on demand, they will always be based on the current system source of truth. These configurations also include any special requirements of the connected devices to network ports. For example, some device types may require a specific FEC[11] setting or a transceiver[12] speed override applied to the connected switchport. Additionally, these deployment methods also make it possible to collect real-time metrics from switches (such as LLDP neighbors[13] and port status) and communicate the data back to the unified system design database for troubleshooting or analysis. The goal of treating infrastructure as code depends on the unified system design database to drive the CI/CD network automation processes and bring more consistency and reliability to broadcast network infrastructure.

## Understanding The System

Systems do not just need to be designed and built. Their functions and complexities also need to be understood by stakeholders and users. The architecture of a new system or facility generally starts with whiteboard sessions and sketches. These high-level designs develop into block diagrams and system architectures. Eventually these plans are refined into detailed designs. The original high-level drawings that outline functionality are still invaluable to communicate the function of a system. Unfortunately, these drawings are not always archived for future reference, or they are locked away in some forgotten folder structure or cloud account, inaccessible to those who would most benefit from them. Unified system design retains these artifacts in a structured, searchable framework and makes them accessible to the users who are charged with maintaining these systems in the future. This standardized access to system architecture(s) helps with the training of new engineers. It also helps bypass those who might attempt to hoard knowledge and improves system visibility throughout the organization.

In the transition to the cloud these agile approaches become even more essential. Media companies that have maintained physical infrastructure for many decades continue to migrate core systems to the public cloud. This trend shows no sign of stopping, but the processes to document these cloud environments has not yet caught up. Many formats of documentation are needed, from high-level architectures to fiber circuits details, to deployment scripts. Unified system design captures all of this. Having a centralized collaborative platform to plan and define the resources that will be required in the

---

[10] Network Operations Center.

[11] Forward Error Correction (FEC) is a digital signal processing technique that introduces additional information to a line to check for errors in transmission.

[12] Transceiver is a network adapter such as a modular optical ethernet adapter or SFP.

[13] Link Layer Discovery Protocol (LLDP) enables network devices to send and receive detailed information about the devices connected to themselves (aka their "neighbors").

cloud makes deployments much easier. When that same data is then able to be used to automate deployment the real power of unified system documentation is unleashed.

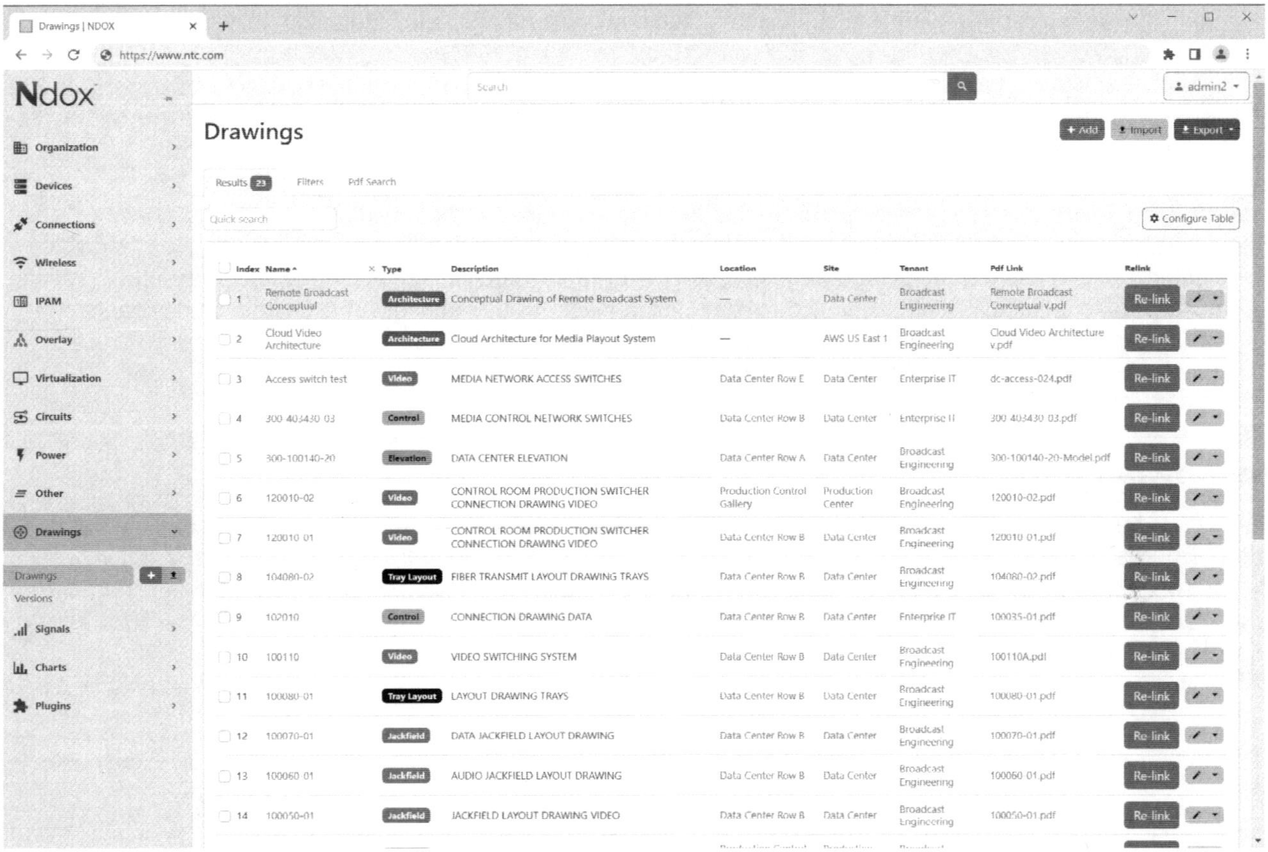


FIGURE 5: DRAWING REPOSITORY PLUGIN.

Deloitte has successfully designed and built world-class broadcast facilities using unified system design approaches that demonstrate the seamless integration of system drawings with a searchable database containing the design details. Depending on the client and system, there are many possible preferences around drawing processes and software, sometimes even using a combination of drawing tools. (For example, the "broadcast" team may use AutoCAD while the "Corp IT" team prefers Lucid Chart.) The unified system design approach is agnostic to drawing software preferences by serving as an integrated catalog of PDF drawings from any software. PDFs are scanned for relevant details and linked directly to the underlying data. Hostnames, racks, locations, cables, and drawings are all automatically linked together using an automated drawings plugin. The result is that existing drawing libraries can be made accessible to all types of users and more importantly these drawings can then be directly linked to an accessible, dynamic data source that serves both the technical and business stakeholders.

## Conclusion: System Design in the Media Industry

Over the past several decades, IP networks have steadily grown to become the universal standard for nearly all global media infrastructure. Documentation standards have failed to keep up with the challenges of managing complex network infrastructure which is why new approaches to broadcast documentation must be employed. Database-centric tools are available to support these new approaches to documentation, many of them open source. The key to unlocking the potential of all these solutions is to unify all system design information—both physical and logical—together in one place. This data can then be used to build the design, manage implementation, and coordinate changes of media systems with a focus on long term maintainability and stability.

These tools do not replace the need for skilled broadcast and network engineers who understand the functionality of a system. Instead, it improves the ability of these individuals to manage larger systems more effectively and efficiently. It is necessary for media organizations to have established documentation processes such as the ones outlined above: to build, to communicate, and to understand the complex systems currently required to support content workflows. When the importance of accurate documentation is understood by business leaders and treated as an imperative, it enables the organization to respond more quickly to changes in technology. Implementing standardized documentation tools across all networks and systems helps to strengthen and protect technical platforms. Equally important, it helps unify diverse teams of people, often with different perspectives, who must work together to build and manage the media systems of the future.

## Acknowledgements

Thanks and appreciation to Dean Hallett, Hallett Leadership and Jeremy Stretch, NS1.
Additional thanks to Deloitte Media Solutions team members: Angie Yarusso, Nick Quigley, Olivia Manousos, Evan Lucchesi, Jason Williamson, Blake White, Frank Albano, Matt Villa, Chris Lansdown, Jake Tejada, William Hooper, Todd Povilaitis, Michael Vovk, John Footen, Laurie Morse, and Peter Adamiak.

# An Open Platform for Media Over IP Network Load Testing with Off-The-Shelf Hardware

**Ievgen Kostiukevych, Pavlo Kondratenko**
**European Broadcasting Union**
**Geneva, Switzerland**
kostiukevych@ebu.ch, kondratenko@ebu.ch

**Thomas Kernen**
**NVIDIA**
**Zurich, Switzerland**
tkernen@nvidia.com

**Willem Vermost**
**VRT**
**Brussels, Belgium**
wim.vermost@vrt.be

**Abstract** – As the media industry continues to transform and adopt media over IP solutions, the importance of proper testing and verification of network performance and timing infrastructures cannot be overemphasized. The SMPTE ST 2110-21 standard sets strict timing and jitter requirements that depend on predictable network behavior. The acceptable network load level limitations for particular video formats used in a facility must be tested and verified before commissioning the facility. However, broadcasters and system integrators often skip this step due to cost and the unavailability of equipment that can generate adequate network traffic load and proper traffic profiles. This creates a need for a cost-effective solution that enables broadcasters to perform acceptance testing of their media over IP networks as close to the real-world load, traffic patterns, and network scenarios as possible. This paper is the first in the series of publications to propose a solution for media over IP network load testing using off-the-shelf hardware and open-source software. The proposed solution allows for generating specific media traffic profiles, ensuring that the performance of the traffic shape and network timing is adequately tested and verified, leading to a more reliable and robust media over IP infrastructure. The paper explores the hardware, software, tuning, and integration needed to build such a testing platform. Future publications will explore that traffic patterns and real-world testing.

## Motivation for Research

As the media industry continues undergoing what is probably the most significant transformation since the introduction of the original Serial Digital Interface (SDI) [1] standard, the work on high-performance uncompressed media over IP is approaching its 10th birthday, with the publication of the first revision of Audio Engineering Society (AES) AES67 [2] standard, followed by the Society of Motion Picture and Television Engineers (SMPTE) ST 2022-6 [3], early European Broadcasting Union (EBU) research in the field of ultra-high definition TV over IP networks [4], Video Services Forum (VSF) Technical Recommendation (VSF TR-03) [5], and finally the SMPTE ST 2110 suite of standards [6]. Traditional broadcasting methods have been replaced with more efficient, scalable, and cost-effective solutions

This paper is excerpted from the Proceedings of the 2023 NAB Broadcast Engineering and Information Technology (BEIT) Conference, © 2023, National Association of Broadcasters, 1 M Street SE, Washington, DC 20003 USA.

based on various flavors of media over IP powered by cutting-edge IP networking technologies. While such systems have numerous advantages, they also come with a new and unique set of challenges. Due to the inherited flexibility of such systems, the predictability, robustness, and deterministic performance of the underlying networking and timing infrastructures are becoming an essential benchmark of overall reliability.

SMPTE has defined the ST 2110-21 [7] standard as part of the ST 2110 suite that imposes strict timing and jitter requirements that depend on predictable network behavior. Additionally, the standard limits the acceptable network load level for particular video formats used in a facility. This may be further impacted by the switch Application-Specific Integrated Circuitry (ASIC) implementation, buffer, and queueing architectures of a switch platform. All this must be tested and verified before commissioning the facility. Unpredictable, unreliable, and indeterministic network behavior due to overloading, inadequate switch platform, or switching behavior may impair the performance of the traffic shape and introduce undesirable behavior in media flows traversing the network forwarding [8].

The network load and performance, as well as the switch platform architecture and components, also affect Precision Time Protocol's (PTP) [9] timing and synchronization performance. PTP is a critical component of media over IP networks and is used to ensure that all devices on the network are in sync. Network overload or generally inadequate performance under load can impact the accuracy of PTP and lead to synchronization issues like network timing and endpoints synchronization degradation [10].

Considering the importance of these fundamental infrastructures, proper testing of media over IP networks is critical to any Proof of Concept (POC) or acceptance testing of a newly built broadcast center that should not be overlooked. However, many broadcasters and system integrators often skip this step for various reasons and rely on the manufacturer's performance claims, reuse of untested design patterns, and gut feeling, which can lead to unforeseen consequences later on.
This step is often skipped due to cost and the unavailability of equipment that can generate adequate network traffic load and proper traffic profiles. From a budget standpoint, the entry barrier to owning the tool required for such testing is too high for most Public Service Media (PSM) broadcasters and system integrators. As a result, there is a need for a cost-effective solution that enables broadcasters to perform acceptance testing of their media over IP networks as close to the real-world load, traffic patterns, and network scenarios as possible.

The authors propose a solution for media over IP network load testing with the possibility of using specific media traffic profiles using off-the-shelf hardware and open-source software. By doing so, broadcasters and system integrators can ensure that their media over IP networks meet the strict requirements of SMPTE ST 2110-21, IEEE 1588, and operate at their peak performance.

In this paper, the authors explore the process of selecting a hardware platform, its tuning and optimization, and the preliminary performance testing results in a controlled lab environment. The follow-up work will focus on real-world media over IP traffic profiling, generation, and further testing and benchmarking.

## Hardware and Software Platform Selection and Tuning

SMPTE ST 2110 is a standard for transporting professional, mainly uncompressed media over IP networks. Therefore, the bandwidth requirements of ST 2110 streams can be quite high, which poses a challenge for testing the networks designed for such applications. High-performance Field-Programmable Gate Array (FPGA) -based devices are often used to generate the traffic needed to test ST 2110 networks. These highly specialized devices can generate the required network load due to the direct access to the FPGAs, outputting the packets directly to the wire. However, this equipment is costly and not readily available to all users. It is also generally tailored for general-purpose networking and often uses so-called "Internet" traffic patterns. While this is fine for lab-based acceptance testing of general ASIC or switch platform performance, it may not be so indicative in the applications where a lot of multicast Real Time Protocol (RTP) [11] traffic is present in the network.

Creating such a system capable of producing an adequate network load and potentially imitating various traffic patterns while using commodity off-the-shelf (COTS) IT hardware components and generic software is not trivial. It requires careful performance tuning and understanding of how the hardware APIs interact with the Linux kernel and the user space.

To achieve this goal, careful system tuning is required to ensure that the components perform at their optimal levels and are configured to interact with the hardware in the most efficient way possible.
A newly released (at the time of writing) server platform was chosen for the initial prototyping. The server used in this experiment is an HPE ProLiant DL385 Gen11 [12], equipped with the following hardware components:

- 2x AMD EPYC 9174F [13] processors, each with 2x16 cores and 2x32 with SMT, operating at a frequency of 4.1 GHz.
- 256 GB RAM consisting of 4x64 PC5-4800B-R modules.
- 2x NVIDIA ConnectX-6 DX MCX623106AN-CDAT (NVIDIA SKU 900-9X6AG-0056-ST1) network interface cards (NICs), F/W ver. 22.35.2000 [14].
- 4x NVIDIA ConnectX-5 EX CX516A-CDAT (PCIe Gen4) (NVIDIA SKU 900-9X5AD-0056-ST7) NICs, F/W ver. 16.35.2000 [15].
- 2x NVIDIA ConnectX-5 CX516A-CCAT (PCIe Gen3) (NVIDIA SKU 900-9X5AD-0056-ST1) NICs, F/W ver. 16.35.2000 [15].

The software used in the experiment is as follows:

- Ubuntu 22.04 LTS operating system [16].
- OFED 5.8-1.1.2.1-LTS [17].
- TREX 3.02 network traffic generator [18].

The AMD EPYC platform offers many PCIe Gen5 lanes directly connected to the CPU [13] [12] without using the PCIe switches in the motherboard. This theoretically allows using all eight dual-port 100G NICs for line-rate egress. The overall system "throughput" assessment was part of the research because the system bottlenecks may not only be in the PCIe bus. Therefore, not all available NICs were installed simultaneously at every experiment stage.

## Server Tuning

Modern server architectures are designed to run a diverse set of workloads ranging from non-specific (i.e., generic) to highly specialized applications. Due to this wide range of diversity, systems need to be capable of accommodating these via allocating system resources both from a physical and logical point of view. This leads to hardware optimization via reconfiguration of the BIOS combined with operating system flags and parameters to assign and allocate resources to different tasks.

The main purpose of the server hardware in this specific use case is to maximize the NIC throughput and minimize the NIC latency, as commonly used in High-Performance computing (HPC) environments. The AMD "BIOS and Workload Tuning Guide for AMD EPYC 9004 Processors" [19] and "High Performance Computing (HPC)" [20] documents detail the recommended settings for all BIOS parameters. We will summarize the key ones below.

Disable Simultaneous Multithreading "SMT Control" to force a single thread per core. This is typically recommended for high-performance workloads so that there is no thread sharing on any given physical core.

Set the Power Profile Selection to "High Performance" or "Maximum IO Performance Mode."

Set to Manual the Determinism Control and Enable the "Performance" determinism profile.

Set NUMA Nodes per socket to 2 or 4 and benchmark performance changes.

Set the xGMI Max Link Width Control to Manual and "x16". Depending on the PCIe NICs used, this may not be supported by some older generations of NICs.

Disable the Algorithm Performance Boost (APB) to set a fixed P-state control. This will force the AMD Infinity Fabric and memory controllers into full-power mode and eliminates latency jitter.

Set the PCIe Speed PMM (Power Management) Control to "Static TLS Gen5". This may only work properly if all PCIe devices (NICs) are PCIe Gen5. Else, they may not be detected correctly or perform in an unexpected manner.

Disable the C2 C-State (Idle and power gated) in the BIOS setting if available. AMD EPYC Core C6 (CC6) States is the name used for the generic APCI C2 state. Verify from the OS that "`cpupower monitor`" the actual state reported to the OS.

The CPU governors should be set to "performance", i.e., the highest-available frequency within the P0 state via the "`cpupower frequency-set -g performance`" command.

Subsequently, the verification of the execution power states (P-States) can be done via the "`cpupower frequency-info`" command.

IRQ is an interrupt request sent from the hardware level to the CPU. While receiving the interrupt, the CPU will switch to the interrupt context known as Interrupt Service Routine (ISR) in order to handle the coming interrupt.

The affinity of an interrupt request (IRQ Affinity) is defined as the set of CPU cores that can service that interrupt. To improve application scalability and latency, it is recommended to distribute IRQs between the available CPU cores. One may disable IRQ Affinity from the default setting via the "`irqbalance`" command to force pinning the IRQ Affinity to specific CPU cores per network interface.

Furthermore, the use of the "`mlnx_tune -p HIGH_THROUGHPUT`" profile may provide additional information and sources of optimization for the host and the NVIDIA/Mellanox ConnectX NIC configuration.

In multi-processor servers, the Non-Uniform Memory Access (NUMA) allows for each processor to be directly connected to a separate and specific set of memory. Indirect access from the other CPU(s) to the (remote) RAM is still possible, but such requests are slower as they pass through that memory's controlling CPU, as seen in Figure 1.

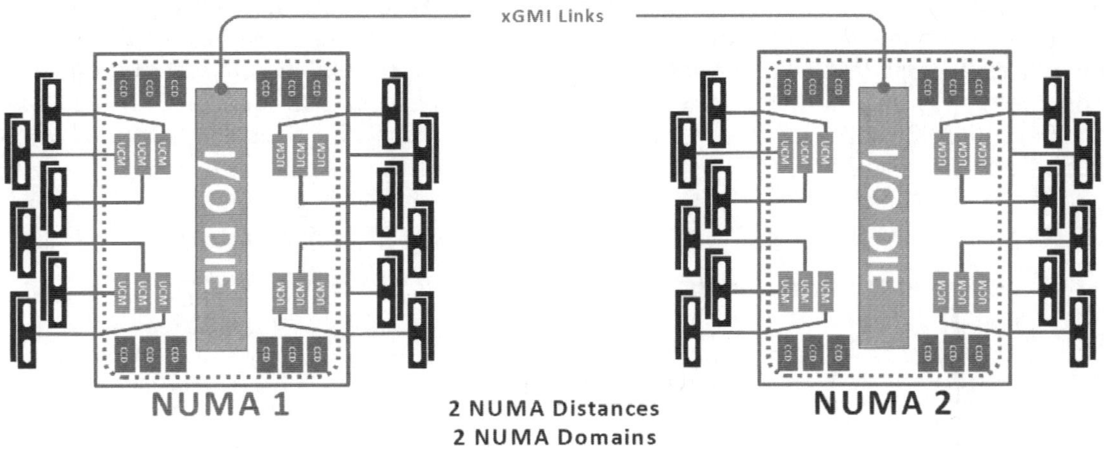


FIGURE 1 NUMA DOMAINS IN AMD EPYC ARCHITECTURE.

The x86 CPU architecture has supported NUMA for many years, and combined with Linux NUMA-aware scheduling, the operating system (OS) attempts to schedule processes to a CPU directly attached to a specific set of RAM.

The "`numactl`" selects scheduling and memory placement to bin the correct resources based on the NUMA architecture of the selected resources. This was previously discussed in [8].

The following commands are commonly used to discover, identify, and set tasks with specific NUMA-related resources.

"`lscpu`" can be used to verify the number of threads per core, cores per CPU socket, NUMA nodes, and CPUs per NUMA node. "`hwloc-ls`" can use used to obtain CPU IDs and PCIe Bridge layouts. "`numactl -H`" lists the CPU cores per NUMA domain.

Additionally, one may wish to verify each PCI bridge, device, port, and NUMA mapping for each NIC via the following commands: "`mst start`" followed by "`mst status -v`".

Note that the "`taskset`" command allows for retrieval or to set the process's CPU affinity to bind a process to a given set of CPUs in the system, mapped to the appropriate NUMA, CPU, RAM, and PCI resources (NIC).

A Linux kernel line of parameters to be passed at boot may look like this: "`isolcpus=0-30 nohz_full=0-30 rcu_nocbs=0-30 amd_iommu=force_isolation iommu=pt default_hugepagesz=1G hugepagesz=1G hugepages=80 intel_idle.max_cstate=0 processor.max_cstate=0 amd_pstate=disable rcu_nocb_poll`" which we will now unpack and expand upon.

The "`isolcpus`" parameter isolates a given set of CPUs from disturbance which, combined with the "`nohz_full`" disables the default 1Hz tick offloaded to work queues. "`rcu_nocbs`" further prevents CPU callback mode from being invoked in a softirq context reducing the OS jitter on the offloaded CPUs. The "`rcu_nocb_poll`" further improves the real-time response for the offloaded CPUs. Note that since we have 2x16 cores in the test server, we wish to isolate 31 of these for the purpose of the application that will be running. The final core will thereby be allocated to the OS to perform all background operations.

Enable "`iommu=pt`" in the Linux kernel command line to provide the best "pass-through" performance. This may sound counterintuitive since Input-Output Memory Management Unit (IOMMU) is a Management Memory Unit (MMU) component that connects a DMA-capable I/O bus to system memory, as seen in Figure 2. It maps device-visible virtual addresses to physical addresses, making it useful in virtualization. By setting it to "`pt`" (pass-through), this capability is disabled, and a 1:1 mapping is created between the resources.

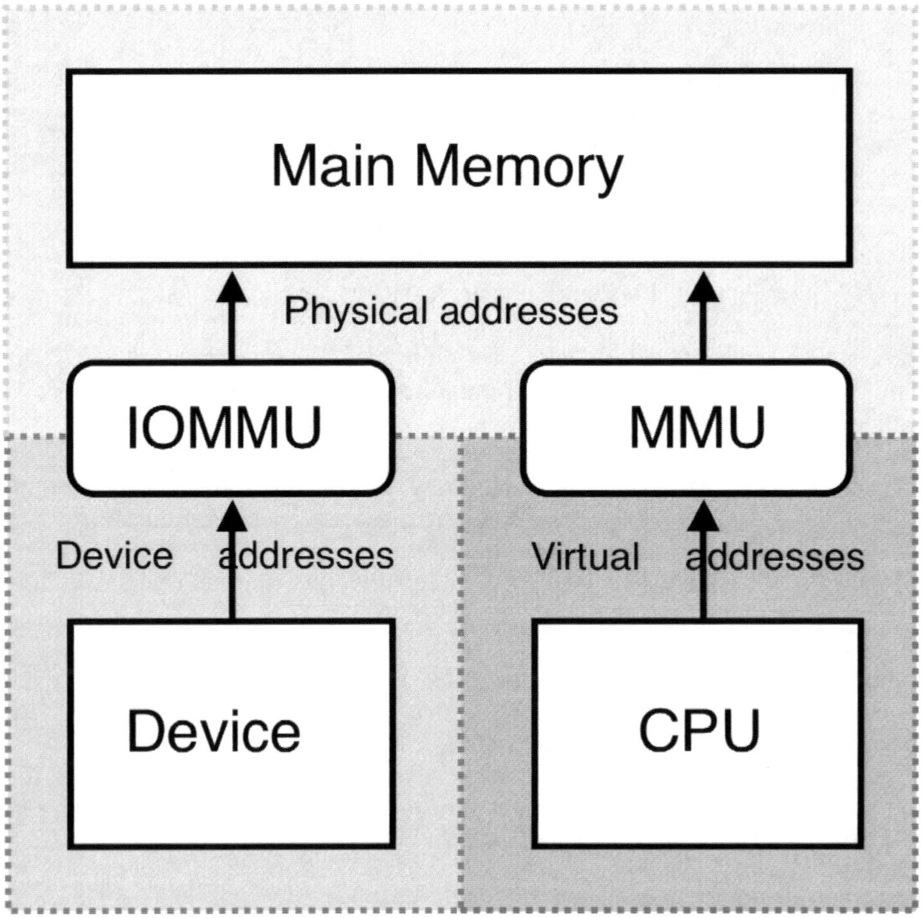


FIGURE 2: COMPARISON OF THE I/O MEMORY MANAGEMENT UNIT (IOMMU) TO THE MEMORY MANAGEMENT UNIT (MMU). (SOURCE: WIKIPEDIA)

The HugeTLB pages [21] builds on top of the multiple page size support provided by the CPU architecture. "`default_hugepagesz=1G hugepagesz=1G hugepages=80`" allows allocating and setting the size of the HugeTLB pages at boot.

Finally, to maximize CPU utilization capabilities, the C-State and P-States need to be disabled by using "`intel_idle.max_cstate=0 processor.max_cstate=0 amd_pstate=disable`"

Further detailed information about these commands can be found in the Linux kernel parameters documentation [22].

## What is DPDK?

Data Plane Development Kit (DPDK) [23] consists of a series of libraries and drivers, running in userspace designed to accelerate packet processing workloads running on a wide variety of CPU architectures such as x86, POWER, and ARM processor and is mainly targeted at Linux.

To accelerate network Input/Output (I/O), DPDK bypasses the Linux kernel, performing packet processing in userspace to maximize networking performance. DPDK achieves this using a Poll-Mode Driver (PMD) running in userspace that continually checks incoming packet queues to see if new data has arrived. This removes the overhead from memory copying without the expense of context switching between user and kernel space, achieving both high throughput and low latency, as outlined in Figure 3.

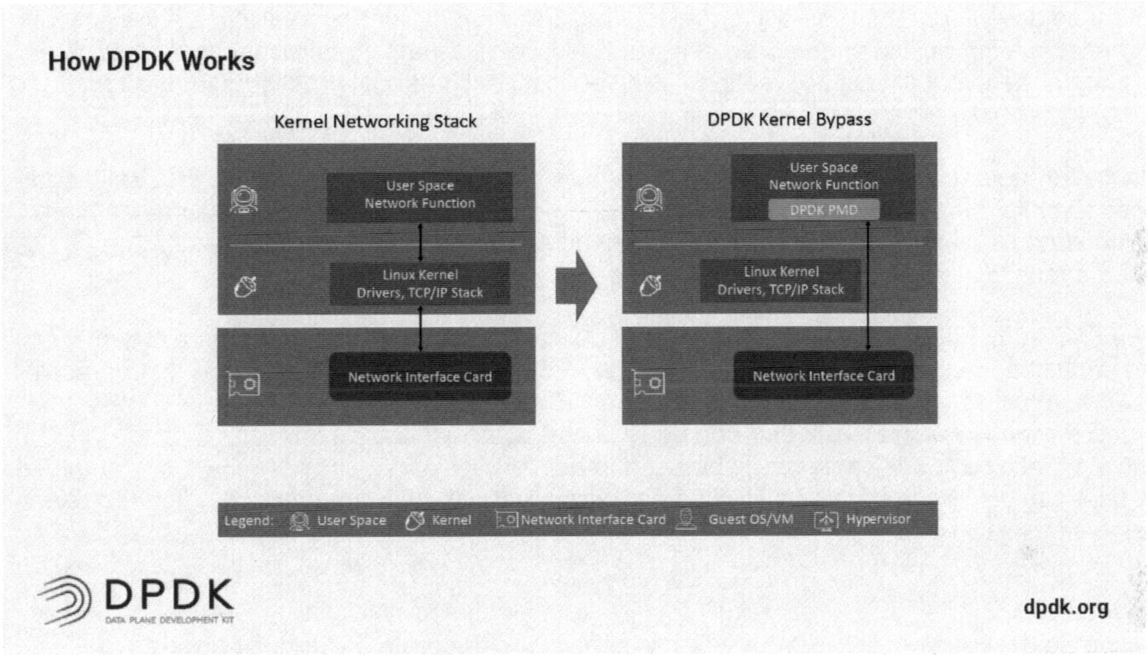


FIGURE 3: HOW DPDK WORKS (FROM MYTH-BUSTING DPDK IN 2020) [24].

A detailed Linux and DPDK configuration guide for performance testing with NVIDIA ConnectX NICs is available in the following Performance Report [25].

## Who is TREX?

TREX [18] is an open-source software stateful and stateless traffic generator based on DPDK supporting layer 3-7 traffic and scale to multiple 100Gbps/sec of traffic with the proper hardware. Supporting the use of YAML [26] and PCAP packet capture library [27] files to define, generate, and playback specific traffic profiles. The tool also provides console and Graphical User Interface (GUI) options to manage the resources. Its main purpose is to provide a COTS-based alternative to purpose-built traffic generators commonly used in the industry to benchmark Device Under Test (DUT) performance from traditional test and measurement vendors such as Keysight Technologies [28] and Spirent Communications [29]. The source code for TREX is hosted by Cisco in a GitHub repository [30].

## Synthetic Payload

In networking, a "payload" refers to the actual useful data transmitted over a network. For testing purposes described in this paper, the payload's content does not necessarily have to be real, but the length of the payload is important.

In an IP network, there are two types of streams: "elephant" and "mice". Elephant streams are large, sustained data flows that consume a significant amount of bandwidth. They are typically created by large data transfers, such as downloading large files or streaming video. On the other hand, mice streams are small, intermittent data flows that consume relatively little bandwidth. They are typically created by small data transfers, such as web browsing or sending emails.

Managing elephant streams is crucial for network administrators as they can potentially congest the network and cause delays for other users. Congestion occurs when there is more traffic on the network than it can handle, leading to slower data transfer rates, dropped packets, and increased latency. This can affect the performance of critical applications and services, such as real-time video and audio streams.

In contrast, mice streams typically have less impact on network performance. However, they still need to be managed to ensure they do not consume more bandwidth than necessary. For example, a large number of mice streams can collectively consume a significant amount of bandwidth, causing congestion and affecting the performance of other network traffic.

Therefore, the desired capability of the testing platform operations is to be able to recreate the ratio of elephant and mice streams in a statistical pattern similar to the one found in a real, loaded, large-scale ST 2110 network, effectively creating and using an ST 2110-like Internet Mix (IMIX) profile. The actual audio and video payloads are irrelevant and can be replaced by an arbitrary synthetic payload.
While generic synthetic payloads can already be used in network testing to simulate the traffic and load the network, they can also be generated with different parameters and bitrates depending on the type of stream being simulated.

### Video Payload

As an illustration, in the case of ST 2110-20 [31], it is possible to generate a synthetic payload to emulate video flows with varying resolutions and frame rates. Specifically, 1080p50 streams typically exhibit a bitrate of roughly 2.2 Gbps, while 2160p50 streams may consume approximately 10 Gbps.

At this point, the particular traffic shape enforced by SMPTE ST 2110-21 is not considered. Previous investigations have demonstrated [10] that the network load can be increased to a point where gapped traffic shapes transform into linear traffic shapes. As a result, the receiver of such video streams may not be able to reconstruct the transported video within an acceptable timeframe. Demonstrating this phenomenon for video traffic is straightforward in both theoretical analysis and practical application.

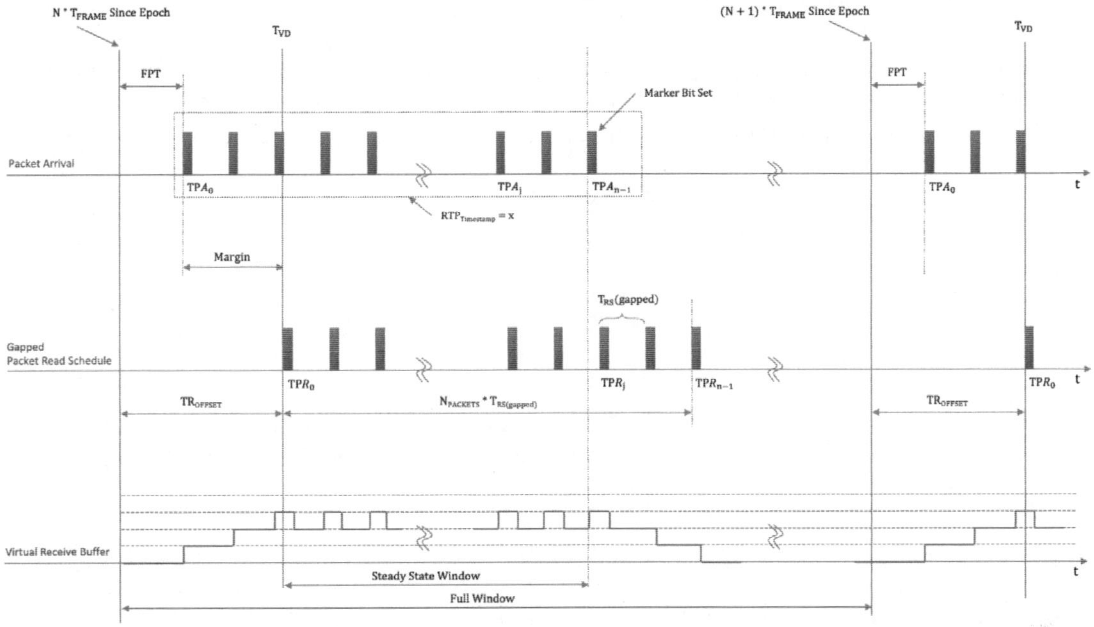


FIGURE 4: DIAGRAM ILLUSTRATING THE GAPPED PACKET READ SCHEDULE.

## Audio Payload

For the ST 2110-30 [32] audio streams, synthetic payloads can be generated with different sample rates, bit depths, and a number of channels. The typical bitrate for an ST 2110-30 single-channel audio stream is around 1.5 Mbps.

## Ancillary Data Payload

For ST 2110-40 [33] ancillary data streams, synthetic payloads can be generated with different data types, such as timecode, captions, and metadata. The bitrate for an ST 2110-40 stream is typically much lower than audio or video streams.

The initial experiment described in this paper uses a generic IMIX [34] profile, with the creation and further experiments with the media IMIX profile being left to the next stages of this research. With the following example, the authors try to show why a continuation of this research may be of interest.

## Example

For a given high-definition video stream, 1080i50 with YCbCr-4:2:2 10-bit color sampling, the needed bandwidth can be calculated as follows:

$$1920 * 1080 = 2073600\, Pixels\ per\ frame$$

Each pixel is described using 20 bits. At least two pixels need to be packetized together for it to be significant. This is called the “pixel group” or pgroup

$$2 * 20 = 40\, bits\ or\ 5\ Bytes\ per\ pgroup$$

Assume that the default MTU size is used minus the necessary bytes for all the headers (Ethernet, IP, UDP, RTP, RFC4175) a maximum of 1446 bytes can be encapsulated per Ethernet frame.

$$1446 / 5 * 2 = 578 \, Pixels \, per \, Ethernet \, frame$$

Knowing the number of pixels needed per video frame and the maximum number of pixels one can transport per Ethernet frame, it is simple to derive the amount of needed Ethernet frames to transport the complete video frame or the two fields in this case. The last Ethernet frame will not have a full payload in this example.

$$2073600 / 578 = 3588 \, Ethernet \, frames$$

Per second of video, 50 fields or 25 frames are transported.

$$25 * 3588 * 1542 * 8 = 1.106.539.200 \, bps \, or \approx 1.106 \, Gbps$$

Imagine a network with an interconnect of 10 Gbps. Assuming there is no other communication but video streams flowing over this link, 9 video streams can be accommodated. This does work for video streams using the linear packet read schedule.

Introducing the gapped Packet Read Schedule (Figure 4) in these equations equals to adding ~4% of bandwidth. This extra bandwidth does not represent any data. It is a specific timeslot for a specific video stream in which no IP datagrams are sent and aren't expected by the receiver.

$$1.1 \, Gbps + 4\% \approx 1.151 \, Gbps$$

If 9 video streams are used, relying on a 10 Gbps network interconnect will not be effective. Although no packets will be lost as the actual data traffic is only 1.1 Gbps, the gap between the data and the maximum capacity of the network will be filled with Ethernet frames. Recent experiments have shown that this gap is shrinking in favor of pushing the data over the network, making it difficult for "Gapped" receivers to reconstruct video frames within a reasonable timeframe.

Using the same network interconnect of 10 Gbps will not work in the case of 9 video streams. No packets will be dropped since real data traffic is still 1.1 Gbps. But the space of the "gap" will be used to fit the Ethernet frames on the wire. Previous experiments have shown that the gap is closing, and the packets are spaced out more evenly. As a result, a receiver will not be capable of reconstructing the video frames in a timely manner.

The comprehension of this experiment is straightforward; however, when there is an amalgamation of disparate traffic categories, it becomes arduous to illustrate in a theoretical manner. Consequently, further research is necessary to transition from synthetic payload to authentic payload. At a minimum, the traffic shape should be authentic.

## PTP Synchronization of The Testing Platform

As outlined in the previous chapter, in real-world ST 2110 networks, the streams are tightly paced per the ST 2110-21 standard, which is critical for adequate utilization of both the buffers in the network devices and the media receivers. This precision is achieved by tightly synchronizing clocks across the network using IEEE 1588, PTP. By locking the testing platform to PTP, it is possible to simulate the traffic patterns of real-time flows accurately, which is critical for analyzing the impact of the network on these tightly synchronized flows.

This also allows for the option to lock multiple testing platforms to PTP for cross-synchronization between them, which, together with higher-level orchestration, can enable multiple network segments to be placed under test to monitor their interaction with each other. This is important, especially when testing large-scale spine-leaf networks or when testing red and blue segments of the ST 2022-7 [35] enabled network. By simulating the traffic patterns across all segments, it is possible to identify potential issues and bottlenecks that may occur in real-world scenarios.

The initial experiment described in this paper is not using PTP for traffic generator synchronization. It is planned for the next stages of this research.

## Initial Platform Testing and Optimization Results

### Pre-Optimization Baseline Factory-Default Results with 4 NICs

The first stage of the experiment was to establish the system's baseline performance before BIOS and kernel tweaking. This would set the starting point to compare the optimized performance gains against the factory-default settings.

```
-Per port stats table
 per port - limited to 4
      ports |               0 |               1 |               2 |               3
-----------------------------------------------------------------------------------------
   opackets |        68500476 |               3 |        68444923 |               3
     obytes |    103983718539 |             525 |    103899389085 |             525
   ipackets |               3 |        68527804 |               3 |        68472862
     ibytes |             537 |    104299313659 |             537 |    104215691935
    ierrors |               0 |               0 |               0 |               0
    oerrors |               0 |               0 |               0 |               0
      Tx Bw |     96.35 Gbps |     872.76  bps |     95.81 Gbps |     972.22  bps

-Global stats enabled
 Cpu Utilization : 7.6  %  314.7 Gb/core
 Platform_factor : 1.0
 Total-Tx        :     384.47 Gbps
 Total-Rx        :     384.95 Gbps
 Total-PPS       :      31.66 Mpps
 Total-CPS       :       0.00  cps

 Expected-PPS    :      32.00 Mpps
 Expected-CPS    :      32.00 Mcps
 Expected-BPS    :     388.61 Gbps

 Active-flows    :     1600  Clients :      255   Socket-util : 0.0100 %
 Open-flows      :     1600  Servers :    65535   Socket :     1600 Socket/Clients :  6.3
 drop-rate       :       0.00  bps
 current time    : 16.0 sec
 test duration   : 4.0 sec
```

FIGURE 5: BASELINE TREX PERFORMANCE BEFORE THE PLATFORM OPTIMIZATION.

Figure 5 shows the traffic generation results using two ConnectX-6 DX and two ConnectX-5 NICs. The generator was configured to simulate traffic patterns with strict packet pacing at a rate of 400 Gbps with 8 cores per interface pair, using an IMIX profile for 1514-byte packets. The generator's performance was evaluated by conducting tests with each NIC in a loopback configuration, with one port connected to the other.

The initial results show some inconsistency issues. The generator reported close to 400 Gbps of generated traffic performance during the test. However, after the test concluded, the Total-Tx

(Transmit) and Total-Rx (Receive) reported ~385 Gbps which may be due to the packet size in the IMIX profile.

A ramp load of about 10 seconds was observed with the bandwidth fluctuating around 387 Gbps going up and down by ~1 Gbps. Therefore the tests were performed for at least 20 sec, with occasional sustained tests of 10-minute test performed to observe the system stability.

It was observed that the CPU utilization remained low, with 7% utilization with 8 cores per interface pair. When the number of interface pairs was increased, the CPU utilization rose to 26%, indicating that the platform's performance threshold may have been approaching.

To further investigate the inconsistencies observed in the test results, the use of different DACs (Direct Attach Cable) was also explored. The first three NICs were connected with genuine Mellanox DACs, while the fourth was connected with a compatible DAC. It is possible that this mix of DACs may have influenced the platform's performance.

TREX is limited to using no more than 48 CPU cores by default, whereas the platform had 64 cores with simultaneous multithreading (SMT) enabled. However, at this point, the benefit of the use of SMT for this application was still to be defined. Therefore, exploring the impact of increasing the core limit in TREX to 64 or disabling SMT altogether in the BIOS was considered to achieve better performance.

Two methods to increase the core limit in TREX have been identified. The first involves modifying the code's corresponding variable value and then rebuilding the TREX from this custom code source. The second method involves using the stateless mode, which requires a different configuration and out-of-the-box work with only one interface pair. For now, both methods were deemed as low-priority solutions to be investigated. The use of custom code would impair the repeatability of the overall proposed solution, and the use of stateless mode may limit the potential use of the media-specific IMIX profiles. This led to the conclusion that due to the lack of specific efficient support of SMT in TREX, the SMT can be disabled to avoid virtual core mappings impacting performance by causing bottlenecks on specific processes.

### Pre-Optimization Baseline Factory-Default Results with 6 NICs

The testing continued by adding two more NICs and changing the HPE server's workload profile to "General Throughput Compute". 6 NICs were distributed symmetrically over 2 risers in 2 NUMAs (1xCX6-DX, 1xCX5, 1xCX5-EX per riser, per NUMA). The resulting logical PCIe configuration is demonstrated in Figure 6. The profile description as per the HPE BIOS is demonstrated in Figure 7.

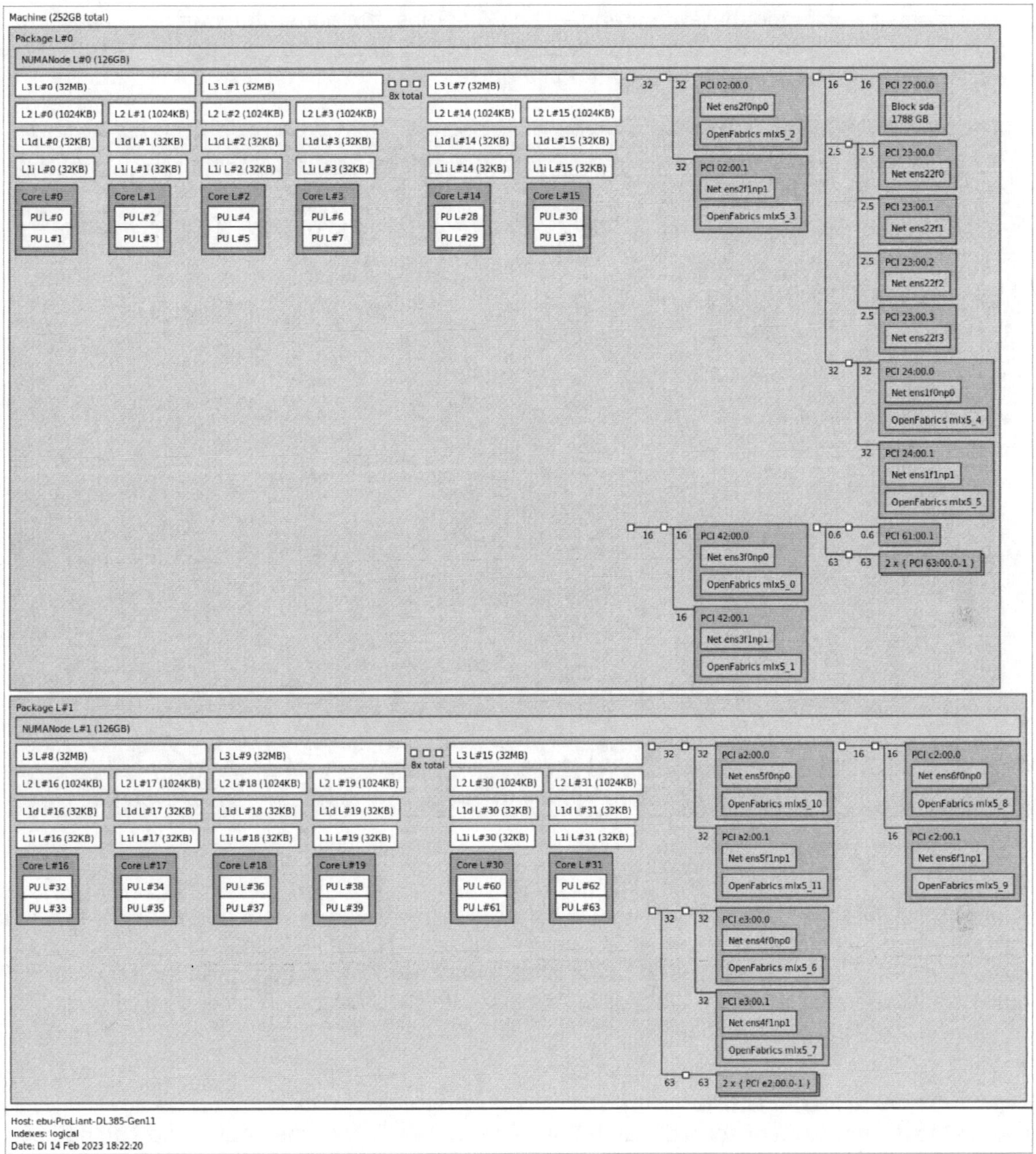


FIGURE 6: THE LOGICAL PCIE SYSTEM CONFIGURATION AS REPORTED BY LSTOPO.

**General Throughput Compute**

Use this profile for workloads where you need the total maximum-sustained workload throughput. When the processor runs at the highest individual core speed, it does not necessarily result in an increased throughput. Rather when the processor is able to perform sustained work across all available cores during maximum utilization, it results in an increased throughput. Power management settings are disabled when they are known to have impact on maximum achievable bandwidth.

Best throughput is achieved when the workload is also (Nonuniformed Memory Access) NUMA aware and optimized, so settings that benefit NUMA awareness are applied.

FIGURE 7: "GENERAL THROUGHPUT COMPUTE" PRESET DESCRIPTION.

After several tests, it was found that when requesting 600 Gbps, the generator was peaking at 582 Gbps. However, the Total_queue_full counters started growing, which is also reported in Total-sw-err in summary stats. These results are demonstrated in Figure 8.

```
-Per port stats table
 per port - limited to 4
      ports |               0 |               1 |               2 |               3
 ----------------------------------------------------------------------------------------
   opackets |       366176083 |               0 |       367356770 |               7
     obytes |    555855293994 |               0 |    557647566034 |            1212
   ipackets |               0 |       366206098 |               7 |       367388173
     ibytes |               0 |    557365681156 |            1240 |    559164788480
    ierrors |               0 |               0 |               0 |               0
    oerrors |               0 |               0 |               0 |               0
      Tx Bw |     96.82 Gbps |       0.00  bps |     97.02 Gbps |       0.20  bps

-Global stats enabled
 Cpu Utilization : 7.3  %  378.0 Gb/core
 Platform_factor : 1.0
 Total-Tx        :     582.09 Gbps
 Total-Rx        :     582.21 Gbps
 Total-PPS       :      47.93 Mpps
 Total-CPS       :       0.00  cps

 Expected-PPS    :      48.00 Mpps
 Expected-CPS    :      48.00 Mcps
 Expected-BPS    :     582.91 Gbps

 Active-flows    :     1600  Clients :      255   Socket-util : 0.0100 %
 Open-flows      :     1600  Servers :    65535   Socket :      1600 Socket/Clients :  6.3
 Total_queue_full : 20911307
 drop-rate       :       0.00  bps
 current time    : 57.2 sec
 test duration   : 542.8 sec
```

FIGURE 8: TREX PERFORMANCE WHEN USING 6 TX PORTS WITH 600 GPS DESIRED.

The reported CPU utilization was still very low (~7%), indicating that a system bottleneck was unrelated to the CPU. Further trials found that the error counters stayed at 0 until ~562 Gbps of desired load, which gave ~545 Gbps of reported Tx/Rx. In the other hand, requesting more than the physical limit of 600 Gbps TX load reported a Total RX/TX of 592 Gbps, with CPU utilization growing to almost 90% and Total-sw-err also growing significantly.

## Occasional Server Boot Failure

During the lab tests, the team observed that the server failed to boot occasionally when going beyond 5 NICs installed. To troubleshoot the issue, first, the Simultaneous Multi-Threading (SMT) feature was disabled. However, the server continued to exhibit boot failure even with 6 NICs once in three attempts with an "Uncorrectable Machine Check Exception" error in the iLO logs. This may also be linked to the novelty of the platform and may be resolved with BIOS updates or a follow-up with the manufacturer. While it is intended for follow-up, it wasn't resolved during the experiments performed for this paper, and the team wasn't successful in running more than 8 NICs simultaneously.

## SMT and Process Core Pinning Optimization

With SMT enabled and 6 NICs, we observed consistent results with a network throughput of 585 Gbps and no errors. However, as mentioned, it was intended to experiment with more granular optimization via pinning the TREX generation processes to the physical CPU cores for more granular control. This required SMT to be disabled.

With SMT disabled and 6 NICs, the results were comparable, but the results started showing more total software errors (total-sw-err). The error-free transmission was only achieved with a requested throughput of around 400 Gbps.

TREX provides native core pinning functionality that was used as an initial option to improve performance. The kernel-provided core pinning was left for future experiments.

The comparison between the SMT modes and TREX-provided core pinning yielded the following results:

- With 600 Gbps requested, an effective 582 Gbps are achieved with or without SMT, and no core pinning but a considerable number of total-sw-err are observed.
- With 600 Gbps requested, the same effective 582 Gbps are achieved without SMT but with TREX-provided core pinning, but significantly lower counts of total-sw-err are observed.

In the case of the 20-second test, the concrete numbers were as follows:

- 20-second test:
  - 960 million packets.
  - 11 million total-sw-err with no core pinning.
  - 4 thousand total-sw-err with core pinning.

While implementing TREX-provided core pinning improved the network performance, we still encountered total software errors (total-sw-err). However, the total-pkt-drop rate remained zero in all scenarios. Further experiments with kernel-based core pinning will be required.

## Bandwidth Validation with External Tools

While the initially generated bandwidth reports were archived via looping back the TX ports of the NICs to the RX ports and the self-reporting of the software, the last concept validation step included the measurement and reporting using an external tool. A high-performance, non-blocking network switch was used to validate the generated packet count and overall bandwidth. The performance of the switch platform was not the object of validation, and it was merely used for providing another data point. Therefore, the make and the model are not quoted as considered irrelevant for the purpose of this paper.

Each port of the NICs was connected with DACs to a 100 Gbps port of the switch, with half of the ports in a TX and another half in the RX mode.

The switch counters showed consistent, sustained performance of both the TX and RX ports, with an average of 97.2 Gbps and 98.4% of link utilization when requesting a total of 600 Gbps of load. Figures 9 and 10 demonstrate the rates reported from the switch for a single port and for all 12 ports used.

```
Ethernet3/1 is up, line protocol is up (connected)
  Hardware is Ethernet, address is fcbd.6786.51f2 (bia fcbd.6786.51f2)
  Ethernet MTU 9214 bytes , BW 100000000 kbit
  Full-duplex, 100Gb/s, auto negotiation: off, uni-link: n/a
  Up 21 minutes, 58 seconds
  Loopback Mode : None
  4 link status changes since last clear
  Last clearing of "show interface" counters 0:52:56 ago
  1 minute input rate 97.2 Gbps (98.4% with framing overhead), 8000409 packets/sec
  1 minute output rate 667 bps (0.0% with framing overhead), 1 packets/sec
     3919250008 packets input, 5949419390563 bytes
     Received 40 broadcasts, 137 multicast
     0 runts, 0 giants
     0 input errors, 0 CRC, 0 alignment, 0 symbol, 0 input discards
     0 PAUSE input
     1086 packets output, 145431 bytes
     Sent 40 broadcasts, 1046 multicast
     0 output errors, 0 collisions
     0 late collision, 0 deferred, 0 output discards
     0 PAUSE output
```

FIGURE 9: SINGLE PORT UTILIZATION AS REPORTED BY THE SWITCH.

| Port | Name | Intvl | In Mbps | % | In Kpps | Out Mbps | % | Out Kpps |
|---|---|---|---|---|---|---|---|---|
| Et1/1 | | 1:00 | 97149.4 | 98.4% | 7999 | 0.0 | 0.0% | 0 |
| Et2/1 | | 1:00 | 0.0 | 0.0% | 0 | 97149.5 | 98.4% | 7999 |
| Et3/1 | | 1:00 | 97153.5 | 98.4% | 8000 | 0.0 | 0.0% | 0 |
| Et4/1 | | 1:00 | 0.0 | 0.0% | 0 | 97153.5 | 98.4% | 8000 |
| Et5/1 | | 1:00 | 97153.9 | 98.4% | 8000 | 0.0 | 0.0% | 0 |
| Et6/1 | | 1:00 | 0.0 | 0.0% | 0 | 97153.9 | 98.4% | 8000 |
| Et7/1 | | 1:00 | 97154.1 | 98.4% | 8000 | 0.0 | 0.0% | 0 |
| Et8/1 | | 1:00 | 0.0 | 0.0% | 0 | 97154.1 | 98.4% | 8000 |
| Et9/1 | | 1:00 | 97154.0 | 98.4% | 8000 | 0.0 | 0.0% | 0 |
| Et10/1 | | 1:00 | 0.0 | 0.0% | 0 | 97154.0 | 98.4% | 8000 |
| Et11/1 | | 1:00 | 97154.0 | 98.4% | 8000 | 0.0 | 0.0% | 0 |
| Et12/1 | | 1:00 | 0.0 | 0.0% | 0 | 97154.1 | 98.4% | 8000 |

FIGURE 10: ALL USED PORTS UTILIZATION AS REPORTED BY THE SWITCH.

## Conclusion and Future Work

Acceptance testing of a large-scale SMPTE ST 2110 network requires careful consideration of various factors. With the increasing adoption of ST 2110, ensuring the performance and reliability of these networks is crucial. The successful testing of such large-scale networks requires a comprehensive approach that considers all relevant factors, from the type of traffic to precise timing. With the right tools and techniques, network architects can ensure the performance and reliability of their ST 2110 networks, both as part of acceptance testing before putting networks in production and as a regular testing and maintenance exercise to make sure that there's no performance degradation in the network over time or due to changes in configuration and/or software versions.

The successful initial testing of the platform architected by the authors shows that it is possible to build a capable traffic generator using off-the-shelf components and open-source software, reaching a bandwidth of almost 600 Gbps in a system with a form factor of a 2-rack-unit server. However, this process requires a deep understanding of the hardware APIs and the Linux kernel to tune the performance of the different components.

Although further testing and optimization are required to achieve the peak performance and potential of the selected platform, it is promising that the platform could predictably and repeatably generate the expected bitrates.

Further work is needed to capture and recreate the statistical media IMIX profile and experiment with the traffic load patterns and the reaction of the various switch platforms. It is the intent of the authors to reach out to a number of public service media broadcasters that are running large-scale ST 2110 networks and gather real-world data to build the media IMIX profile, that would be as close to the real-world implementations as possible.

Additionally, the successful implementation of PTP synchronization on the testing platform allows for a more accurate simulation of the traffic patterns with stricter packet pacing. This will enable an analysis of the impact of the network on the tight tolerances of the precisely paced flows, as well as cross-synchronization between multiple platforms deployed in various network segments.

Finally, the authors intend to produce a detailed and easily-reproducible "howto" guide for the proposed platform covering configuration, optimization, and usage to lower the entry barrier in terms of the technical complexity and enable the wide range of media broadcasters, including but not limited to those that are members of the EBU, to use and benefit from the platform.

## Acknowledgments

These projects would never have been possible without the collaboration between the European Broadcasting Union, NVIDIA, and the Vlaamse Radio- en Televisieomroeporganisatie (VRT).

## References

[1] "ST 259:2008 - SMPTE Standard - For Television — SDTV - Digital Signal/Data — Serial Digital Interface," in ST 259:2008 , vol., no., pp.1-18, 29 Jan. 2008, doi: 10.5594/SMPTE.ST259.2008.

[2] Audio Engineering Society, AES67-2018: AES standard for audio applications of networks - High-performance streaming audio-over-IP interoperability.

[3] "ST 2022-6:2012 - SMPTE Standard - Transport of High Bit Rate Media Signals over IP Networks (HBRMT)," in ST 2022-6:2012 , vol., no., pp.1-16, 9 Oct. 2012, doi: 10.5594/SMPTE.ST2022-6.2012.

[4] F. Poulin, T. Kernen and A. Kouadio, "Technical Review: Ultra High Definition TV over IP Networks," European Broadcasting Union, Geneva, 2014.

[5] "Technical Recommendation TR-03," Video Services Forum, 2015.

[6] "OV 2110-0:2018 - SMPTE Overview Document - Professional Media over Managed IP Networks Roadmap for the 2110 Document Suite," in OV 2110-0:2018 , vol., no., pp.1-4, 24 Jan. 2019, doi: 10.5594/SMPTE.OV2110-0.2018.

[7] "ST 2110-21:2017 - SMPTE Standard - Professional Media Over Managed IP Networks: Traffic Shaping and Delivery Timing for Video," in ST 2110-21:2017 , vol., no., pp.1-17, 27 Nov. 2017, doi: 10.5594/SMPTE.ST2110-21.2017.

[8] T. Kernen, W. Vermost and N. Kerö, "Measurement methodology and real-world compliance results for ST 2110-21 devices," in NAB BEITC, Las Vegas, 2019.

[9] "IEEE Standard for a Precision Clock Synchronization Protocol for Networked Measurement and Control Systems," in IEEE Std 1588-2019 (Revision ofIEEE Std 1588-2008) , vol., no., pp.1-499, 16 June 2020, doi: 10.1109/IEEESTD.2020.9120376.

[10] T. Kernen and W. Vermost, "The art of conforming to SMPTE 2110-21 traffic model," in NAB BEITC, Las Vegas, 2018.

[11] "Request for Comments: 3550 "RTP: A Transport Protocol for Real-Time Applications"," 2003.

[12] "HPE ProLiant DL385 Gen11 Data sheet," [Online]. Available: https://www.hpe.com/psnow/doc/PSN1014689137WWEN.pdf. [Accessed 6 March 2023].

[13] "AMD EPYC™ 9174F General Specifications," [Online]. Available: https://www.amd.com/en/product/12636. [Accessed 6 March 2023].

[14] "NVIDIA ConnectX-6 DX User Manual and Datasheet," [Online]. Available: https://docs.nvidia.com/networking/display/ConnectX6DxEN. [Accessed 6 March 2023].

[15] "NVIDIA ConnectX-5 Ethernet Adapter Cards User Manual and Datasheet," [Online]. Available: https://docs.nvidia.com/networking/display/ConnectX5EN. [Accessed 6 March 2023].

[16] "Ubuntu 22.04.2 LTS (Jammy Jellyfish)," [Online]. Available: https://www.releases.ubuntu.com/22.04/. [Accessed 6 March 2023].

[17] "NVIDIA MLNX_OFED Documentation Rev 5.8-1.1.2.1 LTS," [Online]. Available: https://docs.nvidia.com/networking/display/MLNXOFEDv581121LTS/NVIDIA+MLNX_OFED+Documentation+Rev+5.8-1.1.2.1+LTS. [Accessed 6 March 2023].

[18] "TRex release notes, Release 3.02," [Online]. Available: https://trex-tgn.cisco.com/trex/doc/release_notes.html. [Accessed 6 March 2023].

[19] "TUNING GUIDE AMD EPYC 9004, BIOS & Workload, Publication 58011, Revision 1.1," December 2022. [Online]. Available: https://www.amd.com/system/files/documents/58011-epyc-9004-tg-bios-and-workload.pdf . [Accessed 6 March 2023].

[20] "TUNING GUIDE AMD EPYC 9004, High Performance Computing (HPC), Publication 58002, Revision 1.1," [Online]. Available: https://www.amd.com/system/files/documents/58002-epyc-9004-tg-hpc.pdf. [Accessed 6 March 2023].

[21] "Linux HugeTLB pages," [Online]. Available: https://docs.kernel.org/admin-guide/mm/hugetlbpage.html. [Accessed 6 March 2023].

[22] "Linux Kernel parameters," [Online]. Available: https://www.kernel.org/doc/html/latest/admin-guide/kernel-parameters.html. [Accessed 6 March 2023].

[23] "DPDK – Data Plane Development Kit," [Online]. Available: https://www.dpdk.org/. [Accessed 6 March 2023].

[24] "Myth-busting DPDK in 2020 - Revealed: the past, present, and future of the most popular data plane development kit in the world," [Online]. Available: https://nextgeninfra.io/dpdk-myth-busting-2020/. [Accessed 6 March 2023].

[25] "NVIDIA Mellanox NICs Performance Report with DPDK 22.07," [Online]. Available: http://fast.dpdk.org/doc/perf/DPDK_22_07_NVIDIA_Mellanox_NIC_performance_report.pdf. [Accessed 6 March 2023].

[26] "YAML: YAML Ain't Markup Language™," [Online]. Available: https://yaml.org/. [Accessed 6 March 2023].

[27] "TCPdump & libpcap," [Online]. Available: https://www.tcpdump.org/. [Accessed 6 March 2023].

[28] "Keysite Technologies," [Online]. Available: https://www.keysight.com/. [Accessed 6 March 2023].

[29] "Spirent Communications," [Online]. Available: https://www.spirent.com/. [Accessed 6 March 2023].

[30] "Cisco Systems Traffic Generators," [Online]. Available: https://github.com/cisco-system-traffic-generator. [Accessed 6 March 2023].

[31] "ST 2110-20:2017 - SMPTE Standard - Professional Media Over Managed IP Networks: Uncompressed Active Video," in ST 2110-20:2017 , vol., no., pp.1-22, 27 Nov. 2017, doi: 10.5594/SMPTE.ST2110-20.2017.

[32] "ST 2110-30:2017 - SMPTE Standard - Professional Media Over Managed IP Networks: PCM Digital Audio," in ST 2110-30:2017 , vol., no., pp.1-9, 27 Nov. 2017, doi: 10.5594/SMPTE.ST2110-30.2017.

[33] "ST 2110-40:2018 - SMPTE Standard - Professional Media Over Managed IP Networks: SMPTE ST 291-1 Ancillary Data," in ST 2110-40:2018 , vol., no., pp.1-8, 25 April 2018, doi: 10.5594/SMPTE.ST2110-40.2018.

[34] D. Murray and T. Koziniec, "The State of Enterprise Network Traffic in 2012," in 18th Asia-Pacific Conference on Communications (APCC 2012), 2012.

[35] "ST 2022-7:2019 - SMPTE Standard - Seamless Protection Switching of RTP Datagrams," in ST 2022-7:2019 , vol., no., pp.1-11, 13 May 2019, doi: 10.5594/SMPTE.ST2022-7.2019.

# Redefining The Control Plane

**Daniel Murphy**
**NEP Group**
**Pittsburgh, Pa., United States**
dmurphy@nepgroup.com

**Abstract** – NEP is engineering a global media platform as the convergence of technology rapidly changes all the rules. This paper is a real world look behind the challenges and solutions to modern broadcast architecture that led to the development of TFC (Total Facility Control), NEP's proprietary platform controller. These are unprecedented times as the industry is disrupted throughout the value chain. Consumer technology has exploded the demand for content and is revolutionizing the ways in which it is consumed. Broadcast technology continues to respond, driving faster innovation and more cost-effective solutions. These forces converge at the inevitable embrace of software defined workflows, established IT technology and a growing trend towards COTS hardware. Yet how ready is the industry for this change? The collapsing of the traditional control layer and decentralizing of processing, creates serious burdens for any enterprise efforts. Building a scalable, automated, and secure control plane requires a new approach.

This paper explores NEP's approach to modern broadcast architectures and applies the real-world experience gained in the development of TFC and deployments worldwide for some of the biggest sporting events and broadcast facilities.

## Preface

Since our first deployment of TFC, I've often been asked by customers and technology partners to write a paper on its origin story. I've told the abridged version in countless meetings and training sessions but up until now, we have never told the full story on how it came to be. And you might wonder why we have chosen a technology conference to do this now? The answer is simple. The story of TFC is intrinsically linked to the immense technology and commercial changes in our industry.

TFC was created by engineers working in the field who felt the impact of these evolving market forces every day, and who understood that a new approach was needed to deliver broadcast and media into the future. While ST2110 was the major shift in technology that started NEP's development of TFC, it's only the beginning of the much bigger technology change built on the broader adoption of IT from other industries.

The game is changing for consumers, for content creators, for manufacturers, and for engineers. I've often heard it said that we need a new breed of engineers. And while no doubt retraining and new skillsets are required, what is more important is that we take a radical new approach to the control layer itself. That's why TFC exists - to enable NEP to boldly move into this new era of technology and thrive amongst the challenges our industry faces.

Rethinking the broadcast control plane has never been more important. I hope this paper illustrates why NEP took a fundamentally different approach to control, and how the industry can benefit from an expanded approach to the control layer. I also hope you will allow this paper to deviate a little from the usual format as I weave together the story of TFC while describing the technological challenges and solutions to modern broadcast architecture it was built to solve.

I also want to make a special thanks to all the NEP broadcast engineers, developers and IT professionals that work every day to make TFC a success and help NEP transition to a technology platform of the future. And our customers and partners who see the vision for what we are building and work with us to make it a reality.

## Introduction: Disruption in The Media Technology Landscape

Today there is enormous change within the media and entertainment sector. Consumption of media in ever growing mediums and in increasing volumes is disrupting the traditional broadcast model [1]. A shift in the value of rights and an evolution of programming, with a focus on targeted viewing opportunities to capture and retain customers, is having a trickle-down effect on the value chain. And as the demand for content increases and shifts, creators are searching for new ways to serve this appetite. In response, the broadcast technology industry is rapidly adopting new strategies for product development. Manufacturers are under pressure to develop products faster and enable networks, facilitators, and integrators to meet the demands for exploding content by delivering scale at a lower cost. The move away from bespoke hardware into software, based on commercial off the shelf (COTS) hardware, is the inevitable outcome as these forces converge.

Underpinning the technology change is the rapid adoption of IT from other industries. We are moving away from an exclusively hardware paradigm to unlock the potential for software defined workflows. However, while there is a focus on a new approach to delivering the engine room (video and audio processing, networking, storage, rendering, transmission/delivery, etc.), the role of the control layer has largely remained unchanged.

Yet the biggest challenges in technological innovation exist in the control layer. The adoption of NMOS[1] and other control initiatives lag behind ST2110 processing. Implementation of the JT-NM technology pyramid [2] has been slow, as evidenced by the little progress between Version 1 (2018) and Version 2 (2020), as shown in Figure 1. The control layer seems to have taken a back seat. The industry is focused on processing as we drive towards cloud computing and COTS processing engines.

FIGURE 1A: JT-NM TR-1001-1:2018

FIGURE 1B: JT-NM TR-1001-1:2020

[1] https://www.amwa.tv/nmos-overview

The theory of adopting existing commercially available technology is compelling, and there are many examples of success, such as the adoption of COTS network switches. However, in practice, this transition has been messy. The focus on technology has not been equaled with a focus on easing the adoption of this new technology for the operational engineers responsible for managing it. And success for this technological shift requires significant consideration be given to usability for operational engineers within the control layer.

Today, the challenge of recruiting, training, and retaining qualified broadcast engineers remains a major issue for our industry. And the introduction of this new, highly complex IP technology and software defined workflows happening in tandem only works to exacerbate staffing issues. The solution must be to redefine the control plane and increase automation to build a service layer that manages the complex orchestration of software and networking on-premise and in the cloud.

This paper examines how redefining the control plane and expanding the role of the control system to include configuration, provisioning, orchestration, and granular monitoring of broadcast, IT and network systems can help to overcome the challenges our industry is facing and ensure success of the modern scalable broadcast system.

## Section 1: Collapsing the Traditional Control Layer in The Era of ST2110

The control layer of a traditional broadcast system is made up of several disparate systems including, but not limited to:

- broadcast controller
- tally and logic manager
- individual device controllers (e.g.: routers, switchers, cameras, glue)
- management network
- timing and reference system
- IP switch control plane
- scheduling and automation systems
- monitoring systems (e.g., scopes, probes, sensors)

In traditional system architecture, the broadcast controller (controller) provided a unified interface across the control layer. The controller sits over the top of these various systems using abstraction protocols to communicate with primary responsibilities of router crosspoint control, tallies, GPIOs and device parameter control.

Over time, controllers have become more sophisticated incorporating parts of the control layer directly. For example, many modern broadcast systems do not have a separate tally and logic manager but use the broadcast controller exclusively. Some controllers handle scheduling and automation natively without directing a separate underlying system. This collapsing of the control layer provides a seamlessly integrated and more cohesive user experience while reducing total system cost and complexity.

Typically, broadcast controllers were designed around a small number of monolithic routers that provided centralized electrical switching of signals. The move from traditional baseband to IP, and even more acutely ST2110, had major impacts on the control plane: a significant increase in the number of devices in any system; the separation of media essences (video, audio, meta) resulting in an increased number of signals or flows that a controller must manage; the decentralization of control to devices at the edge; and the enabling of systems to scale far beyond the capacity of baseband solutions. This decentralization introduced additional challenges in network configuration and security.

Manufacturers responded by implementing new ways of controlling IP, adding drivers to support more external orchestration, and increasing performance to handle the demand. However, in 2018 these controllers' fundamental role was not expanding to deal more with these underlying challenges. And so, NEP began development on a next generation controller designed to collapse more of the control layer. This new approach took learnings from large scale online platforms and cloud providers, to redefine the way to think about control and how to develop and build a broadcast control ecosystem in a scalable, flexible, and resilient way.

## Infrastructure as Code

The first solution for the control challenges ST2110 introduced is to take a different approach to provisioning and managing devices by adopting the IT datacenter philosophy of Infrastructure as Code (IaC). IaC is the process of managing and provisioning infrastructure through software, instead of physical hardware configuration, or interactive configuration tools such as UIs [3].

Consider the difference between a monolithic router and an ST2110 gateway. There are many more parameters required to be configured on an IP gateway and it is easy to create a conflict, for example by programming the same IP or multicast address into different devices, as shown in Table 1.

| Baseband Router | IP Gateway |
|---|---|
| Mgmt IP Address<br><br>Labels<br>Format*<br>Frame store*<br>Spigot/IO indexes<br><br><br><br><br><br><br><br>** optional* | Mgmt IP Address*<br><br>Streaming IP Address(es)<br>Labels<br>Format*<br>Frame store*<br>Multicast Address(es) (up to 6 per spigot)<br>Multicast Port(s) (up to 6 per spigot)<br>Payload ID(s) (up to 6 per spigot)<br>PTP Domain<br>Network interface(s)<br>VLAN*<br><br>** optional* |

TABLE 1: OUTLINING THE DIFFERENCE IN PARAMETERS REQUIRED FOR BASEBAND ROUTERS AND IP GATEWAYS.

This impact was felt acutely during the build of the Andrews Hub in NEP Australia. Each endpoint would take between five and 15 minutes to configure. The original installation had 90 gateway devices each with 20 inputs and outputs across IP and SDI. That equated to 1,800 signals, 5,400 essences and 10,800 flows that needed to be configured uniquely to prevent a conflict, amounts that, already on a relatively small scale, exceed the efficiency of spreadsheets. It is easy to see why greater automation is required. Manual configuration was not only time consuming, but prone to error. TFC began as a configuration utility to automate this, first by generating scripts and then eventually by actively configuring and managing configuration on the devices in real time.

At the time, NEP considered whether this provisioning belonged in the broadcast controller or to take a different approach to using Continuous Configuration Automation (CCA) [4] tools such as Ansible or Terraform. While these tools are a step in the right direction, and inevitably have a role in modern broadcast commissioning, NEP saw the need for the broadcast controller to maintain real-time configuration control of the devices it orchestrates.

The broadcast controller should be the single source of truth for the appropriate state of any given device, to ensure the signal is propagated everywhere it is needed, in the right format, and at all times. To do this effectively the controller must monitor for configuration changes and react accordingly. In some cases, these changes may be unauthorized and require reverting to force state, and in other cases the controller might need to react to an external change.

## Handling The Scale

As the control plane itself grows and the role of the broadcast controller expands, traditional monolithic applications that rely on vertical scaling struggle to handle the performance demand. A modern software development methodology and architecture is necessary to handle the scale.

A microservices architecture is a suite of independently developed software services, where each service maintains a specific process and communicates through a well-defined mechanism to serve a specific business requirement. The methodology focuses on building single-purpose modules with specific interfaces and operations. The popularity of microservices has increased dramatically over recent years due to enterprise organizations looking for methods to become more agile and move towards a DevOps and continuous delivery pipeline [5].

The benefits of development with microservices are:

- Easy to deploy: Each microservice is deployed individually without affecting other services.
- Easy to understand: Each application serves a specific business domain, is isolated and has few dependencies. Because the applications are smaller, they are easier to understand.
- Increased re-useability: Services can be shared across the business. Generic services such as login, user management and rights management can all be shared and reused.
- Minimize the risk of change: As systems are small and interfaces between services are well-defined the system can be frequently updated after automatic test runs. Small, frequent changes are less risky and time consuming than big bang changes that require a lot of regression testing.
- Isolation of defects: When a test fails or a problem occurs in the live running system, the problem can be isolated and solved without affecting other services.
- Scalability of individual services: When one of the services needs to handle increased workload during peak usage, multiple instances of that service can be automatically started.
- Upgrade seamlessly: enable services to be upgraded and downgraded with limited or no downtime, which is especially important for 24/7 facilities and critical infrastructure.

One major driver on the scale requirements is that all parts of the control layer should be API driven, to ensure maximum automation. Traditionally many external broadcast controllers have been stateless, for example where they read back the internal state from a router. There was no need to control every configuration value on every device and so protocols that exposed a limited number of parameters and basic X-Y switching was sufficient.

However, as systems scale and the need for automation grows, API access to every parameter is critical. To effectively implement infrastructure as code, engineers cannot be required to use native interfaces to configure devices. Devices need to expose all their configuration via API and the controller needs southbound drivers that can effectively manage configuration of the device, not just real time routing or select parameter control.

Likewise, automation of the controller itself is required via APIs, for example linking to enable a scheduling system to populate information or 3rd party control. Traditionally northbound APIs have been limited to routing protocols, label protocols or select parameter control using protocols such as Ember+, TSL, SW-P-08 or NMOS. However, to fully take advantage of the controller and ensure that it can effectively remain the source of truth for state in the system, the controller should expose all its configuration and real time control over APIs.

TFC can be externally controlled using its native APIs for advanced configuration and real time control of routing and device parameters. For compatibility, TFC also supports classical routing protocols like Ember+, SWP-08 and TSL 5.0.

Finally, when dealing with the scale, a different approach to identifying and categorizing signals is required. Traditional control systems abstract signals as crosspoints represented in a flat "X-Y" matrix. This works efficiently with hundreds or even thousands of crosspoints. However, with tens of thousands of crosspoints or more, it starts to become overly complex, with finding and managing signals becoming a needle in a haystack.

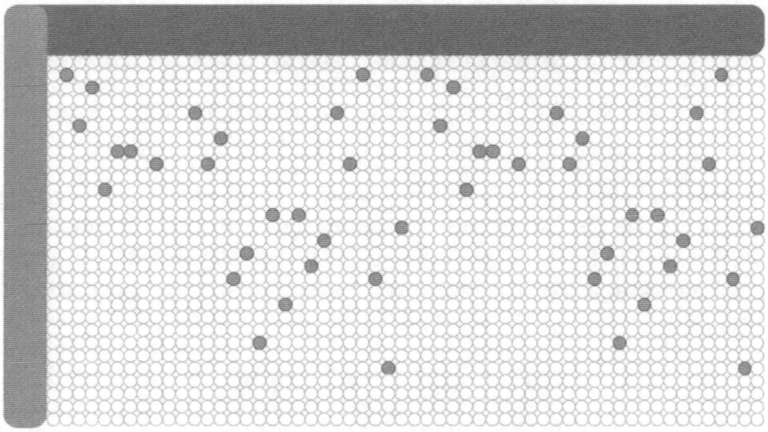

FIGURE 2: EXAMPLE OF CROSSPOINTS REPRESENTED IN AN X-Y MATRIX.

As ST2110 systems have enabled scale beyond the reasonable levels of a single matrix there have been different approaches to solve for management.

Other industries dealing with large data sets of relationships, such as social media platforms and search engines, use "tagging" as a common method of storing logical associations in a collection which makes finding and handling data easier. As part of the development of TFC, NEP discovered a novel way to implement "tagging" to make a more logical approach to signal management.

In TFC, tagging allows users to identify signals quickly and easily in both logical and physical domains. And further, using familiar web interface standards enables users to learn quickly and reduces the need for understanding of complex underlying virtual signal routing workflows.

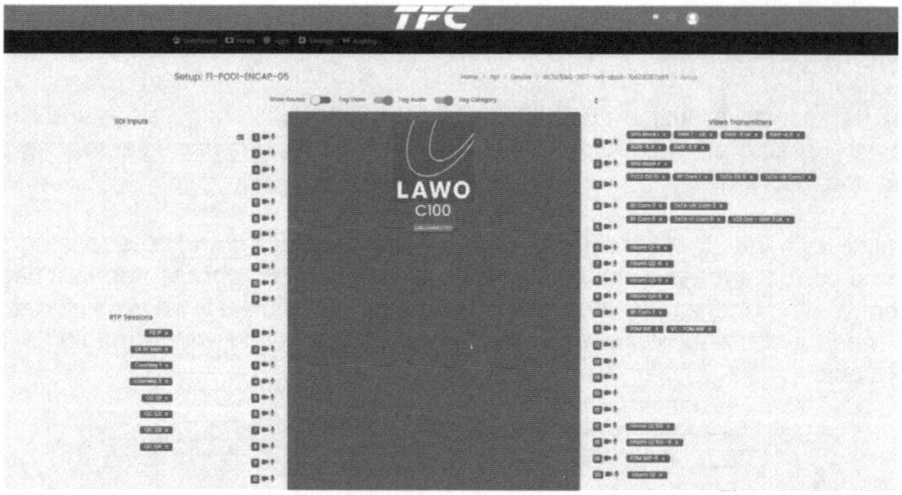


FIGURE 3: EXAMPLE OF TAGGING SIGNALS IN TFC.

## Centralized Production

There are unique demands on the control plane in a centralized production environment. The primary driver for centralizing processing is to increase utilization by pooling devices that can be dynamically assigned to productions. To manage this assignment efficiently, scheduling systems need to be integrated into the control layer.

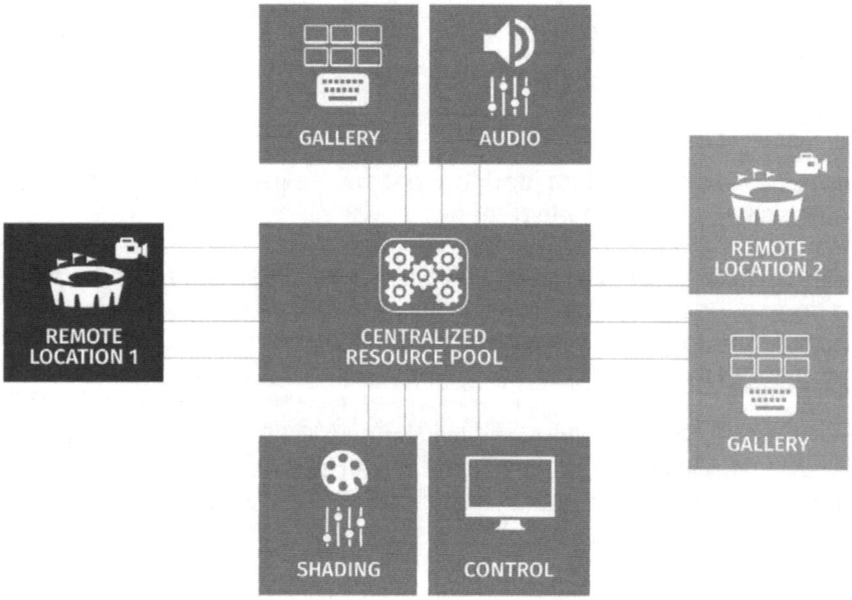


FIGURE 4: DIAGRAM ILLUSTRATING HOW A POOL OF RESOURCES CAN BE ACCESSED BY MULTIPLE BROADCAST FACILITIES.

The broadcast controller needs to divide up endpoints from a single underlying pool of resources while ensuring segregation between productions. Traditional controllers did not have the concept of this segregation and while you could feasibly create logical separation using filters or separate matrixes, this did not extend all the way to user permissions. When looking at global signal lists there would still be similar signals across multiple OBs (e.g., Camera 1 in multiple control rooms simultaneously) that could easily be mistaken one for another.

TFC introduced the concept of productions and a pool. Resources normally begin life in the pool where they can be checked out to a production either permanently or for a period of time. Within TFC, users must switch between productions where they have access to the resources only for that production or the pool where they can control where resources are assigned. User permissions can restrict access to the pool and individual productions, ensuring that operators only have access to what they are assigned.

The benefits of pooling are:

- Creates redundancy across different hardware (even different brands and models) - in the event an assigned resource fails the system can dynamically assign a different compatible resource.
- Flexibility to allow resources at any moment in time to be securely shared across different productions according to a schedule or at manual instance rather than being constrained by the limits of a given facility.
- Provides safe control of devices across multiple simultaneous productions - productions on air have their resources "locked" from unwanted automation and network access from other productions.

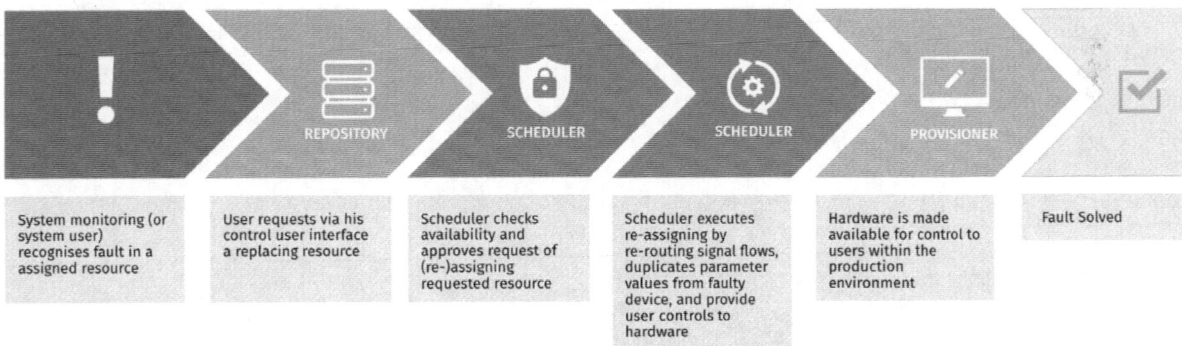


FIGURE 5: DEPICTION OF HOW A CENTRAL POOL OF RESOURCES CAN BE USED TO RECOVER FROM AN EQUIPMENT FAULT.

Centralized production also creates a multi-tenant environment where different customers might be using the same backend pool of resources. The controller needs to be able to assign devices and signal paths to the correct production and importantly ensure that one customer's content cannot be accidentally exposed to another customer, especially when the content is sensitive; for example, game shows or reality television programs where it is important for the results not to be leaked.

For this reason, the production concept within TFC was further developed to include the ability to create "Ephemeral Productions" that only exist for a short time while that production is in use. With Ephemeral Productions, a template is created that defines the required resources (e.g., cameras, multiviewers, vision switcher size, audio console). When a user launches an ephemeral production, an environment (e.g. a specific studio and production control room) are automatically connected to backend devices assigned from the pool of available resources. Once finished the production is terminated and destroyed. Devices that were streaming are automatically stopped, receivers are blinded, multiviewers cleared to blank and all resources are returned to the pool.

This makes it impossible for a multicast flow from a previous production to accidentally be left assigned to a monitor or destination that is being used by different production. As the template defines what resources are required in an abstracted way, productions can also be easily migrated between different physical environments such as studios, stadiums, production control rooms and voice booths.

## Software Defined Networking

IP control systems, in contrast to baseband systems, not only need to route and control devices, but they also need to understand what is happening in the network. SDN features were developed by NEP to enable the broadcast controller to have a truly symbiotic relationship with the network.

To answer the question on why an SDN is required let's examine the alternative. Non-blocking switch topologies running PIM and IGMP might be seen as an adequate solution. However, relying on devices to only request joins to a sum of flows that will not exceed the bandwidth limitations of the port, is inherently risky, especially when the receiving device has no visibility on the actual bitrate of the senders. And while it might be possible for receiving devices to use SDP information, this is not the intended responsibility of the device and the device is not aware of any network limitations upstream, such as the uplink between the spine and leaf. Consider how that device would manage the format flip of a camera from 1080p to 2160p. There will always be a propagation time for the SDP which means that risk of over-subscription still exists. It is the SDN controllers' responsibility to ensure that ingress traffic is policed, and joins are only made within the constraints of any given link in the path. This is why SDN is critical for even networks built on a single chassis, non-blocking network.

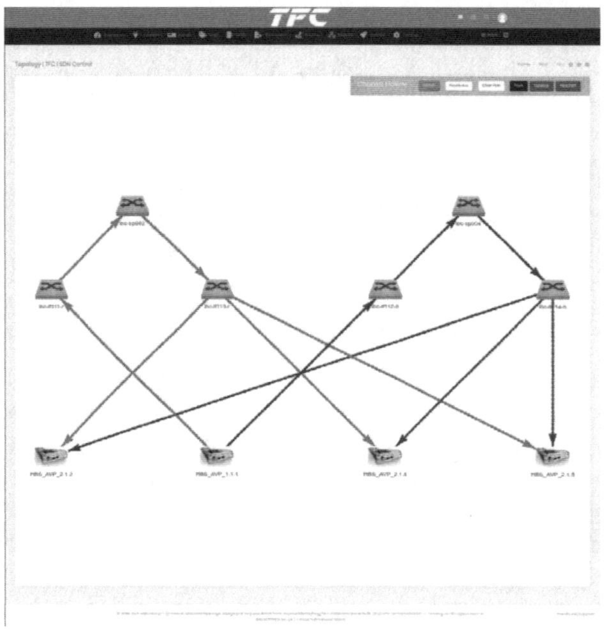

FIGURE 6: VISUALIZATION OF PATH ENGINE IN TFC.

There are four main functions that an SDN needs to deliver:

- **Configuration**: allows users to configure and provision the network fabric. Users should be able to apply or roll-back network configuration. The configurator can take advantage of CCA tools like Ansible.
- **Path Engine**: programs real-time multicast routes into fabric for media flows and provisions layer 2 data services. It applies dynamic policing based on the format of the transmitter. It load-balances based on business logic such as flow priorities.
- **Monitoring**: ensures compliance between the path engine and switches. This engine responds to topology changes and can effectuate automatic recovery or reprovisioning due to degraded links or events in the network.
- **Scheduler**: allows automated routing and service provisioning against a calendar. This can be synchronized with external scheduling systems.

But why then should the SDN and the broadcast controller be combined? External SDNs are limited in their visibility to flows and switches in the network. This is just the beginning of the story. SDN needs to do more than just prevent over-subscription and manage links. It should enable a lean architecture that delivers efficiency, a reduced footprint and maximum utilization of both network and broadcast resources.

Consider the advantage for the SDN in having inside information from the broadcast controller, and vice versa, in the following use cases.

## Use Case: Dynamic Flow Priorities

Setting priorities on flows enables automated recovery actions to account for the value of different signals. For example, the main center camera of a field of play might have a higher priority than a beauty shot of the city used occasionally for overlaying graphics.

Imagine that fiber is accidentally cut along the path leading to a serious degrading of service and a restriction to the amount of bandwidth now available. If that beauty camera is currently to line/in program on transmission, then sacrificing it to enable the field of play camera could create an on-air incident. But the broadcast controller knows this camera is on air to provide tallies.

By combining controllers, SDN business logic can call upon internal broadcast business logic to ensure that cameras that are to line or preview are automatically given the highest priority of the remaining bandwidth.

## Use Case: Localized Leaf Processing

In a spine leaf network, managing back pressure on the spine is critical. By distributing processing horizontally along the leafs, resources can be allocated in a more efficient way. Rather than having all the distributed multiviewer input stage processing on one leaf and all the replay machines on another leaf, imagine you stripe the processing so that a leaf has both multiviewer processing and replay. The burnt in timecode outputs are rarely routed directly to monitors but are frequently only used in the multiviewer.

If the broadcast controller can call upon the SDN to determine multiviewer inputs available on the same leaf as the replay, the controller can limit the amount of traffic egressing from the leaf up to the spine. As most of the monitoring in the truck is served from multiviewers, this efficiency can significantly reduce total utilization of leaf to spine bandwidth.

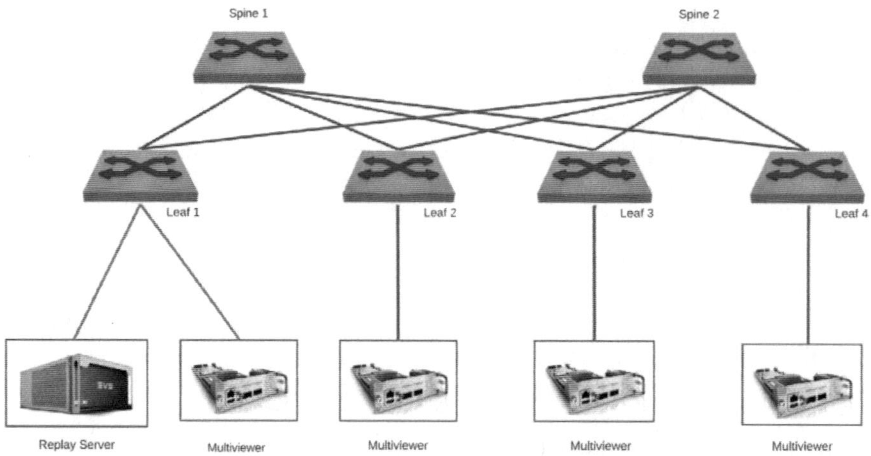


FIGURE 7: ILLUSTRATION OF LOCALIZED LEAF PROCESSING AVOIDING TRAFFIC TO THE SPINE.

## Managing WAN (Wide Area Network) Connections

The SDN should also be able to orchestrate flows over a WAN or service provider network. The ability to automate and control the network was the second catalyst for developing TFC. Prior to TFC, a senior network engineer needed to safely connect each mobile broadcast facility to the centralized production hosted at the Andrews Hub and balance bandwidth across incoming lanes of IP traffic from across the country. TFC allows broadcast engineers to provision, connect, and disconnect safely and instantly at the touch of a button.

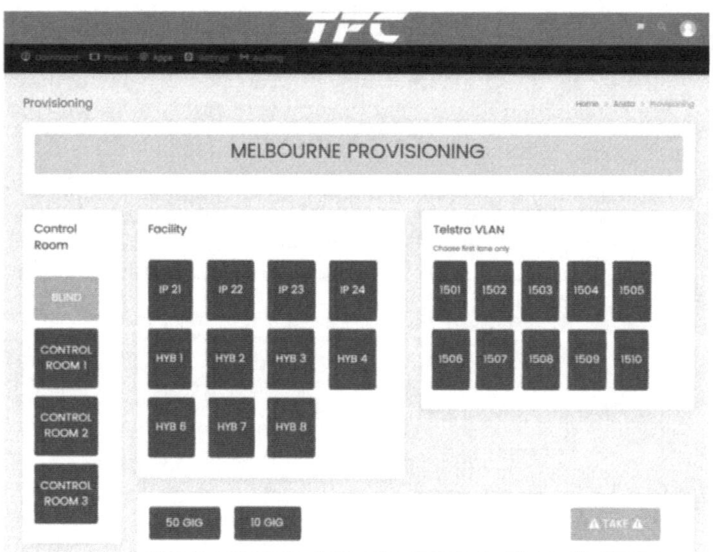


FIGURE 8: EXAMPLE TFC PANEL FOR PROVISIONING WAN CIRCUITS AT THE ANDREWS HUB, AUSTRALIA.

# Section 2: Orchestration of Workloads, Not Devices

As ST2110 matures, the industry is shifting its technology focus to software processing running on COTS servers and cloud computing. The decoupling of hardware from software enables manufacturers to build solutions faster and shrinks the footprint of the technology stack. The utilization of hardware can be greatly increased as software workloads can be interchanged on the same hardware.

This will have a profound impact on the control layer. Currently, broadcast controllers manage devices that have defined inputs, processing, and outputs. A device has a personality and capabilities that can be built into the business logic of a controller's driver to enable users to take advantage of what that device is capable of. However, as this moves into the purely software world, a controller will be responsible for instantiating applications with capabilities. This fundamental shift requires a deeper level of orchestration and provisioning.

Yet, the constraints around the processing have not changed. For the same reasons, the control layer needed to be collapsed, and a central broadcast controller put in charge of both the network and devices, now the controller needs to be in the single source of truth that assigns processing to hardware inside the system. The industry needs an open approach to orchestration of processing that allows broadcast controllers to direct how hardware resources are assigned, both the servers hosting the processing and the network.

## Software Processing On COTS

This transition will take some time. To begin with, manufacturers will likely adopt a lift and shift strategy to simply move existing hardware products to applications running on assigned servers, for example replacing a vision mixer not on a dedicated appliance but bare metal on a COTS server. However, some products will need to scale across multiple nodes and some products will only consume a fraction of the processing on a single node.

The real advantage is being able to separate the hardware from the product altogether. Running applications that provide some discreet processing on any given worker node, products are then just the combination of processing applications running on servers that work together to solve a problem.

For example, a multiviewer is a combination of video scalers and graphical elements rendered on a raster of a given format. You could see these as individual processes that could be orchestrated across nodes. As we see manufacturers start to adopt this microservices approach to product development, the traditional control needs to expand into more of a service layer.

The long-term vision for NEP is to create a glass-to-glass unified media technology platform, where these products are connected and served from scalable, worldwide automated datacenters, seamlessly hosted in a hybrid public, private and mobile cloud. TFC will provide the foundations to manage the control layer, but in an elastic, scalable platform. There is a need to redefine this control layer as more of a service layer, responsible not just for devices but for the applications and resources consumed on them.

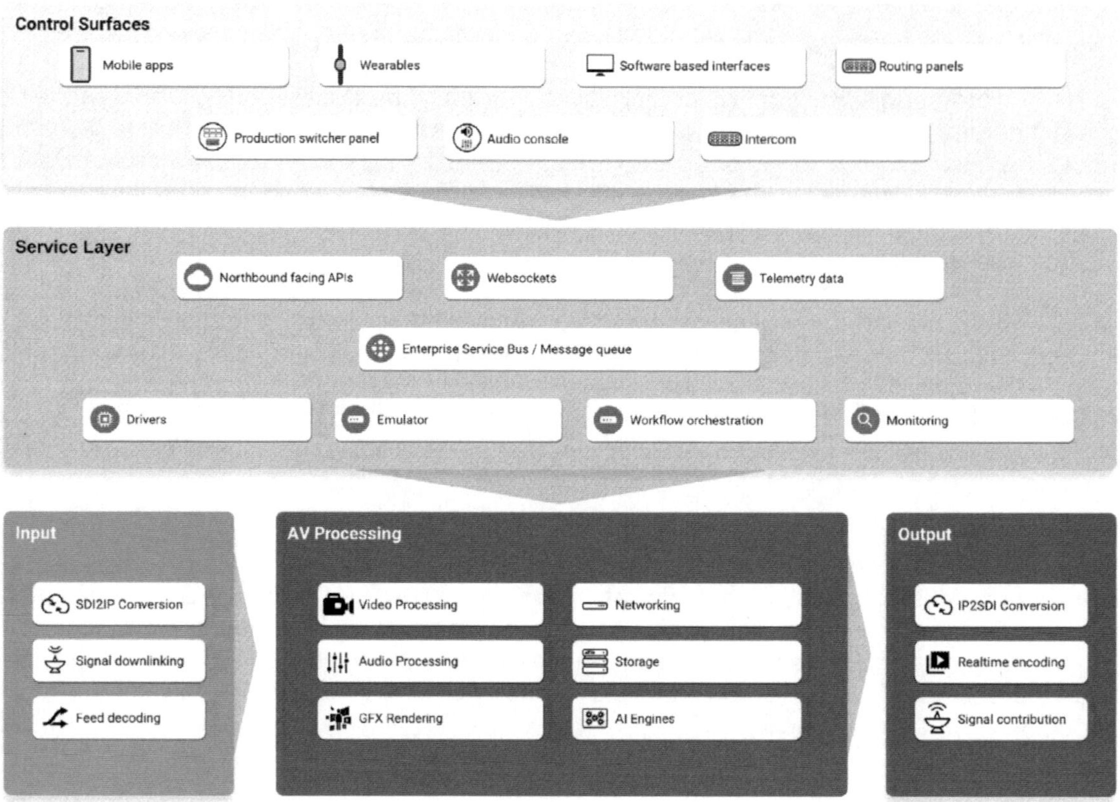


FIGURE 9: DIAGRAM SHOWING THE CONTROL PLANE AS A SERVICE LAYER BETWEEN PROCESSING COMPONENTS AND CONTROL SURFACES.

Manufacturers will provide the north (control surfaces) and south (processing) components, while the control platform will be responsible for the service layer in the middle, providing orchestration, monitoring, APIs, drivers, and an enterprise service bus.

The promise of this efficiency relies on the ability of workloads to scale up and down. The service layer needs to provision and deploy the applications required by any given production, operation, or facility. But how do applications get provisioned and who is responsible for this provisioning? Should this be the responsibility of individual manufacturer controllers or a centralized broadcast controller?

## DevOps and the "Cattle Not Pets" Principle

The successful provisioning of applications requires functional DevOps: the joint effort between developers and operational teams. "DevOps is the combination of cultural philosophies, practices, and tools that increases an organization's ability to deliver applications and services at high velocity" [6]. This is required both from the manufacturer and the facilitator where collaboration between DevOps teams will be a crucial part of system delivery.

The main objective of DevOps is to provide applications with high availability, automate the provisioning and scale to the requirements of any given production. This is fundamentally different to the approach integrators and facilitators currently take to commissioning systems or rigging productions.

The broadcast industry can leverage from the IT industry an established principle for how DevOps provisioning should occur: cattle not pets. Pets can be thought of as "indispensable or unique systems that can never be down. Typically, they are manually built, managed, and "hand fed"" [7]. Cattle can be thought of as "arrays of more than two servers, that are built using automated tools, and are designed for failure, where no one, two, or even three servers are irreplaceable. Typically, during failure events no human intervention is required." [7]

Currently broadcast devices are treated as pets. They have names and assigned functionality. As these devices are replaced by applications running on an underlying pool of COTS servers, they become cattle that are ephemeral – they only exist for the period of time they are needed. This more efficient approach is required to achieve higher utilization. Each hardware node will host different applications at different times according to the controller's business logic.

The assumption that failures will occur also helps architect systems where individual components can fail without compromising the whole system or transmission. The focus on automation also ensures system instantiation and recovery during failure is fast. But the best advantage is that it takes the burden of building and maintaining systems away from broadcast engineers. We need to learn from the adoption of ST2110 and the retraining of skillsets that was required in our engineering workforce. To be only a few years later, requiring our engineers to learn a whole new IT skillset, that is more fundamentally different than the jump from baseband to IP, will place an undue burden on any facilitator. This needs to be solved by software.

## Who Should Provision Applications?

It is clear that an orchestrator needs to "herd the cattle." But should manufacturers provide this orchestration, or should this be part of the platform's native service layer? There is a debate brewing over who should be responsible for provisioning. Manufacturers have a role to play, and some have expressed the need to manage their application's provisioning. The arguments for manufacture orchestration can be summarized as:

- support: they need to control the hardware to guarantee performance and reliability of their software.
- administration: they need to know what is installed, for how long and with what features to enable licensing – especially in an OPEX pricing model.
- ownership: they understand the requirements of their software better and can determine the best hardware node to assign software processes.

These are compelling arguments, however the concern for integrators and facilitators, like NEP, is how this will evolve into enterprise system design in a multi-vendor environment. While the trend towards vertical integration among manufacturers continues, it is unlikely that any single manufacturer will provide the entire processing requirements for many systems. From a business risk perspective, it is also likely that many companies will not choose a single manufacturer for all their processing requirements.

The challenge is if multiple manufacturers inside a system each want to have their own orchestration systems, a blocking architecture is required where hardware is assigned to specific manufacturers. This will impact scaling and erode utilization benefits. Additionally, without a single source of truth, the complexity of managing multiple orchestration layers places an undue burden on the controller.

So how can the controller address the concerns of the manufacturers?

On support, there needs to be a level of maturity between software development and operational expectations. Traditionally, the industry has expected manufacturers to provide appliances with the hardware and software fully supported. And software will always have hardware specifications that must be met to guarantee delivery. Both operators and manufacturers need to move beyond a "one throat to choke" mentality and find a way to handle the demarcation of responsibility between the infrastructure (being the responsibility of the controller and facilitator) and software (being the responsibility of the manufacturer).

Manufacturers need to provide ways of describing the resources a given application requires to achieve what is asked for by the controller. The controller needs to ensure these resources are deterministically assigned. Monitoring services therefore become critical for support, as described in Section 3.

The licensing and administration component is a difficult challenge to overcome. It is unreasonable to assume every manufacturer will adopt standard technology for licensing as the model is complex and likely to be unique to their business. The controller therefore needs to be able to integrate with multiple external licensing systems and manufacturers need to provide APIs for the controller to assign and revoke licenses when deploying workloads.

The question then ultimately comes down to ownership. The platform controller stands as the best orchestrator to choose on which hardware to provision an application, as it is responsible for the entire system, including hardware, network, monitoring, and security. The best assignment of resources is intrinsically linked to the state of the network and the context of the application. Applications need to be deployed to localize processing on leafs for the same reason devices are currently configured to localize processing. By having more control over where processing is instantiated, the controller can ensure a more efficient allocation of resources from a network bandwidth perspective. The platform controller understands the latency in different locations of hardware and can assign a given application to a location according business logic that the manufacturer cannot be expected to manage. For example, assigning localized audio processing at a remote venue to ensure IFB mix minuses have no audible latency for talent.

Notwithstanding all the above, there is a role of manufacturers to develop their own platforms that may even host applications from different manufacturers. Not every company has the scale and enterprise capabilities of NEP to create an entire platform. NEP will deliver this as a service, as a new paradigm of the facilitation that we provide to many customers today. But manufacturers will likely also offer their own platforms to customers, especially where a turnkey environment is desired. Nevertheless, the principles remain the same. The modern broadcast controller needs to evolve and extend the control plane beyond its current boundaries. A successful platform needs one centralized controller responsible for orchestrating the network, hardware, and software applications in the system.

## Kubernetes Clusters in Broadcast Environments

When managing hundreds or thousands of microservices in a system, orchestration of the applications will require a new control layer. Running these applications on bare metal without automating deployment, scaling and management will not scale. Kubernetes, while not the only choice, will be popular due to its ubiquity in other industries, wide support from CPU, GPU and FPGA manufacturers and current adoption in the broadcast market [8] [9].

Yet there are significant challenges to using Kubernetes in a broadcast environment. NEP uses Kubernetes as the container orchestration for TFC including in fly packs and outside broadcast mobile units. Container orchestration is essential for scalable deployment of a microservices application such as TFC. The challenges in adopting Kubernetes led to the development of "NEP Illuminate" which manages the Kube clusters and applications deployed on them.

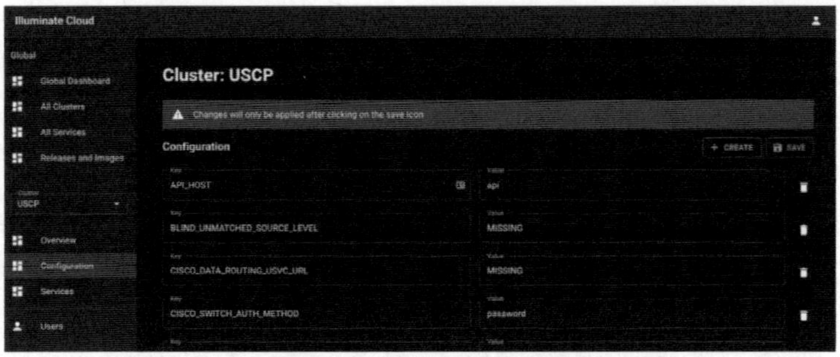


FIGURE 10A: TFC ILLUMINATE CLUSTER CONFIGURATION.

Illuminate exists as a tool in two forms:

- **Illuminate Cloud**: AKA the mothership, where infrastructure clusters are defined, and environments can be configured. Services and applications are assigned to specific clusters. The current version and diagnostic information about the cluster is collected and stored so that the delivery team has visibility on all deployments, even when that deployment is offline (e.g.: a mobile unit or fly pack that is powered off).
- **Illuminate Agent**: this runs on the local Kubernetes cluster and communicates with the cloud to get instructions on what services need to be deployed and the configuration required. The agent does all the heavy lifting to manage the underlying cluster and can work entirely independently from the cloud. The only requirement for cloud connection is for downloading of software updates, manifest changes and reporting back of status.

The greatest challenge is in the knowledge and experience required to set up and maintain Kubernetes itself. Automating the setup with Terraform and Ansible is easy enough, but there are many moving parts. Monitoring the health and responding to faults requires a combination of software automation and engineering expertise. Running Kubernetes on premise is less common than in the cloud and even less common in environments where the system is air gapped from the internet altogether. These skillsets are hard to find in DevOps engineers let alone broadcast engineers.

To begin, NEP used Rancher as UI and management layer over Kubernetes. Rancher is a popular software stack with a lot of useful tools, but it still requires an in-depth knowledge of how Kubernetes works. For example, while Rancher helps take care of underlying components (e.g., etcd, apiserver, kublets, coredns) you still need to understand how Kube objects work, and which objects an application uses (e.g., pods, deployments, stateful sets, services, ingresses).

Before Illuminate, developers would write manifests for the objects required for any microservice in the application. However, as the number of deployments scaled over 20 this became unmanageable and cost too much development time. Illuminate enabled the management of clusters to shift to broadcast engineers who could use a simple UI.

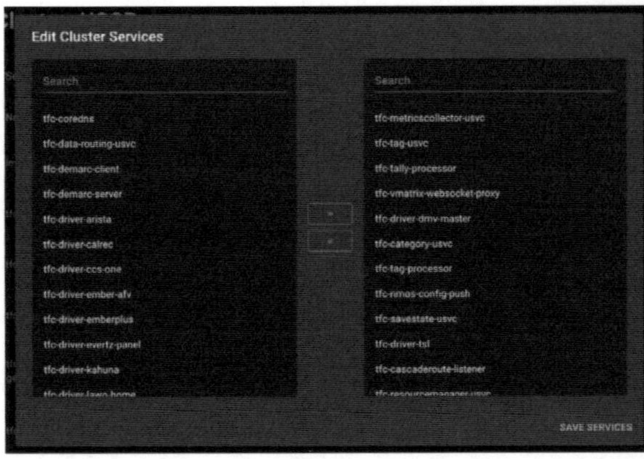

FIGURE 10B: TFC ILLUMINATE ASSIGNING SERVICES TO A CLUSTER.

FIGURE 10C: TFC ILLUMINATE MANAGEMENT OF RUNNING SERVICES.

By far the greatest problem experienced running Kubernetes was mobile units and fly packs that constantly were powered off and moved between jobs. This is an exceedingly rare use case and consequently Kubernetes is not inherently designed to be turned off frequently. The underlying components need to find quorum as part of their high availability architecture. Without a deterministic boot sequence many problems were encountered ensuring that these components (e.g.: databases, message queue, etcd) had quorum and were running redundantly.

Illuminate Agent creates a start and stop button for the facility that automates the boot process, ensuring that components are brought online in the right order to find quorum and dependencies are running before progressing to the next stage of boot.

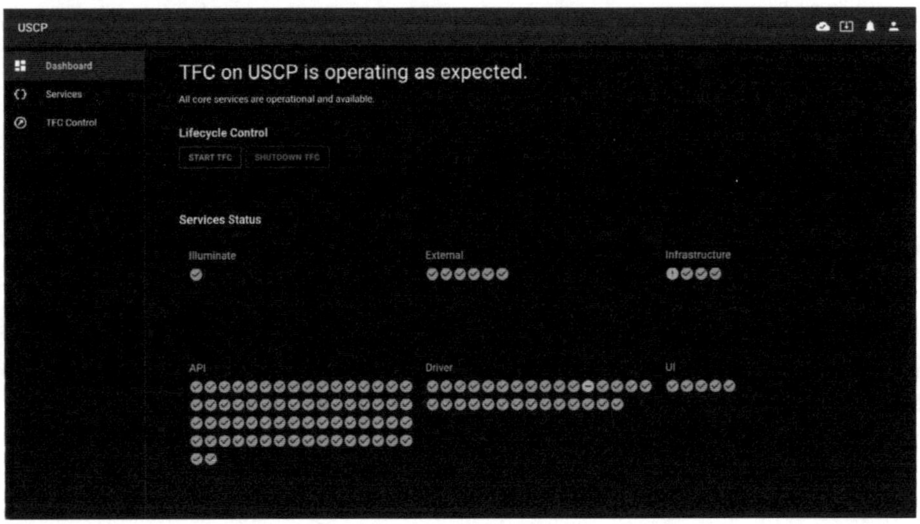


FIGURE 10D: TFC ILLUMINATE DASHBOARD WITH START AND SHUTDOWN CONTROLS.

Container images for each microservice are built during Continuous Integration [10] stages and hosted centrally in the cloud. As running Kubernetes air gapped from the internet is rare, Illuminate handles the edge case for fetching container images and storing them locally for use by Kubernetes across each node, even when offline.

Illuminate can be configured for Continuous Delivery where updates can be automatically deployed on release. However, this is generally only enabled for lab facilities. Versions of software are listed in Illuminate and can be marked as General Availability (GA). Engineers at the facility can upgrade to the latest GA version or downgrade to previous GA or any specific version.

## Section 3: Monitoring

The approach to monitoring and alarming in many traditional broadcast environments has been as a side mission and unfortunately very often is not fully configured or properly maintained due to time constraints. Monitoring is designed to allow engineers to discover problems and visualize what is happening inside the system. However, as we move towards more enterprise IT systems the line between monitoring for diagnosis and monitoring for control is blurred.

A modern controller should integrate monitoring that automates scalable data collection, storage, and presentation tools. The manual configuration, deployment and maintenance of monitors is time-consuming and error prone. If a device is added or removed from the controller, it should be added or removed from the monitoring system. Additionally, if workloads are spun up and down then the monitoring collectors for those systems also need to be spun up and down.

### Architecture of Monitoring

The main objectives of a monitoring service should be:

- Overall network integrity
- Optical hardware, SFP, Link Budgets, errors
- Device hardware health - CPU, disk, memory, fans, temperature, agents, etc
- Device network health - packet counters, flow states, error counters
- Prefix, routes, and ACL (Access Control List) counters
- Vxlan overlay states
- Buffers - Microburst detection
- Bandwidth and link consumption
- QoS policing
- ACL rule matching
- PTP PDV and Offset monitoring (switches and hosts)
- Aggregation of logging from all devices (formatted as Syslog, preferably RFC5424)

A wide set of collectors need to work 24/7 to gather logs, metrics, and configuration parameters. This enables the system to detect unauthorized changes and report abnormalities. These collectors should feed a time-series database to ensure easy aggregation of data.

FIGURE 11A: EXAMPLE DEVICE DASHBOARD FOR MONITORING OPTICAL HEALTH.

Logs are critical in diagnosing what is wrong during or after an incident. But aggregating logs can be useful for monitoring in real time to prevent logs. Syslog is the most commonly used format for logging and is a solid basis for this aggregation. But as syslog began as a de facto standard, and there are multiple published specifications (e.g.: RFC 3164 [11], RFC 5424 [12]) not all syslog messages are interoperable. To improve indexing and aggregation it is necessary to harmonize syslogs across devices. The broadcast controller should, in the same way it manages device drivers for control, manage the deployment of harmonization. TFC implements regex conversion via Datadog Vector.[2]

TFC has chosen a suite of open-source tools, well supported by the IT community, to build into its underlying monitoring platform:

- InfluxDB[3]: time-series database
- Grafana Loki OSS[4]: Log aggregation, indexing, searching and storage
- Grafana OSS[5]: Dashboard and graph visualizations and alarming
- Promtail[6]: Log ingesting agent
- Influx Telegraf[7]: Telemetry ingesting agent

The greatest challenge to effective monitoring is to create a scalable way to collect, process and store metrics. These tools are deployed as containers running inside a Kubernetes cluster that enables redundancy and allows scaling of parts of the monitoring system as appropriate. These tools have proven to provide reliable and high-performance monitoring at the largest events NEP services.

## Case Study: International Sporting Event

At a recent international sporting event, TFC was deployed as the SDN and ST2110 routing solution. The network extended between IBC and 42 locations with more than 8.3 Tbps of traffic, with 403 devices and 150 switches under control. More than 30,000 individual telemetry metrics were collected. Over 30 days, more than 5TB of logs and telemetry were stored.

---

[2] https://vector.dev/
[3] https://www.influxdata.com/products/influxdb/
[4] https://grafana.com/oss/loki/
[5] https://grafana.com/oss/grafana/
[6] https://grafana.com/docs/loki/latest/clients/promtail/
[7] https://www.influxdata.com/time-series-platform/telegraf/

## Telemetry Driven Control

Monitoring should favor streaming telemetry (e.g.: gRPC, websockets, raw listeners) over polling approaches (e.g.: SNMP, HTTP endpoints) as telemetry enables:

- Push instead of polling for increased resolution
- Incremental updates for greater efficiency
- Faster decision making for automation based on business logic
- Less overhead with lighter collectors

Telemetry should not just be ingested into time-series databases but also be available and processed by broadcast drivers. For an SDN to function correctly, it must monitor active links and, for example, respond when a link is degraded by rerouting traffic via a different path in the network. While using telemetry is standard practice for most SDNs, this same level of diligence has not traditionally extended to the whole control plane.

For example, in a transmission chain an engineer might set up monitoring and fail over, either automatic or human intervened, to ensure the integrity of the transmission path. While this is effective for protecting specific transmission paths, this special treatment is not practical to extend to every signal if relying on engineers to manually configure.

As established above, the controller's responsibility should go beyond merely monitoring and routing flows between devices. It should be responsible for provisioning and instantiating these devices and flows. Therefore, it should be able to automatically respond to malfunctions by instantiating services on working nodes.

## Anomaly Detection

Anomaly detection is technology used to identify when a metric value or event rate deviates from its normal behavior [13]. These technologies allow systems to predict incidents before they happen or decrease time to resolution by focusing engineers on usual behavior in a system that might lead to diagnosis faster.

This is especially important for devices that have variable telemetry under normal operating conditions. For example, a network link can be baselined after a production is provisioned and then alarms can automatically generate if traffic drops above or below normal for that production.

For this to be effective the monitoring system needs to be integrated with a controller that understands the production template that is running. The system enters a learning phase to plot what is "normal" for that production. There can be several learning phases for different stages of the broadcast process that are known to the controller, such as rigging, on air and derigging. Once normal behaviors are learned, anomalies, such as system or component failures, operator errors or security breaches, can now be identified for review.

Whilst this seems like a relatively simple use case, for this to be successful the monitoring system needs to collect a large amount of data and rely on complex unsupervised machine learning algorithms and statistical modelling, so they are robust and accurate.

These metrics also become invaluable data that can continuously be fed back into future design and architecture.

## Visualizing Monitors and Alarms

There are many commercially available visualization tools that are sensible to integrate into the broadcast controller. These can be embedded into web UIs, linked from admin panels, or used standalone. Due to this flexibility and the quality of open-source solutions it was concluded for TFC that using and off the shelf visualization was better than building monitoring and alarming natively into the controller UI. The only exception is for integrating the SDN path finder and network maps, where for performance and custom functionality, such as people able to reroute flows via different paths, a proprietary interface was built.

NEP chose Grafana for visualization due to its wide adoption and support for plugins as well as a combined interface for alarms and monitoring. Grafana allows you to share queries for graph elements on a dashboard and alarms.

A successful monitoring setup will provide visibility of essential metrics (e.g.: ptp, temperature, memory and cpu usage, bandwidth, optical levels) at a point-in-time, trending over time and alarming whenever reaching thresholds.

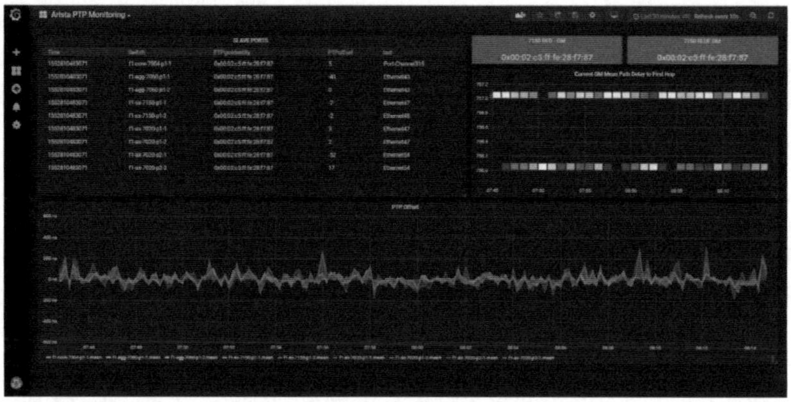


FIGURE 11B: EXAMPLE DASHBOARD FOR MONITORING PTP HEALTH IN THE NETWORK.

Dashboards for specific device types can be created to give engineers visibility on device state over time and diagnose issues. However, this can lead to hundreds of dashboards showing thousands of metrics. The best approach to proactive monitoring is to monitor by exception. In most dashboards NEP creates "Penalty boxes," also known as a "Dark Cockpit," that show urgent actionable issues up front. For example, rather than show optical levels of every transceiver in the network, only show when they meet a given threshold. This kind of dashboard then becomes a kind of checklist for engineers to work through to get a system into the optimal state.

FIGURE 11C: EXAMPLE DASHBOARD SHOWING DEVICE PTP STATUS AND STREAMING BITRATES.

In addition to engineering monitoring, TFC configures simplified monitoring dashboards for end users. These can show device status, fiber levels and allow users to quickly see potential issues in the system.

Visualizing data and comparing logs and telemetry across multiple systems at the same time is critical for investigating incidents and ensuring compliance with SLAs (Service Level Agreements) and risk management plans.

### Learning Lessons to Avoid Repeat Incidents and Regression

When an incident occurs there are nearly always warning signs, logs or telemetry that could have alerted engineers or automation systems to prevent the incident from happening. An important part of the incident management process is the root cause investigation that should identify ways the incident could have been avoided. Nearly always this requires additional monitoring and alarming to prevent future recurrence.

It is important that this additional protection is rolled out to all other deployments to make sure that lessons learned from an incident in one facility are communicated and remedial action is taken in all facilities.

TFC maintains a library of metrics and rules that are used for error monitoring/alarming. This has been built up over time from the experiences at facilities across NEP Group. Across deployments of TFC, dashboards and alarms can be pulled and pushed to ensure that updates to the monitoring system are propagated to every deployment. The controller can act as an oracle, drawing experience from across whole NEP Group to continually build on this and make sure that lessons learned from previous jobs are applied to every job.

Additionally, these alarms and dashboards provide excellent training opportunities for new engineers, enabling continuous improvement.

## Section 4: Security

The need for IT Security in broadcast to be taken more seriously is apparent. The 2020 published version 2 of the JT-NM technology pyramid [2] still lists its security recommendations, such as EBU R 148 [14] and EBU R 143 [15], as “rarely available.” For a long time, the industry has relied on physical security and obfuscation as the main forms of defense. Yet the attack surface has grown due to the increase in the number of devices, the size of local area networks and the use of wide area networks to facilitate centralized production and cloud computing.

Security for controllers has been primarily about encrypting communication in transit between the controller and devices and clients. While external security systems and auditing are essential, securing the control plane and enabling the broadcast controller to be responsible for key elements of security is critical. Security should be baked into the system design and therefore be a prime concern of the controller, especially as it facilitates more automation.

As the controller itself is media software, it should comply with the Cybersecurity Recommendation For Media Vendors’ Systems, Software & Services (EBU R 143) [15]. Many of the recommended tools listed in Cybersecurity Recommendation On Minimum Security Tests For Networked Media Equipment (EBU R 148) [14] should be adopted or integrated into the controller. The best way to ensure that a device or application is secure is to enable security testing automatically when it is added to or instantiated by the controller.

For best practice, all systems should include a vulnerability scanner capable of analyzing security threats and creating vulnerability reports. Currently this needs to be carefully managed in regular maintenance windows as these scans can impact systems, especially where devices and applications are vulnerable to DDoS attacks. The controller should automate the configuration of scans to enable these scans to be executed by broadcast engineers.

While the industry continues to move towards an overall improved security posture there are key concerns for that controller that should be prioritized.

### Shrinking The Attack Surface

The controller should work to shrink the attack surface by limiting exposure at the edge and managing device admission to the network.

One of the most ubiquitous security issues in the industry is open network ports. Most engineers know the risks associated, and yet, if you went to the tailboard of many broadcast trucks in the world you will find RJ45 wired to open network ports. If this is a known risk and still happens, the question is why? A major contributing factor is having no easy and automated solution for closing and opening the ports. The broadcast controller needs to assume this responsibility as part of device discovery and authorization.

While using DNS-SD and NMOS might simplify discovery, this approach priorities convenience too highly over security. Perhaps this is a controversial assertion, but NMOS does not go far enough to protect networks from unauthorized, misconfigured, or malfunctioning devices connecting to the network.

TFC prefers to use an agent running inside the switch to negotiate directly with the device and register it with the controller. Devices that have not been explicitly authorized by an administrator should be quarantined. A quarantined device should not be able to reach any other host or system in the network except the local discovery agent. Streaming devices should operate inside single host subnets, preferably 31 bit for efficiency. They should have their address assigned by DHCP.

Before a device is admitted to the network, ACLs should automatically be applied to the port to prevent undesired traffic. Too many networks have been impacted by unwanted traffic from one device affecting other devices. These ACLs should open only secure and essential traffic. If the multicast network has IGMP and PIM enabled, then these ACLs also should explicitly allow multicast groups and ports to protect against conflicts. Without automation, this task is impractical to deploy and maintain for a network engineer. In an SDN network where IGMP and PIM are disabled, static multicast paths should only be stitched to ports with an active and authorized device.

### Authentication and Auditing

As cloud computing and centralized production are adopted, the need for role-based access and enforcing stringent authentication is critical. Users should only have access to the productions, devices, signals/flows that they need to perform their role. It is also important to audit all user activity to enable the ability to trace changes in the system.

Public panels should be avoided and over time replaced with convenient but secure authentication methods. Hardware panels in the future should be accessible with NFC or one-time pin code access. Soft panels should require full authentication to the application or one-time pin code access. Panels should time out with a reasonable amount of inactivity, for example no longer than the length of staff shift. Operators should be trained to lock their panels and workstations as is common practice in IT environments.

To adopt these recommendations, production operators will need to be willing to endure some inconvenience compared to the open and ready panels they arrive to today. This will require a shift in thinking, and it is important that the industry socializes the importance of adopting security changes even at the expense of minor inconveniences.

All datacenter driven environments, such as centralized production, studios and cloud hosted facilities should adopt a managed identity service as part of a Privileged Access Management (PAM) strategy. External users and operators should be federated into identity management services. Access should be automated as much as possible. Onboarding and offloading processes should be well documented and followed. Regular auditing of user access should be performed.

For mobile units and fly packs, a managed directory service can be complex as they frequently must operate without any external connections. However, this can be managed in the same way a corporate network manages satellite offices that might have unreliable WAN connections. Over time all facilities should have centrally managed identity services according to the PAM strategy.

## Demarcation Using NMOS Between Connected Facilities

The need to connect multiple facilities together is relatively common. Traditionally this has been effectively achieved using SDI. ST2110 provides the ability to exchange many flows on a small number of network connections to greatly reduce rigging time and add flexibility. This is extremely advantageous especially on major international sporting events, where lots of facilitators, rights holders and host broadcasters need to share feeds. In the US particularly there are also several events each year with large compounds with multiple vendors.

To successfully connect networked facilities together, a secure demarcation was developed by NEP. There are two important services that the demarcation must provide, PTP and ST2110 multicast, each with its own security and resilience issues.

PTP should be distributed on separate PTP-only ports and not in-band on the media ports. The controller should enforce security policies and enable broadcast engineers to configure PTP distribution ports. A unique PTP domain should be selected so that local facility master clocks can synchronize northbound with the centralized PTP and then provide PTP as normal southbound to the facility. PTP should ideally be handed off from the demarcation switch directly to the facility master clocks. Redundant paths should be provided for main and backup clocks. The controller should ensure PTP is forced in one direction so that PTP can never be leaked from one facility to another using the centralized PTP service.

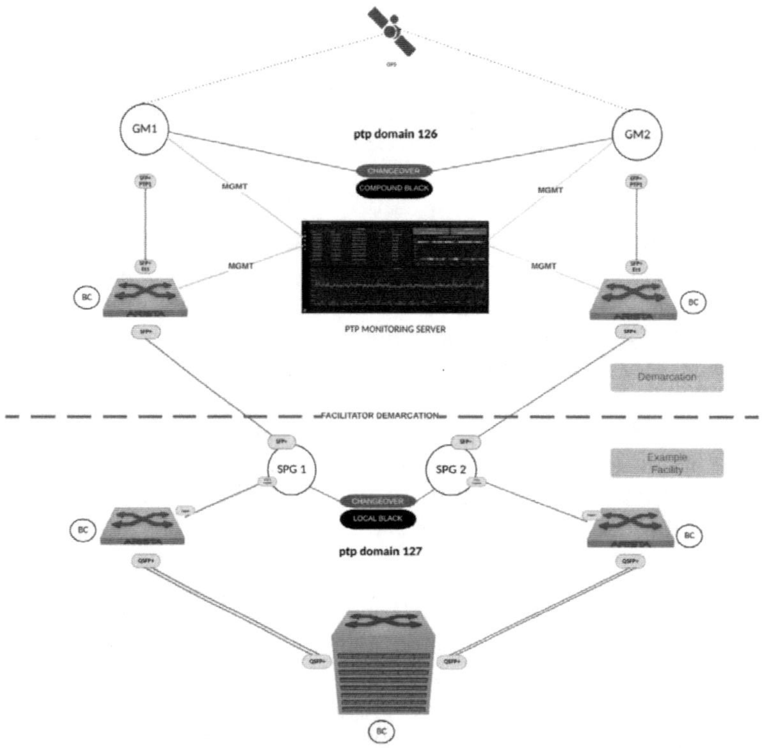


FIGURE 12: DISTRIBUTED DELIVERY OF PTP USING SECURE DEMARCATION ACROSS LOCAL NETWORKS.

This setup is most appropriate for directly connected local facilities in the same area and it is advised to consult a network architect for other use cases. Additional considerations like distance, latency, risk of loss of GPS and other environmental factors may be important. For example, connections of a WAN or service provider network may not be suitable for PTP and instead of distributing PTP, local clocks synchronized with GPS may be more appropriate.

There are three objectives for the demarcation of ST2110 across facilities:

- Secure network ports to ensure traffic is firewalled and only authorized traffic is allowed.
- Provide an NMOS IS-04 node and IS-05 connection service to enable easy routing between networks.
- Enable s,g mNAT for traffic that might in conflicting network ranges (both unicast and multicast). This can be optional if connecting between facilities from the same vendor, however it should always be used when connecting a foreign entity.

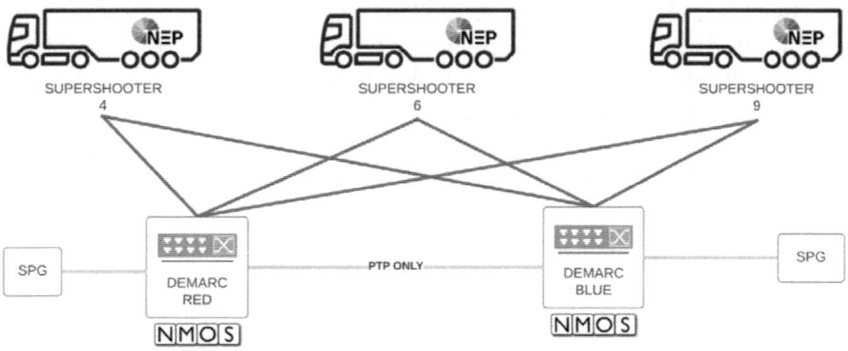


FIGURE 13: ILLUSTRATION OF DEMARCATION OF ST2110 USING NMOS.

For security reasons the main controller will never be directly exposed to the foreign network. Instead TFC automatically generates custom service containers (agent) for each foreign network that runs inside the switch and only contains the available functionality and permitted sources and targets for that connection. This reduces the exposed attack surface and creates a 'hard' border forming a Software Defined Perimeter. The agent is the only management access the foreign network should have access to. All other traffic is explicitly denied.

The agent exposes itself as an NMOS node that can be automatically discovered by the foreign network controller. Within the local controller, senders and receivers can be created that will be advertised to the foreign controller.

To send flows to the foreign network, the local controller routes into a receiver that is advertised on the NMOS node to the foreign controller. If mNAT is enabled, this will automatically be programmed through the switch and SDPs translated. All flows to the foreign network are statically joined, so IGMP requests are ignored, and PIM is disabled.

To receive flows from the foreign network, the foreign controller patches into the advertised receivers. The NMOS agent will then advertise that flow back to the local controller so that it can be tagged and routed as if it was any other NMOS device in the network. Again, if mNAT is enabled the agent will automatically program this in the switch and translate the SDP advertised. To support foreign networks with IGMP/PIM, ports can optionally have IGMP host proxy enabled.

This demarcation service allows facilities to connect and within minutes safely exchange ST2110 flows without risk that issues in one network affect the other network.

## Conclusion: NEP Core and The Future Service Layer

The industry is in the middle of profound technological change that began with the move to IP and ST2110 but is fast becoming a wider adoption of COTS hardware in all parts of the broadcast ecosystem. This is exacerbating the challenges with recruiting, training, and retaining broadcast engineers.

A new approach to broadcast control is required with a focus on more automation and adopting DevOps methodologies. The controller needs to do more than orchestrate hardware and devices but deliver application configuration and provisioning, manage the network, provide monitoring and alarming, and enforce security standards.

NEP is investing in the development of the service layer, NEP Core, to create a scalable global platform that will host the broadcast technology of the future. There is also a role for manufacturers to develop their own platforms to meet the needs of their customers. It is, however, critical that manufacturers work together with all platform developers to provide open ways to serve applications without the need for stacking multiple layers of orchestration within a system.

It is time to redefine the control plane and adopt a new service layer fit for the future.

## References


[1] A. Vignelles and D. Marshall, "Broadcast in the Age of Disruption," SMPTE15: Persistence of Vision - Defining the Future, Sydney, NSW, Australia, 2015, pp. 1-6, doi: 10.5594/M001600

[2] Joint Task Force on Networked Media Technical Recommendation TR-1001-1:2020 v1.1 System Environment and Device Behaviors For SMPTE ST 2110 Media Nodes in Engineered Networks

[3] Wittig, Andreas; Wittig, Michael, "Amazon Web Services in Action", ISBN 978-1-61729-288-0, p. 93.

[4] https://en.wikipedia.org/wiki/Continuous_configuration_automation

[5] J Guntenaar; NEP Group. 2020 Broadcast Control System Architecture & Vision Document. Unpublished internal company document.

[6] AWS, "What is DevOps", https://aws.amazon.com/devops/what-is-devops/#:~:text=DevOps%20is%20the%20combination%20of,development%20and%20infrastructure%20management%20processes.

[7] Bias, Randy, "the History of Pets vs Cattle and How to Use the Analogy Properly", https://cloudscaling.com/blog/cloud-computing/the-history-of-pets-vs-cattle/.

[8] https://github.com/intel/intel-device-plugins-for-kubernetes

[9] https://github.com/RadeonOpenCompute/k8s-device-plugin

[10] https://aws.amazon.com/devops/continuous-integration/

[11] Gerhards, R., "The Syslog Protocol", RFC 5424, DOI 10.17487/RFC5424, March 2009, <https://www.rfc-editor.org/info/rfc5424>.

[12] Gerhards, R., "The Syslog Protocol", RFC 5424, DOI 10.17487/RFC5424, March 2009, <https://www.rfc-editor.org/info/rfc5424>.

[13] https://aws.amazon.com/what-is/anomaly-detection/

[14] EBU R 148 Cybersecurity Recommendation On Minimum Security Tests For Networked Media Equipment (https://tech.ebu.ch/docs/r/r148.pdf)

[15] EBU R 143 Cybersecurity Recommendation For Media Vendors' Systems, Software & Services (https://tech.ebu.ch/docs/r/r143.pdf)

# Filling The Gaps in Video Transcoder Deployment in The Cloud

**Vibhoothi[1], Daniel Joseph Ringis[1], Xin Shu[1], François Pitié[1], Zsolt Lorincz[2], Philippe Brodeur[2], Anil Kokaram[1]**

**[1]Sigmedia Group, Department of Electrical Engineering, Trinity College Dublin**
**[1]Dublin 02, Ireland**

**[2]Overcast HQ**
**[2]Dublin 02, Ireland**

vibhoothi@tcd.ie, ringisd@tcd.ie, xins@tcd.ie, pitief@tcd.ie, zsolt@overcasthq.com, philippe@overcasthq.com, anil.kokaram@tcd.ie

**Abstract** – Cloud based deployment of content production and broadcast workflows has continued to disrupt the industry after the pandemic. The key tools required for unlocking cloud workflows, e.g., transcoding, metadata parsing, streaming playback, are increasingly commoditized. However, as video traffic continues to increase there is a need to consider tools which offer opportunities for further bitrate/quality gains as well as those which facilitate cloud deployment. In this paper we consider pre-processing, rate/distortion optimization and cloud cost prediction tools which are only just emerging from the research community. These tools are posed as part of the per-clip optimization approach to transcoding which has been adopted by the large streaming media processing entities but has yet to be made more widely available for the industry.

## Introduction

Video transcoding is a critical engineering component in broadcast systems today. As encoders mature, mechanisms to squeeze even more quality at lower bitrate continue to emerge that exist outside the standardization effort. Per-clip transcoding or content-aware transcoding, deployed at scale by Netflix in 2015 [1], exploits the idea that adapting transcoder parameters to each clip allows substantial gains over generic parameter sets. This is only one aspect of content adaptive treatment.

Taking a wider perspective, we admit consideration of pre-processing tools and, from a customer standpoint (particularly in cloud deployment [2]), tools that can predict the compute load about to be incurred. However, i) per-clip content adaptation provides huge gains in compression but comes with substantial compute cost; ii) pre-processing of media is well known to improve compression behavior, but the control of that pre-processor is difficult; and iii) users cannot yet assess or predict the costs of these modules in the cloud when applied to their datasets without actually launching the job and making a crude prediction as the job unfolds. In this paper we address these gaps as follows.

1. **Optimized Pre-processing:** The video denoiser is one of the simplest pre-processing tools that has a direct impact on video quality and bitrate. Since the late 1990's [3, 4] the potential was recognized for video denoisers to reduce bitrate in compression and improve picture quality especially for User Generated Content (UGC). But controlling the interaction of the denoiser with the encoder remained a challenge especially if there was no integration of the two

This paper is excerpted from the Proceedings of the 2023 NAB Broadcast Engineering and Information Technology (BEIT) Conference, © 2023, National Association of Broadcasters, 1 M Street SE, Washington, DC 20003 USA.

processes. Too much denoising drives the bitrate down, but it destroys picture quality. In this paper we introduce a simple, empirical experiment which allows a user to directly measure the interaction and so parameterize the pre-processor optimally for a particular codec/denoiser combination. We show as much as 2dB gains as compared with ignoring this interaction.

2. **Optimized Transcoding:** Discovering those optimal parameter sets is computationally challenging [5]. In the asymmetric world of the large, high-quality streamer, the compute cycles spent in transcoding are expected to be recovered many times over in streaming to the end user. But as a commodity process, per-clip transcoding needs to be managed to control the compute cycles required. This is especially acute with more recent standards like H.265 and AV1 which are notorious for cycle consumption in default configurations. We present in this paper a computationally efficient strategy for optimizing the rate distortion criterion in a codec to adapt it to a particular piece of content. The objective gains are measured in terms of Bjøntegaard-Delta (BDRATE) percentage. Gains are modest on average (2% BDRATE) but per-clip gains can hit over 14.89%. Our proxy-based approach can achieve 80% of these gains with over 10x improvement in compute load.
3. **Compute Load Prediction:** Finally, we consider a process for predicting the compute load required to complete a transcoding job. It is true that the problem of predicting "time to complete" is a fundamental challenge in a general software reliability sense. However, in the context of cloud deployment the community is missing a dependable tool for allowing a customer to allocate appropriate budget for a transcoding job, perhaps at scale. Efforts to build such a tool using ML approaches have already been undertaken in the research community [6]. But an examination of datasets shows that it is a challenge to collect enough examples of encode feature/duration pairs so that the feasible space is covered. In this paper, we take a different approach, based on classification and non-linear quantization of encode durations. Our results show good performance over a wide range of compute loads but still require careful attention to training data and deployment scenarios.

## Pre-Processing for Improved Compression Performance

Denoising as a pre-processing module has been explored since the 1990's [3, 4]. It is proposed to mitigate the impact of degraded input video on transcoding (e.g., User-Generated-Content (UGC) input content). It is also used to massage input clips so that they become more amenable to encoding and therefore result in less encoding artefacts (e.g., treatment of film grain). The problem is that encoders themselves act as denoisers because of the coring effect of Discrete-Cosine Transform (DCT) quantization. Van Roosmalen et al [3] were among the first to spot that the effect changed with target bitrate. That means that for effective pre-processing, the denoiser settings should be related not only to the input measured noise level but also to the target bitrate of the encoder. The nature of the encoder itself is also a factor. For example, H.264 will quantize in the DCT space in a different way compared to AV1.

Ideally, this relationship can be implicitly resolved by constraining the denoiser to optimize the quality of the output pictures from the encoder as a function of noise level and target bitrate, and not w.r.t. the quality of the pictures from the denoiser itself. This is an important point. Given an input degraded video sequence $G_n$, we do not care about the output quality of the denoised picture from the pre-processor, i.e., $\hat{I}_n = P(G_n)$ where $P$ is the pre-processor. We only care that the output quality of the denoiser/encoder cascade is high, i.e., $\hat{I}_n^T = T(P(G_n), r)$, where $r$ is the target encoding bitrate and $T()$ is the transcoding operation. The resulting cost function for the denoiser $(I_n - \hat{I}_T)^2$ is therefore highly non-linear because of the influence of the encoder.

Recent efforts using a deep neural network (DNN) as a pre-processor [7, 8, 9, 10] have employed differentiable simulations of the essential parts of an encoder. This offers a fully adaptive module which could adapt to transcoder target bitrate and input noise level. In that case, the DNN functions as much more than a denoiser, acting to enhance details which might be otherwise lost in encoding.

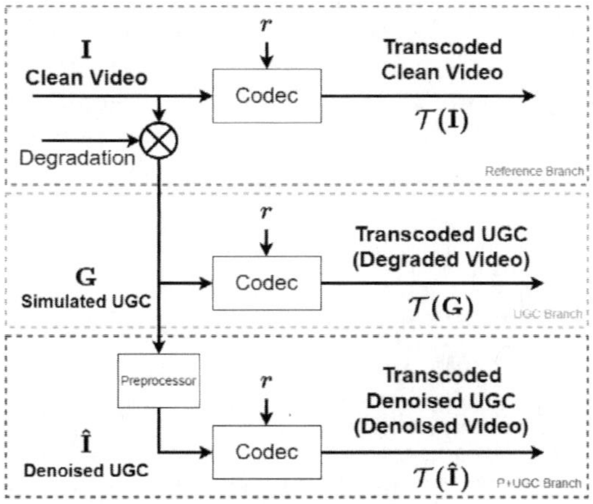


FIGURE 1: WORKFLOW FOR MEASURING OPTIMAL PREPROCESSOR PARAMETERS.

While effective, the computational cost of that module is of course a challenge. In addition, the efficacy of those systems relies on the goodness of fit of the simulated encoder. Instead, we take an empirical approach to the problem. Rather than design a fully adaptable pre-processor, we evaluate its performance using $(I_n - \hat{I}_n^T)^2$, i.e., in tandem with the encoder for a large UGC test set and over all our denoiser parameter settings and target bitrates. This gives us a mapping from input noise level $\sigma^2$ and target bitrate $r$ to the optimal parameter setting for our chosen denoiser and codec combination.

Figure 1 illustrates our experimental setup. A Clean video $(I_n)$ is artificially degraded with gaussian noise to create simulated UGC content $(G_n)$. This UGC is denoised through the action of a pre-processor resulting in an estimate $(\hat{I})$ of the clean data. At a target bitrate $R$ we require the encoded, preprocessed content output from the P+UGC workflow, to be as close as possible to the reference workflow output. The output of the UGC workflow (middle) is expected to be the worst output content in this workflow model. For the simulations, we use the MCL–JCV (USC MediaComm Lab Set) [11] corpus of 30 clips at 720p in a variety of framerates. We assume the data to be relatively clean from degradation and hence simulate UGC by adding noise to generate PSNR of $G_n$ from 20 to 40 dB. We evaluate both the 3D Wiener filter [12] and an example of a DNN Denoiser fast DVDNet [13] in cascade with both AV1 and VP9 encoders. Further details are available in [14].

Figure 2 shows average PSNR over our dataset of $\hat{I}_n^T$ w.r.t the clean original source using two different preprocessors with AV1, and input degradation level at 27.5 dB. Each curve shows the output quality with varying filter strength at a particular bitrate. In all cases, even with no filtering, the output quality is higher than the input, but there is clearly a different optimal filter strength (corresponding to max PSNR) depending on the target bitrate. The gain in PSNR over no filtering is about 1-2 dB for > 512 Kbps. The denoising effect of the encoder is shown at the left edge of each curve where the filter strength is 0. The curves are not flat but with a clear maximum showing that there is an optimal filter strength for a particular bitrate at this level of input degradation. Gains are almost 2dB over no filtering, for a midrange of bitrates 2-4 Mbps.

The decision surface is smooth enough to use a polynomial for fitting. Given a measured degradation noise level $\sigma$ and the target bitrate $r$ we fit a 5th order polynomial $f(\sigma, r)$ yielding the required optimal filter strength. We employ different models for each codec/filter combination and the resulting prediction reduces the possible PSNR gains by at most 17% for the worst degradation level 20dB. Otherwise, there is little impact of errors in prediction. Figure 3 shows visual results from one filter/codec combination.

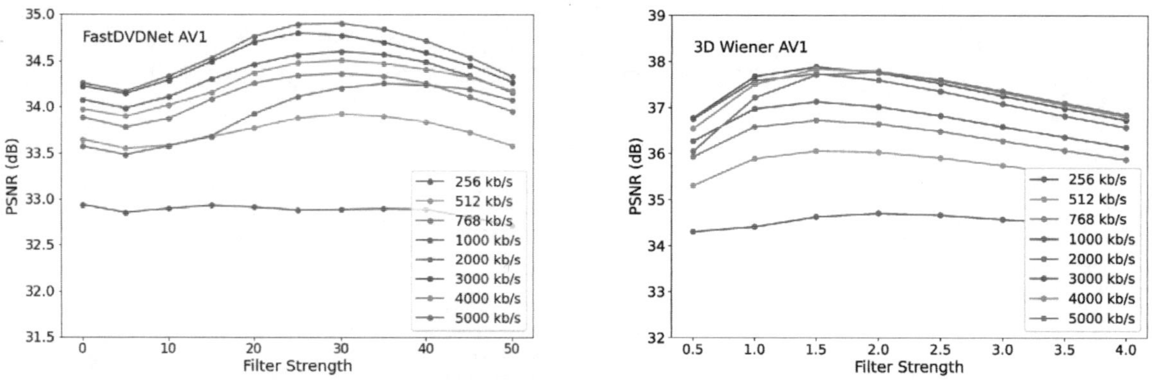


FIGURE 2: PERFORMANCE OF TWO DIFFERENT PRE-PROCESSORS FOR VARYING FILTER SETTINGS AT DIFFERENT BITRATES.

## Content-Adaptive Transcoding for Reducing Bitrate

Streaming services such as Netflix have relatively small libraries of video for distribution to users at high quality and low bitrate [1]. Aaron et al [1] recognized that by choosing codec parameters per clip, significant gains could be achieved. This is because the statistics of video clips vary greatly over any corpus. Hence, tuning for average improvement does not achieve the best compression performance possible for a given clip. Their work in per clip encoding focused on adjusting input parameters of video transcoding, primarily optimizing the bitrate ladder for Dynamic Adaptive Streaming over HTTP (DASH) streaming.

In the work on content-adaptive transcoding, it is typical to adjust parameters like quantization step size and the resolutions used in the design of the bitrate ladder [15]. Parameters that affect the rate/distortion trade-off are typically left untouched. In this work we investigated per-clip optimization of the Lagrangian multiplier used in the Rate Distortion Optimization module of video codecs.

### Rate-Distortion Optimization

Rate-distortion optimization is a constrained optimization problem in which the goal of the encoder is to minimize distortion, D, while ensuring that the bitrate, R, remains below some bitrate, $R_{max}$. This problem can be solved using Lagrangian optimization [16]. In this approach the codec transforms the constrained optimization problem into an unconstrained problem by introducing a cost function, J, in the rate distortion equation as follows:

$$J = D + \lambda R \quad (1)$$

This essentially combines distortion and rate through the action of the Lagrangian multiplier ($\lambda$). This technique was adopted in video codecs through empirical experiments starting early as H.263 as it is effective and conceptually simple. However, in practice there are several interactions between coding decisions which make this problem less straight forward, resulting in a number of empirical approximations for transformation of $\lambda$ between different tools in practical encoder implementations. While theory suggests that the selection of $\lambda$ in the encoder should be optimal, in practice it is not optimal for a given clip. There exists a limited amount of work on adaptation of $\lambda$ for this purpose [17]. The idea is typically to adjust lambda away from the codec default by using a constant $k$ as follows:

$$\lambda = k * \lambda_o \quad (2)$$

where $\lambda_o$ is the default Lagrangian multiplier estimated in the video encoders, and $\lambda$ is the updated Lagrangian. In this work we estimate $k$ per clip by directly maximizing BDRATE [18] gains. BD-rate [18] measures the % difference in area between two Rate-Distortion (RD) curves and hence quantifies the improvement in encoding over a range of Quantization-parameters (QPs) /Bitrates. We use 6 QP points here to characterize the RD function for a clip. BDRATE for a particular clip is therefore used as a cost function in standard canned numerical routine (like Brent's [19] or Powell's algorithm [20]). The optimizer then simply iterates until changes in the cost function become small enough. See [5, 21, 22, 23] for more details.

Our previous work [5, 21] targeted VP9 and HEVC, treating all frames in the same way. Using the YouTube-UGC dataset [24] (~10k clips), we reported average BD-rate (%) gains of 1.63% for VP9 (libvpx-VP9) and 1.87% for HEVC (x265). Later in 2022 [22, 23], we recognized that most of the gains could be due to effects on keyframes and this effect was different for different codecs. By optimizing $\lambda$ only in the higher priority frames (Keyframes, highest level B-frames, Golden-frames) we gained a 4-fold increase in BD-RATE for AV1: from 0.41% to 1.63%.

For this work, we deploy a similar strategy but optimize with respect to BD-rate (%) of Multi-scale Structural Similarity Index (MS-SSIM). Instead of a single multiplier, we estimate two different $k$ for two different keyframe types in AV1 seeking to improve gains further. Two different optimizer methods are used in this work, a) Brent's method for single $\lambda$ multiplier (x264, x265); and b) Powell's method for the 2-dimensional search for two $\lambda$ multipliers (different frame-types) for AV1 variants (libaom-AV1, SVT-AV1).

## Results

Details about the dataset and encoder settings used can be found in the Appendix. Table 1 summarizes the gains for optimized transcoding in our proposed process. Gains with this process are modest for AV1 (2%) but significant for selected clips, i.e., 10% of clips achieve gains of over 5% in AV1 for example, and 4% achieve similar gains in X264/5. Treating keyframes differently results in much improved average BDRATE gains with the per-clip gains of more than 10% for AV1. This shows that the per-clip approach can make a significant difference.

| *Video Encoder* | *Tuning Method* | $k$ | *Average Iterations* | *BD-Rate (%) MS-SSIM Gains* | | | |
|---|---|---|---|---|---|---|---|
| | | | | *Average* | *Best* | *Clips with >1% gains* | *Clips with >5% gains* |
| ***X264*** | All frames | 1.20 | *9.8* | -1.54 | -9.89 | 40 | 4 |
| ***X265*** | All frames | 1.17 | 11.7 | -1.50 | -9.67 | 42 | 4 |
| ***Libaom-av1*** | K1 = KF; K2 = GF/ARF | (9.83, 1.70) | 48.27 | -2.49 | -14.89 | 68 | 12 |
| ***SVT-AV1*** | K1 = GF/ARF; K2 = Interframe | (1.44, 1.20) | 44.41 | -2.00 | -9.16 | 40 | 10 |

TABLE 1: BDRATE GAINS WHEN OPTIMIZING UGC-SUBSET (100 VIDEOS), FOR DIFFERENT ENCODERS WITH DIFFERENT TUNING METHODS.

## Reducing Computational Costs

Clearly the main drawback of this kind of direct optimization technique is that for each iteration of the optimizer, we require the evaluation of 6 RD points which implies 6 encodes. To make this process more practical we can instead perform the optimization on a proxy of the original clip at a lower datarate or use a proxy encoder, e.g., the encoder at a faster preset. These ideas (applied to bitrate ladder design) were first presented by Katsavounidis et al at the Meta Industry workshop at ICIP in Taiwan 2019. In this case, the $k$ estimated from these proxies is then applied to the actual encoder/datarate clip. We expect to lose optimality at the higher resolution or actual encoder preset of course but choosing the datarate and/or faster preset judiciously can reduce this loss.

1. **Method A: *Downsampling***. We estimate $k$ at a lower resolution and apply it to the original resolution clip. For videos <=720p we recommend using a proxy at 144p. For videos above 720p, we recommend downsampling the spatial resolution by 2.
2. **Method B: *Using a faster preset.*** We use the fastest preset for the encoder proxy (speed-6 for AV1)

Table 2 reports on results over our YT UGC set. We measure impact of the proxy strategies on reducing the compute time per iteration of the optimizer. There is a substantial speed-up with fractional loss in gains. For x264/x265, we deployed Method (a), and for AV1 variants (libaom-av1, svt-av1), we deployed Method (b). We achieved 80-100% of the possible BDRATE gains with compute time improvement of 20-200 in all cases except SVT-AV1, where we achieved only 50% of the possible gains with a x6 speed improvement, perhaps showing the efficiency of SVT-AV1. Given 40 optimisation iterations, the overall speedup for AV1 is a substantial 8000x!

| ***Video Encoder*** | ***Method*** | ***BD-rate MS-SSIM (%)*** | | ***Avg encoding time per optimisation iteration (mins)*** | |
|---|---|---|---|---|---|
| | | ***Default*** | ***Proxy method*** | ***Default*** | ***Proxy method*** |
| X264 | Downsample | -1.54 | -1.31 | 0.898 | 0.049 |
| X265 | Downsample | -1.50 | -1.23 | 3.246 | 0.148 |
| Libaom-AV1 | Proxy preset | -2.49 | -2.53 | 5817.10 | 25.28 |
| SVT-AV1 | Proxy preset | -2.00 | -0.87 | 27.73 | 5.487 |

TABLE 2: BDRATE (%) MEASURED IN TERMS OF MS-SSIM BETWEEN DEFAULT AND PROXY-METHOD FOR OUR DATASET.

There is an additional overhead required to downsample the videos, an overhead that was excluded from the encoding time calculation. It is expected that other resolutions of video content would already be available in most content delivery systems. One explanation for the dramatic effect with libaom-av1 is due to the encoder preset configuration from AOM-CTC where we have controlled encoder settings in static GOP conditions.

### ML for Computational Efficiency

Although DNNs are not discussed in the same room as low computational cost algorithms, the previous class of traditional ML techniques are quite computationally efficient. So, it is possible to propose that we can extract features from the original input clip and use those to predict an optimal $k$. Covell et al [25] were the first to try this approach; we use a feature set derived from their proposed set. It includes measures of complexity based on relative P/B frame bitrates measured from a first pass encode with default settings. See Appendix for details of the feature set. With this approach, we only need one RD operating point to be calculated, followed by assembly of the feature vector. We used a random forest regressor with squared error cost function to predict $k$. The computational complexity was therefore reduced by a factor of 60X. With the same dataset as used above, we achieved 67 % of the expected BDRATE gains with an average BD-rate improvement of 1.01% for H.265.

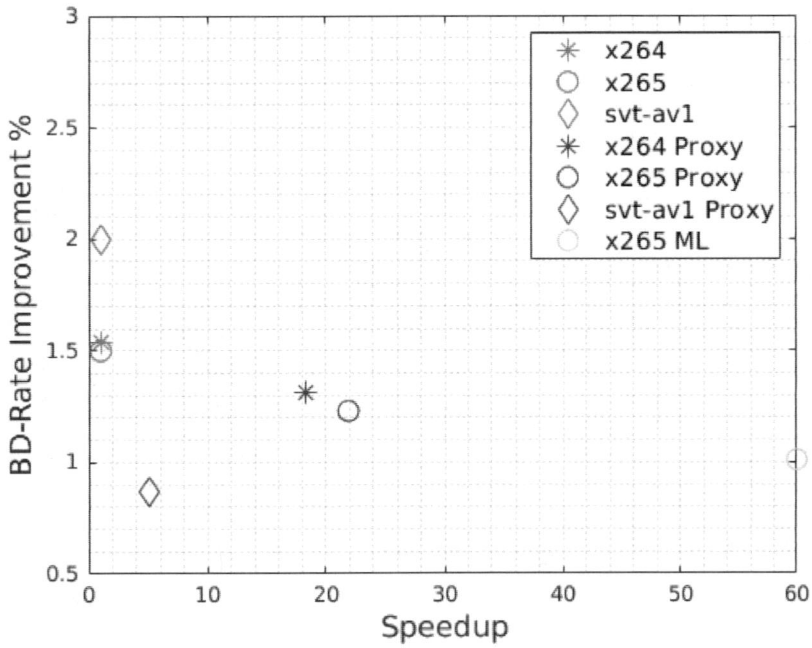


FIGURE 3: SPEEDUP IMPROVEMENT OF DIFFERENT METHODS. X-AXIS DENOTES SPEED-UP FACTOR OVER BASELINE; Y-AXIS DENOTES THE BD-RATE (%) IMPROVEMENT.

**Workflow**

An important point to note here is that we consider these optimisation modules to be best deployed as a 2nd pass action in a transcoding pipeline. That is because in all of these methods we always begin with a default encode pass from which inference begins. Hence we can easily track whether optimisation is worth it and terminate early on the basis of bitrate performance or computational load. Figure 3 shows the tradeoff between computational performance in terms of speed improvement and BD-Rate gains. As expected, computational load is proportional to bitrate gains. For x265, the ML technique is the fastest but worst performing, while the use of downsampled proxies perhaps yields the best tradeoff. Even though reduction in compute load is important, assessing the compute load ahead of time could also mitigate the pain of large compute loads from a user point of view. We discuss that functionality next.

## Cloud Cost Calculator for Budgeting Cloud Deployment

Current cloud based transcoding workflows facilitate predefined encoding settings e.g., AWS MediaConvert. These are billed according to a) framerate b) resolution c) encoder type d) standard encoding preset (Basic vs Professional Tier), and e) region of the cloud server. There is also reserved pricing for transcoding slots. For example, for a 10-minute HD 30 fps video, encoding with 2 different encoders (H.264 and H.265), in predefined AWS MediaConvert settings at US-East, will cost $0.15 for basic tier or $0.24/$0.42 (Speed/Quality variants) in professional tier. HEVC (only in professional tier) costs $0.48/$3.3 for the same options. Reserved pricing is $400 and upwards. Note: These costs are measured at the time of writing this work in February 2023. Custom encoder binaries (via FFmpeg software or standalone encoder binary) can also be deployed. In AWS, users can either use a custom AWS Lambda instance for jobs under 15 mins or deploy in an AWS Fargate instance for longer jobs.

The point is that against this backdrop of heterogeneous cost/compute profiles, given a large set of clips, it is unclear how a user can reliably assess the compute load required to execute the encoding jobs without performing the operation. A simple approach to cost prediction is to run a sample of the encoding jobs and measure the cost, hence predicting the overall cost by scaling by the number of clips. But that might incur unjustified costs itself. Since 2015 [26], there has been increasing attention to modelling and predicting encoding time for a given video based on the intrinsic properties of the clip. The essential idea is that the encoding time must be related in some way to the content of the clip and so features extracted from the clip should be able to help provide a good prediction. Initial proposals use video metadata as features [26] while later work ([27] circa 2020) used spatial and temporal statistical measures of clip complexity. The work by Amirpour et al [5] used a measure for spatial and temporal complexity derived from DCT coefficients (which we also use here) and an additional set of features generated by the MobileNet classification network [28]. Figure 4 shows the process flow which is common to most approaches to this problem so far. In our case the feature set consists of video properties like size, framerate together with statistical measures of spatial and temporal complexity and target encoder settings. The effect of training data on the performance of the final cost prediction almost swamps any effect from the particular classifier chosen.

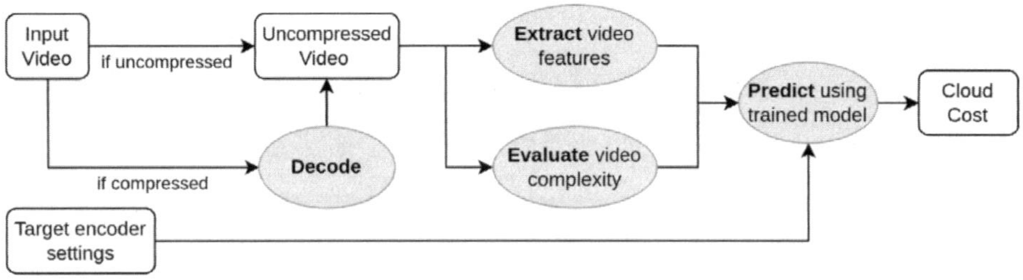


FIGURE 4: FLOW DIAGRAM OF A VIDEO-INTRINSIC CLOUD COST CALCULATOR. FEATURE EXTRACTION ALONG WITH COMPLEXITY ESTIMATION IS CARRIED OUT FOR PREDICTION.

In previous efforts, the prediction algorithms directly predicted the transcoding time based on these features using regression approaches [27]. However, the datasets tend to be quite unbalanced with more data at the low compute load end rather than the high compute load end. The heavy tailed distribution of the resulting encoding times encourages the use of log scales for building regression models. Another approach to deal with this is to quantize clip encode durations in bins with increasing bin widths and use a classifier. A class then refers to a range of durations and not to a single execute time. We deployed a simple Support Vector Machine (SVM) classifier for this purpose and found that it improved recall by about 20% c.f. linear bin width. However other effects were more important and those are discussed in the next section in the context of a regressor. Our feature set is assembled from data extracted using the existing VideoComplexityAnalyzer (VCA) [29] toolkit. See the Appendix, Table A.4 for details. The compute time for executing this ML process is negligible w.r.t. to the time to encode.

## Analysis

Table 3 reports the overall performance of our system (H.264 over 6 CRFS 22:5:47) using a well known regression framework (XGBoost). Our various test setups are in Table A.5. The rows show performance of different test sets, while columns show the impact of linear and log scales for time measurement. R2 scores show that using the log space improves fitting across all the sets. From a customer standpoint however, it is more interesting to report on % error in the estimation of the actual encode time. We use the MAE and symmetric MAE (sMAE) which is less biased to errors in small numbers. On the face of it, we appear to be able to achieve an error of 5-13% with this regressor on our training set using the log-scale. The "Generalised" row shows the performance when we ensure that the content sources in train/test are different. That is the usual approach to generating models which generalize well. However, from a cost budget standpoint the linear scale is more appropriate. Measuring that error in linear space, the sMAE is about 12% (Generalised) and MAE at 25%. So, in fact whether we use linear or log time transformations we are over 10% in error.

| | | Linear | | | Log | | | Log →Linear | |
|---|---|---|---|---|---|---|---|---|---|
| Test Set | Split Method | R2 | MAE (%) | sMAE (%) | R2 | MAE (%) | sMAE (%) | MAE (%) | sMAE (%) |
| Validation Set | Overfit | 0.987 | 40.09 | 13.09 | 0.998 | 13.83 | 5.11 | 10.25 | 5.04 |
| | Generalised | 0.762 | 98.22 | 25.43 | 0.969 | 26.92 | 8.69 | 24.56 | 12.05 |
| YT-UGC Set | Overfit | -0.058 | 225.41 | 40.65 | 0.847 | 65.82 | 18.01 | 44.67 | 17.45 |
| | Generalised | -0.074 | 181.79 | 35.79 | 0.818 | 115.95 | 16.99 | 54.77 | 18.90 |

TABLE 3: PERFORMANCE OF VARIOUS ML ALGORITHMS TRAINED WITH DIFFERENT DATASETS INCLUDING TRANSFORMATION OF TIME TO LINEAR SPACE.

With an error rate potentially as high as 25% the customer can be confident only of estimates in orders of magnitude. For example, if the cost of the actual encode was 100 cycles, we would be able to confidently predict the range was 75 – 125 cycles. At a cost of 10,000 cycles our prediction range increases to 7,500-12,500. The effect in real terms of cycles is therefore exaggerated for more compute intensive jobs. This is not necessarily as poor as the numbers might imply. Whereas without this tool, the customer had no information, now we can be confident of some range based on the actual data.

To show how important the influence of content is on the performance of these models, we change our training set so that clips from the same long form content appear both in the holdout and training set. This is the "Overfit" row. In that case we can achieve 5% (log) or 13% (linear) sMAE in training and test. By including samples of the target data in the training set, we have reduced the error from about 25% to about 10%. That means prediction is significantly improved. Our 10,000 cycle count can now be predicted as within a range of 9000 – 11,000 cycles. This is a well-known phenomenon in ML, but in this application, overfitting does have a use case. When presented with a large corpus, it means that it is possible for a small training set created using a random selection of clips from that corpus, can yield good prediction performance. That is a reliable workflow.

When we use this model on a new corpus which was not part of the training/testing (YT-UGC), performance degrades across the board. In this case "Overfit" and "Generalised" just refers to the model trained on data exhibiting "crosstalk between train/test" or not accordingly. In that case error rates increase dramatically. Further insight about the nature of this holdout test set as compared to the training data is shown in the distribution of Spatial and Temporal Energy (SE/TE) for the clips in Figure 5. The YT-UGC set seems to be approximately distributed in the same space as the training set but not at the higher end of the scale, yet the prediction error is higher than we would expect. This means that SI/TI may not correlate well enough to encode time and that more useful intrinsic information needs to be extracted. Essentially, the ability of these ML approaches to generalize remains a question. For example, by retraining different models for each preset/target CRF combination (not shown in table) for 4K resolution videos, we can reduce the final MAE (%) to as low as 3.8% (with CRF27, and very-slow preset). This also indicates a significant body of work left to be done to determine how best to sample this space.

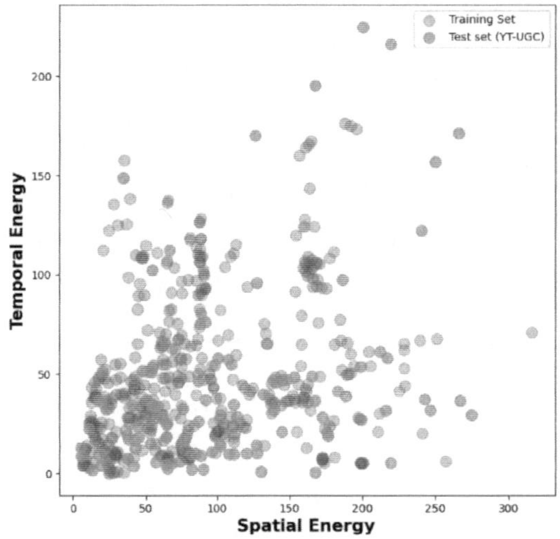


FIGURE 5: DISTRIBUTION OF SPATIAL AND TEMPORAL ENERGY FOR OUR TRAINING AND TEST CLIPS MEASURED USING VCA [24].

## Conclusion

In this work, we examined 3 tools addressing gaps in the development of transcoder pipelines: optimization for pre-processing, encoder parameterization, and a tool for compute load prediction. We also proposed low-cost solutions in each case which are appropriate for cloud deployment. Our use of proxies was able to reduce the compute load for RD optimization by a factor of 200 without loss of quality. The pre-processing module relies only on a simple 2D polynomial fit to data that can be gathered offline. Finally, our cloud cost calculator is more reliable in an overfitting mode than in a general "blind" mode. There is still substantial room for improvement in these tools, and we expect that the class of ML cloud cost predictors has enormous potential for customer management.

## Acknowledgements

This work was supported by Enterprise Ireland's (EI) Disruptive Technology Innovation Fund (DTIF) with Grant Number DT-2019-0068 (VISP), The Adapt SFI Research Centre SFI Grant Number (13/RC/2106), Google/YouTube Faculty Awards and the Ussher Research Studentship from Trinity College Dublin.

## References

[1] Aaron, A., Li, Z., Manohara, M., De Cock, J., & Ronca, D. (2015). "Per-title encode optimization." *The Netflix Techblog.*

[2] Reznik Y., J. Cenzano and B. Zhang, "Transitioning Broadcast to Cloud," in SMPTE Motion Imaging Journal, vol. 130, no. 9, pp. 18-32, Oct. 2021, doi: 10.5594/JMI.2021.3106162.

[3] van Roosmalen, P. M., Kokaram, A. C., & Biemond, J. (1998, September). "Noise reduction of image sequences as preprocessing for MPEG2 encoding." In *9th European Signal Processing Conference (EUSIPCO 1998)* (pp. 1-4). IEEE.

[4] Segall, C. A., Karunaratne, P. V., & Katsaggelos, A. K. (2000, December). "Preprocessing of compressed digital video." In *Visual Communications and Image Processing 2001* (Vol. 4310, pp. 163-174). SPIE.

[5] Ringis, D., Pitié, F., & Kokaram, A. (2020). "Per Clip Lagrangian Multiplier Optimisation for HEVC." *IS&T International Symposium on Electronic Imaging Science and Technology*, *32*(10), 136–137.

[6] Amirpour, H., Rajendran, P. T., Menon, V. V., Ghanbari, M., & Timmerer, C. (2022, September). "Light-weight Video Encoding Complexity Prediction using Spatio Temporal Features." In *2022 IEEE 24th International Workshop on Multimedia Signal Processing (MMSP)* (pp. 1-6). IEEE.

[7] Guleryuz, O. G., Chou, P. A., Hoppe, H., Tang, D., Du, R., Davidson, P., & Fanello, S. (2022, December). Sandwiched Image Compression: Increasing the resolution and dynamic range of standard codecs. In 2022 Picture Coding Symposium (PCS) (pp. 175-179). IEEE.

[8] Chadha, A., & Andreopoulos, Y. (2021). Deep perceptual preprocessing for video coding. In Proceedings of the IEEE/CVF Conference on Computer Vision and Pattern Recognition (pp. 14852-14861).

[9] Chadha, A., Anam, M. A., Treder, M., Fadeev, I., & Andreopoulos, Y. (2022). Toward Generalized Psychovisual Preprocessing For Video Encoding. SMPTE Motion Imaging Journal, 131(4), 39-44.

[10] Andreopoulos, Y., "Neural Pre and Post-Processing for Video Encoding With AVC, VP9, and AV1," in AOM Research Symp, 2022.

[11] Wang, H., Gan, W., Hu, S., Lin, J. Y., Jin, L., Song, L., ... & Kuo, C. C. J. (2016, September). "MCL-JCV: a JND-based H. 264/AVC video quality assessment dataset." In *2016 IEEE international conference on image processing (ICIP)* (pp. 1509-1513). IEEE.

[12] Kokaram, A. (1994). 3D Wiener filtering for noise suppression in motion picture sequences using overlapped processing. *Signal Processing VII, Vol3*, 1780-1783.

[13] Tassano, M., Delon, J., & Veit, T. (2019, September). "Dvdnet: A fast network for deep video denoising." In *2019 IEEE International Conference on Image Processing (ICIP)* (pp. 1805-1809). IEEE.

[14] Hanooman, V., Kokaram, A. C., Su, Y., Birkbeck, N., & Adsumili, B. (2022, October). "An Empirical Approach for Optimising the Impact of a Preprocessor in a Transcoding Pipeline." In *2022 IEEE International Conference on Image Processing (ICIP)* (pp. 2201-2205). IEEE.

[15] Katsavounidis, I., & Guo, L. (2018, September). "Video codec comparison using the dynamic optimizer framework." In *Applications of Digital Image Processing XLI* (Vol. 10752, pp. 266-281). SPIE.

[16] Sullivan, G. J., & Wiegand, T. (1998). "Rate-distortion optimization for video compression." *IEEE signal processing magazine*, *15*(6), 74-90.

[17] Zhang, F., & Bull, D. R. (2018). "Rate-distortion optimization using adaptive lagrange multipliers." *IEEE Transactions on Circuits and Systems for Video Technology*, *29*(10), 3121-3131.

[18] Bjontegaard, G. (2001). "Calculation of average PSNR differences between RD-curves." *ITU SG16 Doc. VCEG-M33*.

[19] Brent, R. P. (2013). *Algorithms for minimization without derivatives*. Courier Corporation.

[20] Powell, M. J. (1964). An efficient method for finding the minimum of a function of several variables without calculating derivatives. *The computer journal*, *7*(2), 155-162.

[21] Ringis, D. J., Pitié, F., & Kokaram, A. (2020, August). "Per-clip adaptive lagrangian multiplier optimisation with low-resolution proxies." In *Applications of Digital Image Processing XLIII* (Vol. 11510, pp. 40-51). SPIE.

[22] Vibhoothi, Pitié, F., Katsenou, A., Ringis, D. J., Su, Y., Birkbeck, N., Lin, J., Adsumilli, B. & Kokaram, A. (2022, October). "Direct optimisation of λ for HDR content adaptive transcoding in AV1." In *Applications of Digital Image Processing XLV* (Vol. 12226, pp. 36-45). SPIE.

[23] Vibhoothi, Pitié, F., & Kokaram, A. (2022, October). "Frame-Type Sensitive RDO Control for Content-Adaptive Encoding." In *2022 IEEE International Conference on Image Processing (ICIP)* (pp. 1506-1510). IEEE.

[24] Wang, Y., Inguva, S., & Adsumilli, B. (2019, September). "YouTube UGC dataset for video compression research." In *2019 IEEE 21st International Workshop on Multimedia Signal Processing (MMSP)* (pp. 1-5). IEEE.

[25] Covell, M., Arjovsky, M., Lin, Y. C., & Kokaram, A. (2016). "Optimizing transcoder quality targets using a neural network with an embedded bitrate model." *Electronic Imaging*, *2016*(2), 1-7.

[26] Deneke, T., Lafond, S., & Lilius, J. (2015, December). "Analysis and transcoding time prediction of online videos." In *2015 IEEE International Symposium on Multimedia (ISM)* (pp. 319-322).

[27] Zabrovskiy, A., Agrawal, P., Mathá, R., Timmerer, C., and Prodan, R. Complexcttp: Complexity class based transcoding time prediction for video sequences using artificial neural network. In 2020
IEEE Sixth International Conference on Multimedia Big Data (BigMM) (2020), pp. 316–325

[28] Howard, A. G., Zhu, M., Chen, B., Kalenichenko, D., Wang, W., Weyand, T., Andreetto, M., & Adam, H. (2017). "Mobilenets: Efficient convolutional neural networks for mobile vision applications". *arXiv preprint arXiv:1704.04861*.

[29] Menon, V. V., Feldmann, C., Amirpour, H., Ghanbari, M., & Timmerer, C. (2022, June). VCA: Video complexity analyzer. In *Proceedings of the 13th ACM Multimedia Systems Conference* (pp. 259-264).

## Appendix

### Experimental Setup

We demonstrate performance with 4 different implementations of three coding standards: x264 (H.264), x264 (H.265), libaom-av1 and SVT-AV1 (AV1). More information on the configuration is shown in Table A.1.

| Video Encoder | Version | QP | Tuning used | Encoder Configuration |
|---|---|---|---|---|
| **x264** | 0.157.x | {22, 27, 32, 37, 42} | All frames | CRF mode single threaded, single pass, medium preset (default) *$x264 –threads 1 --crf $QP --output OUT.264 $INPUT.Y4M* |
| **x265** | 3.0+28-gbc05b8a91 | {22, 27, 32, 37, 42} | All frames | CRF mode single threaded, single pass, medium preset (default) *$x265 –threads 1 --input INPUT.y4m --crf QP --output OUT.mp4$* |
| **libaom-av1** | 3.2.0, 287164d | {27, 39, 49, 59, 63} | K1 = KF; K2 = GF/ARF | AOM-CTC Random Access@P6, Static GOP, Single-threaded. *$AOMEMC --cpu-used=0 --passes=1 --lag-in-frames=19 --auto-alt-ref=1 --min-gf-interval=16 --max-gf-interval=16 --gf-min-pyr-height=4 --gf-max-pyr-height=4 --limit=130 --kf-min-dist=65 --kf-max-dist=65 --use-fixed-qp-offsets=1 --deltaq-mode=0 --enable-tpl-model=0 --end-usage=q --cq-level=$QP --enable-keyframe-filtering=0 --threads=1 --test-decode=fatal -o output.ivf $OPTIONS $INPUT.Y4M* |
| **SVT-AV1** | v1.4.1-17, gf0efc5fa | {27, 33, 39, 46, 52, 58}, | K1 = GF/ARF; K2 = InterFrames | CRF mode with 1 LogicalProcessor@P9 *$SVTAV1ENC -lp 1 --crf $QP --preset 9 -I $INPUT.Y4M -o output.ivf* |

TABLE A.1: VIDEO ENCODER CONFIGURATIONS, QP SETTINGS, AND SAMPLE COMMAND-LINE OPTIONS.

## Dataset

We implemented our direct search optimization scheme on one hundred clips from the YouTube-UGC [24] dataset. These videos were selected to provide a robust sample of modern video. This list can be found in Table A.2.

FIGURE A.1: SCREENSHOT OF THE UGC-SUBSET1 DATASET CONTAINING 100 VIDEOS USED IN THE STUDY.

| # | Video Group | Number of videos | Video count (resolution, count) |
|---|---|---|---|
| 1 | HDR | 2 | {(2160, 1), (1080, 1)} |
| 2 | HowTo | 4 | {(720, 1), (360, 1), (1080, 1), (480, 1)} |
| 3 | VR | 4 | {(720, 1), (2160, 1), (960, 1), (1080, 1)} |
| 4 | LyricVideo | 4 | {(720, 1), (360, 1), (1080, 1), (480, 1)} |
| 5 | NewsClip | 4 | {(720, 1), (360, 1), (1080, 1), (480, 1)} |
| 6 | Vlog | 5 | {(720, 1), (360, 1), (480, 1), (2160, 1), (1080, 1)} |
| 7 | VerticalVideo | 7 | {(720, 1), (1280, 1), (360, 1), (480, 1), (2160, 1), (960, 1), (1080, 1)} |
| 8 | CoverSong | 8 | {(1080, 2), (480, 2), (720, 2), (360, 2)} |
| 9 | Animation | 8 | {(1080, 2), (480, 2), (720, 2), (360, 2)} |
| 10 | Lecture | 8 | {(1080, 2), (480, 2), (720, 2), (360, 2)} |
| 11 | MusicVideo | 8 | {(1080, 2), (480, 2), (720, 2), (360, 2)} |
| 12 | TelevisionClip | 8 | {(1080, 2), (480, 2), (720, 2), (360, 2)} |
| 13 | LiveMusic | 8 | {(1080, 2), (480, 2), (720, 2), (360, 2)} |
| 14 | Gaming | 10 | {(1080, 2), (480, 2), (2160, 2), (720, 2), (360, 2)} |
| 15 | Sports | 12 | {(1080, 2), (480, 2), (2160, 2), (960, 2), (720, 2), (360, 2)} |
| | **Total** | **100** | **{360, 21}, {480, 21}, {720, 22}, {960, 4}, {1080, 23}, {1280, 1}, {2160, 8}** |

TABLE A.2: TESTING DATASET OF 100 VIDEOS FROM THE YOUTUBE-UGC DATASET FROM 15 DIFFERENT CLASSES CONSISTING OF 7 DIFFERENT SPATIAL RESOLUTIONS.

## Feature Set for Prediction of k

Features from the encoded video were used to predict the optimal k for improved BD-Rate performance for a given clip in x265. These features were collected from encoding the clips at QP = 32 when k = 1. Further details about the model can be found in [21].

| | | | |
|---|---|---|---|
| YouTube UGC Group | P avg-QP | P/B Count | P/B Ratio Y *P/B Size |
| WIDTH | P bitrate | P/B bitrate | P/B Ratio U *P/B Size |
| HEIGHT | B count | bitrate *P/B Ratio Y | P/B Ratio V *P/B Size |
| Bitrate | B avg-QP | bitrate *P/B Ratio U | P/B Count *P/B Size |
| Y-MS-SSIM (for each frame type) | B bitrate | bitrate *P/B Ratio V | P/B Ratio Y *P/B Ratio U |
| U-MS-SSIM (for each frame type) | P/B Ratio Y | bitrate *P/B Count | P/B Ratio Y *P/B Ratio V |
| V-MS-SSIM (for each frame type) | P/B Ratio U | bitrate *P/B Size | P/B Ratio U *P/B Ratio V |
| P count | P/B Ratio V | | |

TABLE A.3: FEATURES USED TO TRAIN RANDOM FOREST MODEL USED TO PREDICT K FOR LAGRANGIAN MULTIPLIER OPTIMIZATION.

## Feature Set for Prediction of Encoding Time

| **Features** |
|---|
| Height |
| Number of total pixels |
| Frame rate |
| Number of frames |
| Spatial Energy [Mean, Max, Median, Std deviation] |
| Temporal Energy [Mean, Max, Median, Std deviation] |
| Mean Brightness |
| Preset |
| Target CRF |

TABLE A.4: FEATURES USED TO TRAIN ENCODING TIME PREDICTOR.

## Experimental Setup for Encoding Time Prediction

| | |
|---|---|
| **Dataset used** | AOM-CTC, AOM-Candidates, Vimeo-Corpus-10s, Xiph-Media Collection (commonly known as *Derf* video set). |
| **Number of videos** | 451 |
| **Resolution** | 4096x2160, 3840x2160: 4K (107); 1920x1080, 1080x1920: 2K (182); 1280x720: 720p (75) 480x360: 360p (66), 480x270: 270p (21) |
| **Duration** | 2s, 4s |
| **CRF** | 22, 27, 32, 37, 42, 47 |
| **Video preset** | ultrafast, superfast, veryfast, faster, fast, medium, slow, slower, veryslow |

TABLE A.5: EXPERIMENTAL SETUP FOR ENCODING TIME PREDICTOR.

# Zero Trust Network Access Considerations for Remote Live and Post Production

**Karen D. Gondoly**
**Leostream Corporation**
**Boston, Mass., United States**
kgondoly@leostream.com

**Abstract** – As virtualization and GPU technologies evolve, the Media & Entertainment industry is discovering that adopting a remote access strategy with a hybrid cloud approach is a strategic imperative. The challenge of securing a hybrid environment for live and post production workflows requires organizations to understand and implement Zero Trust Network Access (ZTNA) concept. By understanding the importance and pitfalls associated with authenticating, authorizing, connecting, and tracking access to a hybrid environment for a remote workforce, organizations can ensure the security and productivity of its data and staff.

## Introduction

In days of yore, the IT department was staffed by knights. Prior to the wide adoption of the laptop in the 1990s, IT venerably defended their castle - also known as their corporate network, data, data center, and computing resources - against attackers from without. This network security strategy, appropriately known as "castle-and-moat", was rooted in the belief that no one on the outside could access an organization's intranet unless specifically invited in. Anyone allowed to cross the moat, however, had access all resources on the network.

An effective moat required significant dedicated resources to defend the perimeter, including staff, firewalls, intrusion detection and protection systems, and more. When an enterprise's employees were located on-premises, IT dedicated their resources to building and defending their moat. The introduction of the laptop in the 90s, posed the first challenge.

With laptops in hand, employees became mobile, as did the data and corporate assets on those mobile devices. Now, IT had the simultaneous tasks of securing the laptops (essentially each device became a user's personal castle) and maintaining the corporate moat, while also designing new methods for users to traverse the moat while they were away. For the latter use case, corporations began to deploy VPNs.

Corporate VPNs allowed traveling users to access their organization's intranet from anywhere. While a VPN does allow remote work, organizations more recently realized the inherit pitfalls in using them. First, any employee who crosses the moat via the VPN now has access to the entire network. For traveling users with laptops or accounts that could be compromised, this level of access posed a serious security risk. Second, users that perform graphics-intense tasks noticed that connections via a VPN had poorer performance, lowering productivity. Finally, for IT, VPNs were difficult to scale and costly to implement.

This paper is excerpted from the Proceedings of the 2023 NAB Broadcast Engineering and Information Technology (BEIT) Conference, © 2023, National Association of Broadcasters, 1 M Street SE, Washington, DC 20003 USA.

In order to support a remote workforce without a VPN connection to the corporate data center, organizations began leveraging the public cloud. However, not all use cases are appropriate to host in a public cloud. As organizations selectively moved data and workloads into public clouds, they bifurcated their data center into on-premises and hosted components. With multiple hosting locations, IT's task of securing environments and providing adequate access multiplied, the moat metaphor failed, and the VPN became a relic.

To adequately secure a hybrid on-premises and cloud-hosted environment, accessed by a hybrid on-premises and remote workforce, organizations must incorporate zero trust network access concepts.

## Zero Trust Network Access for Remote Access

Zero trust network access comprises a large set of concepts and technologies. This paper focuses on zero trust network access as it relates to a remote access environment for live and post production workflows. That environment typically includes data and applications hosted either on-premises or in one or more public clouds, and on workstations or virtual machines. Editors and end users need to connect and log into those machines in order to perform their work.

ZTNA as it applies to that environment covers the following four concepts:

- **Authentication:** Indicates how to trust the identity of users who have access to remote production environments.
- **Authorization:** Improves content security by implementing strict access control rules.
- **Connections:** Ensures adequate performance and security by replacing VPN technology and leveraging display protocol technology.
- **Tracking:** Audits access and usage to ensure security.

Before covering these concepts, the remainder of this section provides a quick introduction to Zero Trust Network Access and the benefits and challenges associated with implementing it.

### Introduction to and Benefits of Zero Trust Network Access

Gartner® defines Zero Trust Network Access (ZTNA) as "Zero trust network access (ZTNA) is a product or service that creates an identity- and context-based, logical access boundary around an application or set of applications. The applications are hidden from discovery, and access is restricted via a trust broker to a set of named entities. The broker verifies the identity, context and policy adherence of the specified participants before allowing access and prohibits lateral movement elsewhere in the network. This removes application assets from public visibility and significantly reduces the surface area for attack." [1] In summary, zero trust network access requires IT to trust no one and constantly verify a user's identity.

Gartner more recently defined ZTNA as "a security paradigm that explicitly identifies users and devices, and grants them just the right amount of access so the business can operate with minimal friction while risks are reduced." [2] As a paradigm, implementing ZTNA in an organization requires not only technology, but a buy-in from the organization and a commitment from IT.

The benefits of including well-architected zero trust network access solutions as part of a remote access environment are clear, including:

- Better protection for users and data.
- Increased visibility into what users and devices are accessing on the network.
- Simplified IT when automated privileged access management is implemented.
- Streamlined user access, when combined with SSO solutions.

Reaping these benefits requires IT to consider the challenges inherit in ZTNA as they design their remote access solution.

### Challenges of Zero Trust Network Access for Remote Access

Organizations often experience the following five common obstacles when implementing ZTNA.

- **Cost:** Implementing ZTNA potentially requires an investment in new technologies, such as multi-factor authentication providers or VPN replacements. In the context of a remote access solution, the additional insight and control that IT gains over user access can allow them to recoup ZTNA costs in other aspects of the environment.
- **Limited support:** Not all methods for connecting users to hosted resources support all applications and operating systems. IT can mitigate this limitation by building an environment that automatically selects the appropriate method based on the user, what type of client device they are using, and what they are connecting to.
- **Weak identity management:** Not all organizations are currently outfitted with a federated identity solution in the cloud. Enterprises that have standardized on identity providers, either in the cloud or on-premises, can easily mitigate this challenge and improve the end-user experience by leveraging their corporate identity provider, as users are already familiar with that login process.
- **No on-premises trust broker:** Organizations that decide to leverage a hosted trust broker risk outages or breaches dependent on that broker's security stance. IT can maintain complete control over their environment and data if they invest the time and resources to host a trust broker in their environment, either on-premises or in their public cloud account.
- **Complex policies:** Building adequate and accurate access control rules can be daunting and time consuming. To alleviate this burden, IT can invest in a trust broker that helps automate tasks as much as possible.

## Key Considerations for ZTNA for Remote Access

The following sections cover the four concepts related to ZTNA for remote access and discuss ways to address the challenges outlined in the previous section.

### Authentication

Authentication is the first consideration for any ZTNA implementation and is particularly important as the gatekeeper for a remote access solution. How an organization chooses to verify their user's identity is crucial in a never trust, always verify architecture.

Different authentication methods to consider include the following.

- **Password:** Password authentication requires a user to select a strong, unique text string to enter along with their username. While historically the most common type of authentication, remote access systems that use password authentication should set strong minimum requirements for passwords and enforce multi-factor authentication, to ensure that malicious attackers with stolen passwords cannot access the network.
- **Physical tokens:** Physical tokens allow users to authenticate using an object in their physical possession, often in conjunction with a PIN or other value that the user knows. Leveraging physical tokens may allow end users to authenticate into a remote access solution using the same method used to, for example, enter the studio building.
- **Smart cards and proximity cards:** A common form factor for physical tokens, smart cards and proximity cards can be leveraged to authenticate users into a remote access solution. Smart cards store cryptographic keys (digital certificates) that are used to identify the user and,

therefore, provide greater security that proximity cards. Proximity cards typically store a simple ID number that must be associated with the user via an external system.
- **Digital certificates:** Digital certificates are electronic files that are tied to a cryptographic public/private key pair. Digital certificates are often considered to be phishing resistant, however they have overhead associated with them in the cost and time required to create and rotate them.
- **Multi-factor authentication (MFA):** MFA includes any authentication method that requires two or more forms of identification. In many cases, a second authentication factor based on something the user has (their mobile device, a physical token, etc.) is used to enhance the security of the username and password authentication used for the first factor. Multi-factor authentication is a requirement when building zero trust into a remote access solution.

To reduce the impact of designing zero-trust concepts into the authentication process for a remote access environment, organizations that have standardized on a corporate identity provider should leverage that solution to authenticate users into their remote access environment. This increases adoption by providing a familiar authentication experience for end users, and also gives organizations stronger identity management.

Zero trust environments also require continuous authentication and, therefore, after users are authenticated into the remote access solution, they must be continually authenticated as they access corporate resources. Leveraging single sign-on or identity orchestration solutions can provide a more seamless end-user experience while ensuring security.

## Authorization

After the user's identity has been established and authenticated, the next consideration to ensure content security is authorization. Zero-trust remote access environments must implement a principle of least privilege in order to provide users with access to the minimum set of resources and data required to perform their job function. Implementing least privilege allows organizations to limit attack vectors by restricting access, plus can help organizations prioritize resource usage for the correct users.

Authorization rules, or access control rules, should leverage the identity of the user as well as other factors, such as the user's location, client device, job role, etc., to determine the appropriate resources to offer to the user each time the user requests access. Therefore, authorization rules need to be adaptive and dynamic, changing what resources are offered to the user at every login, as appropriate.

For example, a user logging into the production environment while on-premises may be directed to an editing resource in the corporate data center. That same user logging in while at a job or client site may be directed to an editing workstation in the cloud.

Access control rules for a remote access environment need to be developed not just on the basis of least privilege, but also with an eye on ensuring end-user productivity. By building a hybrid remote production environment that spans the on-premises data center and the public cloud, adaptive rules can direct users to the appropriate resources based on where the user is physically located, in order to lower the latency of their connection. The rules can also take the user's current tasks into consideration to direct them to an appropriately sized resource, to ensure adequate performance.

The type of device that a user logs in from is another important factor in adaptive access control rules. The rules may need to change what type of resources the user is connected to and how they are connected based on the user's device.

To alleviate the challenge of developing adaptive access control rules, organizations should leverage a trust broker that provides adequate flexibility based on the types of workflows the organization needs to implement. For additional security, consider a trust broker that is installed in the organizations network, instead of leveraging a hosted solution. This gives the organization full ownership of their data and access control. Trust brokers can be bundled with security gateways to provide remote access, as described in the following section.

## Connections

Authenticated users who have been offered a list of authorized resources next need to connect to those resources. For remote editing in live and post production environments, that typically entails connecting users to GPU-enabled physical, virtual, or cloud-hosted workstations.

As previously discussed, in the past, end-users would launch a VPN connection to a corporate data center in order to connect to a remote editing environment. In a zero-trust architecture, the VPN is replaced by an intelligent security gateway that opens access only to the authorized resources.

These security gateways are typically controlled by the trust broker used to implement the access control rules. They open access to the network when the user requests the connection and automatically revoke access when the user has completed their task.

There are several key considerations when choosing a security gateway for remote access, in order to address the previously mentioned challenge of limited support.

- Ensure the security gateway supports the types of desktop connections, known as display protocols, required to connect the user to their offered resources.
- Determine if it supports the various types of end-user client devices.
- Research in-browser client-less options, to avoid installing software on end-user devices.
- Review that the security gateway can be architected for high-availability across a hybrid environment.

A carefully selected combination of trust broker and security gateway can help organizations mitigate the challenge of the cost associated with a remote access environment. For example, the management plane of the environment can automate capacity in a public cloud to help organizations minimize cloud costs. It can also help maximize resource usage by intelligently managing access to shared pools of resources, which may allow organizations to purchase less hardware or fewer cloud instances.

## Tracking

The final step after securing user authentication, authorization, and connections, is to track all user activity in the remote production environment. Adequate monitoring not only ensures security, but allows organizations to plan for the future growth of their remote production environment by monitoring usage trends.

Organizations should put systems in place that log user activity in order to answer the following questions.

- Which users authenticated into the remote access environment, as well as which users failed to authenticate, in order to identify potentially compromised credentials?
- What resources and data does each user access, and for how long?
- Where are users physically located when they are working with corporate assets via the remote production environment?
- What client devices are users connecting from and, based on that, are there some devices that should be prohibited?

- Are there any outliers in user behavior, such as users logging in from unusual locations or times, which may indicate a security breach?

As previously mentioned, the tracking system can also be leveraged to monitor usage patterns in order to plan for the required capacity in the remote access environment. For example, track the number of users connected to resources over time to help determine when to purchase new hardware or spin up additional cloud-hosted resources.

## Conclusion

A robust remote access environment for live and post production workflows allows organizations to increase the productivity of their editors and modernize their workforce. The key is to ensure content security in an environment that encourages users to access content from outside of an organization's castle walls. Incorporating zero trust network architecture concepts into a remote access solution is a necessity. When done correctly, organizations can realize ZTNA without compromising end-user experience or productivity.

## References

[1] Gartner IT Glossary "Zero Trust Network Access (ZTNA)", as of February 28, 2023.

[2] Gartner, Watts, John, D'Hoinne, Jeremy, Koeppen, Dale, and Winckless, Charlie, "Predicts 2023: Zero Trust Moves Past Marketing Hype Into Reality," ID G00780267, 6 December 2022, p. 3.

# Reconfigurable Manifold Combiner

**Derek Small**
**Dielectric**
**Raymond, Maine, United States**

**Abstract** – Traditionally, when looking at expanding a filter system for the addition of new channels, the use of a Constant Impedance Module (CIF) would be used. This paper will examine a new combiner technology that allows for expansion without the use of the CIF and showcases additional attributes that make it a viable solution for broadcasters moving forward. The groundbreaking technology helps pave the path for future channel combiners, especially when space and economics demand something other than the CIF.

## Introduction

The new technology being introduced incorporates a Manifold combiner, which is not new to the industry. However, the combination of features added to the Manifold, and described in this paper, make it a more economical option moving forward for systems requiring expandability and less floor space in the transmitter building. Manifold combiners have one filter per channel and are combined/phased on a coaxial Manifold to provide enhanced electrical characteristics for each channel but lack flexibility in expansion for additional channels. Directional filter modules, or constant impedance filter modules, CIF's, are cascaded and easily expandable due to the constant impedance seen at each module output. CIF modules are less efficient, significantly more expensive and require more space due to the extra components within the modules. Tube transmitters prefer constant impedance modules to operate properly making CIF combiners popular. Today's new solid-state transmitters are smaller, more efficient, and easily operate into bandpass filters with high out-of-band reflection making smaller, more efficient Manifold combining more beneficial for the broadcaster's budget.

## Reconfigurable Manifold Description

Introducing the addition of unused ports on the Manifold spline allows for future expansion. This in combination with an analysis to compute the line lengths for the output spline (all while keeping the I/O's in the same location) is what makes this package unique. One benefit of a typical Manifold combiner is that the overall footprint is much smaller than the CIF. The Manifold allows for the most compact configurations, which is beneficial given each transmitter building is unique and space is often a limiting factor. The Manifold has advanced electrical characteristics over the CIF. By eliminating the hybrids, the peak power rating can be increased. These advantages will be discussed in more detail further in this paper.

## Mechanical Advantages

The reconfigurable Manifold combiner incorporates a streamline design with a footprint that is half the size of an equivalent CIF. A Manifold has 60% fewer components than the CIF. The reduction of components equates to better reliability as shown in the following failure rate formula:

$$\lambda = \sum_{i=1}^{n} N_i \lambda_i \pi_{Qi} \tag{1}$$

Where n is the number of part categories, $N_i$ represents the quantity of the i[th] part, $\lambda_i$ is the failure rate of the i[th] part and $\pi_{Qi}$ is the quality factor of i[th] part [1]. From equation (1), we conclude that reliability is directly proportional to component count. The simplicity of the Manifold inherently makes it more reliable than other complicated combiner styles. A comparison between a Manifold and equivalent CIF is shown in Figure 1.

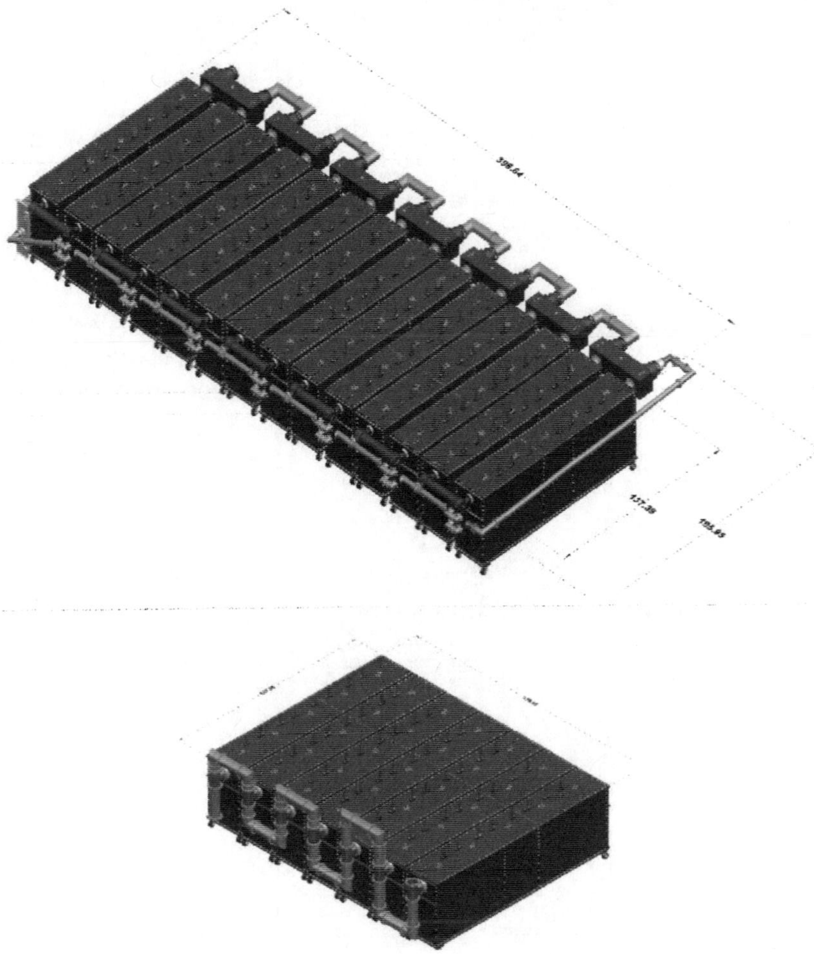

FIGURE 1: CIF (TOP) VERSUS MANIFOLD (BOTTOM).

The unique output U-links on the Manifold have a significant advantage as new channels are added into the system. It allows for easy removal of the spline to make phase modifications without disrupting the physical location of the existing filter inputs thereby eliminating the cumbersome rerouting of the transmission line inputs when new stations are added. When new channels are added to the Manifold design, it is simply a matter of verifying electrical data of the system. Figure 2 below depicts how the output U-links are configured to keep the footprint as small as possible while leaving the input ports in the same location.

FIGURE 2: OUTPUT U-LINKS DESIGNED TO KEEP INPUTS IN SAME LOCATION.

Each channel requires a filter module whereas a CIF requires an input and output hybrid and a second bank of filters. In addition, the Manifold combiner does not utilize any reject loads or a ballast load for the combined system output.

Once the number of stations to be combined is defined the overall footprint of the Manifold remains constant after installation. In contrast, with a CIF filter, space needs to be planned and reserved for future expansion. Any future expansions of a CIF system will take considerably longer than the Manifold design.

## Ports for Future Channels

The example being used for this paper is a 7-channel Manifold combiner. Five of the channels are defined and two open ports are dedicated for future channel expansion. Reference Figure 3.

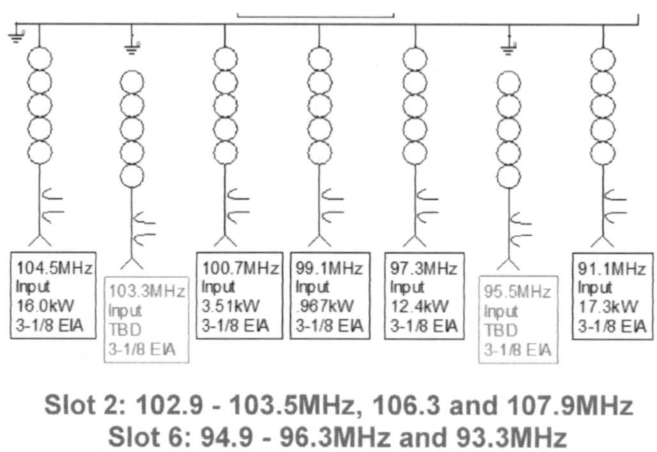


FIGURE 3: FIVE CHANNEL MANIFOLD WITH THE FUTURE EXPANSION OF TWO CHANNELS SHOWN IN RED BOXES. FREQUENCIES THAT CAN BE ADDED FOR THIS EXAMPLE SHOWN IN BLUE.

## Spare Filters

When manufacturing and testing the system all 7 filters are incorporated. The frequency matrix, based on the anticipation of future channels, is confirmed using 3-dimensional electromagnetic simulation software (HFSS) and circuit simulation. The two additional filters are delivered to site and utilized for the future channels or as backup filters. A field technician can tune the two spare filters to the required new channels and place them in line by removing the shorting cap and adding the new channel. If a new channel is being added, the Manifold spline will need to be adjusted and retuned before going back into operation. This procedure is relatively simple and typically takes less than 4 hours to complete. This approach is notably quicker than adding a new CIF module to an existing CIF combiner system.

Or in the rare event a filter requires maintenance, the filter can be removed, and the spare put in its place. If a spare filter is utilized to replace a failed main filter, the damaged filter should be visually inspected for issues while spare parts are ordered to get the original filter back in operation. The repaired filter can continue to be utilized as a spare or to be used as a new station in the system in the future. Spares are a fraction of the overall costs when compared to today's CIF topology. The Manifold concept equips the station for all future scenarios, whereas CIF systems simply are not equipped with spare parts or expedient, economic expansion capability.

## Electrical Shorts for Unused Ports

Continuing with the 7-channel system with 5 defined channels example, the unused ports are capped with an electrical short that have the equivalent short distance as the filter itself. The output spline is defined for each filter configuration. To accomplish this, a channel matrix is defined. The filter configurations are defined by the broadcaster in advance of the combiner production. Alternately, a new channel can be defined and added after shipment. Analysis of the new spline is completed using HFSS and circuit simulation. See Figure 4 showing the two blank locations where the future channels will be added to the Manifold.

FIGURE 4: FIVE CHANNEL MANIFOLD SHOWING TWO SLOTS FOR FUTURE STATIONS. TWO SLOTS WILL BE ELECTRICALLY SHORTED AND USED IN FUTURE WHEN STATIONS ARE DEFINED.

## Electrical Characteristics of Spline Defined in HFSS

At time of order the HFSS tool defines the S-parameters of each tuned filter. In addition, S-parameter data is taken on the elbows and tees in the output spline. This data is then entered into a circuit simulator to calculate the line lengths for each configuration. Figure 5 shows the possible changes to output U-links. Depending on the scenario, changes to a few or all U-links may be necessary.

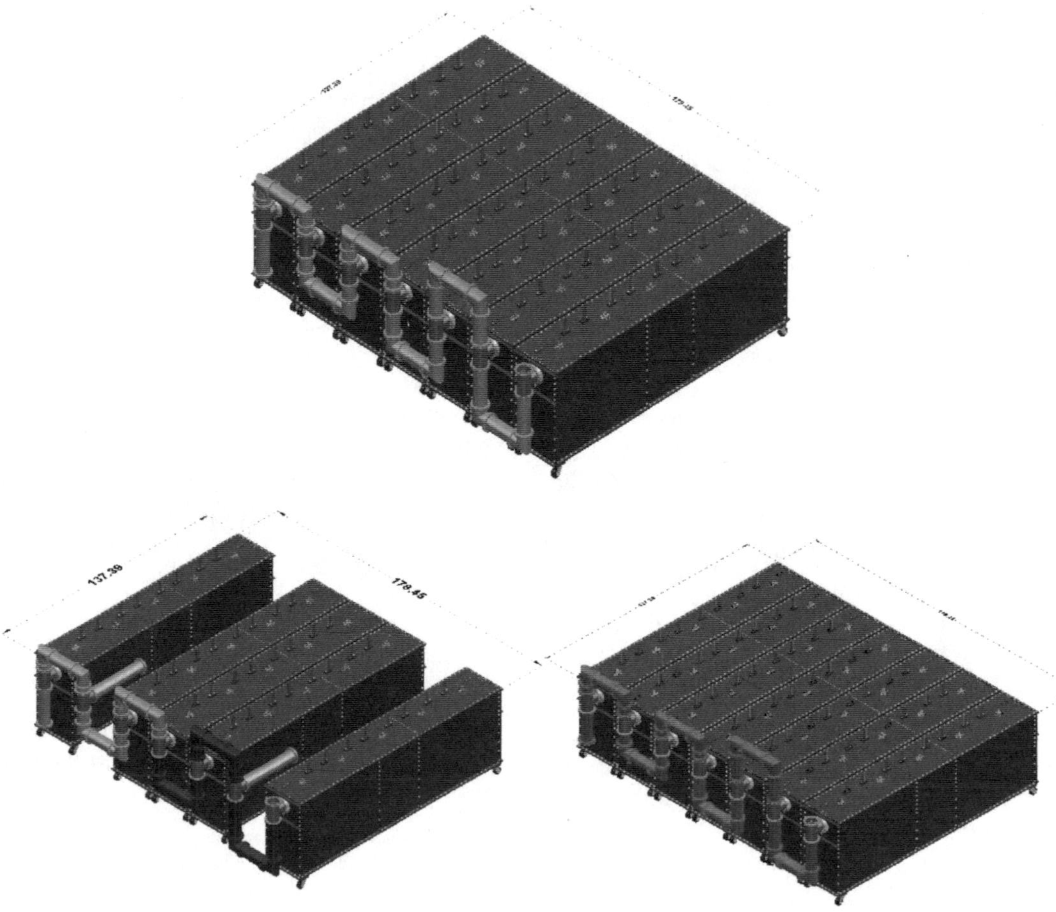

FIGURE 5: SHOWS ORIGINAL SPLINE VERSUS TWO SCENARIOS OF ADDING NEW CHANNELS. OUTPUT SPLINE CHANGE COULD BE PARTIAL U-LINKS AS SHOWN IN BLUE OR ALL U-LINKS SHOWN IN RED.

HFSS is a powerful tool that has advanced technology for Broadcasters. Time to market and implementation costs are minimized by the advancements with HFSS or other 3D electromagnetic programs. Obviously, these programs can only be managed by subject matter experts.

## Manifold Enhanced Electrical Characteristics

The Manifold combiner has enhanced electrical characteristics over the CIF. The 7 channel CIF combiner will have increased loss in the chain further away from the antenna. Typically, the station at the ballast load end of the chain will experience a degradation in performance over the other channels in the system. The optimum location is at antenna side due to the degradation in electrical specifications as you get farther away from the antenna. This is an advantage of the Manifold design, there are no compromised positions in the chain. All channels have similar loss, VSWR, and group delay characteristics. The loss tables in Figure 6 illustrate the loss/efficiency between Manifold and CIF.

| Manifold Combiner | | | |
|---|---|---|---|
| Station | Freq, MHz | Loss, dB | Eff, % |
| 1 | 104.5 | 0.43 | 0.91 |
| 2 | TBD | | |
| 3 | 100.7 | 0.41 | 0.91 |
| 4 | 99.1 | 0.4 | 0.91 |
| 5 | 97.3 | 0.39 | 0.91 |
| 6 | TBD | | |
| 7 | 91.1 | 0.36 | 0.92 |

| CIF Combiner | | | |
|---|---|---|---|
| Station | Freq, MHz | Loss, dB | Eff, % |
| 1 | 104.5 | 0.5 | 0.89 |
| 2 | 100.7 | 0.55 | 0.88 |
| 3 | 99.1 | 0.61 | 0.87 |
| 4 | 97.3 | 0.67 | 0.86 |
| 5 | 91.1 | 0.71 | 0.85 |
| 6 | TBD | | |
| 7 | TBD | | |

FIGURE 6: MANIFOLD AND CIF INSERTION LOSS COMPARISON.

VSWR in a Manifold combiner is also improved over a CIF combiner. Each station in the Manifold can easily be tuned to under a 1.06:1 VSWR, regardless of the station's location in the chain. A CIF has higher VSWR closer to the load side due to the addition of the output hybrids. Low VSWR is a desired specification in any system as it results in a more efficient system. Having a system with equivalent specifications for all channels and an advantage for all the tenants in the master system.

Hybrids on the output side of a CIF module are the weakest voltage link in the system. Hybrids inherently require a large capacitance at the coupled strip junctions. This junction capacitance must be carefully constructed to maximize peak power rating of the hybrid. The Manifold combiner can take advantage of system peak power rating since hybrids are eliminated from the system. Of course, the power ratings of the filters will be burdened since only one is used as opposed to two in a CIF, however, with proper sizing of the I/O's and filter the burden is easily reduced.

## Intermodulation Suppression (IM)

The prime function of a channel combiner is to combine power from multiple transmitters into a single transmission line for broadcasting on a common antenna. A secondary but important function is to suppress 3$^{rd}$ and higher order intermodulation byproducts generated in the high-power amplifier of each transmitter. Figure 7 shows the generation of a third order intermodulation product from a high-power amplifier. F1 is the frequency of the amplified channel and f2 is the frequency of power applied to the output of the amplifier due to lack of perfect isolation. The frequency assignments of FM broadcast are such that the intermodulation products can fall on other FM frequencies, causing interference, or more significantly on airport communications and radar frequencies that can cause life critical interference. The FCC mandates the IM suppression from a high-power FM transmitter be -80 dB below the carrier in the FM band.

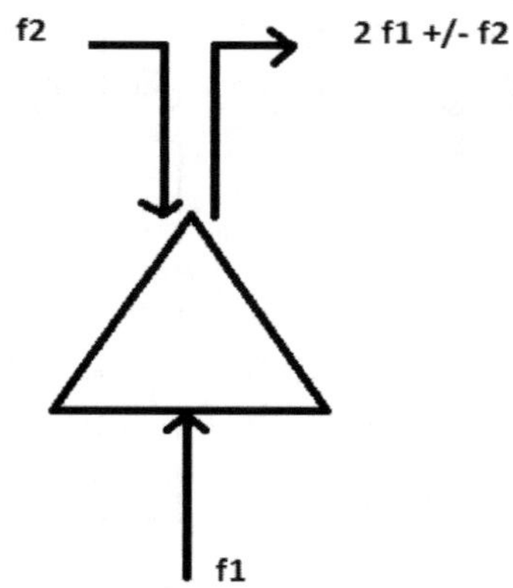


FIGURE 7: IMD PRODUCT GENERATION.

Figure 8 shows filter rejection at 800kHz for the 4-pole cross-coupled filter used in the Manifold combiner. Looking at the 3rd IMD product, f2 is reduced by:

- 35dB passing through CH filter to transmitter
- 24dB transmitter turn around loss (Solid State Transmitter)
- 3rd IMD reduced another 35dB passing through CH filter

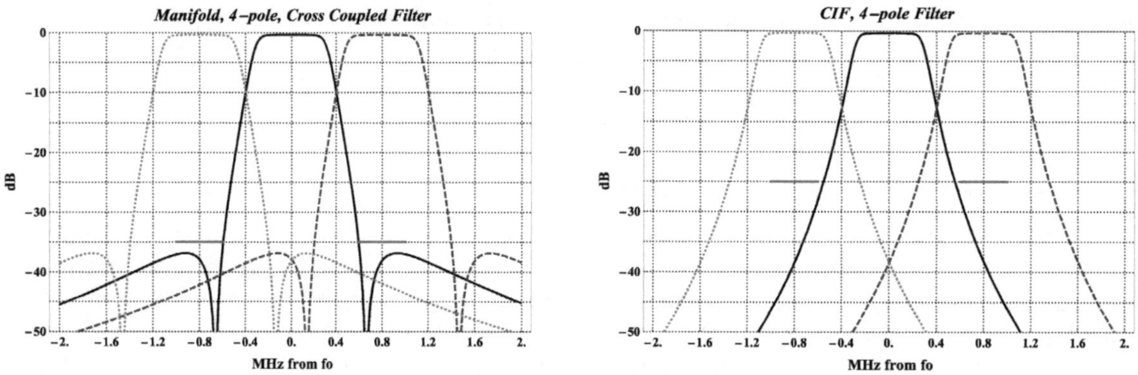


FIGURE 8: MANIFOLD AND CIF FILTER FREQUENCY RESPONSE.

Total IMD reduction in the Manifold combiner design is 94 dB, well below the 80 dB specification. The total IMD shown above is for closely spaced channels and will improve with larger the channel spacing. Additionally, 5 pole filters with cross coupling would increase the IMD reduction and gain headroom on the FCC -80 dB specification. If ample IMD headroom is achieved, you can consider reducing the number of poles within the filter and or remove cross coupling to widen the filter response. Note: The wider the filter the better the insertion loss.

## Market Analysis

In reviewing how complex the solve matrix is for any site, we start with identifying there are 100 stations on the FM spectrum. Even though the analysis is simplified and optimized with software it can still be daunting to consider the possibilities that must be solved. However, knowing that the minimum spacing for stations is 800 kHz the potential for the maximum stations in one market can be defined by (2),

$$\frac{F(t)}{F(e)} \quad (2)$$

Where F(t) is total number of stations available on the FM dial or 100 and F(e) is the number of stations eliminated each time one is selected due to 800 kHz spacing, or 4.

This suggests that the market maximum potential size is 25. For example, the Boston market has 21 stations. Once low power stations (less than 4kW ERP) and directional patterns are eliminated only 9 stations remain. See Figure 9.

| Status | Calls | Freq | Power | City | State |
|---|---|---|---|---|---|
| LIC | WERS(FM) | 88.9 | 4 | Boston | MA |
| LIC | WGBH(FM) | 89.7 | 100 | Boston | MA |
| LIC | WJMN(FM) | 94.5 | 9.2 | Boston | MA |
| LIC | WBQT(FM) | 96.9 | 22.5 | Boston | MA |
| LIC | WBZ-FM | 98.5 | 9 | Boston | MA |
| LIC | WZLX(FM) | 100.7 | 21.5 | Boston | MA |
| LIC | WBGB(FM) | 103.3 | 8.7 | Boston | MA |
| LIC | WWBX(FM) | 104.1 | 21 | Boston | MA |
| LIC | WMJX(FM) | 106.7 | 21.5 | Boston | MA |

FIGURE 9: HIGH POWER OMNI BOSTON CALLS.

When breaking down the Boston market the possibilities of an Aux or Main site with multiple different stations is quickly minimized. The stations in conjunction with their vertical real estate organization can analyze the Manifold combiner design and available ports for future stations. As an example, assume 5 out of the 9 stations in Figure 9 incorporate into a shared antenna system for economic purposes, while taking advantage of expandability with spare parts, the end user may decide to build a 7 channel Manifold giving two of the 4 remaining stations the ability to join the system. If the 4 stations not going into the system are A, B, C & D then solutions are needed to solve the following spline scenarios:

- 5 known stations with A & B
- 5 known stations with A & C
- 5 Known stations with A & D
- 5 known stations with B & C
- 5 known stations with B & D
- 5 known stations with C & D

The total possible combinations would be defined by (3):

$$C(n,r) = n!/[r! * (n-r)] \quad (3)$$

Where n is number of stations not included in the Manifold, for Boston that is 4. And r is number of spare ports going into the Manifold, for Boston that is 2.

The solve for the output spline and validation at time of test would be minimized to the 6 possible solutions for the Boston market, the point here is the analysis is simplified when you break down the possibilities by market.

Another example is the St. Louis market. See Figure 10:

| Status | Calls | Freq | Power | City | State |
|---|---|---|---|---|---|
| LIC | KDHX(FM) | 88.1 | 42 | St. Louis | MO |
| LIC | KWMU(FM) | 90.7 | 100 | St. Louis | MO |
| LIC | KSIV-FM | 91.5 | 85 | St. Louis | MO |
| LIC | WIL-FM | 92.3 | 100 | St. Louis | MO |
| LIC | KSD(FM) | 93.7 | 74 | St. Louis | MO |
| LIC | WFUN-FM | 96.3 | 92 | St. Louis | MO |
| LIC | KYKY(FM) | 98.1 | 90 | St. Louis | MO |
| LIC | KEZK-FM | 102.5 | 100 | St. Louis | MO |
| LIC | KLOU(FM) | 103.3 | 90 | St. Louis | MO |
| LIC | KSLZ(FM) | 107.7 | 100 | St. Louis | MO |

FIGURE 10: ST. LOUIS HIGH POWER OMNI ANTENNAS.

When breaking down St. Louis, the possibilities of an Aux or Main site with multiple different stations is again quickly minimized. The stations or vertical real estate companies can then analyze the Manifold combiner design and how many unused ports for future stations should be in the said design. Again, as an example, assume 4 of the stations above agree to go on a shared antenna system. Like Boston, the end users in St Louis may decide to also build a 7 channel Manifold giving three of the six remaining stations the ability to jump into the system. If there are 6 unknown stations and three possibilities going into Manifold, using (2), gives a total of 20 iterations that need to be solved.

The solve for the Manifold output spline and validation at time of test would be minimized to the 20 possible solutions for the St. Louis market. The point to be made is it is still a simple engineering analysis.

Another scenario may be that over time this Manifold configuration gets completely occupied and an $8^{th}$ station needs to be added. A new analysis that includes an $8^{th}$ channel into the system can be done. In this case additional space would be needed to make it happen, but still can be designed so all existing I/O's remain in the same location.

Note: When looking at any potential market it is key to get an FM consultant involved to make sure the market is analyzed to its fullest. Other factors like HAAT, station moves, ERP changes, etc. should be considered and may give more options than examples in this paper. The key here in this paper's analysis is that the number of possible stations on any one master combiner is not significant when you start looking at site specific data. A Reconfigurable Manifold with all the benefits listed in this paper should be considered at sites where a CIF combiner would have been traditionally used.

## Conclusion

Historically, typical channel expansions of multiple channel configurations utilize the CIF combiner. However, with the advancements in simulation software in combination with other construction techniques, the Manifold provides a viable alternative to the CIF. The Manifold is known for its equality in electrical specifications for all stations and the considerably smaller footprint, but until now was not expandable. When future master sites are being built, the Manifold provides a superior, economical solution to other traditional systems.

This groundbreaking technological advancement will give future multi-station systems a better choice moving forward. As technology continues to evolve, the choice between a Manifold over a CIF system may become even more clear.

This paper covers an example in the FM frequency band, but the technology discussed can also be deployed for UHF television channels.

## References


[1] MIL-217 Standard.

[2] Small, D. J., “Technical Proposal for FM Channel Combiner,” RF TP_083022, August 2022.

[3] Schadler, J. L., “Changing the Landscape of FM Broadcast Antenna Technology,” NAB BEITC Proceedings 2022.

# ENG and DoD: Update on 2 GHz Sharing


**Robert J. Russell, CPBE, ATSC3[1]**
**Technical Broadcast Solutions Inc.**
**Dover, DL, United States**
rj@technicalbroadcast.com

**Robert D. Weller, P.E., CPBE[2]**
**National Association of Broadcasters**
**Washington, D.C., United States**
rweller@nab.org



**Abstract** – Broadcasters' spectrum is valuable. In the run-up to the AWS-3 auction, Congress, NAB, SBE, the Pentagon, NTIA, and the FCC reached a handshake agreement to share the band 2025–2110 MHz, provided broadcasters and the military could reach agreement on the technical details. As a result, nearly $45 billion was raised from auction of spectrum freed by military and other Federal users. In May 2022, DoD, NAB, and SBE concluded a memorandum of understanding (MOU) that allows routine military access for terrestrial and airborne systems at certain locations as well as procedures for coordinated access at other locations. Bench and field testing were conducted of compatibility between military and ENG systems to determine sharing parameters. Technical negotiations have set interference thresholds and coordination mechanisms. A web-based system for tracking military frequency coordination requests has been implemented. This paper summarizes the current state of ENG/Military spectrum sharing in this band.


## Background: The AWS-3 Auction and FCC Rules

In 2010, President Obama directed the National Telecommunications and Information Administration (NTIA) in collaboration with the Federal Communications Commission (FCC) to make 500 MHz of spectrum available for fixed and mobile wireless broadband over ten years [1]. In partial fulfilment of this Presidential Directive, on January 29, 2015, the FCC completed an auction of Advanced Wireless Service licenses in the 1695–1710, 1755–1780, and 2155–2180 MHz bands, collectively called the "AWS-3" bands. This auction raised (in net bids) a total of $41,329,673,325 [2]. Thus, the 65 MHz of auctioned spectrum had an average value of $2.06/MHz-pop [3]. Based solely on the results of this auction, the value of the 85 MHz of broadcaster's 2 GHz spectrum would be 57.7 billion dollars [4].

Most of the AWS-3 bands were formerly allocated to the Federal government and were used by a number of military systems, both terrestrial and airborne. Among the most challenging tasks leading up to the auction was identifying comparable spectrum bands in which to relocate Federal incumbents. While some Federal systems remain in the AWS-3 bands under sharing agreements with the AWS-3 licensees, most were relocated to other spectrum. Federal agencies can be reimbursed out of auction proceeds for costs of relocating to different spectrum and maintaining comparable capability of systems. Agencies are also allowed to enter into sharing arrangements and receive funding to

[1] The author is President of TBSI, PO Box 712, Dover, DE 19962
[2] The author is Vice-President for Spectrum Policy, NAB, 1 M St. SE, Washington, DC 20003

accommodate those arrangements. Monies are held in a "spectrum relocation fund," administered by the Office of Management and Budget.

As part of the AWS-3 proceeding, the FCC adopted an Order adding primary Federal fixed and mobile service allocations to the 2025–2110 MHz band, limiting Federal use of these allocations to military use, specifying coordination requirements in accordance with a Memorandum of Understanding (MOU) between Federal and non-Federal fixed and mobile operations (*i.e.*, broadcast auxiliary services and systems, "BAS"), and providing interference protection and priority to the non-Federal fixed and mobile operations (including BAS) under Footnote US92 to the US Table of Frequency Allocations [5]. Specifically, Footnote US92 states [6]:

> In the band 2025-2110 MHz, Federal use of the co-primary fixed and mobile services is restricted to the military services and the following provisions apply:
>
> (a) Federal use shall not cause harmful interference to, nor constrain the deployment and use of the band by, the Television Broadcast Auxiliary Service, the Cable Television Relay Service, or the Local Television Transmission Service. To facilitate compatible operations, coordination is required in accordance with a Memorandum of Understanding between Federal and non-Federal fixed and mobile operations. Non-Federal licensees shall make all reasonable efforts to accommodate military mobile and fixed operations; however, the use of the band 2025-2110 MHz by the non-Federal fixed and mobile services has priority over military fixed and mobile operations.
>
> (b) Military stations should, to the extent practicable, employ frequency agile technologies and techniques, including the capability to tune to other frequencies and the use of a modular retrofit capability, to facilitate sharing of this band with incumbent Federal and non-Federal operations.

While frequency coordination is required in accordance with an MOU, the particulars of that document were not part of the 2014 FCC Order. Following adoption of the Order, the Department of Defense (DoD), National Association of Broadcasters (NAB), and Society of Broadcast Engineers (SBE) began negotiations to describe and define the sharing arrangements between the military and broadcast uses (including CARS and LTTS). The MOU became effective when it was signed by all parties on May 4, 2022 [7]. The MOU is binding on all parties but can be modified by mutual agreement. While not part of Footnote US92, the DoD has stipulated that military systems will be limited to the four systems identified in its proposal for replacement spectrum for the 1755–1780 MHz band [8].

## Uses of 2025–2110 MHz in the United States

The principal non-Federal use of 2025–2110 MHz in the United States is by broadcasters for electronic newsgathering (ENG), which is considered a mobile service. Some number of fixed stations are also used by broadcasters to provide point-to-point links, typically over long distances where higher frequency bands are not well suited. The 85 MHz of 2 GHz spectrum is officially divided into seven 12 MHz channels, numbered A1 through A7, with the remaining 1 MHz set aside for "response channels" in the lower and upper 500 kHz of the band [9]. ENG operations often involve a "news truck" with a mast-mounted directional antenna, transmitting program material to a central receive site with a high-gain antenna, where it is relayed (typically using a fixed point-to-point microwave link or fiber) to the station's master control. This remote-truck configuration is typical for news crews covering breaking stories and can involve path lengths of up to 50 miles.

ENG operations can also involve a low-power 2 GHz "camera back" transmitter integrated with a video camera that transmits using a non-directional antenna to a nearby low-gain receive antenna. This hand-held configuration is typically used to provide sideline coverage of sports events and other situations where the camera may move during the broadcast. Most ENG operations use a digital transmission standard, such as DVB-T, with bandwidths, error correction, and modulation appropriate for the situation. In television markets with many stations, each 12 MHz channel is further divided into lower and upper sub-channels, providing up to 14 six MHz "split" channels. Because of interference from AWS systems above 2110 MHz and to a lesser extent below 2025 MHz, channels A7U and sometimes A1L may be reserved as guard bands.

The 2025–2110 MHz band is also allocated for Federal use in the U.S. for Space Operation, Earth Exploration-Satellite (EESS), Space Research, Fixed, and Mobile services on a primary basis with a number of restrictions to avoid interfering with or constraining the non-Federal uses including broadcast ENG. These Federal uses are broadly termed satellite operations (SATOPS). SATOPS applications typically consist of intermittent telemetry, tracking, and control (TT&C) uplinks to satellites from fixed ground terminals, often with narrow bandwidths (less than 1 MHz). While broadcast users refer to this frequency band as the "2 GHz band," SATOPS users tend to use the terms "Unified S-Band" (USB) or simply "S-Band."

In addition to Federal use, many commercial satellite operators seek special temporary authority (STA) or experimental authorization to operate telemetry, tracking and control (TTNC) uplinks in the 2 GHz band either through the FCC's Office of Engineering and Technology or its International Bureau. The frequencies assigned for these uplinks are coordinated globally through the International Telecommunications Union to ensure compatibility with other satellite operations. These authorizations are conditioned on prior coordination with ENG operations (typically through the local SBE frequency coordinator) and must operate on a non-interference basis.

There is currently an FCC Notice of Inquiry regarding opening the 2 GHz band for commercial space launch operations on a routine basis [10]. If such operations are ultimately authorized by the FCC, they may directly affect those coordination efforts and existing sharing agreements.

## DoD Uses of 2025–2110 MHz in the United States

### Tactical Radio Relay (TRR)

Some elements of the U.S. military use the 2 GHz band to support a network backbone that provides connectivity from command-and-control locations to mid- and lower-level battlefield commanders. Such systems are typically called "Tactical Radio Relay" (TRR) and provide a secure, point-to-point digital microwave circuit using transportable base stations that can be set up and relocated easily and quickly as shown in Figure 1. While TRR radios can also tune to other spectrum, 2 GHz spectrum is often used for training activities in the U.S. While the precise characteristics vary, typical TRR radios transmit at 1.6 watts with directional antennas having a gain of 23 dBi with a transmit bandwidth of about 2.5 MHz [11].

FIGURE 1: TYPICAL TRR DEPLOYMENT. SOURCE: ULTRA ELECTRONICS TCS (2011).

## Small Unmanned Aircraft Systems (SUAS)

Four services of the U.S. military field unmanned aircraft systems (UAS). The Army uses the 2 GHz band to support certain small UAS (SUAS) for reconnaissance and other purposes. “Small” in this context means aircraft that can be handheld, or hand carried by one person as shown in Figure 2. The SUAS consists of an aircraft and a ground control station (GCS). The transmit power levels of the SUAS systems are not publicly reported but the nature of these small, battery-powered aircraft should suggest that the power levels are no more than a few watts.

FIGURE 2: RQ-11B “RAVEN” SUAS. SOURCE: US ARMY ACQUISITION SUPPORT CENTER.

## Other DoD Uses

The Department of Defense initially proposed to use the 2 GHz band for High Resolution Video (HRV) and Tactical Targeting Network Technology (TTNT) systems, but shared use of BAS spectrum for these systems has not yet been negotiated or authorized. Military SatOps in this band are covered by Footnotes US222, US346, and US347 and are beyond the scope of this paper.

## 2 GHz BAS Sharing Parameters

### Baseline Interference Protection Criterion for Co-channel Sharing With ENG

ENG systems are typically opportunistic and may operate very close to the threshold sensitivity of the receiver. An interference level of -108 dBm/1 MHz has been agreed upon as a baseline criterion for assessing whether detailed analysis is required. An interfering signal that falls below the -108 dBm threshold should not noticeably degrade the ENG system, and DoD systems that demonstrate compliance with that value can be coordinated under the MOU without further study.

While ENG receiver performance varies between models and also with different bandwidths, types of modulation, use of error coding/correction, etc., a Nucomm Type CR7 Newscaster receiver was selected for bench-testing as a representative model. A NuComm CamPac2 was used as a companion test transmitter. Bench tests were conducted using QPSK, 16 QAM and 64 QAM modes at bandwidths of 6 and 8 MHz using a variety of forward-error correction (FEC) and guard interval (GI) settings [12]. The measured threshold sensitivity ranges from -89.4 dBm (6 MHz, QPSK) to -74.7 dBm (64 MHz, 64 QAM). [13] Taking the lowest threshold value of -89.4 dBm (6 MHz) to ensure conservative results, the equivalent sensitivity normalized to a 1 MHz bandwidth is -97.2 dBm/1 MHz.

The effect of interference from digital DoD systems can be modeled by the presence of additive white gaussian noise (AWGN) at the ENG receiver – that is, noise in addition to the receiver's established noise floor. Degradation in the ENG receiver sensitivity is equivalent to increasing the noise floor of the receiver – that is, reducing the signal-to-noise (S/N) ratio or increasing the interference-to-noise ratio (I/N). While there are no "official" protection requirements specific to ENG, it is considered a primary allocated mobile service and for such services both NTIA and the ITU recommends the interference-to-noise (I/N) power ratio should not exceed -10 dB [14] [15]. The amount of interference, I, that increases the noise floor, N, by some amount, ΔN, is called the interference-to-noise ratio or I/N ratio. For I/N = -10 dB, the permissible level of interference is 10 dB below the receiver noise floor. The resulting degradation in the receiver sensitivity, ΔN, is calculated from:

$$\Delta N = 10\log_{10}\left[1 + 10^{\left((I/N)/10\right)}\right] \tag{1}$$

Thus, for I/ N = -10 dB, ΔN = 0.4 dB. A 0.4 dB degradation in receiver sensitivity would not be detectable in practical ENG operations. For the assumed ENG receiver sensitivity of -97.2 dBm/MHz, the allowable level of interference would be 10 dB lower or -107.2 dBm/MHz. For this agreement, this figure was rounded down to -108 dBm/MHz.

### D/U Ratio for Fixed BAS Links

BAS fixed links at 2 GHz are assumed to be properly engineered with significant fade margins. Thus, some level of co-channel interference from a DoD system might be tolerated, accounting for the relatively strong desired BAS signal level. A D/U value of 60 dB has been agreed upon as an alternative criterion (to the -108 dBm interference threshold figure) for assessing interference to fixed BAS links. Measurements were conducted to determine the D/U ratios required to achieve zero uncorrected errors on the CR7 receiver under various conditions. The median D/U was found to be 11.3 dB [16]. To this D/U ratio is added the necessary fade margin to achieve good reliability. An assumption of "five-nines" reliability for the ENG link is assumed, corresponding to an annual outage of about five minutes. Link reliability, R, is the inverse of the probability that a fade will exceed the design fade margin, $L^2$, over a path and is given by [17]:

$$R\left(\frac{p}{p_o} > L^2\right) = 1 - Cd^3L^2\frac{f}{4}10^{-5} \tag{2}$$

where:

- *C* is the climate and terrain factor or "Radio-climatic Zone"
- *d* is the path length in miles
- 20log(*L*) is the fade depth in decibels
- *f* is frequency in GHz

C typically ranges from 0.25 for rough terrain in dry areas to 6 for smooth terrain (or over-water) paths and tropical areas. In terms of geographic area, most of CONUS is considered Radio-climatic Zone 1 (*i.e.*, C = 1). For a 60-mile path in Zone 1 at 2.1 GHz, a fade margin of 51 dB is needed. Thus, the D/U ratio should exceed 62.3 dB under those conditions. For a 50-mile path in Florida (C = 6) the required fade margin is 56 dB to achieve the desired reliability of 99.999%, yielding a D/U requirement of 67.3 dB.

For 596 fixed 2 GHz BAS paths studied from the FCC engineering database, the median path length is about 27.5 miles. That length implies a necessary fade margin of 48 dB in Radio-climatic Zone 6, falling to 41 dB in Zone 1, implying a D/U requirement of 51.3 to 59.3 dB. For this agreement, the upper D/U value was rounded up to 60 dB.

## Criteria for Split-Channel and Adjacent-Channel Sharing

Measurements were taken of various interfering signals at the ENG receiver with a desired signal at 3 dB above the sensitivity threshold. Interference was considered to occur when uncorrected errors result in disturbance of the demodulated picture [18]. One test placed various 8 MHz ENG signals in the center of the channel with a 2.4 MHz interfering signal at the lower channel boundary (*i.e.*, 6 MHz below the ENG signal) as shown in Figure 3. The minimum interference threshold was found to be about 21.3 dB stronger than the desired ENG signal. Thus, for the minimum receiver sensitivity of -97.2 dBm/MHz, an interfering signal in the adjacent channel could be allowed at levels up to -75.9 dBm/MHz. For this agreement, a value of -77 dBm/MHz was agreed upon for adjacent-channel interference.

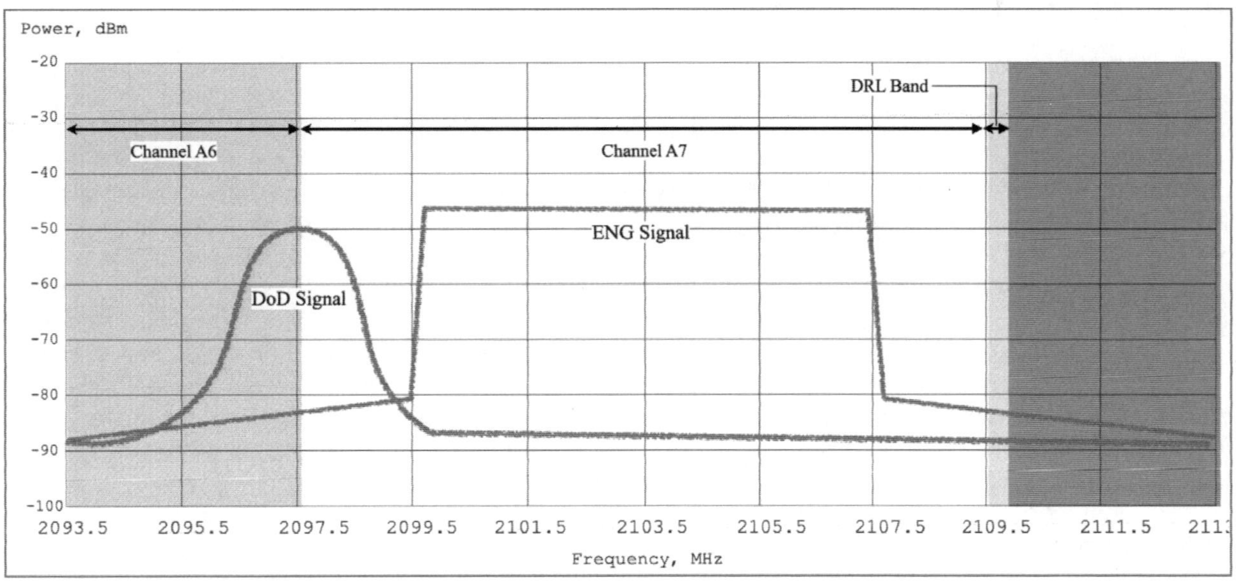


FIGURE 3: ILLUSTRATION OF ADJACENT-CHANNEL INTERFERENCE TEST.

Another test placed a 6 MHz ENG signal in the upper portion of a channel and a 1 MHz interfering signal 3 MHz below (*i.e.*, in the center of the overall channel) as shown in Figure 4. That is, a "worst case" split-channel arrangement. The minimum interference threshold was found to be about 14.4 dB stronger than the desired ENG signal. Thus, for the minimum sensitivity of -97.2 dBm/MHz, an interfering signal in the adjacent split could be allowed at levels up to -82.8 dBm/MHz. For this agreement, a value of -82 dBm/MHz was agreed upon.

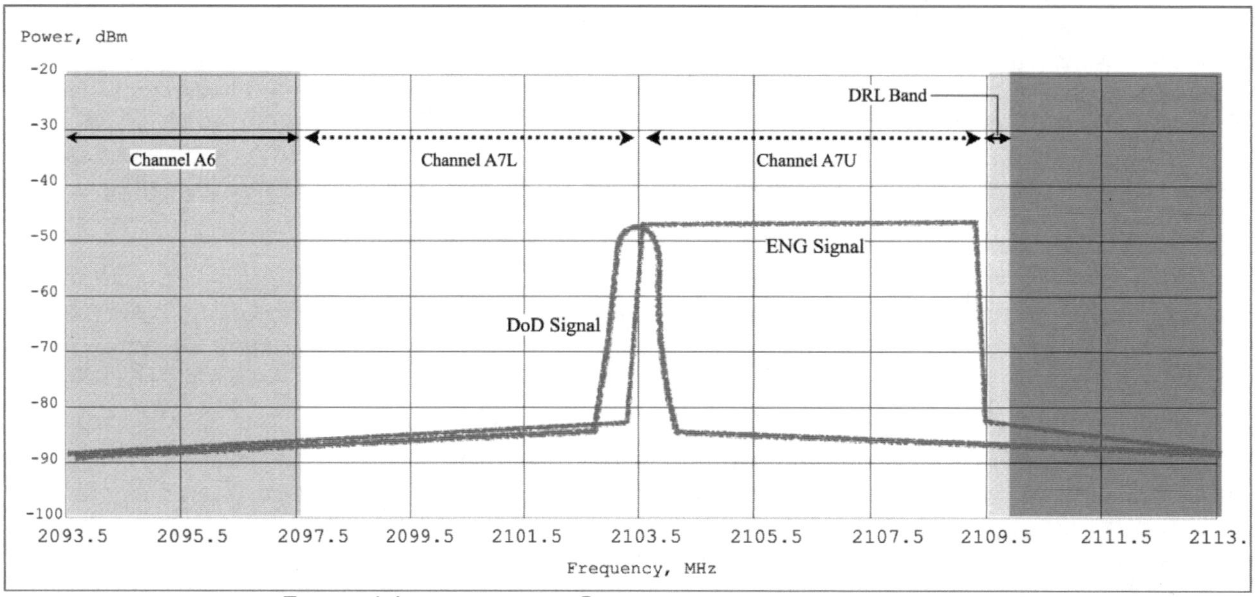


FIGURE 4: ILLUSTRATION OF SPLIT-CHANNEL INTERFERENCE TEST.

No D/U ratio criteria have been agreed upon for adjacent-channel and split-channel operations at this time. So, threshold interfering signal level values of -77 and -82 dBm/MHz will apply.

## Processes for Channel Access

### Prior Channel Coordination

Prior channel coordination (PCC) is one of the coordination methods defined in the memorandum of understanding. This methodology allows the local frequency coordinator to evaluate the existing "home channel" plan in a given television market and assign a home channel for the local military installation to use. In this scenario, the Department of Defense is treated just like any broadcaster in the market with a specific channel(s) assigned for their use. This type of coordination is used mainly for high-priority military installations that wish to access 2 GHz spectrum on a frequent basis. Since the spectrum is broken into seven 12 MHz standard channels or 14-6 MHz narrow ("split") channels a DoD user can be assigned a single standard channel or, more commonly, two narrow channels, which are typically A1L and A7U. Those two narrow channels are often disfavored by broadcasters due to out-of-band interference from Advanced Wireless Services (AWS) operating below and above the 2 GHz band. Prior Channel Coordination allows nearly unfettered use by both the broadcast and military communities. When the Department of Defense is assigned a home channel, they are still required to notify the broadcast community a minimum of 24 hours before beginning operation. This allows the local frequency coordinator to be aware they are operating in the event of interference so appropriate action can be taken.

### Active Coordination Request

Active coordination requests (ACR) are another coordination method that is defined in the memorandum of understanding to allow DoD access to the 2025–2110 MHz spectrum. This method is used in television markets where broadcaster use of the spectrum is congested and a home channel cannot be assigned to the requesting military installation. With this type of coordination, a multistep process is used to facilitate successful coordination if possible. The requesting military installation submits a request via an online tool (SMCS, described in the next section) to allow the local frequency coordinator to evaluate the interference potential of the request. The initial request includes all necessary details of the military's intended use, including the system type, use dates, and DoD's interference analysis of all possibly affected receive sites. The local frequency coordinator then has 96 hours to acknowledge the request at which time the request is moved to "review" status. If the request is not acknowledged within 96 hours, it will automatically move to review status at the end of that time. Once the request is placed into review status, the coordinator will have 30 days to review the request with local broadcasters to determine whether a 2 GHz channel is available for the dates requested. Once that review has been completed the local coordinator can make one of the following decisions:

- **Recommend Approval** – This allows the request to move forward to the SBE National office for final approval to ensure that the request fully complies with the conditions defined in the MOU.
- **Recommend Denial** – This allows the request to move forward to the SBE National office for denial. The SBE National office requires a reasoned explanation for the denial before making a final decision.
- **Recommend Negotiation** – This allows the request to move into a negotiation period where the broadcast community can recommend alternatives and/or conditions to facilitate an approval. These conditions could be limitations on time of use, alternative frequencies, altitude restrictions, azimuth restrictions, etc. The SBE National office will work with the local coordinator to complete these negotiations and work towards a final approval. Another outcome of the negotiations could be identifying a single station in the market that could coordinate in real time directly with the military user. This alternative is burdensome on the affected station and so would be used only in rare instances.

Once the review is complete the SBE National office will place the active coordination case into one of the following states.

- **DoD Use Approved** – This status allows the military installation to move forward with their use of the spectrum and can also be notated with any restrictions noted during negotiations. An approval still requires a notification a minimum of 24 hours before planned use of the spectrum. DoD can propose alternative restrictions, leading to additional negotiations with local broadcasters.
- **DoD Use Denied** – This status is only used if there is no possible way to allow sharing with DoD anywhere in the 2 GHz band.

## SMCS

The Spectrum Management Coordination System, SMCS, is an online tool developed by the Department of Defense and their contractors with local frequency coordinator input to facilitate and track all DoD coordination requests and military planned use notifications in the 2025–2110 MHz spectrum. SMCS tracks all PCC notices and is used to complete active coordination requests. This system includes a database with all known broadcast uses of the 2 GHz band. The database is updated monthly using a combination of FCC ULS data and local coordinator databases. The technical parameters in this database are used to analyze potential interference to broadcast auxiliary facilities as part of the ACR submission.

SMCS is available for all local frequency coordinators once training has been completed. The training for this system is comprehensive and includes both the military and broadcaster roles to ensure full understanding of the tool.

An illustration of the SMCS user interface is shown in Figure 5 and an illustration of the BAS sites considered in an ACR interference analysis in Southern California is shown in Figure 6.

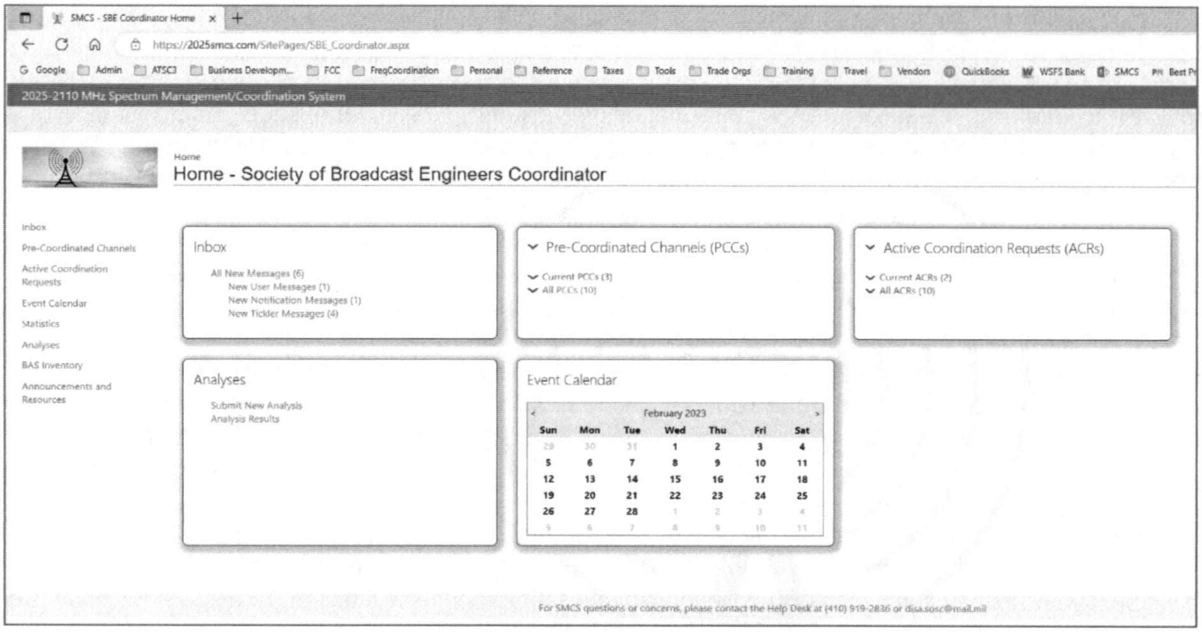


FIGURE 5: SMCS USER INTERFACE.

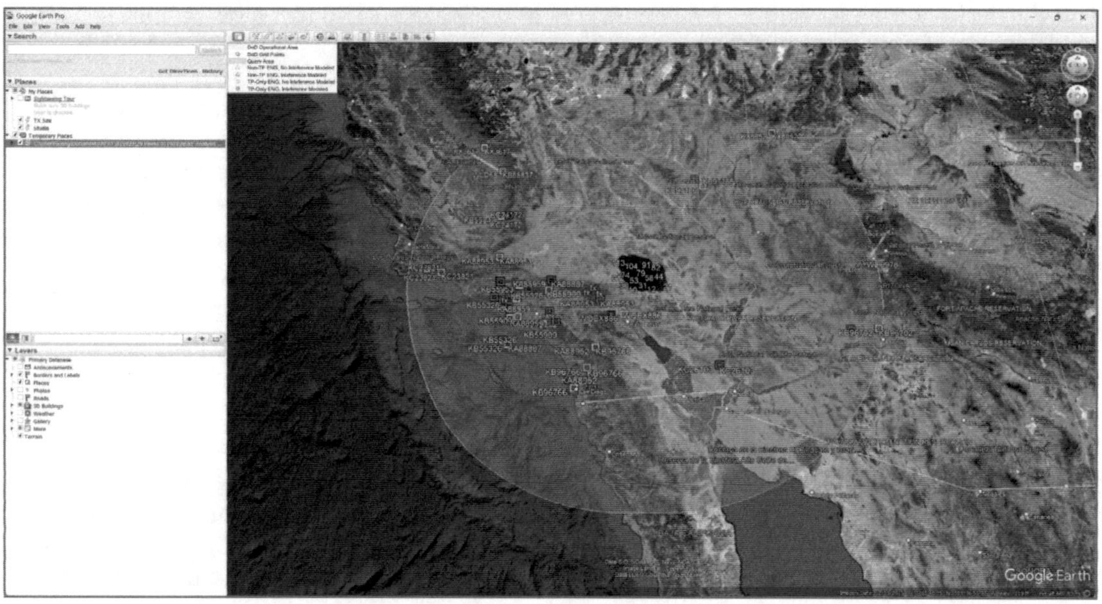


FIGURE 6: ILLUSTRATION OF ACR INTERFERENCE ANALYSIS. DOD OPERATIONS ARE PROPOSED IN THE BLACK AREA. THE AREA CONSIDERED FOR INTERFERENCE ANALYSIS IS SHOWN IN THE GREEN. BAS SITES ARE IDENTIFIED BY EITHER GREEN OR RED PINS. NO INTERFERENCE IS PREDICTED TO THE GREEN SITES WHILE INTERFERENCE IS PREDICTED TO THE RED SITES.

## The Stop Buzzer

Every Department of Defense coordination is required to provide a "stop buzzer" (cease-operations) contact for interference reporting. This contact includes a phone number and email address that must be able to be reached at all hours during operations. Once the stop buzzer has been contacted their operations must cease until the source of the interference has been confirmed.

## Summary

A Memorandum of Understanding between broadcasters and the Department of Defense allows certain military systems to access the 2 GHz BAS band. BAS operations have priority over military use and all military uses must be coordinated with broadcasters. The potential for interference to broadcast receivers is minimized either by assigning a "home" channel to the DoD facility (with notification required prior to the commencement of operations) or by conducting an interference analysis on a case-by-case basis (resulting in possible restrictions placed on the military system). The coordination parameters include limiting co-channel military systems to -108 dBm/MHz at the BAS receiver, by limiting military systems operating in an adjacent channel (*i.e.*, at least 6 MHz from the BAS center frequency) to -77 dBm/MHz, and by limiting military systems operating in a "split" channel (*i.e.*, 3 to 6 MHz from the BAS center frequency) to -82 dB/MHz). A web-based system, SMCS, is used to track notifications of operation and active coordination requests.

## References

[1] Memorandum for the Heads of Executive Departments and Agencies, "Unleashing the Wireless Broadband Revolution," released June 28, 2010, 75 Fed. Reg. 38387 (July 1, 2010).

[2] FCC, "Auction of Advanced Wireless Services (AWS-3) Licenses Closes – Winning Bidders Announced for Auction 97," Public Notice DA 15-131 (January 30, 2015).

[3] The U.S. population in 2010 (the latest available census at the time of the auction) was approximately 309.3 million people.

[4] The US population in 2020 (the latest available census at this writing) was approximately 329.5 million people.

[5] FCC, "Amendment of the Commission's Rules with Regard to Commercial Operations in the 1695-1710 MHz, 1755-1780 MHz and 2155-2180 MHz Bands," Report and Order, GN Docket 13-185 (March 31, 2014) ¶211.

[6] 47 CFR §2.106.

[7] "Memorandum of Understanding Between U.S. Broadcasters and U.S. Department of Defense Concerning Spectrum Sharing in the Band 2025-2110 MHz," April 12, 2022.

[8] Letter from Chuck Hagel, Secretary of Defense, Penny Pritzker, Secretary of Commerce, and Martin Dempsey, General U.S. Army to Sen. John McCain, January 16, 2015.

[9] Channels A8, A9 and A10 are in the 2450-2483.5 MHz band and are shared with unlicensed (Wi-Fi) and mobile satellite services.

[10] FCC, "Allocation of Spectrum for Non-Federal Space Launch Operations," Report and Order and Further Notice of Proposed Rulemaking, ET Docket 13-115, FCC 21-44 (April 22, 2021).

[11] Commerce Spectrum Management Advisory Committee (CSMAC), Working Group 4 Final Report, July 24, 2013.

[12] Army Spectrum Management Office, "Electromagnetic Compatibility Evaluation of TRR Equipment to ENG Equipment – Characterization Results," August 30, 2016. (CIO/G-6 Report).

[13] Measurements taken at the receiver input. At the input to the LNA found on many receivers, sensitivities would be better, ranging from about -83.4 to -96.9 dBm, depending on configuration.

[14] ITU-R Recommendation F.758-7, “System parameters and considerations in the development of criteria for sharing or compatibility between digital fixed wireless systems in the fixed service and systems in other services and other sources of interference,” November 2019.

[15] NTIA, “Interference Protection Criteria – Phase 1 – Compilation from Existing Sources,” Report No. 05-432, October 2005, p. 6-15.

[16] CIO/G-6 Report, *op cit*.

[17] Bell Laboratories, “Transmission Systems for Communications,” Fifth Edition, p. 462.

[18] Alion Science and Technology, “SATOPS/ENG Radio Frequency Interference Bench Testing,” November 2018.

# "Generative AI:" Supercharging Humans, Transforming Creativity

**Naveen Narayanan**
**Quickplay**
**Toronto, Ontario, Canada**

**Abstract** - "Generative AI" is the next-level process of using machine learning algorithms to create new content based on "intelligence" gathered through training on a large corpus of text (even code!), images, audio, and video files. The broad category of Generative AI utilizes many different types of models, including Large Language Model (LLM). LLM is an AI model trained on a large corpus of text to predict the likelihood of a given sequence of words using statistical techniques. Companies such as OpenAI and Midjourney or open-source communities such as Stable Diffusion have invested millions of dollars in productizing groundbreaking AI papers and pre-training on large datasets available on the Internet. Once available, individuals and companies can utilize these large, pre-trained models to solve domain-specific problems, through transfer learning, without the significant computational overhead.

This paper describes some of the early applications of Generative AI and LLMs models in media broadcasting and streaming. One of the demonstrated applications is the ability to generate actionable video descriptors/tags, such as identifying a scene where a woman is standing in front of the Eiffel Tower or on a moving train.

## Relationship Between LLM and Generative AI

LLMs fall under the category of Generative AI, which pertains to AI systems capable of producing novel content, such as images, music, or text. Generative AI systems utilize machine learning algorithms to learn patterns from large datasets and then apply those patterns to generate new content that is similar to the training data.

In particular, LLMs focus on creating natural language text. These models typically undergo training on extensive amounts of text data and use statistical models, neural networks, and other machine learning techniques to understand the structure and patterns of language. Once trained, LLMs can generate new text that bears similarities in structure and style to the original training data.

Generative AI systems, including LLMs, have practical applications in various fields, including media broadcasting and streaming. In media, LLMs can be used for tasks such as video summarization, scene recognition, and content recommendation.

For example, a Generative AI system using LLMs could analyze a movie and automatically generate a summary of its plot, or it could recognize and tag specific scenes in the movie, such as action scenes or scenes that feature a particular actor. This information could then be used to recommend similar movies to viewers based on their preferences.

This paper is excerpted from the Proceedings of the 2023 NAB Broadcast Engineering and Information Technology (BEIT) Conference, © 2023, National Association of Broadcasters, 1 M Street SE, Washington, DC 20003 USA.

Another media-specific use case for Generative AI and LLMs is image generation. These models can be trained on large datasets of images and then used to generate new images that are similar to the training data. This technique has been used to create realistic-looking images of people, animals, and even entire scenes.

Overall, the use of Generative AI and LLMs in media can improve the content discovery and recommendation process for viewers, as well as provide more efficient and accurate ways to analyze and understand media content.

## Evolution of LLMs

The evolution of LLM has been a significant area of research in natural language processing (NLP). Here is a more detailed overview of its evolution:

1. **Early models:** The earliest LLMs were based on statistical models, such as n-gram models, which predicted the probability of the next word based on the preceding n-1 words. However, these models were limited in capturing long-term dependencies in text. Long-term dependencies in language processing models refer to the challenge of capturing the relationship between words or phrases that are far apart from each other in a sentence or a document.
2. **Neural language models:** In the 1990s, researchers introduced neural network-based language models, which used feedforward neural networks to predict the probability of the next word based on the preceding words. However, these models still had difficulty capturing long-term dependencies.
3. **Recurrent neural networks (RNNs):** In the mid-1980s, RNNs were introduced [1] to model longer-term dependencies in text data. RNNs use a feedback loop to pass information from one time step to the next, allowing them to maintain information about the context of the sentence.
4. **Sequence-to-sequence models:** In the late-1990s, sequence-to-sequence models were introduced.[2] These use two RNNs (an encoder and a decoder) to translate one sequence of text into another. These models were used for machine translation, text summarization, and other NLP tasks. Long Short-Term Memory (LSTM) and Gated Recurrent Units (GRUs) are examples of this type of model.
5. **Pre-trained models:** The real breakthrough in LLM and Generative AI came in 2018 with the development of the first Large Language Model (LLM), GPT-1 (Generative Pre-trained Transformer 1), by OpenAI. GPT-1 was trained on a massive corpus of text data, including books, articles, and websites, and could generate new text almost indistinguishable from the human-written text. This breakthrough opened the door to various new applications for Generative AI, such as text completion, creative writing, and chatbots.
6. **Advancing pre-trained models:** Since the development of GPT-1, researchers have continued to refine and improve Large Language Models. In 2019, OpenAI released GPT-2, which was even more powerful than its predecessor, and was capable of generating long-form text. GPT-3, released in 2020, took this a step further and was capable of generating text in multiple languages and styles and performing a wide range of other tasks such as translation, summarization, and question-answering.

Overall, the evolution of LLMs has been characterized by a shift towards more powerful models that can capture longer-term dependencies and generate more coherent and natural language. Introducing pre-trained models has also allowed for faster and more efficient training of models for specific tasks.

## Advantages of LLMs

LLMs offer a range of advantages for developers, particularly those working in media-related fields. Here are some key benefits:

1. **Pre-trained models:** One of the biggest advantages of LLMs is that pre-trained models are available for developers to use. These models have been trained on large amounts of text data and can be fine-tuned for specific tasks, such as sentiment or image analysis. This saves developers time and resources; they don't have to start every new project from scratch with an army of experienced AI developers.
2. **Faster Content Creation:** LLMs and generative AI can help developers create media content quickly and efficiently, saving development time. For example, generative AI can create new and original content, such as music, art, videos, and even entire stories or scripts, allowing developers to automate the content creation process and generate more diverse and innovative content.
3. **Improved Efficiency:** Developers can optimize various workflows, such as optimal ad insertion points, scene-based encoding, celebrity recognition, and thumbnail generation, using LLMs and generative AI to improve the efficiency of their media-related products.
4. **Enhanced Personalization:** LLMs and generative AI can help developers create more personalized experiences for end-users by generating content that matches their interests and preferences. For example, thumbnail generation based on user persona or generating personalized images based on textual prompts in any style can improve the user experience and engagement.
5. **Improved Accessibility:** LLMs and generative AI models can help improve accessibility by generating captions and subtitles automatically, making the content more accessible to people with hearing impairments. Additionally, text summarization can help users quickly and easily consume content, making it more accessible to people with limited time or attention.

Overall, developers building media-related products can leverage the capabilities of LLMs and generative AI to create engaging, personalized, and efficient media experiences for their users, ultimately leading to increased revenue and user satisfaction.

## Multimodal AI

Multimodal AI (Artificial Intelligence) refers to the field of AI that focuses on developing models and systems that can process and understand multiple modalities, such as images, text, speech, and video [3].

Traditionally, AI models have been designed to work with one specific modality, such as natural language processing (NLP) for text or computer vision for images. However, with the increasing availability of multimodal data, there has been a growing interest in developing AI systems that can understand and combine information from multiple modalities.

Multimodal AI models typically use deep learning techniques, such as convolutional neural networks (CNNs) and recurrent neural networks (RNNs), to process and extract features from each modality. These features are then combined to create a unified representation of the data, which can be used for various tasks such as image captioning, video analysis, and speech recognition.

One of the key advantages of multimodal AI is that it can enable more natural and intuitive interactions between humans and machines. For example, a virtual assistant that can understand text and speech can provide a more seamless and efficient user experience.

Multimodal AI has many applications, including healthcare, autonomous vehicles, entertainment, and education. For example, in healthcare, multimodal AI can analyze medical images and patient records to provide more accurate diagnoses and treatment recommendations.

Multimodal AI represents an exciting and rapidly growing field of AI research, with the potential to revolutionize how we interact with machines and process complex information.

## CLIP Model

Contrastive Language-Image Pre-Training (CLIP) is a multimodal deep learning approach developed by OpenAI in 2021 [4]. It is a neural network trained to understand the relationship between images and their associated text descriptions.

The CLIP model is trained using contrastive learning, which involves comparing pairs of images and their corresponding text descriptions. The goal is to learn a representation that captures the underlying semantics of both the image and text, allowing the model to understand how they relate.

One of the key innovations of the CLIP model is its ability to perform zero-shot classification. This means the model can classify images based on text descriptions it has never seen before. For example, if shown an image of a giraffe and asked to classify it as an animal or a plant, the CLIP model can correctly classify it as an animal without additional training.

The CLIP model has many potential applications, including image and text search, content moderation, and creative writing. It has already been used in several real-world applications, such as creating a language model to answer questions about images and generate captions for images.

Overall, the CLIP model represents a significant breakthrough in the field of deep learning, as it demonstrates the ability to learn complex relationships between different modalities (e.g., images and text) and perform high-level tasks without the need for task-specific training.

## Use Cases of LLMs in the Media Industry

Here are a few potential use cases for applying LLMs in the media industry.

1. **Celebrity Recognition**
   LLMs can be used to identify and recognize celebrities in videos for various purposes, such as identifying actors in a movie or TV show, recognizing musicians in a music video, or spotting athletes in a sports broadcast. This can be useful for social media and influencer marketing campaigns, where brands may want to identify and collaborate with celebrities.
2. **Search and Discovery**
   In addition to detecting objects and landmarks, AI models can detect moods, genres, and actions in videos. These video descriptors can be used to index the catalog for search and discovery use cases and detect changes in moods and genres over time. For example, one might search for scenes where a celebrity appears in front of the Burj Khalifa or inside an airplane.
3. **Optimal Ad Insertion Points**
   AI can detect black frames, scene transitions, and silences to find optimal locations to insert ads within a video. This is a powerful capability for OTT content distribution when paired with Dynamic Ad Insertion, which allows service providers to generate new ad inventory and monetize via targeted advertising.
4. **Scene-Based Encoding**
   Scene-based encoding is a technique used in video compression that considers the characteristics of individual scenes in a video to optimize the compression ratio and video quality. In scene-based encoding, the video is divided into segments with similar characteristics, such as lighting, motion, and content. The encoding process then analyzes each scene separately and adjusts the compression parameters to best match the characteristics of that scene. AI can help divide the video into individual segments that can be the encoder's input.
5. **Thumbnail Generation**

LLMs can identify images that contain objects, landmarks, and moods, which can be grouped into clusters to personalize the experience for content discovery. For example, images/thumbnails that are high-action versus romantic versus thriller.

6. **Start/End Credits and Video Segment Detection**
   LLMs can identify the scenes in a video with start and end credits, recaps, and intros. These markers can be used for building application features such as "Skip Intro" and "Watch Next".
7. **Content Creation**
   Generative AI can create new and original content, such as music, art, videos, and even entire stories or scripts. Specifically, AI can be optimized for image-generation tasks, and models can generate high-quality images from textual descriptions. This can generate personalized images based on textual prompts in any style, such as pixel art, oil painting, polaroid photo, watercolor, and more.
8. **Restoration and Remastering**
   Generative AI can be used to restore and remaster old media content, such as films or photographs, by removing noise, enhancing colors, and improving resolution.

9. **Text Summarization**
   The AI transformer model can also be used for text synopses, automatically summarizing long articles into shorter, more readable versions. This is particularly useful for creating summaries of news articles or generating social media posts from long-form articles.

## Use Case Demonstration

The following section provides an overview of the utilization of various models, such as Open AI's CLIP and Facebook's DETR [5], in a use case that was executed by Quickplay. A visual representation of the workflow can be found in Figure 1.

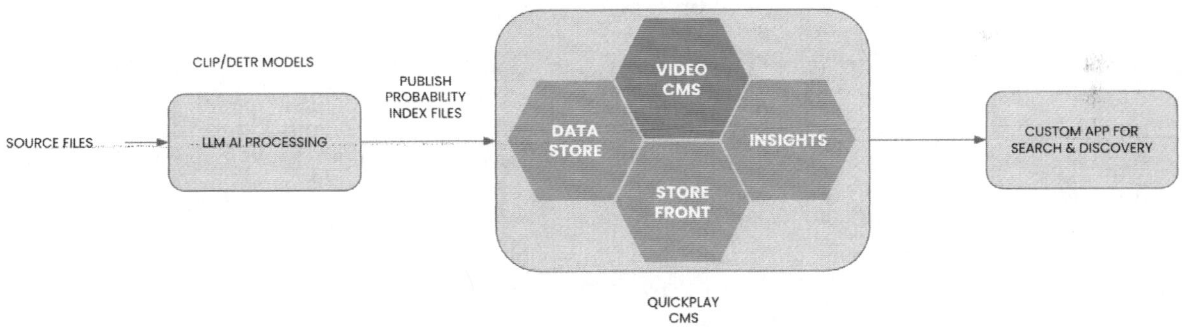


FIGURE 1: WORKFLOW USED BY QUICKPLAY FOR USE CASE DEMONSTRATION.

The Quickplay video ingestion workflow breaks the source video file into constituent images/frames. Images are then sampled once every second to keep the processing overhead under control for this demonstration. Each image is fed into an AI workflow utilizing the DETR model to identify black frames and images without objects. This is an essential first step because it was seen that CLIP models do not work well on black frames and images without any objects. Next, we utilize the CLIP model to determine the probabilities associated with critical textual descriptions provided as inputs to the process. Descriptions include celebrity names (Tom Cruise, Tom Hanks), action types (driving, fights, prison escape, fishing, etc.), landmarks (Burj Khalifa, Budapest Station, Kremlin), genres (thriller, war, romance) and objects (text, watch, guns). As discussed before, CLIP is a multimodal pre-trained model that can accept natural language descriptions/phrases as inputs, analyze the frame, and generate the probabilities of each phrase appearing in the image. For example, we can determine images where Tom Cruise appears near Burj Khalifa or where Tom Cruise is climbing. Similarly, we can get the AI model for identifying the probabilities of the occurrence of landmarks in the scene - Burj Khalifa, Budapest train station, and more.

The output of the CLIP model is a matrix (number of images x number of text phrases). The probability values in each row indicate the model's confidence in the occurrence of each phrase in the corresponding image. The matrix is stored alongside the video metadata associated with the video within the Quickplay CMS. Figure 2 below is a sample matrix of probabilities generated by the above ingestion process.

| Frame | Tom Cruise | Jeremy Renner | Woman Spy | Prison Escape | Gunfight | Submarine | Girls with Guns | Russian Agents | Man |
|---|---|---|---|---|---|---|---|---|---|
| frame0 | 0.294 | 0.038 | 0.036 | 0.587 | 0.062 | 0.015 | 0.017 | 0.138 | |
| frame24 | 0.277 | 0.621 | 0.216 | 0.243 | 0.075 | 0.012 | 0.006 | 0.042 | |
| frame48 | 0.519 | 0.421 | 0.098 | 0.132 | 0.279 | 0.019 | 0.011 | 0.006 | |
| frame72 | 0.868 | 0.081 | 0.042 | 0.07 | 0.312 | 0.01 | 0.011 | 0.002 | |
| frame96 | 0.922 | 0.063 | 0.067 | 0.074 | 0.803 | 0.013 | 0.017 | 0 | |
| frame120 | 0.608 | 0.279 | 0.22 | 0.402 | 0.252 | 0.019 | 0.099 | 0 | |
| frame144 | 0.816 | 0.053 | 0.187 | 0.47 | 0.147 | 0.016 | 0.005 | 0.152 | |
| frame168 | 0.752 | 0.125 | 0.032 | 0.046 | 0.798 | 0.043 | 0.021 | 0.001 | |
| frame192 | 0.968 | 0.005 | 0.057 | 0.03 | 0.221 | 0.039 | 0.015 | 0.1 | |
| frame216 | 0.985 | 0.003 | 0.041 | 0.066 | 0.634 | 0.032 | 0.006 | 0.027 | |
| frame240 | 0.954 | 0.003 | 0.036 | 0.077 | 0.197 | 0.005 | 0.005 | 0.027 | |
| frame264 | 0.77 | 0.007 | 0.039 | 0.063 | 0.073 | 0.004 | 0.005 | 0.116 | |
| frame288 | 0.987 | 0.002 | 0.071 | 0.056 | 0.532 | 0.04 | 0.043 | 0.001 | |

FIGURE 2: SAMPLE PROBABILITY MATRIX GENERATE BY CLIP MODEL FOR FRAMES FROM THE MOVIE "MISSION IMPOSSIBLE - GHOST PROTOCOL."

A custom web portal was built to list all images from the video file in a grid and to provide the ability for the user to search and discover images that meet specific criteria. For example, if the user wants to see all images with Tom Cruise, the system will scan through the column that lists the probability of Tom Cruise appearing across all images. The resulting images are rendered using a pre-configured probability cut-off value (> 0.99) and sorted in descending order to ensure high-confidence images are displayed at the top. A similar approach is applied for landmarks (e.g., Burj Khalifa) to display resulting frames. In this case, the system would scan through the column that lists the probability of Burj Khalifa appearing across all images and would pick up images that meet a high cut-off value (high confidence).

## Web Portal for Search and Discovery of Celebrities/Objects/Genres Within a Film

In Figure 3 below, a list of all images (frames) present in the video file is displayed, revealing a total of 7,969 frames.

FIGURE 3: STARTING WITH ALL SCENES FROM A MOVIE.

The user can filter frames by selecting specific celebrities, landmarks, and genres. Figure 4 below displays the results when Tom Cruise is selected, showing all frames in which he appears. As a result of this filtering, the number of frames displayed is reduced to 1265.

FIGURE 4: SELECTING SCENES WHERE TOM CRUISE APPEARS.

Users have the option to further narrow down their search by selecting a specific landmark. For instance, if the user chooses the Burj Khalifa, the system will display results containing scenes where Tom Cruise is either near or inside the building. The refined results are presented in Figure 5, which includes 24 filtered images.

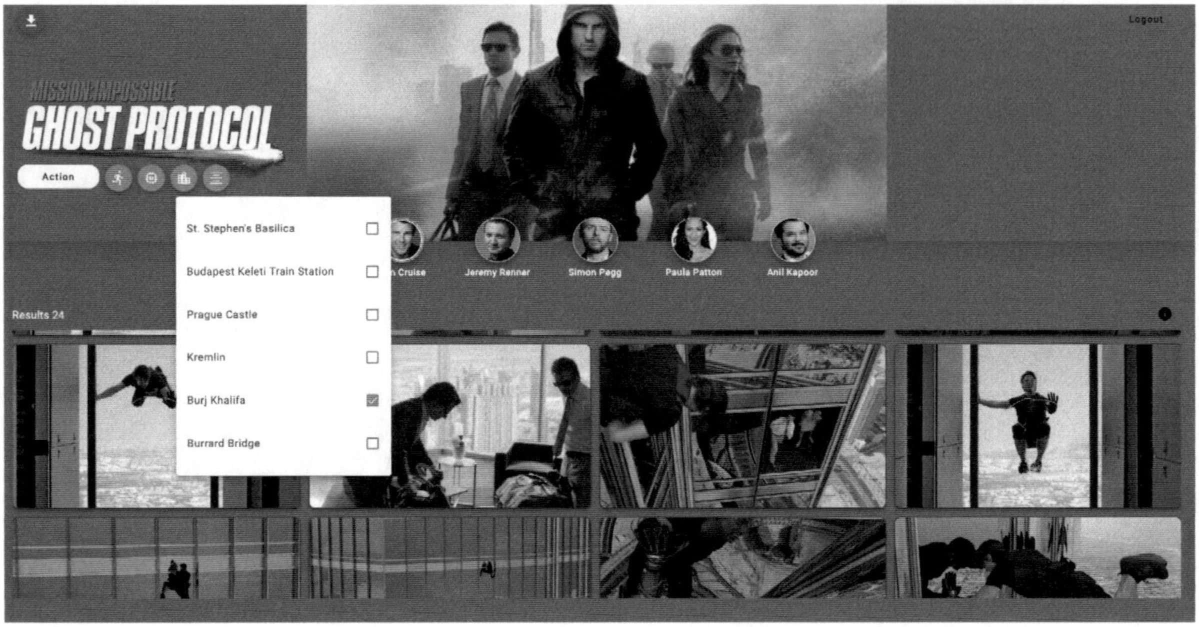


FIGURE 5: SELECTING SCENES WHERE TOM CRUISE APPEARS AT BURJ KHALIFA.

If the user selects Kremlin while keeping Tom Cruise selected, the results are further filtered to display images where Tom Cruise is near or inside Kremlin. See Figure 6.

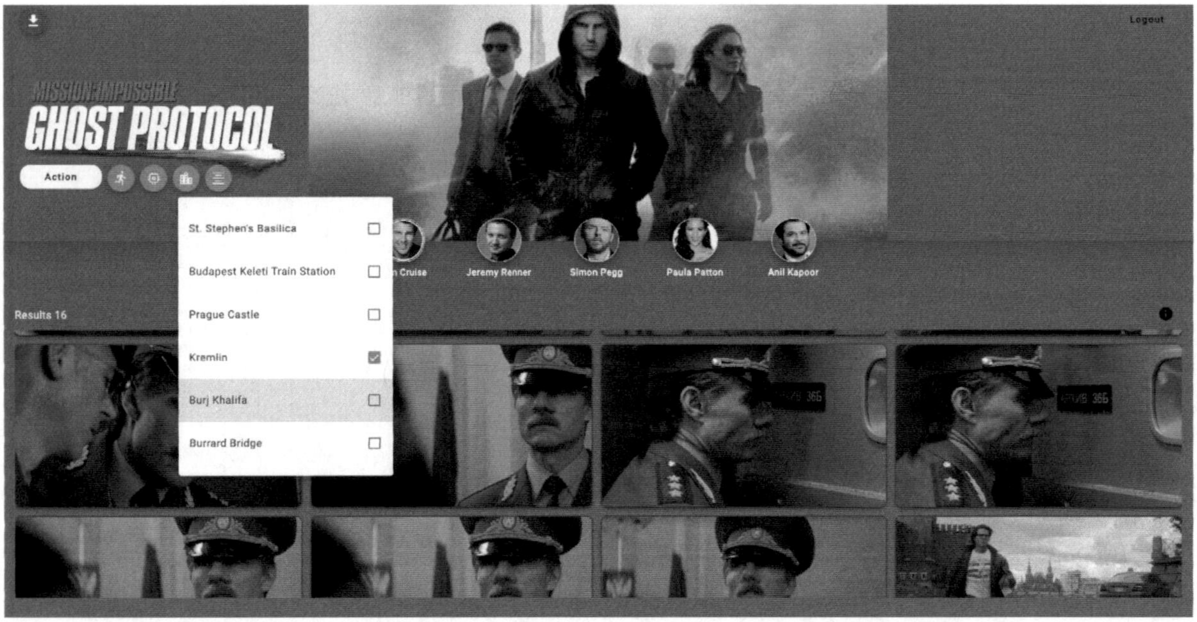


FIGURE 6: SELECTING SCENES WHERE TOM CRUISE APPEARS AT KREMLIN.

Users can select any image to create a poster thumbnail for the movie. Multiple poster thumbnails can be generated and attached to the film in the Quickplay CMS, an essential aspect of providing a personalized discovery and browsing experience. An example of this step is depicted in Figure 7.

FIGURE 7: CHOOSING THE THUMBNAIL AS A POSTER.

The portal offers a few additional capabilities, including the ability to filter content by keywords such as Women Spy and Prison Escape, as demonstrated in Figures 8 and 9.

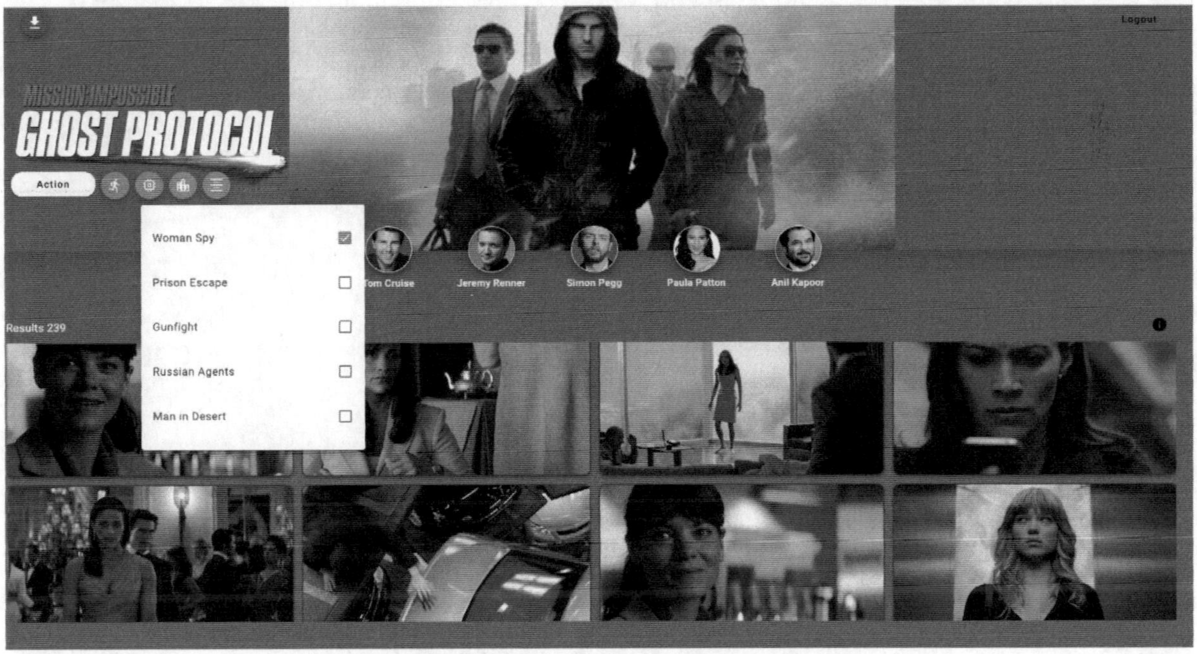


FIGURE 8: SELECTING SCENES WITH WOMAN SPY.

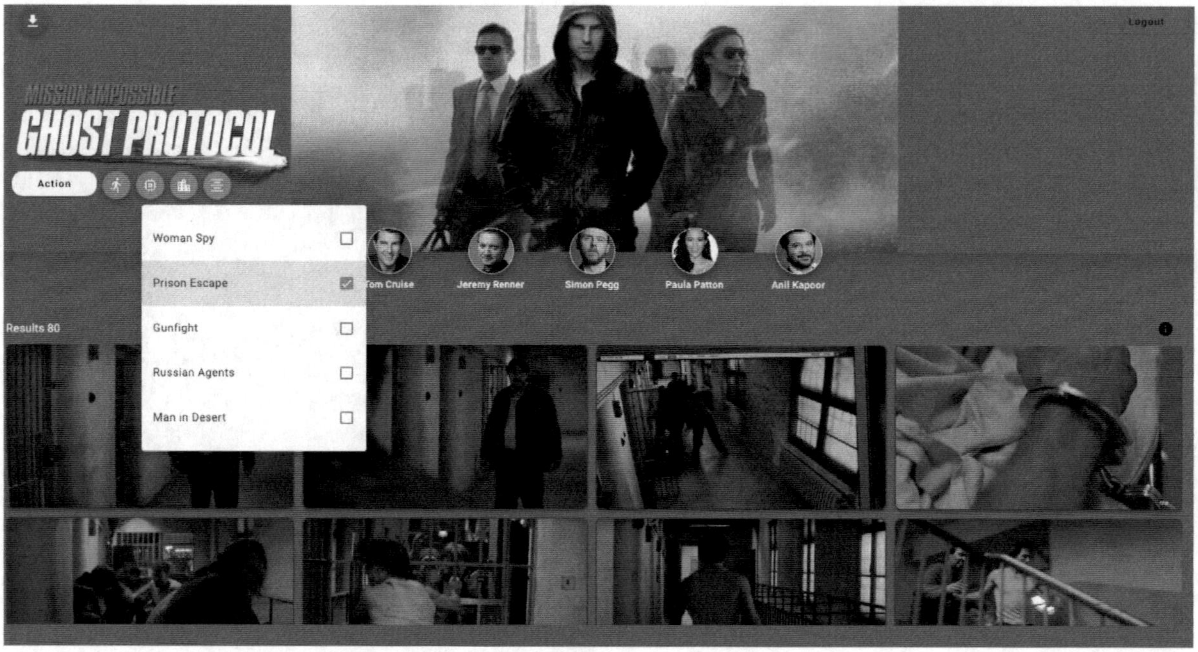


FIGURE 9: SELECTING SCENES WITH PRISON ESCAPE.

The user can filter images or scenes based on specific actions such as driving, jail fight, retina scan, and more. It is important to note that these actions are free-form natural language phrases used to query the AI against the images/scenes. An example of this is shown in Figure 10 below, where the user can filter scenes involving driving. Additionally, Figure 11 from the movie Forrest Gump demonstrates an example of detecting an action, where images containing anti-war rallies are displayed.

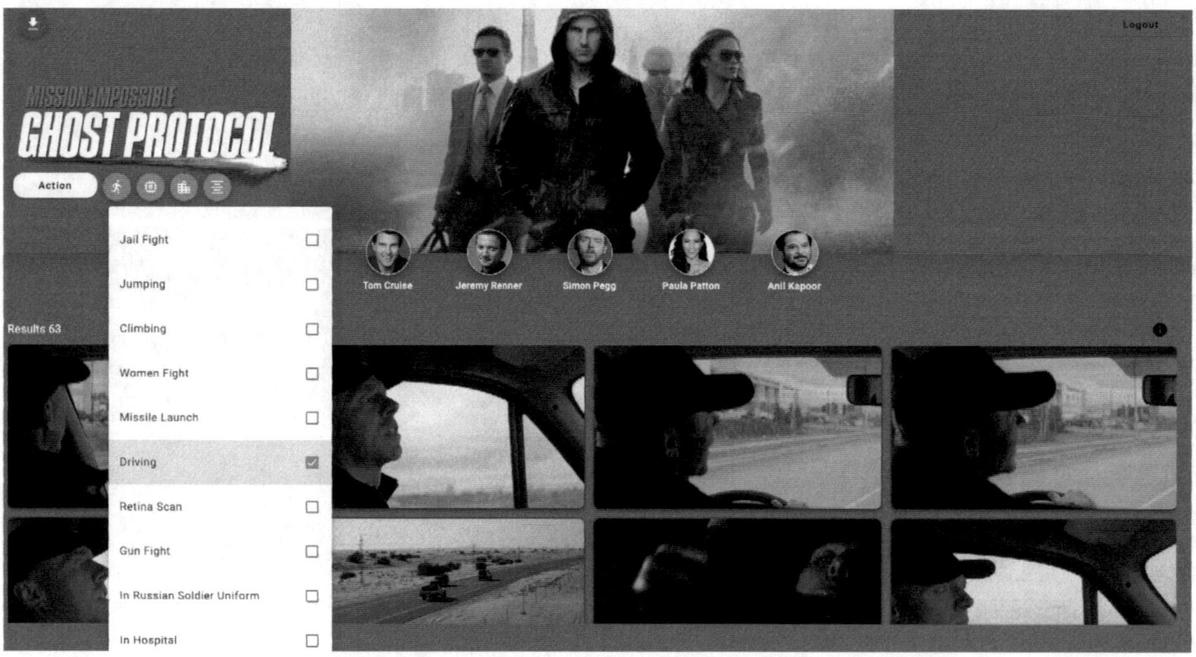


FIGURE 10: SELECTING SCENES WITH DRIVING.

FIGURE 11: SELECTING SCENES INDICATING ANTI-WAR RALLY.

The web portal showcases a few other exciting use cases, one of which is the detection of start and end credits. This is accomplished by querying the AI model for the occurrence of text in images and selecting frames with a high probability of credits. See Figure 12. Successive frames with high probabilities of text indicate either start or end credits, depending on their location within the movie. Figure 13 displays the probabilities versus frame numbers, visualized as a graph. The beginning and end of the movie show similar patterns of high-probability frames.

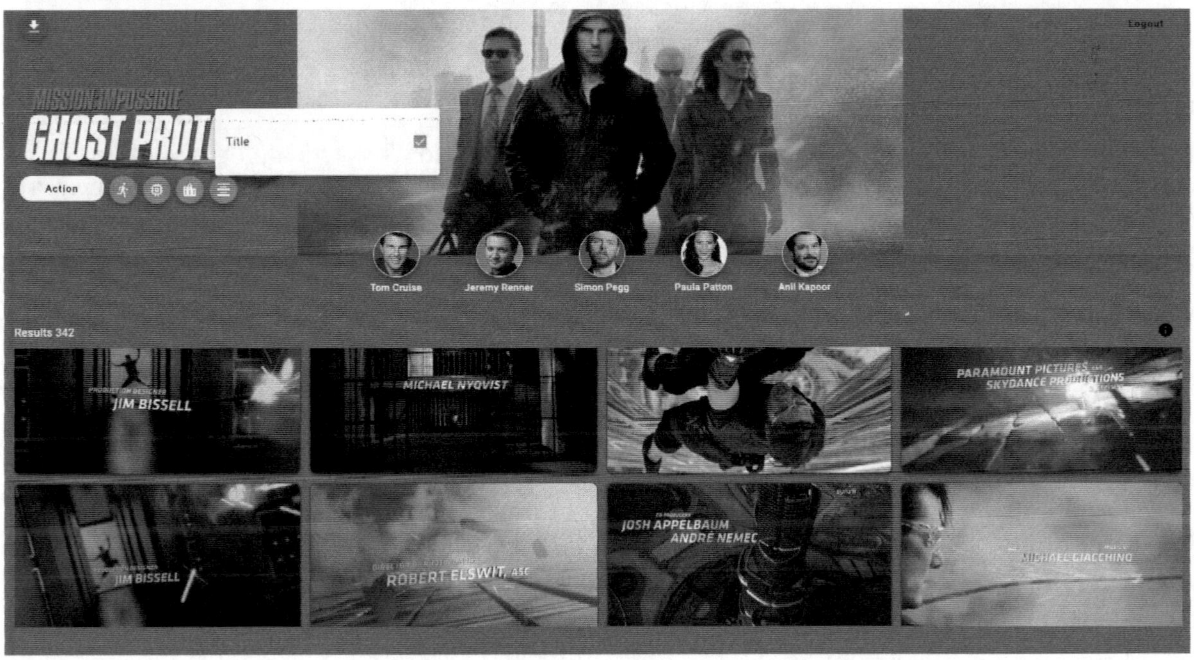


FIGURE 12: SELECTING SCENES WITH START/END CREDITS.

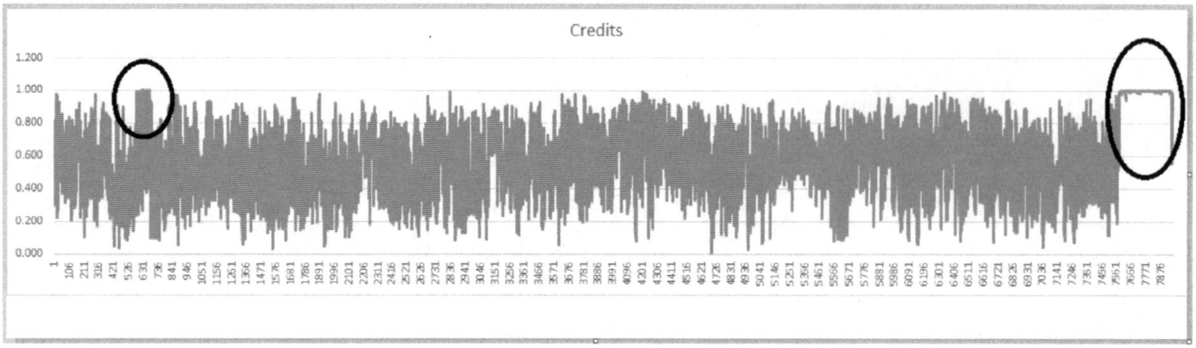


FIGURE 13: DETECTING PATTERNS FOR START/END CREDITS.

Additionally, a time-series plot of genres across the video timeline demonstrates how the genres change throughout the film. Figure 14 displays a section of the time-series plot for the movie Forrest Gump, which starts with comedy as the prevalent genre but shifts to drama and war as time progresses. This provides an excellent opportunity to create specific segments within a movie that can be used for generating mood/genre-based video clips, targeted advertising, and more.

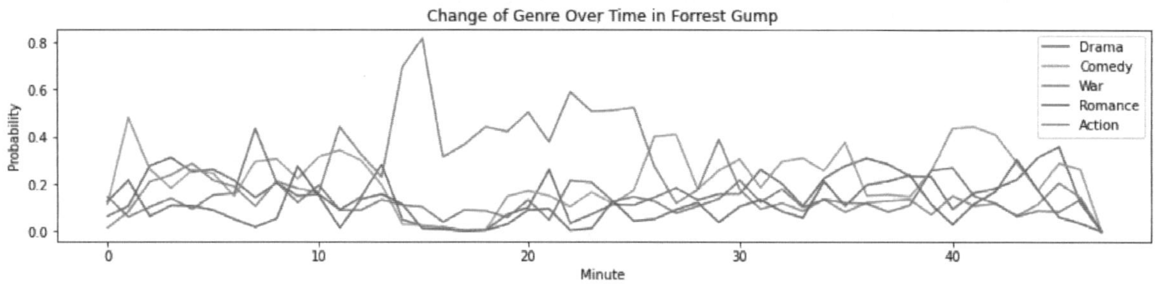


FIGURE 14: CHANGE OF GENRE OVER TIME.

## Conclusion

As the television content landscape becomes increasingly crowded with a multitude of streaming applications and content options, media companies need to find ways to differentiate themselves from their competitors and attract more customers. One solution for media organizations is to leverage the tools and products enabled through large language models (LLMs) and generative AI. We are witnessing the start of a significant technological shift as cloud and AI technologies converge. With AI tools, media companies can generate content, enrich and extract metadata, personalize the user experience, and automate tasks without the need for a significant investment in AI-model training or hiring a team of expert AI developers. The application built by Quickplay demonstrates how pre-trained AI models can be used to experiment quickly with different use cases, potentially providing a competitive edge over competitors.

## References


[1] RNN, https://en.wikipedia.org/wiki/Recurrent_neural_network

[2] LSTM, https://en.wikipedia.org/wiki/Long_short-term_memory

[3] Multimodal learning, https://en.wikipedia.org/wiki/Multimodal_learning

[4] OpenAI CLIP Model, https://github.com/openai/CLIP

[4] Multimodal AI Research, https://openai.com/blog/tags/multimodal/#:~:text=A%20long%2Dterm%20objective%20of,to%20better%20understand%20the%20world.

[5] Facebook Research's DETR Model, https://github.com/facebookresearch/detr

# Delivering Broadcast Quality, Fully Automated Sports Production Through AI-powered Sports Action Tracking and PTZ Cameras

**David Edwards, Siddhi Imming**
**Vislink**
**Colchester, Essex, United Kingdom**

**Abstract** – With consumer expectations of viewing experience set through watching tier 1 sports productions, sports programmers are searching for solutions that deliver an engaging experience for a cost that reflects the budgets available.

Artificial Intelligence-driven sports production solutions have been available for some time. But to date, the ability to accurately track the sporting action combined with visual clarity has been a challenge.

This paper describes how a panoramic camera system can be implemented to monitor the entire field of play, to feed an Artificial Intelligence (AI) system that identifies the sporting action. Further, this paper describes how the AI engine can drive a high-quality pan-tilt-zoom (PTZ) camera to follow the action to deliver the program feed.

The paper will also discuss how the AI engine can accurately point the PTZ camera - taking into account video and AI processing delays, how those processing latencies can be measured, to forward predict directional vectors and correctly point the program feed camera irrespective of distance from the camera and the variation in angular velocity realized.

## Introduction

Live sports is a major draw for viewing figures for linear broadcasting with such events holding places in the top 10 most watched programs each year across the globe[1].

Sporting programming delivers high-end production values, achieving a visceral experience that plays to the tribal needs of watching their team win.

There are many sporting events that are yet untapped and a demand amongst the public to consume this content.

With expectations of viewing experience set through watching tier 1 sports productions, sports programmers are searching for solutions that deliver an engaging experience for a cost that reflects the budgets available to produce new sports programming.

---

[1] For example, UK Top 10 TV shows 2022 - TV since 1981 | Barb, US Top 10 TV Shows 2022 - Most watched TV shows in the U.S. 2022 | Statista

Artificial Intelligence driven sports production solutions have been on the market to offer automated production of sports games for some time. But to date, their impact has been limited. The ability to accurately track the sporting action combined with visual clarity has not yet matched the classic production values that viewers have become accustomed to.

To deliver a similar viewing quality experience, the desired sporting action needs to fill the majority of a high-quality, full frame rate camera sensor. Pan-Tilt-Zoom lenses provide a good solution to deliver visual quality and to automate control of where to point the camera.

With a PTZ camera closely following the sporting action, challenges arise in delivering accurate tracking of sporting action across the entire field of play. As human camera operators do, an automated system must monitor the events beyond the field of view of a single, closely zoomed camera lens.

With data processing being required to identify the position of the sporting action within a 3D space, the processing period creates inevitable delays. Technical and predictive measures may be utilized to ensure that the PTZ camera is pointed at the correct area.

## AI Action Tracking – More Than Just Follow the Ball

Automated action tracking in sporting events is a complex task. Simple logical rules cannot accommodate the complexities that arise in following the action played out by sentient humans competing and making rapid decisions to achieve a win. Artificial intelligence technology is however well placed to achieve good accuracy with this task.

Different sports have many different properties and no single coded or learned behavior can be directly transferred from one sport to another. However, there are similarities within different types of sport – ball games, track races, etc.

Within ball-based sports games the best productions are associated with more than just a simple follow the ball action tracking. The play is complex. The ball may go out of play in one location and may come back into play at a different location. The ball may get obscured from camera view whilst the action proceeds. Different on-field players exhibit different behavior – goal keepers, referees.

The gameplay can often involve a cluster of players in the region around the ball for many sections of play. For other segments in a match, if the ball approaches the goalkeeper, it may be best to ensure that both the ball and goalkeeper remain in shot. Consequently, there can be advantages for the AI director engine to have the ability to recognize different types of players and players from different teams.

FIGURE 1: IN BALL SPORTS, MACHINE LEARNING AI ALGORITHMS CAN DETECT THE AREA OF SPORTING PLAY AS A GROUP OF PLAYERS NEAR THE BALL.

For track sports, it can again be important for the AI engine to differentiate between different on-track people. A bike race or a horse race may involve assistants who participate in the start or end of the race. The AI engine may need instruction to ignore those people. In short, the AI engine will give a better, more immersive production if it is context aware of the start and of the race.

## When Is a Ball Not A Ball? When It Is a Head

Achieving accuracy in tracking the sporting action is of key importance in televising an event. Missing a goal in a soccer game or the winner crossing the line in a track event would be bad. Care needs to be taken to ensure that it can differentiate between key action elements and false objects.

In soccer, some on-screen objects can be mistaken for the ball – the penalty spot for example, or the head of the coach standing on the sideline. For track racing sports, the sporting action takes place on the track. By including positional rules into the AI director, false positives of sporting action can be reduced and accuracy of action improved.

FIGURE 2: IN BALL SPORTS ADDITIONAL WORK IS NEEDED TO ENSURE THE AI SYSTEM CAN DIFFERENTIATE A BALL FROM A HEAD, OR, FOR EXAMPLE A PENALTY SPOT.

## The Quality Problem

### Lens Quality Matters

For many years the general public has been exposed to marketing messages from smartphone and camera manufacturers that more pixels deliver greater quality images. For AI sports systems, as with consumer imaging products this can be true. With digital camera systems there must be at least one pixel spacing between two objects for the objects to be resolved as separate elements. For this reason, existing AI sports production systems have moved to high resolution cameras.

Should the pixel resolution of the image sensor greatly exceed the resolution of the lens, further increases in the number of image pixels can deliver few additional resolution benefits. Driving to ever higher pixel resolution is not the only answer.

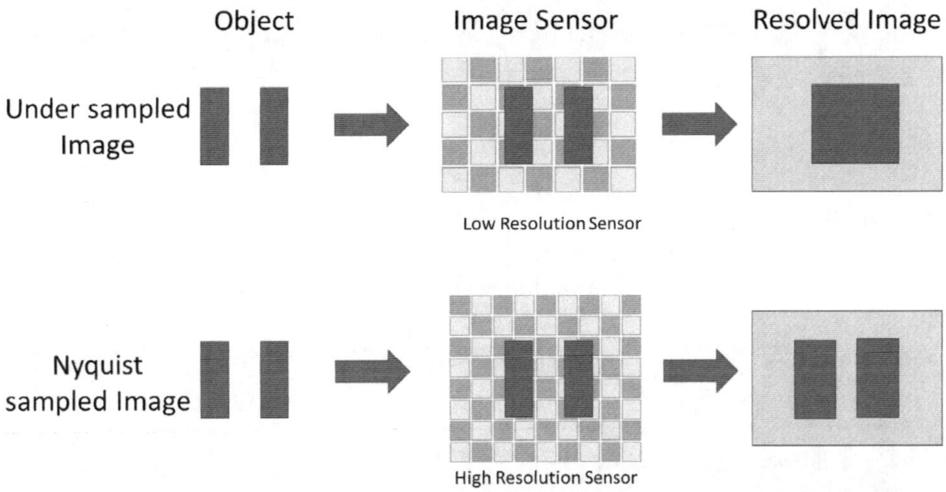


FIGURE 3: IMAGE QUALITY CAN BE IMPROVED WITH HIGHER RESOLUTION SENSORS.

There are limits to image quality gains that increased pixel increases can deliver to the benefit of image clarity. The drive to increased pixel resolution images for AI sports production systems can create their own problems. More image data requires more computational power - potentially driving up image processing latencies or system cost.

Lens quality can be vital in delivering high-quality images. Lower quality lenses are likely to deliver softer images containing greater levels of distortion and diffraction effects, which can limit the usability of closely digitally zoomed (cropped) sections of the image.

The Rayleigh Criterion, dealing with diffraction effects, expressed with the equation:

$$\theta = 1.22 \frac{\lambda}{D} \tag{1}$$

tells us that two objects can be better resolved, related to their angle of separation θ if the lens aperture or lens diameter is larger.

A larger lens can also allow use of a larger image sensor. A larger image sensor with less densely packed pixels can deliver reduced camera noise and a sharper image – particularly in lower light conditions. With many sporting events scheduled for evening fixtures or inside arenas, it is not always possible to provide TV studio light levels. Low light performance from the camera system can be important.

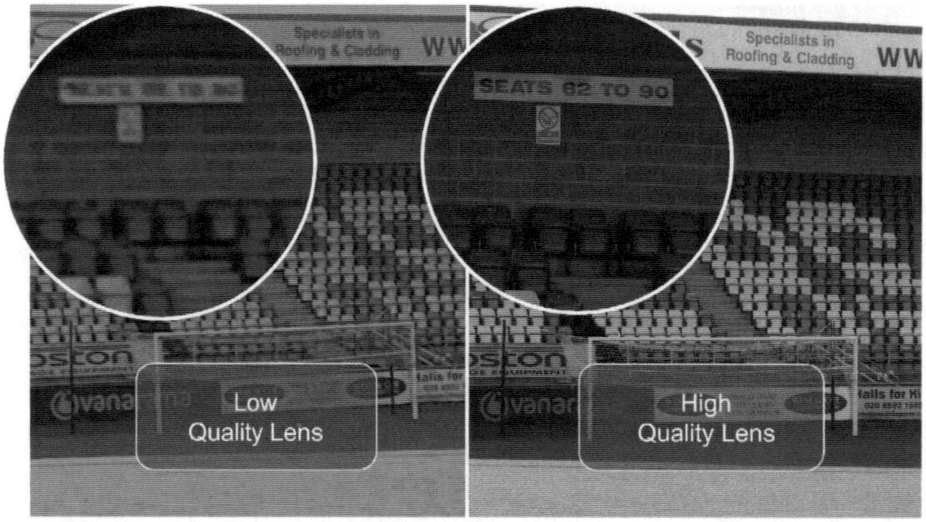


FIGURE 4: OBSERVING THE DIFFERENCE IN IMAGE CLARITY BETWEEN A LOW QUALITY AND A HIGH-QUALITY LENS.

## Creating a Composite Image

Multi-lens panoramic cameras equipped with smaller sized lenses are very capable at delivering individual images that are suitable for being digitally stitched together into a panoramic image.

FIGURE 5: A STITCHED MULTI-LENS PANORAMIC IMAGE PRIOR TO DE-WARPING. BLENDING AFFECT CAN BE OBSERVED IN THE HIGHLIGHTED AREA.

The lenses can be physically spaced close to each other. With minimal parallax effects, it is possible to stitch together overlapping images to create a single multi-image that does not suffer from large parallax discontinuities – but they can still be present, especially for objects close to the camera.

FIGURE 6: A VISLINK MVP XCAM MULTI-LENS PANORAMIC CAMERA.

FIGURE 7: PARALLAX ERROR – OVERHANGING ROOF OF THE STAND CLOSE TO THE CAMERA DOES NOT GIVE QUITE THE SAME PERSPECTIVE BETWEEN TWO CAMERA LENSES IN THIS COMPOSITE/STITCHED IMAGE.

Parallax errors risk becoming greater when accommodating larger lenses and larger image sensors because the lenses need to be physically spaced with greater separation. It therefore becomes more difficult to create stitched images when seeking to use larger lenses in search for image quality gains.

A different approach is therefore required.

**In Search of Better Quality with a PTZ Lens**
One can learn from experience gained from years of manned sports productions that make use of broadcast/studio cameras equipped with large image sensors and high-quality optics to deliver sharp, high contrast images with good color saturation.

With the goal of delivering engaging sports production without carrying the cost profile of a full tier 1 production, the AI driven solution needs to find an intermediate position between high-end studio cameras and multi-lens panoramic cameras.

A Pan-Tilt-Zoom (PTZ) lens is an appealing compromise in delivering a larger, higher quality image sensor capturing content in broadcast native 1080p50 or 60fps video formats in combination with a multi-element zoom lens, which together have the potential to provide sharp images even in lower lighting conditions.

FIGURE 8: PAN-TILT-ZOOM LENS USED BY VISLINK AS PART OF THE AI ACTION TRACKING SYSTEM.

But a single PTZ lens cannot accomplish the task of observing the entire field of play – to identify the progress of the sporting action, and simultaneously provide a close-up shot of the action as it unfurls. An overall view of the entire field of play is also required.

## Integrating a PTZ Camera

In order to deliver on the ability of a PTZ camera to produce AI controlled high-quality, close action of sports events, the AI director needs to have visibility of the entire field of play.

A hybrid system can be used where a wide angle/panoramic view is deployed to find the action whilst a high-quality PTZ camera can be used to capture the action for the program feed.

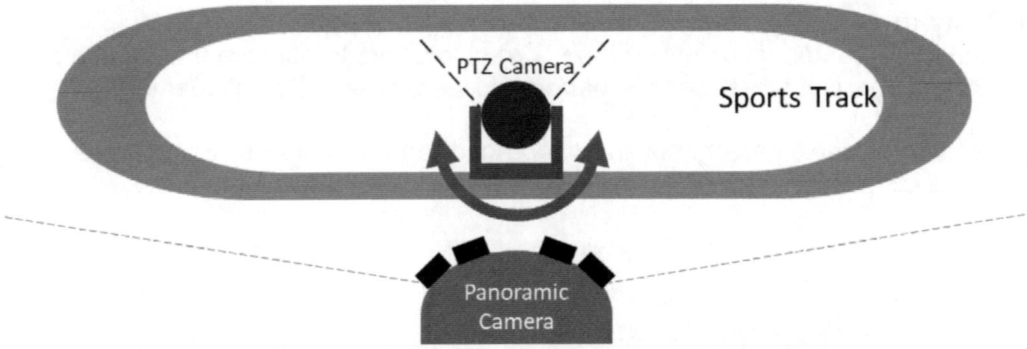


FIGURE 9: SCHEMATIC OF COMBINING A PANORAMIC CAMERA AND PTZ CAMERA.

FIGURE 10: INSTALLATION OF COMBINED PTZ CAMERA (TOP) AND PANORAMIC CAMERA (BOTTOM).

Using this hybrid, dual-camera architecture, the AI director, which identifies the sporting action, can operate through the panoramic image and steer the PTZ camera to produce the program feed.

There are however issues that arise from identifying sporting action through one camera and capturing the program feed through a different camera. Data processing latencies become a critical issue. Time is needed for the image processing to stitch together the multi-camera panoramic image to create a composite picture. Time is needed for the AI director to identify the sporting action, calculate the position where the action is taking place and command the PTZ camera to that location. By this time the sum of the time taken to process all these actions often means that the action may have moved on to a different position on the field of play.

## Managing Delay in AI-Controlled PTZ Camera Positioning

To ensure that the PTZ camera is pointing at the correct location, to observe the wanted object, one needs to relate object positions between the panoramic camera and the PTZ camera.

Positioning of sporting objects detected by the panoramic camera and AI system can be referenced using the spherical coordinates system for a 3D space.

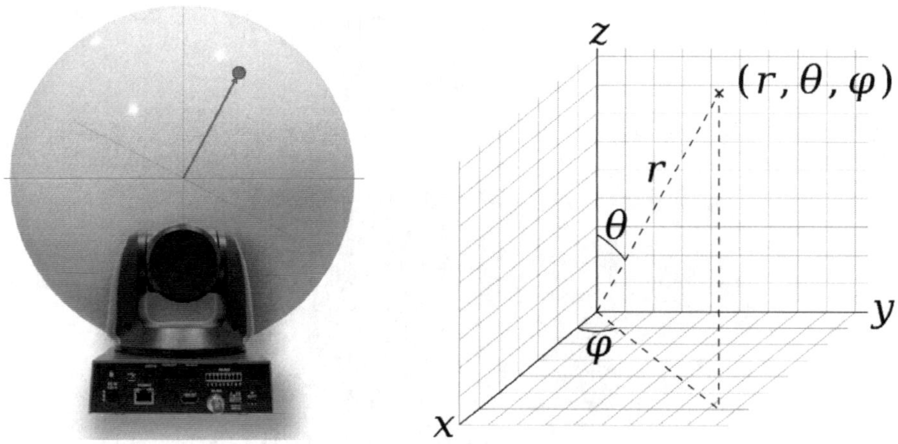


FIGURE 11: OBJECT POSITIONING USING SPHERICAL COORDINATES.

In order to perform positioning prediction and accommodate AI processing delays, the velocity or motion vector of the object needs to be calculated. Vislink has found that these calculations are best performed in the cartesian geometry space. A translation from spherical to cartesian co-ordinates is performed.

Where:

$x=\rho\sin\varphi\cos\theta$
$y=\rho\sin\varphi\sin\theta$
$z=\rho\cos\varphi$

There can be challenges in identifying the precise position of the sporting action. With a camera viewing across the sporting arena, there is a spatial variation in pixel resolution per meter between objects close to and far away from the camera. A reduction in the number of pixels per object can lead to inaccuracies or noise in position estimation.

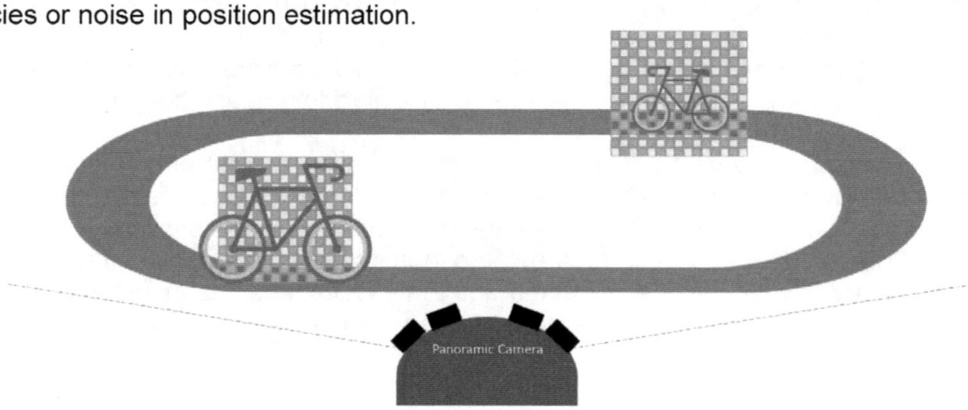


FIGURE 12: REDUCED POSITIONAL RESOLUTION FOR FAR-AWAY FROM THE CAMERA.

Objects, for example bicycles on a velodrome racetrack, are viewed with different perspectives and can be interpreted to have different centers depending on their position as they traverse a racetrack. This difference in viewing perspective can also introduce uncertainties in the object's center and introduce noise into the precise positioning identification and motion estimation.

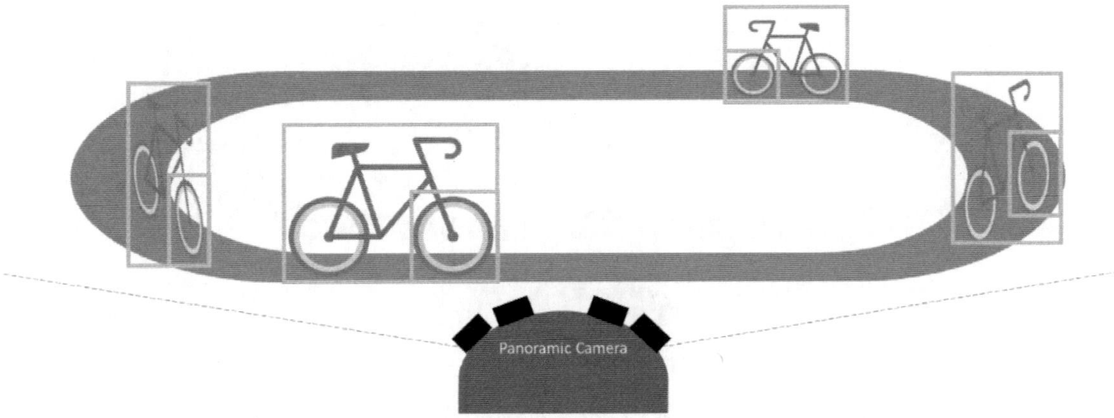


FIGURE 13: RESOLVING POSITIONAL ACCURACY CHANGES WITH DIFFERENT PERSPECTIVES AS AN OBJECT MOVES ACROSS THE SPORTING AREA.

FIGURE 12: EXAMPLES OF DIFFERENT OBJECT POSITIONAL ESTIMATION IN RESPONSE TO DIFFERENT PERSPECTIVES.

Using a predictive algorithm making frequent positional measurements, it can be possible to create a continually updated, accurate estimation of the sporting object motion vectors, which accommodate for the "noise" of variations in velocity and inaccuracies in positional measurement, from the panoramic camera.

With a knowledge of the inherent delay in the panoramic camera image processing and a noise-free AI-based object detection, one can calculate the position of the sporting object.

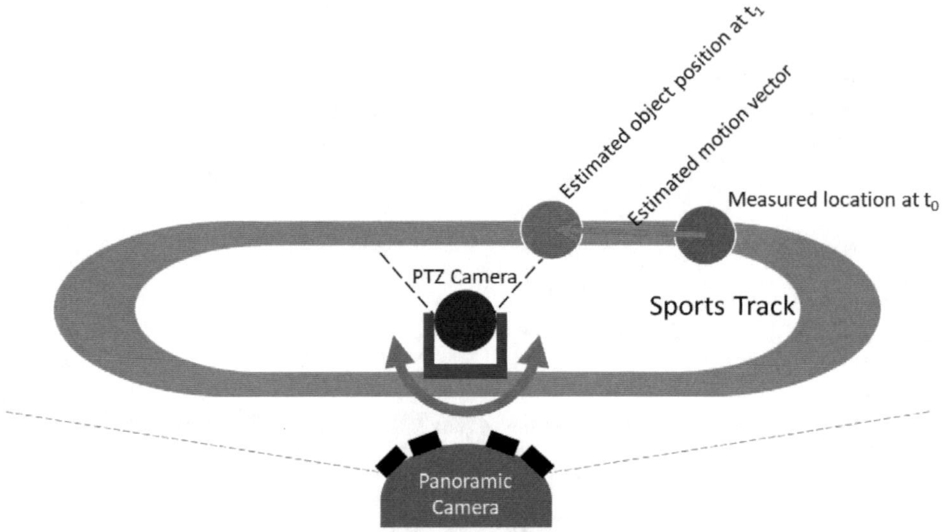


FIGURE 13: CALCULATING OBJECT POSITION FOR A DELAY OF $T_1 - T_0$.

Having estimated the position of the sporting object, compensated for the data processing delays, it becomes possible to map the predicted object location back into spherical coordinates needed for the camera pointing system.

The combination of regular measured object position - through the panoramic camera, plus a regularly refreshed estimated motion vector ensures that PTZ camera pointing accuracy is maintained. As a control system this acts as the measured (delayed) panoramic camera system acting as a feedback loop into the pointing algorithm and the motion vector estimation acting as a feed forward control.

## Managing Angular Acceleration and Velocity

In tracking a moving object with a PTZ camera it is important that the motorized control can keep pace with the action.

Laws of angular velocity and acceleration result in objects moving close to the camera requiring faster tracking than objects further from the camera lens.

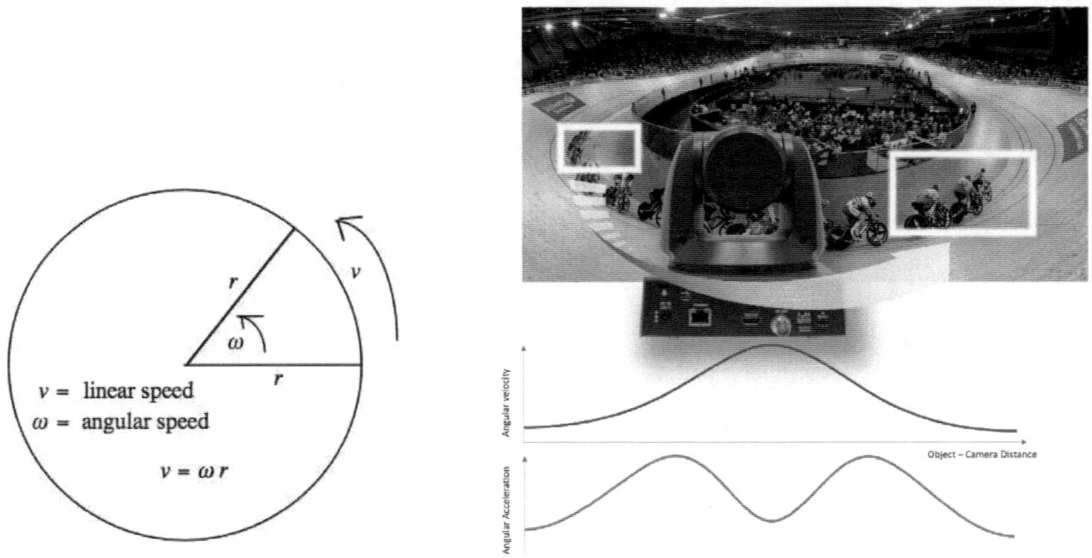


FIGURE 14: ANGULAR VELOCITY AND ACCELERATION.

To accommodate high speed tracking, the gearing mechanisms and speed of PTZ tracking motors need special attention. The ability to pan (and tilt) a camera at speed can create difficulties in enabling rapid pan acceleration and maintaining smooth and accurate tracking.

Camera positioning choice can partly alleviate the issue of finding the best balance of pan speed and acceleration. Positioning the camera further from the action can of course reduce the angular velocity that the camera needs to accommodate. For image quality reasons though, closer is often better. In practical installations however, their choice of camera position is rarely a free choice.

Vislink made some changes to the pan mechanism for its PTZ AI solution to get the best balance of tracking speed, acceleration and smoothness. By transitioning from stepper motor technology to control the pan and tilt of the camera to AC powered servo motors, it becomes possible to get very fast, low inertia motorized positioning in combination with high positional accuracy.

FIGURE 15: VISLINK PAN-TILT CAMERA MOUNT UTILIZING HIGH-SPEED, VERY LOW INERTIA AC SERVO MOTORS.

FIGURE 16: CLOSELY TRACKED SPORTING ACTION UTILIZING AI ACTION TRACKING AND PROGRAM DIRECTION, ORIGINATING FROM A PANORAMIC CAMERA WITH THE PROGRAM FEED CAPTURED BY A PTZ CAMERA.

Should the angular velocity required to capture the sporting object still prove too high for the PTZ camera to perform accurate tracking, the option exists to perform a digital pan across the image-plane of the panoramic camera image. One should note that in this situation where the sporting object has maximum angular velocity, the sporting object is likely to be closest to the hybrid panoramic and PTZ camera system, where the panoramic camera is delivering greatest resolution and image clarity.

## Conclusion

Through machine learning, with guidance from production rules, it is now possible to accurately identify sporting action and mimic the production style of human directed sports events. However, to create compelling content the AI generated production not only has to achieve accurate action tracking but also needs to deliver good quality video imaging.

Good quality lenses that allow the viewer to be presented with a high-resolution close-up of the sporting action are essential to viewer enjoyment of the production. PTZ cameras are a good price/quality compromise to deliver providing high quality images. However, since a PTZ is not capable of simultaneously delivering a close-up of the action and observing the entire area of play, a linkage needs to be made between the program feed PTZ camera and a panoramic view, which the AI engine can use to scan to determine the area where the sporting action is taking place.

With intrinsic delays in a panoramic image and computational delays through the AI action tracking algorithms, issues arise in being able to steer the PTZ camera to the location of the sporting action in real time. By linking together action tracking and motion vector estimation algorithms, it is now possible to future predict the location of sporting action.

Sporting action can move rapidly around the field of play. There are challenges in achieving motorization of a PTZ camera that can achieve rapid movement and acceleration of the camera in combination being able to command accurate positional pointing. Replacing traditional stepper motors with AC powered very low inertia servo motors is now being trialed as a camera pointing solution that provides responsive and accurate results.

# AM Radio FCC NRSC Compliance Reports

**James (Jim) Dalke, CPBE, CBNT, 8-VSB, AMD**
**Dalke Broadcast Service, Inc.**
**Bellevue, Wash., United States**
jim@dalke.com

**Martin Hadfield, CPBE**
**The Hadfield Group, LLC**
**Seattle, Wash., United States**
mdhadfield@aol.com

**Abstract** – Every year, each of the more than 4,000 FCC-licensed AM radio stations in the US are required to make and document "NRSC measurements" and place the reports in the station official files. While these measurements can be done by local station engineers, the measurements are relatively complex and can require sophisticated equipment to be completed properly. Compiling the measurements into a document that meets FCC requirements can also be difficult. The number of contract engineers capable of making the making the measurements and providing professional reports continues to decline. The cost of providing these reports is increasing, making it even more difficult for station management to meet the FCC report requirements. This paper discusses some history behind these measurements, reviews the details as specified in the FCC rules and NRSC Standards, and offers suggestions on how to compile the measurement data to create professional reports.

## Introduction and Summary

The authors have been making AM NRSC field measurements and providing professional reports for Pacific Northwest broadcasters.[1] They have been developing procedures and processes to make the necessary field measurements and efficiently compile the data into Federal Communications Commission (FCC) compliant reports.

There are two FCC rule of interest here. The first, CFR 47 Part 73, §73.1590, requires that the licensee of each AM station must make equipment performance measurements for transmitters annually with not more than 14 months between measurements. Next, measurements for spurious and harmonic emissions must be made to show compliance with the transmission system requirements of the second rule of interest, §73.44, AM transmission system emission limitations. At the end of this paper is an example NRSC Compliance Report as prepared for station records and reprints of the FCC rules which require these reports.

## History

Equipment performance measurements have long been an important part of the radio engineer's responsibilities. These measurements have also been referred to as proof of performance measurements. Performance measurements for AM radio stations have been required by the FCC in

[1] The National Radio Systems Committee (NRSC, www.nrscstandards.org) is a technical standards-setting body co-sponsored by the National Association of Broadcasters and the Consumer Technology Association.

This paper is excerpted from the Proceedings of the 2023 NAB Broadcast Engineering and Information Technology (BEIT) Conference, © 2023, National Association of Broadcasters, 1 M Street SE, Washington, DC 20003 USA.

the United States for many decades. The specific requirements and procedures for these tests have evolved over time as the technology and regulatory environment has changed.

One of the earliest examples of proof of performance testing dates back to the early days of radio broadcasting in the United States. In the 1920s, the Department of Commerce (and later, the FCC) required all radio stations to regularly test their equipment to ensure that it was operating within specified parameters. Since then, the FCC has continued to require periodic proof-of-performance testing for AM radio stations as part of its regulatory oversight of the broadcasting industry.

In 1991, the FCC adopted rules requiring AM radio stations to conduct proof-of-performance testing using procedures recommended by the NRSC. Since then, the NRSC has continued to play an important role in developing and updating technical standards and testing procedures for AM radio broadcasting. The NRSC works closely with the FCC and other industry stakeholders to ensure that its recommendations are effective in promoting high-quality and reliable broadcasting while also reflecting changes in technology and industry practices, in particular with respect to the development of HD Radio AM band and FM band digital radio systems.

## FCC Rule Requirements

FCC rule §73.44 defines the spectral limits of the signal coming from the AM station transmitter as well as the limits of the harmonics and intermodulation products of the AM transmission system.

The rule specifically states that "Emissions 10.2 kHz to 20 kHz removed from the carrier must be attenuated at least 25 dB below the unmodulated carrier level, emissions 20 kHz to 30 kHz removed from the carrier must be attenuated at least 35 dB below the unmodulated carrier level, emissions 30 kHz to 60 kHz removed from the carrier must be attenuated at least [5 + 1 dB/kHz] below the unmodulated carrier level, and emissions between 60 kHz and 75 kHz of the carrier frequency must be attenuated at least 65 dB below the unmodulated carrier level. Emissions removed by more than 75 kHz must be attenuated at least 43 + 10 Log (Power in watts) or 80 dB below the unmodulated carrier level, whichever is the lesser attenuation, except for transmitters having power less than 158 watts, where the attenuation must be at least 65 dB below carrier level."

This rule was developed through the efforts of the NRSC and has been published in NRSC-2-C, *Emission Limitation for Analog AM Broadcast Transmission Standard*, April, 2018. Table 1 and Figure 1 are from this publication.

## Making the Measurements

FCC rule §73.44 provides, in part (a), the required setup for the use of a "swept frequency RF spectrum analyzer" (SA) for making the measurements to show compliance with the emission requirements. It states that the SA be set at 300 Hz resolution bandwidth (RBW) and no video filter (or with the video filter set to at least three times the RBW, see NRSC-2-C section 4.3.2). The SA is to be set for peak hold for 10-minute minimum durations.

The authors recommend that two SA scans be made, one with a 50 kHz span and the other with a 200 kHz span. Typically, SAs provide an option to save as a screen capture or save as a data set. To provide a simple graph with the report, the authors suggest saving the data set as a comma separated value (CSV) file and importing it to an Excel spreadsheet which can then be used to generate a graph of the results.

| Frequency band relative to carrier (± kHz) | Minimum Attenuation relative to carrier (dB) |
|---|---|
| 0 to 10.2 | 0 |
| 10.2 to 20 | at least 25 |
| 20 to 30 | at least 35 |
| 30 to 60 | at least (5 + 1 dB/kHz) from carrier † |
| 60 to 75 | at least 65 † |
| Beyond 75 | at least 80 † |

*† For carrier power levels between 158 and 5000 watts, the minimum attenuation from carrier reference level for emissions more than 75 kHz from carrier frequency shall be (43 + 10logPW) dB (where PW is the carrier power in watts) or as indicated in Table 1, whichever is lesser attenuation. For carrier power levels less than 158 watts, a 65 dB minimum attenuation shall apply.*

TABLE 1. RF MASK FOR ANALOG AM BROADCAST STATION SPECTRUM OCCUPANCY. SOURCE - NRSC-2-C.

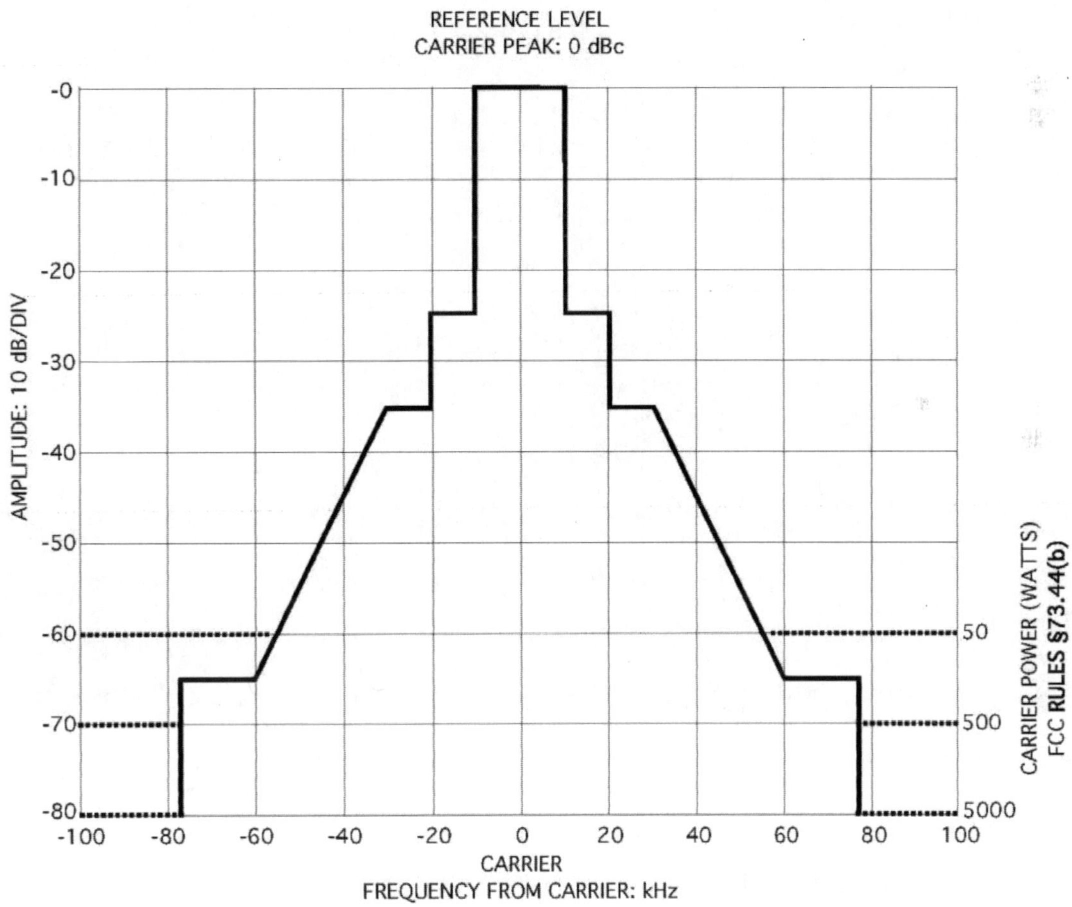


FIGURE 1. ANALOG AM BROADCAST RF EMISSION LIMITS. SOURCE: NRSC-2-C.

Part (d) specifies that the measurements should be made at ground level approximately 1 kilometer from the center of the antenna system. For directional stations, the authors suggest that the measurements be made in a major lobe of the directional pattern. There are times the distance to the transmitter needs to be adjusted because of high noise levels and terrain obstructions. In general, the measurement location should be far enough away to eliminate near-field distortions and produce maximum signal-to-noise ratio. A photo of author Jim Dalke making an NRSC measurement is provided in Figure 2.

FIGURE 2. AUTHOR JIM DALKE PREPARING TO MAKE THE NRSC FIELD MEASUREMENTS FOR THE STATION IN THE BACKGROUND. THE FIELD METER NEXT TO THE SA IS USED TO CHECK HARMONICS.

## Harmonics and Intermodulation

While the spectral scans for the 50 kHz and 200 kHz graphs are the primary object of the emission report, emissions beyond ±75 kHz must be attenuated from about 63 dB to 80 dB below the unmodulated carrier level, depending on the transmitter power output. There are two major sources of these unwanted emissions, harmonics, and intermodulation products. Regarding harmonics, in an AM transmitter, the modulated signal is applied to the carrier wave to produce the modulated radio signal. However, the process of modulation also produces harmonics, which are frequencies that are multiples of the carrier frequency. These harmonics can cause interference with other radio signals, so it's important to minimize them. Harmonics are relatively easily detected on an AM receiver tuned to multiples of the carrier frequency. The second and third harmonics can usually be detected and measured with a standard Potomac Instruments FIM-41 field strength meter.

Intermodulation (IM) is an interference phenomenon that can be created by AM radio stations. IM occurs when two or more signals with different frequencies interact in transmitters and transmission systems or in a listener's receiver. Intermodulation can easily occur in multiplexed stations (two or more stations sharing a tower or array of towers) or from different stations with antennas or antenna arrays located in close geographic proximity.

The formula for intermodulation products calculates the IM frequencies produced by the nonlinear mixing of two or more frequencies in a system. The formula can be expressed as

$$f_{IM} = Mf1 \pm Nf2 \tag{1}$$

Where: $f_{IM}$ is the intermodulation product frequency, f1 and f2 are the frequencies of the two signals which are mixing (in this case the AM carrier frequencies), and M and N = 0, 1, 2, 3,... For example, if two AM stations operating on frequencies of 1050 kHz and 1250 kHz are mixing in a nonlinear manner, the third-order intermodulation products can be calculated as:

$$f_{IM1} = 2f1 - f2 = 850 \text{ kHz} \tag{2}$$
$$f_{IM2} = 2f2 - f1 = 1450 \text{ kHz} \tag{3}$$

Third-order IM products are of particular interest because they are usually the strongest (*i.e.*, highest in amplitude) and it happens that the third-order IM products of transmitters in the AM broadcast band fall typically fall within the AM band making them relatively easy to detect using the FIM-41 field strength meter.

## Sample NRSC Emissions Compliance Report

The following pages represent a sample report which satisfies the FCC rule requirements and can be stored with the stations' official records. The report consists of the first page documenting how, where, and who made the measurements, while the second page shows the graphical results of the spectrum measurements (there would be two sets of graphs for stations operating different modes day and night). A final page is included which is a copy of the related FCC rules pertaining to the measurements.

# <Company name here>

PO Box 4321, Anytown, USA 12345

<Today's date>

RE: <station call sign> NRSC Compliance Measurements

The attached spectrum analyzer graphs are records of measurements taken to demonstrate compliance of station <station call sign>, Anytown, USA with the transmitter system emission requirements specified in §73.44 of the FCC Rules and Regulations. These measurements were taken on <measurement date> at location <latitude>, <longitude> (WGS84) using a <model name and number> Spectrum Analyzer and a <model name and number> Loop Antenna. The spectrum analyzer was adjusted as specified in §73.44(a).

***<Engineer's signature here>***

**<engineer name>, <qualifications such as PE or SBE certification>**

<engineer name> is a Society of Broadcast Engineers Certified Professional Broadcast Engineer and FCC GROL License <example credentials shown>

## NRSC SPECTRUM ANALYSIS

50 kHz Span

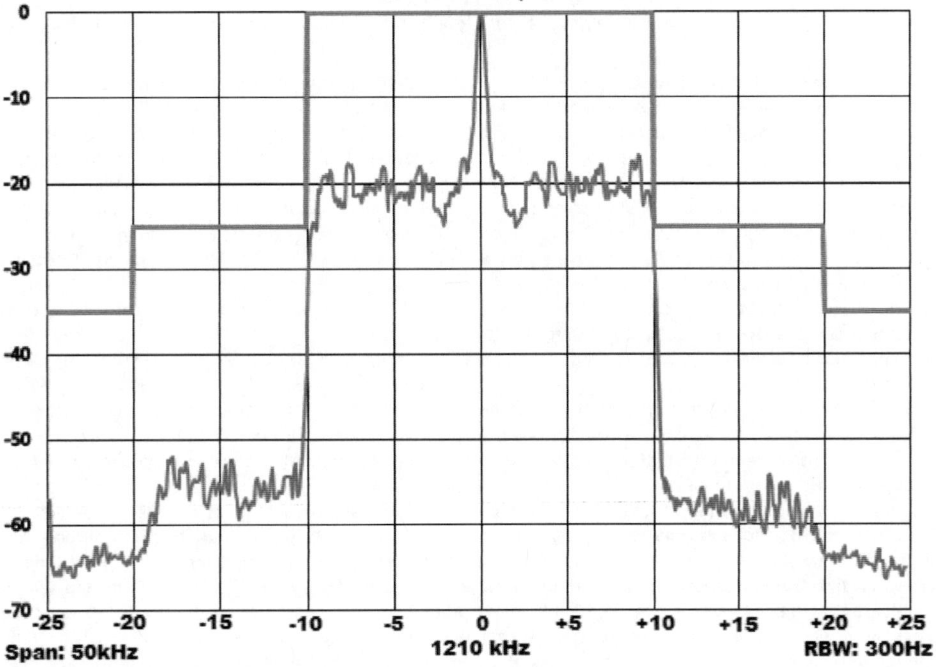


200 kHz Span

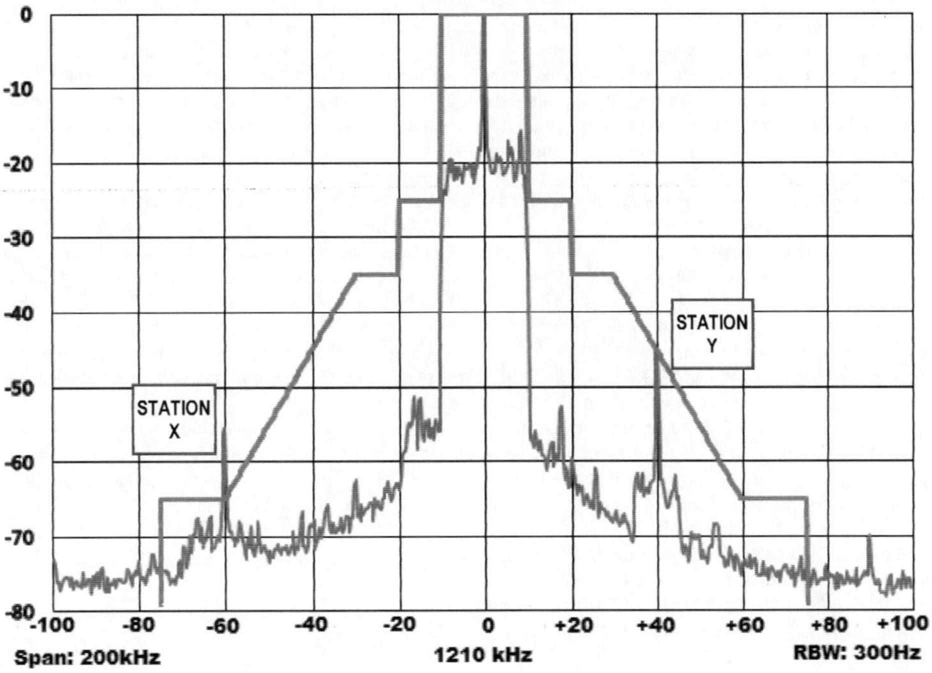

*The following excerpts from the FCC regulations are related to the required AM Emissions Measurements in this report.*

# Code of Federal Regulations Title 47

Telecommunication, Parts 70-79

Revised as of October 1, 2021

**§ 73.44 AM transmission system emission limitations.**

(a) The emissions of stations in the AM service shall be attenuated in accordance with the requirements specified in paragraph (b) of this section. Emissions shall be measured using a properly operated and suitable swept-frequency RF spectrum analyzer using a peak hold duration of 10 minutes, no video filtering, and a 300 Hz resolution bandwidth, except that a wider resolution bandwidth may be employed above 11.5 kHz to detect transient emissions. Alternatively, other specialized receivers or monitors with appropriate characteristics may be used to determine compliance with the provisions of this section, provided that any disputes over measurement accuracy are resolved in favor of measurements obtained by using a calibrated spectrum analyzer adjusted as set forth above.

(b) Emissions 10.2 kHz to 20 kHz removed from the carrier must be attenuated at least 25 dB below the unmodulated carrier level, emissions 20 kHz to 30 kHz removed from the carrier must be attenuated at least 35 dB below the unmodulated carrier level, emissions 30 kHz to 60 kHz removed from the carrier must be attenuated at least [5 + 1 dB/kHz] below the unmodulated carrier level, and emissions between 60 kHz and 75 kHz of the carrier frequency must be attenuated at least 65 dB below the unmodulated carrier level. Emissions removed by more than 75 kHz must be attenuated at least 43 + 10 Log (Power in watts) or 80 dB below the unmodulated carrier level, whichever is the lesser attenuation, except for transmitters having power less than 158 watts, where the attenuation must be at least 65 dB below carrier level.

(c) Should harmful interference be caused to the reception of other broadcast or non-broadcast stations by out of band emissions, the licensee may be directed to achieve a greater degree of attenuation than specified in paragraphs (a) and (b) of this section.

(d) Measurements to determine compliance with this section for transmitter type acceptance are to be made using signals sampled at the output terminals of the transmitter when operating into an artificial antenna of substantially zero reactance. Measurements made of the emissions of an operating station are to be made at ground level approximately 1 kilometer from the center of the antenna system. When a directional antenna is used, the carrier frequency reference field strength to be used in order of preference shall be:

(1) The measure non-directional field strength.

(2) The RMS field strength determined from the measured directional radiation pattern.

(3) The calculated expected field strength that would be radiated by a non-directional antenna at the station authorized power.

(e) Licensees of stations complying with the ANSI/EIA-549-1988, NRSC-1 AM Preemphasis/Deemphasis and Broadcast Transmission Bandwidth Specifications (NRSC-1), prior to June 30, 1990 or from the original commencement of operation will, until June 30, 1994, be considered to comply with paragraphs (a) and (b) of this section, absent any reason for the Commission to believe otherwise. Such stations are waived from having to make the periodic measurements required in § 73.1590(a)(6) until June 30, 1994. However, licensees must make measurements to determine compliance with paragraphs (a) and (b) of this section upon receipt of an Official Notice of Violation or a Notice of Apparent Liability alleging noncompliance with those provisions, or upon specific request by the Commission.

[47 FR 8588, Mar. 1, 1982, as amended at 49 FR 3999, Feb. 1, 1984]

**§ 73.1590 Equipment performance measurements.**

(a) The licensee of each AM, FM, TV and Class A TV station, except licensees of Class D non-commercial educational FM stations authorized to operate with 10 watts or less output power, must make equipment performance measurements for each main transmitter as follows:

(1) Upon initial installation of a new or replacement main transmitter.

(2) Upon modification of an existing transmitter made under the provisions of § 73.1690, Modification of transmission systems, and specified therein.

(3) Installation of AM stereophonic transmission equipment pursuant to § 73.128.

(4) Installation of FM subcarrier or stereophonic transmission equipment pursuant to § 73.295, § 73.297, § 73.593 or § 73.597.

(5) Installation of TV stereophonic or subcarrier transmission equipment pursuant to §§ 73.669 and 73.1690.

(6) Annually, for AM stations, with not more than 14 months between measurements.

(7) When required by other provisions of the rules or the station license.

(b) Measurements for spurious and harmonic emissions must be made to show compliance with the transmission system requirements of § 73.44 for AM stations; § 73.317 for FM stations and § 73.687 for TV stations. Measurements must be made under all conditions of modulation expected to be encountered by the station whether transmitting monophonic or stereophonic programs and providing subsidiary communications services.

(c) TV visual equipment performance measurements must be made with the equipment adjusted for normal program operation at the transmitter antenna sampling port to yield the following information:

(1) Field strength or voltage of the lower side-band for a modulating frequency of 1.25 MHz or greater, (including 3.58 MHz for color), and of the upper side-band for a modulating frequency of 4.75 MHz or greater.

(2) Data showing that the waveform of the transmitted signal con-forms to that specified by the standards for TV transmissions.

(3) Photographs of a test pattern taken from a receiver or monitor connected to the transmitter output.

(4) Data showing envelope delay characteristics of the radiated signal.

(5) Data showing the attenuation of spurious and harmonic radiation, if, after type acceptance, any changes have been made in the transmitter or associated equipment (filters, multiplexer, etc.) which could cause changes in its radiation products.

(d) The data required by paragraphs (b) and (c) of this section, together with a description of the equipment and procedure used in making the measurements, signed and dated by the qualified person(s) making the measurements, must be kept on file at the transmitter or remote control point for a period of 2 years, and on request must be made available during that time to duly authorized representatives of the FCC.

[47 FR 8589, Mar. 1, 1982, as amended at 51 FR 18450, May 20, 1986; 65 FR 30004, May 10, 2000]

# How AI Can Reduce Energy Consumption and Drive Sustainability in FM Radio Broadcasting

**Daniel Werbrouck**
**WorldCast Systems**
**Bordeaux, France**

**Abstract** – With energy costs soaring across the globe, reducing energy consumption is increasingly a top priority among radio broadcasters, to reduce operating costs as well as to meet the world's growing need to implement greener solutions. In the broadcasting chain, the transmitter represents the most impactful device from an energy-usage perspective, as it continuously delivers a fixed output power to the antenna. In the FM chain, transmitters go from a few watts to dozens of kilowatts depending on the coverage area, landscape and radio listeners' profile. To support broadcasters in meeting their sustainability goals and economic challenges, a technique called SmartFM is described in this paper that enables up to 40% lower energy consumption.

## Project Genesis

Frequency modulation (FM) radio broadcasting, using VHF band II (87.5 MHz to 108 MHz), is one of the few broadcasting standards adopted by all the countries in the world, with some relatively minor variations. The adoption of a single worldwide standard has allowed manufacturers to develop very low-cost receivers, accessible even to the populations of emerging countries which as a logical consequence have adopted FM radio as an essential means of mass communication. FM technology was originally deployed in 1955 / 1956; standards and recommendations quickly established the technical rules defining the conditions of transmission and reception.

Today, other than in very exceptional cases, FM broadcasting stations transmit 24 hours a day, 365 days a year; this implies continuous operation of all the transmitters that make up FM radio networks. The cost of energy is constantly increasing, and very unlikely to decrease or even stabilize in the short and medium term, constituting an increasingly significant item in the management of operating expenses.

This paper describes the results of a study using different assumptions based on the technological evolution of FM transmitters and the actual performance of modern receivers in order to develop a breakthrough concept in the broadcast and qualitative analysis of an FM signal.

## The Problem at Hand

A transmitter is made up of different stages including one or more power blocks capable of supplying from a few watts to 10 kW, for standard models. The efficiency of a 10 kW transmitter is about 75% (an average of the better transmitters on the market), meaning that 75% of the prime electrical power provided to the transmitter is emitted as desired RF energy. This translates into a direct electrical power consumption of about 13.3 kW per hour, 24 hours a day. Additional power consumption attributable to the FM transmission also includes indirect consumption, such as the forced ventilation of the transmitters' amplifier stages and a portion of the air conditioning of the premises housing the transmitters; these collateral costs are directly proportional to the dissipation of the transmitters, which is directly related to the output power of each transmitter.

Moreover, the reliability of a transmitter is also closely linked to the operating temperature of the power components (*i.e.*, transistors): this reliability decreases according to a geometrical progression in relation to higher temperatures of the RF block (amplifier and power supply).

Purely technological efforts have made it possible to significantly improve the efficiency of transmitters over the years but it is not expected to improve significantly beyond the current state, as the theoretical limits of physical optimization of components have almost been reached.

In order to obtain significant additional energy savings, designers must therefore focus on the structural fundamentals of FM, by imagining a concept that combines the tremendous progress made by transmitters and receivers in terms of performance, with "intelligent" transmission management. This idea, which has many benefits, raises a major concern: the listening comfort of the listener cannot and must not be altered in any way. This is the achieved design goal of SmartFM.

## State-of-the-Art and Current Status

The International Telecommunication Union - Radiocommunication sector (ITU-R), based in Geneva, Switzerland, is the organization responsible for the definition and evolution of international technical rules, with each member country being responsible for adopting them through its own regulatory body. The ITU-R has 193 member countries.

The basic standards for the transmission of an FM sound broadcasting program were established in the 1950s and 1960s. They have evolved very little on the fundamental level, nor on the minimum intrinsic performance required to meet optimum specifications; when defining a project to set up a station or a network of FM stations.

Over the years, rules have been added defining the broadcasting of sound programs in stereo, the insertion and management of associated digital data in the baseband signal (using Radio Data System, RDS, technology), the definition of adjacent channel protection, the measurement and management of the modulating signal power of the complete FM baseband signal (MPX, consisting of the main audio program and FM subcarriers) and several methodologies concerning the measurement of the field strength received at a given point. (For additional information on FM modulation and standards, see [1]-[6].)

One of the first recommendations written by the ITU-R [7] defines the minimum RF field strength required for nominal listening comfort, according to three types of reception areas (rural, urban and dense urban) and two types of broadcast modes (monophonic and stereophonic). These minimum field strengths were calculated according to the characteristics of the consumer receivers of the time, the noise levels observed in VHF band II and, of course, signal attenuation as a function of distance.

From these minimum field strengths, engineers can define the service areas of each transmitter with complex formulas (nowadays using powerful algorithms for simulating the terrain and exact propagation conditions of the VHF wave, for example, Longley-Rice propagation studies). They can establish the effective radiated power (ERP) needed to obtain these recommended field strengths over a defined service area. It is then very simple to calculate the required output power of the transmitter by subtracting the gain of the selected antenna system.

This ITU-R recommendation was born in 1956, the last revision being in 1998. But for more than 60 years, many technical advances have changed the application of these rules, without the ITU-R changing in-depth the minimum characteristics required for the broadcasting of a sound broadcasting program in FM, VHF band II. What has changed?

## The Positive Points

### The Receivers

Various technological leaps have allowed receivers (in particular, low-cost, entry-level receivers) to increase sensitivity and selectivity performances very significantly. The arrival of semiconductors and specialized integrated circuits with very high gain explains this progress. It can be estimated that the average gain in sensitivity of an entry-level FM receiver is about 10 dB between a model manufactured in 1965 and its counterpart in 2022 [8].

In addition, the front-end RF stages benefit from active components allowing the implementation of a large-amplitude AGC before saturation; the intermediate frequency (IF) amplification stages also have a very important gain function for an operation in permanent saturation which results in a nearly constant signal-to-noise (S/N) ratio on the audio outputs no matter the level of the received field, as soon as these stages reach their effective sensitivity threshold.

Figure 1 below shows received audio S/N ratio as a function of RF signal power for 1965 and 2022 generation FM receivers. The blue curve shows the 1965 receiver performance; this is consistent with ITU-R BS.415-2 [9] which specifies that an FM receiver should have a minimum sensitivity of -75 dBm (32 dBµV or 40 µV) for a signal-to-noise ratio of 30 dB.

The orange curve shows the performance for the 2022 receiver. It is 11 dB higher than that of its predecessor but this receiver benefits above all from a very significantly higher listening comfort (*i.e.*, increased S/N ratio, of +17 dB) in the "standard" working area, *i.e.*, for RF levels above 45 dBµV.

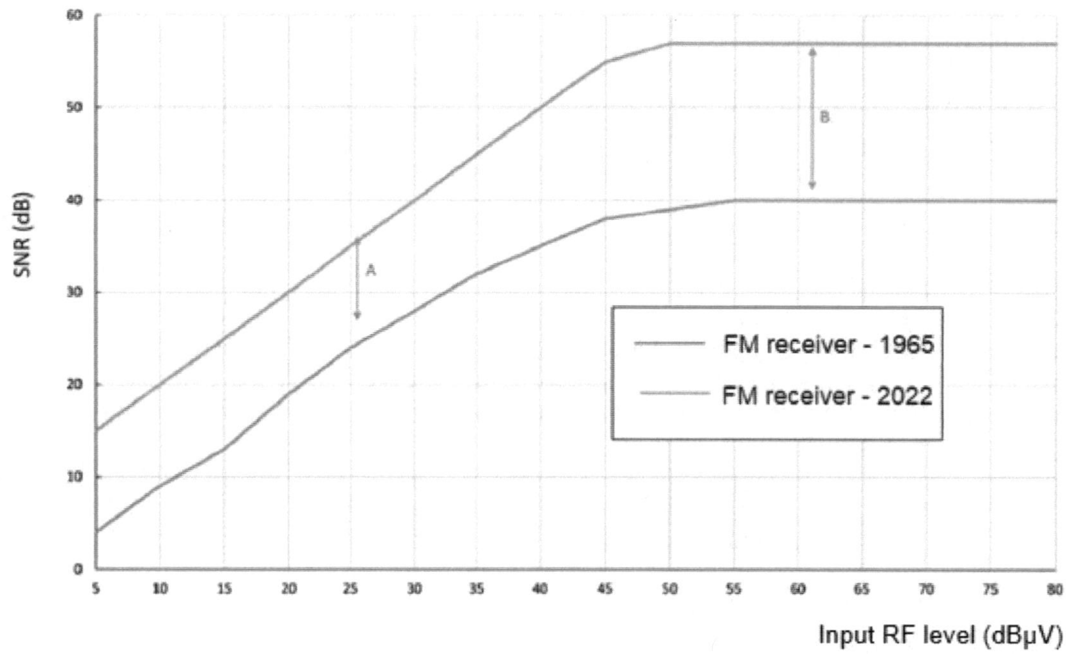


FIGURE 1: LABORATORY MEASUREMENTS ON TWO ENTRY-LEVEL RECEIVERS: ONE MANUFACTURED IN 1965 (TRANSISTORIZED) AND ONE MANUFACTURED IN 2022 (FET + DEDICATED IC). MEASUREMENTS MADE USING AN UNWEIGHTED 30 DB RF SIGNAL-TO-NOISE RATIO, ON A CENTER FREQUENCY OF 98 MHZ, WITH A SINUSOIDAL REFERENCE SIGNAL F = 1 KHZ @ ±40 KHZ OF DEVIATION.

## Sound Processing

From the beginnings of FM until the 1970's and 1980's, the sound signal broadcast by an FM transmitter had a dynamic range almost identical to that of the incoming audio source, *i.e.*, the variation between pianissimos and fortissimos was usually greater than 30 dB, especially for voice, which made background noise perceptible as soon as the RF S/N ratio fell below 40 dB, *i.e.*, as soon as the receiver left its zone of best performance (RF level < 50 dBµV).

From the 1980s onward, tools for processing the sound program (called audio processors) appeared, first in AM and then in FM. This equipment consists of filters that "slice" the spectrum of the audio signal into several frequency bands (generally between 3 and 6); each frequency band of the signal thus obtained then passes through a separate compression/band-limiting tool.

At the audio processor output, the signal is reconstituted by summing the different slices and typically, subcarrier elements are added, as well. This type of processing is now present on almost all FM networks, with more or less depth depending on the type of program and allows, according to the opinion of the station managers, to mark the content with a sound identity recognizable by the listeners with the goal of increasing their loyalty to the station. This audio and multiplex processing drastically limits any transient variation of the sound signal above an absolute threshold (due to compression and limiting) that can vary from -30 dB of the absolute threshold to -6 dB for stations with a very high amount of processing. This reduction in dynamic range can considerably increase the listening comfort by masking the received noise in borderline reception conditions.

It should be remembered that the masking effect over a relatively wide audio spectrum means that a sound signal A that is 10 dB higher than a second sound signal B superimposed onto it is enough to completely mask the latter. In theory, if the received noise is only 10 dB less than the sound signal, this noise is not perceived by the listener. Of course, altering the original dynamics of the sound signal has an impact on fidelity. Used to the extreme, compression can result in a loss of audio quality for the listener.

### FM Transmitters with Digital Modulator

A new technological step has been taken with the design of fully digitally-synthesized FM transmitters, from the modulation input to the generation of the RF FM frequency. This translates into total precision and stability over time of the modulation settings, so that no deviation between two different transmitters operating on the same frequency is possible. This is important in booster overlap areas where a receiver can quickly switch several times from one transmitter to another depending on the reception conditions, without any audible alteration of the sound envelope (assuming that the audio delay differences between the two different transmitters is negligible).

### The Radio Data System (RDS)

In an FM broadcast network, engineers would establish the service area based on the station's target audience. The network was then based on a series of main transmitters and re-transmitters, whose overlaps were supposed to ensure optimal listening comfort.

To achieve this, the transmitter powers were determined so that the electromagnetic field would be at least equal to the recommendations over the entire service area. With the advent of RDS in the 1990s, European listeners largely lost manual control over the choice of the transmitter/frequency to be received in favor of an automatic optimization of listening comfort using the Alternate Frequency (AF) switching feature of RDS. However, the AF function does not generally apply in the US or many other places around the world.

## The Negative Points

The radio environment of the FM band has deteriorated over the years. The success of this broadcasting medium has given rise to numerous networks that have occupied all possible channels in the frequency band, creating a higher level of residual noise across the entire VHF band II spectrum, through the combination of spurious frequencies structurally accompanying each broadcast on a fundamental frequency. Furthermore, the systematic use of sound program processing tools has significantly degraded the level of protection between adjacent channels and generated interference and intermodulation problems in the receivers. Finally, overall radio frequency "noise" has increased (due to, for example, appearance of GSM networks, polluting industrial equipment, etc.), reducing the effective sensitivity of receivers, especially in dense urban areas.

## The Takeaway

The continuous evolutions of FM broadcasting and the related technologies pave the way to an innovative approach of FM broadcasting. Indeed, reducing permanently the RF power of FM transmitter will cause a loss of listeners due to reception issues. Optimizations are only possible if the listeners experience is at the center of these changes. Global efficiency can then be improved.

## The SmartFM Concept

The only technical objective of a radio broadcast chain is to obtain a satisfactory and constant listening comfort over the whole service area of a signal or many signals. Listening comfort is defined above all by the notion of audio S/N ratio, which can be summarized as follows:

When listening to the program, is the listener disturbed by any interfering noises (static, interference and any other sounds that do not belong to the broadcast content)? If the answer to this question is no, it does not mean that there are no interfering noises present, but simply that they are not audible. It is easy to understand that if the listener listens to very soft music, or to a debate made up exclusively of voices, with silences between the various statements, the unwanted noise will become audible or even annoying, compared to listening to modern music made up of electronic instruments covering almost the entire audible spectrum, with a constant level that is almost always maximum. In this case, unwanted noise will be masked and there is little risk that the listener will perceive it. In short, by adapting the audio S/N ratio to the program content, there will be no change in overall listening comfort.

The audio S/N ratio is essentially determined by the amount of field strength received by the receiver antenna, which is partly determined by the transmitted signal power. This radiated power is itself defined by multiplying the RF power of the transmitter by the amplification factor of the antenna array (*i.e.*, antenna gain). Changing the output RF power has a direct impact on the receivers located out of the comfort zone, *i.e.*, the coverage area where the reception quality is not depending on the RF signal received. Nevertheless, depending on the audio signal components and tessitura, these disturbances are not necessarily heard by the human ears. It is then possible to dynamically change the RF output power, with no impact on listeners experience.

The SmartFM process is a non-intrusive system that does not remove, ad or modify the composition of the audio signal, but is essentially based on the proven principle of the time and frequency masking effect of a sound signal, combined with the analysis of the real dynamics of the multiplex signal. The higher the MPX power of the station, the more effective SmartFM usually is.

## The Technical Solution

The SmartFM process involves a device controlling the RF output power of the transmitter according to the expected audio perception from listeners as determined by time and frequency masking effects. The masking effect is the ability for a listener to prioritize specific sounds ahead of others, depending on the environment. Based on this principle, the noise perception may vary a lot depending on the conditions which alters the overall quality for the listener. SmartFM analyzes the masking effect but unlike perceptual audio compression systems, SmartFM does not cause any loss of audio data.

Overall, the denser the sound signal, the more it masks noise and sounds of lower amplitude sounds. Thanks to the presence of audio processing tools, the multiplexed signal reaches density levels never seen in other areas of sound broadcasting. The dynamic range is thus inscribed between two immutable limits only a few decibels apart, whose high threshold is always located at or near the maximum of the authorized deviation (commonly ±75 kHz depending on the country). The masking effect is then maximized with respect to the non-essential and undesirable noises likely to be part of the global signal demodulated by the receiver.

The ear is also insensitive to a small portion of the interfering sounds produced after the disappearance of the masking sound, for durations between 50 and 100 ms, according to the frequency and the amplitude of the masking and masked sounds [10]. This post-masking effect is used here to perform calculations and determine the actions to be taken via the SmartFM algorithm.

### The Implementation Process

The core of the SmartFM invention is based on the following essential points:

- Detailed analysis of the characteristics of the sound signal encapsulated in the composite multiplex signal;

- Real-time measurements of modulation indices, multiplex signal strength, loudness, duration of rapid change in audio signal dynamics;
- Development of algorithms based on audio program format and instantaneous measurements of parameters representative of the audio spectrum.

The data from these processes then enters a processor whose calculations are based on the principle of artificial intelligence (AI), considering the learning and predictive aspect of the actions to be taken, determined according to the behavior of the data analyzed and the presets of the operation.

Once calculated, the power control action is applied to the transmitter's power supply and RF power stage control circuits. The output power is thus "modulated" in accordance with the decided actions.

Figure 2 shows the general organization of the SmartFM process in the FM signal generation and amplification chain.

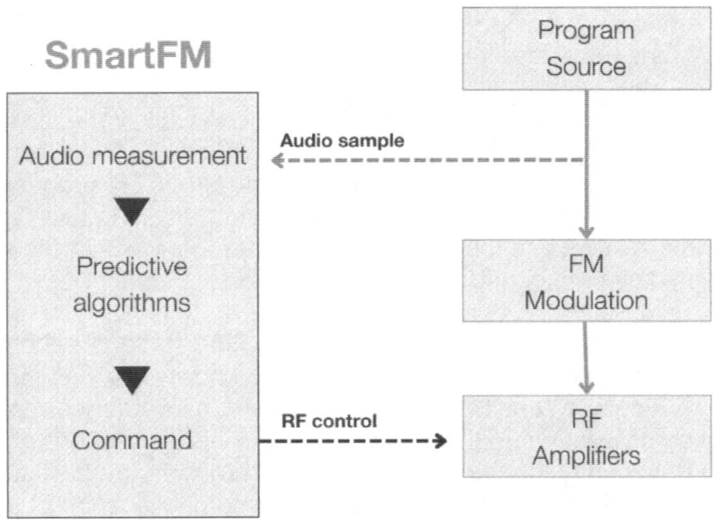


FIGURE 2: GENERAL ORGANIZATION OF SMARTFM PROCESS IN THE FM SIGNAL GENERATION AND AMPLIFICATION CHAIN.

The invention of the SmartFM process is the subject of a patent registered worldwide, under the name EPM (Efficient Power Management) [11].

## On-Air Operation

Deploying SmartFM on an FM broadcast station or network does not require any changes in infrastructure or operating habits. The system is fully autonomous and operates within the scope of the operator's instructions. The RF power of the transmitter can be limited within a maximum configured variation range.

The variation of the power applied to the transmitter has no consequence on the quality of the transmitted signal and does not cause any measurable side effect on the behavior of the receiver that could lead to a degradation of the sound signal. Indeed, the SmartFM algorithm analyzes the audio content without altering it through a sampling line separated from the broadcast chain. The transmitted signal is then identical with and without SmartFM (MPX deviation, MPX power, etc.).

During the analysis of the audio signal, the technology measures key parameters to evaluate the possible power reduction to apply to maintain the same quality of reception for the listener.
At this stage, SmartFM only acts on the RF parameters. Modern FM transmitters are designed to maintain their specification for a given power range. SmartFM power variation range is configured depending on transmitter power capabilities. The specifications of the transmitter remain consistent with and without SmartFM.

In the end, over an average of 24 hours, the apparent power consumption (APC) of the transmitter is reduced by 0 to 40% depending on the sound characteristics of the program broadcast. This means a very real and significant reduction in the energy bill.

Among the other positive effects of SmartFM are the following:

- Overall reduction of transmitter power component temperature rise resulting in longer transmitter life and improved MTBF;
- Reduction of the electrical bill of the cooling equipment due to the reduction of the heat dissipated by the transmitters;
- Reduction of $CO_2$ emissions - by reducing energy consumption, SmartFM contributes to reducing $CO_2$ emissions generated during power generation.

Numerous objective tests and subjective "blind" listening sessions with professional and non-specialist audio listeners of different age groups were conducted in WorldCast Systems' laboratories, following rigorous procedures, to qualify and validate the relevance of the SmartFM process. All the confidential studies performed by WorldCast Systems in the early age of SmartFM showed that the system was completely transparent and that it was impossible for the listener to detect whether the technology was on or off. No alteration of the listening comfort could be detected.

But laboratory tests are not enough to fully validate SmartFM. Pilot stations set up by WorldCast partner customers have made it possible to deploy SmartFM on a few test networks to observe the behavior of the system in particularly sensitive situations. The measurements and listening of these emissions in a real operating context were entrusted to an independent expert to avoid any risk of conflicts of interest and to truly certify the results. These expert reports are particularly positive and confirm all the conclusions already validated in the laboratory: no degradation of listening comfort and no modification of the sound range when SmartFM is activated. Below is graph showing the results from these reports of subjective listening, during drive tests, with and without SmartFM.

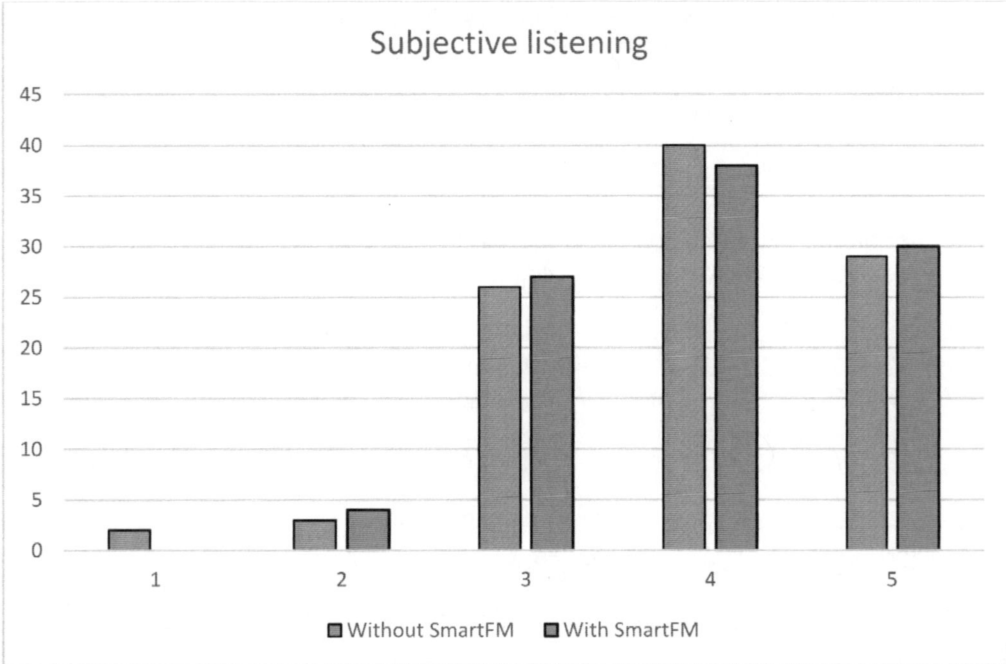


FIGURE 3: SUBJECTIVE LISTENING COMPARISON WITH AND WITHOUT SMARTFM DURING DRIVE TEST. LISTENING GRADE IS SHOWN ON THE X-AXIS (1-POOR TO 5-EXCELLENT) AND PERCENTAGE OF LISTENERS IS SHOWN ON THE Y-AXIS.

To date, major national broadcasters have tested and deployed SmartFM on their networks (for example, see [12]). Very significant savings were immediately observed on the energy consumption of their broadcasting equipment. As an example, Uplink Network (Germany broadcaster) has deployed SmartFM on their network of 850 FM transmitters from 100W to 10kW, resulting in 12% energy savings and 400 tons of CO2, according to Thomas Weiner, COO of Uplink.

## References


[1] ITU-R Recommendation BS.641 – "Determination of radio-frequency protection ratios for frequency-modulated sound broadcasting", International Telecommunication Union Radiocommunication Sector, 07/1986

[2] ITU-R Recommendation BS.704 – "Characteristics of FM sound broadcasting reference receivers for planning purposes", International Telecommunication Union Radiocommunication Sector, 06/1990

[3] ITU-R Recommendation BS.1770-4 – "Transmission standards for FM sound broadcasting at VHF", International Telecommunication Union Radiocommunication Sector, 10/2015

[4] ITU-R Recommendation SM.329-12 – "Unwanted emissions in the spurious domain", International Telecommunication Union Radiocommunication Sector, 09/2012

[5] White paper WHP 202, "Terminology for loudness and level dBTP, LU, and all that", Andrew Mason. BBC, 08/2011

[6] ITU-R Recommendation SM.1268-5 – "Method of measuring the maximum frequency deviation of FM broadcast emissions at monitoring stations", International Telecommunication Union Radiocommunication Sector, 08/2019

[7] ITU-R Recommendation BS.412-9 – "Planning standards for terrestrial FM sound broadcasting at VHF", International Telecommunication Union Radiocommunication Sector, 12/1998

[8] ITU-R Recommendation BS.415-2 – "Minimum performance specifications for low-cost sound broadcasting receivers", International Telecommunication Union Radiocommunication Sector, 07/1986

[9] ITU-R Recommendation BS.450-4 – "Transmission standards for FM sound broadcasting at VHF", International Telecommunication Union Radiocommunication Sector, 10/2019.

[10] Herre, Jurgen, *Psychoacoustic Models for Perceptual Audio Coding—A Tutorial Review*, 2019.

[11] Werbrouck, Daniel, US Patent No. US10985851B2, Method and device for optimizing the radiofrequency power of an FM radiobroadcasting transmitter, April 20, 2021

[12] "Case Study – El Conquistador deploys SmartFM on their Network, WorldCast System, June 2020, https://www.worldcastsystems.com/en/c115d420/category/el-conquistador-chile-deploys-smartfm-on-their-fm-network

# Integral Broadcast Filter Switch

**Anthony Travaglini**
**RF Engineer – Dielectric LLC**
**Raymond, Maine, United States**

**Abstract** – In a typical television or radio RF system, a switch is introduced between the transmitter output filter and transmission line, isolating the external part of the system (transmission line and antenna). The switch provides the capability to proof the transmitter into an RF load or troubleshoot if a problem exists in the transmission line or antenna. In this paper, a new filter technology that allows the integration of the switching into the filter itself will be discussed. There are potential benefits offered by this technique that can be expanded upon to contribute to simplified systems.

## Introduction

Broadcast RF systems consist of 5 very basic components: transmitter, filtering, switching, transmission line run and antenna, as shown in Figure 1. Each of the basic components adds cost and complexity to the overall system. Integrating one or more of the RF components into a single component can help to reduce this cost and complexity.

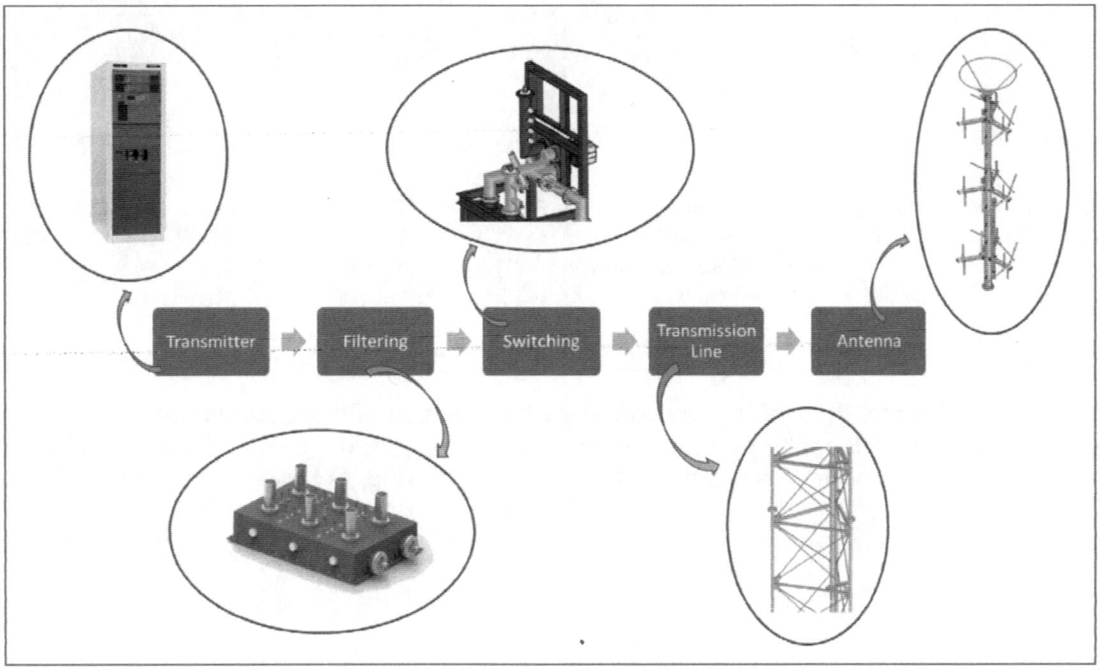


FIGURE 1. BASIC BROADCAST RF SYSTEM.

This paper is excerpted from the Proceedings of the 2023 NAB Broadcast Engineering and Information Technology (BEIT) Conference, © 2023, National Association of Broadcasters, 1 M Street SE, Washington, DC 20003 USA.

Switching provides the flexibility to route RF signals to multiple ports such as the transmission line and antenna or an RF load. Most switches are based on mechanical rotary systems, as shown in Figure 2. The rotary systems can be manual or motorized, each complex and involving a sizeable number of parts.

Filtering is used to remove unwanted signals that lie outside of the RF mask of a licensed channel. The filter, in some cases such as low power television and radio broadcast, is less complex and less expensive than a switch. The purpose of this paper is to introduce a new device that integrates both the filtering and switching functions. The concept provides an economical solution to expensive switches in both high power and low power applications as well as technical benefits in high power combining systems. The device will be referred to as the "filter switch."

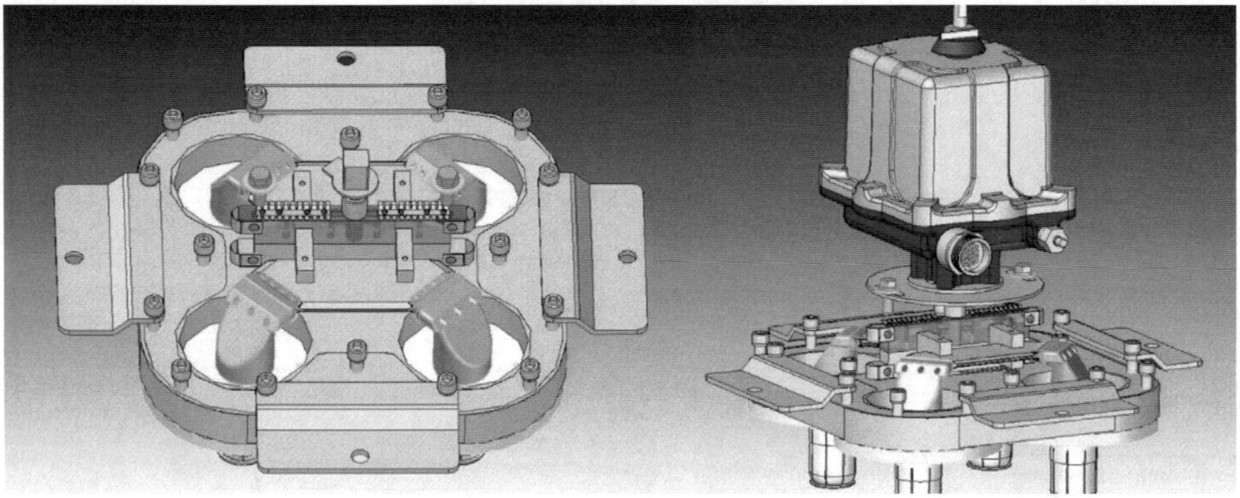

FIGURE 2. BASIC INTERNAL DEPICTION OF A BROADCAST RF ROTARY SWITCH. THE DRIVE SHAFT, CENTERED ABOUT ALL FOUR PORTS, TURNS THE VANE AND PLATES TOGETHER. EACH PLATE CONNECTS TO ONLY TWO PORTS. THE DRIVE SHAFT ROTATES 90° TO CHANGE SYSTEM CONFIGURATION.

## Filter Switch

As suggested by the name, the filter switch combines the function of the filter and switch into a single component. The design philosophy includes adding a secondary output cavity in parallel with the main output cavity as shown in Figure 3 and Figure 4. For proper filtering, only one output can be active at a time.

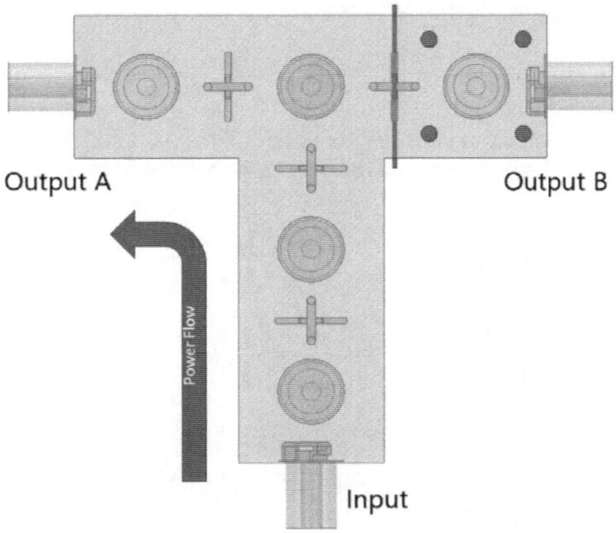


FIGURE 3: BASIC ARCHITECTURE OF THE FILTER SWITCH WITH MULTIPLE OUTPUT CAVITIES. ONLY ONE OUTPUT CAN BE FUNCTIONAL AT ANY TIME. RED PARTS DETUNE THE CAVITY TO REDIRECT POWER TO OPPOSITE OUTPUT.

The goal was to design a detuning mechanism for each cavity to block signal flow in that path when needed without altering the main resonator/coupling features. In other words, detune the un-used path in such a way that the used path yields the desired characteristics of the filter. Figure 4 shows the reversal of outputs as well as a three-dimensional view of the detuning mechanism. High-frequency Structure Simulator (HFSS) analysis proved this would not only be mechanically intensive, but more importantly, this technique would not satisfy the isolation requirements of a typical rotary switch which is upwards of 60 dB. It was determined that the "detuning" needed to be moved external to the resonating cavity. This approach utilizes a strategically located RF short.

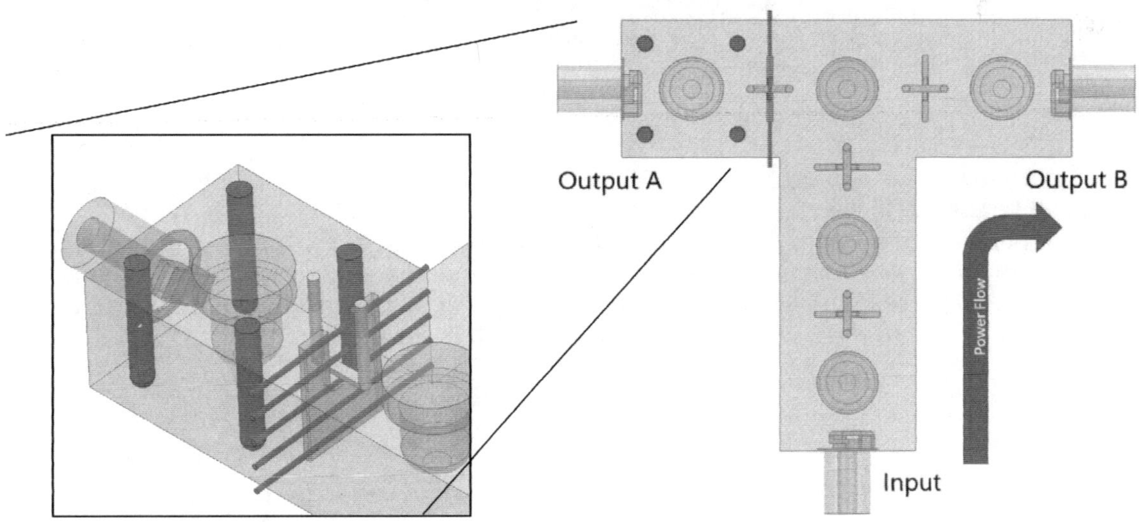


FIGURE 4: POWER FLOWING TO OUTPUT PORT B. RED PARTS ARE DETUNING ELEMENTS.

The concept can be reversed to incorporate two ports in a single cavity. Rather than detuning the cavity of the undesired path, a mechanism situated at each port would control the power flow. Investigations started with an open or short for each port. Each branch of the output occupies either one of two states, open or closed. By manual or motorized means, the RF path can be switched from one output to another using these states.

Depending on the filter style (folded, inline, etc.), the arrangement of ports becomes vital. For example, a folded filter has the input and output on the same plane. The additional port would be 90° offset, causing internal asymmetry in the coupling/resonance to each port, as shown in Figure 5.

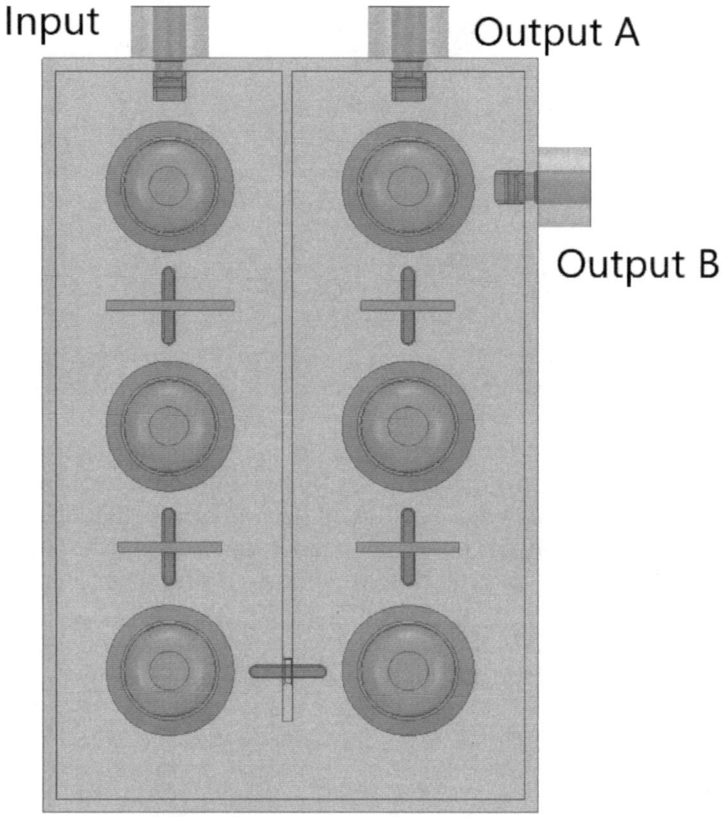


FIGURE 5: BASIC ARCHITECTURE OF A FILTER SWITCH WITH MULTIPLE ASYMMETRIC OUTPUT PORTS.

This equated to a difference in return loss and filter response between each port. To overcome the asymmetry, the entire layout is optimized for symmetrical performance at each port. Figure 6 shows the basic architecture of the device which has a single input and more than one "selectable" output of the filter or vice versa. The current mechanism to short one of the outputs is an RF lockout tagout unit. This ensures there is ample isolation between filter input port and the unused output port.

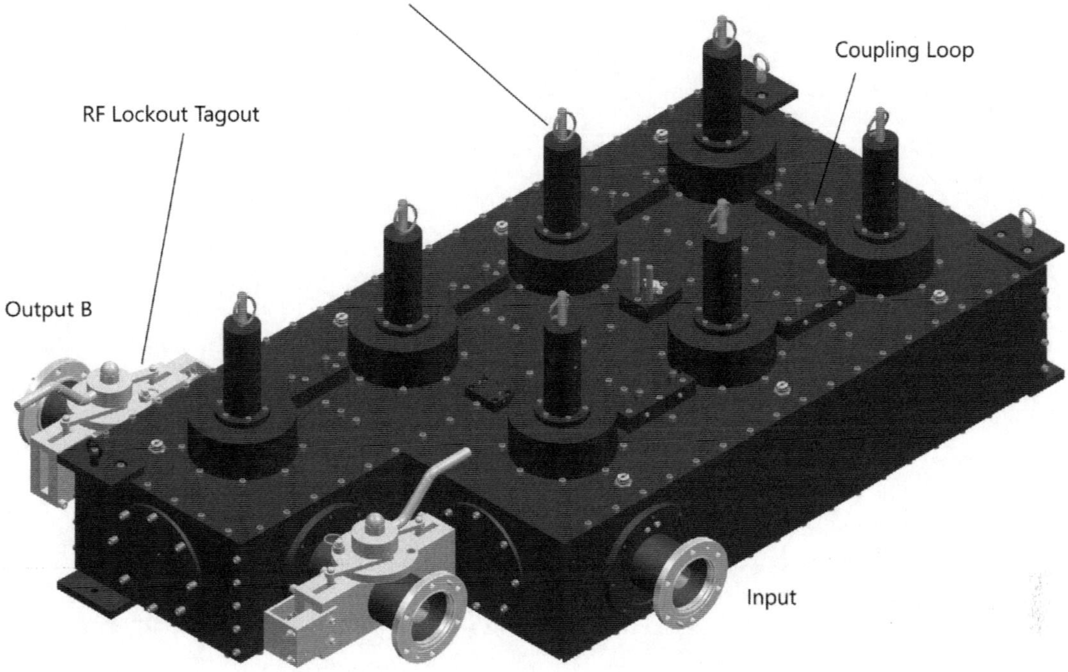


FIGURE 6: BASIC ARCHITECTURE OF A FILTER SWITCH WITH MULTIPLE OUTPUT PORTS IN A FOLDED CONFIGURATION. RF LOCKOUT TAGOUTS CREATE THE SHORT AT EACH OUTPUT.

For this example, the redesign is a seven pole, folded box layout with the option for cross coupling if more rejection is required. A seven-pole filter without cross coupling and a six-pole cross coupled are both capable of achieving the FCC full-service mask requirement. Figures 7 and 8 show each response with the FCC mask overlaid. While the addition of the 7th cavity may lead one to assume the cost of the filter has been increased, this cost is offset by the elimination of the cross coupling and subsequent tuning time. It is arguable the seven-pole has better performance versus the traditional 6 pole largely due to the rejection being greater at the band edges and beyond.

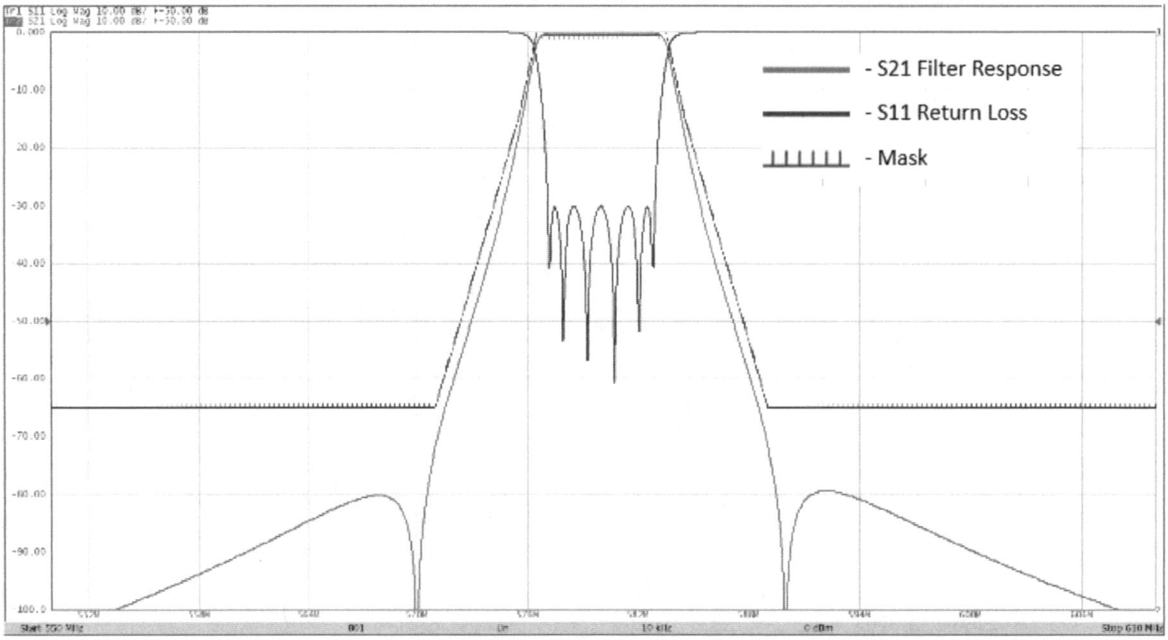


FIGURE 7: SIX-POLE CROSS COUPLED FILTER S-PARAMETER DATA (X-AXIS UNITS ARE DB).

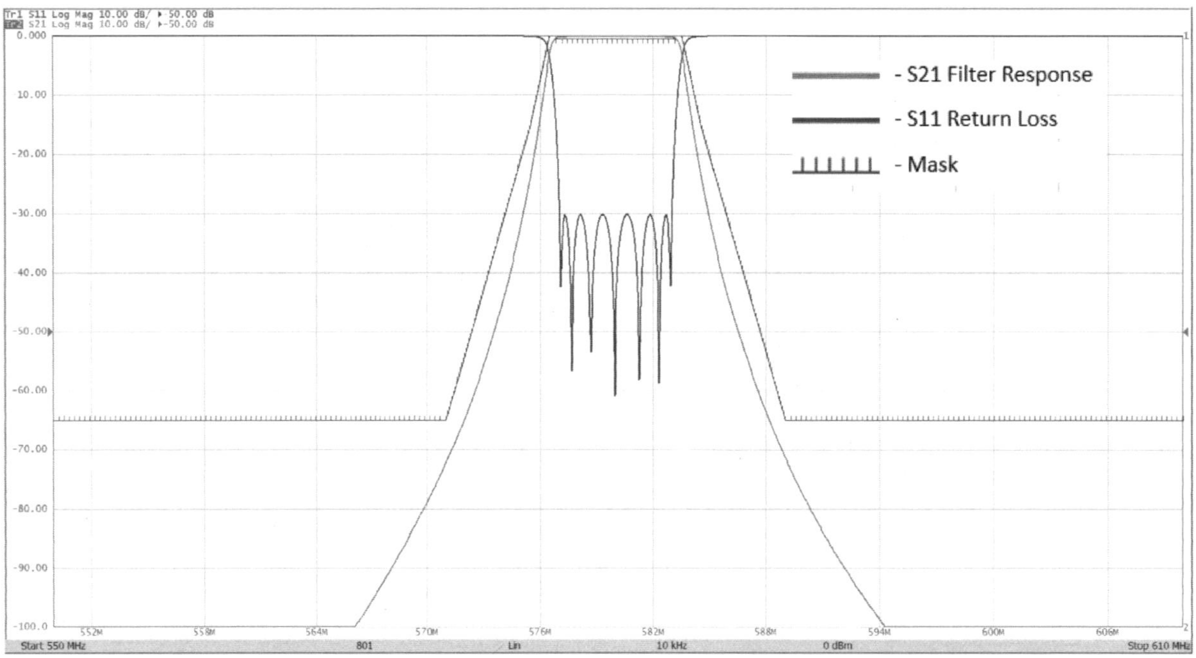


FIGURE 8: SEVEN-POLE INLINE FILTER S-PARAMETER DATA (X-AXIS UNITS ARE DB).

## Filter Switch Performance

Output port symmetry is one key to the success of a device utilizing the concept. Not only does the use of multiple output cavities yield poor isolation figures, it also increases the chances of an arc event. If not executed properly, the detuning features introduce conductive elements which decreases distance to ground in certain areas. Progressing to the next step of introducing two ports at the output cavity, a proper short at one port eliminates the potential for breakdown. The key is that the location of the short at each port needs to be optimized to maintain the required loading and resonance in the frequency band of operation.

Recall the asymmetrical orientation of the output ports of the folded 6 pole filter (as shown in Figure 5). With the ports 90 degrees apart, the internal geometry of the cavity is now unbalanced. As a result, keeping the tuning components constant and changing which port is shorted now yields an undesirable effect in the filter response. The performance differences can be seen in the plots in Figures 9 and 10.

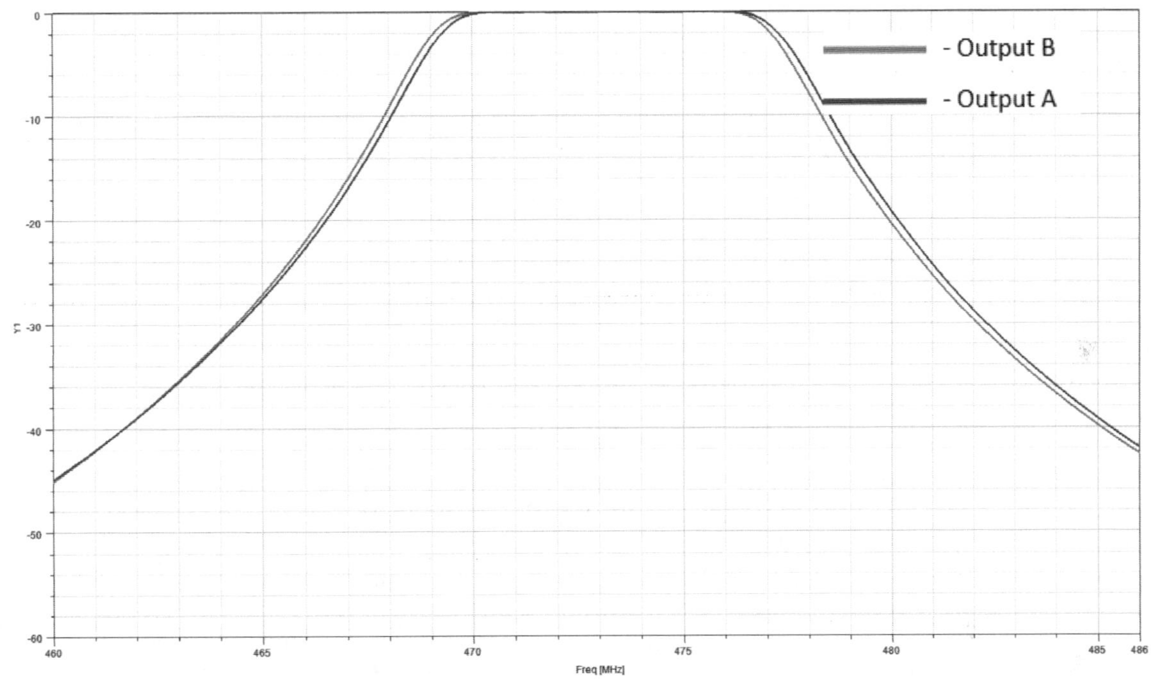


FIGURE 9: S21 FILTER RESPONSE WITH ASYMMETRIC OUTPUTS IN DECIBELS.

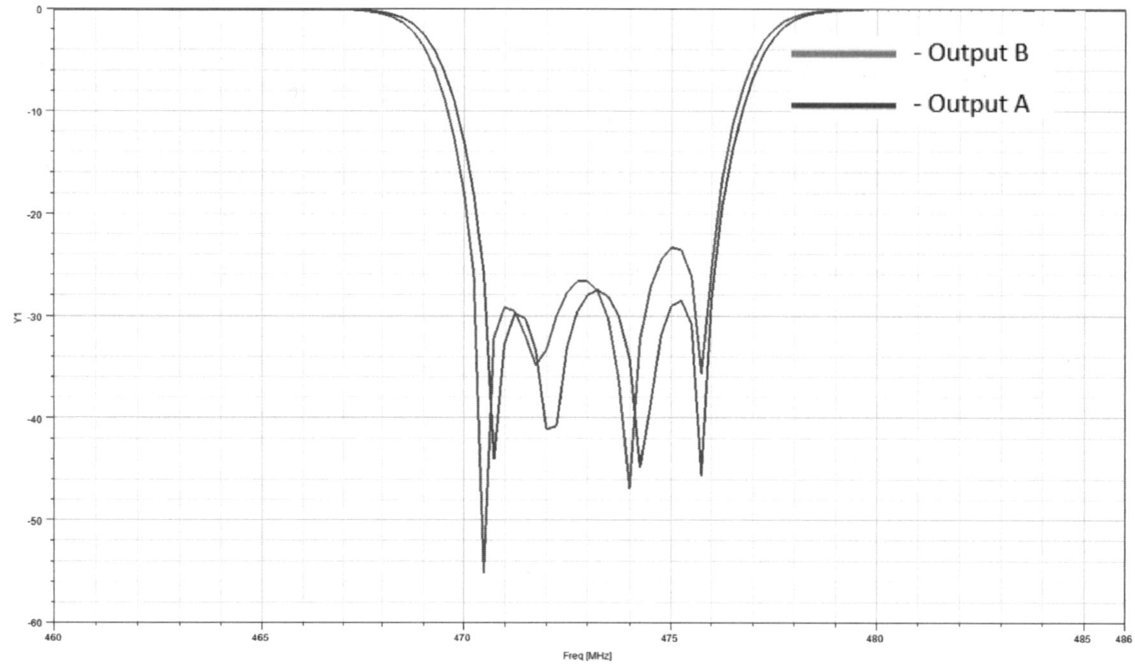


FIGURE 10: S11 RETURN LOSS WITH ASYMMETRIC OUTPUTS IN DECIBELS.

It is shown in these figures that the filter response has shifted slightly in frequency but more importantly, the return loss of the filter is negatively affected and no longer meets desired specifications. To compensate for the asymmetry, the filter would need to be slightly retuned every time the output port is changed. This is not feasible without a vector network analyzer and an experienced technician.

To overcome this, a modification of the folded filter layout is necessary to create a cavity that allows for symmetrical outputs. Keeping in mind FCC mask requirements, an additional cavity was added to a six-pole filter resulting a seven-pole folded design. Remaining folded saves space and allows for optional dual cross coupling to achieve even more rejection.

## Filter Switch Simplicity

An advantage of the filter switch is its simplicity. Failure rate is defined as:

$$\lambda = \sum_{i=1}^{n} N_i \lambda_i \pi_{Qi} \tag{1}$$

Where n is the number of part categories, $N_i$ is the quantity of the i$^{th}$ part, $\lambda_i$ is the failure rate of the i$^{th}$ part and $\pi_{Qi}$ is the quality factor of i$^{th}$ part [2]. From equation 1, one can conclude that reliability is directly proportional to parts count [3]. The total number of parts in a filter switch component is over 25% less than an equivalent separate filter and switch configuration, not including hardware, as indicated in Table 1. Along with less parts, the shorting mechanism utilizes contact surfaces that are not as crucial as those in a rotary switch.

| Component | Filter Switch (7-Pole Inline) | Filter w/Switch & Frame (6-Pole Cross Coupled) |
|---|---|---|
| Filter body | 136 | 134 |
| Control unit | 15/each (LOTO) | 128 (Switch/Frame) |
| 5-Port directional coupler | 58 | 29 |
| Total | 224 | 291 |

TABLE 1: PARTS COUNTS - FILTER SWITCH VS. EQUIVALENT SEPARATE FILTER SWITCH UNITS.

While the economic appeal is real, the assimilation of multiple components does not come without its disadvantages. Typically, between the filter output and the switch is a set of directional couplers for total power output (TPO) measurements. This new architecture will include a set of couplers at each port, doubling the quantity needed.

## Motorized Controlled Filter Switch/Interlocks

The use of actuators to remotely control RF switches has been common practice for decades. Since the position of the internal rotary veins need to be extremely accurate and repeatable over time in order to maintain good electrical performance, precise mechanisms must be used. This of course comes at a cost. The actuators on the filter switch will always be accurately positioned since the short will be a linear movement in or out of the coaxial line.

In order to make this foolproof, the ports cannot be both open or both closed at the same time. "Smart" interlocks will need to be employed at each port/lockout tagout. The interlock would need to utilize an "XOR" gate for the transmitter to respond correctly. Another option is a lockout tagout with "dual" throws. This would allow the control of both ports with a single movement.

For the purpose of this exercise, commonly used and known parts were used to prove out the sensitivity, accuracy of placement, and impact on isolation. More development is underway to determine as a means of creating a more simple, even more cost effective, repeatable, and durable mechanical solution to incorporate the short into the construction of the filter switch.

## Further Integrations

From a top-down perspective, the next step is to investigate what other components can be consolidated. The most beneficial integration would be a directional coupler from the output cavity, eliminating the need for dual external couplers. Another possibility is for the use in combiner systems. The potential for the filter switch topology would introduce the load at the filter level.

Broadcasters using multiplexed facilities could potentially increase their troubleshooting capabilities and allow the other stations in the combiner chain to remain on the air while the transmitter is getting proofed on a new station. There are various other factors to consider when looking to apply this to combined systems, however the primary factor is the shorts proximity to the filter cavity.

VHF and FM applications may prove to be more successful as a result of the wavelength being applied. The filter switch concept was developed and analyzed at the low end of the current UHF TV band. More analysis is required to determine the feasibility and sensitivity of the short position and construction at higher frequencies. If the distance from the filter to the combiner is correctly optimized, the option of switching ports on the filter may not change the performance of the entire combiner system.

## Conclusions

The advantages of integrating the filter and switch of a broadcast RF system into a common component have been discussed. The new solution allows the high-power and low-power broadcaster both technical and economical benefits. This solution eliminates the need to purchase an expensive switch, associated elbows, and plumbing, as well as extra framework in order to route the RF path to a load. The smaller footprint of the filter switch saves space and allows for easier installation. The filter switch is a simple design utilizing fewer parts and connections, which increases reliability.

## References


[1] Javier Ossorio Garcia, Juan Carlos Melgarejo Lermas, Vicente E. Boria, Marco Guglielmi, "On the Integration of Microwave Filters and Waveguide Switches", IEEE Microwave and Wireless Components Letters, Vol. 31, No. 3, March 2021

[2] *MIL-217 Standard*

[3] Schadler, J. L., "Changing the Landscape of FM Broadcast Antenna Technology", BEITC Proceedings 2022.

# Cybersecurity "Proof of Performance" for the Broadcast IT System

**Wayne M. Pecena CPBE, CBNE**
**Texas A&M University – KAMU TV & FM**
**College Station, Texas, United States**
w-pecena@tamu.edu

**Abstract** – The broadcast station today relies on an Information Technology (IT) infrastructure based upon the Internet Protocol (IP) whether a small radio station or a state-of-the-art ATSC 3 TV facility. Protecting the infrastructure against cyber threats grows more challenging each year for the broadcast IT engineer. Threats are constantly evolving, and the cybersecurity precautions implemented must evolve as well. New Federal Communications Commission (FCC) regulations will likely add EAS focused cybersecurity compliance requirements in 2023.

It is essential to know your vulnerabilities and potential exposure to cyber criminals before implementing the necessary precautions. Penetration testing or pen testing provides a proof-of-performance of the broadcast IT infrastructure through proactive identification of cybersecurity holes and vulnerabilities. Precautions thought to be in place can be verified and any missing protections implemented before exploited by the cybercriminal.

This paper and presentation will explore the concepts of penetration testing, the value of use and tools available to apply to the broadcast IT environment as an approach to validating the cybersecurity readiness of the broadcast IT infrastructure against cyberattacks.

## Introduction

The broadcast station today relies on an Information Technology (IT) infrastructure based upon the Internet Protocol (IP) whether a small radio station or a major market state of the art ATSC 3 TV facility. Protecting the infrastructure against cyber threats grows more challenging each year for the broadcast IT engineer and is a constant cat and mouse game with threat actors. Threats are constantly evolving and the cybersecurity precautions implemented must evolve as well. New Federal Communications Commission (FCC) regulations will likely add Emergency Alert System (EAS) focused cybersecurity compliance requirements later this year. With or without FCC intervention, the broadcast station must address cybersecurity upfront rather than as an afterthought.

The threats to the broadcast IT infrastructure that exist today are numerous and widespread. From a high-level view, threats can be categorized into malware or network focused threats. Malware threats focus upon the host operating system and applications they execute. Common industry sub-categories of malware include:

- Ransomware
- Viruses
- Worms and Trojans
- Spyware

This paper is excerpted from the Proceedings of the 2023 NAB Broadcast Engineering and Information Technology (BEIT) Conference, © 2023, National Association of Broadcasters, 1 M Street SE, Washington, DC 20003 USA.

Network focused threats focus upon the network infrastructure components and exploiting the IP protocol(s) that include threats such as:

- Address Resolution Protocol (ARP) spoofing
- Rogue service advertisements
- Denial of Service (DoS) attacks
- Distribute Denial of Service (DDoS) attacks
- Man in the Middle attacks

The Cybersecurity & Infrastructure Security Agency (CISA) tracks cyber vulnerabilities through their Known Exploitable Vulnerability (KEV) catalog. A quick glance at the KEV reference resource will put into perspective the number of potential vulnerabilities faced today. In February 2023, the KEV contained over eight-hundred and eighty (>880) individual vulnerabilities. [1]

Today, the DDoS attack and ransomware likely offer the greatest threat to any IT system, broadcast focused or not. Sources of these threats can originate from many sources or threat actors. Threat sources may include:

- Nation states
- Terrorist groups & organized crime
- Hacktivists and individual hackers
- Disgruntled individuals

The sheer number of potential threats combined with the diversity of threat sources often ends in a feeling of a hopeless situation and results in throwing one's hands up admitting defeat. Cybersecurity is and can be extremely complex and countless financial resources can be consumed in attempts to prevent and mitigate the impact upon our broadcast plant. Hope should not be lost, as there are effective and often inexpensive steps can be taken to prevent a cybersecurity event from occurring or to minimize the impact if an event occurs.

Cybersecurity is often defined as "focused upon the protection of computers, networks, programs and data from change, destruction or unauthorized access and/or change". A first step in the elimination of the cybersecurity helpless mindset can be found in an understanding of a few cybersecurity principals followed by a structure approach to implementing prevention measures.

Cybersecurity is based upon several principals that are applied as actionable tasks to protect the IT infrastructure. Principals form the basis of best practices that guide cybersecurity precautions in practical implementation steps. Key cybersecurity principals include:

- The NIST Cybersecurity Framework
- The CIA Triad
- Defense-in-Depth
- The Principal of Least Privilege

The National Institute of Standards and Technology (NIST) Cybersecurity Framework provides structured guidelines and steps to implement and maintain ongoing cybersecurity programs in any organization. [2] The framework is comprised of five functional categories describing the following high-level functional areas of a cybersecurity program: Identify, Protect, Detect, Respond and Recover.

Each of the five functional categories are further sub-divided into levels of further detail leading to implementable steps through an extensive set of reference documents. These references provide the implementation detail appropriate for the specific level. Figure 1 illustrates the five functional categories and the first level of sub-categories of the framework.

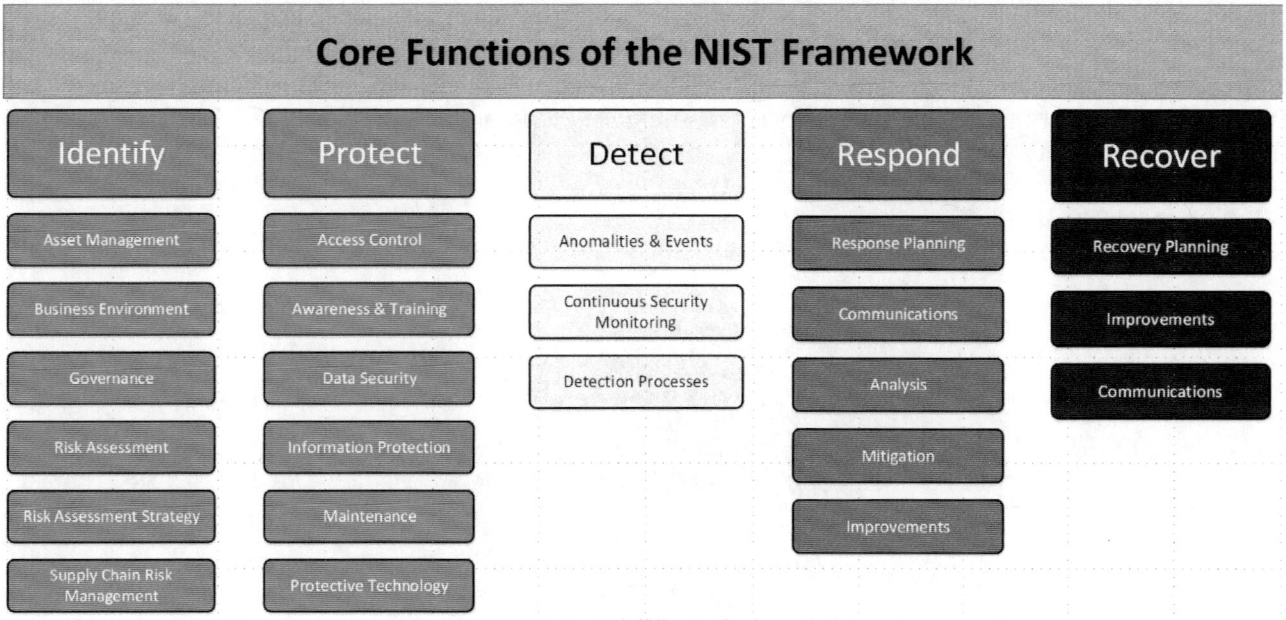


FIGURE 1: THE NIST CYBERSECURITY FRAMEWORK

The Identity function begins with an accurate account of all IT assets involved. IT assets include hardware, software, networks, and data. From the inventory produced, the assets are in turn prioritized based upon the organization's business context. Reliable delivery of program content is likely a high-priority business context for any broadcast station. The identity process is the first step of implementing a risk-based plan and the first step in dispelling the helpless mindset by bringing structure and dividing a complex undertaking into manageable steps. A risk-based analysis approach does not seek to address every IT cybersecurity risk that may exist at the same priority level. It seeks to identify and assign a high priority to the high impact and high likelihood potential threats. Less priority is assigned to the lower impact and lesser likelihood threats. A numerical rating scale is often used to describe the overall cybersecurity health of an organization's IT systems. Areas found deficient can then be used to prioritize resources to remedy or bring them into compliance in situations where regulatory requirements or organizational policy exists.

The Protect function utilizes the previously compiled IT asset inventory to create a policy or approach of what to protect and how to protect an asset. Asset protection is addressed in terms of physical asset protection as well as establishing access control for users and applications. The concept of least privilege required is utilized.

The Detect function is focused upon IT asset monitoring in terms of knowing what is normal and alerting when an anomaly occurs. In this functional area, the systems are identified that are required to monitor system activity or user activity alerting when a possible cybersecurity event occurs.

The Respond function focuses upon a plan of action when a breech occurs. The scope ranges from a physical event such as a facility break-in to a malware incident occurring. Recovery steps are identified in advance such that recovery can be as efficient as possible as opposed to developing a plan after an event occurs. The post-analysis aspect of any event occurrence is also an important step in the continued improvement process.

The last functional area addressed is Recovery in scope with the Response action plan, the Recovery function outlines steps to restore compromised assets and return to normal operation.

The CIA triad [2] is often considered the classic model of IT security. The model utilizes three objectives to be achieved within any IT system ranging from the network to the server storage systems to the applications. The three objectives are illustrated in Figure 2 and are comprised of:

- Confidentiality
- Integrity
- Availability

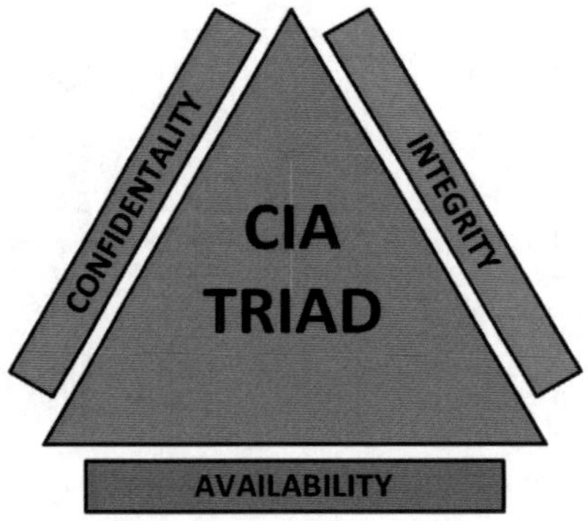


FIGURE 2: CIA TRIAD

Confidentiality can be equated to privacy or preventing information reaching undesired hands or unauthorized users. Access by users and applications is restricted or limited to a "need-to-access". Other IT system implementation techniques include encryption, authentication and off-line data storage.

Integrity seeks to prevent data from being changed as it moves through a network, is processed through an IT workflow or as stored at rest in a data storage system. File access controls, checksums and encryption are common implementation mechanisms. An important aspect of the Integrity objective is to have detection mechanism(s) to know if tampering or altercation has occurred.

Availability seeks to ensure that IT resources are available to legitimate users or applications and not available to those that are not authorized to access or utilize. Implementation techniques include network infrastructure redundancy, server redundancy and attack detection systems.

Network architecture is critical to implementation of cybersecurity precautions and should be considered the starting point. The network should be segmented in lieu of the traditional flat design. The segmented or layered network breaks down a larger flat network into smaller individual networks, or independent segments. Each of these segments is an independent subnet or broadcast domain. Perimeter security was once the norm for network resource protection, however in today's threat landscape internal network protection techniques are required. The segmentation reduces the attack surface by limiting the reach that an infected host has to reach other host devices often referred to as "east-west" movement throughout the network.

The architecture of a castle can best illustrate the DiD concept. Often surrounded by a moat, an attacker might be faced with armed guard towers and an outer barrier wall if the moat as the first barrier is breeched. If the outer wall is breeched, the attacker is likely to find a higher inner wall to conquer. All of these barriers are in place to protect the treasures stored in the most inner core of the castle.

The National Security Agency (NSA) developed the principle of Defense in Depth (DiD). [3] DiD provides the concept of multi-layered coordinated security mechanisms to implement. The goal is to have redundancy in protection mechanisms. The concept is based upon the premise that if one security protection mechanism fails or is breached another obstacle is in place.

The architecture of a castle can best illustrate the DiD concept. Often surrounded by a moat, an attacker might be faced with armed guard towers and an outer barrier wall if the moat as the first barrier is breeched. If the outer wall is breeched, the attacker is likely to find a higher inner wall to conquer. All of these barriers are in place to protect the treasures stored in the most inner core of the castle.

The Principal of Least Privilege (PoLP) establishes that a security architecture should be designed to grant the minimal resources required for a user or an application to perform the desired system function. PoLP is implemented through access controls for allowing authorized users to access specific systems or an application to have file modification permissions as examples.

These cybersecurity principles are the basis for actionable or practical security precautions that are created as best-practices, regulatory requirements or company policy. Precautions often include steps such as:

- Creating physical access barriers
- Implementing a segmented (layered) network architecture
- Utilizing Ethernet switch port security & snooping services
- Packet filtering (stateless) through an Access Control List (ACL)
- Packet filtering (stateful) via a firewall
- Encryption & Virtual Private Networks (VPN) for remote access
- Authentication & access control
- Protection systems (antivirus, malware, intrusion detection)

## Penetration Testing as the IT Proof of Performance

The tenured broadcast engineer likely had a love-hate relationship with the annual Proof of Performance ritual required by FCC regulation up until de-regulation in the 80's. According to the 1975 Broadcast Engineering magazine's "FM Proof of Performance Manual' [4], the annual proof is "is probably the most important piece of engineering that most radio station chief engineers are exposed to" [x]. FCC part 73.254 required stations to perform audio frequency response (50 - 50,000 Hz) measurements and harmonic distortion measurements for specified fundamental frequencies at 3 modulation levels wrapping up with an end-end system noise measurement.

The de-regulation of broadcast engineering in the mid 80's eliminated many compliance requirements (as well as eliminating the FCC First Class Radiotelephone license), although some annual measurements are required such as National Radio System Committee (NRSC) emission measurements for AM radio. For the most part, the broadcast engineer is responsible for compliance and is free to perform whatever measurements they may deem needed at whatever intervals. Compliance with technical performance regulations is still required with the broadcast engineer determining the best course of action to ensure. In most cases, routine periodic measurement and documentation of critical technical operating parameters continues as a best practice to ensure compliance.

For the broadcast IT engineer today, once cybersecurity precautions are in place, verification of those precautions thought to be in place is likely one of the most important tasks the station engineer must perform. Penetration testing or pen testing is the last step in your cybersecurity prevention plan and should be viewed as the "proof of performance" of the broadcast IT system. It is time to adopt the mindset of a threat actor or "hacker. Not that mindset of a malicious or "black hat" hacker but become a "white hat" or an ethical hacker commonly known as a penetration tester. The same tools that a malicious hacker might use are used to verify the proper cybersecurity precautions are in place, functioning as intended and to seek cybersecurity vulnerabilities or holes so that proactive corrective action can be taken.

For the threat actor or the penetration tester, the CIA Triad goals become the goal of the Disclosure – Alteration – Denial (DAD) Triad [4] as illustrated in Figure 3. Confidentiality becomes a target to be breached to disclose valuable information or expose sensitive data through techniques such as social-engineering or spyware. Integrity becomes a target of Man-in-the-Middle attacks, malware and data record manipulation to alter data whether in-transit, in a workflow or stored at rest. Availability becomes the primary objective of a ransomware infection or a Denial of Service (DoS/DDoS) attack to deny access to legitimate users or applications.

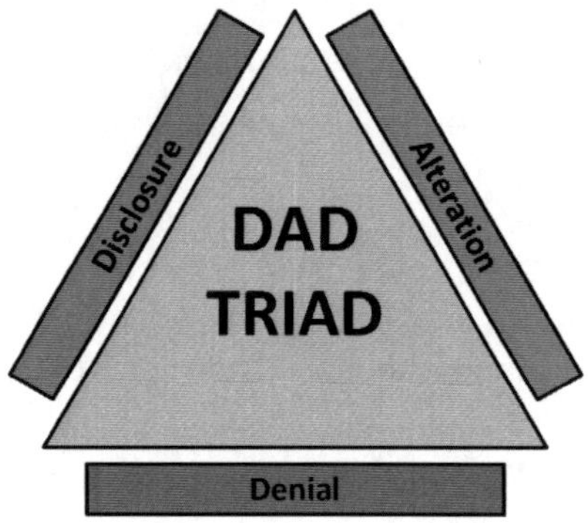


FIGURE 3: DAD TRIAD

## Penetration Testing Process

Penetration testing is often referred to as a Pen Test or an action by a pen tester serving as a “white hat” hacker or as an “ethical hacker”. Penetration testing is the process to confirm the validity of cybersecurity protections or the insecurity of an IT infrastructure. It is an evaluation of an organization's capability to defend against attempts to circumvent cybersecurity protections of a network infrastructure, software applications, hardware, and endpoint devices and users. Penetration testing is a proactive process to seek and exploit real-world threats and should not be considered a vulnerability test that seeks to be non-invasive, seeking only potential vulnerabilities.

The scope of the pen test can be relatively simple to complex. The scope of a pen test may focus on one specific aspect or take into account several factors depending upon the desired environment assessment. Scope factors may include physical security, network infrastructure, software applications and users. Pen tests approaches are classified in one of three ways: black box, white box or gray box testing.

The black box test is one where the pen tester has no knowledge of the IT environment to be tested. Any required information to perform the test must be gained through network reconnaissance or exploration or the mining of public information often through the Internet. White box testing provides the pen tester with complete knowledge of the environment they are testing and are often given access to the internal infrastructure. Gray box testing occurs when the tester has some knowledge of the IT environment to be tested.

Pen testing [6] begins with a plan that defines the scope of the desired test. The next step gathers the necessary information to perform the test. Information can be gleamed from a number of sources often involving the public Internet or through a simple Google search or tools such as Whois (https://lookup.icann.org) search. Next is the actual execution of the test where attempts are made, or vulnerabilities are actually exploited. The process ends with the reporting of findings from the test and the follow-up documentation. The findings are often used to specify the proactive steps to resolve any potential vulnerabilities discovered during the test. Figure 4 illustrates the overall process.

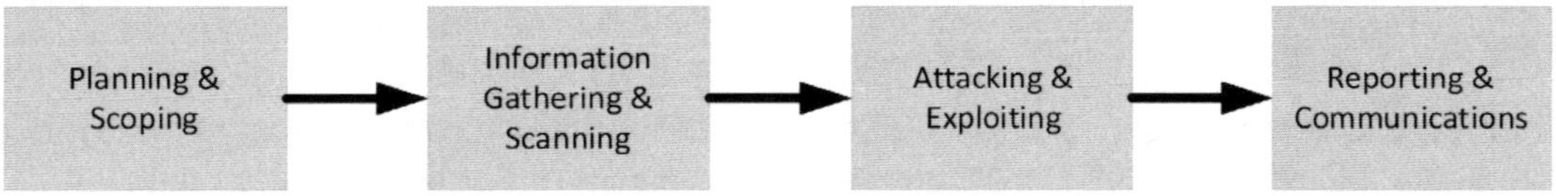


FIGURE 4: PENETRATION TESTING STAGES

The actual penetration testing is performed with various tools that are readily available as commercial products or as open-source software. Figure 5 illustrates a selection of the most popular open-source tools in 2022 [7]. Each of these tools offers specific advantages depending upon the scope and the environment to be tested. An extensive evaluation of the available tools is well beyond the scope of this paper. However, it is useful to call attention to a few of the tools that may be useful to the broadcast IT engineer.

**10 Most Popular Penetration Testing Tools 2022**

Aircrack-ng

Burp Suite

Cain & Abel

CANVAS

John the Ripper

Kali Linux

Metasploit

SQLmap

W3af

Wireshark

Source: Spiceworks.com

FIGURE 5: PENETRATION TESTING TOOLS

## Penetration Testing Tools

Commonly referred to as a port scanner, open-source tools such as Network Mapper or "nmap" (www.nmap.org) can be used to seek and find potential cybersecurity vulnerabilities by identifying host devices visible on a network, determine services enabled by active port identification, identify versions of services being executed and operating system utilized by the host. Enhanced capabilities of nmap include the ability to script or automate the testing process through the nmap scripting engine (NSE). Advanced detection techniques can be utilized such as determining firewall or packet filtering implemented and firewall evasion and avoidance to avoid prevention system detection.

Nmap as a port scanner determines if a User Datagram Protocol (UDP) or a Transmission Control Protocol (TCP) port is open. An open UDP or TCP port indicates that a specific service is being executed on the host being scanned. Ports are categorized into one of three categories:

- Well Known Ports (port # 0 – 1,023)
- Registered Ports (port # 1,024 – 49,151)
- Dynamic Ports (port 49,152 – 65,535)

By default, nmap scans the most popular 1,000 ports, although all 65,535 TCP ports and 65,535 TCP ports can be scanned by specifying the proper option syntax. Figure 6 illustrates a basic nmap port scan of a broadcast specific host device that returned four (4) open or active well-known TCP ports.

```
Discovered open port 80/tcp on 128.194.247.138
Discovered open port 443/tcp on 128.194.247.138
Discovered open port 22/tcp on 128.194.247.138
Discovered open port 631/tcp on 128.194.247.138
Completed SYN Stealth Scan at 10:29, 4.91s elapsed (1000 total ports)
```

FIGURE 6: NMAP PORT SCAN

The discovered well-known ports suggest that the following services are available or are being executed on this host device:

- Port 80 is the well-known port for Hypertext Transfer Protocol (HTTP) used for web services
- Port 443 is the well-known port for secure or encrypted HTTP (HTTPS)
- Port 22 is the well-known port for Secure Shell encrypted communications (SSH)
- Port 631 is the well-known port for the Internet Printing Protocol (IPP)

Further host information discovered by nmap indicates the specific version of the services executed upon the host device as illustrated by Figure 7.

```
Not shown: 995 filtered ports
PORT      STATE  SERVICE  VERSION
22/tcp    open   ssh      OpenSSH 6.9 (protocol 2.0)
| ssh-hostkey:
|   1024 b7:24:25:72:89:f1:d3:8b:5a:82:44:0b:86:58:89:4c (DSA)
|   2048 e4:96:eb:de:a0:b5:65:b5:30:ab:aa:57:f5:09:5e:f8 (RSA)
|_  256 e2:54:4a:21:b2:66:c0:b6:46:ec:17:7b:ae:1e:f3:63 (ECDSA)
80/tcp    open   http     Apache httpd 2.2.26-31 ((Unix))
| http-methods:
|   Supported Methods: GET HEAD POST OPTIONS TRACE
|_  Potentially risky methods: TRACE
| http-robots.txt: 1 disallowed entry
|_/
|_http-server-header: Apache/2.2.26-31 (Unix)
|_http-title: *******The Digital Alert Systems DASDEC Base Page*
443/tcp   open   ssl/http Apache httpd 2.2.26-31 ((Unix))
```

FIGURE 7: NMAP DISCOVERED SERVICE VERSIONS

The nmap command set [8] is comprised of over 125 individual commands in addition to numerous command line switch characters to invoke desired scan options yielding hundreds of command line syntax combinations. The following default nmap scans in Figure 8 maybe useful to the broadcast IT engineer:

| | |
|---|---|
| Scan Individual Host: | nmap [ip address]<br>nmap [domain name] |
| Scan an IP Range: | nmap [ip address] – [ip address] |
| Scan a Subnet: | nmap [ip address] / CIDR |
| Service Scan: | nmap -sV [ip address] |
| Scan All Ports: | nmap [ip address] -p- |
| Port Scan by Service Name: | nmap [ip address] -p HTTP<br>nmap [ip address] -p SSH |
| TCP Port Scan: | nmap [ip address] -sT |
| UDP Port Scan: | nmap [ip address] -sU |
| Discover Host Op System: | nmap -O [ip address] |
| Fast Port Scan: | nmap -F [ip address] |
| Discovery (no ping): | nmap -Pn [ip address] |

FIGURE 8: DEFAULT NMAP SCANS

## Web Based Tools

In addition to host based executable penetration tools, web-based search tools are available. Search engines focused upon the discovery of IP host devices available on the public Internet offer a basic penetration test that can be quickly executed from a public network external to the IP host of interest. Two such web-based search engines are: Shodan (www.shodan.io) and Censys (www.censys.io).

Shodan was introduced in 2009 as the first search tool to search for and discover IP hosts devices on the public Internet. Searches can be performed by IP address, a device host name or several other keyword categories. In addition to the discovery of host devices, Shodan will discover open TCP ports. The following Shodan screen image in Figure 9 indicates that no open ports are available via the public Internet for IP address 100.92.118.27.

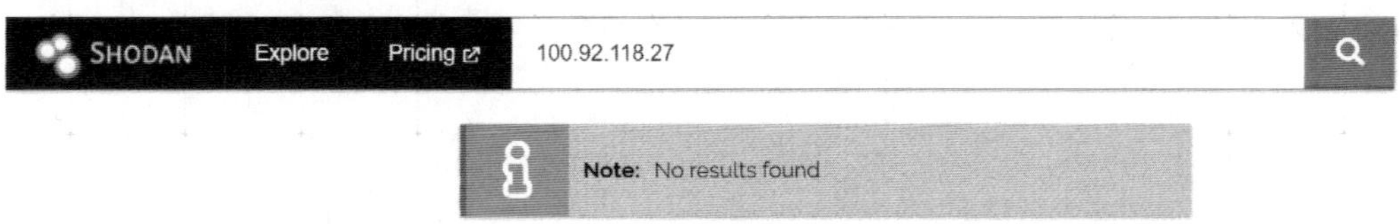


FIGURE 9: SHODAN SCREEN IMAGE

Shodan [9] also allows a custom query to be entered via a browser such as:
www.shodan.io/host/100.92.118.27

Censys offers similar search functionality as Shodan, but acts as a continuous monitor to proactively discover when potential vulnerabilities occur in an organization's IT infrastructure. The following Censys screen image indicates that no open ports are available via the public Internet for IP address 128.194.247.201.

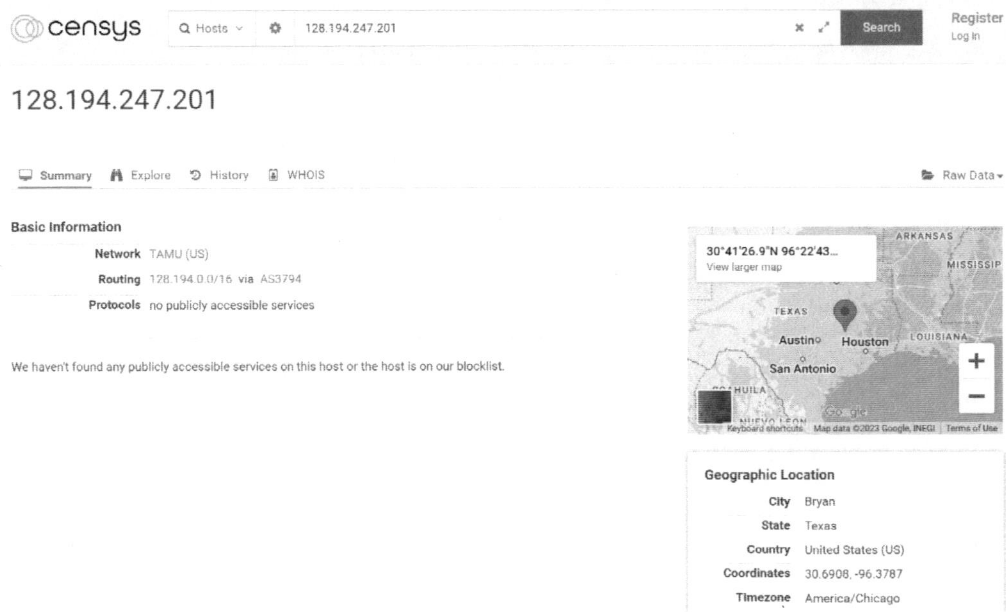


FIGURE 10: CENSYS SCREEN IMAGE

Censys also allows a custom query to be entered via a browser such as: www.censys.io/ipv4/128.194.247.201

## Conclusions

Now that the broadcast infrastructure is entrenched as an IT infrastructure, there are new challenges that must be embraced. Cybersecurity is one front and foremost challenge faced by the broadcast IT engineer. The broadcast industry has been relatively untouched for decades even as the technology employed migrated from analog to digital. The infrastructure traditionally employed baseband signals of analog audio and video, digital audio and video that were built on dedicated infrastructure. The dedicated infrastructure might be shielded twisted-pair cabling, coaxial cable or even fiber optics. A key attribute that it was dedicated in a point-point arrangement for interconnection rather than a shared infrastructure utilized among multiple devices and functions. With everything now IP based, we have a common infrastructure that transports packets regardless of the payload they might contain.

One cannot create or claim an absolutely secure IT environment. However, you can take reasonable and implementable steps to minimize the attack surface of your IT infrastructure and to minimize the impact if a cybersecurity event should occur. Penetration testing should be considered the final stage of your overall program to verify the precautions you believe to be in place are in fact in place and functioning as expected. If not, protections can be corrected in a proactive manner before a threat actor takes advantage of a vulnerability.

It is yet to be seen what the adopted FCC EAS cybersecurity regulations will require. The proposed requirement requiring the EAS participant to certify that they have created and implemented a cybersecurity plan might include a penetration test as a demonstration of the validity of their plan and implementation.

## Summary of Cybersecurity Precautions

A cybersecurity to-do list for the broadcast IT engineer should include the following at minimum:

- Utilize the DiD approach to provide redundant precaution implemented in a structured and coordinated manner
- Segment your network as the right architecture is an important first step in cybersecurity precautions (and performance enhancement)
- Use encryption & Multifactor Authentication (MFA) for any remote access
- Apply PoLP to users and applications
- Limit or control access by packet filtering and/or firewalls
- Disable (or block) any unused services to minimize the attack plane
- Keep IT network hardware and operating systems updated and current
- Ensure default login credentials are changed to strong & unique credentials
- Maintain system backups following the 3-2-1 rule & know how to restore those systems
- Utilize network equipment capabilities such as Ethernet switch port security
- Monitor your infrastructure and know what is normal
- Educate users regarding the dangers & tactics of social engineering & phishing

## References

[1] Cybersecurity & Infrastructure Security Agency, Known Exploitable Vulnerability catalog, https://www.cisa.gov/known-exploited-vulnerabilities-catalog.

[2] National Institute of Standards and Technology, 2018, Cybersecurity Framework Version, https://www.nist.gov/cyberframework/framework.

[3] Chapple, M. & Seidel, D., "PenTest+ Study Guide", 2022, pp.2-3

[4] Broadcast Engineering Magazine, "FM Proof of Performance Manual", 1975, p.7, pp. 9-10 & p.28.

[5] Chapple, M. & Seidel, D., "PenTest+ Study Guide", 2022, p.3.

[6] Chapple, M. & Seidel, D., "PenTest+ Study Guide", 2022, p.10.

[7] BasuMallick, C., "Top 10 Penetration Testing Tools in 2022", 2022, www.spiceworks.com.

[8] Marsh, N., "nmap 6 Cookbook", 2010, pp.45-97.

[9] Horowitz, M., Router Security. Shodan and Censys Queries, 2022, https://routersecurity.org/shodan.php.

# Fighting Misinformation with Authenticated C2PA Provenance Metadata

**Dr. Nigel Earnshaw**
**The British Broadcasting Corporation**
**London, United Kingdom**
Nigel.Earnshaw@bbc.co.uk

**Jonathan Dupras**
**CBC/Radio-Canada**
**Montreal, Quebec, Canada**
jonathan.dupras@radio-canada.ca

**Bruce MacCormack**
**Neural Transform**
**Lunenburg, Nova Scotia, Canada**
Bruce@NeuralTransform.com

**Abstract** – Over the last three years, teams from Microsoft, The New York Times, CBC/Radio-Canada and The BBC have come together as Project Origin. This group has participated as part of a wider community in the standardization of provenance signaling technologies to attach authenticated metadata to media content. The Coalition for Content Provenance and Authenticity (C2PA) specification was the result of these collaborative efforts. This paper will outline the features of the C2PA specification, and the work being undertaken to add this functionality to existing media production workflows to add transparency and counter disinformation and malicious use of synthetic media.

## The Growing Threat to the News Ecosystem

The widespread availability of powerful generative media tools has challenged the fundamental "seeing is believing" basis of much of our modern news ecosystem. A need for a higher level of validation will be required for publishers to maintain the trust of our audiences. Established media organizations are at risk of being fooled into using illegitimate content. Brands can be impersonated and have their credibility used to amplify both disinformation and misinformation. The long-established practices for fact checking and defending the veracity of news content are at risk of being overwhelmed by the growing volume of unsubstantiated content in the system.

The emergence of generative AI tools for creating media has led to a call for the development of AI tools to detect this new form of content. This approach will always be faced with a cat and mouse dilemma. The advances in creation will outpace the ability to detect. Worse, detection tools when used with Generative Adversarial Networks will dramatically improve the ability of misinformation to avoid detection. It is anticipated that detection tools in general use will have usable life spans measured in weeks.

This paper is excerpted from the Proceedings of the 2023 NAB Broadcast Engineering and Information Technology (BEIT) Conference, © 2023, National Association of Broadcasters, 1 M Street SE, Washington, DC 20003 USA.

As an alternative, media provenance uses well understood cryptographic technology to validate the identity of a publisher and the technical integrity of the content. It is a solution that can operate at scale in a mechanized approach. The challenge will be to come to a universally accepted method of using provenance manifests across unrelated organizations and industries.

## Building a Coalition

In 2019 teams from Microsoft, the New York Times, CBC/Radio-Canada and the BBC came together as Project Origin to focus on protecting the integrity of content when consumed over any platform. Rather than think about detecting which content might have been 'faked' the more straightforward approach of being able to determine in a cryptographically secure way the organization or individual which claims to have published content was felt to be more stable and practical. In addition, this approach does not create any uncertainty or imply judgment and so enriches the media ecosystem in a positive way.

At the same time another consortium, the Content Authentication Initiative (CAI), led by Adobe, had been considering this challenge from a creator perspective and had made the same observations. Together the combined membership of these two groups, along with ARM, Intel, Truepic and Sony and others, formed an open standard body – the Coalition for Content Provenance and Authenticity (C2PA). The C2PA open technical standard (V1.0) for authenticated provenance metadata was published in January 2022. This has been updated and maintained over the last year [1].

The current membership of C2PA reflects the way provenance data can originate at different points in the media value chain and can, if permitted, be carried along the contribution and distribution networks in a way that preserves the chain of provenance through to the end consumer. Participation in C2PA includes well known and substantial organizations representing camera designers and manufacturers, content infrastructure companies, broadcasters and news organizations, content tool and application vendors, human rights advocates, and social media platforms.

## The C2PA Specification - A Common Core Approach

### Design Goals

The C2PA process began by articulating its Guiding Principles for the C2PA Designs and Specifications. These include the overarching goals of providing a way for producers and custodians of any given content to assert provenance data in a verifiable manner. A second goal is that the "C2PA specifications should not provide value judgments about whether a given set of provenance data is good or bad, merely whether the assertions included within can be verified as associated with the underlying asset, correctly formed, and free from tampering".

Throughout the whole process much emphasis has been placed on the design goals of ensuring privacy, responsibility, scalability, extensibility and interoperability among others.

### Overview of the C2PA Technical Features

The C2PA technical approach is to authenticate provenance related metadata in the form of a manifest data structure which includes a unique impression of the content bits in the form of a secure cryptographic hash. Having then 'bound' the content impression within the metadata manifest, the manifest is then cryptographically signed using public credentials recognized by validators in the field. In this way a validator can determine the technical integrity of the received manifest and content by validating the signature on the manifest and checking that the received content matches the content impression within the manifest.

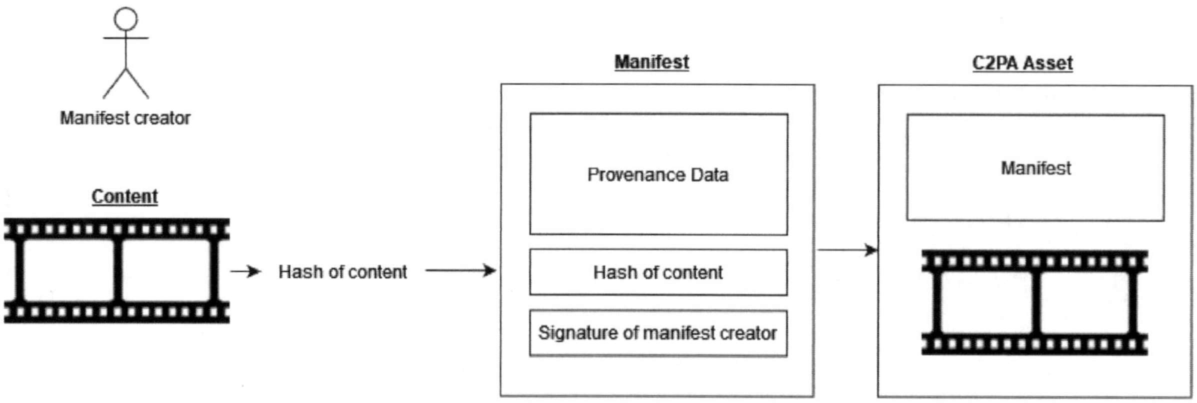


FIGURE 1: SIMPLIFIED SCHEMATIC OF THE C2PA ASSET.

The simplified schematic above shows the relationship between the provenance metadata, content manifest and the C2PA asset. The first consideration is the binding between the bits that make up the content and the provenance metadata. In the simplest case as shown above, the cryptographic hash of the content is included in the manifest. The exact parts of the file included within the scope of the hash are carefully chosen according to the specification and signaled within the manifest.

The next consideration is the integrity of the manifest as a whole. This is assured through well-known and established digital signature algorithms being used to protect the critical parts of the manifest to prevent any changes to either the manifest or the content being made without invalidating the overall structure.

Finally, the specification describes how to include the manifest within the well-known container formats commonly used today. These include JPEG, PNG, SVG, PDF amongst others and for audio/video presentations the base media file format (BMFF) [2] is included. Note that being able to insert the manifest into the data file container to form a C2PA asset is a practical consideration only and does not imply any added security. The C2PA specification anticipates the separation of manifest from content and the possibility of services to discover manifests from content alone. When considering validation, no assumption is made that the co-located manifest is the correct manifest authored for the accompanying content.

When a validating client, e.g., a browser validates a C2PA asset as shown in the simple case as above, then the following steps are taken.

1. The validator locates and extracts the manifest from the file format.
2. The validator verifies the data in the manifest is valid according to the signature. This paper discusses the trust model and acquisition of trusted public keys below. Note that some intermediate security credentials such as x.509 certificates are conveyed in the manifest structure to facilitate the conveyance of a signing certificate related to a known trust anchor. Details of signature and hash algorithms are also conveyed within the signed data.
3. The validator independently determines the hash impression of the content using the hash algorithm signaled in the manifest and verifies this matches the hash embedded within the manifest.
4. The validator matches the assertions included in the manifest with the signed representation of these assertions in the manifest claim. This 'claim' structure is described later in this paper.

Once these checks have been performed, and if all are passed, the manifest can be accepted as provenance data about the content as authored by the party who signed the manifest.

## Metadata and Security Information Standards

The metadata contained within the manifest is described in the specification and allows for proprietary schema. In addition to the C2PA defined terms, guidance is provided for the inclusion of EXIF data [3], IPTC Photo and Video metadata [4] and the use of Schema.org [5].

C2PA manifests use the JUMBF standard [6] to create the various boxes described in the next section. The schema that define the inner data structures are specified using the CBOR Data Definition Language (CDDL) [7] and represented in the data as Compressed Binary Object Representation (CBOR) [8]. In this way the manifest structure is conveyed in a compact format to reduce the size of the manifest within the file, in line with the design goals.

Security data structures which facilitate signing and transport of credentials are represented using CBOR Object Signing and Encryption standard (COSE) [9]. Presently the only security signing credentials specified are the X.509 certificates [9] which use their customary ASN.1 specification rules and Distinguished Encoding Rules (DER) binary format.

## The Components of a Manifest

This section describes in a little more detail the internal component parts of a manifest. This enables an understanding of how elements within a manifest are related to each other, how manifests within a manifest store relate to each other in a chain of provenance and how updates can be added without breaking an established chain. This section will also describe how endorsements may be used to allow those parties who may have to interrupt the provenance chain to demonstrate agreement with a previous signer.

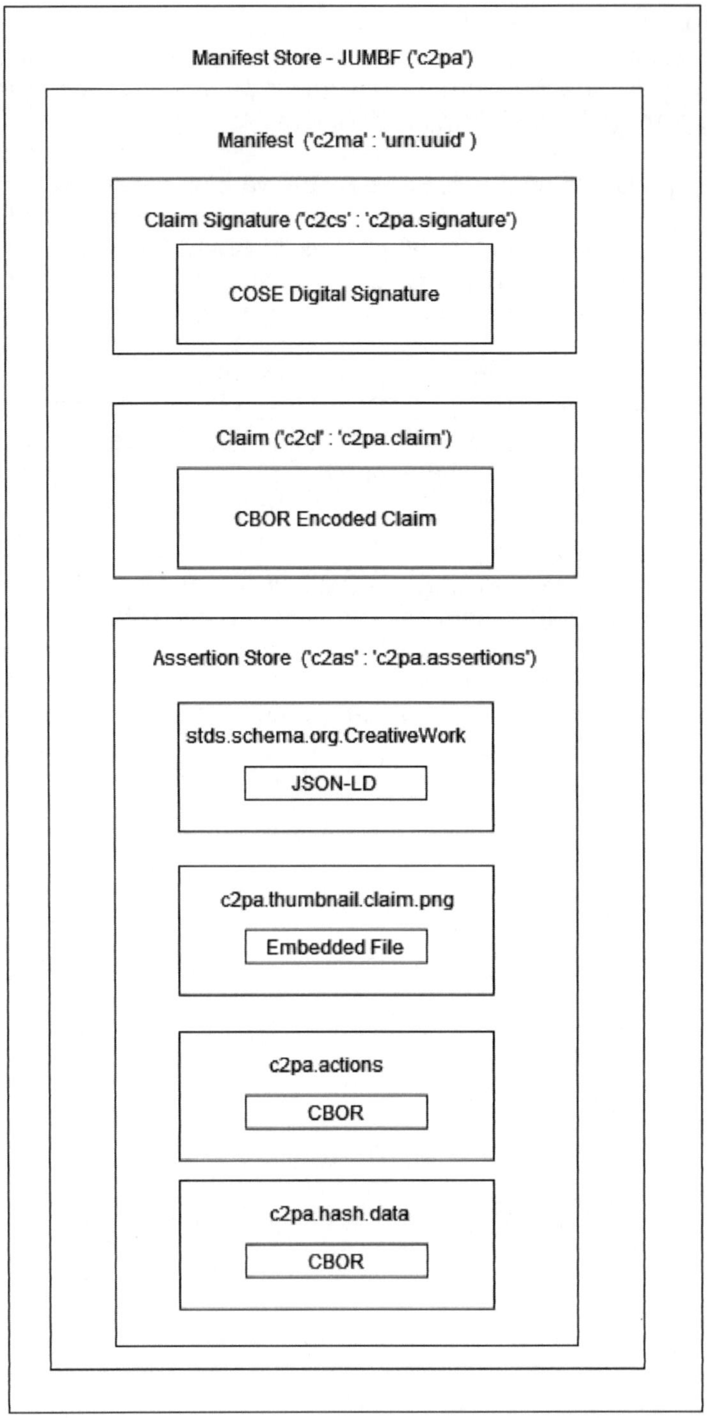


FIGURE 2: THE COMPONENTS OF A MANIFEST.

The schema above shows a visualization of the manifest store. This JUMBF box represents the self-contained unit that conveys the C2PA authenticated provenance metadata. All JUMBF boxes are shown with both their 4-character reference identifier and a dot delimited label encoded into the JUMBF box structure.

From the above we see that this outer manifest store JUMBF box contains within it a series of functionally related JUMBF boxes. As the name suggests, the manifest store can contain a number of independently verifiable manifest structures, though only one is shown above for clarity. Note that in the case where more than one manifest structure is included in the store, each will play a specific role in the provenance history of the content and there will be a signaled relationship between them as described later in this paper.

The inner structure of the manifest shows the core C2PA concept of assertions. Assertions are where the creator of the manifest, which may be an editing tool, expresses actions or includes data about the content for consumption by subsequent actors in the value chain. Assertions may be expressed as a predefined metadata schema or be one of the C2PA defined standard assertions. The data for each assertion is held within its own defined structure and may be encoded as CBOR, JSON or Embedded File content type. CBOR is most typical for the native C2PA standard assertions, JSON is typically where an external schema has been adopted and a thumbnail jpeg image would be an example of an assertion using Embedded File content type.

In many cases metadata about assertions can be optionally included, expressing additional information about the assertion such as date and time associated with that assertion. For example, if the assertion expressed an edit, the metadata could indicate the date this was made. This makes for a comprehensive vocabulary of provenance data.

## Assertions

The standard C2PA assertions include amongst others:

- Assertion metadata - to further describe assertions.
- Cloud data - serving as a reference to any data hosted on the cloud.
- Thumbnail - allowing inclusion of a thumbnail image.
- Actions - a multivalued assertion to describe typical editing actions.
- Ingredient - to reference an included ingredient manifest.
- Endorsement - to describe the endorsement of some actions by another organization.
- Claim review - to describe a review of a third-party claim.
- Creative Work - a schema to describe a creative work in detail.
- Various bindings - discussed below.

## Binding The Content to The Manifest

As listed above, the standard assertions include a special assertion responsible for capturing the appropriate content binding data which cryptographically ensures the logical relationship between the content data and the manifest. C2PA refers to these techniques of using cryptographically unique representations of content as “hard bindings”. This contrasts with additional data that might assist such a process in a less precise manner termed “soft bindings”. The way in which these hard bindings are formulated depends to some extent on the file format of the content, just as the specification for how to embed a manifest within a file has to be file specific. To this end C2PA has defined how to assemble the content data into an input of a secure cryptographic hash for the case of the base media file format (BMFF) the common box-based format for audio and video presentations. Additionally, the case for non-BMFF-based file formats, typical for images, is covered through the ‘Data Hash’ assertion. Finally, for those formats which are ‘box like’ but not compatible with BMFF, a ‘General Box Hash’ is specified.

Note that the choice of cryptographic hash algorithm is part of the specification, as are all choices of cryptographic algorithms including signature algorithms. These are currently well known and trusted algorithms used in many applications today and include for example SHA-256 as a cryptographic hash and signatures based upon ECDSA using well known curves.

Focusing in on the BMFF binding which has been designed with audio/video presentations in mind, there are currently two techniques fully specified. The first relates to situations in which an entire file can be downloaded before playback begins. In this case the manifest contains a hash of all the data except for specific boxes, or parts thereof, which may safely be subject to change during transit. Additionally, the position of the boxes within the file is included in the hash algorithm input data to prevent manipulation of the overall structure by an adversary.

There is a second technique for forming hard bindings over BMFF file formats for those cases in which the data is likely to be downloaded in a progressive or fragmented way, that is, for cases where playback is expected to begin before the whole file has been downloaded by the client. In these cases, the data representing those parts of the file not relating to the audio/video samples can still be verified before playback. However, the content samples themselves are hashed not as one monolithic block, but as a series of hashes relating to each sample chunk of data held within the BMFF mdat box and addressed through the BMFF format. This leads to a requirement to validate many individual hashes separately. To make this manageable these hashes are prearranged within a Merkle tree structure when preparing the manifest. In this way, only the root of the Merkle tree needs to be included within the BMFF assertion structure of the manifest since this relates in a precise mathematical way to all individual hashes.

Validation of individual chunks can be made by the client on download through the associated timely download of data about that hash in relation to the overall Merkle tree structure. This additional Merkle data, which represents the unique list of siblings of each element in the path between the hash and the row element included in the manifest, allows the client to evaluate and process each individual chunk hash to determine whether this cryptographically aligns with the declared value in static manifest. In this way each chunk can be verified independently of each other and without waiting for all the data.

A simplified example of how to validate content data without associated adjacent data is shown in the schematic below. In this case the manifest contains the representation of the root of a Merkle tree, though the validator does not have access to all the Merkle elements at one time. The missing elements are marked in dotted boxes and arrows. However, the Merkle tree elements represented by the boxes marked A, B and C have been delivered with the data in a format that makes their position within the tree structure known. In the figure below the validator can verify the data by first calculating the hash and then using the data at A, B and C to recalculate the root of the Merkle tree. Matching this against the authenticated root value in the manifest allows the data to be verified.

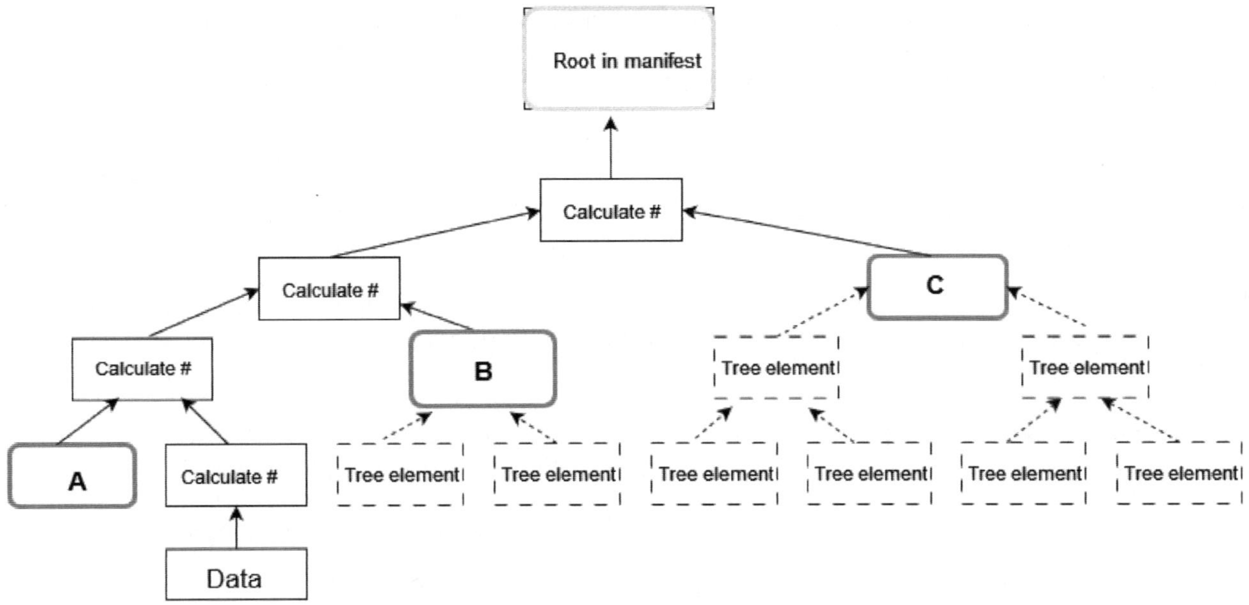


FIGURE 3: DATA CHUNK HASHES ARRANGED INTO A MERKLE TREE STRUCTURE.

## Claims

The claim box is also shown as a component of the manifest structure in Figure 2 above.
The claim is where a cryptographic hash of each assertion is collected together by the claim generator responsible for the manifest. This list of hashes and references can be enriched with other data such as data describing the claim generator itself, a title of the asset, its format, or some housekeeping data indicating the algorithms involved.

The claim box, represented in the manifest as CBOR data, ultimately forms part of the payload of the signature algorithm. Having this indirection between assertion and the signature payload enables assertions to be hosted in the cloud, since it makes it possible to know the manifest has not been tampered with even without retrieving the cloud assertion. This structure also allows a chain of manifests to be created and verified without requiring access to the underlying content associated with the earlier manifests. A description of a chain of manifests is given in a later section.

## Signature

The signature box contains a representation of the signature of the claim payload. The COSE signature data structure used also conveys data about how the signature is formed. All signature algorithms defined use well known public key cryptography and C2PA uses x.509 certificates to allow a public signing key to be cryptographically chained via intermediate certificates to a trust anchor known to the validator. In addition, the data structure can optionally convey a countersignature from a third-party time-stamp authority, witnessing the existence of the manifest at a specific time. Again, there is capacity to convey the PKI credentials associated with the time-stamp authority to a known trust anchor residing in the validator.

## Types and Special Uses of Manifests

The most straightforward application of the C2PA standard is as described with a single actor authoring provenance data for content they wish to create or publish. However, a strong use case is when a creator wishes to take already existing content with its own C2PA manifest and modify this or create something based on this, either exclusively or with other content items.

*Ingredients*. To meet this use case the C2PA manifest store can include one or more component manifest as an 'Ingredient' manifest. These ingredient manifests cannot be altered since that would invalidate their signatures which protect their integrity.

Inclusion of ingredients means that the manifest being authored is now known as the 'active manifest' to designate that this is the manifest at the head of the chain and must be validated first. Note that the inclusion of an ingredient is represented cryptographically by adding a reference into the assertion store of the parent active manifest, thereby cryptographically binding these items together logically.

This concept can be extended again when a creator uses the composite item and includes the active manifest of the original composite item and its associated ingredients as a chain of ingredients in the new items with a new active manifest.

Note that the original content represented by the ingredient manifests is not conveyed with the composite manifest which is bound to the composite content. Therefore, the content bindings assertions in the ingredient manifests cannot be verified. However, due to the indirection of the claim box, the signature of the ingredient manifests can be validated along with the remaining assertion values.

*Endorsement.* A further feature of manifest signaling is when a party wants to acknowledge or 'endorse' permitted actions of specific downstream parties as they transform the content in specific technical ways.

This can happen for example when a publisher provides a direct content feed to a social media platform or content distribution network for wider distribution. There are use cases where the downstream platform will wish to transcode the incoming content to provide a service to many different client devices with different technical parameters but would not wish to change the meaning of the content in any way. However, with C2PA hard bindings any such change will invalidate the original manifest by changing the content bits.

To handle this case a downstream party can be endorsed to publish, transcode or repackage content by obtaining an authenticated endorsement from the content originator that contains the downstream party public key. In this way the downstream distributer can issue a new active manifest and place the original as an ingredient. The new manifest should include the endorsement assertion to signal to the validator that this content transformation is limited and by arrangement with the originating party.

## User Experience Recommendations

The power of provenance data resides in the signaling of the received authenticated data to the asset consumer after processing by the validator. In this way the asset consumer can be assured of the source of the content, which may or may not coincide with the appearance, and whether it is 'as sent', or has been tampered with. More likely any changes have been recorded along the path and so there is a requirement to consider how this information can be conveyed to the asset consumer and how effectively it can be managed by the content creators. This is a matter for the creators of the validator and content creation tools and will provide a point of discrimination in the market as this technology evolves further.

The C2PA has developed clear recommendations and guidance [11] for implementers of provenance-enabled user experiences (UX). The guiding principles are:

- provide asset creators a means to capture information and history about the content they are creating, and
- provide asset consumers information and history about the content they are experiencing, thereby empowering them to understand where it came from and decide how much to trust it.

These principles and the work done are particularly important so as not to overload the user. To avoid this the C2PA considers 4 levels of disclosure to guide the designs

- Level 1: An indication that C2PA data is present and its cryptographic validation status.
- Level 2: A summary of C2PA data available for a given asset. This level should provide enough information for the particular content, user, and context to allow the consumer to understand to a sufficient degree how the asset came to its current state.
- Level 3: A detailed display of all relevant provenance data. Note that the relevance of certain items over others is contextual and determined by the UX implementer.
- Level 4: For sophisticated, forensic investigatory usage, a tool capable of revealing all the granular detail of signatures and trust signals is recommended.

FIGURE 4: FOUR LEVELS OF DISCLOSURE (FROM C2PA USER EXPERIENCE GUIDANCE DOC).

### Trusted Public Key Infrastructure

As described above, the manifest achieves integrity and security through public key cryptography. This in turn assumes the use of Public Key Infrastructure (PKI) to create an ecosystem of appropriately managed private keys and certificates containing the corresponding public keys which can be cryptographically chained in the classic way to a trust anchor known to validators. Validators may contain one of more trust lists of trust anchors depending on which provenance ecosystem they participate in. Validators will have been provisioned with trust lists out of band with respect to online operations. Currently C2PA specifies how to use X.509 certificates to achieve this aim.

C2PA does not mandate or even suggest particular trust lists or public key infrastructure (PKI), and instead takes them and other related configuration as inputs. This is because each application built using the C2PA standard that operates within its own ecosystem will have unique requirements and relationships amongst the participants of that ecosystem. Application implementers may be tempted to take existing trust lists used in other applications, such as those used for validating secure web sites or signed documents and adopt such lists without due consideration. To this end C2PA is developing guidance on the establishing and operating of an application's trust model and identity ecosystem.

### Considerations of Harms, Misuse and Abuse

The C2PA has considered harms modelling and analyzing how a socio-technical system might negatively impact users, stakeholders, broader society, or otherwise create or re-enforce structures of injustice, threats to human rights, or disproportionate risks to vulnerable groups globally. This work has been carried out to understand and offer guidance on the creation and use of C2PA in such a way as to prevent accidental harm through oversight or misuse. This work is described in the C2PA Harms Modelling guidance document [12].

## Adoption into News Workflows

The interdependence of news publishers requires a broad alignment of approaches at key points in newsroom workflows to allow easy interoperability of media files.

The framework for doing this includes:

1. Digitally signing and securing output when it is published. This can first be done at the organizational level, and ultimately at the show or reporter level.
2. Validate media on ingest. This will aid in sorting valid files from AI generated noise. The value of this function will gradually increase as provenance methods gain wide acceptance and the amount of signed content grows. Eventually, the absence of provenance information will be a signal that the content requires greater skepticism.
3. Adding reputational assertions. The optional ability to embed secured endorsements can assist in adding credibility to media exposed outside of its usual markets.

All of the activities will facilitate mechanized validation of content at scale.

It is also important to note that the inclusion of C2PA based secure meta-data will not break existing workflows, and the absence of this data will not, in itself, be a sign that the information is false. These two attributes will allow for a gradual introduction of the technology into the established ecosystem.

After a period of transition, when C2PA signals are widely adopted, the absence of secure metadata will become a suspicious signal, much the same way the absence of a HTTPS lock on a purported corporate website is today.

## The BBC Learnings

The BBC is one of the Origin partners who have participated in the technical working groups of C2PA with a focus on media distribution from a broadcaster's perspective. This has involved testing the specification by coding basic manifest generators and coordinating with other members of the C2PA to ensure interoperable content files can be independently created and verified, thereby strengthening the specification and helping bring the concept to life within the organization.

This early work is being further reinforced through work on a more robust and complete local demonstrator, built within our R&D facility. This will help experiment with user experience as we develop further ideas around the presentation and use of this technology and build upon the original work done by our colleagues and partners within the BBC and C2PA members.

Like all new technologies within a fast-moving news technical landscape, there is now a process of education, evangelizing and assessing how the technology can be integrated into the newsroom workflows. This process takes on a number of forms, from looking at the top-level strategic threat from synthetic content and how this might be countered, through to the exact nature of the current systems and where we might add C2PA functionality in a robust way to our pipelines to ensure secure use. In our experience this touches not only the engineering capabilities, but also journalistic practices and corporate policy and all these areas are now being developed.

Work is now planned on a formal technical analysis of systems integration whilst at the same time exploring the technology from the point of view of a journalist tool, including understanding how using these signals will affect content ingestion and be used with third party contributions. Further questions are also being considered around how provenance data will engage the audience - not least by making it clearer how journalists select and process the material they use. This is a new and exciting area for news practitioners to explore.

## CBC/Radio-Canada Learnings

CBC/Radio-Canada is a founding member of Project Origin and an early advocate for the use of the C2PA specification within its news infrastructure. The initial proof of concept used C2PA to securely sign the output emitting from the central distribution hub. This is the point of highest value creation and is compatible with the currently available C2PA tools. This simple intervention allows the signing of the corporation's content, helping to maintain the credibility and reputation of our work. This trial also allowed us to confirm that the addition of C2PA manifests did not disrupt the downstream flow of media.

Starting early 2022, along with Microsoft and Ravnur, the corporation has participated and completed multiple proof of concepts that allowed us to gain much needed experience with the specification along with determining a target architecture on how to ideally deploy the specification to position the corporation to sign our output.

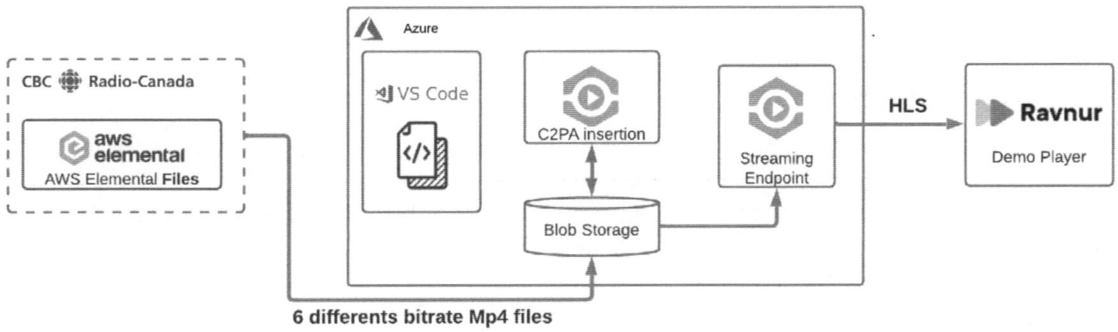


FIGURE 4: SCHEMATIC OF THE CBC/MICROSOFT/RAVNUR PROOF OF CONCEPT OUTPUT SIGNING.

Our initial proof of concept was to sign a piece of content and play it back while displaying it, along with provenance in a video player. These trials were quickly successful.

The implementation of these concepts in our current production environment is challenged by the current lack of universal adoption of the C2PA standard. While it is possible to implement the standard now, it would involve adjusting current workflows to send content to service providers who are leading in C2PA adoption. It is hoped that broader adoption of the standard by current suppliers will allow us to avoid this disruption.

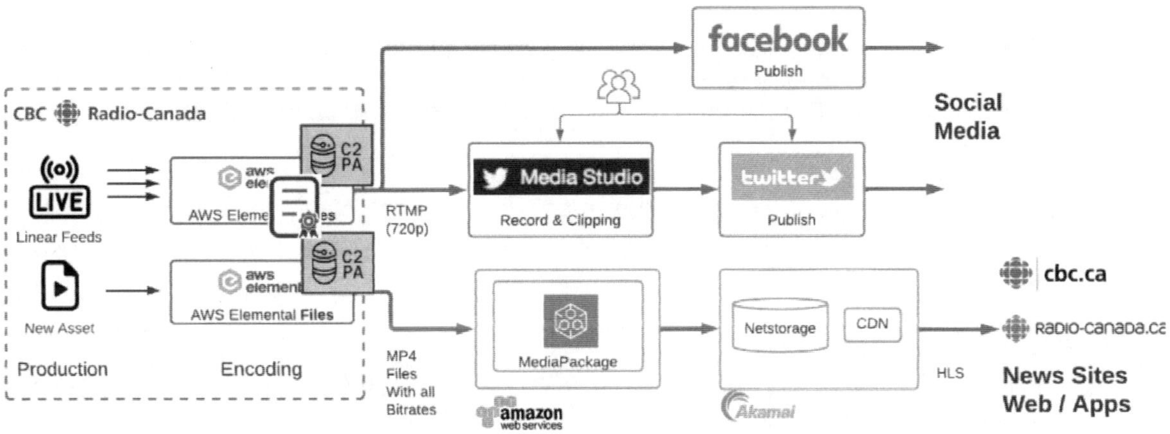


FIGURE 5: IDEAL ARCHITECTURE FOR OUTPUT SIGNING.

In a separate trial, CBC/Radio-Canada is participating in an effort to validate photos coming into its news infrastructure. This assists in confirming the veracity of the content coming into the news systems and will determine how and where the C2PA manifests are accessible in the current workflows.

By validating inputs and signing outputs the corporation is beginning the process of building an end-to-end provenance-based production chain. This is being done to establish the technical experience with provenance tools, and to socialize the use of provenance data within the internal operations of the organization.

This work is also being done to be shared with the wider news and technical communities. Provenance requires broad industry adoption. The corporation will continue to share its learnings with other publishers. In order to signal the importance of media provenance to potential vendors, the corporation has added criteria to its RFP technical compliance grid to emphasize the value of supporting the C2PA specification.

## Growing The Community

Media Provenance is a viable way to protect the news ecosystem from the threat of powerful synthetic media-based disinformation attacks. A large community of media and technology companies and subject matter experts have come together to define a common approach to the problem. The key to making it work is community adoption of common provenance practices.

Widespread adoption of signed and secured news media will make authentic content stand out in a sea of misinformation and synthetically generated noise.

As a broadcaster you can help by:

1. Adding C2PA secure digital manifests to your output at your point of origin.
2. Ask your vendors what their roadmap is to add C2PA functionality to their products.
3. Add a provenance validation step to your newsroom ingest function.
4. Join the growing community of practice to inform others of the need for updated media provenance processes.

Adding C2PA secure media manifests to our outputs is a necessary step to protect the integrity of the global news ecosystem. The Project Origin team is working to develop best practices for the common use of this technology in newsrooms. We look forward to working with you.

For companies that build media technologies, the Coalition for Content Provenance and Authenticity is a diverse and dedicated cross industry effort. Your participation in furthering the development of the specification or implementing this open standard into your product roadmap is welcome and encouraged.

However you chose to participate, the open secure media provenance community welcomes you to join our efforts.

## Acknowledgements

The authors would like to acknowledge the work of the C2PA in creating the technical specification described in this paper. In particular we would like to acknowledge the ongoing work of the C2PA Technical Working Group chaired by Leonard Rosenthol of Adobe and thank them for their permission to present this paper. The authors thank Laura Ellis of the BBC and Kevin Kane of Microsoft for their expert review of this paper and would like to acknowledge the support of the Project Origin members in the production of this paper.

## References

[1] *C2PA Specifications.* https://c2pa.org/specifications/specifications/1.2/index.html

[2] *ISO/IEC 14496-12:2020 Information technology — Coding of audio-visual objects — Part 12: ISO base media file format* https://www.iso.org/standard/74428.html

[3] *Exif. Exchangeable image file format for digital still cameras: Exif Version 2.32* https://www.cipa.jp/std/documents/download_e.html?DC-008-Translation-2019-E

[4] *IPTC Metadata standard.* http://www.iptc.org/std/photometadata/specification/IPTC-PhotoMetadata

[5] Schema.org vocabularies. https://schema.org/

[6] *ISO/IEC 19566-5:2019 Information technologies — JPEG systems — Part 5: JPEG universal metadata box format (JUMBF)* https://www.iso.org/standard/73604.html

[7] Birkholz H, Vigano C, Bormann C. *RFC 8610. Concise Data Definition Language (CDDL): A Notational Convention to Express Concise Binary Object Representation (CBOR) and JSON Data Structures.* June 2019. https://datatracker.ietf.org/doc/html/rfc8610

[8] Bormann C, Hoffman P. *RFC 8949 Concise Binary Object Representation (CBOR).* December 2020. https://www.rfc-editor.org/rfc/rfc8949

[9] Shaad J. *RFC 8152 CBOR Object Signing and Encryption (COSE).* July 2017. https://www.rfc-editor.org/rfc/rfc8152.txt.pdf

[10] Cooper D, Santesson S, Farrell S, Boeyen S, Housley R, Polk W. *RFC 5280. Internet X.509 Public Key Infrastructure Certificate and Certificate Revocation List (CRL) Profile.* May 2008. https://www.rfc-editor.org/rfc/rfc5280

[11] *C2PA User Experience Guidance for Implementers.* https://c2pa.org/specifications/specifications/1.0/ux/UX_Recommendations.html

[12] *C2PA Harms Modelling.* https://c2pa.org/specifications/specifications/1.0/security/Harms_Modelling.html

# Real Radio Hosts Working Virtually: How Real Humans Work with Containerized Broadcast Systems

**Kirk Harnack**
**Telos Alliance**
**Nashville, Tenn., United States**
kirk.harnack@telosalliance.com

**Abstract** – Some radio broadcasters are anticipating their deployment of broadcast software as part or most of their virtualized studio and broadcast infrastructure. A few radio stations and radio networks have already moved to a largely virtualized infrastructure while others are beginning the process now. The virtues of virtualization have been the topic of several dozen professional presentations ranging from manufacturers' revelations to scholarly presentations.

With several systems on-air now, it's time to ask, "How is working with virtualized broadcast systems either different from or similar to traditional broadcast gear?"

This NAB BEITC presentation asks that question and presents answers from broadcast engineers, broadcast IT professionals, and on-air talent.

## Change Brings Pain or Opportunity

In business and our personal lives, circumstances arise that lead to change. Perhaps a broadcaster's office and studio space become more valuable to a different tenant, so the landlord doesn't renew the broadcaster's lease, forcing a studio move. Or a transmitter site's property, once considered quite rural, is now highly desired for commercial development, thus pressuring either dual-use, moving the transmitter, or co-locating with another station. Or maybe an on-air talent must choose to end a long-running morning show partnership because his spouse's employment opportunities lie in a different city or state.

We've considered these business and life changes to be part of the challenges – and opportunities – of living and working. "Town to town, up and down the dial," from the WKRP TV show theme song perfectly summarized the often nomadic nature of broadcast employment. And, whether changes stem from the technical, business, or personnel realms, they often impact each other.

While we strive to see the opportunities in forced change, we must admit there are often downsides. Families are uprooted, separated, or even dissolved through divorce. Business plans are delayed or thwarted as opportunities are lost through unplanned expenses. A leading factor in these upheavals has been a lack of options for continued or improved operations.

This paper is excerpted from the Proceedings of the 2023 NAB Broadcast Engineering and Information Technology (BEIT) Conference, © 2023, National Association of Broadcasters, 1 M Street SE, Washington, DC 20003 USA.

Broadcasters have been tied to fixed studios and offices for the last century. Our technologies and business practices have required that radio stations have these fixed facilities and employees work almost exclusively in those brick-and-mortar locations.

The pandemic of 2020 greatly accelerated our industry's move toward work location flexibility, i.e., working from home. Given the broadcast tool sets and training available early on, contribution often suffered, both in audio quality and in workflow smoothness.

## Broadcast Workflows

Other business sectors have encouraged non-traditional work environments for quite some time. Have you interacted with technical support employees lately? Whether working for an airline, a VoIP provider, an insurance company or even a medical professional, as often as not these employees are working from home.

Until the worldwide Covid epidemic and attendant lockdowns, broadcasters had less need or desire to work from home. Indeed, working from home wasn't typically considered an option. There had been a few high-profile on-air talents working from home more than a decade prior to the pandemic. Robin Quivers, Rush Limbaugh, Neal Boortz, Herman Cain, Michael Savage, and Doug Stephan to name a few. Yet these early radio home-workers were enabled by a board operator and perhaps a producer and a call screener back at the studio. The talent may work from home, but that talent has been supported by staff members usually working in a traditional studio and using traditional radio hardware.

Broadcasters have been looking and waiting for technical solutions allowing remote workflows. While remote voice tracking has been around for over 20 years, broadcasters needed a convenient and satisfying solution to originate full-fledged broadcasts. Finally, a collection of technologies is available to realize the dream of working from almost anywhere and creating meaningful, live content, just as they would from purpose-built studios.

When we consider a list of tools and technologies that can make this happen, we should include the following:

- Audio over IP technology (Livewire, AES67, etc.)
- Software containers (Docker or other OCI-compliant functional blocks)
- Internet connectivity that's fast and reliable
- Software-based audio console with multi-user remote control via browser
    - Built-in audio monitoring and contribution via WebRTC
- Software-based on-air phone system
- Remote-capable phone screening software
- Software audio codecs (WebRTC, Opus, etc.)
- Automation/playout systems with remote control
- Traffic, billing, music scheduling all networked
- Program download/ingest software
- Audio logging, network-connected via AoIP
- Software-based audio processing for streaming, FM, HD, DAB, etc.
    - Internet-friendly FM & HD signal transport

While not every radio station requires all these functions, this list covers the needs of most broadcasters, no matter the station format.

One of the technologies making these software deployments possible is "Containerized Software." While most of us are familiar with Virtual Machines (or "VMs"), software containers are considered more efficient and certainly more manageable than VMs. Indeed, a management system such as Portainer or Kubernetes allows for management and quick failover to backup systems, automating key redundancies and thus keeping broadcasters on the air.

Software container standards are promoted by the Open Container Initiative, or "OCI". Containers were developed as a lighter-weight alternative to bulky Virtual Machines. Software containers more efficiently use a computer platform's resources, enabling a potentially large number of containers to run on a multi-core server. Each container enjoys a high degree of independence from other containers running on the same platform.

## Two Case Studies for Virtual Audio Mixing and Control

It's been said, "Necessity is the mother of invention." During 2022 two broadcasters were in real need of some invention. Fortunately, the technologies needed for averting disaster and disappointment were coming together, providing possible solutions.

Would they work as hoped?

In the following case studies, we've asked the broadcasters to tell much of the stories in their own words.

### Case Study #1: Homeless Radio Stations

Jeff McGinley is Director of Engineering and IT for a group of radio stations in the United States Pacific Northwest. He relates the circumstances leading to their deployment of virtualized studio infrastructure in the form of containerized software.

According to McGinley, "We decided to move out of a studio facility that we were in for 25 years. The infrastructure was old and the building was kind of falling apart. We found a new facility that we were going to move into. The problem is we ran out of time to build out the new facility before we had to be out ... of the old facility. And so it became a big crush to figure out how we were going to keep our seven radio stations on the air ... without having professional studios."

McGinley recalls providing a bare-metal, rack-mount server to Bryan Jones, Senior Support Specialist at Telos Alliance. Upon return, the server now had containerized software installations. The functionality installed included Livewire and AES67 audio connectivity, a full-featured audio console controlled remotely via browser, and supporting software to provide live, remote audio contribution and monitoring using the WebRTC protocols and functionality. The cluster of stations was already using Audio over IP (AoIP) for audio connections with their automation playout systems as well as their on-air phones, hardware audio codecs, and hardware audio processing.

Next these essential broadcast functions could be connected together on an AoIP network and placed in a controlled environment. Remember, they had to vacate the old studio facility and the new space wouldn't be ready for occupancy for several months. The best location for these virtual studios turned out to be one of the cluster's transmitter sites. It has reliable power and excellent Internet connectivity. The stations' automation/playout systems were placed there along with the all-important virtual audio consoles. These were a beta version of the Axia Altus software audio mixer, deployed as OCI-compliant software containers.

To enable convenient remote control, real-time audio monitoring and live audio contribution, a set of protocol servers was also deployed. This included a beacon server, STUN server, and TURN server.

These servers are used to traverse firewalls such that no firewall configuration is needed for end users, and WebRTC works seamlessly via a simple and secure invitation process [1].

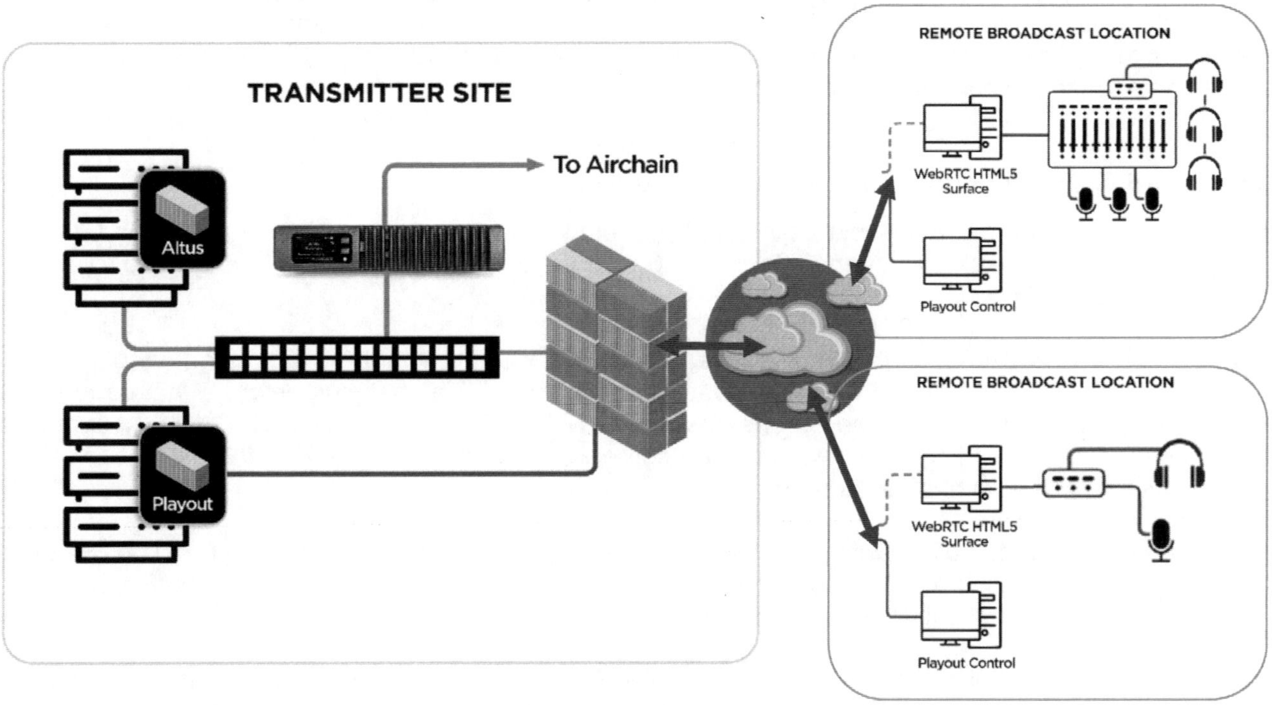


FIGURE 1: MULTIPLE USER / CONTRIBUTION SITES, CONNECTING TO VIRTUAL AUDIO MIXING.

McGinley describes how on-air talent, working from their homes or temporary offices, remotely connects to their virtual studio gear, "We've got full control over our virtualized studios. Everyone can reach into that using VPNs. They can access our automation systems, import media as needed to the file server, and access the audio loggers. Most importantly, they can use the Axia Altus virtual audio console to mix their shows live."

Jeff McGinley's seven-station cluster needed up to five simultaneous virtual audio consoles available, so five Axia Altus containerized audio mixers were deployed.

IT security was part of the design from the beginning. McGinley says, "We have a VPN client that's easy to use and provides two-factor authentication. For the end users it's very simple; it's really easy. For the networking team it was a little complex to set up, but now it just runs."

When considering an audio mixing console that's controlled with a computer browser, either via mouse or touchscreen, one may think that older users would balk at not having real knobs and faders to touch. Jeff McGinley assumed this as well. But to his surprise he learned something new about the more senior on-air talent. "I was pretty anxious to have them start using a mixer with a screen interface, but those people have been the most reliable and have needed the least amount of hand-holding. They've really gotten used to dragging the fader with a mouse or clicking on and off the source. They picked it up within the first air shift; no problem."

In this use case the radio stations already enjoyed the modern conveniences of an Axia Livewire AoIP networked environment. Jeff McGinley and other engineers were already familiar with the techniques involved and were quite comfortable with the technologies. We'll soon look at another use case where the studios were – and still are – almost entirely analog.

Just recently Jeff's stations have moved into their permanent home, having installed their hardware AoIP audio consoles in the new studios. With the immediate need gone for remote-controlled virtual mixing, McGinley is keeping two of his five virtual audio consoles online. He notes, "This is a perfect way for us to go on remote without having to use a board-op back at the station. The person at the remote broadcast can connect directly into the air chain on go live.

## Case Study #2: The Miles Can't Keep Us Apart

Jeff Kingman and Jeremy West host a legendary morning show together on KZOZ-FM, in San Luis Obispo, California. The show's been on for over 20 years, and the two have been doing radio together since their college days.

However, in early 2022 the longtime friends were forced to consider their breakup. Our story begins with Jeff Kingman, half of the morning show duo, revealing some life-changing news. "What happened was Jemery's wife got an awesome job offer in an area with a significantly lower cost of living. Jeremy and I were faced with ending the show or finding some way to continue on. And that's where this new remote audio console technology comes in."

Jeremy continues, "So, I talked with one of your engineers and told him what we wanted to do. He said, 'Well, I'm actually working on a project, because of Covid, where we could actually control the studio from your house with a monitor and a touch screen.'"

Jeremy replied, "Well, that's exactly what we're looking for, because over the course of the 20 years that Jeff and I have been working together, I run the board, and I wanted to make it as easy as possible to transition. So I was thinking if I could control the studio just like I normally do, and Jeff could just show up and talk into a mic like he normally does, that would be the easiest."

Jeff Kingman says that this virtual console setup is giving him flexibility as well. "I, myself, don't have to be in the studio, either. I just log into the codec, and I could be anywhere. In fact, on many occasions, I've done the show from home. Nobody that listens can tell a difference. It's crazy; I'll run into people here – and we only do our show for this market – and people still think Jeremy lives here. There are people who I consider pretty close contacts who have no idea that Jeremy's moved away."

Other than a few startup growing pains of being beta users, the morning show has no change to their workflow. Jeremy West runs the virtual board from his new home in Washington State, while Jeff Kingman is the other half of the morning show, working either from the old studio at the station, or from home – or even on the road.

While the first use case happened at a station cluster that already used Audio over IP networking, this second use case has been in an older facility that's completely analog. The analog outputs from their automation system were split to also feed an Axia xNode. The new "digital" audio console resides in a server running Linux and a Docker runtime engine and the audio console software container. That system is simply paralleled to the old analog console. Either system can be put on-air at the touch of a button.

Phone callers are an important part of Jeff and Jeremy's morning show, so a Telos VXs on-air phone system is also deployed on the same server running the Altus audio console. This containerized phone system is simply paralleled with the old Telos One-x-Six still in the analog studio.

The Axia Altus virtual audio mixing console and virtual Telos VXs phone system at KZOZ-FM demonstrate that old and new technologies can cohabitate. Indeed, for stations not ready to replace everything it's worth noting that parallel operation is easily possible during a transition period that could last as long as desired. Implementing virtual broadcast infrastructure doesn't have to be an all-or-nothing proposition.

## Virtual Takeaways

Jeff McGinley concludes that having available one or more virtual audio consoles is not only part of the operational planning for his employer's other markets, it's also part of their contingency and disaster recovery plans. According to McGinley, "Having a solution like this where you can centralize some broadcast infrastructure and not have to have such a big footprint for your traditional radio studios, this is the easiest thing ever. This should be the number one option when flexibility is required."

For KZOZ-FM, the staff, management, and engineers realize that software-based broadcast functionality has real benefits when life throws curveballs. A morning team with a 20-year history of solid entertainment and audience interaction gets to stay together on-air, despite being physically separated by over a thousand miles. Additionally, the station didn't have to upgrade the entire facility. They were able to upgrade just the equipment needed to keep the morning show together and provide better quality phone calls for contests and listener interaction.

In both use cases, the efficiency of containerized software, running on hardened computer platforms is proving the value of our virtual future.

## What's Next for Radio?

Many IT-centric businesses have already switched from virtual machines to containerized software. From everyday financial transactions to online commerce to cloud-based video conferencing and more, software containers are the environment where these functions are running. Real-time audio and video production are moving this way. The IT sector continues to develop and deploy tools, techniques, and technologies that are applicable to us in the broadcast and content creation industries as well.

## References

[1] "Introduction to WebRTC Protocols." Mozilla Developer Network https://developer.mozilla.org/en-US/docs/Web/API/WebRTC_API/Protocols

# Pop-up 5G Standalone Non-Public Networks (SNPNs) for Live Broadcast Production

**Samuel R. Yoffe, Malcolm Brew, Douglas Allan, Kenneth Barlee, Dani Anderson, Odianosen Ighagbon, Cameron Speirs, and Robert Stewart**
Neutral Wireless Ltd. and StrathSDR, University of Strathclyde
Glasgow, Scotland

**Ian Wagdin**
BBC R&D
London, United Kingdom

**Morten Brandstrup**
TV 2 Danmark
Copenhagen, Denmark

**Jack McGill and Gareth Gordon**
QTV
Glasgow, Scotland

**Don Mullane and Liam Murray**
RTÉ
Dublin, Ireland

**Mark Smith and Muki Kulhan**
IBC
London, United Kingdom

**John Canning and Aaron Behman**
AMD
Santa Clara, California, United States

**Matt Stagg**
BT Sport
London, United Kingdom

**Jonathan Hale**
Warner Bros. Discovery
London, United Kingdom

**Abstract** – A portable, pop-up private standalone 5G network has been developed and deployed around the world in a series of successful proof-of-concepts for outside broadcast production in remote locations. The flexible software-defined radio (SDR) allows us to rapidly customise the network to the environment and requirements, with low-latency configurations and heavy uplink biasing in the bi-directional RF channel to support multiple wireless camera feeds. We used shared spectrum available in the n78 and upper n77 bands (3.3 – 4.2 GHz) in UK, Ireland, Kenya and New Zealand to deliver live-to-air footage. We explored the use of bonding multiple low Earth orbit (LEO) satellites and cellular backhaul, which allowed us to broadcast the Pitlochry Highland Games live from rural Scotland into the IBC 2022 show in Amsterdam. This paper will discuss the critical technical capabilities of the pop-up private 5G network and how broadcasters have rapidly deployed the technology to support historic and sporting events, including the final journey from Scotland of Queen Elizabeth II and the Danish parliamentary elections. We will also explore how to configure connectivity for optimum performance.

## Introduction and Motivation

The use of 5G technology is of great interest to the broadcast industry, as it can offer the low latency and high bandwidth requirements for outside broadcast (OB) program making.

There are two main scenarios that should be considered in the deployment of 5G technologies for program making. The first are contribution feeds, which are characterized by the current use of bonded cellular devices on a public network, that are typically constrained in terms of latency and bandwidth but offer advantages in ease of deployment and large coverage areas. The second scenario is the use of production links that are characterized by low latency, high bandwidth local connectivity dedicated to a single wireless camera channel. Private 5G networks have the ability to impact on both of these scenarios. The main focus of this paper is to look at the production links workflow, but the technology has also been deployed to support contribution workflows at large scale events.

There are many deployment options for 5G Radio Access Networks (RANs). The most well-known implementations are those used commercially as public networks by Mobile Network Operators (MNOs). These nationwide networks generally have good coverage and capacity all throughout urban and suburban environments. While the use of public networks offers a straightforward and readily-available connectivity option in, there can be challenges with real-world implementation of bonded cellular approaches when thousands of people with mobile handsets flood a venue or in areas with poor coverage (resulting in network congestion). Moreover, much 5G network infrastructure runs as non-standalone (NSA), where it actually relies on a 4G LTE core. These networks cannot support the low latency and uplink bandwidth advantages offered by 5G New Radio (NR).

In addition, existing MNO infrastructure is almost entirely hardware based – custom silicon chips that define and run the mobile network hardware and are capable of supporting thousands of attached devices. Public mobile networks are fantastic at serving their customer base, but this hardware-defined approach does not allow for much flexibility to modify network configuration or performance. Many of the newer 'midband' cellular bands use a Time Division Duplexing (TDD) approach, where base stations transmit and receive in the same frequency band. MNOs are required to deploy a permanent TDD downlink bias (*i.e.,* more downlink resource slots than uplink slots) in order to satisfy their customers' data consumption requirements and not interfere with neighboring networks. While these are suitable for fast deployment contribution use cases, they are not really suitable for the uplink-heavy demands of the production workflow, particularly as we move towards a cloud-based workflow where all video feeds need to be available in remote or cloud-based production studios.

In contrast, a standalone non-public (private) network (SNPN) can be deployed that is totally independent of the MNOs [1]. These can be customized to meet the coverage, capacity, latency, or quality of service and performance requirements at specific geographical locations. A detailed discussion on NPNs can be found in the white paper produced by the 5G PPP Technology Board [2]. In the future, it may be possible for MNOs to offer private network slices using their RAN infrastructure or Public Network Integrated Non-Public Networks (PNI-NPNs).

Due to the limitations of hardware-based networks, we are particularly interested in the development and deployment of software-defined SNPNs with highly flexible configuration that can be popped up in a location to rapidly provide connectivity for devices in a hyper local area. Unlike conventional broadcast wireless cameras using COFDM radio technology, where spectrum licenses must be applied for and managed for each camera as well as all of the telemetry and additional communications channels, the IP connection established by 5G not only allows for two-way communication and control, but it also allows for multiple cameras (and other devices, for example microphones) to be connected under a single spectrum license. Additional cameras can be added *ad hoc*, within the constraints of the bandwidth available in the allocated channel.

With that in mind, one of the key factors for the deployment of a SNPN is spectrum access. In the UK, and a growing number of other countries, the upper n77 frequency band (3.8 – 4.2 GHz) has been reserved for shared access. While the licensing models are not currently in place for spectrum access similar to program-making and special events (PMSE) to allow for 5G SNPNs to be readily deployed, we have conducted a number of trials using test and development licenses in the UK and abroad, which we discuss presently.

In order to demonstrate the readiness and use of 5G SNPNs for the broadcast industry, since August 2021 we have undertaken a series of proof-of-concept trials exploring the deployment and performance of private 5G networks for the challenging use of video transport.

## Early Proof-of-Concept Trials

The use of 5G networks for video feed contribution was attractive, but MNO network slicing had not sufficiently matured commercially and broadcasters are concerned about the available uplink bandwidth and spectral efficiency, where unused downlink capacity would need to be deployed in order to achieve suitable uplink bandwidth. Moreover, production feeds often need to sit alongside traditional OB productions and would therefore need output to be available on location [3], and the latency penalty for going up to the cloud and back needed to be carefully considered. With the emergence of viable 5G SNPNs and shared access spectrum made available in the UK, there was an interest in using these SNPNs for production links (as well as contribution feeds), but the technology needed to be tested and contrasted with existing COFDM solutions.

### MotoGP (Silverstone, UK)

***Aim:*** *Demonstrate the use of a pop-up 5G SNPN for video contribution.*

In August 2021, the University of Strathclyde and its spin-out company, Neutral Wireless Ltd., were invited by BT Sport and Dorna to deploy a SNPN at the Silverstone racecourse in the UK, in a trial to connect wireless cameras for a MotoGP race. A single-cell gNodeB was used to flood the pitlane from a high-gain 60-degree sector antenna, with a 50 MHz channel centered on 3870 MHz using 30 kHz subcarrier spacing. The cell ran in SISO with 26 dBm transmit power, and the antenna gain was 17 dBi giving a downlink EIRP of 43 dBm. While running SISO in the transmit path, 4 receive paths were configured to exploit receive diversity and increase performance. The AW2S Panther remote radio head was collocated with the antenna and connected to the gNodeB using single mode fiber. The system ran using the Amarisoft standalone 5G core and vRAN implementation on a single machine with an Intel i9 processor. The flexible software-defined radio allowed for the physical layer TDD configuration to be biased slightly more to uplink, with the frame structure configured to use 5 slots for uplink and 4 for downlink.

FIGURE 1: VISLINK 5G-ENABLED ENCODERS IN THE PITLANE AND MOUNTED TO A SAFETY BIKE.

Multiple cameras provided by Vislink were connected to the SNPN, including the HCAM5 and a motorbike-mounted camera shown in Figure 1. Cameras capturing full HD (1080i50) were connected by SDI to 5G-enabled H.264 encoders connected to the SNPN using modems configured to transmit at 23 dBm, where they were compressed to 12.5 Mbps streams delivered over the 5G network to the corresponding decoder situated in the production gallery, which provided SDI back out into the broadcast chain. End-to-end (SDI-to-SDI) latency was estimated to be around 200 ms. The 12 Mbps video feeds were easily accommodated even at low signal-to-noise ratios (SNRs) ~15 dB and low modulation depth (16-QAM).

This trial was intended as an internal test that ran alongside the tradition OB production. However, the director was impressed by footage coming back from the pitlane, and the cameras were used as part of the live-to-air production, capturing interviews and imagery live from the pitlane. We believe this is the first live-to-air video contribution using a SNPN.

## UK Premiership Rugby (StoneX, UK)

***Aim:*** *Demonstrate multiple low latency 5G-connected cameras with direct COFDM comparison.*

Following some internal development work by Neutral Wireless, the 5G technology used at Silverstone was integrated into a wheeled rack flight case to make it more suitable for transportation and rapid deployment at events. The Neutral Wireless "Network-in-a-box" (NIB) featured the AW2S software-defined radio head and a new compute platform, which was configured to run the Amarisoft 5G core and vRAN software. The first outing for the NIB was at the Saracens versus Northampton Saints Gallagher Premiership Rugby match (at the StoneX stadium, UK) where two cells running 50 MHz channels in n77 were configured to increase coverage range (although it was found that the pitch was sufficiently covered by a single cell). Neutral Wireless also developed a heavily uplink-biased 2:7 (DL:UL) frame structure to significantly increase uplink bandwidth and support more camera feeds.

FIGURE 2: NEUTRAL WIRELESS NIB PITCH-SIDE AT STONEX (LEFT), AND THE 5G AND COFDM CAMERA FEEDS (RIGHT).

Working with BT Sport, BT Media and Broadcast, Vislink and Broadcast RF, the n77 NIB was deployed at the stadium, and integrated into the wider OB that was provided by Broadcast RF. Two wireless pitch-side cameras were fitted with Vislink encoders with COFDM and 5G transmitters, and 12 Mbps feeds were simultaneously sent back over both COFDM and 5G radio links to Vislink decoders to allow for a comparison of the technologies, side by side, as can be seen in Figure 2 (right). There was a latency of a few frames with the 5G feed, as would be expected for the IP-based network. The OB producers used the video carried over the 5G network as part of the live feed, in a UK first. Never before had key match day cameras used as part of a consumer broadcast been enabled in this way.

## IBC Accelerator Project – Remote Production in the Middle of Nowhere

Based on the successful early trials discussed above, the University of Strathclyde and Neutral Wireless pitched an IBC Accelerator project exploring 5G-enabled "remote production in the middle of nowhere". The concept was to take a pop-up 5G SNPN to remote locations around the world where internet connectivity was not assured, and use it to explore new production models based on HD wireless camera feeds and tailored to available backhaul.

The goals were to explore the use of an SNPN to provide the communications backbone for high-bandwidth and low-latency media broadcast applications, and to demonstrate that the technology could be made highly portable and low power for rapid deployment anywhere in the world, including off-grid. In addition, the trials aimed to investigate different backhaul connectivity (and bonding) using fibre, cellular, and low Earth orbit (LEO) satellites infrastructure.

The project was very successful, and recently received the **IBC 2022 Accelerator Project of the Year award.**

### Fleadh Cheoil – Traditional Music Festival (Mullingar, Ireland)

***Aims:***

- *Demonstrate multiple SNPN-connected camera feeds;*
- *Investigate SNPN bonding.*

In August 2022, the Neutral Wireless NIB was deployed at the Fleadh Cheoil Traditional Music Festival in Mullingar, Ireland. The 32kg flight case was transported by car and ferry from Scotland. Working with the national broadcaster RTÉ, two LiveU wireless encoders (LU300 and LU600) were equipped with SIMs for the SNPN and used around the streets of Mullingar. The production ran out of an RTÉ OB van, with the 5G antenna and a Starlink for backhaul mounted on the roof as shown in Figure 3.

FIGURE 3: LEFT: RTÉ OB VAN WITH RADIO HEAD AND ANTENNA MOUNTED WITH STARLINK TERMINAL ON THE ROOF. RIGHT: CAMERA OPERATOR ROAMS THE STREETS TESTING THE COVERAGE PROVIDED BY THE SNPN.

A 20 MHz channel was used in the lower n77 (n78) band with an uplink biased 2:7 (DL:UL) frame structure. The 12 Mbps FHD HEVC video streams broke out on the local user plane where there was an LU2000 server on premise. The feeds were routed through an SDI video distribution switch before being re-encoded at 6 Mbps using an LU600 and streamed back to a decoder at RTÉ headquarters in Dublin to enter their live production chain. The backhaul was bonded over Starlink and dual 4G SIMs. The LiveU encoders were using a latency of 2 s. Full network and signal workflows are shown in Figure A1 in the Appendix.

LiveU video encoders are regularly used to bond multiple MNO connections to maximize uplink bandwidth by intelligently splitting the video stream over multiple routes and recombining on the decoder – something possible due to the high-latency workflow. In this trial, we explored bonding using two SIM cards *on the same SNPN*, and the results were better than expected. While the camera with a single modem could maintain its video feed while in line-of-sight of the cell antenna, we found that the bonded camera was able to go much further including exploring the streets of Mullingar *without* line-of-sight. Since frequencies up at 4 GHz can scatter widely in an urban environment, we could actually make use of the reflections off buildings to maintain connectivity. Since the stream is split over two interfaces with their antenna physically separate spatially, and the load on each dynamically adjusted to accommodate the available bandwidth, the bonded solution was very stable and robust.

## Ol Pejeta Conservancy (Kenya)

***Aim:*** *Demonstrate NDI|HX workflow with YouTube Live stream production using renewable energy.*

FIGURE 4: SNPN DEPLOYED IN THE BACK OF A VAN IN THE OL PEJETA CONSERVANCY WITH THE HOSTS OF SHENG TALK.

Also in August 2022, the Neutral Wireless NIB made its way by aeroplane to Kenya, where it joined WhatsGood Studios in the Ol Pejeta Conservancy – a large nature conservation area in central Kenya.

Spectrum was agreed with the Communications Authority of Kenya for a 50 MHz channel in n77 with a 2:7 (DL:UL) frame structure.

Production ran in the back of a 4x4, using solar panels through an inverter to provide power. Two Magewell Ultra Encode SDI NDI|HX encoders were connected to the 5G SNPN through a 5G-ethernet bridge configured by Neutral Wireless, which streamed 16 Mbps H.264/HEVC to their counter-part Magewell Pro Convert SDI decoders to feed into a Blackmagic ATEM. An NDI Discovery Server ran on the baseband unit that allowed the decoders to discover the encoders, or the NDI|HX feeds could be configured by manually specifying the source IP address on the private 5G network. The cut feed was presented to an Apple Mac mini computer via USB, and was then streamed live to YouTube. As seen in Figure 4, the presenter drove around the conservancy, showing their large YouTube audience the wildlife there and discussing the 5G workflow they were using. The SDI-to-SDI latency in this workflow using the off-the-shelf Magewell encoders and decoders was around 150ms. In this case, fibre backhaul was available at a nearby mobile cell mast, while the production was powered using solar panels feeding a 600W inverter. Full network and signal workflows are shown in Figure A2 in the Appendix.

### Interim Māori Spectrum Commission and Whakaata Māori TV (New Zealand)

***Aims:***

- *Rural deployment for live newsgathering;*
- *Full NDI over 5G.*

To complete the trip around the world, Neutral Wireless worked with the Interim Māori Spectrum Commission (IMSC) to deploy a NIB in rural New Zealand. Spectrum was made available in the n78 band (3.4 – 3.8 GHz) for a 50 MHz channel.

FIGURE 5: SNPN DEPLOYED AT A SCHOOL IN RURAL NEW ZEALAND, WITH MĀORI CHILDREN PERFORMING A MAU RĀKAU TRADITIONAL MĀORI MARTIAL ARTS CLASS.

The 5G SNPN was set up at a rural school, where cameras captured live video feeds of the schoolchildren performing a Mau Rākau traditional Māori martial arts class, as shown in Figure 5. LiveU LU300 encoders were used, with the 6 Mbps feeds backhauled over Starlink to a decoder at the Māori TV in Auckland studios for post-production and live broadcast. Full network and signal workflows are shown in Figure A3 in the Appendix.

In this trial, a BirdDog NDI encoder was used to send an 80 Mbps full NDI video feed over the 5G SNPN to a decoder on the user plane. Again, the NDI Discovery Server ran on the baseband unit. We believe this was the first time that full NDI video has been delivered over a private 5G network.

### Pitlochry Highland Games (Perthshire, Scotland)

***Aims:***

- *Multiple camera OB at rural location with programme feed produced on site;*
- *Programme feed (and multiviewer) delivered live to IBC show floor (cloud distribution);*
- *Talkback over 5G;*
- *Bonded Starlink terminals and MNO SIMs for backhaul.*

The traditional Highland Games are a long-standing celebration of Scottish culture. The Pitlochry Highland Games is one of the busiest weekends of the year for the small rural town in Perthshire, Scotland. The Pitlochry Highland Games were inaugurated in 1852, and we were welcomed by the Chieftain to use the 170$^{th}$ anniversary Games as a testbed for 5G production in a remote location.

This trial aimed to demonstrate a full multiple camera production with an on-site vision mixer to deliver a cut program feed from a location with poor backhaul connectivity. While rural Pitlochry has partial 4G coverage from public networks, the arrival of several thousand people made this unfeasible as a backhaul option. We therefore wanted to test the performance when bonding multiple Starlink units, in principle attached to different satellite flights, to combat the video drop experienced at handover when using a single terminal.

Working with the Scottish production company QTV, a four-camera production was deployed with the Neutral Wireless NIB to Pitlochry. The 5G antenna was mounted on the pavilion overlooking the Games field, along with the two Starlink terminals. The network ran a 100 MHz channel in n77 with a 2:7 (DL:UL) frame structure. Production ran out the back of a Land Rover parked next to the pavilion, shown in Figure 6.

FIGURE 6: LEFT: QTV CAMERA OPERATOR WITH 5G-CONNECTED ENCODER AND ANTENNA MOUNTED ON CAMERA.
CENTRE: ON SITE PRODUCTION IN THE BACK OF A LAND ROVER.
RIGHT: THE MULTIVIEWER FEED RECEIVED AND DISPLAYED AT THE IBC 2022 SHOW IN AMSTERDAM.

The four JVC cameras captured full HD 1080p50, which was passed to H.264 encoders provided by Open Broadcast Systems. These small form factor encoders were powered from a battery bank and carried in a small satchel by the camera operator. An external 5G modem and dual antenna were connected to the encoders by a 2m USB extension cable, allowing for them to be mounted to the camera well above head height and ensuring line-of-sight visibility with the 5G SNPN cell.

The encoders encoded 4:2:2 10-bit video at 20 Mbps, and these streams were packaged using the Zixi protocol and transported to a Zixi Broadcaster server, which distributed them to the Open Broadcast Systems decoder as well as making stream and 5G network statistics available. The local SDI-to-SDI latency was around 160 ms, including a 50 ms Zixi stream buffer. The four camera feeds passed through a Blackmagic ATEM for local multiview and on to a local vMix instance provided by QTV, where they were cut to produce a live program feed. This was sent from vMix to the Zixi Broadcaster using SRT, before being transported to Zixi ZEN Master using the Zixi protocol with the stream bonded over the two Starlink units and two 4G SIMs. In addition to the program feed, a single static camera feed was sent to ZEN Master, and the multiviewer was encoded and sent to Net Insight (unbonded) using SRT. Full network and signal workflows are shown in Figure A4 in the Appendix.

To demonstrate the flexibility of cloud-based distribution, the program feed was shared from Zixi to Net Insight, before being delivered to the IBC show floor at RAI in Amsterdam using SRT. Unfortunately, during the on-stage live interview from Pitlochry, we experienced some packet loss that degraded picture quality and was originally attributed to the Starlink bonding at such a northern latitude. However, it was later found that the inter-cloud connection between Zixi and Net Insight did not have a sufficient latency buffer to account for the round-trip time and jitter for an inter-continental cloud hop over public internet. This was corrected by simply increasing the Zixi stream buffer by an additional 100ms for the remainder of the show. The statistics available through Zixi ZEN Master for each leg of the stream journey allowed us to identify the source of the packet loss.

In this trial we also demonstrated the use of 5G for talkback. The Open Broadcast Systems C-100 encoders were configured to produce a small protected WiFi hotspot that provided the camera operators with internet access over the 5G network. Since half of the production team were remote (at the IBC show in Amsterdam), we decided to use the low-latency voice platform offered by Discord. This allowed for low-latency communication between the director and camera operators (on site) as well as the remote team. We note that the Blackmagic ATEM could be operated remotely from Amsterdam, but the increased latency when using bonded backhaul meant that cuts made live at the IBC show did not appear in the received program feed for a few seconds.

## Live-to-air Broadcasts

The IBC Accelerator exposed the broadcasters and production companies involved in the events to the capabilities of a pop-up 5G SNPN for program making, and inspired the confidence to use the emerging technology on real-world live-to-air broadcasts that we discuss in this section.

### Her Late Majesty Queen Elizabeth II's Final Departure from Scotland

***Aim:*** *Provide a single 5G wireless camera feed at Edinburgh Airport for a live-to-air world feed.*

On Thursday, 8th September, 2022, Her Majesty Queen Elizabeth II passed away at her Balmoral home in rural Scotland. When this happened, Operation Unicorn – the codename for the transport of Her Majesty's body if she were to pass away in Scotland – came into effect. The plan had originally been that the Royal coffin would be transported by rail from Edinburgh Waverley station, but it had been recently changed to an RAF C-17 Globemaster aircraft from Edinburgh Airport. A shortage of availability of traditional wireless cameras systems – bonded cellular or COFDM – in the UK left BBC Scotland (as the world feed provider) and the Glasgow-based production company QTV, who had been tasked with delivering the outside broadcast, without an option to deploy a traditional wireless camera at the airport. A cable trailing across the runway was not a possibility for an angle shooting towards the congregation, and therefore these significant shots could not have been captured.

At the IBC show in Amsterdam, QTV had partnered with Neutral Wireless, Open Broadcast Systems and Zixi to deliver the multi-camera production over private 5G that was being displayed live on the IBC Accelerator stand. The question arose – why could we not deploy this solution at the airport? The only impediment was spectrum. Working with colleagues at the BBC, a short-term short-notice spectrum license for n77 at Edinburgh Airport was granted by the UK regulator, Ofcom, allowing for the Neutral Wireless NIB to be deployed at the airport on Tuesday, 13th September 2022, as shown in Figure 7.

FIGURE 7: LEFT: NEUTRAL WIRELESS NIB AT EDINBURGH AIRPORT. RIGHT: 5G-CONNECTED CAMERA IS SET UP.

The airport was a very challenging RF environment to operate in, particularly with the high-power radar transmitter operating nearby. The shared spectrum licensing for n77 is low power transmit, which is well suited to the broadcast application where we are primarily concerned with listening for the video stream uplink. We found that our antenna was saturated by the radar signal, significantly reducing our receive sensitivity and leading to a large amount of packet loss at a regular periodic interval. We describe this as trying to listen to our user equipment whispering while the radar shouted at us.

To overcome this challenge, we did three things. First, we reduced our channel to 50 MHz, since the narrower bandwidth increases the power spectral density as the same power is transmitted but across a smaller range of frequencies. This increases the signal-to-noise ratio (SNR) at the receiver and improves the uplink channel quality. Secondly, we turned the antenna architecture “the wrong way round” and used our large high-gain directional sector antenna at the user equipment (UE), and the lower gain omni-directional antenna at the cell. This allowed us to whisper a bit louder and improved our SNR while reducing the sensitivity of the receive antenna to the radar, resulting in less (but still noticeable) packet loss. Finally, we increased the Zixi stream buffer up to 250 ms to allow for sufficient packet recovery between radar bursts. With these changes, we were able to deliver a stable 20 Mbps H.264 1080i50 stream as a contribution to the OB production, with an SDI-to-SDI latency of around 18 frames (360 ms). This was noticeable but very workable in an otherwise entirely wired production. We note that the latency was nothing compared to that of the feed provided by the helicopter, which was delayed by several seconds and suffered from low bitrate artifacts and packet loss.

As a backup option, a second copy of the video stream from the same Open Broadcast Systems encoder was taken out using Zixi bonded over dual 4G dongles to an AWS cloud instance. This was then brought back down to the production using a 4G customer premise equipment (CPE). In our testing, this worked well, albeit with a noticeable delay compared to the private 5G feed. However, as the procession approached the airport, the 4G backup feed dropped and could not be maintained. Interestingly, it was not the uplink that failed, but rather the downlink back to the OB van.

The video feed contributed using the 5G SNPN received around 10% air time in the live world feed provided by the BBC, which is estimated to have been viewed by over 1 billion people around the globe. We believe that this was the first public live-to-air international broadcast using private 5G network technology without a traditional failsafe in place.

## National Ploughing Championships 2022 (Ratheniska, Ireland)

***Aim:*** *Deliver a live-to-air feed at a large event with significant network congestion.*

Neutral Wireless partnered once again with RTÉ and LiveU to deploy a NIB and wireless HEVC encoders at the National Ploughing Championships in Ratheniska, Ireland – an event attended by 300,000 people every year. The workflow was similar to the music festival in Mullingar, with an on-site decoder as well as a feed being delivered to RTÉ headquarters for a live-to-air feed. In this trial, the LiveU LU800 encoder used to re-encode the feed for delivery to the production facility bonded the stream over two Starlink terminals with excellent results. The workflow is presented in Figure A5 in the Appendix. Using the 5G SNPN-connected wireless camera, a live weather report was delivered from the fields at the ploughing championships, as seen in Figure 8.

FIGURE 8: RTÉ WEATHER REPORT DELIVERED LIVE FROM THE FIELDS AT THE NATIONAL PLOUGHING CHAMPIONSHIPS.

With 300,000 people attending the event, MNOs faced significant network congestion issues and, to overcome this, additional temporary cells were brought in to cover the rural location. The presence of this concentrated MNO activity created a challenging RF environment for our low power system, and once again we found that our antenna was being saturated. With TDD, the base station transmits and receives in the same frequency band, with transmit and receive alternating in time. The uplink-biased 2:7 (DL:UL) frame structure that we were running, which used 2 downlink slots followed by 7 uplink slots, clashed with the MNO frame structure of 7 downlink slots followed and 2 uplink slot (7:2). Our send and receive were out of phase, resulting in us attempting to listen to our low power UE while the MNO cells were transmitting.

In order to overcome this, Neutral Wireless engineers reconfigured the network to match the MNO frame structure, and used GPS to frame-lock with the MNOs to ensure that we were all listening at the same time. This really highlights the flexibility of the software-defined radio approach, allowing the network configuration to be readily adapted to local RF conditions. Since we were only attempting to contribute one wireless camera feed, the reduced uplink bandwidth caused by the downlink-biased frame structure was not a problem, but usable range whilst maintaining the modulation coding scheme (MCS) to support the required bitrate was reduced.

## Danish General Elections (Copenhagen, Denmark)

***Aims:***

- *Multi-cell network deployment with cell handover;*
- *Ultra-low latency video contributions;*
- *SMPTE 2110 IP-based workflow to delivery.*

As a final 2022 international outing for the Neutral Wireless NIB, in October the SNPN travelled to Copenhagen (Denmark). Working with Danish national broadcaster TV 2 and Haivision, low-latency 5G wireless cameras were used at the historical Christiansborg Palace to capture the events surrounding the Danish Parliamentary Elections.

Two cells running 50 MHz channels in n77 were deployed at the palace – one outside in the courtyard to provide coverage for the arrival of the new Prime Minister (PM), and a second inside the building to provide coverage as the party made their way through to the PM's new office. The outdoor cell was fitted to a bicycle for portability, as captured in Figure 9. Cameras could move around and handover between cells. However, due to the very low latency encoder being used, cell handover did result in a dropped frame. A small buffer could have prevented this dropped frame occurring, but at the expense of an additional latency of 1-2 frames.

FIGURE 9: LEFT: NETWORK ~~IN A BOX~~ ON A BIKE – OUTDOOR CELL DEPLOYED FOR MAXIMUM MOBILITY.
RIGHT: MEASURING THE RF CONSTELLATION (QAM-16).

The baseband unit was located in the basement of the building, where a fiber patch panel provided connectivity throughout the palace and grounds. The two radio heads were both located with their antenna (to minimize RF cable length) and connected to the baseband unit using single mode fiber capable of supporting the 10 Gbps radio fronthaul. Backhaul to the TV 2 studios was dedicated dark fiber.

Two low latency HEVC video streams were encoded by Haivision Pro 460 units directly connected to the Neutral Wireless SNPN using their internal Sierra Wireless EM9191 5G modems. They were transported over the 5G network to a Haivision StreamHub on the local user plane, which decoded the streams and pushed the video out to the TV 2 production facility over dedicated fiber in a fully SMPTE 2110 IP-based production workflow [4,5]. TV 2 measured end-to-end latency of less than 100 ms from camera to their production studios. The resulting feed was looped back to the palace, where it broke out as SDI for local display. At the palace, the SDI-to-SDI latency (including the trip through the TV 2 production workflow and back) was measured as approximately 115 ms.

## Key Learnings

When we started on this journey, the potential benefits of 5G SNPNs for the broadcast industry were understood, but whether the technology was mature enough to use in practice and whether it ultimately delivered on its promises in real-world application remained to be seen. Our biggest take home from the trials and events described here is that the technology is absolutely ready to find use in broadcasting, and will continue to improve with adoption and experience.

The benefits of the software-defined radio (SDR) approach should also not be overlooked, as it allows for complete network flexibility and rapid adaptation to local RF environments. Without this on-the-fly reconfigurability, several of the events above could have failed to deliver on their desired outcomes. The ability to tune the network for uplink bias is significant for broadcasters trying to support as many cameras onto a private network as they can, especially as we move towards 4K content. The SDR solution used here allows for the frame structure to be highly uplink biased, such as 8 upload slots and 1 download slot (1:8). With this configuration, we have been able to sustain over 400 Mbps in the uplink with round-trip time (RTT) of 10ms in single-input single-output (SISO) mode with a 100 MHz channel (over 4 bits/Hz). This can be significantly improved running in multiple-input multiple-output (MIMO) but requires the UE to support uplink MIMO. The frame structure can even be changed to 2:2 or even 1:1 to support very low latency network transit with extremely low jitter (*e.g.,* for audio workflows).

Receive diversity differs to MIMO as the downlink and uplink transmission are both still SISO, however multiple receive paths are used to listen and aggregate the signal. This can be used to significantly increase SNR. At Silverstone for the MotoGP, this led to an improvement of over 3 dB. Using receive diversity allows for different RF polarizations to be received or different spatial locations, which prevent the (regular) situation where the polarization of a UE's SISO antenna is not well aligned with, or obstacles prevent loss of line-of-sight to, one single-polarization receive antenna. For example, if a UE transmitting with polarization +45° and being well received by a +45° antenna were to turn 180° around, its polarization would now be -45° and orthogonal to the receive antenna. With no receive diversity, the signal quality for this UE will drop drastically. Whereas, with receive diversity using both +45° and -45° polarizations, a good connection can be maintained.

For video streaming applications using protocols with error correction (such as SRT and Zixi) we found that running with unacknowledged mode (UM) on the radio link control (RLC) layer can improve latency and jitter. Since the streaming protocols already include packet recovery (such as forward error correction (FEC) and automatic repeat request (ARQ)) we do not need to do this on the RLC layer as well, and it can actually interfere with the retransmission and in sequence delivery. Acknowledged mode (AM) is typically desirable for TCP-like applications. Retransmission at the medium access control (MAC) layer can be minimized, but we recommend not to disable completely.

Likewise, quality of service (QoS) can be defined to managed resources and reduce latency (as the UE do not need to request resources from the scheduler). Static QoS flow and resource priority for particular traffic or IP addresses can be used to ensure particular UEs take priority over others for resources, or RLC UM bearers to reduce retransmission latency for UDP-based video streams with error correction. These can be mapped to access point names (APNs) to restrict access by SIM card. This can be used to guarantee resources to high priority devices. Indeed, UEs with unprotected resources (not QoS guaranteed bearers) can benefit significantly from variable bitrate (VBR) encoders. When resources become constrained or the UE is close to the cell edge with reduced SNR and MCS, rather than drop frames as the bearer can no longer support a specified constant bitrate (CBR) there is a reduction in bitrate (and quality) to match the available resources. It would be preferable for a live feed to reduce in quality than glitch or drop altogether. Both CBR and VBR devices can be accommodated and coexist peacefully on the network.

NDI-based workflows can be configured to run over the 5G network, either using an NDI Discovery Server or mDNS mirroring across interfaces. Like on a wired IP network, for NDI and NDI|HX it is necessary that both the encoder and decoder have clear IP routes to one another, and this should be borne in mind when designing the wider network topology.

While encoders that perform bonding over multiple interfaces are regularly used to bond over multiple MNOs to maximize throughput and reliability, we have found that bonding multiple UE on the same SNPN provides significant benefits to the stream robustness and reliability. These results have been repeated at the University of Strathclyde's rural 5G testbed on the banks of Loch Lomond using LiveU LU300 encoders with dual external 5G modems and SIMs on the same SNPN.

It is often tempting to run a full 100 MHz channel to maximize uplink bandwidth – more is always better, right? But if the application does not require the full bandwidth, then network performance (including range and reliability) can be improved by reducing the channel width and increasing the power per subcarrier.

We showed how multiple (consumer) Starlink terminals could be bonded and used together to avoid the frame drop often experienced by the hard handover from one Starlink satellite to another. The Starlink units were started up physically separated and offset in time, which appears to be sufficient to coax them into connecting to different satellite trajectors and therefore detaching and reattaching at different times. For the Pitlochry IBC event, we used Zixi to bond over two Starlink terminals and two 4G MNO SIMs, but as the crowds arrived we found that the contribution over the 4G links was almost nothing.

In addition to our own learnings, we would like to highlight the findings of the EBU 5G-RECORDS project [5] that investigated the integration of 5G SNPNs in media production workflows [6].

## Conclusions and Future Outlook

5G offers many potential advantages over traditional wireless camera systems used within the broadcast industry, from its high data rates to low latency. For many of these advantages to be realized, it is necessary to look beyond the mobile network operator (MNO) offerings to standalone non-public networks (SNPNs) that offer the user the ultimate in network configurability to tune the network as necessary, such as highly uplinked biased or low latency frame structures. Software-defined radio solutions, as used here, are highly flexible, and in this paper we have demonstrated many different devices and production workflows.

One of the biggest advantages that 5G brings is the bi-directional IP connection to the user equipment, which in the broadcast market allows for talkback, tally, return video and camera control to all be performed with low latency over the one network connection. In this paper, we have demonstrated carrying two-way audio communication over the 5G network to facilitate an OB with off-site participants. While not used in the trials above, we have also developed and demonstrated tally lights integrated with traditional tally hardware, and performed full camera control (exposure, shutter, iris, white balance, *etc.*) with cameras from Grass Valley and ZCAM. Finally, we have provided return video over the 5G network directly using RTP/SRT or using webRTC to web browser clients. In principle, if a device can be connected and controlled over ethernet, it can be connected and controlled over 5G using a 5G-to-ethernet bridge. 5G is ready to facilitate all of this essential OB functionality.

This two-way connection has a significant impact on licensing, since the successful application for one 5G spectrum license can be used to support multiple cameras and all of the control, comms. and telemetry required. With traditional broadcast systems, these each require dedicated spectrum and therefore around 4 individual spectrum licenses must be managed and maintained *per wireless camera* for each event. However, access to shared spectrum is not straightforward or universal, nor are the procedures and licensing models currently in place to support PMSE-like access for agile and reactionary deployment. Spectrum access may be a major bottleneck to SNPN adoption.

The successful proof-of-concepts that have been undertaken and discussed here have demonstrated that 5G SNPNs are capable and ready to support live outside broadcasts. They can be taken anywhere and be used to supplement on site production resources with multiple wireless cameras at latencies that can be used as part of a traditional cabled production. Over the 5G SNPN, we have successfully run low latency feeds (as low as 70 ms SDI-to-SDI) using encoders from Open Broadcast Systems, Haivision, Vislink and Nulink, as well as high latency bonded cellular devices from LiveU, Haivision, and Mobile Viewpoint. We have run multi-camera productions and demonstrated multi-cell deployment with handover. With a heavily uplink-biased frame structure, we can sustain over 400 Mbps in the uplink with a round-trip time latency of around 10ms, although this can be reduced at the expense of bandwidth using low latency frame structures.

This paper also discusses live-to-air events where this technology was successfully used as part of real broadcasts. Of course, the technology is still in its infancy and will improve with investment and experience. In fact, there are a number of new features in release 16 that will be beneficial but are as yet unsupported by the majority of 5G modems. Some important ones include configured grants, ultra-low latency frame structures, and soft handover.

This is an exciting time for 5G and particularly SNPNs as their potential role in broadcast is explored further, and we will continue to engage and push the boundary of what can be achieved with SNPNs and the ultimate creative freedom that wireless production can deliver.

## References


[1] Gomez-Barquero, D., Gimenez, J. J., Muntean, G.-M., Xu, Y., Wu, Y., "IEEE Transactions on Broadcasting Special Issue on: 5G Media Production, Contribution, and Distribution," *IEEE Transactions on Broadcasting*, 68, 2, June 2022, p. 415 [DOI: 10.1109/TBC.2022.3163818].

[2] 5G PPP Technology Board, "Non-Public-Networks – State of the art and way forward," https://5g-ppp.eu/white-paper-from-the-5g-ppp-technology-board-non-public-networks-state-of-the-art-and-way-forward/

[3] P. Sunna *et al.*, "A Multiple Camera 5G Wireless Studio for Professional Content Production Scenarios," *2022 IEEE International Symposium on Broadband Multimedia Systems and Broadcasting (BMSB)*, Bilbao, Spain, 2022, pp. 1-6 [DOI: 10.1109/BMSB55706.2022.9828740].

[4] Brightwell, P., Ferreira, P., Lohmar, T. and Sunna, P., "Media Gateways in Hybrid Wired and Wireless Media Production," *SMPTE 2022 Media Technology Summit*, Hollywood, CA, 2022, pp. 1-21 [DOI: 10.5594/M001981].

[5] EBU 5G-RECORDS Project Outcomes: https://www.5g-records.eu/index.php/outcomes-2

[6] Brandstrup, M., Brightwell, P., Desirello, D., Ferreira, P., Fuentes, M., Lohmar, T., Rodrigo Castillo, A., Sunna, P., Wagdin, I, "5G S-NPN (Standalone Non-Public Nnetwork) for Professional Media Production", *International Broadcasting Convention Technical Papers*, September 2022 [https://www.ibc.org/technical-papers/ibc2022-tech-papers-5g-s-npn-for-professional-media-production/9229.article].

## Appendix: Workflow Diagrams

This appendix contains the full network and signal flow diagrams for the trials discussed above.

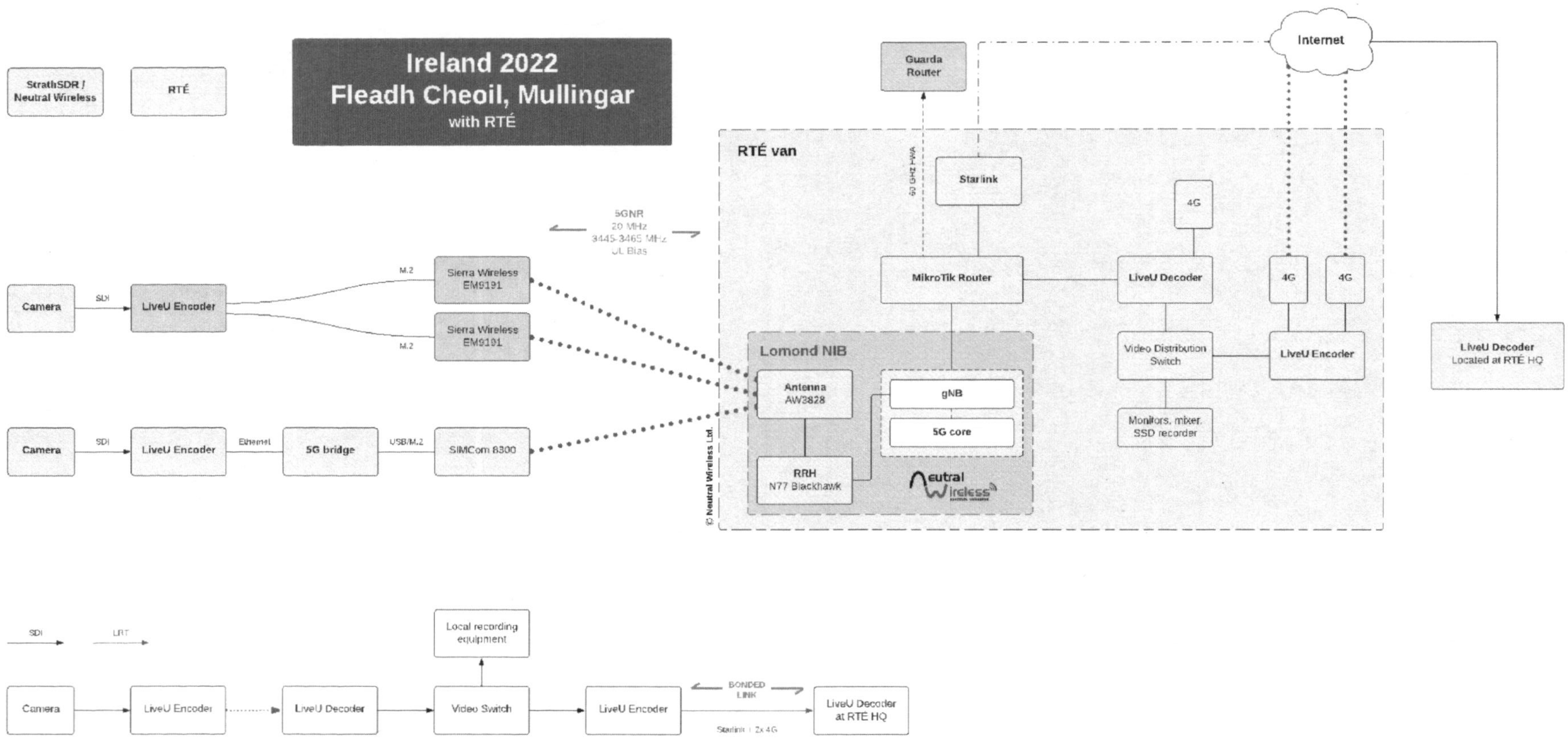


FIGURE A1: NETWORK DIAGRAM FOR THE WORKFLOW USED IN IRELAND (SECTION 3), WITH SIGNAL FLOW DISPLAYED LOWER-LEFT.

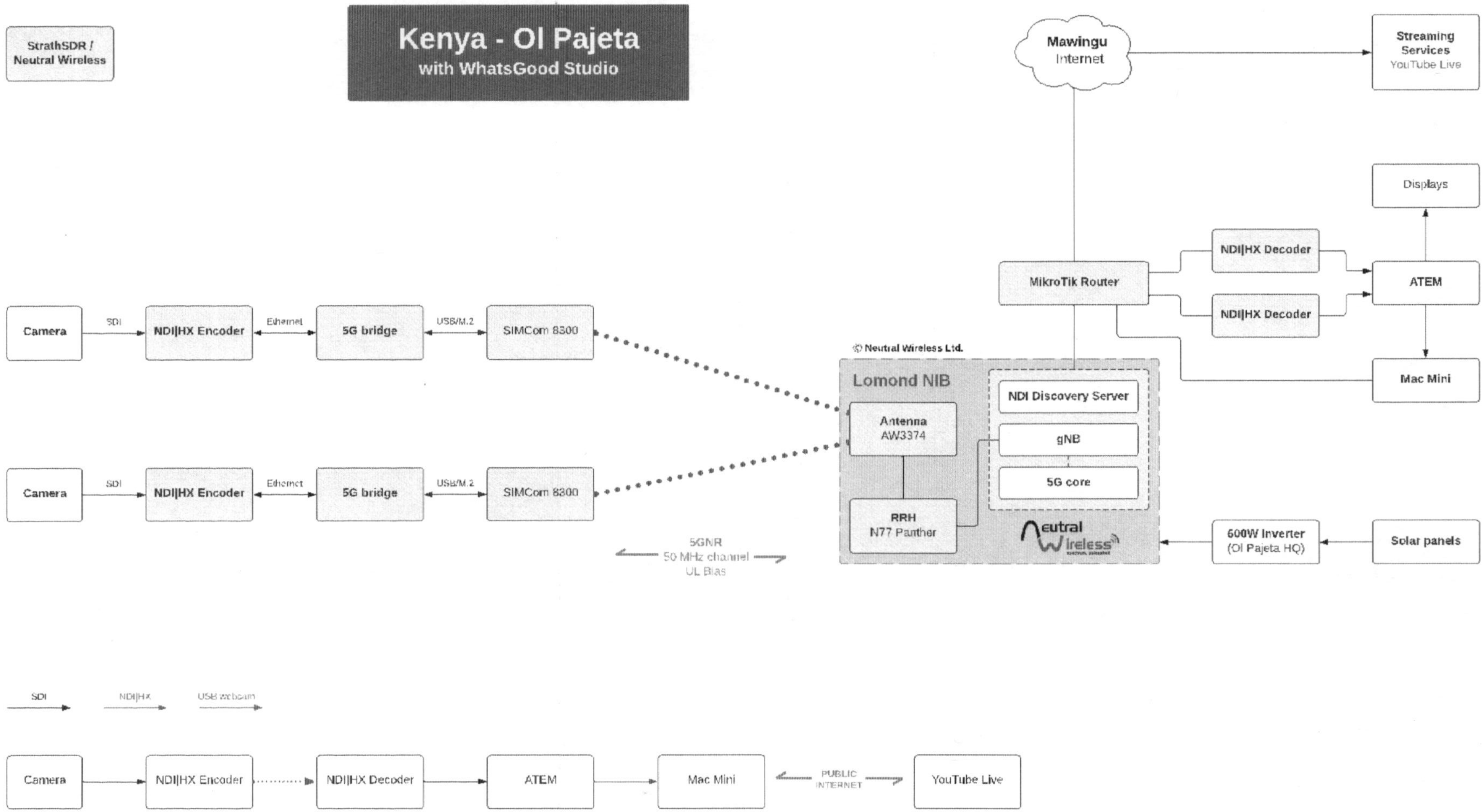


FIGURE A2: NETWORK DIAGRAM FOR THE WORKFLOW USED IN KENYA (SECTION 3), WITH SIGNAL FLOW DISPLAYED LOWER-LEFT.

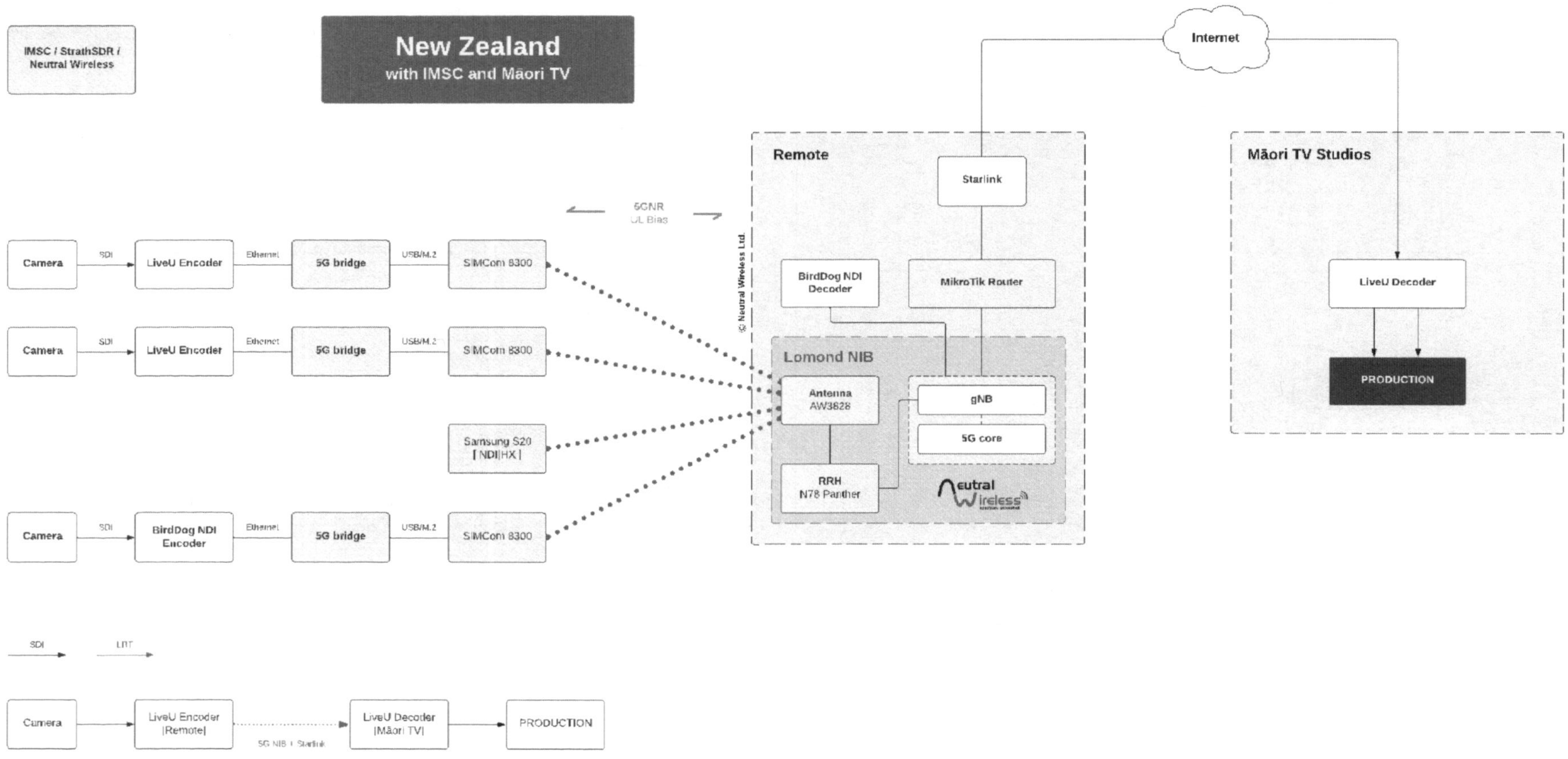


FIGURE A3: NETWORK DIAGRAM FOR THE WORKFLOW USED IN NEW ZEALAND (SECTION 3), WITH SIGNAL FLOW DISPLAYED LOWER-LEFT.

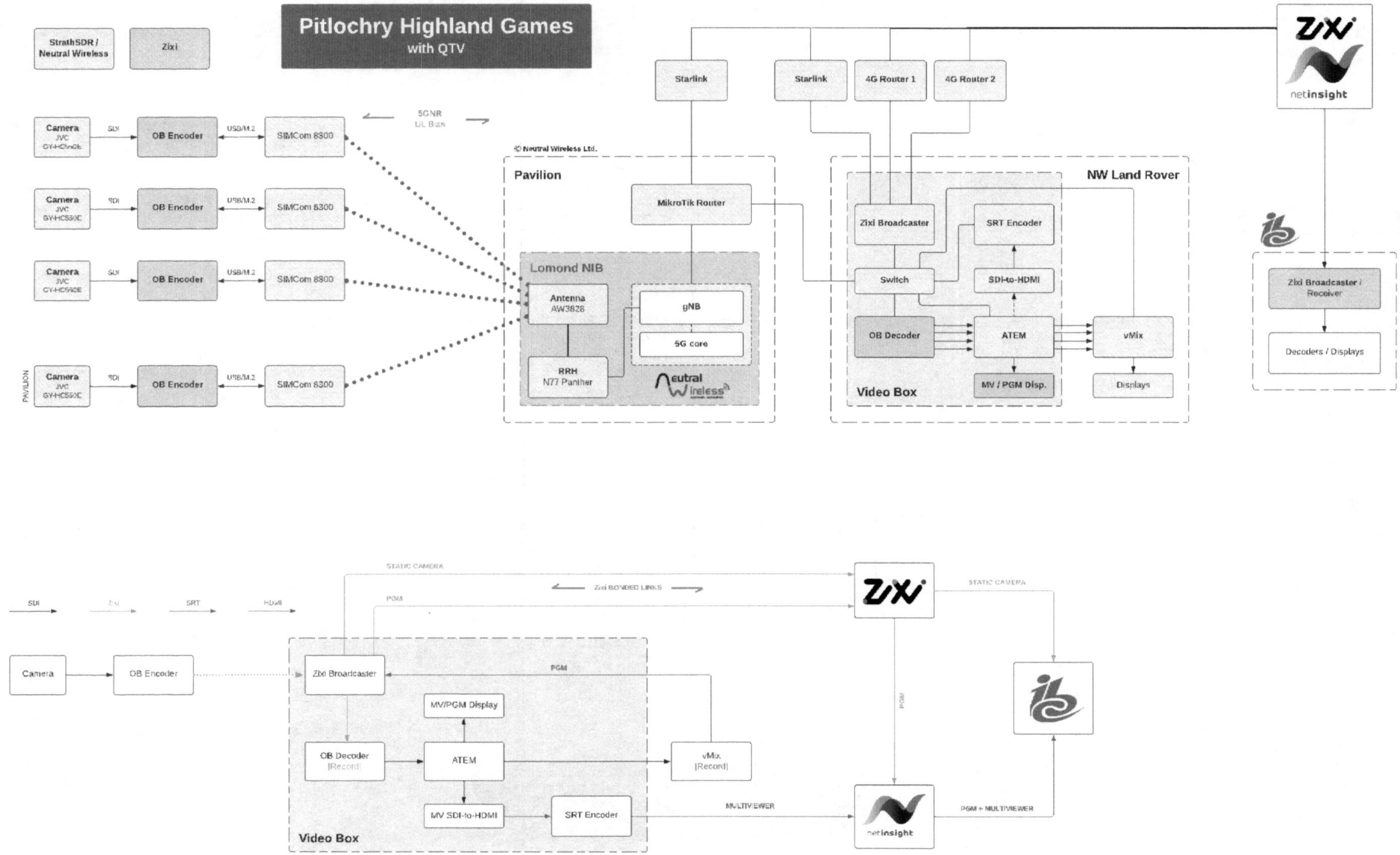


FIGURE A4: NETWORK DIAGRAM FOR THE WORKFLOW USED IN SCOTLAND (SECTION 3), WITH SIGNAL FLOW DISPLAYED LOWER-LEFT

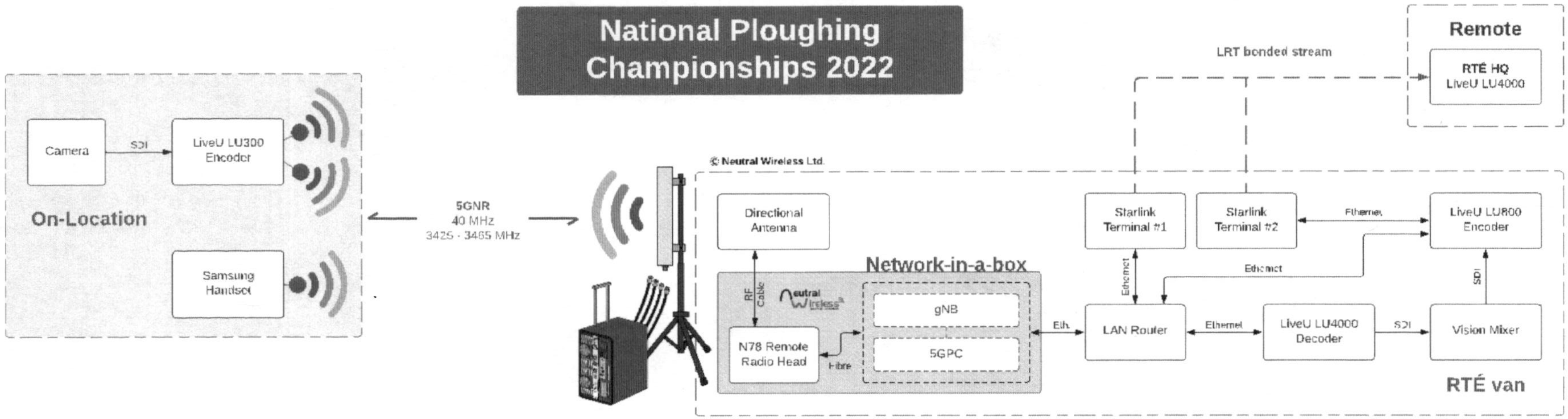


FIGURE A5: NETWORK DIAGRAM FOR THE WORKFLOW USED FOR THE NATIONAL PLOUGHING CHAMPIONSHIP (SECTION 4).

# Hands On Towards Next Generation Media Distribution with the 5G-MAG Reference Tool


**Daniel Silhavy**
**Fraunhofer FOKUS**
**Berlin, Germany**
daniel.silhavy@fokus.fraunhofer.de

**Richard Bradbury**
**British Broadcasting Corporation**
**London, United Kingdom**
richard.bradbury@rd.bbc.co.uk

**David Waring**
**British Broadcasting Corporation**
**London, United Kingdom**
david.waring2@bbc.co.uk

**Dev Audsin**
**British Broadcasting Corporation**
**London, United Kingdom**
dev.audsin@bbc.co.uk

**Thomas Stockhammer**
**Qualcomm CDMA Technologies**
**Munich, Germany**
tsto@qti.qualcomm.com

**Aytac Biber**
**Qualcomm CDMA Technologies**
**Carlsbad, Calif., United States**
abiber@qti.qualcomm.com

**Kurt Krauss**
**Dolby Germany GmbH**
**Nuremberg, Germany**
kkrau@dolby.com

**Jordi Joan Gimenez**
**5G-MAG Association**
**Geneva, Switzerland**
gimenez@5g-mag.com

**Johann Mika**
**ORS**
**Vienna, Austria**
Johann.mika@ors.at



**Abstract**

The 3rd Generation Partnership Project (3GPP) has defined multiple specifications for 5G Media Streaming, allowing operators or third-party service providers to build media services and applications on top of 5G systems. With 3GPP Release 17, these specifications are expanded into the domains of dynamic QoS policies, event exposure, Multicast Broadcast Services, Edge applications, or XR.
3GPP is lacking a reference and conformance program to validate and prototype these specifications. The 5G Media Action Group (5G-MAG) has undertaken the task to accelerate the creation of 5G Media applications by providing the open-source 5G-MAG Reference Tools development program.
In this paper we focus on the implementation of 5G Media Streaming (5GMS) components in the 5G-MAG Reference Tools. Based on a set of industry relevant use-cases, we identify four minimum viable products (MVPs). Starting with a simple implementation of the 5GMS Application Server (AS) and 5GMS-Aware Application for media playback, we move to more advanced features such as media session handling and dynamic configuration of the AS by the 5GMS Application Function (AF). The presented features serve as a foundation for contributors to add more advanced functionalities. An example is a DVB-I Hybrid Service delivered over 5G Broadcast and 5G Media Streaming, enabling the insertion of Premium and Targeted Content on top of it.


## Introduction

The global expansion of connectivity has opened the door for new ways of creating, distributing and consuming content. According to the Ericsson Mobility Report, by 2028, 5G networks will carry 69 percent of the world's smartphone traffic, with the delivery of video content expected to account for 80 percent of the mobile data traffic [1]. Engaging in the development of global technologies, with 5G among them, represents an opportunity for the industry to shape their capabilities and be at the


This paper is excerpted from the Proceedings of the 2023 NAB Broadcast Engineering and Information Technology (BEIT) Conference, forefront of the creation of new services and applications. 5G Media Streaming responds to the growing consumption of multimedia services, with video as its main driver, and the need to open the 5G System capabilities to content providers. This offers new opportunities to manage service provisioning, control quality of service more effectively, develop applications and services in an open API environment, make use of network programmability features, or obtain insight into network and device analytics and reporting, while benefiting from enhanced data rates and lower latencies offered by 5G.

This paper presents an overview of the technologies and features currently being developed as part of the 5G-MAG Reference Tools and the first supported services and applications. This involves, among other tools, the first building blocks for 5G Media Streaming, including baseline features such as content hosting and media session handling, which setup a framework for contributors to add more advanced functionalities.

## 5G Media Streaming

The Third Generation Partnership Project (3GPP) has developed 5G Media Streaming (5GMS), as documented in 3GPP TS 26.501 [2], with the idea of enabling third-party media distribution as a complement to MNO (Mobile Network Operator) managed services. With 5GMS, the 5G network is no longer acting as a bit pipe but providing additional functionalities for collaboration between both mobile operators and content providers. 5GMS offers a framework aligned with modern over-the-top (OTT) media distribution practices and support MNOs and third-party media services to easily access 5G System and 5G Media Streaming features.

The aim is to address several challenges that pure OTT distribution presents, including: (i) quality of experience issues (rebuffering and stall events) that are associated with the operator in the end user's mind, (ii) obscuring of traffic by end-to-end encryption using HTTPS, (iii) unidentified content eating into users' data caps, and (iv) the increasing demand for higher quality, new formats, new immersive and interactive experiences.

### 5G Media Streaming – Protocols and APIs

3GPP TS 26.512 [3] defines the interfaces and protocols that are part of the 5G Media Streaming downlink (5GMSd) System. The basic 5G Media Streaming architecture for unicast downlink media streaming and its components are depicted in Figure 1.

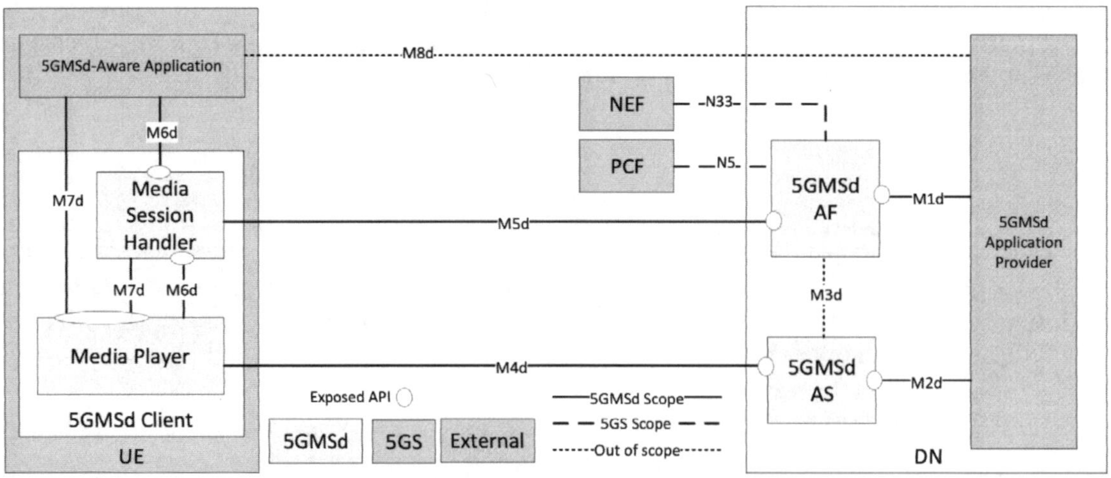


FIGURE 1: 5G MEDIA STREAMING ARCHITECTURE FOR UNICAST DOWNLINK MEDIA STREAMING (ACCORDING TO 3GPP TS 26.501 [2]).

A 5GMSd Application Function (AF), which can be deployed in the 5G Core Network or in an External Data Network, is responsible for managing the 5GMSd System. The AF is a logical function which embodies the control plane aspects of the system, including provisioning, configuration, and reporting, among others. A 5GMSd Application Provider provisions 5GMS functions using a RESTful HTTP-based provisioning interface at reference point M1d. Another RESTful HTTP-based configuration and reporting interface is exposed to UE-based 5GMS clients at reference point M5d.

A 5GMS Application Server (AS), which can be deployed in the 5G Core Network or in an External Data Network, provides 5G Media Streaming services to 5GMSd clients. This logical function embodies the data plane aspects of the 5GMSd System that deals with media content (for instance, a Content Delivery Network). The content is ingested from 5GMSd Application Providers at reference point M2d. Both push- and pull-based ingest methods are supported, based on HTTP. The content is distributed to 5GMS clients at reference point M4d (after possible manipulation by the 5GMSd AS). Standard pull-based content retrieval protocols (e.g. DASH) are supported at this reference point.

A Media Session Handler subcomponent first retrieves its configuration ("Service Access Information") from the 5GMSd AF at reference point M5d and then uses this configuration information to activate and exploit the currently provisioned 5GMSd features.

The 5GMSd-Aware Application controls the Media Session Handler via a UE-internal API defined at reference point M6d. This reference point could, for example, be realized as a JavaScript API in a web browser or via Inter Process Communication (IPC) for native Android applications.

A Media Player subcomponent consumes media from the 5GMSd AS at reference point M4d.

The 5GMSd-Aware Application controls the Media Player via a UE-internal API defined at reference point M7.

## 5G Media Streaming – Extensions

3GPP has considered in Release 17 relevant extensions related to media streaming and, in general, media delivery. The goal is to facilitate and optimize the deployment of media streaming services and applications by offering access to 5G system features and enablers. Extensions include improvements to unicast streaming; integration of 5G Media Streaming with LTE-based 5G Broadcast; and introduction of the 5G Multicast Broadcast Services (MBS) to support efficient multicast and broadcast delivery in a 5G System [4].

A key feature related to the extension of 5G Media Streaming is edge media processing, which leverages edge capabilities of the 5G System to application and content providers [5]. New media transfer protocols, offering content preparation, background data transfer, network slicing, and enhancements to uplink and low-latency streaming according to 3GPP TR 26.804 [6] are also considered. For instance, background data transfer (BDT) enables mobile network operators to incentivize the offloading of traffic into off-peak hours with the aim of reducing network congestion during peak hours. Content preparation is another tool that the mobile network operator may offer to the Application Service Provider to describe the desired processing and delegate the content preparation operation to the 5G system. A new framework for data collection and exposure has been developed in 3GPP TS 26.531 [7] and TS 26.532 [8]. The framework allows an Application Service Provider to provision collection of data and its subsequent exposure, by specifying the metrics and events that a Data Collection Application Function will collect from different data sources [9].

The architecture also considers the delivery of services via different transport means. Examples include broadcast and multicast delivery via LTE-based 5G Broadcast or 5G MBS. This permits media services to be offered simultaneously over multiple delivery networks, referred to as hybrid services. Media

Players are continuously informed about the availability of content on the different data networks along with any operator policy on which network is preferable. Based on this information, a Media Player can make smart content selection decisions by switching between different networks.

## The 5G-MAG Reference Tools for 5G Media Streaming

While 3GPP has completed the enablers for media services on 3GPP-based systems and provides a set of specifications on the radio access layer, the core network as well as on the service layer, the focus in 3GPP is the development of global specifications. However, 3GPP is lacking a reference and conformance program to validate and prototype these specifications.

The 5G-MAG Reference Tools development program was established in mid-2021 with the goal to fill this gap and create common open-source reference tools to support implementation and interoperability of 5G Media technologies [10]. The 5G-MAG Reference Tools are not only used for validating 3GPP specifications but are also intended as a valuable option to build commercial products on. Moreover, the 5G-MAG Reference Tools can serve as a foundation for research projects, papers and field tests.

The initial focus of the 5G-MAG Reference Tools project is the development of Rel-16 and Rel-17 5G Media Streaming and LTE-based 5G Terrestrial Broadcast client components and corresponding 5G unicast and broadcast radio emulators. For that reason, the steadily growing developer community has implemented multiple software components that are publicly available on Github[1].

In the following, we highlight the features of the 5G Media Streaming implementation in the 5G-MAG Reference Tools. For that reason, we first explain the outcome of the development planning program "Target 2023". Next, we focus on specific Minimum Viable Products (MVPs) that deal with various aspects of the 5G Media Streaming chain. Moreover, we introduce a first version of a DVB-I player based on the ExoPlayer[2] library.

### Target 2023

5G-MAG initiated the Target 2023 program to extend the 5G-MAG reference tools based on 3GPP Rel-16 and Rel-17 specifications. Target 2023 was divided into multiple steps as depicted in Figure 2 [11].

[1] https://github.com/5G-MAG
[2] https://github.com/google/ExoPlayer

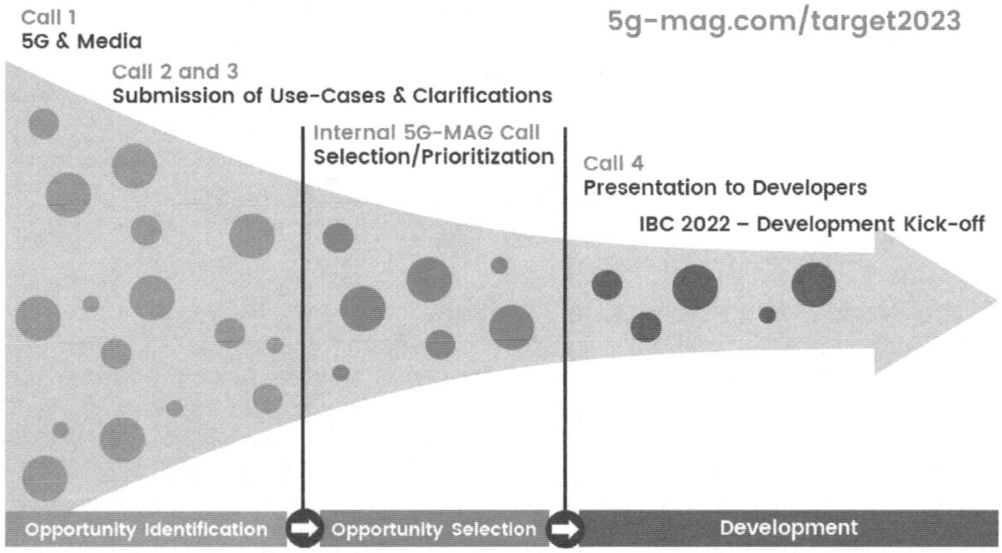


FIGURE 2: THE 5G-MAG TARGET 2023 PROGRAM TO DEFINE THE ROADMAP OF THE 5G-MAG REFERENCE TOOLS IN 2023.

In the first call the 3GPP SA4 experts presented the media-centric 5G technologies and features of 3GPP Rel-16 & Rel-17. Next, 5G-MAG invited its members, and all interested industry partners and individuals to submit market-oriented use-cases in the context of the previously presented 3GPP specifications. After an internal analysis of the submitted use cases identifying the required components' synergies between the uses and taking the available development resources into account, 5G-MAG decided to focus on the following use cases in 2023:

- **Use Case#1 – Reliable Video On-Demand over Mobile Networks using 5G Media Streaming**: Focuses on interruption-free playback of media content on 5G mobile phones. The video and sound quality presented should be the best that can be sustained by the mobile network at any given time. Moreover, metrics about the quality experienced by the viewer and information about the underlying network connection should be reported to the content provider.
- **Use Case#2 – Reliable Personalized Live Radio over Mobile Networks using 5MBS:** A broadcast provided application installed on a 5G-enabled in-car entertainment system enables listening to live radio stations without interruption. The audio stream is delivery via the most efficient method (unicast or multicast/broadcast) to the audience at each base station as the car moves around.
- **Use Case#3 – 5G Broadcast On-Demand with 5G Media Streaming**: 5G Broadcast on-demand enables content providers to offload traffic in high peak times from the CDN to a 5G broadcast based delivery to save costs in CDN distribution. Based on consumption metrics reported by the clients the content provider provisions the 5G Broadcast. The transition between broadcast and unicast is performed seamlessly and not visible on the user's end device.
- **Use Case#4 – Premium and Targeted Content Insertion:** Like the previously presented use case#3 the user's end device can receive media content via broadcast and unicast. One use case leveraging this is targeted advertisement. The advertisements in the broadcast stream are dynamically replaced with targeted advertisements delivered via unicast. Other scenarios exist where other types of relevant content can be dynamically triggered based on location parameters, proximity, and user preferences.
- **Use Case#5 – DVB-I over 5G Media Streaming:** A service provider offers a DVB-I service catalogue that includes live services, on-demand services and catch-up services. The media content is distributed in common formats based on DVB-DASH, HLS and CMAF relying on different components of the 5G Media Streaming architecture such as the Media Session Handler for metric and consumption reporting.

- **Use Case#6 – DVB-I Hybrid Service over 5G Broadcast and 5G Media Streaming:** Like the approach presented in use case#3 the broadcast operator has the ambition to run a hybrid service (integrated broadcast/unicast distribution). Based on the available coverage, the DVB-I services is provided via unicast or broadcast to the user's end device. Additonal use cases such as targeted ad-insertion and delivery of auxilary components (e.g alternative audio languages) via unicast are also in scope of this use case.
- **Use Case#7 – Emergency Alerts and Media Services through 5G Broadcast:** An emergency alert is distributed through LTE-based 5G broadcast.

## Structuring the Work – Minimum Viable Products

The first six use cases presented in the previous section require the implementation of various 5G Media Streaming components. To cope with the complexity of a full-featured 5G Media Streaming system and the resulting implementation efforts, 5G-MAG decided to split the work into multiple minimum viable products (MVPs). These MVPs are not expected to cover all the 3GPP-defined functions and features but focus on building core functions and reference points. Providing these baseline core functions enables the development community to work closely together on different aspects of the 5G Media Streaming chain and extend the 5G-MAG Reference Tools step-by-step with additional features.

## MVP#1 – Starting Point for 5G Media Streaming

The goal of MVP#1 is to implement a starting point for 5G Media Streaming. For that reason, a 5GMSd Application Server (5GMSd AS), a 5GMSd Media Stream Handler and a 5GMSd Aware Application are implemented. The overall architecture of MVP#1 is depicted in Figure 2. It includes first versions of an 5GMSd AS, 5GMSd Media Streaming Handler and 5GMSd Aware Application. The required Service Access Information is provided as a static JSON file.

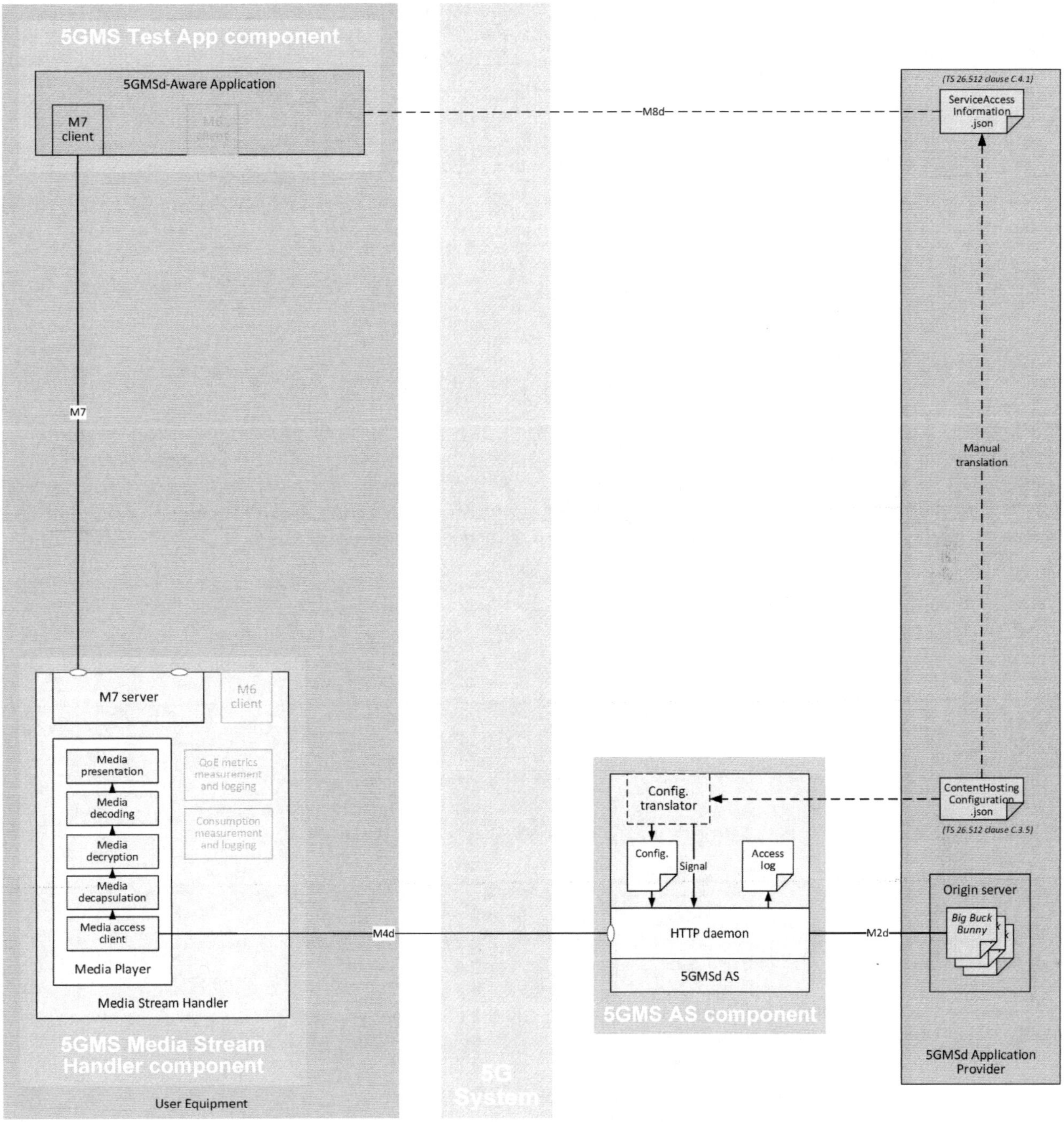


FIGURE 3: ARCHITECTURE OF MVP#1 – STARTING POINT FOR 5G MEDIA STREAMING.

The 5GMSd AS as depicted in Figure 3 is implemented as a Python script that wraps around Nginx. It is configured using a simple JSON file describing a single Content Hosting Configuration based on the syntax defined in TS 26.512 [3]. The test assets are pulled from a CDN or the Origin server at the interface M2d and cached.

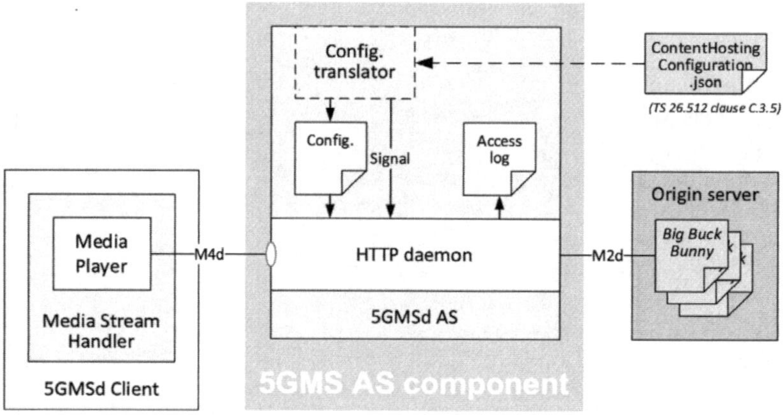


FIGURE 4: ARCHITECTURE OF THE APPLICATION SERVER FOR MVP#1.

The 5GMSd Media Stream Handler is built around the open-source ExoPlayer and invoked by the 5GMSd-Aware Application using the M7 client API, as illustrated in Figure 4. The 5GMSd-Aware Application uses a static Service Access Information JSON file provided by the Application Provider via the private M8d reference point. The Service Access Information file includes a media entry point such as the URL to a DASH MPD hosted by the 5GMSd AS and exposed via M4d.

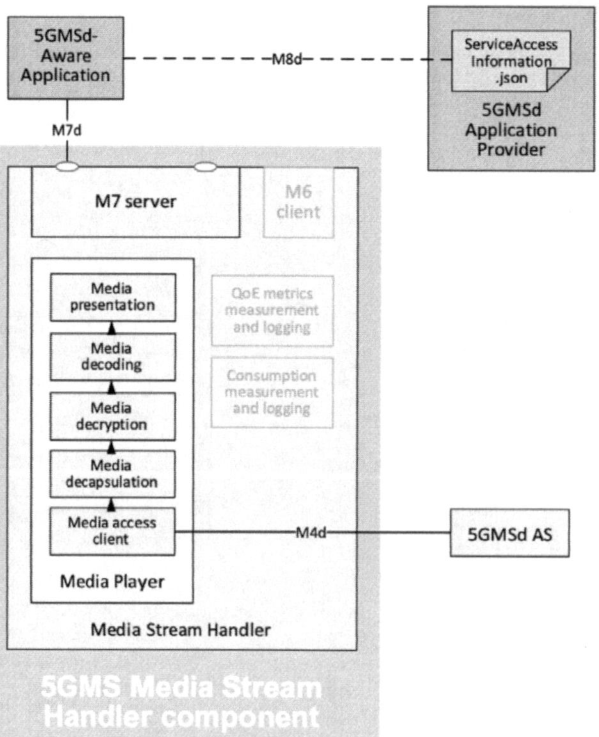


FIGURE 5: ARCHITECTURE OF THE MEDIA STREAM HANDLER FOR MVP#1.

## MVP#2 – Enabling Media Session Handling

For MVP#2, the architecture of MVP#1 is extended by a 5GMSd Media Session Handler and a 5GMSd Application Function (5GMSd AF). The overall architecture of MVP#2 is depicted in Figure 5.

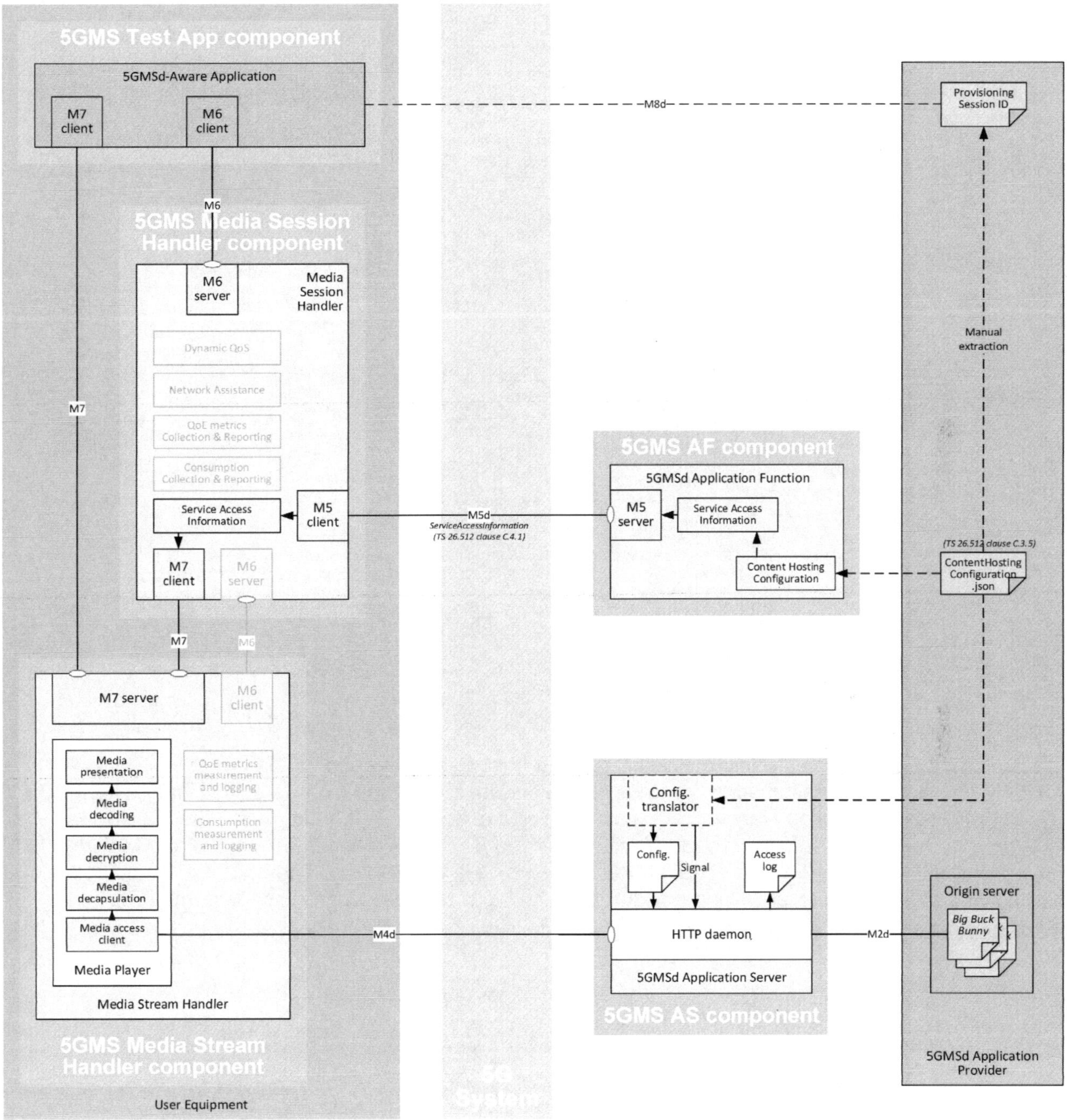


FIGURE 6: THE ARCHITECTURE OF MVP#2 TO ENABLE MEDIA SESSION HANDLING.

The 5GMSd Media Session Handler is invoked by the 5GMSd-Aware Application at the start of each media streaming session via a client API call at reference point M6d as illustrated in Figure 6. The Media Session Handler retrieves the Service Access Information via interface M5d from the 5GMSd AF.

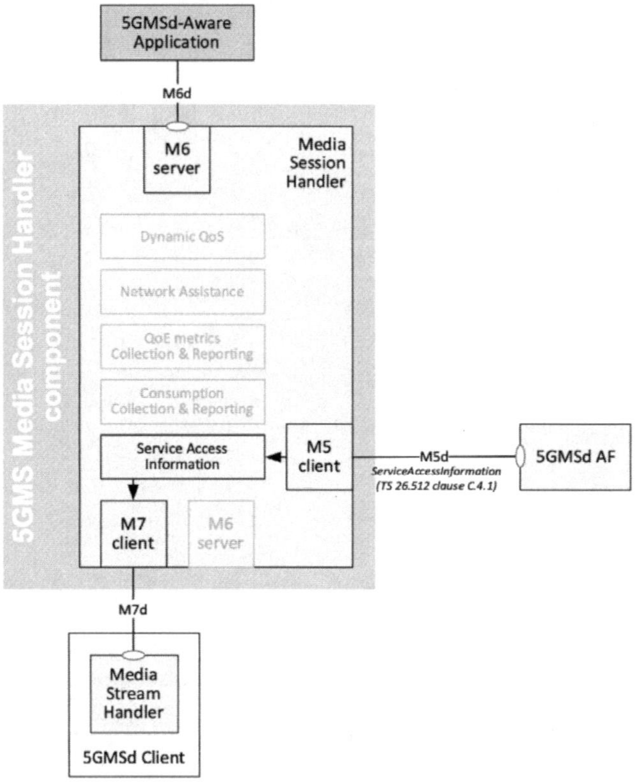


FIGURE 7: ARCHITECTURE OF THE MEDIA SESSION HANDLER FOR MVP#2.

The 5GMSd AF is initialized using the same content hosting configuration JSON as the 5GMSd AS in MVP#1. This information is used to create an internal data model and expose a RESTful API via M5d. The 5GMSd Media Session Handler retrieves the Service Access Information from the 5GMSd-AF via reference point M5d as shown in Figure 7. The returned Service Access Information includes a media entry point, such as the URL of a DASH MPD hosted on the 5GMSd AS. The media entry point is passed to the 5GMSd Media Stream Handler by invoking a client API at reference point M7d.

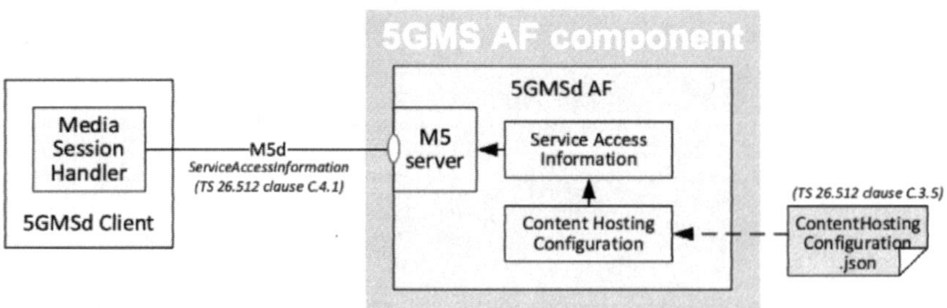


FIGURE 8: ARCHITECTURE OF THE 5GMSd APPLICATION FUNCTION FOR MVP#2.

## Dynamic Configuration of the 5GMSd AS and 5GMSd AF

Having completed the Minimum Viable Product, the next development focuses on the configuration of the 5GMSd AS by the 5GMSd AF. For that reason, the M3 interface with an M3 client on the 5GMSd AF side and an M3 server on the 5GMSd AS side is added. The overall architecture is depicted in Figure 8. The 5GMSd AS is now configured directly by the 5GMSd AF via reference point M3 which is not yet standardized by 3GPP.

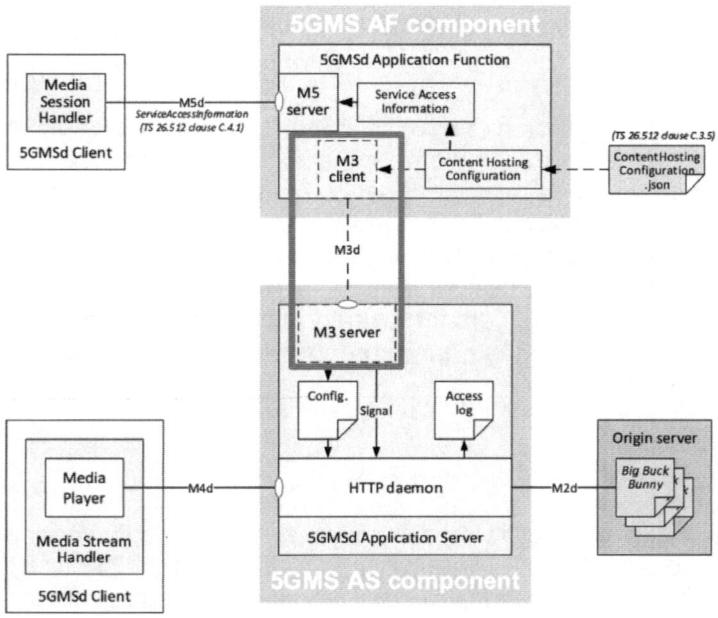


FIGURE 9: THE M3 INTERFACE BETWEEN THE 5GMSd AF AND THE 5GMSd AS FOR DIRECT CONFIGURATION.

Furthermore, the addition of the 3GPP-specified M1 Provisioning API allows a configuration of the 5GMSd AF by the 5GMSd Application Provider as highlighted in Figure 9.

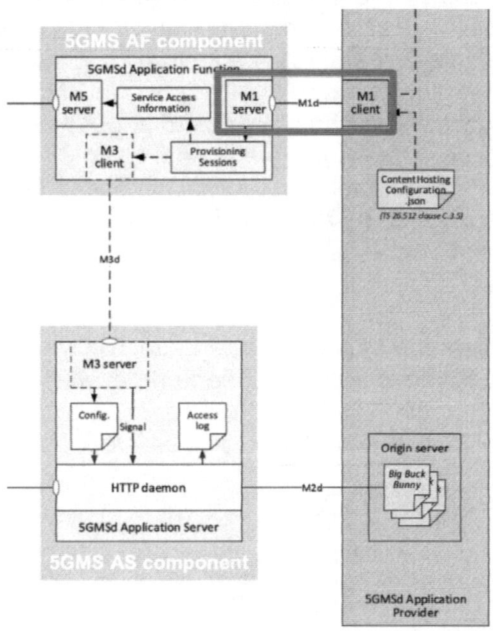


FIGURE 10: THE M1 INTERFACE USED BY THE APPLICATION PROVIDER FOR CONFIGURATION OF THE 5GMSd AF.

### Application-Level Services

Several use cases have been identified as interesting in scope of the work on 5G MAG reference tools. DVB-I and its value for discovery of broadcast and streaming media services has been an early focus of the work in 5G-MAG. Leveraging some work done in DVB to integrate a DVB-I front-end into a 5GMS-Aware Application is another step towards building up a rich tool set for service providers to experiment with service distribution over 5G. It's easy to anticipate discovery of DVB-I media services that are available to consumers via LTE-based 5G broadcast and unicast. There is integration work happening to better understand the requirements for how to integrate the various service components in a meaningful way with 5G.

Enabling personalized content insertion has been identified as another relevant media industry trend. Although advertising is by no means the only category of content anticipated for personalized services, this is a valuable revenue source for a number of service providers, and potentially a key aspect for funding free-to-air services, and members have therefore suggested that 5G MAG addresses the technical challenges of content insertion as part of its Reference Tools activity. Given that the reference toolkit is intended for experimentation with new options for mobile media, other information, like location services, proximity and gaze may be triggers for insertion of any kind of content of interest. Existing and new experiences based on XR may, in the near future, be enabled by the same technical capabilities initially designed for advertising.

## Summary

5G Media Streaming responds to the growing consumption of multimedia services, with video as its main driver and the need to open the 5G System capabilities to content providers. 3GPP has progressed and completed the specifications to build media streaming services on top of 3GPP-based systems. However, 3GPP is lacking a reference and conformance program to validate and prototype the 3GPP specifications.

In this paper, we presented the 5G-MAG Reference Tools, an initiative by the 5G Media Action Group, to provide the currently missing reference implementations for 5G Media Streaming. As part of the "Target 2023" program, a set of industry relevant use cases for 5G Media Streaming was identified. Based on these use cases, multiple MVPs were implemented covering various aspects and components of the downlink 5G Media Streaming architecture. The implementation includes an 5GMSd-AF with support for the M1d and the M5d interface. The 5GMSd-AF configures the 5GMSd-AS via the M3d interface. Via the M4d interface, the 5GMSd-AS exposes MPEG-DASH test assets that are pulled from a CDN. On the client-side, a 5GMSd Aware Application handles the playback by incorporating a 5GMSd Media Stream Handler (Media Player) based on the ExoPlayer library. The 5GMSd Media Session Handler is invoked by the 5GMSd-Aware Application at the start of each media streaming session at reference point M6d. The implemented MVP's serve as a foundation for contributors to add more advanced functionality on top.

Future work includes the extension of the 5G MAG Reference Tools with means for metric and consumption reporting, as well as dynamic policies based on network slicing and downlink network assistance. Moreover, the implementation of 5G Media Streaming over eMBMS and Public Warning Services and Emergency Alerts for LTE-based 5G Broadcast are in the scope of the 5G-MAG Reference Tools.

## References


[1] Ericsson, "Ericsson Mobility Report November 2022", November 2022, https://www.ericsson.com/4ae28d/assets/local/reports-papers/mobility-report/documents/2022/ericsson-mobility-report-november-2022.pdf

[2] 3GPP TS 26.501: "5G Media Streaming (5GMS); General description and architecture".

[3] 3GPP TS 26.512: "5G Media Streaming (5GMS); Protocols".

[4] A. Rico-Alvariño, I. Bouazizi, M. Griot, P. Kadiri, L. Liu and T. Stockhammer, "3GPP Rel-17 Extensions for 5G Media Delivery," in IEEE Transactions on Broadcasting, vol. 68, no. 2, pp. 422-438, June 2022, doi: 10.1109/TBC.2022.3171508.

[5] 3GPP TR 26.803: "5G Media Streaming (5GMS); Architecture extensions".

[6] 3GPP TR 26.804: "Study on 5G media streaming extensions".

[7] 3GPP TS 26.531: "Data Collection and Reporting; General Description and Architecture".

[8] 3GPP TS 26.532: "Data Collection and Reporting; Protocols and Formats".

[9] R. Bradbury, "UE Data Collection Reporting and Exposure", 3GPP Highlights 5, 2022.

[10] 5G-MAG, "5G-MAG Reference Tools", https://www.5g-mag.com/reference-tools , last accessed 27.01.2023.

[11] 5G-MAG, "Target 2023 Projects", https://www.5g-mag.com/target2023, last accessed 27.02.2023.

# Media and Entertainment Sustainability on the Cloud

**Thomas Edwards, Jason O'Malley**
**Amazon Web Services**
**Seattle, Wash., United States**
tedwaa@amazon.com, jasonoma@amazon.com

**Abstract** – Media and Entertainment (M&E) companies are committing to become more sustainable for their employees, customers, and communities. At the same time, M&E companies are seeking to enhance and re-invent their business using cloud computing (the on-demand delivery of compute power, database, storage, applications, and other IT resources via the Internet with pay-as-you-go pricing). Fortunately, the goals of improving sustainability and cloud adoption can be synergistic, as enhanced business efficiency via cloud can also drive sustainability. Cloud providers, through scale and focus on innovation, can achieve higher resource utilization and greater energy efficiency than is possible for typical on-premises or collocated data centers. This paper will examine why M&E companies are seeking sustainability, basic sustainability terminology, M&E sustainability organizations, published sustainability goals of M&E companies, and how M&E companies have actually enhanced their sustainability on the cloud.

## Introduction

The discipline of sustainability addresses the long-term environmental, economic, and societal impact of business activities. The United Nations Brundtland Commission in 1987 defined sustainability as "meeting the needs of the present without compromising the ability of future generations to meet their own needs" [1]. Businesses and organizations can have negative environmental impacts like direct or indirect carbon emissions, unrecyclable waste, and damage to shared resources like clean water.

In particular, the Intergovernmental Panel on Climate Change (IPCC) 2018 special report on Global Warming of 1.5 ºC concluded that: "Human activities are estimated to have caused approximately 1.0°C of global warming above pre-industrial levels, with a likely range of 0.8°C to 1.2°C. Global warming is likely to reach 1.5°C between 2030 and 2052 if it continues to increase at the current rate."[2] Furthermore, the IPCC concluded in its Sixth Assessment Report that "limiting warming to around 1.5°C (2.7°F) requires global greenhouse gas emissions to peak before 2025 at the latest, and be reduced by 43% by 2030." [3]

A Washington Post-ABC News poll conducted in November 2021, found that 67% of Americans felt that climate change represented a "serious problem" facing the country [4]. In a January/February 2020 global poll of 40 countries as diverse as Sweden, Kenya, and the Philippines, 69% of respondents said they consider climate change to be a serious problem [5].

The need for sustainability touches everyone, and multiple sectors of society have expressed interest in sustainability. Many are now using it as a measure for what companies they will work with, invest in, and buy from. Responding to demands from customers, employees, impact investment guidelines, as well as existing or potential future government regulations, companies are increasingly taking sustainability seriously. Media & Entertainment (M&E) companies are now making pledges, developing plans and strategies for sustainability, and are acting on these plans to achieve measurable sustainability goals.

At the same time, M&E companies are also seeking to enhance and re-invent their businesses using cloud computing, defined as the on-demand delivery of compute power, database, storage, applications, and other IT resources via the Internet with pay-as-you-go pricing. Fortunately, the goals of improving sustainability and cloud adoption can be synergistic, as enhanced business efficiency via cloud can also drive sustainability.

## Sustainability Terminology, Goals, and Organizations

The Greenhouse Gas Protocol [6], a partnership between the World Resources Institute (WRI) and the World Business Council for Sustainable Development (WBCSD), establishes comprehensive global standardized frameworks to measure and manage greenhouse gas (GHG) emissions from private and public sector operations, value chains and mitigation actions. In particular, the GHG Protocol defines how to convert other greenhouse gases to CO2 equivalent (CO2e), as well as the three scopes of emissions (diagrammed in Figure 1):

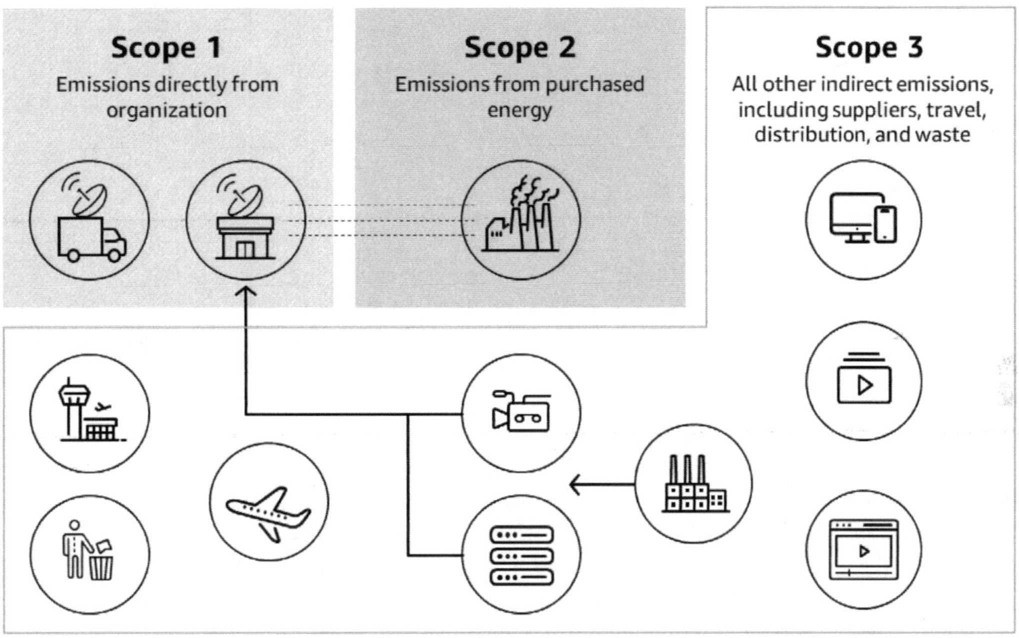


FIGURE 1: GHG EMISSION SCOPES.

- **Scope 1**: All direct emissions from the activities of an organization or under its control. These can include emissions from company vehicles, factory smokestacks, or hydrocarbon powered space heaters. For example, tailpipe emissions from outside broadcast (OB) trucks owned by an M&E company, emissions from backup generators, or emissions from vehicles for transporting sets and equipment on a studio lot may fall under emissions Scope 1.
- **Scope 2**: Indirect emissions from purchased electricity, heat, cooling or steam. For example, electricity used for on-premises data centers, for production control rooms, for set lighting, or for air conditioning.

- **Scope 3**: All other indirect emissions from activities of an organization from sources it doesn't control, such as emissions by other companies due to supply or distribution chains. Thus Scope 3 includes emissions due to all purchased goods and services, employee commuting and business travel provided by outside entities, waste disposal, and leased assets. In the M&E context, Scope 3 would include emissions due to viewing content in movie theaters and on set top boxes and smartphones, as well as any Internet service used to transport the media. It would also include emissions due to media workloads running on a cloud provider.

For most M&E companies, scope 3 emissions are largest, followed by scope 2 and then scope 1. For example, at CBC/Radio-Canada (Canada's national public broadcaster) during the 2019-2020 fiscal year, Scope 1 emissions account for 3% of overall footprint, largely attributed to a vehicle fleet. Electricity consumption accounts for the majority of CBC's Scope 2 emissions, for a total of 9% of overall footprint. Finally, 86% of overall footprint is related to Scope 3 emissions, the main source being from purchased goods and services and the associated supply chain (see Figure 2) [7].

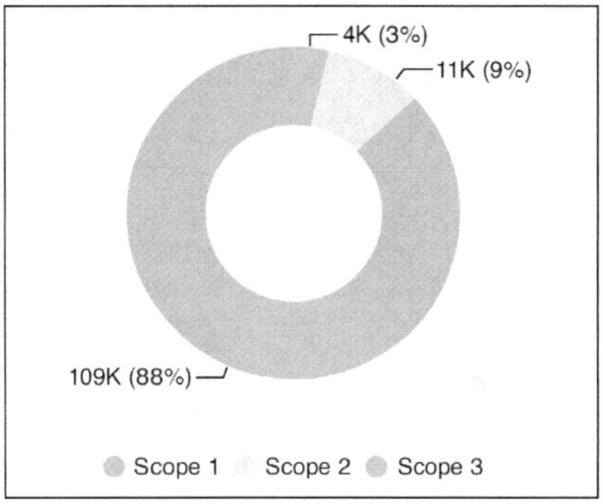


FIGURE 2: CBC TOTAL EMISSIONS (TCO2E) BY SCOPE, 2019-2020 FISCAL YEAR.

### Examples of Sustainability Goals

Although incremental reduction of CO2e emissions is laudable, many organizations seek to identify bolder goals. These include:

- "100% Zero Carbon Energy", when all Scope 2 energy purchases are obtained from zero net GHG emissions sources (such as solar, wind, geothermal, biomass, hydroelectric, and nuclear energy).
- "100% Renewable Energy", when all Scope 2 energy purchases are from a naturally replenishing resource that produces zero net GHG emissions (nuclear and large hydroelectric sources are generally not considered "renewable"),
- "Carbon Neutral", when a company is in balance between emitting carbon and absorbing carbon emissions. Achieving this may include purchase of offsetting carbon credits.
- "Net Zero Carbon", is carbon neutrality when all technologically possible emissions have been eliminated.

Table 1 lists a selection of M&E companies have publicly announced zero carbon energy, renewable energy, or net zero goals.

| M&E Company | Zero Carbon & Renewable Energy | Carbon Neutral & Net Zero Carbon |
|---|---|---|
| Amazon [8] | "powering our operations with 100% renewable energy by **2025**" | "net-zero carbon emissions across our operations by **2040**" |
| BBC [9] | | "Net Zero by **2030**" |
| BT Group PLC [10] | "networks and buildings are all [**currently**] powered by renewable electricity" | "become a net zero business by the end of **March 2031**" |
| Comcast [11] | | "carbon neutral by **2035** for Scope 1 and 2 emissions across our global operations" |
| Disney [12] | "100% zero carbon electricity by **2030**" | "Net zero emissions for direct operations by **2030**" |
| ITV [13] | "Power business with 100% renewable energy by **2025**" | "Net Zero Carbon Emissions by **2030**" |
| Netflix [14] | | "By the close of **2022**, Netflix will achieve net zero greenhouse gas emissions." |
| Sony [15] | "100% renewable energy in its own operations…by…**2030**" | "carbon neutrality throughout the entire value chain, including scopes 1 to 3, by…**2040**" |

TABLE 1: M&E COMPANY PUBLIC SUSTAINABILITY GOALS.

For example, in 2019, Amazon co-founded The Climate Pledge, a commitment to be net-zero carbon across the business by 2040. Over 300 businesses have now committed to The Climate Pledge, including M&E companies ITV and BT Group PLC (the parent company of BT Consumer & BT Sport) [16]. Amazon has also launched The Climate Pledge Fund [17] to support the development of sustainable and decarbonizing technologies and services with an initial $2 billion in funding, and the Right Now Climate Fund [18], a $100 million fund to restore and conserve forests, wetlands, and grasslands around the world.

## Sustainability Goals of Governments

M&E companies operate within the framework of regulations by various governments. The most famous sustainability agreement is The Paris Agreement adopted in 2015, now signed by all countries of the world. This is a legally binding international treaty on climate change, with a goal is to limit global warming to well below 2, preferably to 1.5 degrees Celsius, compared to pre-industrial levels. To achieve this long-term temperature goal, countries aim to reach global peaking of greenhouse gas emissions as soon as possible to achieve a climate neutral world by mid-century. The Paris Agreement requires all Parties to put forward their best efforts through "nationally determined contributions" (NDCs) and to strengthen these efforts in the years ahead [19].

Cities, countries, and regions have also set sustainability goals. For example, Amsterdam has set a goal to achieve a 55% reduction in emissions by 2030, and a 95% reduction by 2050 [20]. 130 countries have now set or are considering a target of reducing emissions to net zero by 2050. For example, Sweden and Germany have legally binding net zero targets for 2045, France, Denmark,

Spain, Hungary and Luxemburg and UK for 2050 [21]. At the super-national level, The European Climate Law sets a goal for Europe's economy and society to become climate-neutral by 2050. It also sets the intermediate target of reducing net greenhouse gas emissions by at least 55% by 2030, compared to 1990 levels [22].

### M&E Sustainability Organizations

Several organizations provide support, guidance, and certification for M&E sustainability:

- **Albert** is an environmental organization to encourage the TV and film production industry to reduce waste and its carbon footprint. Additionally, Albert offers guidance on how to promote and discuss environmental issues in editorial content [23].
- The **Sustainable Production Alliance** (SPA) is a consortium of the world's leading film, television and streaming companies dedicated to accelerating the transformation of the entertainment business into a more sustainable industry. In partnership with the Producers Guild of America Foundation's PGA Green Committee, SPA established the Green Production Guide to provide tools and resources to help implement sustainable plans for production and reduce the industry's overall environmental impact [24].
- The **Digital Production Partnership** (DPP) has established the "DPP Committed to Sustainability" program, which provides a practical tool to assess an organization's progress against key environmental measures, and a common framework for procurement teams to assess the environmental impact of their suppliers [25].
- **Greening of Streaming** is an organization created to address growing concerns about the energy impact of the Internet streaming sector. It provides a forum for the streaming industry to develop better engineering and to foster collaboration through the supply chain to provide a great experience for the consumer without wasting energy [26].
- The **Environmental Media Association** (EMA) is a diverse subsection of entertainment industry influencers, entrepreneurs in business, and green icons dedicated to the mission of promoting environmental progress. The EMA Green Seal is a recognition program honoring progress in sustainable production for movies, television shows, and filmed commercials [27].

## Cloud Sustainability

### Sustainability Shared Responsibility Model

A sustainability shared responsibility model is a framework that outlines the sustainability responsibilities of cloud service providers (CSPs) and customers. Defining the division of labor between a CSP and its customers can help all parties concentrate on the areas where they can bring value to improving sustainability. For example, Figure 3 diagrams the Amazon Web Services (AWS) sustainability shared responsibility model, which can be described as:

- AWS is responsible for optimizing the sustainability of the cloud – delivering efficient, shared infrastructure, water stewardship, and sourcing renewable power.
- Customers are responsible for sustainability in the cloud – optimizing workloads and resource utilization, and minimizing the total resources required to be deployed for workloads.

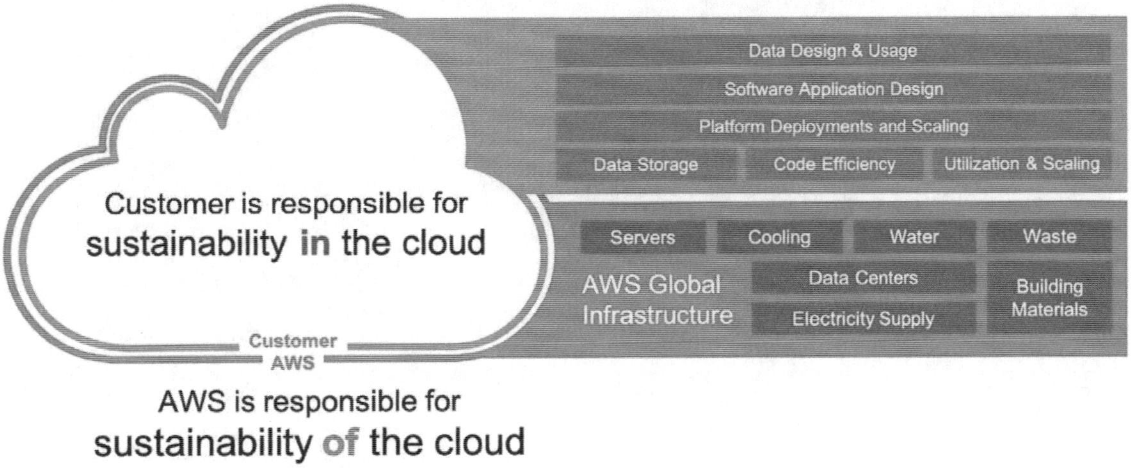


FIGURE 3: AWS SHARED RESPONSIBILITY MODEL OF CLOUD SUSTAINABILITY.

## Sustainability of the Cloud

### *Energy Efficiency*

Cloud providers have a lower carbon footprint and are more energy efficient than typical on-premises alternatives because of scalable investments in efficient power and cooling technology, more energy efficient server populations, and higher server utilization rates. Cloud workloads reduce impact by taking advantage of shared resources, such as networking, power, cooling, and physical facilities.

For example, the results of a study by 451 Research show that AWS infrastructure is 3.6 times more energy efficient than the median of surveyed enterprise data centers in the U.S. [28] and up to five times more energy efficient than typical EU enterprise infrastructure [29]. More than two-thirds of this advantage is attributable to the combination of a more energy efficient server population and much higher server utilization. Average enterprise server utilization rate is only about 18%, leaving a significant amount of capacity completely unused. When carbon intensity of consumed electricity and renewable energy purchases are factored in, AWS executes the same workloads as enterprise data centers with an 88% lower carbon footprint.

Cloud providers also gain efficiency via innovative technologies. For instance, AWS has improved power efficiency and availability by removing the central Uninterruptible Power Supply (UPS) from its data center design and instead integrating small battery packs and custom power supplies into racks. These changes combined reduce energy conversion loss by about 35%.

### *Renewable Energy*

Amazon (the parent company of AWS) is the largest corporate buyer of renewable energy (20 GW), including over 400 wind farms, solar farms, and rooftop solar installations at company buildings in 22 countries [30]. Amazon has reached 85% renewable energy across the business in 2021, and is on a path to powering operations with 100% renewable energy by 2025 [31]. The amount of clean energy produced by these projects will avoid the equivalent of power generation for 5.3 million U.S. homes annually. Specifically, within cloud, 13 AWS Regions were powered with over 95% renewable energy in 2021 [32], as shown in Figure 4.

FIGURE 4: AWS REGIONS POWERED BY OVER 95% RENEWABLE ENERGY IN 2021

***Water Stewardship***

In addition to reducing carbon emissions, cloud providers also seek to reduce water usage. For example, AWS has committed to being "water positive" by 2030, meaning returning more water to communities than it uses in its direct operations [33]. Water positivity is driven by four areas of effort: water efficiency, sustainable sources, community water reuse, and water replenishment.

***Water Efficiency***

AWS is constantly innovating across its infrastructure to reduce water consumption. It's 2021 global water use efficiency (WUE) metric was 0.25 liters of water per kilowatt-hour. This was achieved by using advanced cloud services, such as Internet of Things (IoT) technologies, to analyze real-time water use and identify and fix leaks. AWS further improves operational efficiency by eliminating cooling water use in many of its facilities for most of the year, instead relying on outside air. For example, in Ireland and Sweden, AWS uses no water to cool its data centers for 95% of the year. AWS also invests in on-site water-treatment systems that allow it to reuse water multiple times, minimizing water consumed for cooling.

***Sustainable Sources***

AWS uses sustainable water sources, such as recycled water and rainwater harvesting, wherever possible. Using recycled water, which is only suitable for a limited set of applications such as irrigation and industrial use, preserves valuable drinking water for communities. In Northern Virginia, AWS worked with Loudoun Water to become the first data center operator in the state approved to use recycled water in direct evaporative cooling systems. AWS already uses recycled water for cooling in 20 data centers around the world and has plans to expand recycled water use in more facilities as it works toward becoming water positive.

***Community Water Reuse***

After maximizing the use of water in its data centers, the spent liquid is still safe for many other uses. In Oregon, AWS provides up to 96% of the cooling water from its data centers to local farmers at no charge for use in irrigating crops like corn, soybeans, and wheat.

***Water Replenishment***

To meet its water positive commitment, AWS is investing in water replenishment projects in the communities where it operates. Replenishment projects expand water access, availability, and quality by restoring watersheds and bringing clean water, sanitation, and hygiene services to water-stressed communities. To date, AWS has completed replenishment projects in Brazil, India, Indonesia, and South Africa, providing 1.6 billion liters of freshwater each year to people in those communities. AWS also has several new projects, which, once completed, will provide more than 823 million liters of water to communities each year, including in India, UK, and the US.

Shifting to renewable energy also has environmental benefits beyond lowering carbon emissions. According to the International Energy Agency, the energy sector is responsible for 10% of global water withdrawals used for operating thermal power plants and producing fuels [34]. Unlike thermal power plants, wind and solar plants do not require large amounts of water to operate. In 2020, Amazon's renewable energy generation helped to avoid the withdrawal of about 480 billion liters of water, enough to supply 1 million American households or fill up 190,000 Olympic-sized swimming pools each year.

### *Embodied Carbon*

Embodied carbon consists of emissions associated with materials and construction processes throughout the whole lifecycle of a building or infrastructure. Steel is one of the largest contributors of embodied carbon in the structure of data centers. For example, AWS is working to lower these emissions by working with mills using electric arc furnace production processes. AWS suppliers are using up to 100% recycled content and are powered by electricity only, reducing embodied carbon up to 70%. AWS delivered six projects constructed with recycled steel in 2021 and will expand this to all future U.S. and European data centers moving forward. Concrete also contributes a large share of embodied carbon in data center construction. AWS design standards now require concrete with a 20% reduction in embodied carbon versus standard concrete for new U.S. data centers, and this requirement will be expanded globally [35].

## Sustainability in the Cloud

Sustainability in the cloud is a continuous effort focused on energy reduction and efficiency across all components of a workload by achieving the maximum benefit from the resources provisioned and minimizing the total resources required. This effort can range from the initial selection of an efficient programming language, adoption of modern algorithms, use of efficient data storage techniques, deploying to correctly sized and efficient compute infrastructure, and minimizing requirements for high-powered end-user hardware.

### *Sustainability Pillar of the AWS Well-Architected Framework*

The AWS Well-Architected Framework helps cloud architects understand the advantages and disadvantages of decisions made while building workloads on AWS. The Framework provides a way to consistently measure cloud architectures against best practices and to identify areas for improvement. The Framework is based on six pillars: operational excellence, security, reliability, performance efficiency, cost optimization, and in December 2021, the sustainability pillar was added [36].

The sustainability pillar provides design principles, operational guidance, best-practices, potential trade-offs, and improvement plans to meet sustainability targets for cloud workloads. Design principles for architecting cloud workloads to maximize sustainability and minimize impact include:

- **Understand Your Impact:** Measure the impact of your cloud workload and model the future impact of your workload. Include all sources of impact, including impacts resulting from customer use of your products, and impacts resulting from their eventual decommissioning and retirement. Compare the productive output with the total impact of your cloud workloads by reviewing the resources and emissions required per unit of work. Use this data to establish key performance indicators (KPIs), evaluate ways to improve productivity while reducing impact, and estimate the impact of proposed changes over time. In particular, the AWS Customer Carbon Footprint Tool [37] provides customers with an overview of the carbon emissions associated with their usage of cloud services, an estimation of the emissions reduction resulting from use of cloud vs. an on-premises equivalent, and a forecast of emissions reductions as AWS progresses towards powering operations with 100% renewable energy.

- **Establish Sustainability Goals:** For each cloud workload, establish long-term sustainability goals such as reducing the compute and storage resources required per transaction. Model the return on investment of sustainability improvements for existing workloads, and give owners the resources they need to invest in sustainability goals. Plan for growth, and architect your workloads so that growth results in reduced impact intensity measured against an appropriate unit, such as per user or per transaction. Goals help to support the wider sustainability goals of your business or organization, identify regressions, and prioritize areas of potential improvement.
- **Maximize Utilization:** Right-size workloads and implement efficient design to ensure high utilization and maximize the energy efficiency of the underlying hardware. Two hosts running at 30% utilization are less efficient than one host running at 60% due to baseline power consumption per host. At the same time, eliminate or minimize idle resources, processing, and storage to reduce the total energy required to power your workload.
- **Anticipate and Adopt New, More Efficient Hardware and Software Offerings:** Support the upstream improvements your partners and suppliers make to help you reduce the impact of your cloud workloads. Continually monitor and evaluate new, more efficient hardware and software offerings. Design for flexibility to allow for the rapid adoption of new efficient technologies. New hardware developed especially for cloud can improve energy efficiency of workloads. For example, AWS Arm64-based Graviton3 processors use up to 60% less energy for the same performance than non-Graviton Amazon Elastic Compute Cloud (EC2) instances [31].
- **Use Managed Services:** Sharing services across a broad customer base helps maximize resource utilization, which reduces the amount of infrastructure needed to support cloud workloads. For example, customers can share the impact of common data center components like power and networking by migrating workloads to the cloud and adopting managed services, such as AWS Fargate for serverless containers, or AWS Lambda serverless compute. Use managed services that can help minimize your impact, such as automatically moving infrequently accessed data to cold storage with Amazon S3 Lifecycle configurations or use Amazon EC2 Auto Scaling to adjust capacity to meet demand.
- **Reduce the Downstream Impact of Your Cloud Workloads:** Reduce the amount of energy or resources required to use your services. Reduce or eliminate the need for customers to upgrade their devices to use your services. Test using mechanisms such as AWS Device Farm to understand expected impact and test with customers to understand the actual impact from using your services.

## Sustainability in Specific M&E Applications

### Cloud-based Live Remote Production

One particular application where cloud can enhance sustainability is in live production. Traditionally, outside broadcast (OB) trucks heavily laden with production gear are driven to sports and entertainment venues. Production staff are typically flown in for a day or two for the event. According to the Albert's Annual Review of 2021, "Travel remains the biggest part of a production's carbon footprint, regardless of genre…the data shows us that road and air travel are the most prevalent transport types used by production." [38] Cloud-based remote production minimizes the needed on-site production staff to those only needed for camera and mic set-up and their operators. Live feeds from all cameras and mics are sent to the cloud, where software-based systems are used to produce the event. Directors, engineers, and operators of switchers, graphics, edit, and replay systems can produce the event from any location with adequate Internet connectivity. This reduces the need to transport those systems as hardware in trucks, and reduces the need to fly staff to the venue city.

In addition to a reduction in travel, remote film and television production will commonly chose to utilize portable generators to reliably provide the large amounts of electricity needed to power a remote production. According to Albert, "Most [film and TV] productions will hire a minimum of two high power diesel generators, which each consume an average of 80 litres of diesel per 12 hour period of use, emitting half a tonne of CO2 emissions." [39]. In the 2006 "Sustainability Report in the Motion Picture Industry" from UCLA, diesel fuel is described as "commonly used, despite their environmental drawbacks and the immediate noise and smell; a key advantage of generators powered by diesel rather than natural gas is the fact that they can be refueled while running" [40].

As more of the traditional heavy production hardware becomes virtualized, this allows for more workloads to migrate from diesel-powered on-premises workloads to renewable-powered workloads in the cloud. Production company Media.Monks stated that they developed a cloud-based broadcasting workflow for live sports production that "virtualizes racks of hardware that would have been transported on production trucks and keeps air travel to a minimum...Instead of flying in a 20-person crew from around the world to an event venue with haul gear, we can send a lean team on-site with a portable flypack; we turn on the servers, connect, and we're working with virtually no limitations to innovation" [41].

As part of IBC's Accelerator Media Innovation Programme in 2021 [42], a team of sports broadcasters, rights-owners and technology vendors carried out a workflow trial to produce an English Premier League game on the cloud to support the goal of a net zero carbon future for live productions. The trial included cloud-based video switching, graphics, replay, standards conversion, and editing of a closer for the end of the show.

The project team consisted of BBC Sport, BT Sport, Sky Sports and international rights-holders NBCUniversal and SuperSport, working together with the English Premier League, IMG/Premier League Productions and ALBERT. Technology was provided by Amazon Web Services, Blackbird, Hitomi, Microsoft, M2A Media, Singular.live and Zixi.

Sky Sports took on responsibility for the host broadcast eight-camera match production and the syndication of that feed to partners and international rights-holders. BT Sport produced a four-camera presentation production, along with the domestic UK broadcast wrap at its studios in Stratford. BBC Sport took the host feed to make a file-based highlights production, and Premier League Productions provided the world feed production for international rights-holders.

The Accelerator project highlighted potential fuel reduction that remote/cloud workflows allow. During the trial, the team found that the amount of fuel required on-site was reduced by over 50%. It was learned that the on-site infrastructure could be significantly reduced, which would allow in the future for smaller trucks with less power draw and less carbon impact from resulting from transportation of the equipment. Cloud production reduced the technical infrastructure required for the gallery production. For some broadcasters, this was by up to 70%. Cloud production further reduced the requirements for significant on-site technical facilities by allowing signals to be sent quickly and easily to multiple locations.

In addition to sports, live news events can also be remotely produced. For the 26th Conference of the Parties (COP) to the United Nations Framework Convention on Climate Change (UNFCCC) in Glasgow, also known as COP26, Sky News set up a dedicated news channel produced from London entirely in the cloud [43]. Sky estimated that it reduced its emission footprint by 90%, generating 10kgs of CO2e per 9 hours of programming versus what would have been 119kg by traditional means.

By transporting fewer production staff and using cloud-based production tools, staff can be more efficiently utilized (with less down time from travel) while improving work-life balance. Lead-time on production equipment is removed if it is virtualized using software on the cloud. Productions can be rapidly scaled up or down as needed. Producers can gain easier access to a diverse global talent pool and engineering teams can more freely choose to host workloads in regions adjacent to clean energy sources. And training becomes less burdensome as staff can be trained at home with immediate access to all necessary production systems on-demand, instead of waiting for a production to be over before being able to access a physical switcher, mixer, replay device, etc.

### Cloud-based Media Supply Chain

The content storage, processing, and distribution operations of digital media files and their associated metadata is known as "media supply chain". This is one of the most mature M&E workloads in the cloud. SDVI Rally is an example of a media supply chain platform that enables media companies to optimize the infrastructure deployment and resource utilization associated with running dynamic, responsive media supply chains in the cloud. Since it ensures that cloud infrastructure is always properly sized for the workload requirements, Rally-managed supply chains consume only the resources needed and eliminate the waste associated with underutilized infrastructure. Rally resource management has also been designed so that the platform itself makes utilization more efficient: in 2021, Rally and the supply chains it manages consumed 39% less compute resources per content hour than the previous year of operation. This equates to SDVI's customers using 12,940 fewer dual-quadcore CPU servers running in customer data centers [44]. Furthermore, the company launched its Net-Zero Supply Chains initiative in January 2022, which offsets all GHG emissions associated with the Rally platform, including emissions from operating all third-party application services under Rally management. These offsets take the form of Gold Standard Verified Emission Reductions (VERs) [45].

Cloud-based digital asset management (DAM) tools can allow a globally distributed workforce to share metadata and content over the Internet without requiring emissions from personnel travel or media courier services. Content can be shared directly between production and distribution partner companies using cloud storage "in place" without the need for an explicit Internet transfer. For example, Imagen, a media management platform vendor, works with cloud providers that are committed to renewable energy and elect to use resources in regions which are already running 100% renewable energy [46]. With this approach, despite a 4x growth in the use of cloud services in the past 5 years, Imagen's CO2 consumption is declining, and remaining emissions are offset with carbon credits.

In another example, UKTV, a subsidiary of the BBC, migrated their media asset library to the cloud, which contributed toward their broader sustainability goals to be Net Zero by 2030. This migration used an event driven solution, so that the vast majority of cloud compute resources were consumed only during active tasks. When the tasks have been completed, the asset management solution only required a minimal amount of constant compute resources when idle, reducing compute waste and excess carbon attributable to this workload [47].

### Edit in the Cloud

To assess carbon emissions from video editing, environmental consultancy Green Element compared the impact of three different workflows: "on premises", "cloud based" and "cloud native" [48]. The "on premises" edit workflow required all edit staff to travel to the event, and to use typical editing software there. The "cloud based" workflow was a lift-and-shift migration of typical editing software to cloud virtual instances accessed using remote desktop, and requiring upload, download, and storage of full 50 Mbit/s high resolution files. The "cloud native" workflow (using Blackbird software) transcoded video from live camera feeds or files on-premises into a 2 Mbit/s lightweight proxy version that goes directly into the cloud in real time, and can then be frame accurately edited in a web browser. The workflows were modeled using a two-week event with 4,000 hours of TV and 50 editors. If on premises, the editors would need to fly 2,000km on economy class plane travel to the event.

The on premises model emitted 174t of $CO_2e$ (with 15t due to personnel travel), the cloud-based model emitted 96t, and the cloud native model emitted 15t. Just moving editing to the cloud showed a 44% reduction in emissions, but going further and optimizing use on the cloud showed a 91% reduction.

## Conclusion

M&E companies today are simultaneously planning for sustainability as well as migrating workloads to and re-inventing their businesses on the cloud. Fortunately, these two business directions can work together. The scale and focus on innovation of cloud providers can achieve higher resource utilization and energy efficiency than on-premises computing. The more flexible use of cloud services only when needed by the business reduces wasted energy use. Virtualizing operations in the cloud accessed over the Internet makes operations easier and location-independent, while also reducing the need for transportation energy. Sustainability and cloud enablement work together well for M&E companies.

## References


[1] United Nations, "Sustainability," [Online]. Available: https://www.un.org/en/academic-impact/sustainability

[2] Intergovernmental Panel on Climate Change, "Special Report on Global Warming of 1.5 ºC," 2018.

[3] Intergovernmental Panel on Climate Change, "IPCC PRESS RELEASE: The evidence is clear: the time for action is now. We can halve emissions by 2030.," 2022. [Online]. Available: https://www.ipcc.ch/report/ar6/wg3/resources/press/press-release/

[4] Washington Post-ABC News, "Nov. 7-10, 2021, Washington Post-ABC News poll," [Online]. Available: https://www.washingtonpost.com/context/nov-7-10-2021-washington-post-abc-news-poll/160508a9-cea2-4433-92c8-6dc51838721e/?itid=lk_inline_manual_2

[5] Reuters, "Digital News Report 2020," 2020. [Online]. Available: https://reutersinstitute.politics.ox.ac.uk/sites/default/files/2020-06/DNR_2020_FINAL.pdf

[6] Greenhouse Gas Protocol, "Greenhouse Gas Protocol," [Online]. Available: https://ghgprotocol.org

[7] A. Trastelis, "Greening Our Story: Transforming CBC/Radio-Canada into a World-Class, Sustainable Public Service Media Company," SMPTE Motion Imaging Journal, vol. 131, no. 8, pp. 97-101, September 2022.

[8] Amazon Web Services, "Amazon Sustainability," [Online]. Available: https://sustainability.aboutamazon.com/

[9] BBC, "Environmental Sustainability," [Online]. Available: https://www.bbc.co.uk/sustainability

[10] BT Group PLC, "Sustainable," [Online]. Available: https://www.bt.com/about/digital-impact-and-sustainability/tackling-climate-change

[11] Comcast, "Environment," [Online]. Available: https://corporate.comcast.com/impact/environment

[12] The Walt Disney Company, "Environmental Sustainability," [Online]. Available: https://impact.disney.com/environment/environmental-sustainability/

[13] ITV, "Climate Action," [Online]. Available: https://www.itvplc.com/socialpurpose/climate-action

[14] Netflix, "Netflix Sustainability," [Online]. Available: https://about.netflix.com/en/sustainability

[15] Sony Group Corporation, "Sony accelerates target to achieve a zero environmental footprint by ten years," 18 May 2022. [Online]. Available: https://www.sony.com/en/SonyInfo/News/Press/202205/22-022E/

[16] The Climate Pledge, [Online]. Available: https://www.theclimatepledge.com/

[17] The Climate Pledge Fund, [Online]. Available: https://sustainability.aboutamazon.com/about/the-climate-pledge/the-climate-pledge-fund

[18] Amazon, "Nature-Based Solutions," [Online]. Available: https://sustainability.aboutamazon.com/about/the-climate-pledge/nature-based-solutions

[19] United Nations Climate Change, "Key aspects of the Paris Agreement," [Online]. Available: https://unfccc.int/process-and-meetings/the-paris-agreement/the-paris-agreement/key-aspects-of-the-paris-agreement

[20] Amsterdam, "Policy: Sustainability and energy," [Online]. Available: https://www.amsterdam.nl/en/policy/sustainability/

[21] UK Parliament House of Commons Library, "Global net zero commitments," 12 Nov 2021. [Online]. Available: https://commonslibrary.parliament.uk/global-net-zero-commitments/

[22] European Commission, "European Climate Law," [Online]. Available: https://ec.europa.eu/clima/eu-action/european-green-deal/european-climate-law_en

[23] ALBERT, [Online]. Available: https://wearealbert.org/

[24] Sustainable Production Alliance, "About The Sustainable Production Alliance," [Online]. Available: https://www.greenproductionguide.com/about-the-sustainable-production-alliance/

[25] The Digital Production Partnership, "The DPP Committed to Sustainability programme," [Online]. Available: https://www.thedpp.com/sustainability

[26] Greening of Streaming, [Online]. Available: https://www.greeningofstreaming.org/

[27] Environmental Media Association, [Online]. Available: https://www.green4ema.org/

[28] 451 Research, "The Carbon Reduction Opportunity of Moving to Amazon Web Services," 2019. [Online]. Available: https://sustainability.aboutamazon.com/carbon_reduction_aws.pdf

[29] S&P Global Market Intelligence, "Saving Energy in Europe by Using Amazon Web Services," October 2021. [Online]. Available: https://assets.aboutamazon.com/b0/3e/b0fc6b8a4a85b38ac65a3fbc584c/11061-aws-451research-advisory-bw-cloudefficiency-eu-2021-r5-final-corrected-data.pdf

[30] Amazon, "Amazon sets a new record for the most renewable energy purchased in a single year," 20 April 2022. [Online]. Available: https://www.aboutamazon.com/news/sustainability/amazon-sets-a-new-record-for-the-most-renewable-energy-purchased-in-a-single-year

[31] Amazon, "Delivering progress every day: Amazon's commitment to sustainability," 1 Aug 2022. [Online]. Available: https://www.aboutamazon.com/news/sustainability/delivering-progress-every-day-amazons-commitment-to-sustainability

[32] AWS, "Sustainability in the Cloud," [Online]. Available: https://sustainability.aboutamazon.com/environment/the-cloud?energyType=true

[33] AWS, "AWS Makes Water Positive Commitment to Return More Water to Communities Than It Uses by 2030," 28 November 2022 [Online]. Available: https://aws.amazon.com/local/hongkong/news/water-positive-commitment/

[34] M. Walton, "Energy has a role to play in achieving universal access to clean water and sanitation," 22 March 2018. [Online]. Available: https://www.iea.org/commentaries/energy-has-a-role-to-play-in-achieving-universal-access-to-clean-water-and-sanitation

[35] Amazon, "Amazon's 2021 Sustainability Report," 2021. [Online]. Available: https://sustainability.aboutamazon.com/2021-sustainability-report.pdf

[36] Amazon Web Services, "Sustainability Pillar - AWS Well-Architected Framework," [Online]. Available: https://docs.aws.amazon.com/wellarchitected/latest/sustainability-pillar/sustainability-pillar.html

[37] Amazon Web Services, "Customer Carbon Footprint Tool," [Online]. Available: https://aws.amazon.com/aws-cost-management/aws-customer-carbon-footprint-tool/

[38] ALBERT, "Annual Review 2021," 2021. [Online]. Available: https://wearealbert.org/wp-content/uploads/2022/06/albert-AR-2021_Final.pdf

[39] Albert, "Electric generators powering sustainable sets," 7 Oct 2021. [Online]. Available: https://wearealbert.org/2021/10/07/electric-generators-powering-sustainable-sets/

[40] UCLA Institute of the Environment, "Sustainability in the Motion Picture," Nov 2006. [Online]. Available: https://www.ioes.ucla.edu/wp-content/uploads/mpisreport.pdf

[41] TV Tech, "MediaMonks Uses AWS to Deliver 4K VR to NBA Fans," 8 Jun 2021. [Online]. Available: https://www.tvtechnology.com/equipment/mediamonks-uses-aws-to-deliver-4k-vr-to-nba-fans

[42] F. Ringrose, "Sustainability in Live Production: The Premier League shoots for net zero," 25 May 2022. [Online]. Available: https://www.ibc.org/features/sustainability-in-live-production-the-premier-league-shoots-for-net-zero/8591.article

[43] A. Stout, "Making live productions more sustainable," 16 March 2022. [Online]. Available: https://www.redsharknews.com/making-live-productions-more-sustainable

[44] SDVI, "Net-Zero Supply Chains," April 28 2022. [Online]. Available: https://sdvi.com/net-zero-supply-chains/

[45] Gold Standard, "Gold Standard Emission Reductions," [Online]. Available: https://www.goldstandard.org/articles/gold-standard-emission-reductions

[46] Imagen, "Green clouds ahead - How carbon-neutral cloud storage can meet sustainability goals," [Online]. Available: https://imagen.io/blog/cloud-storage-sustainability/

[47] Amazon Web Services, "UKTV Enhances Media Workstreams and Functions with an AWS Solution | Amazon Web Services," 8 Jun 2022. [Online]. Available: https://youtu.be/cz03AFD1T-c

[48] Blackbird & Green Element, "Decarbonizing Video Production: Removing CO2e emissions from TV and video at source," [Online]. Available: https://www.blackbird.video/wp-content/uploads/2022/06/Blackbird_Decarbonizing-Video-Production-1.pdf?cf_id=6788